# THE PACIFIC STATES

*Author's Travels*

D1327512

# THE

# *PACIFIC STATES*

## OF AMERICA

# THE

# PACIFIC STATES

## OF AMERICA

*People, Politics, and Power*

*in the Five Pacific Basin States*

NEAL R. PEIRCE

W · W · NORTON & COMPANY · INC ·
NEW YORK

FIRST EDITION

*For my wife, Barbara,*
*who shared this odyssey*

Library of Congress Cataloging in Publication Data

Peirce, Neal R.
   The Pacific States of America.

   Bibliography: p.
   1. Pacific States.    2. Alaska.    3. Hawaii.
I. Title.
F851.P43 1972      917.9′03      72–2333
ISBN 0–393–05272–9

1 2 3 4 5 6 7 8 9 0

# CONTENTS

# FOREWORD

THIS IS A BOOK ABOUT the Pacific rim states, part of a series covering the story of each major geographic region and all of the 50 states of America in our time. The objective is simply to let Americans (and foreigners too) know something of the profound diversity of peoples and life styles and geographic habitat and political behavior that make this the most fascinating nation on earth.

Only one project like this has been attempted before, and it inspired these books: John Gunther's *Inside U.S.A.*, researched during World War II and published in 1947. Gunther was the first man in U.S. history to visit each of the states and then to give a good and true account of the American condition as he found it. But his book is a quarter of a century old; it was written before the fantastic economic and population growth of the postwar era, growth that has transformed the face of this land and altered the life of its people and lifted us to heights of glory and depths of national despair beyond our wildest past dreams. Before he died, I consulted John Gunther about a new book. He recognized the need for such a work, and he gave me, as he put it, his "good luck signal."

But what was to be a single book became several, simply because I found America today too vast, too complex to fit into a single volume. A first book, *The Megastates of America*, treated America's 10 most heavily populated states. This volume, together with a companion book, *The Mountain States of America*, begins the exploration of the other 40. Here are Oregon and Washington, the unalike Northwest twins; Alaska and Hawaii, both so different from all the rest of America; and the nation state of California. The California chapter represents an expansion and updating of the version which appeared in *The Megastates of America*, now including more detail on natural regions, conservation battles, and the places where people live—small towns and cities, the neighborhoods of Los Angeles and San Francisco, and suburbia. Succeeding books will view separately people, politics, and power in the Plains States, Deep South, Border South, Great Lakes, Mid-Atlantic, and New England States.

A word about method. Like Gunther, I traveled to each state of the Union. I talked with about 1,000 men and women—governors, Senators, Representatives, mayors, state and local officials, editors and reporters, business and labor leaders, public opinion analysts, clergymen, university presidents and professors, representatives of the Indian, black, and Spanish-speaking communities—and just plain people. Some of the people I talked with were famous, others obscure, almost all helpful.

I went by plane, then rented cars, made a personal inspection of almost every great city and most of the important geographic areas, and must have walked several hundred miles in the process too, insanely lugging a briefcase full of notes and tape recorder into the unlikeliest places. Usually I got names of suggested interviewees from my newspaper friends and other contacts in new states and cities and then sent letters ahead saying I would like to see the people. From the initial interviews, reference to still more interesting people invariably ensued. Rare were the interviews that didn't turn out to be fascinating in their own way; the best ones were dinner appointments, when the good talk might stretch into the late evening hours.

Altogether, the travel to 50 states took a year and a half, starting in 1969; then came more than two years of writing, all too often made up of 15-hour working days. The writing was complicated by the need to review hundreds of books and thousands of articles and newspaper clippings I had assembled over time. And then each manuscript after it had been read and commented upon by experts on the state (often senior political reporters), had to be revised to include last-minute developments, and still once more given a final polish and updating in the galley stage.

Amid the confusion I tried to keep my eye on the enduring, vital questions about each state and its great cities:

What sets it (the state or city) apart from the rest of America?

What is its essential character?

What kind of place is it to live in?

What does it look like, how clean or polluted is it, what are the interesting communities?

Who holds the power?

Which are the great corporations, unions, universities and newspapers, and what role do they play in their state?

Which are the major ethnic groups, and what is their influence?

How did the politics evolve to where they are today, and what is the outlook for the 1970s?

How creatively have the governments and power structures served the *people?*

Who are the great leaders of today—and perhaps tomorrow?

A word of caution: many books about the present-day American condition are preoccupied with illustrating fundamental sickness in our society, while others are paeans of praise. These books are neither. They state many of the deep-seated problems, from perils to the environment to the abuse of power by selfish groups. But the account of the state civilizations also includes hundreds of instances of greatness, of noble and disinterested public service. I have viewed my primary job as descriptive, to show the multitudinous strands of life in our times, admitting their frequently contradictory directions, and tying them together analytically only where the evidence is clear. The ultimate "verdict" on the states and cities must rest with the reader himself.

For whom, then, is this chronicle of our times written? I mean the individual chapters to be of interest to people who live in the various states, to help them see their home area in a national context. I write for businessmen, students and tourists planning to visit or move into a state, and who are interested in what makes it tick—the kind of things no guidebook will tell them. I write for politicians planning national campaigns, for academicians, for all those curious about the American condition as we enter the last decades of the 20th century.

From the start, I knew it was presumptuous for any one person to try to encompass such a broad canvass. But a unity of view, to make true comparisons between states, is essential. And since no one else had tried the task for a quarter of a century, I decided to try—keeping in mind the same goal Gunther set for *Inside U.S.A.*—a book whose "central spine and substance is an effort, in all diffidence, to show this most fabulous and least known of countries, the United States of America, to itself."

# THE
# PACIFIC STATES
# OF AMERICA

*The age of the Pacific begins, mysterious and unfathomable in its*
*meaning to our own future.*

—*Frederick Jackson Turner, in 1914*

IT IS HARD to speak of the Pacific Basin states as a region like others in the U.S.A. First of all, the five states scarcely form a geographically compact unit. From the spot in the desert near Pima, Arizona, where California reaches its southeastern extreme, it is exactly 3,765 miles to the Alaskan island of Attu at the tip of the Aleutians—one-seventh of the circumference of the globe. The distance from the northern extremity of Alaska at Point Barrow to Ka Lea, or South Cape, on the "Big Island" of Hawaii, is only a little less—3,622 miles.*

Second, there is the problem of disparate land areas and population. Alaska is the biggest American state in land area—an astounding 586,412 square miles, 77 percent greater than all the other Pacific States combined. But the Great Land's population of 302,173 in 1970 was only 1.14 percent of the regional total and a distant 50th among the 50 states in the Union. The same Census confirmed that California had, indeed, become the most populous state of the U.S.A. Even if one adds up the population of all Pacific States save California, the Golden State still has three times as many people. The wartime and postwar growth, centered in California, is reflected in these figures:

|  | *1940 Population* | *1970 Population* | *Growth* | *% Increase* |
|---|---|---|---|---|
| California | 6,907,387 | 19,953,134 | + 13,045,747 | + 189 |
| Washington | 1,736,191 | 3,409,169 | + 1,672,978 | + 96 |
| Oregon | 1,089,684 | 2,097,385 | + 1,001,701 | + 92 |
| Hawaii | 422,770 | 769,913 | + 347,143 | + 82 |
| Alaska | 72,524 | 302,173 | + 229,649 | + 317 |

* By contrast, it is only 2,897 miles between the two most widely separated points of the coterminous U.S.—West Quoddy Head, Maine, and Point Arena, California.

With its huge population, California creates its own power and impulses and markets in a way that takes little account of its geographic neighbors. It is like a great nation state on its own, and will be so treated in the California chapter.

The reader will discover other anomalies. The Pacific Northwest states of Washington and Oregon, though they have copy-cat geographies and share a big lumber industry, are totally unalike in character and mood and the dynamic elements of their economies. Alaska and Hawaii share the distinction of being the two newest states of the Union, having joined in January and August of 1959 respectively; but, as everyone knows, they have little else in common.

What then is there to "the age of the Pacific, . . . mysterious and unfathomable" that Frederick Jackson Turner wrote about? What lies beyond the last frontier? The answers must still be very tentative, but some can be suggested:

PHYSICAL SETTING. In sheer beauty, our Pacific States surpass almost all others on the continent. The coastline, unlike the Atlantic, is rough, craggy, dramatic. And behind the seas stand great mountains, many of them mere youngsters in geologic time, the products of upheavals of nature through earthquake and volcano that continue all around the Pacific Basin's "rim of fire." This is no settled Appalachian Range, but a turbulent, still building part of the world.

CLIMATE. The salubrious Pacific winds and currents soften the cold along the shorelines of Oregon and Washington and the Gulf of Alaska but then cool the Hawaiian Islands and the California coast—an almost perfect meteorological combination. Earthquakes in Alaska, volcanic eruptions in Hawaii, fires and floods in California must still be seen as exceptions to one of the most equable climatic belts anywhere in the world. Only "behind" the mountains does fiercely hostile weather sometimes prevail—broiling summers, frigid winters, and often excruciatingly low rainfall, as one may find east of the Coastal Range and Sierra Nevada in California, east of the Cascades in Oregon and Washington. In Alaska the greatest cold is reserved for the area north of the Alaska Range north of Anchorage, though most Americans would consider the weather along the Panhandle, Bay of Alaska, and Aleutians fearsome enough.

MOOD AND PEOPLE. The Pacific states, Alaska excepted, are magnets for population, in part because of the new life style they offer. Poet and critic Kenneth Rexroth has described it well *:

Many students of population believe that the demands of the technological age and the welfare state are such that the centers of civilization will shift back once more to the Mediterranean—but a worldwide Mediterranean that includes Australia, New Zealand, Chile and the Pacific Coast of North America. So in all the West Coast communities the old Puritan ethic, shaped in conflict with an environment of storms and violent changes of weather, of struggle with nature, seems to be withering away, to be replaced, in widely varying degree, by the old *"vie Méditer-*

* In his introduction to *The Pacific States* (New York: Time-Life Library of America, 1967).

*ranée"* of interpersonal laissez faire and *dolce far niente,* of wide tolerance and easy manners.

Clearly, the Hawaiian Islands fit the pattern as well if not better than the Pacific Coast. And this brings us to the theme of the interracial society. Before Watts exploded, there was a Western myth to the effect that the truly tolerant society had sprung up beside the Pacific. That illusion is now shattered, but some fascinating facts remain. The five Pacific Basin states are now home for 78 percent of the Japanese, 72 percent of the Filipino, 54 percent of the Chinese, 7 percent of the Negro, and a high portion of the Mexican-American people living in the United States.* While the process may be slower with blacks, Hawaii is already showing the way toward an intermarried and intermixed multiracial society. One sees the deep black-white and Mexican-Anglo prejudices remaining on the mainland and hesitates to make predictions. But it was only 30 years ago that then despised "Japs" were being deported to concentration camps away from Pacific coastal areas. Today the Orientals, despite the festering problems of San Francisco's Chinatown and its duplicates in a few other cities, are fast approaching full acceptance in American society. It may not be altogether utopian to hope that first acceptance, and then intermarriage, will affect the other racial and ethnic groups as well.

ECONOMY. Since World War II, California, Washington, and Oregon have broken free of the confines of a raw material producing economy to become major centers of service and production. Aerospace contracts enriched California and Washington, and both suffered cruelly when an aerospace recession started in 1970. (With only 13 percent of the U. S. population, the Pacific region was getting enough orders in the late 1960s to hire more than 40 percent of all aerospace workers in the United States.) Oregon, by contrast, has a much more diversified economy.

Alaska's well-being is tied to the U.S. military, lumber, fish, and now her great oil boom. Hawaii lives off sugar, tourists, and troops.

All of the Pacific States take a lively interest in transoceanic trade. Since its resurgence, Japan has become the great and promising market. Already, the vast majority of raw materials produced in Alaska flow directly into the Nipponese market. The total value of U.S. trade with Japan was $2 billion in 1959, $10.5 billion in 1970. So far have things evolved since V-J Day that many Japanese fly to Hawaii for their vacations!

But the specter of labor trouble, hindering trade and adversely affecting the U.S. balance of payments, has risen again in the Pacific Basin following a 23-year hiatus, from 1948 to 1971, in strikes by the powerful International Longshoremen's & Warehousemen's Union. Harry Bridges, now past his seventieth birthday, was considered a militant Marxist two decades ago and the ILWU was drummed out of the old CIO for Communist leanings. But Bridges became more conservative over the years and by the start of the 1970s, on the eve of his planned retirement, was even accused by "Young

* The actual regional totals are 458,681 Japanese, 247,367 Filipino, 236,413 Chinese, 1,514,243 Negroes, and 3,236,455 Mexican-American and other Spanish-speaking peoples. The five states are also home for 155,316 American Indians—20 percent of the national total.

Turks" within his union of being too cozy with management of the shipping lines. A key issue in the strike of 1971–72 was the excess of dock workers as the lines converted increasingly to "containerization." Containers—big metal vans 20 or 40 feet in length—can be prepacked far away from the docks and quickly loaded at the docks, cutting ships' time in harbor to a fraction of the time formerly required. While they save time and money for the shippers, containers threaten to eliminate a large portion of the longshoremen's jobs. Yet unless the U.S. can adapt quickly to advanced new cargo-handling techniques, handling of cargo at its ports may become so expensive that more and more foreign trade shifts to its export competitors. As the 1971–72 strike moved toward its eventual duration of more than four months, for instance, Japan began to shift its orders for wheat to Australia because it could not get possession of the big harvest from the Pacific Northwest states. (Another fruit of the strike was the start of merger negotiations between the ILWU and the Teamsters.)

Another new development in Pacific Basin commerce is the increasing amount of raw capital beginning to flow from the United States across the Pacific, with Australia seen as the great continent of opportunity. Late in the 1960s, for instance, it was announced that the Bank of America, the Bank of Tokyo, and Australia's Bank of New South Wales had formed a joint company to finance Australian development projects.

Though the dollar amounts are never likely to take on cosmic importance, there are interesting possibilities that the two newest states, Alaska and Hawaii, may become trade partners. Hawaii, for instance, could send fruits, vegetables, and dollars north in exchange for natural gas, oil, lumber and seafoods from Alaska. Another "service" Hawaii could provide is a place for Alaskans to thaw out during wintertime vacations. Direct air service between the two states began in 1969, and they envision triangular package deals for tourists from the mainland. The tourists might find an interesting similarity between the two states: prices. Anchorage and Honolulu take turns being the most expensive American city to live in.

POLITICS AND GOVERNMENT. There are no entrenched political machines in the Pacific States. Befitting the newness and volatility of the region, politics tend to be free-wheeling and personality-oriented; party organizations are notoriously weak. In part, this is a result of Progressive-era reforms (as in California, Oregon, and Washington), but one finds the same pattern prevailing in Alaska and Hawaii as well. In terms of partisan preference, only staunchly Democratic Hawaii now seems "safe" for one of the parties, although Washington, at least in terms of its voting for President and Congress, seems to be strongly oriented to the Democrats. As of 1971–72, the region had six Democrats and four Republicans in the U.S. Senate and the House delegations were balanced 31–21 in favor of the Democrats. Starting in 1972, California's share of the U.S. House seats is 43 out of a regional total of 57. And with 54 electoral votes, California's role in Presidential elections will be greater than ever. But in the U.S. Senate, the two most powerful Pacific region Senators may be the duo from Washington state, Henry M. Jackson and Warren G. Magnuson, both chairmen of key committees and expert maneuverers for home-state advantage. Most other Pacific States have been unwilling to keep their men in the Senate long enough to build up power and seniority.

By national standards, the state governments of the Pacific area are extraordinarily progressive—both in structure (clear gubernatorial authority, well informed legislatures, and the like) and in terms of the types of social programs they have enacted. Newness has its virtues; Alaska decided to give its governor more clear-cut authority than any state except New Jersey, and Hawaii has become a virtual hothouse of experimentation in new and responsive government forms, including America's first ombudsman. All five states of the region also have exceptionally liberal abortion laws—in fact, in all the United States, only New York State compares in the progressive nature of its abortion law and the liberality of interpretation.

Will the Pacific, which provided the 49th and 50th states of the Union, furnish still more in time to come? The answer is probably no. There are a number of U.S.-controlled Pacific territories whose future status remains unclear—the 2,000-odd islands of Micronesia, Guam, Samoa, Wake, Midway, Johnston, Palmyra, and others. True independence might well bring economic disaster and would be resisted by the Pentagon because of the high strategic importance of the islands. A nonbinding status of free association with the U.S. is unacceptable to Washington; the Micronesians seem uninterested in a U.S. proposal for commonwealth status. To date, little enthusiasm has been shown for proposals of a new state of the Union built around Guam and Micronesia. But Alaska's former Senator, Ernest Gruening, seems to have a better idea. He proposes that the remaining U.S.-controlled territories be given the option of joining the state of Hawaii, each new area becoming one or more counties of that already far-flung and ethnically diverse state. Gruening's idea would extend the U.S.A. another 3,000 miles toward mainland Asia and 1,000 miles south of the equator.

An even more startling idea is that the Philippines—a nation the size of Arizona, rich in natural resources but with 38.5 million people, almost twice California's total—might choose one day to become a state of the American Union. The yearning for political stability, honesty in government, and heavy capital investment—all of which have eluded the Philippines since the country gained its independence from the U.S. in 1946—has since the late 1960s fostered a strong statehood movement, which now claims close to three million members. Leading Filipino political circles, however, are opposed. Moreover, the U.S. Government might debate long and hard the proposition of assuming responsibility for a country with such severe economic problems and a small but vocal segment of radical youth groups and leftist guerrillas.

But even the idea of Philippine reaffiliation with the United States—an idea amazingly endorsed by over half the Filipino people in a 1971 Gallup Poll—underscores the continuing newness, the push into forms and associations yet unknown, which remains the enduring theme of our Pacific frontier.

# CALIFORNIA

## THE GREAT NATION STATE

## I. THE STATE SCENE

*But in California the lights went on all at once, in a blaze, and they have never been dimmed.*
        —*Carey McWilliams, in* California: The Great Exception

THERE HAS never been a state quite like California. None has ever had so many people—by 1971 over 20 million (up from 9 million in 1945), the new sum greater than that of 20 other states combined or six times as large as the original 13 states in 1790. Every 10th resident of the U.S. is now a Californian. (In 1964, California outstripped New York to become the country's most populous; for most of the postwar era, until a slowdown in the late 1960s, it had grown by more than 1,000 people *a day*.) John Gunther pointed out a quarter-century ago that California was the one that above all others could best exist alone, and the statement is even truer today. If California were an independent country, it would exceed 111 other nations in popula-

tion and 92 in land area. Its gross national product—close to $125 billion—
would be greater than those of all nations of the world save five—the United
States, the Soviet Union, West Germany, France, and Japan. Agriculturally, it would be among the leading nations; in export trade, it would rank
19th. Its per capita income would exceed that of all other countries of the
world, including the United States.

California is so huge geographically—800 miles from corner to corner—
that people have sometimes despaired of running it as a single entity. Two of
the largest cities, Los Angeles and San Diego, are 360 and 470 air miles, respectively, from the state capital at Sacramento, a division greater than that
of any other state. The legislature actually voted in 1859 (nine years after
statehood) to split into north and south states, a proposal frustrated only by
the failure of Congress to approve it. The two-state idea has never died, and
there was a renewed flutter of interest in it during the 1960s, when Northern
California viewed with alarm its loss of voting power under one-man, one-
vote in the state legislature. The suggestion then, as traditionally, was to split
California along the crest of the Tehachapi Mountains, approximately 335
miles south of San Francisco and 115 miles north of Los Angeles. (Fred Ty-
son of the State Environmental Quality Study Council had a different idea—
to split California where the smog from Los Angeles meets the smog from
San Francisco, the idea being that each state would then be in a position to
control its air quality.)

The state-splitting ideas are not likely to come to fruition. Reapportionment gave the vote weight to Southern California, and it is not about to
release it. Water, as we shall see later, may no longer be the great bone of
contention between north and south that it appeared to be just a few years
ago. And there are strong bonds of unity. The expressways between Northern
and Southern California are packed with traffic, and the San Francisco–Los
Angeles air corridor is the most heavily traveled in the world. Even the University of California, for all its campuses, offers unity. There are almost as
many students at Berkeley from Southern California as would be proportion-
ate to the California population (11.3 million people in the south, 8.4 million
in the north, according to the 1970 Census).

But what, one asks, lies at the heart of this peculiar vortex of human energy and desire called California? Theories abound—futurism, *anomie*, boosterism, sun and leisure culture in a beneficent climate, a lemming-like rush to
the precipice of the next great earthquake—and we shall examine some in
turn. Capturing, at any moment in time, the spirit and direction of California
is an almost impossible task; what one records will surely be transmuted by
the time it reaches print. As Gladwin Hill, veteran California correspondent
for the New York *Times*, wrote in his book *Dancing Bear*: "The endless
tide of immigration, peculiarities of geography, and the forced-draft growth
of California's economy have made it a kaleidoscopic succession of states,
changing from year to year, almost from day to day."

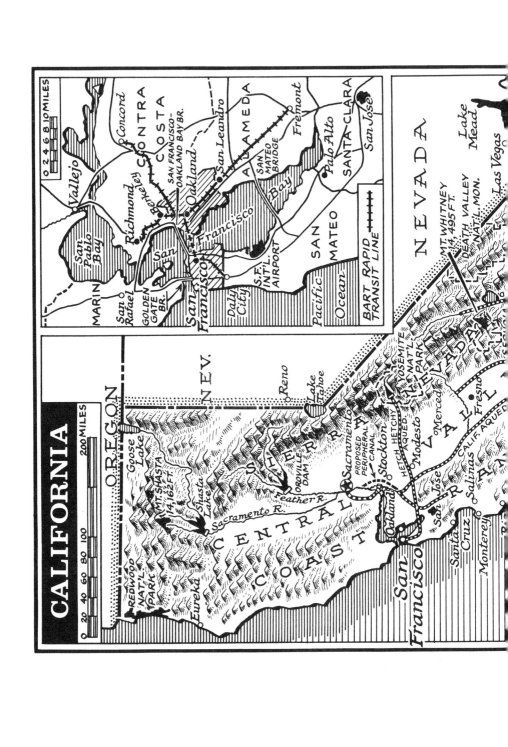

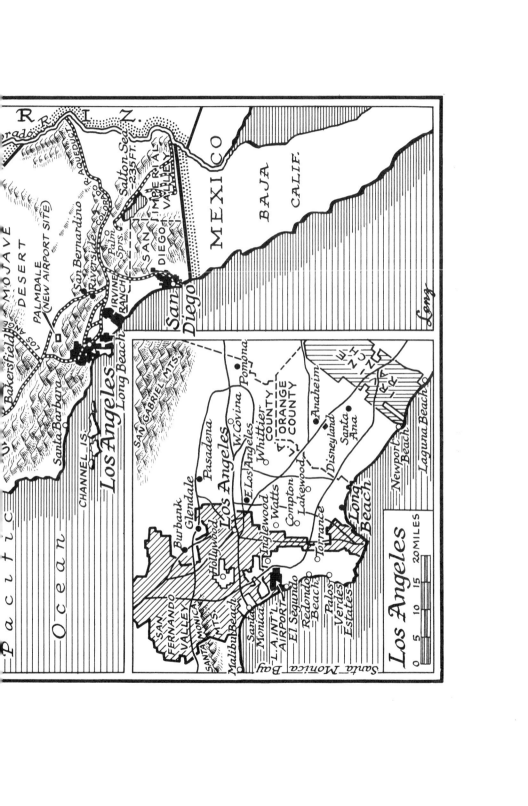

What does seem constant, as Carey McWilliams (a foremost interpreter of modern California) tells the story, is "rapid, revolutionary change":

Just as the energies released by the discovery of gold put California into orbit with one mighty blast-off, so it has been kept spinning, faster and faster, by a succession of subsequent, providentially timed discoveries and "explosions" of one kind or another: the "green gold" of lettuce and other produce crops; . . . the "black gold" of oil; motion pictures, tourism, the aerospace industry. . . . California has raced through the familiar evolutionary cycle—pastoral, agricultural, industrial, post-industrial. . . .

The pace of technological change is matched by the societal. One out of every three California families moves each year (compared to one out of four in the U.S.A. as a whole); Californians change houses as other Americans change automobiles, forever searching for the better life on the other side of the freeway. Telephone and address books are forever out of date, the sense of impermanence overwhelming. California has become an unstratified society made up of communities of strangers; the sociologists speak of *anomie*, the state in which humans find themselves uprooted, drifting, and unfocused. Even the special-purpose communities by interest and age groups—retirement communities, swinging single colonies, college dormitory communities, not to mention income and racial ghettoes—fail to bring real cohesion and may in fact be symptomatic of the ills, since they accentuate the divisions in society. (There is no easier place to become a roaring John Bircher than in a golden-age community where one never has to come to grips with the young or minorities *as persons*; no better place to develop exaggerated hostilities about the whole society than in a student ghetto; no better place to become embittered about all honkies than in a black or Mexican quarter where the only whites seen are police or merchants.)

Californians, Neil Morgan observes in *California Syndrome*, have also built a civilization "quintessentially American," perhaps because they are a cross-section of Americans, or, as some insist, a selection of them. What America is, California is more so. As Wallace Stegner, an adopted Californian, wrote in 1959:

In a prosperous country, we are more prosperous than most; in an urban country, more urban than most; in a gadget-happy country, more addicted to gadgets; in a mobile country, more mobile; in a tasteless country, more tasteless; in a creative country, more energetically creative; in an optimistic society, more optimistic; in an anxious society, more anxious. Contribute regionally to the national culture? We *are* the national culture, at its most energetic end.

A few years later, Stegner was able to add to his list phenomena like air and water pollution, literary despair, increased leisure, the sexual revolution, widespread agnosticism, last-ditch religiosity, and Birchite reaction. "These are tunes that do not change when you cross the border into California," he noted. "Only the volume goes up, the tape spins faster, the tempo accelerates into a hysterical twittering." Today, the catalogue of California firsts and excesses could be broadened to include the age of student revolt and campus violence (dating from Berkeley in 1964), drugs and turned-off kids, alcoholism—850,000 afflicted by last count (the highest rate for any state except Nevada)—anti-university and anti-young politics (pioneered by Ronald Reagan), taxpayer rebellion against the welfare system, law-and-orderism and the political tug to the right, municipal radicalism (Berkeley in 1971), ghetto riots (starting with Watts in 1964) and guerilla warfare between the races, the Mexican-American awakening and organization of the nation's long-downtrodden farm workers, cybernetic politics (à la Spencer-Roberts), and the conservationists' demand to save not only the air and water but the whole natural environment (starting with the pioneer efforts of the Sierra Club).

And in a country swept by self-doubt, California seems to doubt the most. Pollster Don Muchmore told me that in his first surveys after World War II and up to the early 1960s, people were still excited about California and believed in its golden future like an article of faith. Since 1960, this has been replaced by creeping negativism, more doubt about the state's future, discontent with the taxes, and responsibilities that come with the trademarks of success (the bigger car, the lot, the house). "Instead of our state moving toward a cohesive unit, we're breaking into little pieces. There is little common belief of the people—not even in their own state," Muchmore said.

Of the millions who have poured into California in recent decades, a substantial portion has been from the Midwest.* But somehow, the new Californians quickly put Iowa and American Gothic behind them for what seems an easier life in the sun—yet a life, too, of frenetic economic activity. Thus California can at once demonstrate such startlingly different characteristics. This lotus land is also America's aerospace capital. Los Angeles may be the blandest great city ever built; San Francisco, with its wonderful spirit and élan, competes with Manhattan as America's most colorful. California is number one in the U.S.A. in think tanks, psychologists, aeronautical and eletrical engineers, mathematicians, Nobel Prize winners, and, of late, unemployed intelligentsia—a surfeit of the well-educated. It is a land of incredible creative energy. But it is also first or near the top in crime, drug addiction, suicide, divorce (Californians seem to exchange mates as readily as they do houses), homosexuality, and every other form of libidinal indulgence and aberration, not to mention bizarre religious cults and offbeat political movements, Black Pantherism, and hippieism. It may be the capital of the promising "Jesus Revolution" of the 1970s. California has half the backyard swimming pools in all the U.S.A., a fifth of the mobile homes, and is the top national market for pleasure boats, garbage disposals, frozen food, automobiles foreign and domestic, portable barbecues, and king-sized beds and water beds. As if this were not revealing enough, it can also be reported that California led America in the rush to such passing or permanent diversions as surfing, bikinis, topless/bottomless bars and restaurants, wife-swapping, communal living, drive-ins, dietetic foods, triple garages, second-home communities, credit cards, dune

* The North Central region of the country was the birthplace of 3.03 million California residents in the 1960 Census, compared to 2.20 million from the South, 1.07 million from the Northeast, and 1.22 million from other Western states.

buggies, campers, and drag strips. The comment of BBC producer John Morgan after a study of the state: Californians have "seen the future and it plays." There are some dissenters to that future; Nancy Banks-Smith wrote: "With a spot of luck, I hope to die before it happens!"

Wishing the future away won't do the trick, though, since it will come. The question is: Can California (and in turn, the rest of the U.S.A.) turn its brilliance and its playfulness to creative ends? Somehow the playfulness will have to find room for new social cohesion and human cooperation, perhaps abetted by great state leaders of a quality not seen since the days of Earl Warren. As for California's intellectual and technical brilliance, every ounce of it will be needed to cope with the perplexing problems of teeming cities, transportation, the environment. Along the Pacific reaches of the continent, the first and quite tentative steps have been taken to apply advanced systems analysis methods (pioneered in the aerospace industry) to such problems. So far, the payoff has been disappointingly small. But if such efforts fail substantially in the next few years, then not only California but all the U.S.A. could face a grim future in the quality of life it will have to lead in the closing years of this century, or the next. Old hit-and-miss U. S.-style problem solving will no longer do, for there are too many people, too many pent-up demands, and a vanished frontier.

Equally vital are the issues posed by ownership of such large swaths of California's private land by so few gigantic companies, the rapid spread of corporate farming, exorbitantly expensive water projects of principal benefit to a narrow few, ineffective pollution control, "freeway mania," corrupting campaign contributions, and the power of big landholders to compromise government at every level. Long apparent to thoughtful people in the state, these abuses were dramatized in a 1971 report of a Ralph Nader task force entitled "Land and Power in California," prepared under the direction of a 26-year-old Stanford graduate, Robert C. Fellmeth. The report was faulted by many for pejorative language, some factual errors, and lack of historic perspective. But it was filled with documentation. And as newsman Lou Cannon reported to the Ridder newspapers, the practices revealed by the task force are "the stuff of which crusades are made, or better yet, lawsuits. One doesn't have to buy Nader's moralistic view of California to believe that this report may be the best thing that's happened to the state in many years."

## *The Grand Tradition: Hiram Johnson to Earl Warren*

California long ago got the reputation of being a land of loony schemes and political extremes, an image which has stuck and somehow refuses to come unglued. It is common to talk of California as the state with the oddest political structure among the 50, although perhaps that sobriquet should be assigned to New York instead. And Herbert L. Phillips, retired dean of California political reporters, has warned: "The quest for orderliness [in California politics] has tempted many able scholars to undertake huge, solemn and painstaking chronological recitations, in the hope that political symmetry somehow would appear out of the fog. It seldom does."

With the reader properly forewarned, we begin a cursory review of the unfathomable.

The dominant themes of California politics are weak party organizations, the dominance of personalities, wide use of referendum and initiative, and maximum feasible nonpartisanship. All this came about as a reaction to what came before—the era of heavy-handed control by the railroad barons, stretching from 1870 to 1910, a control so complete it has been called "absolute dictatorship." As the state's largest landowner (thanks to the gift of alternate sections of land along the right of way made by the government), the Southern Pacific Railroad exercised monopolistic control of the principal means of transportation. It used every means, bribery the most prevalent, to control California politics for the purpose of enriching the corporate coffers.

The agent of reform was Hiram Warren Johnson, a fiery attorney whose father had been the chief lobbyist for Southern Pacific. Twice elected governor, in 1910 and 1914, Johnson then went on to the U. S. Senate, where he lived out the remainder of his turbulent days (to 1945). "Get the Southern Pacific Railroad out of politics!" Johnson bellowed in his 1910 campaign. When he won, he quickly secured passage of an arsenal of bills intended to cripple political machines and old-style patronage politics. Initiative, referendum, and recall were enacted, as well as nonpartisan election of judges, a cross-filing system for primaries, county home rule, and civil service throughout the state government. Other bills made the railroad commission into an effective regulatory body, controlled utilities and their rates, prohibited child labor, instituted workmen's compensation, and began many flood and conservation projects. Former President Theodore Roosevelt called the work of the 1911 legislature "the most comprehensive program of constructive legislation ever passed at a single session of an American legislature." It was the golden era of Progressive reform, and determined the character of California politics up to the present day. Turbulent California, as much as it has an historic memory, will never forget Hiram Johnson.

But a pleasant or easy man to get along with he was not. A fellow Senator once described him as "a bifurcated, peripatetic volcano, in perpetual eruption, belching fire and smoke." Physically, in Gladwin Hill's words, Johnson was "stocky and jowly, with a made-in-America face and gimlet eyes peering intently through rimless glasses," a man who "compensated for inner insecurity and chronic pessimism with vitriolic belligerence toward any opposition."

Johnson was a Republican but broke with the GOP in 1912 to run for Vice President on Theodore Roosevelt's Progressive ticket, and 20 years later he supported Franklin Roosevelt for President. In 1920, he was offered the Vice Presidency on the Republican ticket with Warren Harding, but refused;

had he accepted, he would have been President. As it was, he stayed on in the Senate, remaining a rabid isolationist, but never losing Californians' affection.

The not unfair criticism leveled against Johnson the reformer is that he threw out the baby of normal two-party operation with the bath water of corruption. "In its place," Hill wrote, "has evolved what might be called a politics of pragmatism—a milieu of opportunism and improvisation, in which party structures are weak, party loyalties are flimsy, 'party responsibility' is unknown, and in which continuity, in personalities and policies, is tenuous and electoral consistency is rare." The wonder is that under those conditions, a large share of able and moderate politicians, both Republican and Democratic, were able to mold in California one of the best state governments in history, remarkably honest and responsive during decades of chaotic growth.

By the 1920s, Progressivism had spent itself and a succession of regular Republican governors kept things on an even keel in Sacramento. The Depression, however, hit California especially hard, with high unemployment and severe strikes. Tens of thousands were on relief, and crops rotted in the field for lack of a market. In 1934, Upton Sinclair, the famous novelist and former Socialist nominee for governor, captured the Democratic gubernatorial nomination and shocked California with his "EPIC" platform—to End Poverty in California. Applying simple Marxist theory, Sinclair advocated turning over to workers some of the means of production—in this instance, the farms and factories of California idled by the Depression. The other elements of Sinclair's platform—graduated income taxes, state support of those unable to work, and a $50-a-month pension for the aged and widows—hardly sound revolutionary today. In desperate, Depression-time Californians, especially the aged without work or hope, they struck an instant spark. The propertied California "establishment" was horrified beyond description and poured a reported $10 million, more money than ever before or since spent on a California campaign, into the effort to stop Sinclair. Among other things, he was charged with being "an anarchist, a free-lover, an agent of Moscow, a Communist, an anti-Christ." In fact, Sinclair was a mild-mannered vegetarian with a searing belief in social justice, preaching ideas a few years ahead of his time. Eventually he was defeated by 259,000 votes, but only after giving the capitalist class the fright of its life.

Sinclair's EPIC was not the only strange idea to hit California in the mid-1930s. Another was Technocracy, a proposal to let the country be run by engineers and technicians; still another was the New England–born Utopian Society, which would have overthrown capitalism for a controlled society in which all work would be done in three hours a day by the working population 25 to 45 years of age. And soon, thousands of California oldsters were being attracted to the Townsend plan, authored by a retired Long Beach physician, Dr. Francis Townsend. He advocated $200-a-month pensions for all citizens over 60, financed by a 2-percent federal sales tax on all business. At one point, Townsend's clubs claimed 2.5 million members. After hitting their peak in 1936, they began a decline, only to be succeeded by the even more politically

potent "Ham & Eggs" movement, which offered pensions somewhat lower—
and thus more realistic—than Townsend's but picked up extra support by
dropping the minimum pension age to 50. The cost of Ham & Eggs would
have been a then-astronomical $30 million a week, but it gained wide support
(including that of organized labor) and was placed on the state's 1938 general election ballot by petitions which were signed by 789,000 voters, a full
quarter of the electorate. The plan was narrowly defeated, but the momentum
behind it helped carry into office the first Democratic governor of the century—Culbert Olsen, a Populist, foe of the oil companies, and party chairman
during the Sinclair campaign four years before. Olsen had visions of being an
historic reform governor like Johnson, but while he began some worthwhile
changes—the penal reform, for instance, which came to fruition under his successor—his record was largely an inept one, most of his ideas being brushed
aside by the legislature. In 1942, he lost decisively to one Earl Warren.

Earl Warren is the watershed figure of modern-day California politics,
the man who took the nonpartisanship of Hiram Johnson (whom he revered)
and gave it its ultimate expression; in a wider sense, he is the man who prepared California to become the nation it is today. No politician of modern
times has been so popular. Warren is the only man ever elected to three
terms as governor of California (in 1942, 1946, and 1950), the only man to
serve so long (almost 11 years), and the only gubernatorial candidate ever to
win the nominations of both parties (in 1946, before cross-filing was abol-
ished). In 1953, he resigned to accept President Eisenhower's appointment
as Chief Justice of the United States.

To the world, Earl Warren offered a wholesome, pleasant exterior, a big,
six-foot, 215-pound man exuding good-willed Americanism. No one ever
accused him of being a deep intellectual. But somehow, the man's basic instincts—political, judicial, moral—proved superb for his times. About the
only incident of a long state career for which Warren is still criticized in
California is his consenting to the wartime incarceration of 110,000 Japanese-
Americans—some 70,000 of them American citizens—in concentration
camps.

Warren showed amazing capacity for growth. For his start in politics, he
owed much to the hotly partisan Old Guard Republican faction headed by
the Oakland *Tribune* Knowland family. But he not only cross-filed when he
ran for state office but seemed to choose his cabinet and other chief officers
on the basis of capabilities, regardless of whether they were Republicans or
Democrats.

Warren's nonpartisanship drove doctrinaire Democrats and reactionary
Republicans to apoplexy, but it never failed at the ballot box. It even drew
the grudging admiration of President Truman, who once said of Warren:
"He's a Democrat—and doesn't know it." The specific list of things Warren
accomplished in California would seem to bear out Truman's assessment.
Among them were major advances in state welfare programs, including increased old age pensions and workmen's compensation, mental hospital and

prison reforms, a state crime commission (predating Senator Estes Kefauver's national investigation by several years), and enthusiastic backing of the Central Valley Project. Warren also showed a willingness to take on some of California's toughest lobbies, including oil and private power. Years before the idea of Medicare was raised in Washington, Warren fought for a general health insurance plan in California, to be financed by joint employer-employee contributions. It was one of the few big fights he ever lost.

One Warren program was peculiarly un-Democratic, however. It involved saving money. During the Depression days, the state treasury had been sorely strapped, and the budget was barely in the black when Warren took office. But the year was 1943, and since aircraft and other defense industries were burgeoning in California, and since the chief revenue methods, sales and income taxes, quickly reflected increases in economic activity, the state suddenly faced the pleasant miracle of tremendous annual surpluses. Herbert L. Phillips describes how Warren met the situation:

> As an alternative to haphazard disbursements, the Governor sponsored a policy of siphoning off into earmarked reserve funds every nickel of wartime treasury income in excess of the state's actual operating needs. . . . [He also] set up special wartime agencies to take inventory of California's accumulated needs, intelligently plan in advance for postwar reconstruction and indicate priorities for a multiplicity of scheduled statewide governmental building programs and public works expansions. Meantime, revenue poured into the treasury at such an unexampled pace that it was possible to authorize a temporary reduction in state tax rates. . . .
>
> In the middle 1940s, after Germany and Japan finally surrendered, releasing men and materials for nonmilitary use, the gigantic California melon was ripe to be cut. Hundreds of millions of dollars in reserve savings were appropriated for the rehabilitation of the state's long-neglected physical plant—the schools, colleges, prisons, hospitals and all the rest. Money was made available for district water projects. . . . Governmental retirement systems were refinanced. Local political subdivisions shared. . . .

Without Warren's hoarding of California's unexpected pot of gold in the 1940s, California might well have been unable to make the quantum jump in services indispensable to accommodating its fantastic postwar population inflow. Had the millions come anyway, one fears, they might have found chaos rather than the semblance of progress in the Golden State.

Even while Warren was scoring these accomplishments in California, some observers wrote him off as a genial extrovert. One of these was John Gunther in *Inside U.S.A.* "Earl Warren," he wrote, "is honest, likeable, and clean; he will never set the world on fire or even make it smoke; . . . he is a man who has probably never bothered with an abstract thought twice in his life . . ."

Yet in 1953, Warren went to the Supreme Court, and within less than a year had persuaded his fellow Justices to agree to a unanimous decision in the school desegregation case, doubtless the single most important decision of the court in modern times. And as the years went on, the "Warren court" assured itself a place in history by altering the basic thrust of American law in the fields of civil rights and liberties, the rights of the accused, and legislative apportionment. Thousands of Americans (including John Gunther) changed their minds about Earl Warren, dividing into camps of strong approval or bitter dissent.

## *Latter-Day Personalities*

Now to review some of the personalities who have crowded the klieg-lit stage of California politics in recent times:

RICHARD M. NIXON. Nixon's name must lead the list, for he was the first Californian since Herbert Hoover to win the Presidency. Nixon's personality and national record will be well known to the reader. His contribution to California is more difficult to discern, for he never held a state or local office. As a successful candidate for the U. S. House (1946, 1948) and Senate (1950), he was mainly known for the skilled way that he suggested communist or other radical tendencies in his liberal Democratic opponents. After his eight years as Eisenhower's Vice President and his defeat for President in 1960, Nixon returned to his native state, ran a race for governor in which he charged incumbent Edmund G. Brown with being less than hard on communists and of bungling the administration of the state, and lost by 296,758 votes. Then ensued Nixon's famous outburst at his "last press conference," his departure for a lucrative law practice in New York City, and Ronald Reagan's eclipse of him as the controlling Republican politician of California. Following his 1968 Presidential election, Nixon shifted his voting residence back from New York (to the "Western White House" at San Clemente). But except, perhaps, in Orange County, he was about as well liked or disliked in California as in any other place in the U.S.A. His intervention in the 1970 Senate campaign, in an attempt to save GOP Senator George Murphy (including a celebrated, disputed "rock throwing" incident at San Jose, which the Republicans tried to turn to their political advantage), proved singularly unsuccessful.

RONALD REAGAN. It is hard to imagine any other state that would take a veteran movie actor, without a day's experience in public office in his life, and elect him governor—and even harder to imagine that the player chosen would turn out to be one of America's most adept politicians, elected once by a plurality of close to one million votes, a second time by more than a half-million, and to be dark horse Presidential candidate of one wing of his party. California did all this with Ronald Reagan, native of Tampico, Illinois; graduate of Eureka College; Des Moines radio announcer; actor in 40 films (mostly B grade); a president of the Screen Actors Guild; onetime liberal Democrat (a cofounder, with Melvyn Douglas, of the state ADA); host for television's "General Electric Theatre"; conservative evangelizer for GE around the U.S.A.; and California cochairman for Barry Goldwater in 1964. From there, it was only two years and a careful cram-course in state government, arranged by Spencer-Roberts & Associates of Los Angeles, for Reagan to become the preeminent citizen politician, and then governor of the nation state.

Reagan's message in his first campaign was that it was time that something be done about runaway taxes, soaring welfare costs, the escalating crime rate, and violence on the campuses. Four years later, in 1970, California was worse off, if anything, in all those areas. The incumbent should have been in trouble, but he was not. For each evil, there was an appropriate villain. Taxes and high budgets were the fault of inflation and spendthrift legislators. High welfare costs were to be blamed on welfare cheaters, permissive social workers, and federal regulations that hamstrung California's cost-cutting program. Crime was the fault of judges, cop haters, bombers and Democratic legislators who resisted Reagan's law enforcement programs. Campus unrest was the fault of undisciplined students, rascally professors, and outside agitators. All these problems remained, but the voter could count on Reagan to stand between him and the unruly ones, to stop the outrage short of the patio gate. The natural political charm and telegenic appeal of the man, an aura of modesty even while being tough, of sounding liberal even while taking terribly illiberal positions, set Reagan apart from other conservative leaders—and in tone, if not in substance, from his wealthy, right-wing backers. The engaging smile, the soft-spoken aura of "how can you question my motives?", of utter reasonableness and occasional put-upon-ness, all superbly transmitted by television, made Reagan a unique commodity among American politicians.

Reagan was fortunate, however, that his reelection to a second term preceded by several months the revelation that he paid no California state income tax for 1970. Someone in the state tax office apparently leaked the fact to the press, and Ronald Reagan, the man who had campaigned against withholding on the ground that "taxes should hurt," and who earned $76,500 in salary and perquisites in 1970, was forced to make a lame explanation that because of "business reverses," he had not paid a penny to the state. But he refused to divulge the nature of his business holdings (saying reporters should be "ashamed" of themselves for delving into personal matters). The New York *Times* reported in June 1971 that Reagan may have been spared tax paying by joining other wealthy persons in using a legal "tax shelter," based on the preferential treatment given by the tax laws to owners of cattle herds.

What actual record, behind the image, was Reagan making? He had appointed some top-drawer men to the judiciary, and his tax reform package, rejected by the legislature, at least incorporated the sound principle of taxing income more and property less. In his first year in office, he had the courage to ask for $946 million in new taxes, though the rapidly escalating budget gave him little choice. Long opposed philosophically to payroll tax withholding for income taxes—he declared early in his administration that he was "locked in concrete" on the issue and only "hot irons" pressed to his feet could make him change his mind—he finally relented and withholding went into effect in January 1972. The fundamental problem of California government has been deadlock between Reagan and the legislature. As Tom Goff, the Los Angeles *Times* Sacramento bureau chief, reported early in 1972:

> Both legislative houses are narrowly and, therefore, ineffectively dominated by Democrats who see state government as an instrument for social and economic change.
>
> They are countered by a determined conservative Republican governor who sees all government as a stumbling block to progress—almost an evil plague which must be fought to a standstill if man is to survive. The governor, Ronald Reagan, has been able to block virtually every attempt by Democrats to expand the role of state government. His weapons have been the veto and an almost unprecedented ability to control the votes of the members of his own party in the legislature.
>
> Most of the cutbacks and economies Reagan has effected have been by administrative edict. Many of those have been overturned by the courts as being contrary to law.

The net result, Goff noted, has been "stagnation" in state government, a state of affairs likely to last until the voters do something to break the deadlock.

In many respects, Reagan seemed like a "breather" governor, as Eisenhower was a "breather" President for the U.S.A. in the 1950s. But where Ike had been a healing influence, Reagan deliberately scorned and alienated minorities in his society—browns and blacks, the students, and the poor—to create his political majority. A widespread feeling that Reagan favored the wealthy over the poor, plus the publicity about his state tax return and adverse reaction to his record on property taxes, welfare, and education, were said to be factors in a precipitous drop in his personal popularity reflected in the public opinion polls in 1971–72. Mervin Field, the state's leading pollster, said: "He has polarized Democrats, the education and welfare people, state employees, and even some Republicans. What he offered was style—the citizen on detached duty—but there was an implied promise that he would solve problems. When he didn't, it created trouble."

A prime example of Reagan's attitude toward the unfortunate in society was his 1970 veto of the federal grant for the California Rural Legal Assistance Agency. CRLA had begun in 1966 after César Chávez and his farm workers' union focused attention on the problems of the rural poor. Tens of thousands of indigent Californians were able to turn to CRLA offices for help. But local power structures and especially the big farmers, which include key Reagan supporters, were enraged, and he exerted heavy political pressure on the Nixon administration in Washington to have the whole program killed. Despite repeated high-level reports exonerating CRLA of wrongdoing and praising its work, its long-term future remained much in doubt.

Discussing Reagan's short supply of creative solutions to California's multitudinous problems, political editor Richard Bergholz of the Los Angeles *Times* commented to me: "Reagan has not been an especially good governor, but then again he has been better than a lot of people thought he would be. What troubles me is that so little has been done specifically about the state's long-range problems. What has the state really done to come to grips with smog and water pollution, transit and parks, open space and land planning?

When the Reagan image is forgotten, what will his actual record look like 20 or 30 years from now?"

EDMUND G. ("PAT") BROWN. A native of San Francisco (where he was born in 1905, a year before the great earthquake and fire), Brown knocked down two great Republican heavies to win two terms as governor—William F. Knowland in 1958, Richard M. Nixon in 1962. On a third-term try, Ronald Reagan proved his nemesis. Brown was a moderate Democrat and often shunned partisanship on the model of Earl Warren and the Republican who succeeded Warren from 1953 to 1959, Goodwin Knight. He rose to power as Warren had done—as a crime fighter and attorney general—but he lacked any measure of the glamour of his more famous opponents. But he was an honest, capable administrator, and the Republicans also obliged by helping to defeat themselves.

With the hindsight of the early 1970s, Brown emerges as the last of California's governors who could or did believe that growth in itself was a desirable end. While Brown was in office, the great (and now, it appears, possibly unnecessary) $1.7 billion California Water Plan was passed. Some 1,000 miles of freeway, now seen as mitigated blessings, were constructed. In terms of Brown's times, these were great achievements. His years in office also saw the first major overhaul of the executive branch in 30 years, abolition of the troublesome cross-filing system in primaries, and creation of California's first fair employment practices commission. The universities and schools made great strides, and the state began to invest more in aid for the needy aged and in mental care facilities.

WILLIAM F. KNOWLAND. Big Bill Knowland, once aptly called "the Lone Moose," still lives in Oakland, publishing his family newspaper, and, by latest reports, taking a conciliatory position on black-white relations in that troubled city. It is a new role for Knowland, former U. S. Senator (1945–59), the inflexible conservative who succeeded Robert Taft as Senate Republican Leader. In 1958, Knowland almost caused the ruination of the California GOP when he returned to California determined to run for governor in a thinly disguised move to position himself for the 1960 Republican Presidential nomination. Governor Knight, planning to run that year, had to be forced out of the race and persuaded to run for Knowland's Senate seat instead. The game of musical chairs offended the voters, as did Knowland's conscious, strong partisanship and his identification with the "right-to-work" proposition on the 1958 ballot. Knowland went crashing down to defeat by a margin of more than one million votes, while Knight, forced into a Senate race he had not sought, lost by 723,000.

JESS UNRUH. Jesse M. Unruh, the man whom Reagan defeated to win a second term as governor in 1970, was born the youngest of five children of an illiterate and impoverished Kansas sharecropper, grew up in Texas, hitch-hiked to California at 18 with five dollars in his pocket, and became the speaker of the state assembly at 39. Unruh has appeared in three quite disparate incarnations since the late 1950s. First, he was "Big Daddy" Unruh, the heavy-drinking, cigar-smoking, 290-pound, five-foot-nine-inch speaker of the assembly, ruthlessly making and breaking bills and other politicians' careers through his absolute power over committee memberships and connections with fund-providing lobbyists. In those early years, Unruh uttered two harsh dicta still remembered: "Money is the mother's milk of politics," and, speaking of lobbyists: "If you can't take their money, drink their booze, screw their women, and look them in the eye and vote against them, you don't belong here."

Starting about 1963, Unruh entered a new stage. During that year, he had foolishly invoked a little-used parliamentary rule to have Republican assemblymen opposing him on a bill locked up in the chamber for 23 hours. "The Lockup," as it became known, generated bales of bad publicity for "Big Daddy." At the same time, Unruh was becoming concerned about his image, especially after a political cartoon that depicted him as a fat Buddha. So he cut way back on the Scotch and martinis and undertook a rigorous non-starch diet that had his weight down 100 pounds in a few months. He remained a powerful politician, but turned his attention increasingly in two directions: shaping the assembly into the most professional, best-staffed legislative house in the United States, and becoming a national authority and lecturer on state legislatures and government. He succeeded brilliantly in both pursuits, acting as a consultant for the Eagleton Institute at Rutgers and winning election in 1966 as head of the National Conference of State Legislative Leaders.

The third incarnation began in the Ambassador Hotel in Los Angeles the night that Bobby Kennedy was shot. Unruh had been an early supporter of John F. Kennedy in 1960 and was heading Robert Kennedy's slate in the 1968 California primary. Unruh was only a few feet away when Sirhan Sirhan shot the Senator, and later said: "I nearly went crazy." He said he found that Kennedy's death taught him "a sense of high-risk politics," persuading him to abandon the "cautious, close-to-the-vest" politics of his middle years in a return to the less cautious idealism of his youth. At the Chicago convention that summer, leading the Kennedy delegation chosen in the primary, Unruh eschewed all strong-arm tactics, ran the delegation in a democratic manner, and won national notice by his clear dissent from the brutal manner in which the convention was run.

That fall, Democrats lost control of the assembly, making Unruh into minority leader instead of speaker. In 1970, came the showdown in the gubernatorial contest with the highly popular—and strongly favored—Reagan. Unruh was strapped for campaign funds—a result of wealthy Democrats' deep resentments about his refusal to support Governor Brown, with whom he often feuded, for reelection in 1966, and his late endorsement of Humphrey in 1968. (Final reports indicated Unruh had contributions of $887,822 to run his campaign, compared to a Reagan total of $2,200,223.) Unruh ran a Populist-style, "give-'em-hell" campaign in the style of Harry Truman in 1948, painting Reagan as the creature of "half-hidden millionaires" who Unruh said were running the state for their own private interest. Lacking money for television, Unruh would take along a busload of TV newsmen to "events" such as an uninvited appearance before the home of Reagan-backer Henry Salvatori, charging on camera that the wealthy oilman would benefit from Reagan's tax reform package. The tactic did get attention, and there was doubtless merit in many of his charges, but may also have detracted from the dignity of Unruh the candidate.* Only time would tell whether his new Populism could really tie together the "little people" of California in a revolt against wealthy, Republican-led government. With unemployment drawing voters back to the Democratic line, Unruh did hold Reagan to half his plurality in the 1966 race against Brown. If the California press had not prematurely discounted Unruh's viability as a candidate, he might have come much closer.

MAX RAFFERTY. In Rafferty, state superintendent of public instruction from 1963 to 1971, California produced an extraordinarily contentious and publicized education chief. California in the postwar era was faced with the problem of creating virtually one school a day, accommodating growing minority group enrollments with special education problems, and cutting down on an alarmingly high school dropout rate. "War babies" reached school age before localities were equipped to deal with them, thousands of school bond issues had to be passed, and a teacher shortage had to be met. At first all the initiatives were left to an in-group of professional educationalists who had formulated state policy under a string of "prestige superintendents," working hand-in-hand with a powerful teachers' lobby, since the early 1920s. In the late 1950s and early '60s, protests began to mount about the way school districts were shortchanging students in favor of high pay for teachers (at average wages second only to Alaska). Sputnik aroused concern about the quality of education, and social tensions in the schools began to mount. So did the percentage of voter rejections of new school bond issues.

Rafferty, a bombastic, ultraconservative, no-nonsense academician, burst onto the scene in the 1962 state superintendent's race on a platform denouncing "permissive, pragmatic progressivism" in the schools. In a close election, he beat a liberal opponent and began a divisive eight years in office during which he dwelt on issues like sex education, drugs, and school busing, adding much heat but little light to solution of California's education dilemmas. Fortunately, the legislature was authorizing a number of innovative new programs and the state board of education moved ahead with new approaches in math, sciences, and social sciences, plus a reform in the training of teachers that culminated with abolition of education as a major in California's colleges.

In 1968, Rafferty made a bid for higher office by challenging liberal U. S. Sen. Thomas H. Kuchel in the Republican primary. The campaign was a right-wing classic, in which Rafferty said Kuchel had failed to deal with "the

---

* Lou Cannon, author of the excellent book *Ronnie and Jesse—A Political Odyssey*, wrote in his *California Journal* column during the 1970 campaign that voters were "not idiots" and couldn't be expected to buy Unruh's "half-hidden millionaires" thesis because "it requires people to distrust Reagan's motivations. . . . Unruh, of all people, should have known better. Only the really bum politicians are used by the very rich. The good politicians, and Unruh used to be a very good one, use the rich to accomplish their own ends, which is one of Unruh's best rebuttals to the criticisms of his own legislative career."

four deadly sins" he saw confronting the U.S.—violence, pornography, drugs, and lawlessness. Among other things, Rafferty said it was time to "stop naming social reformers, political hacks, and child-marrying mountain climbers to the Supreme Court." He narrowly beat Kuchel, but lost the general election.

In 1970, Rafferty ran for a third term as superintendent and was a strong early favorite in a year when the voters were said to be already aroused about busing, drugs, and "permissiveness." But apparently the rhetoric had lost its appeal. Rafferty was challenged and defeated that year by Dr. Wilson C. Riles. Riles for six years headed the multimillion-dollar California compensatory education program, winning the reputation among professionals of being the best administrator of federal "Title One" moneys in the entire U.S. Riles said Rafferty had turned teachers, parents, and school boards against each other with a surfeit of inflammatory rhetoric and demagoguery. Riles's own image was that of a cool professional, who seemed to be talking sense about financing the schools, making them more accountable to the people, and pouring more money and energy into the vital area of early (preschool) education. Many thought the fact that Riles was a Negro would preclude his election. But it did not, as he defeated Rafferty with a plurality of close to a half-million votes (54.1 percent).*

At least a million voters, it appeared, had voted for Reagan and Riles on the same day. The results made one wonder about any neat ideological pigeonholing of the California voter. Even Orange and San Diego Counties —the only two heavily populated counties in the U.S. to go for Goldwater in 1964—gave Riles a respectable share of their vote (46 and 49 percent respectively). Riles carried Los Angeles County by 53 percent and then swamped Rafferty in Northern California with majorities like 63 percent in San Francisco and 65 percent in suburban Marin and Santa Clara counties. In 1968, it may be recalled, Wallace got only 6.7 percent of the California vote, less than in states like Illinois, Michigan, Ohio, and Pennsylvania.

The Rafferty sun seems finally to have set in California; after the 1970 election he went off to Alabama to teach.

The California canvas is so broad one could go on and on with a parade of personalities. In large measure because of their poor Republican opposition, two Democrats now hold the state's U. S. Senate seats—Alan Cranston, first head of the California Democratic Clubs, now in his late 50s, and John V. Tunney, former Congressman and son of the ex-heavyweight boxing champion Gene Tunney, a man in his mid-30s. Both men have served too briefly (Cranston since 1969, Tunney since 1971) to make a major mark in the Senate. Both were suspected of being lightweights when they first arrived in Washington but have begun to establish some legislative specialties and earn respect from their colleagues and the press. They have identical 92-percent favorable ratings on their Senate votes from Americans for Democratic Action, but both also know well how to take a less-than-liberal position to

---

* To Rafferty's credit, it must be recorded that he promoted more members of ethnic minorities to high posts than any previous state superintendent. It was a marvelous irony that one of them beat him.

defend California aerospace or agribusiness. Tunney, many believe, may now be the most powerful single person in the California Democratic party. Now gone from the Senate is Thomas H. Kuchel, a Republican in the Warren tradition, who was Republican Whip until Max Rafferty upset him in the 1968 primary; Cranston then seized the middle of the road and easily defeated Rafferty in the general election.

Considering its size, California's big House delegation (increased from 30 in the 1950s to 43 in the 1970s) has not made a major impact in Washington. Some of its members have stood out on occasion, however. Among Democrats, Chet Holifield, dean of the delegation, has served with distinction as chairman of the Joint Committee on Atomic Energy despite some run-ins with conservationists on the issue of hazards from atomic power generation. In 1971, he took over chairmanship of the Government Operations Committee and proceeded to rule in an arbitrary and highhanded manner by abolishing subcommittees that had taken a special interest in consumer affairs and the invasion of privacy. George Miller has been chairman of the House Science and Astronautics Committee for several years. B. F. Sisk, a powerful member of the Rules Committee, handled the 1970 Congressional Reform Bill on the floor and the next year ran for House Majority Leader; his district, including part of the Central Valley, tends to make him conservative and grower-oriented. Another Central Valley Congressman, John E. Moss, won a measure of fame for the Freedom of Information Act he authored. Phillip Burton, from San Francisco, has been a leader in welfare legislation, and, according to my friend Lou Cannon, who covers Capitol Hill for the Ridder papers, "one of the few Congressmen who'd rather have the bill than the credit." Another Bay Area Democrat, Jerome P. Waldie, is a tough, brainy man with driving ambition who dared early in the game to suggest (while his colleagues maintained discreet silence) that it was time for aging House Speaker John W. McCormack to retire. Waldie is also a major opponent of the State Water Plan because of what he says would be its disastrous ecological effects. He intends to run for governor in 1974, and it should be a colorful campaign. Finally, mention should be made of James C. Corman of Los Angeles, a key operative in passage of several of the major civil rights bills of the 1960s, and Thomas M. Rees, also of Los Angeles, who like Waldie was willing to buck the old House leadership, campaign against the Vietnam war, and take a strong role in environmental reform.

Most powerful among Republicans is H. Allen Smith of Pasadena, ranking member of his party on the Rules Committee. Smith's philosophy of government seems several degrees to the right of Herbert Hoover, but he is a key negotiator with younger members of Congress, even those he disagrees with, and he has taken an interest in some aspects of congressional reform. (Smith has announced his retirement from Congress, as of January 1973.) Charles S. Gubser of the Bay Area is a conservative who believes his party must modernize itself in many areas; he has been active in air pollution control and in parks and rules legislation, and coauthored the proposal to make public teller votes in the House. Craig Hosmer of Long Beach is a leading

Republican hawk and his party's ranking member on Joint Atomic Energy; William Mailliard of San Francisco is considered a leading House authority on maritime issues. San Diego's Bob Wilson, an old Nixon intimate, wields great potential power as chairman of the National Republican Congressional Committee, a group which hands out millions of dollars to Republican House candidates across the country in each election. One of the more liberal Republicans, Alphonso Bell of Los Angeles, will probably become his party's ranking member on the Science and Astronautics Committee in 1973.

Finally, the Republican delegation includes the remarkable figure of Paul N. (Pete) McCloskey, Jr., the ex-Marine who was decorated for "extraordinary heroism" in the Korean War and broke into politics by sinking the good ship *Lollipop*, Mrs. Shirley Temple Black, in a 1967 special election for a seat from San Mateo County, south of San Francisco. McCloskey suddenly became a national figure in 1971 when he announced he might run for President unless President Nixon stopped the "demeaning and cowardly" use of air power in Indochina and "hiring" South Vietnamese "mercenaries to do our dying for us." (He did run in the 1972 New Hampshire primary, receiving 20 percent of the vote; after that he abandoned his active Presidential candidacy.) McCloskey believes that "the American political process depends on people willing to lose their seats and offices to do what's right. I think we have to prove to young people that politics is an honorable profession."

## Innovative Politics

Hiram Johnson invented and Earl Warren institutionalized a lot of devices to make California's politics unique among the states, but even after them California has been busy on innovations the rest of the country may pick up later. Some prime examples of the old and new:

INITIATIVE AND REFERENDUM. California has one of the nation's best legislatures, but the people trust it the least. Since 1911, when initiative and referendum were written into the state constitution, almost 500 consitutional changes and 65 new statutes have been placed on the ballot for the people to decide on, not to mention referendums on about 35 laws already passed by the legislature. Initiatives can go on the ballot by vote of the legislature, or by popular petition of a set percentage of the state's voters. In Johnson's day, it took about 30,000 signatures to put an initiative on the ballot; now close to 500,000 are required, and signature-gathering has become a big business at an average of 25¢ a head. For 500,000 signatures, that is a lot of money. "Whatever its noble origins," L. A. *Times* columnist Art Seidenbaum has written, "the initiative has lately become the most questionable single entry on an interminable ballot; instead of being responsive to the grass roots, it may now be a device for special interests, interests wealthy enough first to buy their way into an election and then to seduce the voters with come-on advertising."

The focus of initiatives on the ballot has changed over time. In the first decade, many proposals dealt with moral and economic problems such as prohibition, prize fighting, compulsory vaccination, and the eight-hour day. In the 1920s, several dealt with public education (in an attempt to get the state to shoulder a greater cost burden). The voters also forced the state to adopt an executive budget, still hailed by many as the initiative's greatest accomplishment. The 1930s saw the focus turn to the various pension plans; Ham & Eggs alone made it to the ballot five times between 1938 and 1948. In 1948, an initiative organized by George McLain and his senior citizen followers was passed; it actually appeared to transfer control of social welfare money to McLain himself, and was undone in the next election. The biggest battle of the 1950s was over "Right to Work," on which proponents reported spending $954,389 to win its passage and organized labor countered with $2,556,037 in the successful effort to defeat it.

In 1964, the people approved two initiatives, only to have them found unconstitutional thereafter. One was the famous Proposition Fourteen to repeal the Rumford Housing Act, an open housing statute the legislature had approved. Out of fear of a black neighbor, perhaps with a dash of free-enterprise, the people approved the proposition by a 2–1 margin. But the NAACP filed suit charging the proposition constituted state action for discriminatory practices, in violation of the 14th Amendment of the U. S. Constitution; the California and U. S. Supreme Courts, in turn, upheld the NAACP. The other, Proposition Seventeen, outlawed pay television. Its supporters, notably movie theater owners who feared empty seats if people could pay to see more sports and theatrical events at home, spent $1.9 million to put it across. For no apparent reason, save their ignorance and confusion, the voters approved the move, but the courts reversed it on constitutional grounds.

A bewildering array of propositions greet the voter each election day. In 1966, there were 16 on the state ballot; in 1970, exactly 20. The subject matter in those elections ranged from regulation of chiropractors to how farmland should be taxed, regulation of boxing and wrestling, and a constitutionally dubious amendment to suppress "obscenity" which the voters, *mirabile dictu*, voted down.

RECALL. Also enacted by Johnson and his followers in 1911, recall has been used frequently in local elections. There have been aborted recall movements against governors, none ever coming to a vote.

LOCAL NONPARTISANSHIP. The state constitution requires nonpartisan elections for all county and municipal offices. The result is quite simple: no local partisan "machines" in the style known to the East and Midwest; rarely, if ever, a serious election fraud; an entrenched civil service often indifferent to elected officials and new policies they may try to effect.

CROSS-FILING. From 1913 until its repeal in 1959, California's partisan elections (Congress, governor, legislature, etc.) were held under this curious device, one that lets members of each party run in the other party's primary as well. Until 1952, party designations did not even appear beside candidates' names on the primary ballots. The most famous of all the cross-filers was Earl

Warren, who thus won both parties' gubernatorial nominations in 1946 and didn't even have to compete in the general election. But Warren was not alone. Between 1914 and 1950, the offices of attorney general, secretary of state, and controller were won in the primary in seven out of 10 elections. Often the nonincumbent party despaired of winning an office and ran no candidate at all; in 1944, for instance, 12 of 20 state senate seats went by default (one candidate only), six were determined in contested primaries, and only two were decided in the general election. But after 1952, when a new law went into effect requiring a "Rep." or "Dem." beside each candidate's name, things changed rapidly. In 1952, with no party designation, 14 out of 30 congressional races were won in the primary by cross-filed or unopposed candidates; in 1954 the number fell to two.

Cross-filing was accused throughout its half-century career of crippling strong or well-organized parties and thus undermining any real party responsibility. It gave rise to auxiliary, or volunteer, party groups, for the purpose of making endorsements (of which more later); perpetuated "incumbent empires"; and, in the words of political scientist Totten J. Anderson, led to the "loss of partisan identification with issues of public policy, since candidates campaigned under a 'middle-of-the-road' banner, often refusing to identify themselves publicly with any party."

And intrinsically, cross-filing worked to the advantage of the Republicans. California has long had many more registered Democrats than Republicans, so a GOP contender always benefited from having any attention removed from the partisan issue. And since Republicans were long able to get preferential press treatment in major California newspapers, they tended to be better known to the voters.

Wisely for their self-interest, the Democrats repealed cross-filing, once and for all, when they had control of both the governorship and both houses of the legislature in 1959. The result, in almost everyone's view, has been to make California politics conform more to a national norm than at any time since Hiram Johnson arrived on the scene. Partisanship, for instance, has been growing by leaps and bounds in California, as voting patterns in recent legislative sessions show.

VOLUNTEER GROUPS. Progressive-era legislation so closely circumscribed the legal activities of the regular political parties—even forbidding them to make pre-primary endorsements—that volunteer or extralegal party groups naturally sprang into being. The first was the California Republican Assembly, formed in 1934–35 by a group including Earl Warren, to improve the party's organizational efforts and make pre-primary endorsements. Part of the goal was to revive the party and wrest control from Old Guard reactionaries, thought responsible for the party's losses. CRA became a kind of elite party organ, always with a fairly limited membership (never over 25,000). In various years it helped Warren get elected governor and gave Goodwin Knight and Richard Nixon their starts in California politics. Warren "willed" CRA to Sen. William Knowland when he left for Washington in 1953, but modern Republicans remained influential. The bitter GOP infighting of 1958 virtually immobilized CRA; in 1964, the Goldwaterites took control, hastening its decline. Gladwin Hill reported in 1968 that CRA had "deteriorated into a strident right-wing splinter claiming 12,000 adherents," competing with United Republicans of California, a right-wing spinoff with 9,000 members.

The Democrats' counterpart—the California Democratic Council (CDC), a federation of Democratic clubs—got started in 1953, 19 years later than CRA. But it made even more of a splash in state and nation. CDC's inspirer was the late Adlai E. Stevenson, its ideology left-wing with a bent for participatory politics, its main activity endorsing candidates for office. Hundreds of clubs were chartered and membership eventually rose to close to 100,000. CDC conventions were never afraid to take controversial positions on public issues, often causing no little embarrassment for Democratic officeholders. But the publicity was magnificent—in many years, CDC conventions were the biggest Democratic gatherings in the U.S., complete with delegates, emotional oratory, and maneuvering. In 1958, CDC hit its zenith when all but one of the statewide candidates it endorsed were elected. One of them was CDC's first president, Alan Cranston, former head of the United World Federalists, who got elected state controller. Now he is a U. S. Senator.

CDC has always had its problems, however. For one thing, professional Democratic politicos like Jess Unruh (until a latter-day conversion) viewed with disdain what they considered CDC's amateurism and ideological excesses. In 1964, Unruh helped fashion a bitter defeat for the CDC by backing for the U. S. Senate former White House Press Secretary Pierre Salinger in place of the CDC's Cranston. Two years later, CDC president Simon Cassady struck out at President Johnson and his war policies with such vitriol that Governor Brown felt obliged to force his removal; some believe CDC never recovered from that internal struggle. By 1970, CDC had declined to less than 10,000 members, a thin shadow of its former self. Its endorsements were scarcely taken seriously by major candidates.

What had happened? Lou Cannon (who believes the CDC "was never as powerful as it thought it was and isn't as impotent now as some critics would like to think") says the demise of cross-filing deprived CDC of its basic reason for existence. Without cross-filing, Democrats no longer needed a special mechanism to keep Republicans from gaining Democratic endorsements.

DECEPTIVE REGISTRATION FIGURES. For decades, Democrats have had a substantial majority of major party registrations in California; the Republicans' recent high-water mark was 42.4 percent in 1967, a figure which has since declined. The January 1972 figures:

| | | |
|---|---|---|
| Democratic | 4,448,986 | 55.2% |
| Republican | 3,127,929 | 38.8 |
| American Independent | 43,376 | .5 |
| Peace and Freedom | 47,785 | .6 |
| La Raza Unida | 20,543 | .3 |
| Miscellaneous, Declined to state | 363,996 | 4.5 |

This does not mean that the Democrats automatically win elections. As someone cracked, California is that state where "party loyalty is about as prevalent as chastity." Many who list themselves as Democrats are Southerners registering in the party of their forefathers; many were New Deal Democrats and remain registered that way out of pure inertia. What's more, California Republicans turn out a much greater share of their registrants on election day (84 percent in the 1966 election, for instance, in comparison to 77 percent of the Democrats). And Republicans have the big business backing which makes it possible for them to outspend the Democrats consistently in state and local elections, although the unions, when aroused, can even the score to some extent. (Labor leaders like Sig Arywitz, who heads the Los Angeles County Federation of Labor, claim they did a major job in converting Wallace votes into Humphrey votes in the closing stages of the 1968 campaign and that labor was "the backbone" of the Humphrey campaign in the state. When unemployment zoomed under the Nixon administration, labor was able to play a crucial role in returning both houses of the legislature to Democratic control in the 1970 elections. But labor's political effectiveness is hampered by the increasing independence of unionists in good times, and also by the low number of unionists registered to vote—only 42 percent of organized labor's Los Angeles County membership, for instance.)

Despite their disability in registrations, the Republicans have done very well for themselves in gubernatorial and state legislature elections over the years. Since the turn of the century, the Democrats have won only three elections for governor (Olson in 1938, Brown in 1958 and 1962). Both houses of the legislature have been under Republican control for most of this century, with three years of Democratic interregnum in the Senate in the late 1930s and then a Democratic sweep of both chambers in 1958 that kept the GOP out in the cold for a full decade. Late in the 1960s, the Republicans made a comeback in both houses, only to lose out again in 1970—a crucial loss, since they were then denied control when congressional and state legislative district lines were being drawn up for the decade of the 1970s. (The 1970 defeat was especially crushing for the Republicans, who had invested years of planning and millions of dollars in a concerted campaign to get control of the 1971–72 legislature, and thus, they hoped, California for the decade of the 1970s. As it turned out, the Democratic-controlled legislature passed a legislative redistricting plan which Governor Reagan promptly vetoed, leading the state supreme court to order use of the old districts until a new plan could be devised and agreed upon before the 1974 elections. A new congressional districting bill, generally protecting the 38 incumbent U.S. House members and dividing the five new seats apportioned to the state between the parties, was also vetoed by Reagan. But the state supreme court ordered it into effect anyway.)

Both California parties—Republicans after the 1950 Census, Democrats after the 1960 Census—have shown themselves masters of the art of gerrymandering. In 1952, for instance, the GOP was able to win 63 percent of the state's congressional seats with 54 percent of the statewide House vote; in 1962, after they had gerrymandered, the Democrats got 66 percent of the seats with 53 percent of the vote.

No matter how carefully a party gerrymanders, however, and no matter how firmly it seems ensconced in the executive chambers of Sacramento, the voters after a while will turn it out. High intrastate mobility upsets the complexion of districts, and "safe" districts rapidly become marginal. A highly competitive, two-party system is alive and well in California today, and seems likely to remain that way.

In fact, California's political behavior is much closer to that of the entire U.S.A. than people recognize. As Richard M. Scammon and Ben J. Wattenberg point out in *The Real Majority:*

> California, viewed psephologically, is not really atypical, screwballs notwithstanding. . . . California is known as an excellent *barometric* state. Among large states, Illinois and California are the two that vote most consistently like America as a whole. Since 1948 California has never been more than two percentage points away from the final national percentage for the Presidential winner.

Will California continue to be a barometric state? The extension of the vote to 18-through-20-year-olds could move it a degree or two to the left, perhaps even more so than the rest of the country because of the state's heavy youth population. Of the 11.2 million new potential voters under 21 in the U. S. A. in 1972, 1.2 million will be in California alone. They will represent 8 percent of the entire California eligible electorate of 14,237,000. A little arithmetic applied to some not impossible assumptions indicates a potentially decisive impact. If 60 percent of the youths register to vote, and two-thirds of them vote Democratic for President, the Democrats will experience a net gain of 233,000 votes in California.* It should be remembered that Nixon carried California against Humphrey by only 223,346 votes in 1968, and against an even more youthful John F. Kennedy by only 35,623 in 1960. Thus the youth vote has the potentiality of wiping out the entire Republican plurality.

PRESIDENTIAL PRIMARIES. Popular election of national convention delegate slates was another one of Hiram Johnson's ideas and early enactments. But despite 60 years of use, the California Presidential primary—up to now, in any event—has rarely played a crucial role in a nomination fight. This is because any Presidential candidate must consent to having a slate of delegates pledged to him entered in the primary. Since California itself so often has a "favorite son," out-of-state candidates hesitate to enter the primary, with the result that the contest is meaningless.

* Organizers of the California Campus Coalition, which has registrars working on campuses throughout the state, claim that 18–20 year olds are registering Democratic in a 3–1 ratio, and 21–25 years olds in a 5–2 Democratic ratio. A rise of general political interest in California was reflected in the total of 1,347,000 new voters added to the rolls in 1971, compared to 406,000 in 1963 and 558,000 in 1967, the last two pre-Presidential election years.

There have been three crucial postwar primaries, however. In the 1956 Democratic primary, Adlai Stevenson's slate defeated one pledged to Estes Kefauver by a margin of better than 2–1. Stevenson's nomination up to that point had been quite uncertain; after California it was almost assured. Likewise, in the Republican primary of 1964, Goldwater got 51.6 percent of the vote, Rockefeller 48.4 percent. This was the primary that knocked Rockefeller out of the Presidential race and insured Goldwater's nomination. But in the fall election, Goldwater lost California to President Johnson by 1.3 million votes.

The 1968 Democratic primary featured a close fight between Senators Robert F. Kennedy of New York and Eugene J. McCarthy of Minnesota. Kennedy, who had lost a key race to McCarthy in Oregon just seven days before, needed a victory to restore his "winner's image" and prepare him for the decisive convention contest with Vice President Hubert H. Humphrey. Kennedy did win, by a margin of 140,000 votes out of 3.1 million cast. But just after acknowledging the cheers of his supporters in a Los Angeles hotel, Kennedy was shot to death.

The assassination of the young Senator, brother of slain President John F. Kennedy, was to be of momentous import. With his death, Hubert Humphrey's nomination was virtually decided—and with it, the possibility of any rapprochement of the Humphrey regulars with the left wing of the Democratic party that might have lessened the violence in Chicago and put the Democrats in better position for the fall election. As it was, Nixon's national lead over Humphrey slipped from 16 points in midsummer polls to practically zero by election day; his final plurality of 510,315 votes (0.7 percent) would be one of the narrowest of the century. California itself went for Nixon by a plurality of 223,346 votes—3.1 percentage points; without the state's 40 electoral votes, Nixon would have lacked the electoral vote majority required for election, thus throwing the election open to bargaining with Wallace's electors or decision by the House of Representatives.

Reagan in 1968 used the "favorite son delegation" device to freeze other candidates out of the Republican Presidential primary. Twice in the late 1960s, bills were passed by the legislature to establish an open Presidential primary along the lines of the Oregon law, with voters permitted to express a preference among all nationally recognized Presidential candidates. Such a shift would automatically make California *the* crucial test of strength in every Presidential nomination fight. Reagan, however, vetoed the legislation each time it reached him.

But the day of "favorite sons" may fast be fading, especially in this state, which a serious candidate for a Presidential nomination simply cannot ignore if he hopes to be a strong factor in his party's convention. David Broder of the Washington *Post* suggests California is "The Political Giant" of the U.S.A. today:

The national political news continues to be written from Washington, but more and more of it is being made in California, a continent away. The increasing dominance of American politics by the giant on the Pacific is one of the significant facts of the 1970s. . . .

In part, it is the sheer size of the state that has given it its dominant role. [In 1972], for the first time, California will replace New York as the No. 1 prize in the election, with 45 electoral votes.

Its wealth, too, commands respect. San Francisco, Los Angeles, Beverly Hills and Palm Springs probably pour as much money into national campaign treasuries now as do New York or Texas.

And the Californians, by accident or design, have achieved a crucial role for themselves by staging their winner-take-all Presidential primary in June— making it nearly the last and by all odds the largest payoff tournament on the road to a Presidential nomination.

With 271 votes in [the 1972] Democratic convention, California has the power to put its favorite candidate more than one-fifth of the way to the nomination.

It is worth noting that when the Democratic party's reform commission tried to persuade California to abandon its "winner-take-all" primary feature, the proposal was flatly rejected. "There isn't a chance of a snowball in hell that we will change this," M. Larry Lawrence, Southern California state chairman, told the *National Journal* in 1971. "We like the power and strength. . . . California is going to be the dominant force at the convention." Nevertheless, the delegate selection procedure was democratized as never before, with persons representing a wide range of age, sex, and race groups nominated for the various candidates' primary-day slates by grass roots caucuses.

CAMPAIGN MANAGEMENT FIRMS. California is the state where the first professional campaign management firms appeared, and where the largest national firms are still located. Granddaddy of the profession is the San Francisco firm of Whitaker and Baxter, begun in 1933 as the professional (and later matrimonial) alliance of Clem Whitaker, a young reporter and public relations man, and Leone Baxter, manager of the Redding chamber of commerce. Their idea was simple, but revolutionary: a public relations firm specializing in politics. California provided especially fertile ground because (a) each ballot was crowded with initiatives and referenda, many so important to certain groups that they would spend up into the millions to ensure their passage or defeat, and (b) professional assistance for candidates was needed to fill the vacuum created by the lack of adequate party organizations. In all, W & B won 70 of the 75 campaigns it managed between 1933 and 1955. In classic PR firm style, a single, preferably emotional issue would be found as the central theme of a campaign, and then driven home again and again. "The average American," Whitaker once said, "doesn't want to be educated; he doesn't want to improve his mind; he doesn't even want to work, consciously, at becoming a good citizen."

Over the years, W & B coordinated the 1934 California League Against Sinclairism, helped Earl Warren warm up his fairly austere public image when he first ran for governor in 1942, helped run campaigns for William Knowland and Richard Nixon, and was retained at $100,000 a year to publicize the American Medical Association's campaign against federal-aid medical programs. Whitaker died in 1961, but his son Clem Whitaker, Jr., carried on in his place. In the mid-1960s, the firm was hired to publicize a national campaign to overturn the one-man, one-vote decisions of the U. S. Supreme Court. Some unwanted publicity accrued from the company's belated entry into the ill-starred campaign to elect former child actress Shirley Temple Black to Congress in 1967. W & B of late seems to have moved, intentionally, into the shadows, taking on low-profile bond and initiative issues and providing services for handsome retainers paid by some large corporations.

As campaign costs soared in California—to $50,000 for a close state legislature race, $100,000 or even more in a tight congressional contest, and up to several millions in a gubernatorial campaign—so did the need for professional campaign management. Firms sprouted up left and right, some fly-by-night, some formidable and permanent. Among the permanent was Baus & Ross, a Los Angeles firm, founded in 1946, that worked for Nixon (1960 Presidential primary and general election), Goldwater (1964 primary) and Brown (1968 campaign for third term as governor). The firm created a stir in 1964 when it signed off the Goldwater campaign after he won the primary; four years later owners Herbert M. Baus and William B. Ross explained that "the money was good in the primary, but it could have been better in the final had [we] been willing to give obeisance to gung-ho Goldwaterism gone rampant."

California's most publicized and effective campaign management group of recent years has been Spencer-Roberts & Associates of Los Angeles. William Roberts was a television time salesman, Stuart Spencer a recreation director in Alhambra when the two met doing volunteer Republican work in the late 1950s and decided "there must be a more scientific way to get our men elected." It was a crucial moment in American politics, with the age of the computer just dawning, traditional party organizations in decline, and campaigns becoming incredibly more complex and expensive than they had been in the past. A kind of systems approach to political campaigning was required, and S-R became a leading U.S. firm in developing the system needed.

Since the mid '60s, Spencer-Roberts has operated by providing the candidate with "all-encompassing" services, starting with counsel on the qualities he should look for in his campaign chairman, "kitchen cabinet," legal adviser, and executive committee. The firm schedules the opening of campaign headquarters, design and distribution of printed brochures, the purchases of advertising in all media, and coordination of volunteer services. (Average fee —10 to 20 percent of the gross cost of a campaign.) S-R also orders one or more polls to show voter attitudes within any district it enters. Issue development and media use are directly related to the survey data.

Roberts of S-R believes that traditional party apparatuses in California, and increasingly across the country, are "almost irrelevant to winning" modern-day elections and can be replaced in large measure by organizations like his own. "If I'm set up to raise money independent of them, and I'm set up independent organizationally, and I'm set up for election-day operation, and I've got a quality candidate, then what the hell do I need them for?" he said in a 1971 Washington *Post* interview. California businessmen, he said, were getting very used to backing candidates independent of the party. "They like to control. They like the direct infusion of money," Roberts asserted. But without parties, Roberts was worried about what device could be used to force emergence of competing candidates "and make us decide what's best." And he did not share Clem Whitaker's old disdain for the people:

I think they make wonderful decisions based on the knowledge they have. I don't say that they are ignorant and stupid and can be led around by the nose. . . .

I'm opposed to putting a lot of rules and restrictions on campaigning. I think I ought to have the right to lie to you if I think it'll help me win. I think you have the right to detect my lie and vote no when you go in the polling booth.

An organization known as Decision Making Information (DMI), which functioned until 1971 as a subsidiary of S-R but then became independent, has concentrated on advanced computer techniques, including sophisticated analysis of the socioeconomic characteristics of each precinct or township within a district, employing Census Bureau reports down to the tract level. Such factors as education, occupation, fertility ratios, race, and ethnic status are all fed into the system. Then they are compared with party registration data and returns from one or more past elections—all weighted as the campaign managers may consider the most relevant, so that in reality an important element of human judgment is part of the "system." The final precinct priority lists should reveal those in which the candidate can anticipate the most support. A cardinal rule is to "deal from strength." Rather than concentrating on hostile areas with minimal gain opportunities for the candidate, all direct mailing, telephone campaigns, and final get-out-the-vote efforts on election day can be concentrated in the most promising precincts.

A well-fed computer, DMI men say, can also suggest names for fund-raising appeals, create walking lists for precinct workers, and suggest, down to fine geographical subdivisions, the areas for targeted mailings on set subjects and themes for appearances and campaign speeches by the candidate. Finally, whether a campaign is won or lost, S-R and DMI try to get the candidate and his manager together for post-mortems on what went right and wrong, and why.

Roberts of S-R has said his firm will direct the campaign of "any reasonable, responsible Republican, without hyphenating him," providing he had adequate campaign finances and seems to hold some affection for the free enterprise system. The S-R clientele of "reasonable, responsible" Republicans has ranged from Congressman John H. Rousselot of Los Angeles (who later became a national spokesman for the John Birch Society) to Nelson Rockefeller in the 1964 California Presidential primary. The company participated in liberal Senator Thomas H. Kuchel's 1962 campaign and ran the 1968 campaign (winning the first, losing the second in the primary). But in 1966, it agreed to take on the campaign of Ronald Reagan, a man it had listed two years before as one of the "right-wing extremists" backing Goldwater. Before accepting Reagan as a client, Roberts and Spencer subjected him to long grillings on his philosophy and approach to government; then they took the account and proceeded to do what seemed like the impossible—to make the public forget all about Ronald Reagan the movie actor and exponent of right-wing causes, and instead think of Ronald Reagan the citizen-politician, the moderate candidate.

S-R succeeded, as its competitors stood back to watch the show in awe. The New York *Times* was upset by the feat, editorializing that "the cool professionalism of [S&R's] operations in California is chilling." Many feared that through sophisticated campaign management techniques, the public mind could be manipulated virtually at will; along with this would come a new cynicism of candidates, an inclination of public leaders to read the polls instead of following their own consciences. Some people had expressed the same concerns after the 1960 campaign, when it learned that Simulmatics, a group of MIT academicians working for John F. Kennedy that year, had tried to forecast voter responses to hypothetical events or policy positions, based on the public's reaction to thousands of polling questions in the past. Simulation may be carried to new heights in the 1970s. DMI board chairman Vincent Barabba pointed out in an interview, for instance, that his company and S-R have now been involved in dozens of congressional campaigns across the U.S.A., using a fairly standardized format of in-depth voter study. Between 30,000 and 40,000 persons are interviewed in an election year, each carefully tabbed by age, race, party, and various socioeconomic factors. With such a huge universe, one is not restricted to analyzing the impact of an issue or development on the whole electorate, but can zero in to see how identifiable subgroups, by region, profession, race, or ethnic group, react specifically. A candidate can learn by simulation how the public, and specific voter groups within it, will react to any given policy position he may take.

Such techniques are on a level of sophistication unknown before. But they are also simply modern-day extrapolations, by infinitely superior tools of analysis and communication, of the seat-of-the-pants, instinctive political sensibilities that successful candidates for public office have demonstrated through history. What's more, the simulators and image-makers are only human, and can make mistakes, and frequently lose elections despite their best efforts. Spencer-Roberts' track record includes many defeats in U. S. House elections, the Rockefeller defeat in 1964, the Kuchel defeat in 1968, and Senator George Murphy's loss in 1970. In many cases of defeat, the candidate made fundamentally wrong decisions despite the campaign intelligence brought him by his managers. "My chief problem," Spencer said in an interview, "is to get clients to use the information—to accept the conclusions of the simulation model or other political intelligence." In addition, many slick television advertising campaigns end up harming more than helping a candidate. One likes to think that the public often sees through them to the true mettle of a man.

But campaign management, with polls, computers, sophisticated use of television, and all the rest, has arrived in the U.S.A., courtesy largely of the

Californians, and is sure to stay. Serious candidates of the future will be simply unable or unwilling to turn down a tool that can give them the extra votes they need to win instead of losing.

John S. Saloma and Frederick H. Sontag, in a study for the Twentieth Century Fund, suggest that two prototype "conglomerates" are developing in the political management field, both dedicated to helping Republican candidates. (Working for a single party, managers insist, is easier on their nerves, fosters client trust, and avoids awkward potential conflicts of interest.) One "conglom" is the Spencer-Roberts/Decision Making Information complex, with a base in the West and South; another is the Detroit firm of Market Opinion Research, allied with Bailey, Deardourff & Bowen of Washington, D.C., and concentrating on the East and Midwest. Both groups of firms have gained access to the innermost circles of the Republican National Committee and many state headquarters. Naturally, such consulting firms reach out to create or acquire other firms with electronic data processing capacity, and then the network of new subsidiaries, subcontracting to other firms, shared facilities, and wide links of professional contacts, grows apace. DMI, for instance, has given seminars or presentations on campaign management information and techniques for dozens of organizations, including the U. S. Chamber of Commerce, the American Farm Bureau, the American Medical Political Action Committee, Republican organizations from local to national level, and university-connected groups across the continent.

Both eastern and western GOP "conglomerates," Saloma and Sontag point out, have an interest in electing a Republican President one day. MOR/BD&B hope to see a swing to the left in Republican policy, enabling them to elect a moderate Republican President by the mid-1970s; Spencer-Roberts/DMI since 1966 have become generally identified with the GOP-conservative wing and seem firmly committed to Reagan and his still unquenched ambitions for higher office.

Democratic-oriented professional campaign management firms have yet to advance so far. But the techniques are not secret, and it seems only a matter of time—and money—until they do.

POLITICAL MONEY. The sources of big political money in California (the kind needed to run expensive operations like Spencer-Roberts) are predictable—wealthy "Wasp" businessmen for the GOP, well-heeled Jewish business figures and organized labor for the Democrats. Big oil, big farm interests, big real estate, savings and loan, and entertainment industry money are all major factors in the political money game; aerospace interests, surprisingly, are not—perhaps because their chief wealth comes from Washington. Most of the political fat cats hail from Southern California. The Democratic sources have never reached comparability with the Republicans'. Organized labor, for instance, is strong in certain areas—Longshoremen in the big ports, UAW in the Los Angeles area, Teamsters everywhere—but with the exception of the Teamsters, the unions' contributions to the Democrats are more in the form of manpower than dollars. Despite membership rolls of about two million,

California unions are still frozen out in large segments of the aerospace industry and pack none of the weight their counterparts do in Michigan, New York, or even Texas.

Thus Democrats often are obliged to look to alternative fund sources like the controversial political fund accumulated by Jess Unruh as speaker of the Assembly in the early 1960s. Unruh milked the money from lobbyists at high-priced testimonial dinners; then he doled it out to Democrats in close election races, a sure-fire way to solidify his own power.

One of the most interesting figures in Republican money-raising circles is Patrick J. Frawley, Jr., chief executive officer of companies with sales of more than $200 million annually—Eversharp, Schick, and, until a few years ago, Technicolor. Along with Salvatori, Holmes Tuttle, and the late A. C. Rubel, Frawley helped get Reagan into the 1966 governorship campaign; the group then provided the financial muscle for victory. Two years before, Frawley served as a chairman of American Businessmen for Goldwater and TV for Goldwater-Miller; in 1968 he helped Max Rafferty defeat Senator Kuchel in the GOP Senate primary. Frawley sees the Communist menace everywhere and has opened his checkbook for many causes like Fred Schwarz's Christian Anti-Communism Crusade. William L. Taylor, an ex-FBI agent specializing in investigative reporting, asserted in a 1970 article that "'Frawley has no compunctions about appointing corporate dilettantes who are political kinsmen to the boards of directors" of the companies he controls; in addition his companies have footed the bills for a number of anti-Red extravaganzas on national television. Frawley also gave freely to the campaign of Senator George Murphy, the first of the California actors to break into big-time politics with his election in 1964. Before becoming a Senator, Murphy was an executive of Technicolor. Everyone assumed the relationship was ended, but in 1970 it became known that for five and a half years while serving in Washington, Murphy had been receiving $20,000 per annum "consultant's fee" from Technicolor. The company also paid the rent on Murphy's Washington apartment and provided him with credit cards. The revelations played a role in the old actor's defeat in 1970, and robbed Frawley of a friend good and true in Washington. Frawley, though, continued to shell out what writer Turner estimated was $1 million a year, personally and through his companies, for right-wing causes. Frawley's case is not altogether typical, however; some of the other Reagan moneybags, Holmes Tuttle in particular, are quite pragmatic men with a clear distaste for ideology. And despite the hope of some big givers for decisions from an officeholder friendly to their economic interests, the picture can be overdrawn. As Bill Roberts puts it:

> Most of these guys don't want a quid pro quo. All these guys love is a little romance of being in with the big guy, being able to pick up the phone and say, "Ron, how are you today? What's doing?" That's worth the five grand they put in the goddamn thing.

Reagan and Murphy are not the only past or present members of the Hollywood film colony to take an active role in politics. On the Republican side, Bob Hope, Jimmy Stewart, Buddy Ebsen, and John Wayne are among the many celluloid personalities who have opened their checkbooks and lined up support; in 1970, Wayne headed a "Golden Circle" club that signed up supporters of the GOP campaign for state legislative races at membership fees of $1,000 to $5,000. Big celebrities and sometimes givers for the Democrats have included Shirley MacLaine, Henry Fonda, Dean Martin, and Frank Sinatra (though Sinatra deserted the reservation in 1970 to back Reagan for governor, reportedly because of a personal distaste for Unruh). But it would be a mistake to think that California politics is entirely supported by big names and big money. There is a lot of small-giver, ideological money in California, ranging from right-wing gun nuts on one side to "peace" givers on the other.

California's Aerojet-General in 1958 kicked off a promising experiment to make candidates less dependent on the fat cats. Under the A-G plan, the corporation itself launches a major bipartisan campaign to encourage employees to register, vote, and contribute to the candidate or party of their choice. Interest is stirred up by inviting big- and small-name candidates to appear at rallies on the factory grounds.

By 1970, the Aerojet idea had been adopted by a score of California corporations, had won wide acclaim, but had failed to raise more than a few hundred thousand dollars, statewide, in any year. Ironically, Aerojet dropped its own payroll deduction plan for political contributions in 1970. The action followed the death of the firm's former head, Dan Kimball, an idealistic man who had been a leading Democratic fund-raiser; the rapid drop in Aerojet's employment totals (from 34,000 in its heyday down to 8,000) led the new management to dismiss political fund-raising as an unnecessary frill.

Perhaps the most impressive program of late has been the Hughes Aircraft Company's "Active Citizenship Campaign." In 1968, over 5,000 employees were registered on company premises, $101,000 was raised in contributions from a quarter of the employees (average gift $16.47), and at rallies held at Hughes plants there were appearances by one Presidential, 23 congressional, and 44 state office candidates. Another big California corporation, Pacific Gas & Electric, is into the business of encouraging interest in politics through a limited bipartisan fund-raising program for employees, big candidate rallies, and an excellent eight-week practical politics training course offered employees on company time, free of charge.

## Governing Nation State

*California spends nearly $2 million a day just building and maintaining highways. It spends nearly $2 million a day operating its state university system alone. It spends more on education than 43 other states spend on all government services. Altogether, it spends more than $125 million a week. California gets close to $3 billion a year in grants from the federal government. But this is a pittance compared with its own resources. The income of its citizens runs more than $1 billion a week.*

—Gladwin Hill, *in* Dancing Bear (*figures updated*)

Despite the quality of California's state government, it is beset with California-size difficulties.

The weakest link may be the state constitution. Last subjected to major revision in 1879, it has been amended about 350 times and presently runs to some 83,000 words. California voters have repeatedly turned down proposals for a constitutional convention to start from scratch. The reason, in the words of Totten J. Anderson: "In no state in the Union are interest group prerogatives more thoroughly impacted in the fundamental law, to a large extent through hundreds of constitutional amendments." One of the more innocent examples: a provision that the legislature "shall have no power to prohibit wrestling and 12-round boxing contests in the State of California."

The most recent effort at constitutional reform started in the early 1960s when Assembly Speaker Unruh pushed through authorization of a blue ribbon constitutional revision committee with citizen and legislature members. The recommended reforms, covering some of the major departments of government and authorizing the legislature, for the first time, to set its own rate of pay and hold annual sessions, got strong bipartisan endorsement. Unruh and Robert T. Monagan, Republican leader of the assembly, campaigned hard for passage, and the people approved by a wide margin in 1966. But a second group of revisions, covering such areas as education, local governments, civil service, and state lands, was turned down by the people in 1968 for reasons still obscure. In net, the reforms effected through constitutional revision have been minor.

There are redeeming features. One is the power to guide and shape state government which a strong governor can exert. For 50 years, California has had the executive budget, which permits the governor, through his department of finance—a highly professional arm of state government, akin to the national Budget Bureau—to guide the operation of state government. Favored programs can be increased, others held at *status quo* levels or reduced, subject to the legislature's approval. More than a financial ledger sheet, the budget is a plan of operation. The governor's authority is enhanced by an item veto authority, permitting him to reduce the dollar amount for any item in an appropriation bill—a power U. S. Presidents would dearly love to have. A vitiating factor, however, is the fact that two-thirds of the budget is locked in by constitutional provisions or statutes, beyond gubernatorial control. Moreover, the constitution requires that most expenditure and tax bills be approved by two-thirds of the members of both houses of the legislature, a situation making for quick deadlock when neither party has overwhelming legislative numbers.

Bypassing cumbersome constitutional amendment, Governor Brown undertook the first comprehensive reorganization of the executive branch in 30 years, consolidating numerous boards and commissions into eight broad-gauged agencies through use of his executive powers. Several of the changes were made permanent by the legislature. Reagan took the process a step further by setting up four superagencies—business and transportation, resources, human relations, and agriculture and services. The creative legislative team of Unruh and Monagan contributed to the process, co-authoring, for example, legislation in the social welfare field that solidified under the secretary of human relations virtually all the agencies dealing with deprived areas—correction, youth authority, rehabilitation, health care, public health, social welfare, mental hygiene, employment, and the like.

The Unruh-Monagan legislative role brings us to the next great strength of California government: its superbly staffed, full-time, well paid legislature. The lion's share of credit for this goes to Unruh, with important help from Monagan, who succeeded him as speaker in 1969–70. Unruh gave the assembly the tools it needed to handle research and program development, largely through high-grade, professional staffs assigned to the committees—probably the best of any of the 50 states. Individual legislators were also given budgets for staff assistance—administrative assistants, secretaries, and field representatives—reminiscent of the U. S. Congress.* And they were accorded a new measure of independence by the highest legislative salaries in the U.S.—$16,000 per annum in 1967, raised to $19,200 in 1970, with another several thousand dollars each year in such fringe benefits as a $30-a-day living allowance in Sacramento during sessions and an automobile with an oil company credit card. Assemblymen—and the state senators, who soon followed suit—became freer of lobbyists and the administration for basic information. When Reagan, a budget-minded governor little interested in new programs, took office, the legislature became the programmatic, innovative branch of state government. In 1971, after his unsuccessful race for governor, Unruh retired—at least for the time being—from active participation in government. But one of his young staff men seemed justified in saying: "If Jesse never does anything else politically he will at least get a line in the history books for what he did with the legislature in California.† That judgment seemed vindicated in 1971 when a nonpartisan national study group, the Citizens Conference on State Legislatures, issued a report and ranking on the procedures and operations of the 50 state legislatures and found California number one in the U.S.A. The executive director of the Citizens Conference, ironically, is Larry Margolis, who was Unruh's right-hand man at Sacramento during the 1960s. But no one doubts that California deserves its number one position.

Have the reforms made the legislature a more honest place? The answer is probably yes, with some major reservations. Things have surely come a long way since the 1940s and the days of Arthur H. ("Artie") Samish, a six-foot, two-inch, 300-pound wheeler-dealer lobbyist who boasted to a writer for *Collier's* magazine: "I'm the governor of the legislature. To hell with the governor of the state. If you get a long enough ladder and put it up against the Capitol dome, you can take a picture of me unscrewing the gold cupola."

---

* By 1971, the legislature's staff numbered 1,500, of which 500 were professionals. Annual cost: about $15 million.
† The Unruh system has also turned out to be a great boon to legislators trying to solidify themselves for the next election. At state expense, they have a television and radio tape service, personalized mass mailings, and, of course, their permanent field staff.

For this indiscretion, Samish ended up being grilled by the Kefauver committee, being barred "forever" from lobbying in the California legislature, and catching the attention of the federal government, which finally sent him to jail for income tax evasion.

The "Third House" of lobbyists still flourishes in Sacramento. Those with great influence are said to include such as the Pacific Gas & Electric Co., Standard Oil of California, the Bank of America, the California Teachers Association, Lockheed Aircraft, Transamerica, the Kern County Land Co., the Bankers Association of California, the California Real Estate Association, the California Growers Association, and the University of California. Lobbyists are supposed to register, but many blandly disregard the law; among these, in 1968–69, were men lobbying on two of the most controversial bills: William Burke for the Catholic Church on abortion reform, and E. F. (Tod) Sloan of the National Rifle Association, when gun-control legislation was being considered. As a part of the 1969 package of constitutional revisions, "conflict of interest" provisions applicable to legislators were included. But the restrictions, Lou Cannon has reported, "were totally platitudinous and frankly designed to ease the qualms of newspapers reluctant to see the legislature with power over its own salary scale." Just how platitudinous they were was illustrated in 1969 when the Los Angeles *Times* reported that state senate president pro tem Hugh Burns had shared with an insurance lobbyist and another associate $500,000 in profits of an insurance company that had profited from legislation Burns sponsored. It turned out that the chairman of the Joint Legislative Ethics Committee created by the 1966 vote of the people was none other than Senator Burns himself. He said he had done nothing illegal, and there the matter rested. In the same year, Unruh introduced and secured passage of a bill requiring quite thorough disclosure of outside income by legislators and all other high state and local officials, but in 1970 the state supreme court struck it down as unconstitutional.

Up to the 1960s, California operated under a "federal plan" of legislative apportionment which divided the assembly by relatively equal population units but required geographic representation in the senate. The formula had been voted for by the people in 1926 and they refused on three subsequent occasions—in 1948, 1960, and 1962—to overturn it for equal population districts in both bodies. Malapportionment in the senate reached such egregious proportions that the six million people of Los Angeles County had exactly the same representation as 15,000 in the eastern Sierra district of Alpine, Inyo, and Mono counties—exactly one senator. The disparity in populations was 450 to 1. Then the courts, in the wake of *Baker v. Carr*, intervened in the California situation and reapportionment became mandatory. Overnight, L. A. County's representation shot up to 14 seats; overall Southern California went from nine to 22 seats, while Northern California slipped from 31 to 18.

The popular expectation was that the old conservative core of the senate—rural, Northern, and close to entrenched business interests like Standard

Oil, PG&E, and the Southern Pacific Railroad, all of whom fought hard against reapportionment—would be immediately dislodged. It turned out not to be so. Senator Burns, the crusty old Fresno Democrat and embodiment of the *ancien régime*, was actually retained as president pro tem when the newly apportioned senate met in 1967. Committees remained tightly locked in control of the Old Guard, and the Third House seemed to be carrying on business as usual. Even in winter 1969, when the Republicans finally broke the decades-old Democratic majority in the Senate, Burns stayed on.* A few months later, however, a group of Young Turks of varied ideological stripes ousted Burns and enjoyed a month of reform; soon, however, an old-guard Republican, Jack Schrade of San Diego, got the job. Schrade quickly became the center of a nasty scandal involving a $5,000 "campaign contribution" which looked suspiciously like a direct payoff by the California Association of Thrift and Loan Companies to get one of its favorite bills approved. The Third House seemed in the saddle again.

A new generation of legislative leaders came to power after the 1970 elections, in which the Democrats took control of both houses. California journalist Mary Ellen Leary has described the new assembly leaders as part of a new political generation, just past 30, "schooled in the tough-minded political drive of the Kennedys, . . . clean-cut and incisive as a crew of aerospace engineers." Robert Moretti, 34, a protege of Jesse Unruh from the same Los Angeles community of Van Nuys, became the youngest speaker in the history of the assembly. Moretti differs somewhat from Unruh in that he is committed more to teamwork than to personality. While in college in 1960, he was drawn into politics by the Kennedy campaign.† He grew up in a Detroit immigrant ghetto, the son of an Italian father and an Armenian mother, and was an honor graduate of Notre Dame.

The Moretti leadership team in the assembly includes Jack R. Fenton of Los Angeles, a close Moretti associate named majority leader; Henry Waxman, from a solidly Jewish Los Angeles district, who is chairman of the Elections and Reapportionment Committee; and the sharp-minded and skillful black attorney from San Francisco, Willie Brown, who helped Moretti win election as speaker and was rewarded with the powerful post of chairman of the Ways and Means Committee. The position makes Brown, 37, as influential in Sacramento as Wilbur Mills is in Washington—a breakthrough of immense importance for American blacks. He quickly showed his muscle by eliminating from the 1972 state budget all funds for the state Office of Economic Opportunity, which had been headed by a Reagan appointee, Lewis Uhler, a former John Birch Society member. Brown conducted an investigation of the state OEO office and concluded it duplicated the efforts of other local and federal agencies; he then persuaded his committee to kill a $70,000

---

* Burns voluntarily retired from the Senate at the end of 1970. His service totaled 34 years.
† It may be that the lasting Kennedy impact on American politics will be in the generation of the very young he attracted into politics, now moving into their thirties and forties and assuming positions of real power. The first generation of John Kennedy's closest associates (men like Pierre Salinger, Kenneth O'Donnell, and Theodore Sorensen), by contrast, has done very poorly in elective politics.

budget request for the Uhler office. (Brown is considered a strong contender for the San Francisco mayoralty when Joseph Alioto's term expires in 1975.)

In the senate, the power figure is now Democratic floor leader and caucus chairman George Moscone, an avowed 1974 gubernatorial candidate who is regarded by many as the Democrats' brightest hope in the state today. Moscone is a handsome, articulate San Francisco lawyer in his early forties who has attracted a "brain trust" of bright young men who advise him on fiscal problems, general legislation, politics, and communications. Another liberal Democrat, James R. Mills of San Diego, was elected senate president pro tem.* And in the senate, too, one black now heads a committee—Democratic caucus chairman Mervyn Dymally, head of elections and reapportionment. Both Dymally and the assembly's Willie Brown preach the need for more black involvement in politics. Dymally puts it this way: "The young bloods say the system is racist and irrelevant. True, . . . [but] if you aren't there when the man is cutting up the pie, you aren't going to get any of it." Brown, who was leading street demonstrations before he got into politics, says: "Blacks who are willing to do the homework and learn the techniques will be able through politics to make just incredible changes in the whole life style of black people in this country."

The new leadership bodes ill for the Third House, especially in view of the young Democrats' intention to redirect government benefits from those who possess to those who are dispossessed. But it would be naive to think that the lobbyists are in a hopeless position. A state Democratic party reaching for power will need money, and since business (especially savings and loan and insurance companies) is an important fund source for the Democrats, a stridently antibusiness tone to new legislation is unlikely. This quickly became evident in 1971 with the defeat of key environmentalist bills.

Campaign contributions—some $5 million in 1968 and again in 1970, by official reports—are the most important conduit of special-interest money in Sacramento today. Direct bribes and similar skulduggery, by most accounts, are much less of a problem than they once were. By 1970, it was reported, Sacramento had an increasing number of "new breed" lobbyists, men with more governmental expertise who are more likely to be effective with the group of legislators increasingly in evidence after reapportionment: men and women generally younger, including many issue-oriented professionals and businessmen. According to the L. A. *Times*'s Tom Goff, the "old breed" is expert in the nuances of the legislative process, trades on old friendships, entertains more heavily, contributes heavily to fund-raising dinners, but rarely testifies before legislative hearings. Goff named Daniel J. Creedon, who was conduit for the controversial $5,000 gift to Schrade, as a typical "old breed"

* Mills is among the potential 1974 Democratic gubernatorial nominees. Others include Moretti, Moscone, Los Angeles industrialist and liberal Democratic moneyman Martin Stone, and Secretary of State Edmund G. Brown, Jr. (son of the former governor). On the Republican side, potential names include State Controller Houston I. Flournoy (a highly regarded moderate), Lt. Gov. Ed Reinecke (a popular conservative who outpolled Reagan in 1970), Robert T. Monagan (who is now minority leader of the assembly), and Robert H. Finch (Presidential adviser, former lieutenant governor and U.S. Secretary of Health, Education, and Welfare, who has announced he will leave the White House and return to California after the 1972 elections).

lobbyist. Like many of the "old breed," Creedon works for multiple clients at one time—in Creedon's case, not only the thrift companies but also beer and racetrack interests, highway patrolmen, funeral directors, consulting engineers, and certainly city governments. He operates out of a well-staffed office in the penthouse of the El Mirador Hotel, across from the Capitol. The California legislature may, as Unruh has often said, be "the finest in the nation." But if New Politics has come to town, Old Politics has apparently failed to get the message.

The California state budget, in the same pattern we have noted across the U.S.A., has shot upward at what seems like a geometric rate in recent years. In fiscal year 1945–46, its budget was $324 million; for 1972–73 the governor submitted a $7.6 billion budget. The increases just over a 12-year period, showing the overall figure and some major components, are illustrative:

| | Fiscal Year 1959–60 | Fiscal Year 1971–72 |
|---|---|---|
| | (Figures in millions) | |
| Assistance to local school districts and community colleges | $ 635 | $1,702 |
| Higher education (University of California, state colleges) | 175 | 675 |
| Assistance to localities for public assistance (aid to the aged, blind, needy children, etc.) | 191 | 563 |
| Division of Highways | 253 | 343 |
| Total budget | $2,200 | $6,789 |

Inflation, higher salaries, and expansion of activity in all departments were responsible for these fantastic increases. Despite Governor Reagan's heroic budget-cutting efforts, the figures would probably not look too different if Brown or another Democrat were still governor. In eight years in office, Brown's budget rose by $2.5 billion; in Reagan's first four years, the increase was $2.2 billion.

To pay these spiraling bills, California has been forced to periodic tax increases of massive proportions. The state has a steeply graduated personal income tax that provides about 23 cents of each dollar of income, but the system as a whole cannot be called especially progressive because much larger revenues come from sales taxes (a 4-percent rate, plus 1 percent for localities) and highway user taxes, which, between them, account for 46 cents of the tax dollar. A variety of other charges, ranging from the bank and corporation tax (nine cents) to horse racing fees (one cent) make up the rest of the revenue dollar.

The fiscal woes of California's counties and cities are just as great as the state's, and localities have the feeling that Sacramento has not gone nearly far enough to help them. Hard-pressed county governments, for instance, find 55 percent of their budgets going for welfare, an expenditure item they have great difficulty controlling. They complain that the state legislature often originates programs with costs shared on a percentage basis, but fails to give the counties money increases in proportion to the mandated expansion of services.

Like most states of the Union, California has paid for the bulk of local school costs through local property taxes, a system that has resulted in gross inequalities since the tax base within the state ranges from a low of $103 per child in the poorest communities to a high of $925,156—a ratio of almost 1 to 10,000. State aid to school districts has been only partially effective in equalizing funds, as it covers only 35 percent of local school costs. But in one fell swoop, the California supreme court in 1971 cut the ground out from under the old system. Ruling on a class action brought by Los Angeles parents, it ruled, 6–1, that raising school funds through local property taxes violates the equal protection clause of the 14th Amendment because it "invidiously discriminates against the poor because it makes the quality of a child's education a function of the wealth of his parents and neighbors." Unless reversed by the U. S. Supreme Court, the decision will force the state to adopt a new method of equalized school financing and could, in the words of M. Carl Holman, president of the National Urban Coalition, trigger "dramatic reform for an increased equal educational opportunity for poor children throughout the country." Wilson Riles pointed out that it would wipe out the existing inequalities that make it possible for the city of Beverly Hills to tax its citizens $2.60 per $100 of assessed valuation and come up with $1,500 per child, while West Covina, also in Los Angeles County, taxes $4.30 per $100 and raises less than $700.

At the end of the 1960s, California's per capita local property tax revenue was $226—highest in the nation, where the average figure was $139. Combined state and local tax collections were $540 per person (trailing only New York); as a percentage of personal income they were 12.3 percent (trailing only Wyoming and Hawaii). Per capita welfare expenditures were third highest in the country. It was true that a federal input of close to $3 billion sweetened the picture somewhat, but the reasons for Californians' outraged resistance to higher taxes were not hard to see.

In the area of welfare, a well-intentioned temporary relief program of the 1930s had become a Frankenstein monster of seemingly permanent dependence for 620,000 Californians by 1961. And by 1969, 1.5 million of the United States's eight million welfare recipients lived in California. In California as in many other states, welfare had become a sizzling political issue, with many politicians (including Reagan) contributing to the false public image of the average welfare recipient as a healthy, husky 26-year-old male sitting in front of a color television set guzzling beer instead of working. But as Spencer Williams, then Reagan's secretary of human relations, pointed out in an interview, the number of cheaters was probably not great compared to the whole. California's welfare rolls carried 300,000 aged—typically, a 77-year-old widow. Then there were 12,500 blind, 150,000 disabled (mostly bedridden), 750,000 children, and 250,000 adults 21 to 65 years old. Of these, only 15,000 were male heads of households—and they tended to be seasonal workers, going on and off the rolls. There were more than 200,000 mothers on welfare who were heads of households. "If we could really reach this group and do a good job with it," Williams said, "we'd take about 350,000 off the rolls, because each head of household would take a couple of kids off with her." The problem was that neither California nor any other state, under excruciating budget shortages, was ready to invest the additional millions in employment counseling and rehabilitation care to do the job.

And as Williams acknowledged, only half the eligibles were on the rolls in 1969, many kept off by ignorance or pride. The activist welfare groups were just beginning to go out and recruit more eligibles to go on the rolls. On top of it all, the recession hit California, and by the time this book was written in 1971, the number of welfare recipients in California had burgeoned to 2.5 million. By 1971, in fact, welfare had emerged as the most controversial single issue of state government. Asserting that welfare was going to many "whose greed is greater than their need," Reagan pressed hard for a number of welfare cutbacks. After protracted negotiations, he and the Democratic legislative leadership agreed on a number of reforms that included Reagan recommendations like tighter residency and eligibility requirements, a pilot work program for welfare recipients, and stronger enforcement of child support payments by absentee fathers (one of the most serious abuses in the system). But he had to back down on a rather cold-hearted proposal to put an absolute lid in welfare spending. The compromise included cost-of-living increases, child care for working mothers, and family planning assistance for welfare mothers. But almost immediately after passage of the new legislation, it was mired in administrative disputes and court challenges.

There are several areas in which California's state government has excelled. Its multibillion-dollar State Water Plan, inaugurated under Brown, was long cited as one of these, though there is now serious questioning of how necessary that full investment may have been, and how damaging the plan may be to California's ecology—a story we will look at in our section on the California Southland.

Perhaps the most brilliant success of recent times has been in the field of mental health, as California has shifted away from the big, custodial type of state hospitals to more responsive community health centers. California had pioneered in community health center development with legislation in the mid-1950s. Then, as a result of a legislative study, came landmark 1968 legislation which shifted the basic responsibility for treatment of the mentally ill from state to local government. The state continued to bear 90 percent of the costs and the counties 10 percent, but the first stop was local government. The state contracted with community agencies, medical centers and children's hospitals to operate regional centers for the retarded. The centers were required to provide comprehensive diagnosis. Where necessary, families were given guidance and financial aid to place children in privately operated, state-approved community residential facilities; others were given help, through visiting nurses, babysitters, or day-care centers, to keep their children at home. The average cost was about half that of state hospital care, with no capital outlay. Finally, the legislation took massive strides to protect mentally ill persons. Involuntary commitment to mental hospitals was made a cumbersome process, subject to mandatory court review each 90 days and continuable only if the hospital could show the person dangerous to others. Patients were guaranteed, except in the most exceptional cases, the right to wear their own clothes, send and receive uncensored letters, have daily visitors, and refuse shock treatment or lobotomy. On their release, they would be guaranteed full civil rights.

By 1969, there were only 13,363 patients in the state hospitals (just over a third of the figure 10 years before), and the number was dropping rapidly. Not only had California saved millions of dollars, but it had created a new system that would respect the rights and interests of the mentally disturbed and keep them in the mainstream of their communities, where the hope for eventual full recovery would be the greatest.

In fields of social legislation, California has moved in the last few years to liberalize its divorce laws (imperiling the divorce mill in neighboring Nevada). In 1967 it relaxed its restrictive, century-old abortion laws, and by 1971 there were around 125,000 legal abortions in the state. In fact, recent court decisions make virtually all abortions in California legal if performed by a licensed physician in a licensed hospital. In the field of consumer protection, the most startling breakthrough was a 1971 law requiring state regulation of all automobile repair dealers to protect the public from fraud and negligent work in a $2.5-billion a year business. Pushed for several years by state senator Anthony Beilenson of Los Angeles, the law was finally passed over heavy opposition from new car dealers and the major oil companies. Eight years before, California had pioneered in the consumer field through creation of its bureau of repair services, which specializes in the television-repair field and has power to investigate and bring criminal charges against unscrupulous repair organizations or to revoke their registrations administratively. The bureau's budget is only $300,000 a year, but it is conservatively estimated to save California citizens $15 million a year. A less glowing record has been made of late by the California Public Utilities Commission, once praised by consumer groups as a model regulator in the public interest. Under Reagan's appointees, the commission has bent over backward to grant water, electric, and telephone companies $500 million in rate increases, compared to a net reduction in charges allowed them in the previous seven years.

California has the dubious distinction, according to FBI statistics, of leading the United States in both the number and rate of crimes (3,764 per 100,000 inhabitants in 1968, for example). But it is also a national leader in advanced police training, and has put into operation a $5 million computerized system to link 450 state law enforcement agencies with crime files in Sacramento and Washington, D.C. It was also a pioneer state (in 1966) in putting into operation a state system of financial aid to victims of serious crimes.

In Washington, Justice Department officials say that California's prisons are the best run in the country. Governor Warren instituted the first major change, from an emphasis on punishment to one on rehabilitation, work programs, and indeterminate sentences. Several new pieces of progressive correctional legislation have come under Reagan, and he personally proposed that the department of corrections try out a system of family visitation for prisoners within 90 days of release. Unlike Mississippi's conjugal visitations, the California program provides for visits of a full family for two-day weekends at cottages outside the prison walls. Inmates within 90 days of release are also given 72-hour passes to go see their families and apply for jobs. And the state has been a leader in the nationally popular work furlough program, in which an inmate goes out to work during the day and returns to prison at night. In 1969, a shocking total of 50,000 California adults were convicted of felonies, but only 13.5 percent of them were sent to state prisons—generally the "repeaters" or those convicted of such crimes as homicide, armed robbery, or drug trafficking. The state pays $4,000 a year to any county which will keep a felon in the community, providing him with professional counseling and job training. The recidivism rate has dropped from 50 percent, an average figure in the U.S., to less than 35 percent. And under progressive parole and probation programs, the prison population dropped from an all-time high of 28,600 in January 1969 to 22,000, a 10-year low, in late 1971.

Part of California's relative success is doubtless based on its variety of prisons. Of the 14 state prisons, two are maximum security, no-nonsense types for hardened criminals—Folsom (near Sacramento) and San Quentin (in the Bay Area). Then there are prison hospitals, a number of "medium security" institutions, and some minimum security installations which are generally conservation camps run jointly with the state department of forestry.

Nevertheless, life for a California convict can be living hell. Some critics suggest that the state's prisons, rather than models of achievement for criminal justice, are merely the best of a frightening lot across the U.S.A. Sweeping reforms were recommended, in fact, in a report to the state board of corrections by a 62-member staff directed by Oakland criminologist Robert Keldgord. Among the salient proposals: that San Quentin and Folsom, which are 116 and 91 years old respectively, be closed down because they are "ugly and depressing" and "not secure or safe"; that conjugal visits be allowed at all penitentiaries; that two-man cells be eliminated to decrease homosexuality; that prisoners be allowed to wear civilian clothes; that mail censorship be abandoned; and that the maximum time allowable for sentences to isolation be reduced from 30 to 10 days. Early in 1972, Reagan acceded to one proposal by announcing that San Quentin—where 409 people were executed over the years, and where the highest prison population outside Russia was once registered—would be closed by the end of 1974. But the acceptance of many of the other reform proposals was much in doubt. "How high on the priority list," one Reagan aide asked me, "can you put improvements in penology, when dollars are scarce for schools, medical care, and social welfare? After all, you're talking about people who have committed a crime against society."

As racial tensions mounted in the country during the 1960s, the effects were felt in California's prisons, first through organization by the Black Muslims behind the prison walls, then by other black prisoners with a political-revolutionary awareness. In 1969, at the correctional training facility of Soledad, a white guard killed three black prisoners during a disturbance in the exercise yard; the guard was quickly exonerated, and soon afterward a white guard was found beaten to death. Three black convicts were charged with the murder; these were the famed "Soledad Brothers" of whom one, George Jackson, would gain national fame through his book, *Soledad Brother*. His brother, Jonathan Jackson, was killed in a 1970 shoot-out at the Marin County courthouse, part of an audacious kidnap plot to force George's release, which ended in the death of four persons, including a judge. (This was the incident for which Angela Davis, the ex-UCLA instructor and Communist party member, was accused of procuring the weapons.) A bloody encore came in August 1971 when George Jackson smuggled a gun into his cellblock at San Quentin and touched off a mutiny in which three white guards and two white inmates were killed. In his book, Jackson had repeatedly prophesied that he would not leave the California prison system alive. The prophecy came true as, in a run for freedom across a yard toward the wall, the hardened and embittered young revolutionary was cut down by gunfire from the guards.

Early in 1972, the vein of essential decency in California government was demonstrated when the state's supreme court decreed that the death penalty "may no longer be exacted" in the state, because of conflict with the California constitution. "We have concluded," Chief Justice Donald Wright wrote, "that capital punishment is impermissibly cruel. It degrades and dehumanizes all who participate in its process. . . . Society diminishes itself whenever it takes the life of one of its members." Governor Reagan vigorously attacked the court, which he said was "setting itself up above the people and their legislators," but there seemed little chance of reversal of the 6-to-1 decision, written by a man—Justice Wright—whom Reagan himself had appointed to the court. The decision was likely to spur similar findings in other states, or before the U. S. Supreme Court, and along with the 1971 decision invalidating property taxes to finance education, made the California high court a vital force for change in America as a whole.

## University of California: Pain and Progress of "Multiversity"

Many things Californian evoke superlatives; no institution merits them more than the University of California. Despite its many tribulations, UC remains the most successful institution of higher education that the United

States, and perhaps the world, has ever known. From humble beginnings as an academy in an Oakland dance hall in 1853, it has developed into a "multiversity" of more than 100,000 students and a staff of 50,000, working and studying in nine distinct campuses. The university has an annual budget of well over $1 billion,* offers in excess of 10,000 courses, operates two nuclear laboratories and close to 100 research and experimental stations. It leads the nation in the number of Nobel laureates on its faculty (14 at last count) and in the number of National Merit Scholars who choose to enroll.

The benefit that has accrued to California's people through their fantastic investment in UC is almost beyond estimation. Without the university's distinction in agricultural research, the physical sciences, technology, and water conservation, California would be, as an economic entity, a weak shadow of what it is today.

And preeminently among the American states, California has given its young people an opportunity to take advantage of higher public education. Under the master plan for higher education, adopted in 1960, every California youngster interested in continuing his education beyond high school has an opportunity to do so under a three-tiered program, which, by latest count, accommodated about 1.2 million students:

COMMUNITY COLLEGES (or junior colleges, as they used to be called). The community college is basically a California model, pioneered by Pasadena City College over 60 years ago. There are now 93 such campuses, located throughout the state, guaranteeing a place to any California high school graduate, or, in fact, anyone over 18 "who can profit from the instruction." Enrollment in 1970–71 totaled 800,000. The community colleges, almost all commuter schools in students' home areas, have a dual mission. The first is to provide terminal education—usually technical or vocational training, on a more sophisticated level than high school. Many technicians for California industries, in fields as disparate as computer programming, medical technology, and auto mechanics, come out of these courses. A second mission is to provide an intensive two-year liberal arts grounding for students who may then choose to go on to four-year colleges.

STATE COLLEGES. There are presently 19 such colleges, with an enrollment of 227,000 students. Their four-year program, leading to a bachelor's degree, is open to any California high school graduate who placed in the upper 33⅓ percent of his class, plus successful community college graduates. The emphasis is on undergraduate instruction, and some of the state colleges —notably San Jose State, San Diego State, and Long Beach State—compare well in program and teaching to the best state universities of the country.

THE UNIVERSITY. UC, at the top of the pyramid, accepts only the top 12.5 percent of California high school graduates, plus a limited number of out-of-state students who placed in the top 6 percent of their class. Academically, the university is intended to be, and is, an elitist institution. It also has

* Of the $1 billion, about three-quarters is paid for by the state of California, the remainder from federal grants and research contracts.

three exclusive and jealously guarded functions within California public higher education: to act as the state's primary agency for research; to grant doctorates; to train students for certain professions such as medicine, dentistry, pharmacy, law, and architecture. The master plan assigned these functions to the university campuses to avoid the cost and chaos many feared if the state colleges tried to duplicate them.

UC's tight admission requirements came under increasing criticism in the late 1960s because of the minuscule numbers of blacks and Mexican-Americans who could qualify under them. (The percentage of these minorities enrolled at the eight campuses was less than 2 percent in the late 1960s —even while they represented 19 percent of California high school enrollment.) Thus a special quota of 2 percent, with an option of up to 4 percent, was set for culturally and economically deprived applicants who, admissions officers believe, could, with proper motivation and counseling, perform satisfactorily at the university level. Early experience showed this 4 percent segment earning grades about comparable with the rest of the university's students.

The nine UC campuses provided a fascinating study in diversity. UCLA, in a posh Los Angeles suburb, did not grant a doctorate before 1938 but now ranks among the nation's top 15 universities; it is strong in community involvement, athletics, and several academic disciplines. San Diego, with four Nobel laureates, has one of the best natural science faculties of the U.S. (Scripps Institution of Oceanography, etc.), plus a unique system of "cluster colleges"—science-oriented Revelle, academically and socially freer John Muir, and a controversial Third College especially for blacks, Mexican-Americans, and independently minded whites. Santa Barbara has been a poor sister on the academic scale, seen by many as a surfboard-and-bikini haven; in 1970 it became a center of the most violent campus discord. San Francisco has no undergraduates, just the prestigious UC Medical Center. Santa Cruz, opened in 1965, tries to conquer academic impersonality by division into physically separated colleges of 650 students each. Davis, in the Central Valley between San Francisco and Sacramento, has outstanding liberal arts and physical science programs but is most famous for its agricultural research. Riverside, outside Los Angeles, a pioneer in citrus research and now smog research, has been referred to as "the most tranquil and conservative outpost in the UC system." Irvine, on land donated by the ranch of the same name in booming Orange County, stresses interdisciplinary courses and individual counseling.

But Berkeley, mother of all the others, is still the brightest light of the UC system. Academically, it may be the most famous for its work in physics (the Lawrence Radiation Laboratory), biochemistry, and English, but scores of its faculty, in widely divergent disciplines, stand at the top of their fields. In 1966, the respected American Council on Education found that Berkeley's graduate departments made it "the best balanced, distinguished university in the country." The conclusion came as a rude shock to Harvard, hitherto considered the finest. In a 1971 sequel, the Council found Berkeley had actually widened its lead. In comparison to Berkeley's 32 top-ranked departments, Harvard had 27, Stanford 16, the University of Chicago 14, Yale 13, Michigan, MIT and Princeton 12 each, Caltech 11, and Wisconsin 8.

Berkeley can also offer a magnificent 3.5-million-volume library, a $4.8 million University Art Museum in which visitors move from level to level in a flow of curving space, and now historic Sproul Plaza (made famous by the inauguration of the Free Speech Movement in what now seems a very long ago 1964). As *Newsweek* summarized this turbulent heartland of UC, "Whatever any campus has, Berkeley can usually match, whether the measure be distinguished faculty, student radicals, lab facilities, 'street people,' or beauty —in its girls and its setting."

At times in the late 1960s, it appeared that the chain of violent events that afflicted Berkeley would begin to drive away some of the university's outstanding faculty. Isolated cases of prestigious scholars packing up to go back East were publicized in the press. But in fact, Berkeley averaged only 24 annual resignations out of a tenured faculty of 1,000 in the years following 1964. In 1969, only 17 resigned. One reason was the immense power and independence still enjoyed by the UC faculty; in 1964, for instance, the American Association of University Professors called UC's academic senate the strongest such organization in the country. Another reason was UC's reserve capital of high prestige, accumulated during the regimes of presidents like Robert Gordon Sproul * (1929–58), who brought many Nobel Prize winners to the university and is credited by many with making it into a great world institution, and Clark Kerr (1958–67), who helped formulate the master plan for higher education, guided development of the innovative new campuses like those at Irvine and Santa Cruz, and sought more independence for students and faculty.

Finally, Berkeley in particular offers an intellectual excitement and sense of currency with its times hard to duplicate elsewhere. As sociologist Robert N. Bellah wrote in his book *Beyond Belief*, explaining why he chose to leave Harvard for Berkeley in 1967:

> As against the magisterial certainty of Harvard, Berkeley stands in sharp antithesis; not the calm order of Protestant tradition but the wide-open chaos of the post-Protestant, post-modern era. For all its inner problems, for all of its tensions with an increasingly unsympathetic environment, Berkeley evinces the intensity, the immediacy, the openness of an emergent social order. For one trying to grapple with and define what that order is, it is a good place to be.

Even scholars less attracted to the societal cutting edge were realizing by the late 1960s that they might as well remain at or seek out UC for its many advantages, since the pattern of campus revolt and discord invented at Berkeley had apparently become a national phenomenon. There were few if any safe islands left.

---

* Sproul, according to Lou Cannon, "was a big, back-slapping Rotarian booster of a man who through hard-sell lobbying of the legislature was no more out of place than a welcoming speech to the freshman class." To deal with a legislative crisis, *Time* reported in 1947, "Bob Sproul always has a secret weapon in reserve: alumni of the Order of the Golden Bears, a pack of onetime Berkeley campus big shots who come out of hibernation whenever Golden Bear Sproul cries for help."

The university regents, traditionally regarded as genial guardians of UC and a buffer between it and the political world, have in recent years been caught in a swirl of controversy unprecedented in America—a story to which we will return later. The state constitution says simply that they shall have "all powers of organization and government" over the university and be composed of 16 members appointable by the governor for 16-year terms, plus eight ex-officio members (all state officials, including the governor). The regents are to be free of "all political and sectarian influences." And otherwise, nothing is said about their qualifications. The state colleges also have their own board, as do the junior colleges.

Ever since the master plan's enactment in 1960, there have been challenges to its effectiveness and proposals to change it. One pressure is from the state colleges, which chafe under the rules that forbid them to grant doctorates or engage in more than limited research activities. At a minimum, they have wanted to have their title changed to "university," a shift they believe will be especially helpful in the recruitment of faculty, even if their basic functions remain unchanged. Culminating a five-year legislative effort, a bill was passed in 1971 renaming the California State Colleges the California State University and Colleges. The trustees of the state colleges and the Coordinating Council for Higher Education were instructed to develop jointly and approve criteria to determine when each of the state colleges may call itself a university.

Heaven for a UC professor, it is said, is to have six or seven graduate students interested in his field of concentration, so that he can do his research using their imagination and talents, even while he is training them. The result is that UC does more research and turns out more doctorates than any other institution of higher learning in America. Much of the work is vital, economically, to the state of California. Even through the years that "liberal" Edmund G. Brown was governor, the all-powerful UC board of regents remained a highly business- and establishment-oriented body. Neither Brown, nor any of his predecessors, nor Reagan, has ever appointed a black, Chicano, Indian, or Oriental to the board of regents. Instead, corporate interests like the Hearst Corporation and Bank of America (both with economic interests ranging far beyond their immediate fields of publishing and banking) have held seats over long periods of years. The age of the average regent has hovered around 60. And through the Brown administration, the board remained essentially noncontroversial; in fact the governor himself rarely attended meetings. (All this changed under Reagan, a forceful and regular participant.) Beneath the lofty, distant regents is the huge bureaucracy needed to administer the gigantic UC empire. And then there is the faculty, preoccupied with prestige- and award-winning research, often oblivious to the interests and intellectual development of all save the brightest and most aggressive students. A UC official told me it was perfectly true that the quiet, nonaggressive, A-average high school student who goes to the University of California will get a worse education than he would at a mediocre college where the faculty have time and interest to work with students.

All these factors played a role in the ill-defined but powerful Free Speech Movement of 1964–65, and remain important today. The students were protesting what seemed to them the impersonality and dehumanization of the university through its bureaucracy, the premium placed on research over teaching, the factory-like approach to producing people for industry, and, above all else, the lack of any real student role in shaping the goals and values of the university. By today's standards, the protests of the Free Speech Movement—entirely student-based, completely nonviolent—seem innocent indeed. Clark Kerr recognized the demands for a greater student voice as having some currency. If he had been permitted to deal in a forthright manner with the grievances of that time, as he sought to do, the university might well have been spared most if not all of the extreme militancy and violent turmoil it has since experienced. By responding with some positiveness to student demands, and beginning some democratization of its own structure, UC could have made an invaluable contribution to constructive university change all over America. Other universities, recognizing UC's preeminent position, would have moved voluntarily to make the same reforms.

But it was not to be so. The broad California public was angered and frustrated by the seeming uprising in the university that public tax dollars supported. The faculty, with its own entrenched privileges to defend, was reluctant to accommodate. The board of regents was not anxious to see fundamental reforms, and was concerned about the public reaction. Kerr found himself almost isolated as an apologist for student unrest, refusing to pander to public opinion. Then came 1966 and Reagan's first gubernatorial campaign, in which he called for an investigation of UC Berkeley, a campus he said was dominated by "a minority of malcontents, beatniks, and filthy-speech advocates." Students must "obey the rules or get out," Reagan said repeatedly.

Once in office, Reagan tried to keep his campaign promises. He announced that the fiscal policy of his administration would be to "squeeze, cut, and trim." And he suggested both a 25 percent budget cut and charging of tuition for the first time in UC's history. Kerr warned that UC would be forced, as it never had before, to turn away qualified applicants. Alarmed over the budget cuts, he suspended all new fall admissions and unwisely sought a vote of confidence from the board of regents. And on January 20, 1967, at the first meeting attended by Reagan, the regents voted 14–8 to dismiss him. The reaction to Kerr's firing—across state and nation—was one of shock. Flags flew at half mast at all UC campuses. The lead editorial in the New York *Times* was entitled "Twilight of a Great University."

Subsequently, it took nine months to find a successor to Kerr. The man picked was Dr. Charles J. Hitch. He has performed creditably if not brilliantly in his terribly difficult job; at one point he told the Los Angeles *Times* that his greatest accomplishment as president was survival.

Even with Reagan in office, working assiduously (through persuasion and appointments) to build a permanent majority of regents favorable to his position on university affairs, it is possible that accommodations between students and administration would eventually have been made, letting the Free Speech Movement fade into history as a fairly isolated phenomenon. But in the same years, the Vietnam war boiled to the surface as a national issue, inflaming campuses everywhere. The plight of the nation's black and Mexican-American minorities was dramatized by the civil rights movement, urban riots, and the war on poverty. Hard-core radicalism took root on the campuses with organizations like Students for a Democratic Society. More importantly, a whole generation of American students became "radicalized" —the vast majority opposed to violence in demonstrations, but still committed to a general restructuring of American society to make it less war-oriented, more responsive to human needs. "The students here," I heard from one UC official, "believe that the last 25 years devoted to physical sciences must be followed by 25 years of advance in social sciences. They see we've developed great technological skills but few social skills to deal with the multiple social injustices of our system. And the students say, if society can't see that, perhaps a little demonstration and rioting will get its attention."

At least in the short term, of course, the rioting can be highly unproductive—and dangerous to the university. In the late 1960s, every public opinion poll showed large majorities of the people in favor of "cracking down" on campus dissent. What the disillusioned "middle American" taxpayers did not know was that only a small minority of students engaged in the most violent forms of demonstration. Nor was it well known that one in 10 UC students was putting idealism into practice through volunteer help in disadvantaged areas, helping in schools, tutoring, and staffing summer camps for needy youngsters. Through 1969, UC-Berkeley accounted for 10 percent of the entire membership of the Peace Corps.

The early Reagan years predictably plunged the university into political turmoil on a scale hitherto unknown in America. At one point Reagan suggested—he later said "figuratively"—that a "bloodbath" might be needed to quell violent campus demonstrations. Students and like-thinking faculty responded in kind, accusing Reagan of trying to "repeal the Renaissance," of replacing "the creative society with an illiterate society." Frederick Dutton, a strong liberal Democrat and chief adversary of Reagan on the board of regents, said: "Reagan came into a fiery situation, but instead of dousing it he threw kerosene on it." After one meeting of the regents, Reagan walked over to Dutton and called him, to his face, "a lying son of a bitch."

What the rhetoric sometimes obscures is what has actually happened to the university in the Reagan years. It has not, as Reagan's enemies predicted, plunged into fiscal chaos, with massive faculty departures and thousands of rejected students. But the budget has been subjected to intense scrutiny by the regents and the legislature. UC is no longer, as Jay Michael, its chief legislative lobbyist puts it, the "sacred cow" it once was. Hitch cannot do what Clark Kerr did—plead emotionally for any and all projects desired by his administration and faculty, practically breaking into tears when any program, however mediocre, was suggested for cutting. The UC operating budget has increased by about 50 percent since the mid-1960s, but most of the increase has been eaten up by inflation, merit pay raises, and the costs of a 28-percent increase in enrollment. Capital construction has been cut back drastically, both by the regents and even more by the legislature. Funding shortages are equally if not more serious within the state colleges. As a temporary expedient, budget cuts for the universities and colleges may not prove to be fatal; were they to continue for several years, however, the situation could become desperate, both in research and teaching.

The omens for California higher education were not bright as the decade of the 1970s began. Still fresh in memory was the 1968–69 uprising at San Francisco State College, in which a black instructor, associated with the Black Panthers, urged students to bring guns on campus and a long strike ensued, with the support of radical factions both among students and faculty. Campus bombings occurred and as many as 700 San Francisco policemen were on duty; the college president resigned, to be replaced by the controversial semanticist-turned-administrator, Dr. S. I. Hayakawa. The pitched battle of 1969 at Berkeley over the "People's Park," marked by one death and helicopter gassing of the main campus, was followed by the 1970 demonstrations against the U.S. invasion of Cambodia, during which some radical faculty members made the inflammatory suggestion that the university be "reconstituted" into a political force. Level-headed moderates on campus faculties had their hands full in restoring and keeping order.

There was danger of public higher education falling into general disrepute in the very state where it had made its greatest achievements in America. Granting a 5-percent pay increase for state employees in 1970, the legislature, with Reagan's blessing, took a gratuitous slap at the universities by specifically exempting their employees. (In 1971, Reagan vetoed proposed 10 percent pay increases for university employees, but in 1972 he did recommend a 7.1 percent pay boost for faculty members.) In the autumn 1970 statewide elections, despite a desperate need for more medical personnel, voters rejected a $246 million health sciences bond issue endorsed by most major officials (including Reagan) and newspapers in the state—the rejection coming, many thought, because that now-so-controversial name "University of California" was attached. (More doctors die in California each year than are trained there, the medical manpower deficit made up by what amounts to parasitizing of other states and foreign countries—most of them poorer than California—which have spent heavily to train physicians, dentists, and nurses.)

The students had reason to bemoan the regents' decision, in 1970, to go along with Reagan on imposing the first tuition fees in the university's history. There were no signs that faculty were giving more time to teaching; quite the reverse, the average UC faculty member's weekly time devoted to teaching of undergraduates fell from 13.5 hours in 1960 to 9.7 hours in 1970.

By 1970 there were signs that the political assault on the universities might have reached the point of overkill. Reagan himself saw his winning election margin cut in half, and Senator George Murphy, who had campaigned fiercely against students, was defeated. Rafferty, the rabid right-winger who had once called Berkeley "a four-year course in sex, drugs, and treason," was defeated for reelection by Wilson Riles. By virtue of his position, Riles became a member of the university board of regents—the first black man ever to serve there.

After 1970, Reagan shifted his fire to a new target of opportunity, the welfare mess, and simultaneously the fires of violent dissent in California's universities seemed to be flickering out. The resistance of established institutions was more than the students had thought, demonstrations seemed to have led nowhere, and more and more students seemed to be concentrating on personal development and private interests. But it seemed unlikely that the campuses would ever revert to the quietism of the 1950s; now students had the vote and knew how to organize, and the portentous legacy of the 1960s was that students, for the first time in American history, had become a factor to be reckoned with in the political life of state and nation.

## *The Environment: Desecration and Hope*

Californians rank among the most determined exploiters, desecraters, and protectors of the natural environment that the world has ever seen. Like its citizens, the state government has a spotty record that began in despoliation, turned in recent years to the possibilities of conservation, and may yet—if there is time—save for future generations much of the magnificent heritage of natural California.

Smog, now a severe national problem, came first to the Los Angeles Basin, later to appear in alarming measure in cities like San Jose, Oakland, and Fresno. For almost two decades, air pollution bills have been winning approval in Sacramento, the most famous being the nation's first serious efforts to control automobile emissions. California's emission standards remain the toughest in the nation, and beginning with 1973 models, carmakers will be fined up to $5,000 for each vehicle that fails to meet the state's standards. In 1969, the state senate surprised the world by passing a bill to prohibit the sale of motor vehicles powered by internal combustion engines. The assembly killed the measure, but it was reintroduced in 1970 and might just be passed one day.

California has been less innovative in water pollution control. In 1969, it passed a water quality control act setting up nine regional boards with clear-cut regulatory powers. But the 1971 Nader task force report included a charge that the act was "written by polluters and for polluters, weakened further by nonenforcement." State authorities, of course, denied the charge. In autumn 1970, voters by a 3–1 margin approved a $250 million bond issue for sewage treatment facilities.

Of California's 100 million acres, the federal government owns about half—largely as national forests, parks, and military bases. Private holdings total 50 million acres, with about 38 million in farming and 6.5 million in commercial forestry. Little more than 3 percent of the land area, in fact, is occupied by cities. But those cities often occupy the choicest locations, and their environs have been in peril ever since the great postwar housing push began. Obviously, there was a need for a state plan to show where open space should be preserved (and purchased by the state, if necessary), where transportation corridors might go, where the cities of the future should be located. Beaches are another critical problem; along the whole coastline from Oregon to Mexico, only 90 miles are open to the public, and real estate billboards march up the coastline in tasteless profusion.

The state planning office spent five years and $4 million on a state plan in the 1960s, but the result was a fiasco, hopelessly unspecific and wrapped up in bureaucratise. Disgusted with the state agency's performance, the San Francisco-based conservation group California Tomorrow announced in 1970 it would go to work on a state plan with private financing, and issue it early in the decade.

The legislature did take a forward step in 1965–66 with passage of its "Open Space Land Program," which seeks to create "green belts" of prime agricultural land near urban areas. When the suburban housing tracts started their hedgehop growth across the orchards and open fields, taxes on nearby farms soared under the "highest and best use" formula of assessment, forcing many farmers to sell out. The new legislation permitted farmers to enter into contracts with county governments to keep their taxes based on agricultural use of the land. But according to the Nader task force, the result has been "the twisting of a legitimate concern over the plight of prime crop land into an unjustifiable boondoggle for rich landowning corporations."

Some notable conservation victories have included bond issues for purchase of new and development of old parklands, defeat of a freeway through virgin redwood forests in the north, and the halt called to filling-in of San Francisco Bay. A scenic roads program got its start in the early 1960s when conservationists became upset by the state highway department's plan to "improve" the twisty, picturesque old Route 1 along the Big Sur coastline into a four- or eight-lane highway, a step which would have taken much of the magnificence away. At the urging of then state senator Fred Farr of nearby Carmel, the legislature agreed to a cooperative effort by state and local governments to select and then protect scenic corridors. This initiative later led to the federal scenic roads program as well. California is also creating what will eventually be a 4,000-mile system of parkways—low-speed, scenic roadways through elongated parks—the antithesis of freeways.

Aesthetics, however, have not been the main point of California's gargantuan postwar freeway development. More than 4,000 miles of freeways have been built since the Pasadena Freeway, California's first, in 1940. In 1959, the state started a 20-year plan to build 12,400 *more* miles of controlled access highway at a cost of more than $10 billion. By 1980, California will have 17 million motor vehicles; in 1970, it already had 12 million, 75 percent more than any other state. Builder and advocate of the great freeway system is the state division of highways and its ruling commission, a combine Wallace Stegner of Stanford has referred to as "having nobody to control it, too much money, too much power, and an engineering mentality."

The highway division has extraordinary powers of eminent domain; even more important, some billion dollars a year are assured it, without the possibility of gubernatorial or legislative review. This stems from a provision of the California constitution, actually an amendment added by popular vote in 1937, which states that highway user taxes (gasoline, oil, vehicle registrations) must be used directly for highway building or improvement. Proposals that any of these huge revenues might be diverted to alternate transportation systems, or air pollution control, are assailed as unconscionable "raids on the highway fund." In 1970, for instance, a modest proposal for diversion of up to 25 percent of locally generated gas taxes for smog prevention and mass transit was overwhelmingly voted down in statewide referendum after a scare campaign (warning of new taxes) launched by the highway lobby with heavy oil contributions.* In addition to petroleum interests, according to *Cry California*, the "Freeway Establishment" includes the trucking industry, automobile clubs (AAA), heavy-equipment manufacturers and dealers, concrete producers, general contractors, the lumber industry, rock and aggregate producers, and, of course, the state division of highways. There is no mightier lobby in California.

Many of the new freeways, like Interstate 5, which cuts north to south through the Central Valley and runs clear from Oregon to San Diego, generate scant opposition and are welcomed by communities along their route. Coastal and urban California have begun to react differently, starting with the now famous revolt of San Franciscans against the unsightly Embarcadero Freeway in the late 1950s. Subsequent revolts against the freeway builders' plans have been noted in such places as Beverly Hills, Laguna Beach, the Monterey Peninsula, and Santa Barbara, with varying results. Under pressure from conservationist and community groups, the highway engineers have agreed to drop hundreds of miles from their planned multithousand-mile network of new freeways. In a portentous 1971 decision, a federal judge ordered a halt to the $100 million, 14-mile Foothill Freeway in southern Alameda County, about 23 miles from San Francisco. A unique alliance, including the Sierra Club and the Mexican-American Legal Defense Fund for La Raza Unida, brought the court action, charging that the new road violated two federal statutes—the Environmental Protection Act of 1969, because no statement had been filed assessing the freeway's impact on the environment, and the Uniform Relocation Assistance Act of 1970, because officials had made no relocation plans for some 5,000 Mexican Americans whose homes would be displaced by the road. The environmental problem included the road's path through the Hayward Botanical Garden and two

---

* In 1971, however, legislation was passed extending the state sales tax to gasoline and earmarking most of the revenues for public transportation.

other parks and its course close to an earthquake fault; without relocation assistance, the displaced families would mostly be forced into the slums of San Jose and Oakland. One of the public interest lawyers in the case asserted that the court's ruling "challenges the validity of the planning process used by the federal government [for new freeways] all over the country."

California has spawned more conservation groups than any other state, the most famous of all being the Sierra Club, founded by the famed naturalist John Muir in 1892 to "explore, enjoy, and preserve the Sierra Nevada and other scenic resources of the U.S." The club still has a lot of hikers, but its principal visibility has come through the great fights to preserve the natural environment. Examples: fighting for a Redwoods National Park, lobbying Congress to prohibit dams that would encroach on the Grand Canyon of the Colorado, trying to halt a six-lane expressway along the banks of the Hudson in New York state, opposing the supersonic transport and the Alaskan oil pipeline. In addition to lobbying (which caused Internal Revenue Service cancellation of the club's tax-exempt status), the club has increasingly resorted to lawsuits to protect the public's right to a clean environment. Naturally, big industries have become highly irate; one criticism is that "the club has gone overboard, mounting irresponsible drives to preserve everything in sight." But the Sierra Club has thrived on controversy, growing from 14,500 members in 1960 to about 135,000 in 1972—although a fall-off in the growth rate necessitated some staff and budget cutbacks in the latter year. In 1969 longtime club executive director David Brower resigned in a dispute over financing and publication of lavish books depicting the glories of the natural environment. Brower went off to form a new group known as Friends of the Earth, another of the plethora of conservation groups crowding the California (and now national) stage.

The lobbying efforts of California's multiple conservation groups, once poorly organized and coordinated, are now served collectively by the Planning and Conservation League, set up in 1966 with a full-time staff in Sacramento. (The Sierra Club also has a full-time lobbying operation in the capital.) PCL programs, reflecting the interests of its 87 affiliated organizations, range over such fields as auto emissions, state planning, low-cost housing, mass transit, scenic highways, billboard controls, underground power lines, and open-space protection. In 1971, PCL was in the forefront of a fight to pass legislation to provide orderly planning and growth along the California coastline—an idea vigorously fought by oil companies, utilities concerned about their power plant sites, and owners of major seashore land developments. But despite backing from some of the prominent new Democratic legislative leaders, the entrenched economic powers and their friends in associations of local governments (hungry for the tax revenue from new developments) were able to lobby the bill to death.

The fight to save the Golden State will doubtless be a difficult one, against entrenched and well-funded interests, inertia, and the continuing effects of damage already done to the natural landscape. But now, at least, the conservationists have become strong in number and more sophisticated in technique, and their efforts will be supplemented in the next years by various activities designed to follow up on the Nader task force report. These include a "public interest corporation" set up by Keith Roberts (author of the Nader study on the State Water Project), and a contemplated new Sacramento lobby, probably to be headed by Robert Fellmeth, to press for reforms on land ownership, water projects and pollution control, using the weapons of legislative persuasion, class action litigation and new investigations. Such efforts to redress the lobbying imbalance in favor of the special interests were scarcely dreamed of a few years past. In the years to come, they may play a vital role in reordering Californian priorities—and values.

## Geographic California

"Of the states subsequent to the original thirteen, California is the only one with a genuine natural boundary," James Bryce observed in *The American Commonwealth*. Westward lies the iridescent Pacific; to the south the Colorado River and the Mexican desert; to the east the high, snowy peaks of the Sierra Nevadas; to the north more mountains and forests of Oregon. Superimposed on the east coast, the outline of California would run from New York City on the north to within a few miles of Jacksonville, Florida, on the south. It is a land of startling contrasts—dense forests, sun-scorched deserts, alpine mountains, fruitful valleys. The most cited contrast is between 14,-494-foot Mt. Whitney, highest peak south of Alaska, and Death Valley, just 60 miles to the southeast, dipping 282 feet below sea level, the lowest point of the Western Hemisphere and the hottest and driest in the United States. Rainfall along the moist northern coast averages 35 inches a year and has gone to a record 190 inches at Honeydew; at Bagdad, a weather station in the Mojave Desert, two years have been known to pass without a drop of precipitation.

Most of coastal California is sunny and balmy, the kind of lotus land that has drawn millions. But nature can play cruel tricks. Californians live in uneasy knowledge, and some in intense terror, of the San Andreas fault, which runs practically the entire length of the state, the longest and most exposed fracture anywhere in the world's crust. It has been in motion 65 million years, with slippage between the two sides of 300 miles. West of the fault, which is 20 miles deep, the land is moving northward about two centimeters a year faster than the land to the east. What concerns geologists is that the two abutting edges of the fault near San Francisco and Los Angeles are presently frozen together. Incredible amounts of restrained energy are thus built up. Eventually, they demand release. More than 20 severe earthquakes have struck California in the past century. In 1857, an earthquake in the Techachapis, north of Los Angeles, caused a 30-foot jump in the western edge. The great 1906 earthquake in San Francisco caused a 30-foot movement. Buildings collapsed, streets sank, fires ravaged the heart of the city, and close to 700 were killed. In February 1971, Californians got another grim reminder that they live atop one of the most active earthquake zones in the world. A tremor officially described as "moderate" occurred near Los Angeles' San Fernando Valley on the line of the San Gabriel fault, which is part of the San Andreas network.* The quake took 64 lives, caused damage that may cost $1 billion to restore, triggered more than 1,000 landslides, and released methane gas from the ocean floor near Malibu Point. This is mere child's play in comparison to the potential destruction of a really serious quake, like that of 1906. Respected seismologists estimate the damage might be $10 billion and cost hundreds of thousands of lives. It is "reasonable" to expect, according to a state legislative committee report, that a great earthquake—7.75 or higher on the Richter scale—may occur "once in every 60 to 100 years." The time frame thus suggested: 1966 to 2006.

Scientists discount the suggestion that all of California west of the San Andreas might slip into the ocean in a great Superquake. But Curt Gentry, in his book *The Late, Great State of California*, makes just that suggestion and calls his book "nonfiction."

Earthquake is not the only threat to naturally pleasant California. The Southern coastal region is caught in a cycle of wind, fire, floods, and mudslides. Over the low hills near the ocean grows a low, dry undergrowth known as chaparral, along with pine forests a few miles further inland. At the end of a long, dry summer, the prevailing wind patterns from the ocean may change and the Santa Ana winds, crackling dry and powerful, come sweeping in from the desert. The slightest spark on the chaparral and a conflagration ensues.

In autumn 1970, after Southern California had gone without significant rain for 200 days, humidity had dropped to 5 percent and temperatures were over 100°. The hot Santa Anas swept in again, often at velocities of as much as 70 mph., starting 10 simultaneous timber and brush fires. In the most extensive fires of California's history, a half-million acres were burned over, eight lives lost, more than 1,000 homes and other buildings burnt, with damage of $170 million.

Fire is not alone in the cycle. In winter, especially after bad fires which have destroyed the ground cover, torrential downpours on the desert-like land may cause mudslides that come down the canyons to envelop houses and cost incalculable damage. In 1969, the worst rains, mudslides, landslides, and damage of modern times hit Southern California. Hundreds of homes built precariously on cliffs or flood-prone areas were destroyed.

For all of California's sweetness and artificiality, the primordial cycles of fire and rain and earthquake continue, nature keeping man in his place.

Befitting California's nation size, its geography may be reviewed in three distinct parts.

---

* The 1971 quake shocked scientists because the precise area struck had been seismically inactive since about the end of the last Ice Age—around 10,000 years ago.

First, there is the California which remains fairly close to its original condition. Here one speaks of the mountain and big timber country of the North Coast and lordly Sierra Nevada, the forbidding southern desert, and the great Central Valley. This discussion follows in the next several pages.

Second, there is the man-made civilization around the shores of San Francisco Bay. This section begins on page 98.

Finally, there is the California Southland, a megalopolis stretching from San Diego to Santa Barbara, with Los Angeles its linchpin. See page 129.

## *North Coast and Sierra Nevada*

We start with the North Coast and the mountains. The rugged, lonely coastline stretching northward from San Francisco is a land of rolling fog, breakers smashing against high bluffs, and of moist, deep forests. The most renowned of these hold the stately redwoods, which soar to 200 or 300 feet in height and endure—where lumbermen spare them—for a lifespan of 400 to 800 years. Few human experiences compare to standing within a grove of these ancient redwoods, where the light is a dim cathedral luminescence broken by occasional beams of sunlight filtering through to the forest floor.

In 1820, when California logging began, there were two million acres of redwoods in a strip extending from the Big Sur Country south of San Francisco into Northern California. Today, less than 270,000 acres of virgin redwoods still stand. And all but a few thousand acres stand in danger of desecration by the end of this century. A great conservationist battle, led by the Save-the-Redwoods League and the Sierra Club, led to establishment of the Redwoods National Park in 1968. The park will preserve 58,000 acres of the most handsome virgin redwood stands, including two older state parks, for posterity. But such compromises had to be reached with the lumber industry that many doubt the viability of the oddly shaped park as it now stands. To reach it, one often has to drive past huge sawmills and tepee burners and fight for highway space—even on roads through the national forest—with big commercial logging trucks. The timber industry is continuing to cut close up to park boundaries, and from many choice spots in the park one can look a few hundred yards and see cruelly cut over hillsides. One writer describes it as "an impoverished little park whose watershed is in enemy hands, whose resources are constantly menaced, whose peace and quiet are reserved for the hard of hearing and whose unspoiled vistas are most impressive to those with tunnel vision." But proposals to increase the park size face a very uncertain future in Congress.

The redwoods fight, some believe, is just the first chapter of a battle to preserve Northern California's treasures, including wilderness areas, the state's few wild rivers, the lush Napa Valley vineyards, and some of the best open land in California. An ongoing battle surrounds the whole lumber industry of Northern California, with the U.S. Forest Service anxious to authorize much more logging than the conservationists believe should be permitted. Counting not only redwoods but other tree species—pine and Douglas fir, incense cedar, mountain birch, and white oak—Northern and Sierra California still have the greatest virgin forest in the United States, about 10 million acres in all. The Forest Service, which has no less than 20 million of California's 102 million acres under its stewardship,* is under constant lumber industry pressure to open up more and more of these lands, not only for domestic lumber needs but so that the industry can get its profits from a yearly exportation of seven billion board feet of logs, lumber, and pulp to Japan. Among the Forest Service's many problems is the unfettered access to public land made possible by 1872-vintage mining law, which—in the words of journalist William K. Wyant—"reflects the rough-and-ready, finders-keepers philosophy of California gold rush days." At the end of 1970, 32,500 "live mining claims" had been made on public land in California. When federal agents went to investigate one of these in Northern California's Shasta Trinity National Forest, one of them was shot and two others attacked, presumably by the irate prospectors.

The biggest city on the entire North Coast is Eureka (pop. 24,337) with the world's largest redwood mills and a superb natural harbor. (I remember having the first radio interview of my life in Eureka, in 1947; in those days even the most inconsequential young tourist was specially welcomed.) For the most part, the North Coast has only small lumbering and fishing villages, some with a distinctly New England flavor reflecting their first settlers. Cape Mendocino, the westernmost extrusion of the coterminous United States, still has virtually no roads or people, though the first developers are now selling off some summer lots among the redwoods.

Moving inland in the region south of the Oregon border, one comes on more thinly populated area including the home of two lonely volcanic mountain peaks, Shasta and Lassen, the southernmost of a chain of volcanic mountains that stretches to the Aleutian Islands. Lassen, which last erupted in 1915, still emits wisps of steam and smoke; Shasta has a snow cover throughout the year and is a winter ski resort. At the northeastern extremity of the state is the bleak lava country of the California plateau, akin to arid eastern Oregon. So unlike Southern Californians, the few people of this remote other California are stern, rugged folk, leading a robust and difficult life. "The towns of Northern California," Irving Stone wrote, "are so old and inbred that if you have an argument with a merchant or city clerk in Alturas you find that you have offended half the families of Modoc County." Modoc County has only 7,469 permanent residents, but until the reapportionment of the 1960s it had, together with two adjacent counties, equal representation in the state senate with Los Angeles and that county's 6 (now 7) million.

---

* Together with the Bureau of Land Management, the Park Service, and other agencies, federal control extends to 45 million acres in California—44.8 percent of the state's total land area.

Ranging southward 430 miles from Mount Lassen are the magnificent Sierra Nevada Mountains, the great granite spine that cracks California from the rest of the continent. The Sierra Nevada play an inextricable role in California history, for at their feet settlers found the gold which touched off the great Gold Rush of 1848 and the state's first great population boom. (Beyond a certain architectural influence, by contrast, the much older Spanish mission civilization of early California has played a minimal role in the development of the California we know today.) It was the Sierras which inspired the poet's words chiseled on the State Capitol at Sacramento— "Bring me men to match my mountains." As Neil Morgan has written, "The Sierra Nevada tends to unite Californians in some sense of community. In its alpine fastness, one cannot escape the feel of history. Here lies an unyielding, unchanging California in contrast to the one below."

The jewel of the Sierras is Yosemite National Park, created in 1890 by a Congress influenced by the writings of John Muir, the great naturalist who spent many years of his life in these mountains that he named the "range of light." The breathtaking Yosemite Valley, with its El Capitan, Half Dome, Bridalveil, and Yosemite Falls, is thought by many to be the most beautiful valley on this continent. But the park—farsightedly created to encompass 1,189 square miles—also contains the great sequoia groves with trees that began their growth as much as 1,500 years before the birth of Christ, and remote highlands filled with alpine meadows, pine stands, rushing streams, and waterfalls. Most of this territory is still accessible only on foot or horseback.

It was only 45 years ago, in fact, that the first automobile road was built into Yosemite. What the automobile did to the Yosemite Valley is a story sad to tell. By the late 1960s, a summer weekend brought as many as 70,000 tourists, all in their private fume-spewing vehicles that added to the smog problem created by the thousands of campfires they built.* Traffic was often slowed to a standstill. In desperation, the National Park Service first instituted one-way roads and then barred all private auto traffic from the valley. Instead, tourists must now park their cars in peripheral areas and are transported about the valley in free open-air sightseeing buses. Now, as in times past, there is room and calm for horseback riding and bikes. Camping spots have also been cut back to reduce air pollution and correct Yosemite's reputation as the worst "tent tenement" among all national parks. Intent on averting a repetition of a 1970 riot, caused when 200 young people refused to break up an unauthorized camp on Stoneman Meadow and mounted rangers charged in, causing many injuries, the Park Service has tightened law enforcement. But rangers' weapons are no longer flaunted, and more young rangers have been hired. They are expert in rock climbing, ecology, Indian lore, astronomy, geology—"whatever it takes to relate to people," according to Lynn Thompson, the new park superintendent.

* The annual visitor figure at Yosemite is presently close to 2.5 million; practically all these visitors are intent on seeing the comparatively small valley area.

"Progress" in another form has also come to Yosemite—the widening into a comparatively dull, broad highway of the narrow old Tioga Pass Road to the east, once undoubtedly the scariest high mountain road (precipitous drops, minimal guard rails) in all the U.S.A.

The next most popular spot in the Sierra Nevada is cold, radiant Lake Tahoe, now pollution-threatened and afflicted by incredibly cheap gambling casinos just over the border on the Nevada side. The federal Bureau of Outdoor Recreation has recommended establishing a "national lakeshore" to protect land in the Lake Tahoe Basin from further development.

Now man-made pollution is even threatening the trails and summit of lordly Mount Whitney, within Sequoia National Park. Whitney is presently being ascended by more than 10,000 people a year, all bringing along bottles, cans, wrappers, and other reminders of the world below that too often get left along the trail. As recently as 1963, only 2,000 people reached the summit; I can remember reaching the top in 1954, gasping for breath in the thin air, but exalted to stand totally alone, without another human in sight, on the highest spot in the 48 states. Now the National Park Service is considering a heliport on the summit to facilitate trash removal!

Not far from Mount Whitney, within the Sequoia National Forest, lies exquisite Mineral King Valley, ringed by majestic snowy peaks with eight vast, natural snow bowls curving upward from the 7,800-foot-high valley floor—one of the finest sites anywhere for a ski resort. The U.S. Forest Service, manager of the land, decided that under its "multiple-use" philosophy (water and watershed management, timber grazing, wild life, and recreation), Mineral King would be an ideal spot for a ski and year-round resort to serve the needs of the burgeoning Los Angeles area, only 228 miles to the southwest. So it invited bids on a carefully controlled development and accepted the proposal of Walt Disney Productions to build a $35.3 million year-round resort, to accommodate skiers in winter and fishermen, hikers, and swimmers in the warmer months. The Disney people intend to construct an "Alpine Village" of steeply pitched and many-gabled roofs with hotels, restaurants, shops, and 22 ski lifts and gondolas. Parking will be in a huge underground garage over a mile away, with an electric cog railway to carry visitors into the village, where only horse-drawn sleighs will ply the streets. Patronage is expected to reach a million annually.

The Forest Service is delighted with the sophisticated Disney proposal, which its developers say will avoid overcrowding traffic jams, and primitive luggage handling which afflicts not only the European ski resorts but many in the U.S. as well. But the preservationists of the Sierra Club decry the project, alleging that it will desecrate and overpopulate the small valley, doing irreparable damage to the delicate alpine ecology. Some also suggest, as free-lance writer Arnold Hano has reported, that the project would be "a transplanted Disneyland—cute, colorful, supercalifragilisticexpialidocious and out of keeping with the rugged setting of the High Sierra." The Disney camp hotly retorts that it will make its development as appropriate to Mineral King as Disneyland was for the recreation needs of Anaheim, that there will be no pollution, no erosion, no desecration, and not even the destruction of a single sequoia, even though an access road to the almost inaccessible site will run through nine miles of redwood groves in the adjacent Sequoia National Park. The Sierra Club went to court to block the project but was turned down flatly by the U.S. Court of Appeals, which said it could not find that government officials had been arbitrary "in determining to make available a vast area of incomparable natural beauty to more people rather than to have it remain inaccessible except to a rugged few."

Predictably, conservative politicians like Governor Reagan and then Senator George Murphy backed the Disney project. But so have former Governor Brown and former Senator Kuchel, an avid conservationist throughout his public career, who said: "If we fail to develop selected areas such as Mineral King, the 50 million people who will be in California before the end of this century will spill over the sides of the coastal cities and ravage the Sierra with unplanned and undirected enthusiasm for the vanishing outdoors."

## The Great Central Valley: Cornucopia of Fruit and Vegetables

The topographic map of the western U.S.A., honeycombed with mountains and outthrusts, reveals no level area to compare with California's Great Central Valley. The dimensions of the valley, covering a sixth of California's land area, are hard to grasp; as Neil Morgan points out, the Appalachian mountain range of the east could easily fit into the valley, and its land area is greater than all of Denmark. Within the valley, the fields are flat and monotonous; the dusty little farm towns click off every few miles with scarcely a distinguishing mark. Great irrigation canals flow soundlessly through the fields, adding mugginess to the hot air. Only occasionally do tall windbreaks of cottonwoods or eucalyptus break the dull infinity of straight crop lines. For Californian and visitor alike, there seems little reason to tarry.

But this great mechanized farm plant is a wonder all in itself. Chiefly because of it, California leads the U.S.A. in the value of farm products—more than $4 billion each year, the heart of an overall state "agribusiness" of some $16 billion. No other California business—not even aerospace—is of comparable magnitude. Within the valley grows every species of temperate-zone or subtropical fruit, vegetable, or field crop known to man, tobacco alone excepted. The astonishing variety, concentrated in various parts of the valley according to soil type and precise climatic conditions, includes grapes, olives, plums, figs, peaches, oranges and lemons, alfalfa, cotton, Irish potatoes, sweetpotatoes, walnuts, almonds, tomatoes, corn, sugar beets, prunes, rice, strawberries, clover, asparagus, celery, lettuce, beans, onions, apricots, pomegranates, avocados, loquats, guavas, artichokes, cherries, honeydew melons, cantaloupes, cauliflower, spinach, dry beans, garlic, wheat, hops, barley, apples, and grapefruit—and this is only a partial list. The valley is also a major producer of beef and dairy cattle, concentrated in its dry borders. The state is second only to Iowa in livestock, second to Florida in citrus, second to Texas in cotton, and the preeminent or exclusive producer of a wide variety of exotic fruits and nuts.

California's great vineyards—in the Napa and Sonoma Valleys, and now more and more in the Salinas Valley near Monterey—produce 85 percent of the U.S.A.'s wine output, a $700-million-a-year business for the state. Wine consumption in America has increased 60 percent just since 1960, five times as fast as the population growth. (The quality is improving through advanced technology. A visiting British wine expert, Hugh Johnson, reported after a 1970 trip that "California is making wine as good as the wine of France. At the peaks not quite so good, but on the average maybe better.") Wine-tasting expeditions to the Napa and Sonoma wineries remain some of the most delectable adventures anywhere, bearing out the prediction of Robert Louis Stevenson, who honeymooned in the Napa Valley in 1880 and later wrote: "The smack of California earth shall linger on the palate of your grandson."

Technically, the Central Valley is two—the valley of the Sacramento River to the north, of the San Joaquin to the south. Both valleys are served by waters flowing down from the Sierras through the most intricate and extensive irrigation system ever built by man. A major portion of the labyrinth of dams, pumping stations, and canals has been financed by federal dollars through the Central Valley Project, which was first approved as a state project in the 1930s. Among other things, the CVP transfers water from the mountainous upper reach of the Sacramento River Valley to the drier San Joaquin Valley, where the combination of water and high temperatures makes possible a phenomenal growing season of nine to ten months.* Already, farm production in the San Joaquin Valley exceeds that of 44 other states, and three of its counties—Fresno, Kern, and Tulare—lead all counties in America. Something over $1 billion has already been invested in CVP, with projected expenditures as high as $4 billion to bring another three million acres of irrigable but still unexploited Central Valley land into production by later in this century. The land will be needed, for freeways and the cannibalization of prime producing farmland for suburban sprawl have taken well over a million acres out of production since World War II, a process that is continuing. (For a time in Los Angeles County, for instance, the bulldozers were flattening 3,000 acres of orange orchard a day.) Several major U. S. food producers

---

* The Central Valley Project should not be confused with the subsequently developed California Water Plan to transfer water from the north as far as Los Angeles and San Diego, which will be discussed later. It should be borne in mind that producing an average acre of crops on desert land requires five acre-feet of water; even with California's huge population, nine-tenths of the water use in the state is still for agriculture.

are also starting operations in Mexico, where labor is cheaper and land more plentiful.

Without the massive technical assistance it has received from the University of California—in development of hybrid strains, fertilizers, mechanical harvesters, pesticides, scientific irrigation, and feeding and extension courses —the state's farm industry would never have attained the heights it now occupies. The university's citrus experiment station at the Riverside campus, for instance, literally saved California's orange trees, afflicted by a rare virus, from obliteration in the 1940s; a disease-resistant variety was discovered and grafted onto trees throughout the state. In the early 1960s, a university scientist suddenly announced he had developed a hormone to double the annual production from an acre of grapes. University scientists invented a lettuce picker with pressure sensors to feel if a head is ready to pick and automatic knives to cut the stem. Pneumatic tree-shakers have been developed to harvest nuts and olives. Men lofted in the cages of scissor-extended booms pick citrus by wielding suction tubes. The university's scientists have worked to breed grapes, melons, asparagus, and other fruits that can be machine harvested; among the most celebrated of these is a new, squarish variety of tomato, developed through computer-controlled genetic breeding, which can be picked without damage by a harvesting machine developed at the university. One reason California made such dramatic inroads on Southern cotton production was that it was able to pick nine-tenths of its crop mechanically before the South had automatic equipment for one-tenth its crop. At Davis, a faculty of 14 offers a three-year course in wine-making—in effect, a free trade school for the California wine industry. University scientists help farmers carry on biological and chemical warfare against more than 100 varieties of insects plus fungi and viruses. (Sadly, many beneficial and harmless insects, birds, and other wildlife die in the process, resulting in a "web of death" documented by Rachel Carson in *Silent Spring*.)

Since the days of the gigantic Spanish and Mexican landholdings, most of which fell into Anglo hands after 1848, California has been preeminently a state of big farms. The number of farms has fallen by more than half since 1950 and is expected to drop to 30,000 by 1980; already two-thirds of the production comes from 15 percent of the farms. The *average* invested value of all California farms is a stupendous $327,000. Big "factory" farm operations are obviously more practical in an economy dependent on massive and expensive irrigation practices, airborne pest control and seeding, and the huge expense of sophisticated mechanical plowing and harvesting equipment. Today millionaire big-city entrepreneurs and giants like the Kern County Land Company, the Di Giorgio Corporation, and Schenley Industries own a substantial portion of Central Valley farmland. Corporations like Standard Oil, Tenneco, Kaiser Aluminum, and Southern Pacific—have diversified into agriculture. According to writer Nick Kotz, just three corporations—United Brands, Purex, and Bud Antle, a company partly owned by Dow Chemical—

already dominate California lettuce production. Tenneco, which had 1970 sales of $2.5 billion, has told its stockholders: "Tenneco's goal in agriculture is integration from the seedling to the supermarket." But *Business Week* reported in early 1972 that Tenneco and some other big corporations were cutting back on their California farm holdings. The problem: profits below expectations, or even cash losses in some operations, occasioned by farm price fluctuations, rising farm labor costs, and the corporations' lack of expertise in tending the land.

California's big farm landholding interests have for decades been favored by subsidization by state and federal governments alike. A principal reason that the state of California moved so rapidly into vast water projects for irrigation was that the big Central Valley landholders would be ineligible to receive water under federally sponsored irrigation projects, which have a 160-acre limitation for a single owner. (The average farm unit in the Central Valley is close to 1,000 acres.) The landowners made sure that California enacts no such restriction on its own projects. Former U.S. Budget Director Charles L. Schultze wrote in 1968:

In many parts of Southern California, irrigators pay $2.80 per acre-foot for water from federal projects. The value of water for other uses is about $35 per acre-foot. A typical 320-acre cotton farm will use about 1,300 acre-feet per year. The opportunity cost of the subsidy to such a farm is, therefore, about $42,-000 *per year*. The same farm may grow 450 bales of cotton per year, receiving an average subsidy of $28,000 on its cotton production. The two subsidies combined are worth $70,000 per year. The subsidy cost of placing one low-income family in decent housing averages about $800 per year.

One celebrated California case is that of the San Luis dam and water distribution system in the San Joaquin Valley, authorized by Congress in 1959 at a cost of $480 million. The Nader California report charges that the project was set up to "benefit" only 130 large landowners and corporations that own 83 percent of the land in the area. Land values in the parched territory served by the system rose by $300 an acre, bringing just one company, Southern Pacific, a reported "windfall" of more than $23 million.

Critics in California delight in calling J. G. Boswell of Fresno "the number one welfare recipient." In truth, his farm received in 1969 the largest subsidy of any in the United States—precisely $4,370,657. Of the 25 U.S. farms getting the largest farm payments under cotton, wheat, and feed-grain programs, 14 (including the top eight) were from California. Profits of the biggest California growers seemed to be endangered by the 1970 farm bill, which limited individual growers to a subsidy of $55,000 for each of the major crop programs (cotton, wheat, and feed grains). Before the bill, 265 California cotton farmers were making more than the new limit. Some of these big growers have been forced to lease out their cotton land (with reduced profits). But some of their number have neatly sidestepped the new law by taking advantage of regulations issued by an obliging Department of Agriculture that permits them to reconstitute themselves as "partnerships" so that each family member or other associate may qualify for the maximum $55,000 payment. Irregularities in the federal subsidy program are rampant; just in Kern County, for instance, investigators in 1971 turned up alleged violations by a third of the farms involved in the cotton subsidy program. Many farmers represented deserted or extremely low-quality land as fertile set-aside in order to qualify for their subsidies—including, it was alleged, farmer Kenneth E. Frick, who also happens to be the administrator of the Agriculture Department's multibillion-dollar annual crop subsidy program.

By contrast, a farm worker in California is ineligible under state law to collect unemployment insurance for those months of the year when he can't get work. In 1971 the legislature passed a bill to extend those unemployment insurance benefits to the state's estimated 245,000 farm laborers. Governor Reagan vetoed the bill.

## *Farm Labor, César Chávez,* La Huelga!

Thus we come to the seamy, often shameful underside of Central Valley life: the condition of those who till the fields. Today mechanization is cutting back sharply on the number of field workers required, and a modicum of laws are being enacted to protect them. Fewer are migrants: more are permanent residents of the valley towns. There is a marked difference between the east side of the Central Valley, where family farms predominate (due to cheap water), and the west side where the big farms dominate. But a huge farm labor pool is still required. In 1967, the last year for which full statistics are available, there were 700,000 laborers in California's fields and vineyards, the vast majority working in the Central Valley. Their average annual income for *all* work (both farm and nonfarm) was only $1,709; their living conditions in many places were still reminiscent of what John Steinbeck described in *Grapes of Wrath.**

As Richard G. Lillard tells the story in *Eden in Jeopardy,* California farmers

face the problems caused by a plantation system that in some ways parallels that of the Old South or the former hacienda system of old Mexico. It means good living for the owners, and a miserable lot for the field and orchard workers and their families. . . . California specialties require much handwork as men and women chop, trim, thin, girdle, top, stoop, bend, feel, dig, pound, cut, pull, walk, climb, reach up and out, lift, carry, amid heat, dust, cold, rain, mud, insects, from dawn to sundown. . . .

Historically the farmers have solved the problem of the labor shortage by encouraging immigrants who felt lucky to have the jobs they had—Chinese in the

* A nonfiction account of the same conditions Steinbeck portrayed in 1939 is *Factories in the Field* by Carey McWilliams, then chief of the state division of immigration and housing who later became editor of *The Nation.* McWilliams' charge of "farm fascism" on the part of the big growers evoked a reply from the Associated Farmers calling McWilliams "California's Agricultural Pest Number One, outranking pear blight and boll weevil."

1850s and later, and then, roughly in order, Mexicans, Japanese, Filipinos, Armenians, Caucasians from the American Dust Bowl, and Negroes from the mildewed lower Mississippi Valley, and last of all, arm and shoulder men, braceros, from Mexico. . . .

While the big farm owners lived well, sent their children to Stanford, and vacationed in Europe, the California farm workers lived in dirty shacks, drank impure water, used filthy privies, and ate poor food. . . . Their town life was amid a world of drunks, prostitutes, bums, degenerates, sadistic police, and "100% Americans," prejudiced county hospitals, segregated churches—and kindness, too, from a few old-stock Americans.

To offset the farm labor shortage as the Okies drifted off to more lucrative wartime jobs in shipyards and aircraft factories, Congress in 1942 approved the *bracero* program to import temporary Mexican laborers, who came by the hundreds of thousands. Many Mexicans, who found low California farm wages opulent by standards in their own country, also stole across the border illegally—the so-called "wetbacks," in honor of the practice of some in swimming or wading across the Rio Grande out of sight of border guards. After the war, the growers' lobbies fought fiercely to retain the *bracero* program while organized labor, frustrated in its earlier attempts to recruit the farm workers into unions, strove to end the program on the grounds that it provided cheap and unfair competition for American workers. Finally, in 1964, Congress killed the *bracero* program; an interim "green card" program to let in smaller numbers of Mexican workers continued for some years.*

Even with the *braceros* gone, though, the Mexican-Americans and Filipinos working the Californian fields were earning an average of less than $1,-400 a year, far below the federal poverty level. Wages were often advertised at $1.40 an hour, then reduced to $1.10 when the workers arrived. Work was unavailable several months of the year, and such amenities as overtime pay, paid holidays, vacation, sick leaves, and pensions were virtually unknown. Indiscriminate grower use of highly toxic pesticides led to illness among many farm workers and their children, whom they were often obliged to bring to the fields to work with them. Workers also found themselves at the mercy of the labor contractors, the middlemen between them, and the growers. Less of them than in the past were living in the growers' sterile compounds, but the housing available was often in the category of dirt-floored, tin and tarpaper shanties. No people ever more clearly needed a savior, a Moses to lead them from the wilderness. In 1965, such a man appeared. His name was César Estrada Chávez.

Chávez had been born in 1927 in Yuma, Arizona, but the stability of his early childhood was shattered in 1937 when his father's farm failed and the family took to the road as migrant laborers, following the crops in Arizona and California. The only home César and his four brothers and sisters often knew

---

* Illegal Mexican aliens, some with forged green cards and Social Security numbers, continue to pose a serious problem in California. Farmers, housewives, and small businessmen often hire them at wages below the U.S. and state minimums, depriving legal residents of jobs. In 1971, Governor Reagan signed the first law in any state stipulating penalties for employers who knowingly hire illegal aliens. Immigration officials estimated that at least a million Mexican nationals were working illegally in California, at least 200,000 of them in Los Angeles.

was a tent or the back seat of the family automobile; education was sporadic, and César made it only through the seventh grade. Later he married, acquired a taste for biography and history, especially of the Mexican people, and began to emerge as a spokesman for his fellow migrant workers in the field.

In 1961, after several years of work with the Los Angeles-based Community Service Organization, Chávez returned to Delano with his wife and eight children to work in the vineyards at $1.25 an hour and to start the long process of community organization that would lead to unionization of farm workers. At that time, he recalled in an interview, he thought it would be "at least 10 years before we had our first contract. But we had one four days short of four years. It was beyond all my wildest expectations." No such prospects for early success were apparent in 1962, however, when he formally organized the National Farm Workers Association. In a battered old station wagon, Chávez drove hundreds of miles through the Central Valley, talking with farm workers. Years later, one of his fervent followers recalled Chávez at that time: "Here was César, burning with a patient fire, poor like us, dark like us, talking quietly, moving people to talk about their problems, attacking the little problems first, and suggesting, always suggesting—never more than that—solutions that seemed attainable. We didn't know it until we met him, but he was the leader we had been waiting for." Chávez has been compared with Martin Luther King, a man whom he corresponded with but never met. "Some of the press," he told me, "say our movement is almost like a religion. And we say, well, it's the religion of fair play and justice." The model, of course, is a truly remarkable one in a day when so many, including young militants among Chávez's fellow Chicanos, are prone to often vengeful and spiteful paths of separatism and self-proclaimed radicalism. Chávez comments:

We consider ourselves, in our own quiet way, to be very radical. It takes a lot of radicalism to be willing to work without a paycheck and it takes quite a bit more to be willing to give up food for 10 days or so and it takes quite a bit to be able to struggle for five years when a lot of people are in doubt whether you're going to win or not. That's the radicalism I think pays off. The desire to get things done is very deep among us, and we're willing to sacrifice and pay the price. We feel the problem is not only a Chicano problem, but a problem of everyone. We're committed to human beings and we don't care what color they are.

Having witnessed the failure of many farm strikes for lack of proper organization, Chávez thought his NFWA should wait several years for a strike or run the risk of being crushed. But in 1965, the previously ineffectual AFL-CIO Agricultural Workers' Organizing Committee made demands of a $1.40-an-hour year-round wage and piece-rate bonuses of the grape growers around Delano, and, when the growers refused to even discuss the matter, called a strike. Some 1,000 workers, mostly Filipino, walked out of the fields. The growers started evicting families, and Chávez immediately offered the strikers the unconditional help of the NFWA. It was a different kind of a strike, and a different kind of a battle, than the growers had ever faced before. At Chávez's insistence, it remained nonviolent (or almost totally so), even when the growers brought in strikebreakers from other localities. And drawing on his contacts from earlier years, Chávez organized broad outside support from minority and antipoverty organizations, clergymen of various faiths (especially the Migrant Ministry of the Northern California Council of Churches), labor unions, students, and liberal political leaders. They gathered contributions, sent food, joined picket lines at the vineyards and at the metropolitan headquarters of the big growers.

That the strike would be a long, difficult one could have been predicted from the first, because the growers are closely associated with the long-dominant power structure of California, ranging from the big banks and oil companies to the Santa Fe Railroad and the ever helpful University of California. In Delano, the local powers were adamantly opposed; Chávez was accused of importing troublemakers, of forcing a union on workers who didn't want one, of having Communist backing.

But Chávez had the right touch of charisma and drama to transform *La Huelga* into *La Causa*. Just six months after the strike had begun, he called a great pilgrimage march, 300 miles from Delano to the steps of the State Capitol at Sacramento, every inch by foot. Down the flat, long black ribbon of Highway 99 marched the farm workers, Chávez's 82-year-old father among them. Chávez decreed it would be a nonsectarian march, and at the forefront went the banner depicting Our Lady of Guadalupe together with a large cross and the Star of David. There were Mexican and American flags, and behind, a dozen brilliant red pennants with the black eagle, symbol of the National Farm Workers Association. Twenty-five days later, on Easter Sunday, the footsore marchers arrived in Sacramento. As they had marched, there had been two great capitulations: Schenley and Di Giorgio. But at Sacramento, Governor Brown was not present. He was spending the weekend at Frank Sinatra's home in Palm Springs.

Support, great and small, poured in—winning for Chávez and the movement press coverage and television exposure worth millions. Once convinced they should visit the valley and view the action first hand at Delano, the most hardened newsmen found themselves turned on and strangely drawn to the movement. United Auto Workers president Walter Reuther came and marched with the strikers through the streets of Delano; later, after Chávez undertook a 25-day fast "as an act of penance, recalling workers to the nonviolent roots of their movement," Senator Robert F. Kennedy came to kneel beside Chávez at the Communion at which he broke his fast. In 1967, the AFL-CIO—which had long been dubious about the wisdom of sinking serious resources into the difficult farm organization field—nevertheless chartered Chávez's group as the United Farm Workers Organizing Committee, merged its own group into it, and dispatched William Kircher, a top organizer, to help Chávez with a $10,000-a-month budget.

At no point was the strike in the fields particularly effective; the labor pool of impoverished migrants the growers could draw on was simply too great. Thus came the boycott of the grapes produced by Joseph Guimarra's

5,000-acre vineyards, which would spread to a general national boycott of all California table grapes after Guimarra started shipping its grapes in the cartons of its competitors. (Guimarra, who came to the U.S. from Southern Europe in the 1920s, built his holdings from scratch and by the late 1960s was California's top grape producer, producing 52 million to 65 million tons of grapes a year. His corporation grossed $5.5 million to $7.5 million. In a 1968 article, labor editor Dick Meister of the San Francisco *Chronicle* reported that "Strikers like to picture Joe Guimarra and his fellow growers as devils. They are not, but they do seem quaintly out of touch with what has been going on beyond the vineyards since they moved into the valley beside the Mexican-Americans three decades ago. They seem sincerely perplexed that anyone would suggest farm workers need—or want—anything but what the *patron* gives them." One of the sad casualties of the boycott was the very small grape owners, many of Yugoslavian or Italian descent, who employ few or no workers.)

The national grape boycott eventually became the most effective boycott in American labor history, with all Americans, in effect, taking a stand for or against La Huelga. The boycott was not without its enemies. Governor Reagan called the strike and boycott "immoral" and "attempted blackmail." During the 1968 Presidential campaign, Richard Nixon publicly condemned it and gleefully ate grapes at a public rally in California. Nixon declared that "we have laws on the books to protect workers who wish to organize, a National Labor Relations Board to impartially supervise the election of collective-bargaining agents"—disingenuously failing to mention that federal law specifically exempts farm workers from protection under the National Labor Relations Act. (Ironically, the grape boycott would have been illegal if agricultural interests had not managed to have their industry exempted in the basic labor law of the 1930s.) Now many growers would like to be under NLRA coverage, since it would deprive Chávez of the right to use his favorite and most effective weapon, the secondary boycott, which was made illegal by the 1947 Taft-Hartley Act. Chávez argues that the industrial unions developed without the antiboycott provision from passage of the Wagner Act in 1934 until Taft-Hartley. They had real protection from the NLRB in those years, and were thus able to organize their industries, build large memberships, and "stand the unfairness of Taft-Hartley when it came," he maintains. "I want those 12 years too. If you give us Taft-Hartley now, you'll kill us."

The boycott was supported by millions, and in 1970, having lost millions of dollars in income, Guimarra and the other great growers capitulated. In an agreement arranged by a high-level committee of Catholic bishops, the growers agreed to recognize Chávez's union and to a sign a three-year contract, with wages going up to $2.05 an hour by 1972—with a 20¢ bonus for each box of grapes at harvest time. Signing the agreement with Guimarra, Chávez said simply: "This is the beginning of a new day."

The new day promised to have many dimensions. On the union front, it suggested that Chávez's union would be the catalytic force in organizing the farm workers of California, and quite possibly in achieving what had seemed forever impossible in the annals of American unionism—organizing the great army of farm workers across the U.S.A. But it would be a long, difficult struggle. By late 1971, the UFWOC had only 80,000 members in California, and of them, only 30,000 under contract. The organization was also signing up members in other great farm labor states, especially Texas, Florida, Michigan, Oregon, and Washington—but a minuscule percentage, to date, of the 1.5 million farm labor pool. Chávez told me the organization struggle would be "a lifetime process," successful first with the large ranches, much later with the smaller farm operations. Even in the Central Valley, opposition to him remained bitter and obdurate among the growers. Salinas Valley lettuce growers rushed to make labor agreements with the Teamsters lest the detested Chávez organize their fieldhands; Chávez responded by calling a successful strike of the lettuce workers and then ordering a national boycott against all non-UFWOC lettuce from California and Arizona. Then he was jailed for pressing the boycott, and again seemed the martyr as famous people like Coretta King and Ethel Kennedy came to Salinas in his support. In spring 1971, an uneasy truce was reached with the Teamsters which would leave the field workers to Chávez's union and the processing workers to the Teamsters.

Chávez's success had immense implications for the traditionally disjointed, seemingly indifferent Mexican-Americans of the Southwest. *La Causa* could be for them what the garment unions were for the Jews of New York or the railway porters' union for the black bourgeoisie—a solid economic institution representing and fighting for their interests, a point of pride. The Chávez union, related directly to the strong family structure of the Mexican-American and cooperative in its spirit and approach, quickly provided a model too for the Mexicans in the urban Los Angeles setting through their East Los Angeles Community Union. Chávez found a way to make Mexican-Americans proud of their heritage, and he could be called the real father of the Mexican-American civil rights movement. There was doubt whether this soulful, almost mystical man, forever clothed in the simple garb of a field worker, would want to bid for status as a leader of all Mexican-Americans. But of them all, he alone seemed to have the promise and the power.

\*    \*    \*

Before we leave the Central Valley, some concluding notes on its cities. The largest, of course, is Sacramento, the state capital, which started in the Gold Rush days around Sutter's Fort. Now, with government, agribusiness, an inland port, and a vigorous injection of defense-space industries, Sacramento has reached a quarter of a million people (metro area 800,592). Palms, verdant lawns, and colorful flowerbeds surround the glistening wedding-cake-like capitol building, but the city has more than its share of dreary, boxlike government buildings packed with civil servants and computers to manage a complex nation state. Across the level valley floor march a monotony of flat, straight streets, fortuitously masked by orange and magnolia trees; of the weather it must be reported it is so murderously hot that the policemen wear pith helmets in the summers. In a 60-square area between the Sacramento River and the Capitol, where flophouses, warehouses, and cheap saloons abounded, a $220 million urban renewal plan is being instituted under a plan drawn up by two distinguished California architects, Richard Neutra and Robert Alexander. Part of the project is restoration of a Chinatown district including a new Confucian temple.

Sacramento's leading newspaper, the McClatchy-owned *Bee*, provides excellent coverage but is liberal-Democratic to a fault; in 1966, for instance, writers were instructed to refer to Reagan in every story as "the Goldwater Republican." The Copley-owned *Union* provides an opposite ideology, but is read by only half as many people.

Miles to the south, approximately halfway between San Francisco and Los Angeles, lies the city of Fresno (pop. 165,972 metro area 413,053), one of the most important centers of agribusiness in the nation. What Fresno has become famed for of late, though, is something altogether different—its handsome downtown mall, stretching six blocks through the center business district, with fountains, cascades, brooks and pools, statuary, a softly ebbing and flowing pavement, islands of trees, light fixtures, small playgrounds, sidewalk cafes, trees, flowers, and shrubs. All of this was done with scarcely a change to the Main Street U.S.A. shops bordering the mall. Cars were banished to out-of-sight lots and little electric trains (a dime a ride) substituted to carry pedestrians to their destinations. The project, engineered by Victor Gruen Associates, cost $1.8 million to build but increased retail sales an estimated $2 million in its first five years of life. Architectural critic Wolf Von Eckhardt credits it with being the "most exciting" pedestrian city center this side of the Atlantic. Fresno also proved to be one of the outstanding cities under the federal Model Cities program; its mayor, Floyd H. Hyde, won such a reputation in city planning and race relations that he was called to Washington as chief of the Model Cities program under the Nixon administration.

At the midpoint of the valley lies Stockton (pop. 107,644), which suffers from excessive unemployment, especially in the winter, when the canneries are out of operation, but can boast a bustling port.

Far to the south, not far from Los Angeles, is Bakersfield (pop. 69,515, metro 329,162), center of about a third of California's $1.1 billion annual oil and gas production and hub of a prosperous farm area. The city has a population that ranges from millionaires who support one of California's most prosperous Cadillac agencies to destitute out-of-work Chicanos and blacks living in ramshackle houses on the fringes of the city. Both the state and federal governments have accused Bakersfield schools of gross discrimination against blacks and Mexicans, including gerrymandering of attendance areas, purposely locating new schools to prevent integration, and failing to provide programs to let Chicano children overcome their cultural and language problems. The conservative power structure of this rather Southern-thinking city has been shocked by militant new demands of the minorities and their liberal white allies, but it tries to keep all change to a minimum. The scene is repeated in many towns, large and small, up and down the Central Valley, where the strong Southern roots of the population still influence behavior. That the great farm revolt started at Delano, a little city (pop. 14,559) just a few miles north of Bakersfield, is mostly happenstance; it could as easily have been in any of the cities we have mentioned, or in scores of others, from Chico or Yuba City in the north to Modesto or Merced in the south.

## Life and Water in Desert California

A great swath of the Southland, covering practically a quarter of the entire Californian land surface, is harsh, unredeemed desert, a land of stark, treeless mountains, baked flatlands, and an infinity of rock and sand. The geographers define two principal California deserts, though the casual traveler will notice little difference between them—the northern, or higher, desert, called the Mojave, and the southern, lower, and even hotter desert, which is named Colorado after the river on its eastern side. Some half million visitors a year now make their way to the otherwordly wasteland of Death Valley, renowned for its great wind-riffled sand flows, the dried lake bottom of lacerated salt crystal, brilliantly hued canyons and mountains, and below-sea-level depths. Wintertime temperatures are in a comfortably moderate range, but the valley maintains its reputation for extreme heat with frequent summer readings of 120 degrees and a record 190 one July day in 1958.

A massive 140-mile-long trough, Death Valley is but a small part of the greater Mojave to which it belongs. The bleak Mojave, formed by truncated mountain ranges and high, arid plains, actually covers 25,000 square miles, an area equal to several eastern states combined. Scattered mining towns, where borax (of 20-mule-team fame), iron ore, tungsten, gypsum, and salts are extracted, account for much of the sparse population. Thousands of acres have been appropriated by the military for bombing ranges and space-equipment test stations; at Edwards Air Force Base the X-15 rocket ship, the fastest self-propelled vehicle ever built by man, conducted its test flights. There are now increasing concerns about what man may be doing to this desert, the most accessible in the world to a large, technologically advanced urban concentration. Philip Fradkin of the Los Angeles *Times* has reported:

The California desert, so vast it once appeared limitless, is starting to look used, almost worn-out in places. . . . Modern man has left strips of asphalt, railroad tracks, power lines, tin cans, motels and gas stations, and waste materials from mines. . . . California's more than 1 million motorcycles, trail-bikes, dune buggies and other off-road vehicles have churned ruts in a desert environment so fragile it still bears the tracks of Gen. Patton's tanks on World War II maneuvers. . . . In

1968, the Bureau of Reclamation estimated recreational use of the desert at 5 million visitor days. . . . Already, on holiday weekends, traffic into the desert is bumper-to-bumper. . . .

Few roads venture to cross the Mojave, but those that do have special interest. An east-west course is cut by famous old U.S. Route 66, traveled by the Okies in the 1930s on their great trek to California. Running northeast from the Los Angeles area, directly through the heart of the Mojave, is the principal road to Las Vegas. The most harrowing auto trip I have ever made was on a Friday afternoon, heading from Las Vegas to the coast. The road was still two-lane and the Vegas-bound horde of pleasure-seeking Californians, gambling with their lives as they would with their money that weekend, insisted on passing in the most dangerous spots, forcing our car off the road time after time. Now, blessedly, the road has been converted into an interstate. Neil Morgan reports on the little town of Baker, a favorite gas- and watering-spot on this stretch. Baker exists on 17 gas stations from which tow trucks head out as far as 100 miles to help stranded motorists. Flat-broke gamblers headed home from Las Vegas swap televisions, radios, jewelry, and guns for gas, and Morgan quotes a local gas station owner as saying that "everybody in town at one time or another has been offered to share a wife in trade for gas or repairs."

The principal feature of the Colorado Desert, filling California's southernmost extremity, is the indefatigable old Colorado itself and the man-made diversions from the river, which have made possible a flourishing agriculture in the steaming desert land of the Imperial Valley. Though its flow is but a fraction of the Columbia and other great world waterways, the Colorado is spoken of with awe by those who know its elemental power and force. It flows from headwaters in Colorado and Wyoming's Green River, slashes across southeastern Utah, then into Arizona and through the unparalleled Grand Canyon, on to southern Nevada where the massive Hoover Dam first tamed it in the 1930s, and along the western boundary of Arizona where it finally touches California. The drainage area of the river is close to a quarter of a million square miles, and in years of high flow its brown, silt-laden waters have carried as much as 170 million cubic yards of earth to its delta in Mexico's Gulf of California.

Since 1939, a principal source of water for Los Angeles and San Diego has been the Colorado River Aqueduct, which crosses the parched Colorado Desert from Parker Dam (several miles below Hoover) to the metropolitan region, its passage facilitated by 42 tunnels through the mountains and five great pumping stations. But long before the aqueduct to Los Angeles was even thought of, the Colorado was shaping the destiny of what would become known as the Imperial Valley along the Mexican border, an area of 3,000-square miles once thought fit only for rabbits and rattlesnakes. Inspired by early visionaries in the use of diverted water for agriculture, the privately owned California Development Company in 1901 built a series of ditches that siphoned off Colorado River water into the valley, which has an elevation lower than the Colorado or, in fact, the ocean itself. Thousands of settlers arrived and phenomenal crop yields were soon being taken out of the desert land. But an unwise cut into the river, followed by roaring spring floods and desert cloudbursts in 1905, brought disaster. The Colorado deserted its normal channel and began to pour its entire flow into the Imperial Valley through the promoters' cut. Following the law of gravity, the water accumulated in the Salton Sink, lowest point (235 feet below sea level) in the valley. Thus it was that the Salton Sea, some 24 miles long and now a familiar feature to air travelers and map studiers, came to be. Only in 1907, at the expenditure of many millions of dollars and heroic efforts by Southern Pacific Railroad crews, were the rampaging flood waters finally turned back to their normal channel.

Thirty-four years later, work was completed on the federally sponsored All-American Canal to link, safely, the Colorado River with the Imperial Valley. Construction of the Hoover Dam also meant that floods would no longer be the problem they once were. The canal, actually a concrete-lined river some 200 feet wide, carries 2 billion gallons of water each day to the thousands of miles of feeder canals built by the Imperial Irrigation District. (A measure of the fantastic water demand of agriculture is that the daily water usage of the 119 Southern California cities and towns serviced by the Colorado River Aqueduct is only half the amount needed to irrigate the Imperial Valley.)

Now one of the most productive farm areas of the country, hot, sun-baked Imperial Valley—sometimes called the Algiers of the U.S.A.—produces rich crops of melon, tomatoes, carrots, cotton, tangerines, asparagus, lettuce, and sugar beets, some even in the dead of winter, and virtually the total U.S. date crop. Feed crops are growing in importance, providing fodder for a growing number of feed lots. Yet every one of the half million acres would quickly return to desert dust without irrigation. And despite man's best efforts, the valley remains less than a hospitable place to live. Temperatures are stiflingly hot, hordes of crickets descend in the summertime and make it impossible to walk about without crunching hundreds underfoot, and the population remains almost static (74,492 in 1970). The Salton Sea, replenished by natural and agricultural runoff, became a favorite fishing, boating, and swimming resort, but now increasing salinity is threatening even that, much to the alarm of the recreationists.

The true power in the Imperial Valley is in the hands of the prosperous growers who sit on the board of and control the Imperial Immigration District (IID). There is no more poignant case in America of government subsidy designed to help the "little man"—in this case, the small farmer—being siphoned off to the advantage of the quite rich and very rich. The federal intent in subsidizing the irrigation systems in the Imperial Valley was to encourage small farming; in fact, a key provision of the Reclamation Act of 1902, which has never been repealed, says that no person owning more than 160 acres may receive federally supplied water, and that the owner must re-side on or near the land to qualify. But in practice, the IID simply ignored the 160-acre provision; the Interior Department, in a questionable 1933 ruling of the lame duck Hoover administration, countenanced the violation, and for years the matter rested there.

Today owners of more than 160 acres control in excess of 50 percent of the irrigated acreage in the Imperial Valley. Two-thirds of the land is owned by absentees, and some holdings are as large as 10,000 acres. Some of the big corporate owners include United Fruit, Purex, Dow Chemical, Tenneco, and the Irvine Land Company. With a pliable local press, the politicians safely in their corner, and the economic muscle on their side, this established order has seemed, until now, totally impregnable. (Not even the Los Angeles *Times* reports fairly or adequately on the land and water issue in the valley, some say because the Chandlers personally own large tracts that benefit from the federal doles.) But there is a gadfly—a valiant, almost pathetic figure who has been fighting the big landowners almost singlehandedly over several years. He is Dr. Ben Yellen, now in his early sixties, a Jewish doctor from Brooklyn who moved to California and runs a small clinic in Brawley where he treats 50 or 60 patients a day, most of them poor Mexican-Americans whom other doctors won't handle. Writer Michael E. Kinsley, who visited Yellen, reports that he sleeps on his cot in his clinic and uses virtually all of his money filing lawsuits against the establishment and issuing periodic mimeographed newsletters clobbering the existing order in Tom Paine-like fashion.

As Yellen sees it, the big owners have perpetrated a massive fraud on the United States and the poorer people of the valley. To their argument that farms as small as 160 acres simply aren't practical because of massive farm machinery investments required, Yellen replies that the irrigated acreage will grow five times as much food as land elsewhere in the U.S., and that a husband and wife, each with 160 acres (which the law permits) "can farm here 320 acres, which is equivalent to 1,600 acres in the rest of the United States." The rich growers, he argues, are being paid huge government subsidies in cheap water * in violation of the law, to farm land on which they don't pay enough taxes, so that they can cultivate crops harvested by Mexican workers imported fraudulently across the border, so that they can be paid huge sums of money by the government not to grow anything at all.

The federal government finally moved to enforce the 160-acre rule in a court suit filed in 1967 while Stewart Udall was Secretary of the Interior. The case languished in district court for several years and was then decided in favor of the big landowners (whose friends include some of the mighty in both parties, including Governor Reagan, President Nixon, and Senator Tunney, whose old congressional district included the Imperial Valley). The Nixon administration inexplicably decided not to appeal the case beyond

* The IID uses 2.8 million acre feet of water each year, 70 percent of the Colorado River water allotted to California. The amount is almost twice the water consumption of the city of New York, sold at but a fraction of cost.

the federal district court level, despite the fundamental issues of law compliance, agrarian democracy, and the use of millions of dollars of taxpayers' money. Yellen then filed another court suit, joined by 123 migrant workers as a class action, and late in 1971 achieved his first great breakthrough: a decision by U.S. District Judge W. D. Murray that most of the land in the Imperial Valley is held illegally by nonresident owners, a violation of the Reclamation Act of 1902. Implementation, however, might be years away; first there was likelihood of an appeal to the Supreme Court; secondly, as Nick Kotz reported in the Washington *Post*, the Nixon administration could "let the case proceed further into a litigation jungle in which the migrant plaintiffs probably will eventually lose or run out of money to pursue their case." Lawyers in the Justice and Interior Departments believe that enforcing the 1902 law would be impractical or romantic, although there is, interestingly, a fresh precedent—the federal government's recent decision to revive another old statute, the Refuse Act of 1899, to stop industries from pumping pollutants into interstate streams. With a will to act, the government could reverse the land monopolization pattern of many decades; as for Ben Yellen, he is in failing health and may not be able to push his lonely fight much longer.

In perennial California style, bright new possibilities for the Imperial Valley always seem to be right around the corner. In 1970, scientists of the University of California at Riverside announced they had discovered seven exploitable geothermal fields in the Imperial Valley, estimated to have the potential to produce 20,000 megawatts of power and up to seven million acre-feet of distilled water annually for up to three centuries. The implications for the Southwest are immense. The electric power generation, involving no air pollution, would be 15 times that of the Hoover Dam, or by another estimate, enough to provide electrical power to run 33 cities the size of San Francisco for a century. The water flow might make the Imperial Valley virtually self-sufficient in irrigating its 400,000 acres of farmland, thus freeing vast quantities of Colorado River water for Southern California or parched Arizona. Yet despite these immense stakes, the U.S. is far behind Mexico in building of pilot power generation stations to exploit the geothermal fields, despite one PG & E station north of San Francisco. And the state of California has refused to invest any of its own funds in a program which might provide the power and the water to make Southern California a viable place to live in future times.

A final note before we leave the never-never world of the Imperial Valley. Its largest city, El Centro (19,272), claims to be the biggest settlement below sea level in this hemisphere; the lowest city of all in the valley, Calipatria (1,824), runs colored lights up a 184-foot flagpole at Christmastime. The top is precisely at sea level.

Miles to the northwest lies the resort of Palm Springs (20,936), set on the desert floor in the lee of Mt. San Jacinto, the steepest mountain escarpment (10,831 feet) in the U.S.A. Conspicuous consumption reaches rare

heights in this town. Famous movie stars and big business moguls, a generation of the proudful self-made, congregate here in half-million-dollar houses,
patronize the expensive golf clubs, and drive the most luxurious autos. Former
President Eisenhower, drawn by the fabulous winter golfing rather than the
rest of the glitter, was probably the most modest resident of recent times.

Nowhere is the swimming pool more rampant; there are some 4,000 in
Palm Springs, some even designed, Stephen Birmingham notes in *The Right
People*, in the monogram form of the owner with whirlpools. Bikini-clad dow-
agers bask in the sun like fat lizards with no more serious concern than the
caloric count; the intellectual interests of the males are said to be truncated
at the level of the dollar.*

Like its Los Angeles parent, Palm Springs is low and slung-out; a shadow
law prohibits any building in the shadow of another. By day, the city can
scarcely be distinguished from the palmier shopping centers of the Los Angeles area; by night, amber floodlights playing on the palms create an atmosphere of warmth and opulence contrasted with the backdrop of gaunt mountains etched against the dark purple desert sky.

But this is not exclusively a town of the very rich, gathered in their
own gentile and Jewish ghettos. The well-to-do must share the scene with
Mexicans and blacks, crowded into an appalling slum called Section 14,
and with the remarkably fortunate Agua Caliente Indians. Less than 100 in
number, the Indians own huge sections of land throughout the city which
they lease out to palefaces for about $860,000 a year. Some of America's
wealthiest Indians live here, but others, unfortunate enough to hold unde-
sirable tracts of land, are virtually penniless. The Riverside *Press-Enterprise*
won a Pulitzer Prize for its exposé on the misuse of some of the lands supposedly reserved for the Indians at Palm Springs.

* For an amusing and caustic commentary on the life of the *nouveau riche* of Palm Springs, the
reader is referred to Chapter 19 of Stephen Birmingham's *The Right People*.

# II. THE BAY AREA

## San Francisco: City and Skyline

*San Francisco put on a show for me. I saw her across the bay, from the great road that bypasses Sausalito and enters the Golden Gate Bridge. The afternoon sun painted her white and gold—rising on her hills like a noble city in a happy dream. A city on hills has it over flat-land places. New York makes its own hills with craning buildings, but this gold and white acropolis rising wave on wave against the blue of the Pacific sky was a stunning thing, a painted thing like a picture of a medieval Italian city which can never have existed. . . .*

*Over the green higher hills to the south, the evening fog rolled like herds of sheep coming to cote in the golden city. I've never seen her more lovely. When I was a child and we were going to the City, I couldn't sleep for several nights before, out of bursting excitement. She leaves a mark.*

*—John Steinbeck, in* Travels With Charley

WHEN THE GALLUP POLL IN 1969 asked Americans what city they would most like to live in, San Francisco won hands down, by a 2–1 margin over its closest rival.* "I like the hills, the ocean and the people," said a 28-year-old technician from Akron, Ohio. "San Francisco's got something all its own."

Clearly, it has. I saw it for the first time myself from the Golden Gate on a summer afternoon some 25 years ago, and in my own unformed, boyish way had many of the same feelings John Steinbeck recorded. The red-orange lines of that high, daring bridge, the sparkling bay to one side, the fog-banked ocean

---

\* The runners-up in the 1969 survey were Los Angeles, Miami, Denver, New York City, Phoenix, San Diego, Chicago, Honolulu, and Portland, Oregon—in that order. Interesting omissions, in this writer's opinion: Boston, Seattle, New Orleans, Atlanta.

to the other, the rows of chalk-white buildings running uphill and down—who can forget them? Walk through San Francisco today, and you find streets filled with life at almost every hour of the day, from center city to the neighborhoods. Most colorful of all is Union Square, faced by the regal old St. Francis Hotel, jammed with secretaries and shoppers, demonstrators and businessmen, walking, sunning, sprawling on the grass, singing songs, playing music, a microcosm of San Francisco. If there is an urban glory in America, here it is.

Much of San Francisco's charm lies in its geographic compactness (46.6 square miles), the water on three sides, the 40-odd hills, the constantly shifting panoramas of hillcrest, blue ocean and bridge, spots of fog, gargoyled houses and towers—a city fashioned to a human scale. In a single morning or afternoon, the walker can stroll from the downtown financial district to Union Square to Chinatown, check the North Beach, swing onto a cable car and wind up at Fisherman's Wharf for a seafood delicacy, and then browse about new Ghiradelli Square (a pleasing complex of ships, restaurants, fountains, and lights fashioned out of the buildings of an old chocolate and spice factory). Many remember San Francisco as the city where you could sit in the lounge at the Top of the Mark at day's end and see the city spread before you, the Bay Bridge arching gracefully across to the East Bay, ships to and from the Orient steaming under the Golden Gate, twilight azure giving way to a million night lights.

Such a city, certainly, needs no massive urban facelifting to make it livable. Its people love it as it is. Sometimes they have risen up to save what gives it character. In the 1940s, a single person, one Mrs. Klussmann, organized a great petition drive to save those dangerous, silly, delightful cable cars—and won. In 1958, a great "freeway revolt" erupted against the ugly double-decked superhighway being built along the Embarcadero. The road was cutting across the face of the venerable Ferry Building and blocking the view to the bay; in an historic bow to people interests, the freeway builders had to stop in midcourse, and today the road ends like a knife-cut where they stopped. Several years later, a freeway route that would have cut through part of Golden Gate Park was successfully blocked.

But inexorable physical change is pressing in on San Francisco, threatening what some call "Manhattanization"—the brutalization of its uniquely delicate skyline with sterile, forbidding monuments of glass and steel twice as high as anything that preceded them and totally out of scale with the existing hills and city setting. The most alarming of these was what Nicholas von Hoffman calls "the Bank of America's sinister black and brown tower which rises up like an emblem of corporate insensitivity, giving the finger to the city's people." The 52-story building was the highest West of the Mississippi, and its darkness contrasted unpleasantly with San Francisco's traditional pattern of white, slim structures. In 1960, the last obstacles were cleared for the Transamerica Corporation to build an 835-foot, spire-surmounted, pyramidal office building on Montgomery Street, the "Wall Street of the West." Such monsters may be welcomed in a flat, plains city like Chicago, fulfilling that city's historic role as an architectural experiment station; in a delicate, hilly city like San Francisco, the result can be disastrous.

During the 1960s, 21 high-rise buildings sprouted in the heart of the city, and 23 more are scheduled for completion by 1975. From the Top of the Mark and other promontories of the city, much of the Bay view is already irremediably blanked out. But San Franciscans are unwilling to accept the theory that they have passed the fail-safe point on the road to Manhattanization. In 1970, public protest thwarted the proposal of U.S. Steel to build a 550-foot office building and commercial structure on public land at the waterfront, a project critics said would be a crass exploitation of a precious community resource—the view of their bay, the Ferry Building, and the Bay Bridge Tower.

Most of the startling new high-rises have gone up in the Montgomery Street–Market Street financial district. Market Street itself, an old commercial thoroughfare, is being made into more of a promenade than a boulevard, with broad walks, sycamore trees, benches, and flowers. Just to the south of it the massive Yerba Buena convention center and commercial complex is going up. The Golden Gateway area used to be a wholesale produce area with narrow streets and alleys; now, with the Rockefellers' 15.4-acre, $100 million Embarcadero Center (to include a huge trade mart, hotels, and the like), development is being spurred all along the northern waterfront area. On the southern waterfront, plans are underway for a $11 million marine terminal at India Basin to be home base for the American President and Pacific Far East Lines.

In a classic case of urban renewal equaling Negro removal, large swaths of the Western Addition—a bay-windowed, gingerbread-trimmed area of Victorian homes miraculously saved from the fire that came with the 1906 earthquake—have been levelled for new apartment houses, most occupied by middle- and upper-class whites. One of the positive results was the new Japanese Cultural and Trade Center, a complex of restaurants, shops, and a hotel which has grown as a tourist attraction. But community groups in the still-standing sections of the Western Addition are fighting further encroachment by the developers' bulldozers. One of San Francisco's most severe problems is the flight of young people with children from the city. This is more acute in San Francisco than some other towns because the city is so small that no one has to live there to work there. In a part of America where rapid population growth has been the norm, San Francisco has slipped in population by 59,683 people in the last two decades (to 715,674 in 1970). It is now 13th largest in population among U.S. cities.

## San Francisco: Mood and Life Style

The diversity of this city of light and color has attracted, from others, words like these: Mediterranean, Renaissance, Athens of America, a place of *joie de vivre*, elegant, witty. San Francisco has a lovely sense of the absurd, preserved in the artful foolishness of old Victorian houses and the ding-dong cable cars, sure cures for depression. It is also like an elegant woman, with an indefinable mystique all its own. As Herbert Gold wrote, it "is still the great city of America where a walker can experience nostalgia for the place while he is still there—a little, even a lot, like the *nostalgie de Paris*."

Among other things, San Francisco also has the best little restaurants, in every ethnic variety imaginable, of any American city except, of course, New York. Its stores, both big and small, are often a joy and delight. It also has the highest suicide rate in the country—two and a half times the national average.

These days, the Golden Gate Bridge is the most celebrated place in the city to commit suicide; every pedestrian is watched by closed circuit television, and a suicide patrol car is on hand to question those who act suspiciously. At least 370 men and women have taken the leap from the Golden Gate, not counting those whose bodies were swept out to sea and never found. But the fact is that less than 5 percent of San Francisco's suicides are from the bridge; most are by swallowing pills, and there is a suspicion that the especially alert city coroner's office, which conducts frequent autopsies in suspicious cases, may identify suicides that would be certified as deaths from natural causes in other cities. The suicide rate is particularly high among the elderly, the homosexual, and the otherwise lonely. Two-thirds of the city's people are single, divorced, or widowed. And the city is also number one in the U.S.A. in per capita consumption of alcohol.

But what is bane may also be blessing. Where else on the North American continent, one may ask, can one find such a fantastic mix of people—singles and oldsters, Caucasian and Oriental, Negro and Mexican, Wasp and old-line Catholic ethnic, and every deviant life style imaginable—*all living together in relative peace?* In what other city could one imagine candidates for public office making an open pitch for the homosexual vote, estimated at 90,000? Where else could I have found a police chief who, with an amused wave of his hand, said: "Sure, we've got our problems with homosexuals, transsexuals, and bisexuals, and all the rest of 'em. You name it and we have it in San Francisco. But it's still one of the great, storied cities in the world." In 1971, San Francisco voters made a unique choice for sheriff: Richard D. Hongisto, a man of Finnish descent, veteran of 10 years on the city police force, about to receive his doctorate in criminology from UC Berkeley, who put the peace symbol on all his campaign materials. Hongisto was opposed by the major newspapers, organized labor, and most establishment forces, but capitalized on a split in the "law-and-order" camp to win with 36.5 percent of the vote. His chief supporters were white liberals, the black and Mexican-American communities, students, women liberationists, peaceniks, and homosexuals. The scope of the sheriff's office is narrow, but Hongisto is using it as a platform to press for police reforms, an end to official action in nonvictim crimes (prostitution, drunkenness, and homosexuality between consenting adults), drug-counseling, medical and psychiatric services in the county's jails, venereal disease treatment for the women's facilities—and longer working hours for the judges, to keep the channels of justice less clogged with unresolved cases.

"The culture of civility," Howard Becker and Irving Horowitz suggested in a 1970 article in *Trans-action*, sets San Francisco apart from its sister cities of the continent. The mix of undigested ethnic minorities, colonies, and societies, they say, creates "a mosaic of life styles, the very difference of whose sight and smell give pleasure." Natives of San Francisco "enjoy the presence of hippies and take tourists to see their areas, just as they take them to see the gay area of Polk Street. Deviance, like difference, is a civic resource, enjoyed by tourist and resident alike." Admittedly, this flies in the face of conventional reasoning that when one sees normally proscribed behavior, there is worse to come. But in the free atmosphere of San Francisco, "we see more clearly and believe more deeply that hippies or homosexuals are not dangerous when we confront them on the street day after day or live alongside them and realize that beard plus long hair does not equal a drug-crazed maniac." And the deviants, when they discover via the culture of civility that they are not regarded as an unfortunate excrescence to be suppressed by police and other authorities, "sink roots like more conventional citizens: find jobs, buy houses, make friends, vote and take part in political activities and all the other things that solid citizens do."

What gives rise to a culture of civility? Authors Becker and Horowitz name these possibilities: San Francisco has a Latin heritage and has always been a seaport that tolerates the vice sailors seek out. Explosive growth at the time of the Gold Rush inhibited conventional social controls. Ethnic minorities, especially the Chinese, were ceded the right to engage in activities like prostitution and gambling. An image of wickedness and high living helps draw tourists, and some minor downtown streets are even named for famous madames of the Gold Rush era. And "a major potential source of repressive action—the working class—is in San Francisco more libertarian and politically sophisticated than one might expect. Harry Bridges' Longshoremen act as bellwethers." * San Francisco is one of the few large American cities ever to experience a general strike; the memory lingers, and workingmen remember the policeman may not be their friend. There is a left-wing, honest cast to trade unionism. And finally, San Francisco's high complement of single people worry a lot less than married ones about what public deviance may do to children.

All of this is not to suggest that the square community in San Francisco does not, on occasion, move to stamp out certain vices or to limit others. When the flower children's dream community of Haight-Ashbury turned into a crashpad ghetto of LSD and speed use (as opposed to mere marijuana) in 1967, the city moved in with the police tactical squad and the city health department orders. Later, there was a crackdown on the users and purveyors of methedrine and other narcotics thought to result in violence and crime. When

---

* The West Coast Longshoremen, economically vigorous, intellectually strong, long past their days of alleged Communist involvement, are San Francisco's most influential union now.

the "Third World Liberation Front" at San Francisco State College tried in 1968–69 to shut the university down unless it yielded to their 15 "nonnegotiable demands," the police intervened and were kept on campus by the new president, S. I. Hayakawa, until permanent order was restored. (S. F. State, a commuter college of 18,000 students stuck on a flat, cramped piece of land in the southwest section of the city, seems somehow to suffer all of California's student problems but has few of San Francisco's glories.)

San Francisco police, in their heart of hearts, differ little from their compatriots in cities across the U.S.A. I spent an evening cruising the city streets with two of their inspectors, hearing opinions such as this: "A police officer's duty has always been to enforce the law and keep the peace. Now they're trying to turn us into social workers, counseling and tutoring—a misuse." Or about the suggestion that police should be more educated and professional: "Look at some of the morons going to the universities; is that what education means? They should learn to obey the law first."

And all the glamour notwithstanding, San Francisco's police have a lot to worry about. Six of their number were gunned down in the streets between 1967 and 1971. Counting the suburban area, San Francisco has the highest crime rate of any city—bar none—in the U.S.A. FBI figures for 1969, for instance, showed a crime index of 5,441 incidents per 100,000 population in San Francisco. New York City had 4,731, Washington 4,019, and Chicago 2,680. (In large measure, high crime rates correlate with high population mobility. Where less of the population lives in close-knit neighborhoods, there may be an open, free, tolerant city atmosphere. But with everyone an island unto himself, it is easier for crime to flourish.)

The story of San Francisco's pioneering in the new and open life style of our times began, some think, with the arrival on the North Beach of Jack Kerouac and his unbarbered street saints in the 1950s. The bohemian-beatniks first encamped on the North Beach, but, eventually, rising rents, throngs of tourists, and some degree of police harassment triggered a move to the Haight-Ashbury district. The colony at first went largely unnoticed because its members preferred to sedate themselves on nothing more unconventional than alcohol and marijuana, their preoccupation was with art, and most lived as couples or alone. The life style was free, joyous, and, in its own way, talking sensitively to America. But all this changed drastically in 1964 "with the popular acceptance of mescaline, LSD and other hallucinogens and the advent of the Ginsberg-Leary-Kesey nomadic, passive, communal electric and acid-oriented life style," according to a *Trans-action* study. Rock groups began to prepare what would soon be known as the "San Francisco sound."

In 1966, a Trips Festival was hosted at Longshoreman's Hall by Ken Kesey. The attendance figure was 15,000, and the word "hippie" was born. A year later, the new community staged a Human Be-In for 20,000 on the polo fields of Golden Gate Park; the movement of the hippie flower people was now a familiar one in the national media. The publicity may have been its undoing, for thousands of young people from California and across the country poured in, and soon the Haight was so crowded that a new living unit—the crash pad—emerged. Hundreds suffered frightening hallucinogenic drug reactions, and in the unsanitary, crowded environment, infectious diseases abounded—influenza, streptococcal pharyngitis, hepatitis, genito-urinary-tract infections, and venereal disease. A free medical center, set up with volunteer doctors and helpers, opened up in Haight-Asbury and fought valiantly to help kids coming off bad trips and to stem the disease rate. But with the city health department's refusal of serious help—and even harassment, in contrast to the customary tolerance of the city government—the problem proved beyond manageable proportions. Gradually all but the most unredeemed hard drug users fled the Haight, its days of flowers and love long past.*

The way of life born in the halcyon days of Haight-Ashbury lives on, reflected in virtually every corner of America, the expression still most intense in Northern California. Its components are radical political action (descending from what happened at Berkeley in 1964), continued free drug use, principally of marijuana; sexual freedom and experimentation; and a modern-day revival of what some religious groups had experimented with in the past century —the expanded family and commune. Enlarging on this theme, young Richard Atcheson wrote in 1970:

> Although Ken Kesey's Merry Pranksters exist today only in Tom Wolfe's brilliant evocation of them, *The Electric Kool-aid Acid Test*, the sort of tribal life they evolved has fired the imagination of many Californians, young and old, drug users and not. Most of the famous San Francisco rock groups are communal, and tribalization has come to the Bay area in an amazing number of forms. In many cases, the tribe may consist only of three people or two couples, and their children, bound together in loose economic ties or in thoroughgoing, total communality. There are tribes of single people, all straight, all gay, and even cross-sexual. . . .
>
> Basically, the dropout economy—or the tribal society, as insiders call it— runs on a combination of odd-jobbing, crafts, marijuana dealing, sharing, trading, scrounging, welfare and unemployment checks and contributions from parents.

In time, communal living spread across the United States, in multitudinous forms but largely dedicated, still, to the ideals of simplicity and love which were first expressed in the Haight. Some communes subsisted by farming, others by sophisticated business efforts. The picture was a mixed one of stable and unstable communes; some supporting persons' individuality, many undermining it; some really free associations and others fanatical and almost fascistic in their regimens. Marijuana remained the sacrament, but the hard drugs, especially heroin, were viewed with increasing repulsion. In many communes, a new and strong religious theme was said to infuse the search for "higher consciousness."

---

* Community leaders of Haight-Ashbury point out that Haight Street, where most of the "action" has taken place, is only a part, and not a central one, of their city section. The district has gradually shifted from white to predominantly black. But there is a good mix of low- and middle-income people, the houses are interesting, the schools decent, and the community has a certain ambience. Since departure of the flower children—many of them highly educated, sensitive, concerned individuals about society, at least on their arrival—the major problems have revolved around improving race relations and the conflicts between motorcycle toughs, black youth, and the drug pushers.

A further word about drugs. Few humans are ever as fragile or helpless as addicts to a drug like heroin, doing irreparable harm, first to themselves and often to the world around them. As this book was written, it seemed that the nation was only at the threshold of finding solutions and committing resources to make them work. Yet all over the country, free clinics, rap centers and methadone maintenance facilities were springing up, staffed by visionaries and often just plain kind people.

One thinks of Berkeley's Free Clinic and Rap Center where many kids will come in each week to "crash," other young people sitting with them hour after hour, talking them down. Or some of the newer approaches, like the Center for Special Social and Health Problems—also called Fort Help—run in an abandoned bakery in San Francisco by Dr. Joel Fort, the controversial author of *The Pleasure Seekers*. Dr. Fort would "decriminalize" the drug problem and relate it to others in young people's lives. So his center offers programs not only in drug abuse but in sex problems, compulsive gambling, violence and uncontrollable rages, suicide, crime, obesity, and insomnia.

In Berkeley, Dr. William P. Soskin runs the Ford Foundation-backed Project Community, which he calls a "head school." The totally informal school is intended to give young people training and awareness about themselves in a multiplicity of ways, making unnecessary the false escape of drugs. For instance, there are "guided dream" sessions in which students let an instructor lead them mentally through value systems.

And in Haight-Ashbury, where so much of it all began, there is a house for dropouts and runaways, for kids fearful of going home but not so far gone as to turn to heroin. Drugs are not permitted inside. Nothing sets the house apart from others on the street. It is called Walden.

## San Francisco: Society, Culture, Counterculture, Press, and TV

San Francisco has its Social Establishment, a modern gentility descended in large measure from the rough-hewn capitalists of the Gold Rush and railroad-building eras; there are even a select few whose families came *before* 1849. Social arbiter Stephen Birmingham lists eight of the 19th-century names as the core of the present-day San Francisco *Social Register*—Crocker, Huntington, Stanford, Hopkins, Flood, Fair, Mackay, O'Brien; then he adds a group whose money comes from only more slightly recent mercantile, banking, and shipping fortunes, and a number of wealthy Jewish families, well accepted in their cosmopolitan city. High-society life revolves around institutions and events like the "Monday lunch" in the St. Francis Hotel's Mural Room; the opening of the San Francisco Opera; traditional old clubs like the Pacific Union, the Burlingame, and the Bohemian; and the still-by-invitation-only Debutante Cotillion. The disdain with which the San Francisco blue-bloods regard the upstart Society of the California Southland has, of course, no bounds. In fact, there is a marked provincialism to San Francisco and a closed character to its old society and highest business positions which explains why many Californians are much less enthusiastic about the city than eastern and foreign visitors. An ambitious young man can "make it" much faster in the go-go world of Southern California, which may be one reason why so many more of them have chosen to live there.

In almost narcissistic measure, San Francisco prides itself on the brilliance of its arts. "I'm a nut on culture," Mayor Joseph Alioto effuses: "I think cities have souls. There's a special uniqueness to San Francisco. We spend public money on our Opera, and it's second only to the Met. We have a great Symphony Orchestra and Ballet and American Conservatory Theatre . . ." But the base of support may not be as wide as it seems; much of the city's cultural life has been sustained by a relatively narrow group of brilliant Jews plus Italians interested in music. Los Angeles has certainly done much more in recent times. Even some of San Francisco's own accuse it of being too self-contented, of having only passable opera and symphony. Writes San Franciscan author Herbert Gold: "The theater is as bad as New York's, but there is less of it. The three scattered major museums add up to less than Cleveland's magnificent art institute, nor does the music equal Cleveland's."

Of the city that fostered Mark Twain, Ambrose Bierce, and Bret Harte, Gold says: "Maybe the major arts are literature, painting, sculpture, and music. Maybe some minor knockoffs of the major arts are posters, street and improvisational theater, happenings and the sound of rock. Maybe San Francisco majors in the minors."

The literary flames have never been extinguished in the Bay Area, a tradition carried on today by countless starving young poets and by writers of substance including the likes of Herbert Gold and Wallace Stegner, Barnaby Conrad, Paul Jacobs, and Jessica Mitford. North Beach is a gaudy carnival for tourists by night but still a light-hearted bohemia with film-makers, Hare Krishna beggars, poets, runaway kids, and local Italians and Chinese thronging the street by day; here, at the flowery bower of the Minimum Daily Requirement Cafe, the artists and literati gather with regularity, finding comfort in their numbers. Bookstores abound, as do small presses like City Lights, the Four Seasons Foundation, and the Grabhorn Press. America's greatest poster-makers—Satty and Mouse and Wes Wilson—work around the Bay; so do underground figures making films that range from the political to the pornographic. Dance troupes and little theaters keep emerging and dying. There is even guerrilla park theater under R. G. Davis' San Francisco Mime Troupe, which adapts classical comedies to local themes and goes on, usually free, with masks and rock improvisations to audiences of enraptured children and adults—by Gold's account—"grooving in the open air." The amplified joyrock of the San Francisco sound offers such as the Jefferson Airplane, the Grateful Dead, the Quicksilver Messenger Service, and, until her early death by drugs in 1970, Janis Joplin.

As for the press, it goes without saying that the Bay Area has more than its share of underground papers—the San Francisco *Oracle*, *Good Times*, the Berkeley *Barb* and its competitive offspring, the *Tribe* (published, literally, by a tribe of one-time *Barb* reporters who objected when publisher Max Sherr refused to share the wealth), and *Dock of the Bay*.

But for several years, San Francisans have not needed to look to the underground press for counsel about the world of counterculture and sympathy for new life styles. They have found it right there on the front page of the once rather staid and responsible San Francisco *Chronicle*. One young *Chronicle* reporter is said to have boasted: "If there was a wholesale pot bust in San Francisco tomorrow, 80 percent of the city-side reporters and copy-desk would be in jail." One of its editors called the paper's formula one of "fact, truth and fun"; executive editor Scott Newhall, who managed the transformation of the *Chronicle* between 1962 and 1971, once likened the front page to a circus barker saying, "Hurry, hurry, hurry, the girls are just about to take off their clothes." Once lured inside, the reader, in theory, gets serious coverage. But as the *Columbia Journalism Review* reported in 1969, what one got "often seemed to add up to little more than a ton of feathers"—even if spiced with the writings of two of America's cleverest newspaper columnists, Herb Caen and political satirist Art Hoppe. The political tone is superficially liberal, but two-minute stories, breezy headlines, and lots of sex are (after Caen and Hoppe) what most readers remember.

The evening *Examiner*, part of the Hearst chain, has a totally different editorial face, condemning almost everything associated with youth culture, hippies, drugs, and deviance. Its quality is not outstanding. In fact, the truth is that urbane, cosmopolitan San Francisco, this great world city, has no newspaper of stature.

San Francisco also has a peppery independent monthly, the *Bay Guardian*, edited by Bruce Brugmann, one of America's most skillful muckrakers.

One San Francisco television station gets practically all kudos, no brick bats. It is KQED, a public broadcaster supported in major part by 42,000 audience-members who annually pay from $14.50 to $100. Reaching a maximum audience of 400,000, the station pioneered in such new approaches to television news as its "Newsroom" program, in which expert journalists sit around a U-shaped table to report on and discuss the day's events—a device later copied widely by other noncommercial stations. KQED has received several broadcasting industry awards and was praised in the Columbia University *Survey of Broadcast Journalism* for having done the most extensive job of local coverage in the 1968 election of any station in the U.S.

## San Francisco: Economics, Government, Minorities

San Francisco, it has been said, has two establishments—a Big Establishment peopled by industrialists and financiers whose interests run beyond the Bay Area to the nation and the world, and a Small Establishment of those whose activities are almost exclusively city- or at most Bay Area-oriented. Among the latter are the multitudinous ethnic group leaders, and, of course, the politicians.

First a word on the Big Establishment. Trading off the initial advantages of its port and the Gold Rush, San Francisco for more than a century has been a great commercial, banking, and managerial center. "We're the shipping, financial, and great headquarters city of the West—the place where the boards of directors, the chairmen, the underwriters, the big money are to be found, the place where the big decisions are made," an official of Pacific Gas & Electric, itself headquartered in San Francisco, told me. The statement ignores the strong shift of headquarters cities to Los Angeles, noted throughout the 1960s. By 1970, metropolitan Los Angeles had 120 headquarters offices of California's largest businesses, San Francisco and nearby Bay Area cities only 61.

Nevertheless, San Francisco—by the standards of any other American city —must be considered a financial giant. Its annual bank clearings rank sixth among all cities of the nation. Here is the home office of the Bank of America, the world's largest nongovernmental bank, with assets of $25 billion and almost 1,000 branches in the state of California, plus many overseas. (Founder Amadeo Peter Giannini, the son of an Italian immigrant laborer, rose to the pinnacle of American banking in the great Horatio Alger story of the 20th century. He has been dead since 1949, but his heirs and followers at the Bank of America still finance great portions of California agriculture and underwrite a major share of California's public bonds. Their latest triumph is the BankAmericard, a new form of instant credit—at an annual interest rate of 18 percent—now in the hands of 30 million Americans.) Other great San Francisco banks include Wells Fargo (assets $5.7 billion, fathers of "Master Charge") and Crocker-Citizens National (assets $5.3 billion). California's two largest transportation firms—the Southern Pacific Railroad (revenues $1.1 billion) and Consolidated Freightways (revenues $451 million, largest truck common carrier of the U.S.A.)—are in San Francisco. The city also has California's biggest industrial corporation, Standard Oil of California (1969 sales $4.4 billion).

Pacific Gas & Electric has annual revenues of more than $1 billion, more than any other power company in America; its territory covers two-thirds of California, an area as large as Pennsylvania and New York combined. P.G. & E. has scored a moderate success in holding at bay the Sierra Club and other conservationist groups which blame it for environmental blight through its $300 million annual investment in new facilities; a new power substation in Monterey, for instance, has been built to look just like a mission. Blocked several years ago by the conservationists in developing one site it had chosen for a nuclear power plant, P.G. & E. wisely included the Sierra Club and every environment-related agency of the state government in its deliberations on an alternate site, finally set at Diablo Canyon on barren oceanfront south of San Luis Obispo. The company has also opened up to vacationers some 48 recreation sites near its hydroelectric facilities in the Sierra and Cascade mountains, and it even puts out bulletins on where the fishing is best.

Except for the huge corporate complexes and its port, the city of San Francisco has little industry-related activity; one good reason is that its land area is simply too limited. Together with other Bay Area cities, the port leads the West Coast in general cargo shipping; oil cargoes make Los Angeles–Long Beach greater in overall tonnage. The suburbs are the locale of the Bay Area's manufacturing growth; just in the peninsular suburbs south of the city, for instance, 200 electronics firms have set up plants, including national leaders like IBM, ITT, Ampex, Western Electric, Raytheon, Remington Rand, Sylvania, Sperry-Rand, Zenith, Motorola, Philco, and General Electric.

The visible involvement in city politics of San Francisco's corporate giants, their interests focused out into the state and nation, is not great. There is, however, a fairly active chamber of commerce which works behind the scenes in city elections, reflecting big business interests. The real estate operators, benefiting from the great construction boom, are also very powerful beneath the surface, and the thriving tourist industry plays an important role. Such interests share influence (in differing coalitions, dependent on the issue) with the old propertied class and Brahmin Jews (Zellerbachs, Magnins, and Swigs), the unions, and the assorted ethnics who sturdily resist amalgamation. There are the Chinese in their own great Chinatown; Japanese in the Western Addition; Italians in North Beach, Russians and Poles along Clement Street; German, Irish, and Mexicans in the Mission; and blacks in the Fillmore and Hunters Point districts—the most polyglot, unassimilated assortment of nationalities and races in California. The Italians and Orientals have made perhaps the deepest imprint on San Francisco's style and cultural life, but the Irish have traditionally been more successful politicians. Mayor Alioto, an Italian elected in 1967, won office—like every other successful San Francisco politician—by assiduous courting of the whole panoply of ethnic groups.

In 1971 the San Francisco *Chronicle* asked a jury of 20 distinguished citizens to name the city's 10 most powerful people. Interestingly, the 10 chosen included no woman, no Chinese or Chicano, no labor leader or banker. But it did include these figures: "Joseph L. Alioto, the mayor; Willie L. Brown, the assemblyman; Herb Caen, the columnist; Justin Herman, the boss of redevelopment; Cyril Magnin, the merchant prince; Joseph T. McGucken, the archbishop; Alfred J. Nelder, the police chief; William Matson Roth, the benevolent aristocrat; Ben Swig, the hotelman; and Charles de Young Thieriot, the publisher."

In state and national politics, San Francisco is a liberal bastion and strongly Democratic. The two Burton brothers—Congressman Phillip Burton and state Assemblyman John L. Burton—have long been the acknowledged leaders of the Democratic left wing, one of the few radical city political families in the nation. (A third brother, Robert, teaches English to the convicts at San Quentin.) San Francisco's powerful labor unions, traditionally in the same mold, have been swinging some to the right in recent years in a fit of enthusiasm over the jobs generated by all the new downtown construction. Municipal politics are officially nonpartisan and hard for an outsider to follow; in 1967, for instance, Alioto incurred the disafavor of the Burtons but won election by coalescing the conservative and usually more affluent Irish, the labor unions, upper-middle-class intellectuals, and many blacks whom he was able to lure away from his more liberal opponent. George Christopher, the energetic mayor of the late '50s and early '60s, was a Republican, but of such liberal-to-moderate image that he could peel away thousands of normally Democratic votes.

Met privately or seen in public, San Francisco's Alioto almost overwhelms the beholder with his rapid-talking eloquence, enthusiasm, and imagination. The son of an immigrant Sicilian fisherman, he made his fortune as an aggressive attorney, building the country's largest civil antitrust practice. He was also active in business and banking. By the late 1960s, by Alioto's own acknowledgement, he was "bored with making money." When the man whose mayoralty campaign he was managing suddenly died of a heart attack, Alioto jumped in and won in a whirlwind 56-day campaign. At his inaugural, he played the violin and quoted Jeremy Bentham, Heraclitus, Edmund Burke, Matthew Arnold, Will Irwin, and Gertrude Atherton in an address which called for a pulling together of San Francisco's disparate ethnic groups and an effort to correct the sad living conditions of the Negro ghetto.

Early in his mayoralty term, Alioto helped settle newspaper and symphony strikes, and tried to alleviate the financial pinch on City Hall through new business levies and a commuters' tax. He took a stiff line with the Black Panthers—whom he calls "a bunch of cons, ex-cons, narcotics and gun pushers who not only practice violence but exhort children to violence." But Alioto also met frequently with other young black militants, trying to foster programs that would give them, as he described it to me, "some status, credentials, position in their own community. We couldn't have taken on the Panthers if we didn't work with the young, nonviolent militants."

With his persuasive style and successful mixture of rapping with minorities while suppressing violence, Alioto soon drew national attention and was actually given serious consideration as Hubert Humphrey's Vice Presidential running mate on the 1968 Democratic ticket. He was considered a strong early contender for the 1970 Democratic gubernatorial nomination. And he might well have been nominated, and conceivably have been elected, if it had not been for a September 1969 article in *Look* accusing him of being "enmeshed in a web of alliances with at least six leaders of La Cosa Nostra." Alioto responded with a $12.5 million libel suit, and a first trial, in which careful observers believe *Look* failed to substantiate its charges well, ended in a hung jury. In 1971 an even more serious blow fell. A federal grand jury in Seattle indicted Alioto on nine counts of bribery, conspiracy, and mail fraud. The indictment was based on the way Alioto, as a private attorney in early 1960s, had shared with John O'Connell (then the Democratic attorney general of Washington state) some $925,000 of a $2.3 million fee Alioto received for successfully suing, on Washington's behalf, electrical equipment manufacturers who had overcharged the state. Alioto charged the indictment was "a 14-karat fake" initiated by a Republican-run Justice Department to harass a popular Democratic mayor up for reelection.* The scandals did not, as many expected, mark Alioto with a political death certificate; in fact he charged to a clear-cut victory in November 1971, carrying 37.7 percent of the vote in a field of 11 candidates. In the same election, a ballot proposition to ban all new buildings over six stories was overwhelmingly rejected.

San Francisco now seems to be shifting from a Wasp-Catholic citadel into a heavy minority city, particularly yellow, black, and brown (Mexican and Central American).† And as more and more middle-class whites depart for the suburbs, the city's societal mix is more and more one of the very rich and the welfare poor. Ethnic conflicts seem to escalate, with militants gaining more and more powerful voices. The housing shortage (in a city with less than a 1-percent vacancy rate) gets worse and the tax load heavier—the typical ailments of almost every great American city today.

Conditions remain deplorable among the two minority groups now strongest and fastest-growing in San Francisco—Negroes and Chinese. The blacks are crowded into the shabby inner-city Fillmore district and into Hunters Point, a depressed and isolated shantytown of "temporary" World War II housing on the southeastern edge of the city. In 1940, there were 4,000 Negroes in San Francisco; in 1970, 96,078. The familiar litany of black ghettos, ranging from broken families and menial jobs to police harassment, are evident. (A hard-working police community relations unit has had only moderate success. In 1969, blacks still numbered only 4.5 percent of the police force. But the newly-formed "Officers for Justice" was developing into probably the most militant and political of the nascent black police officer associations around the U.S.) In 1966, San Francisco had its own black riot at Hunters Point; the damage and bloodshed were minor compared to Watts, but the pervasive despair of ghetto residents which caused it was just the same.

Chinatown—America's greatest Oriental population concentration and oldest ghetto—lies squeezed into 42 square blocks of land between elegant Nob Hill and Montgomery Street.‡ Tourists throng Grant Avenue, the main drag, packed with colorful curio shops, banks, and savings and loan associations, tile fronts, bright signs and colors of gold and turquoise, yellow and red. There are some 80 restaurants and numerous food import stores selling everything from quail eggs, squid and shark fins to bamboo shoots, dry fungus, rice, and tea. Daily Chinese newspapers flourish, along with Chinese movies, Chinese radio stations, and Chinatown's own telephone exchange (in a pagoda on Washington Street). Chinatown also has its own unofficial government—the

* Alioto and O'Connell, in March 1972, won a civil case filed by Washington state and utilities seeking return of the $2.3 million. The federal criminal charges were still pending, however.

† In 1970, Orientals were 13.5 percent of the city population, blacks 13.4 percent. California, of course, has more people of oriental ancestry than any other state: 170,131 Chinese, 213,280 Japanese, and 138,859 Filipinos in the latest Census.

‡ Many of the specifics of this account are from an article, "San Francisco's Chinatown," by Mary Ellen Leary, *Atlantic Monthly,* March 1970, as well as other sources cited in the bibliography to this book.

Chinese Consolidated Benevolent Association. Better known as the Six Companies, this is an institution complex, obscure, and still powerful, though not as powerful as it once was, since Chinese youth now seeks its own way and rejects a feudalistic structure that leaves all decisions to an aged elite. The Six Companies still seek to represent the Chinese to the white world and to function as a court in disputes between district or family groups.

The old-time image of the coolie, the shuffling Chinese houseboy, and the corrupt opium den having dissipated, most Americans in modern times have regarded the Chinese in their midst as hard-working, frugal, and the most uncomplaining ingredient of the melting pot. For the thousands of Chinese who have moved out into the greater society, landing good jobs and living in comfortable communities, the middle-class stereotype is true. For most of Chinatown's people, it is highly misleading. By any normal standards, Chinatown is a slum—perhaps the most or only glamorous slum in America, but still a slum:

- Three-quarters of the families earn less than $6,000 a year, one-third are below the federal poverty level.
- The 1969 unemployment rate was 12.8 percent, versus 6.7 percent for San Francisco and 3.9 percent for the country as a whole. Workers are often so desperate for work that they will stay on the job 10 hours a day, seven days a week, and not complain for fear of being blackballed.
- The population density ranges up to 231 people per acre, several times the city average. (In all, the city has 58,696 Chinese people.)
- Of the housing, 51 percent is substandard; 60 percent of the families share a bathroom with another or have none at all.
- In the Chinatown "core" area, median schooling is 1.7 years; in surrounding "greater" Chinatown, the level is 8 years—versus 12 years for the city as a whole. (Yet in 1971, when citywide school busing was ordered, Chinese parents were strongly opposed, fearing a disruption in community life if their children no longer received a unique education in Chinese culture. At the start of the school year, there was a highly effective Chinese boycott of the schools and a group of private "Freedom Schools," named for their Southern predecessors, were formed. But the great majority of Chinese children returned to the public schools, and the freedom schools encountered severe financial problems. Min S. Yee, a Chinese-American freelance writer and former *Newsweek* staffwriter, reported that the anti-busing crusade was "crumbling" in part because the Six Companies and the community's conservative power structure were trying to identify the freedom schools and anti-busing with the increasingly unpopular cause of political unity in Chinatown for the cause of supporting Chiang Kai-shek's "return to the mainland.")
- The number of people needing medical care—but unable to afford it—is 16,000. The tuberculosis rate is three times that of Caucasians in the city. The suicide rate is far above the already-spectacular city rate.
- In crowded sewing-factory sweatshops, 3,000 seamstresses produce gar-

ments for major American firms on a piece-rate basis, sometimes earning only half California's $1.65 minimum wage. They lack all medical, health, vacation, overtime, or sick-pay benefits.

All of these problems are being aggravated by a heavy influx of new Chinese immigrants, the great bulk of whom speak no English, feel frightened and insecure in their new country, and almost inevitably head for the seeming protection of the Chinatown ghetto. The Chinese exclusion laws, enacted in 1882 on a wave of fear about the "yellow peril," were first modified in 1943, further liberalized under the terms of the 1952 McCarran-Walter Act, and substantially removed by abolition of the old national origin quota system in 1965. Now up to 20,000 Chinese may enter the U.S., and the city of San Francisco estimates it is getting as many as 8,000 a year.*

Many of the immigrants are teenagers whose language problem makes them high-school dropouts and unemployables. At the same time, many of the more intelligent young Chinese have begun to challenge the family-based, hierarchical authority imposed on them by the old Chinatown power structure. Petty criminal gangs and a rise in individual acts of delinquency began to appear by the early 1960s; by the latter part of the decade, the hostility of youth to the system was coalescing into a movement of ideological proportions. Militant young "Red Guards" adopted a platform and tactics almost identical to those of the Black Panthers—whom they frankly copied. San Francisco could hardly believe that traditionally docile Chinese youth would resort to such tactics, but the first sporadic acts of social violence were there for all to see. Without concentrated city- and federally-supported programs for employment, language training, housing, and health, the outlook was for a new and bitter chapter in Chinatown's history.

## San Francisco: Saving the Bay and Building BART

The city of San Francisco itself accounts for only 15 percent of the 4.6 million people scattered through the nine counties surrounding San Francisco Bay, living in countless suburban towns plus big cities like Oakland and San Jose. In terms of votes and thus power, San Francisco's weight has been declining steadily since 1940, when it had 37 percent of the Bay Area population.

The great population spurts have come in sprawling suburban counties like Santa Clara (up 500 percent since 1946), a pattern all too reminiscent of Southern California. With the unremitting and inadequately guided growth have come the inevitable problems. The air over San Francisco itself is constantly cleansed by strong offshore winds, but around the interior bay perim-

---

* The 1965 immigration law also resulted in a five-year doubling of San Francisco's Filipino population, to a total of 24,694 in the 1970 Census. In the city's predominantly Mexican-American Mission District, theaters showing films in Tagalog, the Filipino language, are proliferating. A majority of the new Filipino immigrants are professionals looking for better income opportunities.

eter, smog now builds up to alarming levels many days of each year; in Oakland and San Jose, air pollution has reached L.A. proportions. Massive traffic congestion is noted in San Francisco and other heavily built-up areas. Subdivisions and highways gobble up thousands of acres of farmland and green space each year. No sound regional development plan has been enacted; in fact the dedication to local self-government is so strong that almost 575 local governments have sprung up in the Bay Area. Without strong regional (as opposed to local) government, the area is often at a loss to deal with regional-scale problems like waste disposal, air- and water-pollution control, mass transit, and open space.*

Perhaps the region's greatest problem is the protection and preservation of San Francisco Bay, a priceless asset well described by writer Judson Gooding as "an immense, extraordinarily lovely series of inland seas stretching 50 miles from north to south, and extending inland to the great Sacramento delta where the waters from 16 rivers flow down from the Sierras." Over a century, diking and filling by developers has reduced the water area of the entire bay by a third, from 680 to 400 square miles. By the 1960s, conservationists became highly alarmed by the rapidity with which landfill operations were proceeding; one of them predicted that unless a halt were called, the bay within 50 years would be nothing more than a filthy river surrounded by housing tracts and freeways. Conservationists also pointed to the uncontrolled way the 276-mile shoreline was being gobbled up by industry, from docks and shipyards to oil tank farms and salt-manufacturing lagoons, not to mention the dumping of garbage into diked-off areas. Dire peril was seen for the chain of life dependent on the bay—its fringe of estuarine marshland, with fish, plants, and shorebirds—and for every recreational and aesthetic enjoyment of the bay waters.

Added to this, there were run-of-the-mill problems of raw or inadquately treated sewage pouring into the bay from the cities around its rim. San Francisco itself was the prime offender, discharging about 487,000 gallons a day into the bay from a rudimentary treatment plant near the famed Fishermen's Wharf restaurant complex. In the background, there were two proposed government projects which could inflict even greater damage. One was the San Luis Drain to bring in agricultural waste waters—heavy in nutrients from fertilizers, pesticides, and boron that leaks from the soil—from the Central Valley. The other was the Peripheral Canal, a suggested $480 million, 43-mile-long conduit to divert Sacramento River water that normally flows into the delta and carry it on down to Central Valley farms and Los Angeles as part of the California Water Plan. Ecologists argued that lowering the water in the delta would allow salt water to flow "upstream" into the verdant delta region, threatening its ecological balance, and that disruption of the normal westerly water flow would disrupt the natural flushing action which cleanses the bay of industrial and agricultural wastes.

* An eight-county Association of Bay Governments was created in 1966 and produced a preliminary area plan; to date, however, its powers are not great and it acts primarily as a conveyor of federal sewer grants.

The conservationists scored one spectacular victory when the "Save Our Bay" campaigners, spearheaded by some determined women who had worked in Paul McCloskey's congressional campaigns, got the legislature to pass and Reagan to sign a 1969 bill establishing permanent controls over landfill and dredging in the bay. "Save Our Bay" was not only a conservationist victory but perhaps the most determined and effective demonstration of woman-power in California history. And it helped to transform San Mateo County (just to the south of San Francisco) from one dominated by on-the-take, reactionary politicians into one of California's most progressive political seedbeds. For the change, McCloskey can take a lot of the credit.

The outlook for the bay's future has been brightening up in other ways, too. In 1970, both San Francisco and Oakland passed large bond issues for high-grade sewage treatment plants. Limping after fervent attacks by Bay Area Congressman Jerome R. Waldie and others, both the San Luis Drain and Peripheral Canal projects were in deep trouble in Congress, which would have had to bear a major share of the expense of each. With the moratorium on landfill operations, San Francisco had to find a new place to dump its 1,800 tons of garbage each day. The final solution: to haul the waste 375 miles in 30-car freight trains to a remote desert location in Lassen County in northeastern California, where it is dumped in a cut-and-cover operation.* Hardly anyone can mourn for that particular location, so heavily alkaline that sagebrush scarcely survives there. And the site is big enough to accommodate refuse for several hundred years.

Except for the saving of its bay, no modern development has been so important to the Bay Area as a whole as the authorization and construction of BART—short for the San Francisco Bay Area Rapid Transit District, the first major subway system to be built in the United States since 1906. Construction of the 75-mile system, linking San Francisco with the East Bay counties of Alameda and Contra Costa, began on a June day in 1964 when President Johnson touched off a small charge of dynamite in an onion field in far-out suburban Concord. After many delays, the system was finally to begin regular operations in 1972; it is the United States' most advanced modern transit system, both in its technological and aesthetic aspects. The sleek aluminum cars are fully automated, their start-up, speed, and braking controlled by a central computer bank, so that the attendant on board has little to do except attend to the psychological well-being of the passengers and make station announcements. From zero, the cars can accelerate to a top speed of 80 miles per hour in 45 seconds; average speed is 45 to 50 miles per hour, including stops. With seats like those of a commercial airliner, air conditioning, carpeted floors, big windows, and good lighting, the cars are a world away from the screeching underground horrors of the New York system.† The stations are

---

* Lassen County, strapped for funds, welcomes the garbage because it gets paid about 21 cents for every ton dumped. For hauling and dumping, San Francisco pays the railroad $6.50 a ton.

† BART's cars were manufactured by the Rohr Corporation of San Diego, which outbid two veteran car builders—Pullman and the St. Louis Car Division of General Steel industries—to get the job. Rohr used aerospace techniques and a systems approach to construction, but nevertheless (or perhaps one should say appropriately) the first test cars presented a myriad of problems, especially in their automated control functions.

designed with a careful eye to aesthetics, well lighted and attractively decorated at underground locations, landscaped at above-ground stops. About the
only old-fashioned element of the system is that it still rides on rails.

BART had a host of engineering problems to overcome. One was laying
down the world's largest underwater tube—3.6 miles long, as deep as 130 feet
below the bay surface, sitting in the soft bay muds and away from rock so
that in case of an earthquake, the double-barrelled tube can just move about
like a rubber hose. But in the words of B. R. Stokes, the former Oakland
*Tribune* urban affairs reporter who went aboard as BART's first employee in
1958 and remained as general manager throughout the construction of the
system, "all our engineering problems, however great, were simpler than getting adequate financing, and then dealing with the officials of 27 cities, three
counties and at least 50 other governmental agencies, ranging down from the
federal to local districts." A quarter-century, Stokes points out, elapsed between the first germ of the idea of a Bay Area rapid transit system in 1947
and completion in the early 1970s—perhaps a harbinger of what the country's
other cities will face in improving their public transportation.

The first impetus for BART came not from a single person, but rather
from a group of prestigious businessmen and civic leaders who were concerned
about the city's congestion and the need to knit the Bay Area together. San
Francisco's obstacle-ridden topography—water, hills, and narrow connecting
points—provided a greater feeling of crisis in the Bay Area about continued
reliance on the automobile; Los Angeles, by contrast, is like Kansas, where
there are (or were) seemingly unlimited amounts of ground, from a highway
engineer's point of view, to lay out concrete. While the first pressures for mass
transit were local, the state legislature took the initiative in 1951 to set up and
finance a study commission on the problem, to which the nine Bay counties
—in an unusual demonstration of regional cooperation—then lent their cooperation and more financial support. In 1957, the legislature created BART
as a political subdivision of the state.

Two of the biggest counties—San Mateo and Marin—withdrew from
BART before a specific plan could be put to a popular vote in 1962. San
Mateo opted out under pressure from its local merchants, who were afraid
BART would siphon shopping traffic to San Francisco. Marin withdrew after
a petulant Golden Gate Bridge authority refused to allow tracks to run across
the bridge's span. Finally, only three major counties—San Francisco, Contra
Costa, and Alameda—voted on the $792 million bond issue. The affirmative
vote was 61.2 percent—just over the 60 percent required. BART thus became
the largest locally or regionally financed public works project in U.S. history.
And local approval triggered operation of a state law authorizing $180 mil-
lion in bridge toll funds to finance BART's bay tube (the theory being that
the tube would eliminate the need for at least one additional future bridge).

Seattle civic leader James Ellis, who has battled unsuccessfully to get
approval of rapid transit for his area, speaks of the action "of the people of
the San Francisco area in voting upon themselves almost the entire cost of

the BART system" as "one of the most courageous acts ever taken by a local government in the United States." Without mass transit, Ellis says, the Bay Area would "have faced the inevitability of destruction by freeway." This is essentially the message BART's backers took to the people in the 1962 campaign. They acknowledged that the system was terribly expensive —and at that time there was no talk of federal mass transit subsidies. But they conveyed this message: "What will it cost us if we have no mass transit system? How many freeways will we need, how many bridges? What will the cost be in highway accidents? What time will commuters save? How about the disabled and the young and old people who don't drive cars?" Such inducements as the promise of nine minutes riding time from downtown Oakland to downtown San Francisco, a run that takes from 30 to 60 minutes by existing transportation, doubtless helped to sell the case. Another plus was strong business backing, many businessmen seeing direct benefits for their firms in mass transit. And there was scarcely any really organized opposition.

By 1967, runaway inflation and increased costs in aesthetic design had put BART $150 million beyond its budget. Jealous automobile and highway lobbies in the state legislature were not anxious to help, but eventually a one-half-percent sales tax increase in the three counties was authorized. By then, BART was well along with its urgent program of real estate acquisition (some 3,600 pieces of property, with thousands of condemnations), and construction could move ahead to scheduled completion. Final cost: about $1.5 billion.

Now BART's lines throw out three great spokes on the East Bay Side— south to Fremont near the foot of the bay, east to Concord, north past Berkeley to Richmond. In San Francisco proper, the first station is at the Embarcadero; then the line moves southwest, one spur going down to Daly City (site of the Cow Palace), two others out toward the Pacific. Some critics have suggested BART will further the "Manhattanization" of San Francisco as more and more commuters come in just for working hours in the downtown, leaving few tax dollars or other benefits for the city behind. (The proven fact is that BART stimulates office construction. Some $1 billion worth has gone in during the past decade in locations within five minutes' walking time of BART stations.) But the line will have other functions. It passes through or close to ghetto areas of Negroes, Mexican-Americans and others in San Francisco and Oakland, giving the people of those areas new mobility and a chance to get to better-paid jobs in the thriving suburban factories. It provides rapid access to major universities, including San Francisco State and the University of California at Berkeley. And what's more (as if San Francisco needed another), it's sure to be a grand tourist attraction.

BART alone, however, will not be enough to prevent disastrous auto congestion as the number of commuters in San Francisco rises a projected 100 percent in the next 20 years. The city has undertaken an unparalleled number of projects to stop one-man, one-auto commuting, including express lanes or a waiver of bridge tolls for "car pool" vehicles, an extra tax on downtown parking, and use of bridge revenues to subsidize modern commuter buses and to revive the delightful ferry boats that were so foolishly abandoned after the Golden Gate and Bay Bridges had been constructed.

## *In San Francisco's Orbit: From Marin to Monterey*

What San Francisco represents among cities, Marin County—just to the north over the Golden Gate—represents among suburbs. Still fairly light on people (206,038 in 1970), its geography is varied and a pleasure to the eye—a place where mountains, ocean, and bay meet, known for its canyons, loamy farmland, lagoons, and streams. Here are some of San Franciscans' favorite relaxing spots, including Stinson Beach and beautiful Point Reyes, where Congress created a national seashore in 1962. Many towns have strong personalities—one thinks of elegant Tiburon or Riviera-like Sausalito with its delightful harbor location and artists and hippies on houseboats. Mill Valley has a rural quaintness and houses that reflect good upper class taste. But along with the old, cozy communities, Marin has dull, flat newer subdivisions low on both planning and architectural quality.

Primarily, Marin is a commuter county for San Francisco's well-heeled, a place that has changed suddenly from rural backwardness like most of the North Coast to a sophisticated and urbane community. Politically, the county is normally regarded as Republican, but in 1964 it registered the strongest vote in the state against the proposition to abolish fair housing laws, and in 1970 it gave Wilson Riles his highest percentage in defeating Max Rafferty. San Rafael (population 38,977) is the closest thing to a city in Marin County and also has a newspaper—the *Independent-Journal*, superior to any San Francisco paper.

The two counties of "the Peninsula"—directly south of San Francisco—are San Mateo and Santa Clara, living in major degree off the heavy modern-day concentration of aerospace industries. San Mateo (pop. 556,234), has boomed from the population flow of San Francisco to the north, the employment at San Francisco International Airport on the bayside, and the research overflow from Stanford University, just beyond its borders on the south. Generally regarded as one of the more affluent suburbs, it has been reported to have an extraordinarily high divorce rate. Many of the towns are rich, flowery bowers of gardened California at its most attractive; in contrast, the county has huge ticky-tacky row housing developments climbing up over its hills, destined to be the slums of tomorrow. As an example of the desecration, developers have gone in for "mountain cropping" in which they convert what could otherwise be interesting hillside building locations into ordinary flatland so that they can cram in more houses and build more cheaply. The major cities are San Mateo (pop. 78,991), Redwood City (55,686), and Daly City (pop. 66,922, home of the Cow Palace where the Republicans nominated Barry Goldwater for President in 1964 and Eisenhower for President in 1956).

Santa Clara County, at the foot of the bay, is an area of explosive growth in which the population has risen from 290,547 in 1950 to 1,064,714 in 1970. William Bronson, one of California's leading environmentalists, wrote in his book, *How to Kill a Golden State*:

> The Santa Clara Valley in my childhood was a vast forest of prune and cherry and apricot trees. When spring came we drove to see the endless sea of blossoms. After the war, developers moved in and did their best to wreck it all. Some day the full story of the greed, corruption, and incredible shortsightedness that accompanied the valley's destruction may be told.

And in a 1970 issue of *Cry California*, part of the story was told by Karl Belser, a man whom Bronson has hailed as "perhaps the nation's outstanding regional planner." After 16 years of struggling with the local powers-that-be, Belser in 1967 quit as director of planning for Santa Clara County. What had been a "beautiful productive garden," he charged, was "suddenly transformed into an urban anthill" in this fashion:

> Speculators took over and in effect pushed the county into the uncontrolled development. The behavior of all elements of the community during the time from 1950 to 1965 can best be described as pandemonium. Wild urban growth attacked the valley much as cancer attacks the human body. . . . Thousands of cracker boxes were thrown up, all so poorly constructed that they began to fall apart before they were completed. . . .
> Government sold out to business and industry by making many concessions inimical to the public interest as inducements for development investment, while the power structure, led by financial institutions, the media, the wealthy urban property owners, and the business community, exploited the situation to make huge profits.

Local government, Belser said, was chiefly responsible for permitting the "slurbanization," though state and federal governments were also partly to blame. When critics suggested that Belser himself should assume part of the blame, he responded that he was unable, as county planner, to prevent the cities from burgeoning and taking over the great farm areas for which the county was once renowned.

Santa Clara County's governmental structure is indeed a nightmare—crazy-quilt boundaries, 15 local governments and 38 autonomous special districts sprinkled around a county 1,321 square miles in size, extending 55 miles south of San Francisco Bay. The county planners were simply unable to stop the gush of subdivisions marching thoughtlessly out through the groves. As more and more electronic and aerospace firms flocked in, the pressures to find homes for the people proved irresistible. In recent years, the county has been a showplace of all the ills of uncontrolled growth: monotonous tract development, arteries clogged with gas stations and taco stands, glaring lights and gaudy signs, traffic congestion, noise problems, and air pollution.

The fulcrum of Santa Clara's growth has been the city of San Jose, a quiet farm capital of 95,280 souls in 1950, today a sprawling boom town of 445,779 (fourth largest in California). After years of rapacious annexation and new development at any price, the city switched to an approach of controlled growth in the late 1960s, selecting as city manager the capable former city manager of San Diego and deputy mayor of Washington, D.C., Thomas Fletcher. Residents of a big barrio are said to live in the most miserable conditions, but San Jose can boast one of California's most progressive school administrations and best newspapers, the *Mercury News*. In 1971 it elected as mayor Norman Y. Mineta, who had spent two years of his boyhood interned with other Japanese in a World War II relocation camp. Mineta said his election was a "breakthrough for his people, showing that "political success is not just a possibility for Japanese-Americans in Hawaii but on the mainland as well." He is a youthful 40 and intensely concerned about giving the many new residents of his city a sense of identity with their community.

Farther north, close to the San Mateo line, is Palo Alto (55,966), the pleasant university city (Stanford University), which has had the foresight to annex and protect as green space—at least for a time—thousands of acres of the wooded foothills on its western flank. But Palo Alto also has a satellite, East Palo Alto (17,837), a teeming black ghetto that the militants tried to rename "Nairobi."

Stanford, founded by one of the railroad tycoons of the 1880s who hoped it would become the Harvard of the West, has indeed risen to a position of prominence, along with CalTech, in a state where public higher education is so preeminent. Up to 20 years ago, the verdant, quiet campus with its mission-like buildings was affectionately known as "the farm," a place for genteel young Californians to get a superb liberal arts education. Since then its graduate schools have advanced so brilliantly that the American Council on Education ranks them behind only Harvard and Berkeley.

Stanford has also become the centerpiece of a scientific and military-industrial complex spreading across the Southern Peninsula, ranking with Route 128-Cambridge and Los Angeles as one of the most important in America. Its entry into the field began with founding of the Stanford Research Institute in 1946 to "aid and supplement scientific research at Stanford," and later the establishment of the SRI Industrial Park on part of the 8,833 acres of land which Stanford owns but cannot sell under the terms of its founding charter. By 1970, 600 acres of land had been leased to 77 tenants, who employed 17,000 workers—many of them highly paid engineers and technicians. The mix was highly diversified, including companies like Computer Data Corporation, Dow Jones & Company, the Bank of California, IBM, Lockheed Aircraft, and Lockheed Electronics. In countless ways, strong ties were built between the tenants and the university faculty and research activities.

As for SRI itself, it launched into research projects on a global scale. Some of its work was in social and domestic policy fields, but the principal thrust was defense-related, together with activities to further American interests in the Pacific. In the late 1960s and 1970, the attention of the university's militant antiwar student groups inevitably turned to SRI and its deep involvement in military-oriented projects. (In 1968, 50 percent of SRI's $64.2 million income came from the Defense Department). The students were able to demonstrate fairly convincingly the close links between SRI research goals, Stanford's on-campus military research, and trustees of the university and board directors of SRI who were officers of companies producing war materials. They revealed that SRI was deeply involved in chemical and biological warfare research and "counterinsurgency work for the Pentagon on Southeast Asia." Under strong and general student pressure, SRI agreed to stop all chemical and biological warfare research, and the university formally relinquished legal ownership and control of SRI. But SRI's priority on defense work, as opposed to social problems, seemed likely to continue.

Stanford was long spared the tragic excesses of Berkeley, Santa Barbara, and Kent State because, in the words of Peter Stern, a visiting scholar reporting in *The Nation*, there was "a tacit understanding, a 'community of consent' between the protest movement and the administration." Student antiwar groups with high-grade leadership tried to prevent "trashing" (destruction of property); university officials permitted sit-ins, as long as they were peaceful, to continue for limited periods of time and held back the local police. But in spring 1970, sparked by the Cambodian invasion and continued disputes about academic credit for ROTC courses, the consent gave way to attacks on property, two nights of virtual warfare with local police, and arson which destroyed the offices and research materials of scientists at the nearby Center for Advanced Studies in the Behavioral Sciences. President Kenneth S. Pitzer, a soft-spoken liberal who had tried to follow a moderating course, resigned in despair.

In the 1970–71 academic year, while most campuses cooled off, Stanford remained tense with a major dormitory arson, bombing of the president's office, a number of gun firings, sabotage, and vandalism by unidentified "crazies." The new president, Richard Lyman, said the incidents were a relic of the past: "Terrorism tends to be the tactic of a protest movement that has no mass following," he said. The *Stanford Daily*, whose editor that year was a spunky 20-year old girl with a liberal-left editorial policy, joined the condemnation of senseless and life-endangering violence. The paper itself was subjected to ugly threats from extremists and also the Palo Alto police, who searched its files in a fruitless hunt for pictures of protesters. Gradually, tensions cooled, partly the result of the economic pressures on students from increased tuitions. Early in 1972, when the university dismissed 37-year-old Professor H. Bruce Franklin, a respected student of Herman Melville who had become a self-proclaimed Maoist and publicly urged students to resort to violent protest at the time of the U.S. incursion into Laos, the vast majority of both students and faculty seemed to approve of the administration's harsh action. (The Franklin case had received long public hearings, and his dismissal was recommended by a 5–2 vote on a faculty committee. Franklin became one of very few tenured professors to be fired by a major U.S. university for political activism in recent years.) But a return to the carefree days of the '50s at Stanford was not likely; instead attendance was up in student-designed courses in ecology, rapid transit, and health, and interest was growing in women's liberation meetings.

The gulf of ideologies is aptly illustrated by the continued existence at Stanford of the Hoover Institution on War, Revolution, and Peace. Herbert Hoover, a Stanford graduate, wrote the institute's statement of principles: "The purpose of this Institution must be, by its research and publication, to demonstrate the evils of the doctrines of Karl Marx—whether Communism, Socialism, economic materialism, or atheism—thus to protect the American way of life from such ideologies, their conspiracies, and to reaffirm the validity of the American system." The present director of the Institute, Dr. Glenn W. Campbell, is, appropriately, one of Governor Reagan's appointees to the board of regents of the University of California.

In contrast to the beehive of activity along the bay side, the ocean side of the San Francisco Peninsula is quiet and low-keyed, a place where gentle mountainsides go down to beaches and the settlement is still remarkably light. Here one finds massive Fort Ord and the weathered beach-resort community of Santa Cruz (32,076), which combines one of the highest percentages of retired oldsters in the country with a new-life-style campus of the University of California.

Just below Santa Cruz is Monterey Bay and the famed town of Monterey (26,302), steeped in ancient Spanish and Mexican history. This is the town that John Steinbeck loved and made popular in novels like *Cannery Row*, *Sweet Thursday*, and *Tortilla Flat*. Cannery Row no longer gathers innocent sardines into their tin coffins; the reason is that gross overfishing upset nature's balance and swept Monterey Bay, where annual crops of 250,000 tons had once been brought in, clean of sardines by the late 1960s. But the Row has had a revival as an artist colony and spot for atmospheric restaurants and bistros. More flavor is added by Monterey's annual jazz festival, one of the West's great events. I once lived in Monterey for half a year and think always first of those lusty Pacific winds, blowing in great fog covers not vanquished by the sun until late in the day; as one writer has commented, "It is always early spring or late winter in Monterey." There are few more beautiful ocean stretches than Seventeen Mile Drive along the coast with its incomparable golf courses, poetic cypress trees, the sea, cliffs, sand dunes, and sea otters barking on the rocks. Quaint little Carmel-by-the-Sea (4,525), packed with rich retirees, scene of an annual Bach Festival, is called by some a tourist trap (artificial artiness, high prices), but it's the kind of trap we need more of.

A few miles inland lies Salinas, a great vegetable capital and center of the 100-mile-long Salinas Valley where César Chávez and his followers have been writing some new chapters in the saga of the American field hand—encountering hostilities not unlike those that greeted the Okies in the late 1930s. Steinbeck was born in Salinas when it was a town of 3,300; today it has 58,896 "spreading like crab grass toward the foothills," as he reported in *Travels With Charley*.

South of Monterey is Big Sur country, a wild and sparsely inhabited stretch of the coast visited by wise tourists and a semi-permanent home for a number of escapees from the plastic civilizations of urban California. California Route 1, an old two-lane highway, blessedly unimproved, winds along the coastline, offering incomparable views. Here the land drops precipitously from towering cliffs and mountains down to the raging sea, one of America's most awesome and exhilarating sights.

## San Francisco's East Bay: Oakland, Berkeley, and Beyond

Across the bay from San Francisco lies Alameda County, dominated by Oakland (pop. 361,561) and Berkeley (116,716), both old and established cities now afflicted by thorny problems of race, poverty, and student revolt. The East Bay also has a boom county, Contra Costa, whose population rose from 100,450 in 1940 to 558,389 by the 1970 Census count. William Bronson charges that Contra Costa "has undergone perhaps the worst-planned growth in the state," relinquishing its shoreline and most of its land with a view over water to industry and permitting half its rich agricultural land to be taken over by crowded and undistinguished tract housing.

The city of Oakland suffers from two hang-ups, each serious enough in itself but fatal in combination: self-identity and race.

There is still a lot of truth to the comment of Gertrude Stein, who was raised in the city but left for good at 18. "The trouble with Oakland," she said, "is that there's no *there* there." Oakland labors under what observers of such things call the "second-city syndrome," much like Newark or East St. Louis. Across a body of water, easily reached, there is the glittering core of the metropolitan area, offering good restaurants, theater, the business center, and a vibrant street scene. Thus the second city becomes increasingly dreary and commonplace and suffers from an acute feeling of communal inferiority. One young Oaklander put it to me this way: "I can go to San Francisco and stand on the corner and know something's going to happen; I can stand on a street corner in Oakland and know nothing will." On first impression, downtown Oakland has a clean, antiseptic look with its wide streets, brutalizing freeways, and a scattering of modern buildings—a bit reminiscent, shall we say, of Tulsa, Oklahoma. On closer examination, one notes how many empty lots there are, where decayed and unoccupied buildings were bulldozed. Only one central park—occupied by beautiful Lake Merritt—relieves the monotony.* There are few quality stores—mostly discount houses, tattoo stores, and

* The Kaiser Building, which overlooks the lake, is architecturally outstanding and perhaps the most eye-catching building of the Bay Area.

the like. The antithesis to San Francisco's warmth, variety, and color could scarcely be greater.

With completion of the transcontinental railway in 1869, Oakland became the great western terminus. The city boomed especially in the two decades following the 1906 earthquake and fire that almost demolished San Francisco. Excellent urban parks and transit systems were developed. And Oakland remained the principal metropolis for commerce and culture on the East Bay through the late 1930s, because San Francisco could only be reached by a nostalgic but rather inefficient ferry system. But then the Bay Bridge was completed. It became easy for any East Bay people, even those from Contra Costa County, to reach San Francisco by automobile. The airplane began to eclipse the trains, and Oakland became a semi-ghost town. The city has, to be sure, continuing economic strengths. These include the prosperous and progressive Port of Oakland (second only to New York on containerized cargoes), a new international airport (which may begin to steal passengers from San Francisco's because of direct BART service), University of California payrolls, the Alameda Naval Air Station and Oakland Army Terminal, lots of nuts and bolts manufacturing, and major rail and trucking facilities. But it has also suffered from levels of unemployment often *twice* the national average. Few of Oakland's "leaders" live in the city, thus depriving it of normal civic leadership.

Completion of the BART system may, if anything, make the situation worse. "Why should anyone get off in Oakland if Rome is only nine minutes away?" the question goes. In the long run, however, this might reverse, especially as the overcrowding in downtown San Francisco becomes less tolerable. The same BART trains that will take passengers from Oakland to San Francisco in nine minutes will do the reverse, too. Big corporations may opt for Oakland, with its lower real estate costs, as a place for runover office space, computer installations, and the like, since they can all be a few minutes from Montgomery Street. Or at least some people in Oakland hope so. Already there are claims that $50 million or more of construction in Oakland is due to the BART stimulus.

There are some other glimmerings of hope in Oakland. It has a new $30 million coliseum complex for shows, sports, and exhibitions which puts to shame anything San Francisco can offer. Three major league professional teams are based in the city. Jack London Square on the waterfront has been turned into a delightful seafood restaurant area. And high on the hills overlooking the city is the $10 million museum Oakland's people financed with a 1961 bond issue. With separate levels on ecology-environment, California history and culture, and California arts today, the museum is a superb evocation of the state past and present. An authority from New York's Museum of Modern Art has called it "the most brilliant concept of an urban museum in America."

Oakland has had a substantial number of Negroes ever since they first came a century ago as railroad construction men or porters. Then, with World

War II, came a major influx of blacks to work in the shipyards and in defense industries like Kaiser Steel. Since then the black percentage has risen steadily, with the familiar flight of whites to the suburbs. Negroes now account for 34.5 percent of the population. By 1980, blacks are expected to be in the majority.

Oakland has an oligarchic, historically unresponsive establishment, led by the person and family of Oakland *Tribune* publisher (and former U. S. Senator) William Knowland, together with Edgar Kaiser of Kaiser Industries, and unusually powerful real estate interests. The powers-that-be have traditionally treated Oakland's blacks like invisible people. Nevertheless, Oakland's black community has become nationally famous as the original spawning ground of the Black Panthers—founded, as the story goes, over expresso coffee one day in early October 1966 by Bobby G. Seale (who became chairman) and Huey P. Newton (minister of defense). The brief but complex history of the Panthers—Newton's conviction and imprisonment for the shooting of an Oakland policeman, and his subsequent retrial, ending in a hung jury; the role of the brilliant and later self-exiled Eldridge Cleaver; the phenomenon of black-bereted street bloods risen up against the established order; the bloody shootouts with often repressive police, Maoism, and flagrant racism ("Off the pigs!"); breakfasts for little black children with an admixture of hostile racial propaganda; the effort to write a new constitution for America after the inevitable revolution; Huey Newton's amazing decision in 1971 to abandon the rhetoric of the gun, seek allies in the world of black capitalism and the black church, and organize like any other political force in American life—is too long to be told here, and may change fundamentally at any time.

It does seem proper to ask why Oakland, of all places, gave birth to the Black Panthers, who took the place of the late Malcolm X and Stokely Carmichael and H. Rap Brown at the hard edge of black militancy in America. The conscious and unconscious racism of Oakland's white leadership may be considered part of the answer, but it is certainly not unique. A second, though only partial answer, may be the fact that the Oakland Negro community has long had a segment of especially intelligent and imaginative leaders, sensitive to the city's indifference and aware of the abject poverty and hopelessness of many black youths living close at hand. Many of the black leaders, I heard in the city, come from Louisiana, where they had received more basic education than most Alabama or Mississippi blacks. Huey Newton, for instance, was named after Huey Long, and many French names are noted among Oakland Negro leaders.

The Panthers have been at the forefront of those trying to keep the Oakland situation cool, on the simple grounds that they lack the firepower to win if a real riot breaks out. Black-white tensions have also been relieved to a degree by the remarkably progressive administration of police chief Charles R. Gain, a veteran member of the force who took over in 1967 and set out to make the Oakland police department "a model of 'due process.' '' Gain issued new orders to prevent unnecessary clashes with the black community and tripled the black enrollment on the force—a startling turnaround for a police department once renowned for its tough, brutal tactics in dealing with minorities. Some reforms have come to the once demoralized Oakland school system, the work of a new superintendent, Dr. Marcus A. Foster, recruited after major accomplishments with black schools in Philadelphia. There has also been a marked change in the Oakland *Tribune,* which used to take stands almost deliberately designed to exacerbate tensions. By 1970, publisher Knowland seemed to have had at least a partial change of heart. His paper began to give more coverage to black demands, and Knowland moved quietly to form a coalition between white businessmen and black leaders. (Knowland, remembered as a stony and forbidding figure in earlier years, also sprouted a very with-it mustache; the resultant image was almost grandfatherly.)

Next door Berkeley, once known as "the Athens of the West," differs from Oakland as day from night. Knowledgeable Californians insist that Berkeley's government is the most responsive in the state, with high-grade political leadership and a well trained civil service open to creative solutions of problems. Because the level of services has been consistently high, so have the city taxes, among California's highest. But there is a big, wealthy outfit in town with a payroll of $11 million a month. Its name is the University of California, providing jobs for a third of the city's people.

The prime example of Berkeley's creativity is its school integration scheme. What the city has done since the mid-1960s is to institute citywide busing to achieve racial integration. Thousands of children are transported daily from the wooded, hillside suburbs of white affluence to the once heavily Negro schools in the flatlands near the bay. Thousands of Negro children are transported in the other direction. After several years of trial, the system seems to be a clear success. Part of the reason is small classrooms, guidance counselors for troubled students, and sophisticated audio-visual aids—in short, quality education at the end of the bus ride. The long-term benefits may be immense. Unlike other cities with a strong black population (23.5 percent in 1970), Berkeley is not experiencing further white flight from its schools. And it is one of the few cities of the U.S. with a large minority population where student scores on achievement tests rank above national averages. The Berkeley plan was put through by a liberal board of education, which survived a recall attempt in 1964, and Dr. Neil V. Sullivan, a powerful innovator as school superintendent. Sullivan later went on to become commissioner of education in Massachusetts.

Since the Free Speech Movement erupted in 1964, Berkeley has been a city in turmoil, the scene in the first six years of 67 major rallies, riots, bombings, and demonstrations. Sproul Plaza, the crossroads of the university, and Telegraph Avenue, once a quiet half-mile of quaint shops adjoining the campus, have become the scene of as weird a collection of youthful counterculturites as the continent has ever seen. The "street people" are in large part not students but a wild collection of youthful dropouts and runaways, pot smokers, and tear-down-everything political theorists drawn from all over America—and abroad as well.

The unlucky Berkeley police, some 275 men strong (150 of them patrolmen), members of a department long regarded as one of California's best, have shown skill and restraint in dealing with the street people. Occasionally some members of the force will rough up a protestor, and some of the street people's charges of misconduct probably have good basis. But the fact is that in all the violence since 1964, no Berkeley policeman has drawn his revolver.

In 1970, 15,027 of Berkeley's staid and conservative regular citizens petitioned the city to find "ways and means for preventing the proliferation of revolutionary and subversive organizations in the city and on the campus." Their protest, following a wave of "trashing" (breaking of windows and other irrational destruction) that year, included a complaint that since 1964, Berkeley had been subjected to 22 days of curfew, 20 days of street fighting, and over $2.7 million in extra police costs, "not to mention the terror struck into the hearts of old and young alike." A few months later, in what the street people called the "big bust," hundreds of the young drifters from across the continent were rounded up by the police and sent home.

Despite its concerns about street rioting and destruction, Berkeley's politics make it perhaps the most liberal, leftward-oriented community in America. In 1970, it helped elect one of its city councilmen, Ronald V. Dellums, to Congress. Dellums, a black who refuses to shun the description of "radical," sided with the youths involved in the People's Park incident and the San Francisco State strike, and often defended the Black Panthers. Putting together a coalition of blacks from Oakland and Berkeley, students, university intellectuals, and war opponents, he unseated six-term Congressman Jeffrey Cohelan, a staunch—but not extreme—liberal in the Democratic primary. Perfectly in character, Dellums greeted his supporters at a victory celebration with the black radicals' familiar clenched-fist salute. Then he went on to win the general election with 25,021 votes to spare. Not in decades—perhaps not since the late Vito Marcantonio (American Labor Party, 1939–51)—had a man regarded as so far to the left of the American political mainstream gone to Congress. There Dellums began to speak for a black–New Left constituency often voiceless in the past.

Building in part on the organization that sent Dellums to Congress, a group of acknowledged radicals (three blacks and a white) took control of the Berkeley City Council in April 1971 elections. But the simultaneous election as mayor of then-councilman Warren Widener, a 32-year-old black attorney, actually left the radicals with only four of the eight occupied council seats, leading to deadlock on most issues. And while the voters put four radicals on the council, they overwhelmingly defeated a radical-backed ballot proposal to split the city police force into three autonomous units to operate in "the black community, the campus community, and predominantly white community."

Two prominent radical groups—a Black Coalition and a gathering of liberal-leftists called the April Coalition—unified to elect the new Berkeley office-holders. Groups of poor people, antiwar organizers, students (some 10,000 new voters were registered, mostly in the university community), feminists, ecologists, and skilled young professionals all took part in the drive. It is a combination unlikely to reach a majority in many American communities, but it could be the model—especially with the advent of the 18-year-old vote—for contained university communities across America. "Haven't you heard?", Mrs. Ilona Hancock, one of the newly elected council members, asked the New York *Times*'s Steven V. Roberts, "Berkeley is at least five years ahead of the rest of the country." But as the new Berkeley Council distinguished itself by more rhetoric and wrangling and more interracial and intersexual conflict than practically any other governing body in North America, it looked like a model of what the rest of the country would want, at all costs, to avoid.

# III. THE SOUTHLAND

## Growth for Growth's Sake

RICHARD G. LILLARD * tells the story of Earl G. Gilmore, who died in 1964 in the adobe ranch house at Third and Fairfax in Los Angeles where he had been born in 1887. In Gilmore's lifetime, he had seen the land around his home change from dairy ranch to oil field to Gilmore Stadium and Pan-Pacific Auditorium and Television Studio and the million-dollar Farmer's Market, where one finds everything but farmers. "Anyone who has lived his whole life in metropolitan Southern California," Lillard notes, "has seen some such series of transformations, as if the history of civilization were passing in quick review." I recall a 1955 drive along Wilshire Boulevard with a Los Angelan great-uncle already in his eighties, he pointing ruefully to pieces of property now worth millions that he could have snapped up for a song short decades before. Here is the legendary city of the Angels, the city of palms and mountains and the ranch house and the easy life and the benign climate, the city of movie stars and aerospace, the largest heavy-industrialized, semitropical area in the world, beckoning so many new settlers in a generation that its population has more than doubled.

And so it is in Los Angeles (1970 population 2,816,061) a city variously described as "40 suburbs in search of a city," or conversely, "The Ultimate City" (title of a delightful little book by Christopher Rand, based on articles he wrote for *The New Yorker*). The story is much the same throughout megalopolitan Southern California, where some 11 million people lead their lives

* In his book *Eden in Jeopardy* (New York: Knopf, 1966).

within a narrow coastal strip some 210 miles in length, from San Diego in the south to Santa Barbara in the north. In Los Angeles County alone, there are now 24 cities of more than 50,000 population—any one of which, set alone, would qualify as a metropolitan area. (Have you ever heard of Norwalk or Torrance? Each has more than 90,000 people and would be big news indeed set in the midst of most American states. In L. A. County, they are just part of never-ending suburbia.) On a population map of the U.S.A., the big black blotch for the Los Angeles urban conglomerate is sharply set off from the relative nothingness between it and metropolitan Texas, 1,200 miles to the east. The westward tilt is amply illustrated by the growth figures of Southern California in the past three decades:

| County | 1940 | 1950 | 1960 | 1970 | % Change 1940–1970 |
|---|---|---|---|---|---|
| Los Angeles | 2,785,643 | 4,151,687 | 6,038,771 | 7,032,075 | +152 |
| Orange | 130,760 | 216,224 | 703,925 | 1,420,386 | +986 |
| San Bernardino* | 289,348 | 556,808 | 1,033,011 | 1,357,854 | +369 |
| San Diego | 161,108 | 281,642 | 503,591 | 684,072 | +325 |
| Riverside* | 105,524 | 170,046 | 306,191 | 459,074 | +335 |
| Ventura | 69,685 | 114,647 | 199,138 | 376,430 | +340 |
| Santa Barbara | 70,555 | 98,220 | 168,962 | 264,324 | +275 |
| Regional total | 3,612,623 | 5,589,274 | 8,953,589 | 11,594,215 | +221 |
| Percentage of U.S. population | 2.7 | 3.7 | 5.0 | 5.7 | |

* San Bernardino and Riverside counties actually stretch across the desert to the Nevada and Arizona lines, but all save an infinitesimal part of their population is concentrated in the territory just over the mountains from the Los Angeles Basin.

To general astonishment, the Southern California population boom began to level off in the mid-1960s, and in the year ending June 30, 1971, Los Angeles County actually *declined* in population by 91,600. As California headed into the 1970s, in fact, the state's great population boom had suddenly halted; whether it was simply the aerospace and general economic recession that began in 1969, or a permanent shift because California finally was "filled up," no one was quite sure. But the figures were there to see: from a net immigration rate that was close to or over 300,000 annually in the early 1960s, the rate was almost zero in 1970 and projected to stay there for at least two or three years. If one is to believe the projections of the state department of finance, however, the net migration rate will climb back to 100,000 a year by 1974–75 and maintain a steady 150,000 a year for the final 20 years of the century. That would mean a year 2000 population of 32.3 million. The population experts say the counties of heaviest growth will be Ventura, Orange, San Diego, and Santa Barbara in the south and Santa Cruz, Solano, and Sonoma in the north. Los Angeles County is projected to grow another 37.4 percent, to a new total of 9.6 million, by 2000.

The recent pause in population growth may discourage California boosters but be just the medicine Southern California, in particular, now needs.

One looks at what the bulldozers have done to accommodate new population in the quarter-century since World War II and shudders at the prospect of more. There are of course thousands of new homes and larger developments, mostly for the privileged classes, that have been creative and earth-respecting. (Some excellent samples are Rancho Santa Fe near San Diego and the Hope Ranch at Santa Barbara.) But this is not the mass market. In most instances the land developers, unguided by any master plan, have snapped up land parcels of opportunity (especially near freeways), staked out rectangular blocks because they are the easiest to plot, and then built tight-pressed little houses, superficially smart but often of flimsy construction, each with just enough space for their inevitable California backyard "patio." "The only saving grace of these houses is their expendability," according to one local architect; indeed, at such locations as Santa Monica and the southern end of the San Fernando Valley, whole housing tracts of the 1940s and 50s are being torn down for higher density and (hopefully) higher quality construction.

What has been done to the natural landscape in many of the Southern California housing tracts is probably beyond repair, however. As Lillard points out, "Everywhere [the rectangular block] has ignored the natural varied lines of hills and beach fronts, ignored watercourses and barrancas, rocky landmarks and noble old trees. Its monotonous, unalluring pattern has encouraged expansive, ugly grading and filling, and a disdain for the ancestral landscape." A thousand transplanted palms cannot correct such damage, as the visitor will quickly see when he speeds through the Southern California "slurbs" *—endless rows of pastel-colored boxlike homes, occasional industrial parks, low-lying shopping centers filled with stereotyped branches of the big chains, and strips of neon-beckoning honky-tonk gas stations, hot dog stands, and pizza parlors. Often the very land where all this stands was occupied until a few years ago by lovely orange and lemon groves, the very symbol of the semitropical good life that lured so many to California in the first place.

## Auto Culture Extraordinary

A few years ago, columnist Art Hoppe of the San Francisco *Chronicle* ventured south of the Tehachapis in search of the typical Los Angeles resident. He found him to be "a well-preserved, middle-aged, middle-class, two-door Chevrolet sedan." Nowhere in the motorized U.S.A., and indeed nowhere in the world, is there a civilization so shaped to automobile culture as Southern California. In Los Angeles County, a motor vehicle is registered every eight seconds. If all the vehicles in the county were lined up bumper-to-bumper on a four-lane freeway they would stretch from downtown L.A. to Fairbanks, Alaska. Of the workers in the Los Angeles area, 80 percent drive their cars to work, averaging an hour and 36 minutes each day in their private

* "Slurb" is a word coined by California Tomorrow, an environmental protection group, to describe "sloppy, sleazy, slovenly, slipshod demi-cities." The slurb is becoming as common to Northern as Southern California.

little transportation systems, which are also handy if not absolutely necessary tools in reaching the far-flung centers of their metropolitan area, the beaches and the mountains.*

Virtually all Southern Californians own automobiles; the ratio of people to vehicles in the region is 1.5. (In 1967, for instance, the region had 11.2 million people, 5.9 million autos, three-quarter-million trucks, a quarter-million house trailers, and a like number of motorcycles.) The automobile is also the prime killer of California, at least for everyone up to age 36 (when cancer and heart disease take over). More than 4,000 Californians die on the highways annually, with several times that number maimed and wounded. The pedestrian is strictly *persona non grata* in Southern California; in fact several areas have dispensed with sidewalks altogether. Pedestrians or bicyclists will be ticketed if they venture onto a freeway.

The motorist, by contrast, can engage in a dazzling variety of activities without even emerging from his car. California pioneered in, and still leads the U.S., in drive-in movies, drive-in restaurants, drive-in banks, and yes, drive-in churches. People have been seen necking or getting dressed at 60-plus miles per hour, not to mention shaving, telephoning, and dictating letters; there is even the story of a two-girl whorehouse on wheels, with the girls taking turns at driving and servicing their customers in the back of their camper. Of course there is no place in the world where so many people live in mobile homes, some of which qualify as the ultraluxurious, semipermanent type, others less formal and ready at a moment's notice to head back onto the freeway. Californians delight in apocryphal stories like that of the Los Angeles family that decided to skip all the discomforts of credit-installment debt by abandoning its house and living in a mobile home forever in movement on the freeways, always a ramp ahead of the bill collectors.

At ground level, the millions of automobiles, by their sheer numbers, provide any visitor's first and overwhelming image of Southern California. But only from the air can one fully grasp the auto's full land-devouring impact. In downtown Los Angeles, for instance, a concrete and asphalt jungle of freeways, feeder streets, gas stations, and interminable parking lots covers 55 percent of the land area; as one moves toward the suburbs the arresting sights are the football-field sized parking lots of black asphalt encompassing the shopping centers. Thus the automobile, heralded as a device to conquer space, has come to fill it. At the start of World War II, there were eight miles of controlled access highway in all of California; since then, in Los Angeles County alone, 325 miles of freeway have been built, at a cost of $1.5 billion. The freeway juggernaut is scheduled to expand within this single county by an incredible 1,127 additional miles, covering 55 more square miles, at a cost of $5 billion, by 1985. Slicing cruelly across mountains, elevated for mile after mile across the basin areas like a labyrinth of Chinese walls, the freeways represent the points of reference in a far-flung region. A given spot, one is told,

* There are several thousand Southern Californians who live in the San Diego area but commute daily to jobs in Los Angeles—a round trip of more than 200 miles.

is just west of the Harbor Freeway where it meets the Santa Monica Freeway, or two exits east of the Long Beach Freeway interchange on the San Bernardino—and suddenly a hard-to-grasp location has meaning, and one knows how to get there. Without these vital arteries, travel time across the vast Los Angeles basin, or between the cities of Southern California, could be many times what they are today. That the freeways also pose almost impenetrable barriers between communities seems to be but the necessary price of "progress." And it is hard not to be awed by such wonders as the main downtown Los Angeles interchange with its rising and falling concrete ribbons on four levels, a scene that has been likened to an exquisite watchworks in action. (The cloverleaf, someone has suggested, should be declared California's official "state flower.")

A few bright spots should be reported. Los Angeles has installed the country's best advance warning street signs (halfway down the block before the intersection), an innovation most American cities would do well to emulate. (The country's worst street signs happen to be found at opposite poles from Los Angeles—in Portland, Maine, and Honolulu, Hawaii.) Under pressure, the freeway builders are showing more concern than they did for many decades over the siting of freeways. And here and there, as businessmen learn how self-defeating the garish, sign-clogged, traffic-clogged, county-long streets of stores and restaurants and gas stations can be, they have turned to well-designed pedestrian malls where the autos are out-of-sight on the periphery. Some fine examples are to be found in Pomona, Riverside, San Diego, Anaheim, and the San Fernando Valley.

The inevitable question raised by Los Angeles' auto and freeway snarl is: why not mass transit? The irony is that the region once had an extensive, successful interurban rail system, the Pacific Electric. The big red cars of the PE ran outward from downtown Los Angeles to reach the mountains and the ocean, doing much to develop such far-flung communities as Pasadena, Hollywood, Long Beach, Santa Ana, and San Bernardino. By 1930, with 1,200 miles of track, it was the longest city rail system in the U.S., and in 1945, it was still carrying 109 million passengers in a year. But then competition from the automobile, and PE's own failure to improve its equipment and lines, led to rapid decline. The last big red car ran in 1963.

Now the only public transit Los Angeles has left is a quite minimal and universally scorned bus system. And Los Angeles is toying with the idea of investing billions in a replacement for the PE system it so blithely neglected. More than $2 million has been invested in transit studies in recent years. In 1968, a proposed 89-mile network of electric-powered, air-conditioned trains, to cost $2.5 billion, was put on the ballot, but only 47 percent of Los Angeles voters approved (with 60 percent needed for approval). High- and low-income voters approved, but the proposition lost in an avalanche of negative votes from tax-conscious middle-income taxpayers. Thus Los Angeles, with the worst public transportation system of any major U.S. metropolis, and most in need of rapid transit because of its huge distances, is left with none. Early in 1972, there was hope that revenue from the sales tax applied to gasoline would give the city and county enough money to get federal matching funds to build an initial rapid transit line from downtown to South Los Angeles (total cost: about $420 million). The success or failure of San Francisco's BART system may influence what Los Angeles finally decides to do about mass transit; so may an experimental federally funded 19-mile air-cushioned passenger train line between the L. A. Airport and the San Fernando Valley, scheduled to be built in the early 1970s on guideways elevated 20 to 60 feet above the San Diego Freeway.

### Air to Breathe . . .

There are still days when the wind flows in briskly from the Pacific, across the Los Angeles basin, and up into the surrounding hills. And if, on such a day, there has also been a rain to cleanse the air, the ring of the hills stands out with startling clarity, the city takes on a scrubbed luminescence, and suddenly the "city of the angels" seems worthy of its name.

Unfortunately, the occurrence is rare. Air-traffic controller John Roger, who works up in the tower at the International Airport, describes a typical summer morning this way: *

When I come to work at 6 A.M.., visibility is often 15 miles or better; you can see the mountains rimming the basin. But when the commuting hour starts, a wave of grey smoke fans out from the freeways. It's like watching a science-fiction movie. The stuff billows thicker and thicker, starts turning yellow, then brown. By 9 A.M., visibility is down to two miles, and then we have to start landing planes on instruments, just to get them down through the smog. A lot of times we can't even see from the tower to the end of the runway, so we have to watch touchdown on our closed-circuit television monitors.

The scientific explanation for the bane of Los Angeles, its smog, is now well known. Set in a poorly ventilated saucer-like basin, the city has the lowest average wind velocity of any major U.S. city. Cool Pacific air, moving in low over the city, becomes trapped in the basin by higher, warm air, creating a classic "air inversion" that can last for days. On the basin floor, some four million automobiles each day burn eight million gallons of gasoline and spew forth 12,000 tons of noxious chemical compounds—hydrocarbons (unburned gasoline) and nitrogen oxides (created by high-temperature combustion). The hydrocarbons and oxides react to the ultraviolet radiation of the sun to produce ozone, a photochemical smog which irritates eyes, disturbs respiratory systems, and casts its hazy pall across the basin—the workings of a veritable chemical factory in the sky.

Up through the 1950s, automobile-loving Angelenos could assume that the smoke pall over their city came from the thousands of factories scattered across the city. But in that decade, a phenomenal effort was made to control

---

* Quoted in "Los Angeles Has a Cough," by Roger Rapoport, *Esquire*, July 1970.

industrial pollution, one without precedent in the U.S. Enforcing its own tight rules, the Los Angeles County Air Pollution Control District took tens of thousands of cases of pollution violation to court, and won some 95 percent. By the early 1960s, virtually every type of industrial polluter—from oil refineries, incinerators, chemical plants, open-hearth furnaces, and auto assembly plants to restaurants, crematories, and housing developers who cleared acreage with open fires—were under tight control. But still the pollution increased each year, and it became all too obvious that the automobile was the chief culprit. (Today the internal combustion engine is blamed for 90 percent of Los Angeles' pollution problem.)

Starting in 1961, the state of California, followed later by the federal government, began to impose standards for motor vehicle emissions and requirements for devices to reduce pollution. The effectiveness of the control devices, however, was questionable from the start. Los Angeles really achieved nothing more than a precarious status quo in its air pollution problem (marginal control effectiveness balanced out by vehicle population increases). Future hope must lie in radical alterations or a replacement of the internal combustion engine. In the meantime, reports emerge of smog attacking San Diego or Santa Barbara, slipping over the mountains to Riverside or even to Palm Springs in the once inviolate desert far to the east. A thousand acres of towering ponderosa pines in the San Bernardino Mountains are fatally afflicted with smog and must be cut down. California agriculture reports losses exceeding $100 million a year from smog: citrus trees producing only half their normal yield; growers of crops like spinach, celery, and beets forced to flee the L. A. area; the production of such cut flowers as orchids, roses, snapdragons all but impossible in polluted territory. Effects of smog on humans are less well known, but throat and chest irritation is well proven, the death rate from emphysema doubles every four years, and Los Angeles physicians, according to their own medical association, counsel at least 10,000 people a year to leave the area for their own health. Several days each year children up to high school age are not allowed to exercise at all, for fear their lungs might be harmed by the high ozone level in the air. And occasionally, doomsday warnings begin to surface. In 1970, a study council of the state legislature, citing the urban sprawl and air pollution of the Los Angeles basin, suggested it may already have more population than it can properly sustain.

Each great public interest fight has its heroes, and Los Angeles, first with the smog problem, was also the first to try to do something about it. For this, major credit goes to Dr. A. J. Haagen-Smit, a CalTech biochemist now in his early seventies who was the first man to prove just how smog is chemically created in the atmosphere; later, as chairman of the California Air Resources Board, he did royal battle with the auto companies over the effectiveness of their antipollution devices—and won. The tough, uncompromising chief air pollution control officers of Los Angeles County—Smith Griswold and later Louis J. Fuller—provided examples of law enforcement against polluters so straightforward and fearless that they were a class to themselves.

But the problem outpaces the solutions, and the U. S. Environmental Protection Agency has set air quality standards so stringent that the EPA's administrator, William P. Ruckelshaus, says they will make "drastic changes" in urban California life styles. Under present laws and policies, Los Angeles would not meet the new standards until the mid-1980s. But now the federal government requires compliance, including a reduction of 50 to 66 percent in carbon monoxide levels, by 1975. To reach the goal, Los Angeles may have to make a quick transition to rapid transit, stagger its work hours, and resort to extensive car pooling. Ruckelshaus even suggested the necessity of closing sections of Los Angeles and similarly affected cities to all motor vehicle traffic.

The situation is not to be taken lightly. Without rapid, effective countermeasures, according to Kenneth Watt, a respected University of California ecologist, smog in the Los Angeles basin may be bad enough to cause mass deaths by the winter of 1975–76.

## . . . and Water to Drink

With an annual average rainfall of about 15 inches—and virtually all of that in the winter months—Southern California is technically a desert and has no natural way to support the water needs of its millions. The region has 60 percent of California's people but only 2 percent of its water; by contrast, almost 40 percent of the state's water originates in the high mountains of northwestern California, where a meager 2 percent of the state's people live. Only through massive amounts of water importation has Southern California been able to grow into the formidable megalopolis it is today.

In its early years, Los Angeles depended for water on the unpredictable Los Angeles River (a torrent in winter, a trickle in summer, and still a major flood problem), plus hundreds of artesian wells. Capitalizing on a drought in 1904, a young Irish immigrant named William Mulholland, who had worked his way up to the position of chief engineer of the L. A. Water Department, set out to find new water sources. Traveling by buckboard through the desert and mountains, he finally discovered what he was looking for some 240 miles northeast of the city, in the fertile Owens Valley, irrigated by runoff from the Sierra Nevada. Secretly, Los Angeles interests bought up Owens Valley land to which control of its water was attached, and a great aqueduct to Los Angeles was begun—but not until some of the Owens Valley farmers, furious over the loss of water that turned their own fields into parched wastelands, had tried to dynamite the dams.

Owens Valley water is still an important source for Southern California, but the region's burgeoning population has made necessary the creation of vast new supplements. In the 1930s, as the first shortages loomed into view, the region's aggressive Metropolitan Water District proved itself willing and eager to undertake the complex negotiations with other western states and federal departments to get a share of Colorado River water. The point of origin would be the new Parker Dam, some 150 miles below the new Hoover Dam along the Arizona border. Those great dams and the amazing Colorado River Aqueduct (of which we have spoken before) completed, Colorado River water began to flow into the Los Angeles basin in 1941.

Soon it appeared that even this would not be enough, especially as Californians read and began to believe the demographers' extravagant projections of tens of millions of additional people by the end of the century, and projections of a water shortage by the early 1970s. For close to a century, some had dreamed of a massive water diversion program from watery Northern California to its arid south. Now the plan began to take shape. Along the Sierra-fed Feather River above Sacramento, it would be possible to build one of the continent's largest dams—the Oroville, a mile wide and 730 feet high, impounding more than a trillion gallons of water for hydroelectric production, flood control, and especially storage of the water for thirsty Southern California and agricultural irrigation along the way. Numerous other dams and storage reservoirs would also be included. To transfer the huge water load (4¼ million acre-feet), a new California Aqueduct was planned to run 444 miles down the heart of the Central Valley and over the Tehachapis into the south. Under Governor Brown's leadership, most disputes over the California Water Plan (except for hard-core Northern California resistance to theft of its water) were ironed out. The issue was sent to the voters of the state, who in 1960 obligingly authorized $1.75 billion in bonds to get the construction underway. The whole episode was typical of California: the largest bond issue ever voted (up to then) by the voters of any state; a guarantee of delivery of a phenomenal 1.8 billion gallons a day, over hundreds of miles, to Southern California's Metropolitan Water District; a scope to the project which simply dwarfed all earlier water-transfer agreements in American history. "By the time our astronauts reach the moon," the state water resources director grandly proclaimed, "the California Aqueduct of the State Water Project will take its place with the Great Wall of China and become one of only two man-made things on earth the moon visitors are expected to be able to see with the naked eye." (California reporter Lou Cannon appropriately calls this the "monument complex.") Yet even this stupendous project, Californians were told, would only provide enough water to last until the year 2020; by then it would be necessary to develop economical ways of desalinating sea water or to import water from afar (perhaps the Columbia River basin).

Inauguration of the California Water Plan seemed to be all the more farsighted when the U.S. Supreme Court in 1963 ruled against California in the long litigation with Arizona over the allotment of Colorado River Water. The decision, in effect, meant less Colorado River water for Los Angeles.

But as the 1960s wore on, the crucial question became not whether Southern California might run dry, but whether the State Water Plan was not an ill-advised extravagance to provide more water than the Los Angeles area really needed. Several factors contributed to the change in attitude. One was the dropoff in California's phenomenal population growth, thus lessening water demand. The second was the rapidly developing technology of waste-water recycling and reclamation, which some experts suggested would provide a source great enough to satisfy Southern California water needs for another half-century with use of ground water. It was pointed out that Southern California coastal areas were dumping a billion gallons of waste water into the Pacific each day, water of better chemical quality than that being imported across the desert from the Colorado River. Finally, angry voices were raised about the ecological damage that full implementation of the State Water Plan might inflict. The wild rivers of California's North Coast (the Eel, Klamath, and Trinity) would be dammed up, diverted, and in effect ruined. It was charged that diversion to the south of water from the Sacramento–San Joaquin delta, just east of San Francisco, would permit encroachment of seawater and incalculable damage to aquatic life in the delta.

In 1971, just as the State Water Plan was delivering its first water south of the Tehachapis, new controversy broke out as a result of the Nader report charges that the project was "the largest special interest boondoggle in history." It was alleged that state water officials had misrepresented the actual cost of the project, using a $2.8 billion figure when the actual cost (including finance costs on bonds) will be close to $10 billion. And while Southern California property owners will pay from 48 to 65 percent of the costs through taxation, the report said, the heaviest users of the water—corporate farms and industries—would receive water far below its actual cost. To these charges, the general manager of the Metropolitan Water District of Southern California, Henry J. Mills, replied that "the Nader report can only be termed a highly irresponsible and slapdash compilation of inaccuracies, untruths, malicious rumors, unsupported charges, distortions, and headline-hunting generalizations."

Even when one discounted the rhetoric on both sides, it was clear that the Metropolitan Water District, largely through property taxes, would be obliged to spend $6 billion by the year 2050 in paying its obligated share of aqueduct construction costs and necessary additions to its own system to use the water. Southern Californians, once thought to have scored a great victory over Northern California in approval of the plan, would be bearing a heavy tax burden to finance the growth they themselves demanded—the same growth that pollutes their air, crowds their beaches, clogs their freeways, and defiles their natural landscape. And the argument was strong, if not conclusive, that they might have gotten along well enough without any California Water Plan at all.

## Suddenly, a Downtown Los Angeles

Downtown Los Angeles, 1,000 acres of real estate wedged in between four freeways, is perhaps the least "swinging" center city of any large American metropolis. Except for the start and end of the commuting day and the lunch hour, its streets tend to be deserted; at nighttime, when a city with soul would pulse with life, downtown L.A. is positively moribund. Until a few years ago, all that motorists whizzing by on the elevated freeways could see were a few civic center buildings, including the City Hall (then L.A.'s only claim to a skyline), rows of down-at-the-heels stores, a handful of oil company offices and banks, newspaper offices, cheap bars, and dowdy hotels. Fashionable Los Angeles had long since passed downtown by in a westward rush along the elegant Wilshire Corridor, and the old core was populated principally by low-income Mexican-Americans, blacks, and old people. The ultimate sprawl city seemed to have neither interest in nor need for a downtown.

But starting in the early 1960s, and gathering increased momentum in recent years, a great building boom has hit downtown L.A. An essential prerequisite was the 1959 repeal of a 34-year-old limitation of 13 stories on building heights, which had ostensibly been enforced to protect against earthquake damage. (Many believed its true reason was the influence of fringe landowners who wanted to keep down density to insure horizontal rather than vertical growth of the city.) No sooner had the height limitation been lifted than the United California Bank put up a new 18-story building downtown. Since then, the momentum has never stopped. The long-discussed 136-acre Bunker Hill Redevelopment Project moved forward between the old business district and the Music Center site, with skyscraper apartment and office buildings; despite warnings of skeptics that suburban-minded Angelenos would never forsake their ranch houses to live in urban rabbit warrens, former residents of distant suburban communities began to move in to be close to work. One huge new steel-and-glass tower after another rose in the city, and early in 1970, the United California Bank announced it would build a 62-story downtown office tower, the tallest building west of Chicago. By that time, more than $1 billion of construction was underway in downtown L.A. It was enough to assure that this core area would be not only western GHQ for many of America's largest corporations, but the financial, legal, governmental, and cultural center of the far-flung Los Angeles metropolitan region. At last, Los Angeles would have a real downtown—and, by 1971, its first office-space glut.

Unfortunately, there has been precious little planning for the new downtown, despite a belated start under joint business-city funding. No one yet knows how to funnel the hundreds of thousands of additional automobiles off the freeways and into L.A. each day without traffic jams of historic proportions. And the skeptics wonder if the final result will include the kind of things that make cities a delight for people—coffee shops and good restaurants and bookstores and theaters, a relief from sterile suburbia. What many fear is that downtown L.A., when completed, may be gray, a chrome-and-steel wonder of modern construction but a city without a soul.

There are some elements that could be built on to humanize a new downtown. Olvera Street, for instance, is a colorful block-long slice of Old

Mexico in downtown, selling foods and giftwares of the native country. Logically this could be expanded to provide not only a tourist attraction, but a cultural and handwork center for the thousands of Mexicans in the city.

The downtown section includes Little Tokyo, where many Japanese found themselves restricted in ghetto-like fashion before World War II. It remains the daytime center of life for many of Los Angeles County's 104,078 Japanese, but less of the housing center it once was. Recovering from the humiliation of the forced evacuations from the West Coast to inland relocation camps after Pearl Harbor, the Japanese, by dint of hard labor and through the respect they won through their wartime loyalty, have been able to move into almost any L.A. area neighborhood they choose, and to branch out professionally. A significant number, for instance, hold highly skilled positions with aerospace firms; many of the less highly educated are expert freelance landscape gardeners, a lucrative profession in garden-conscious Southern California. With succeeding generations, the Japanese become more culturally attuned to American life, less bound to ancestral ways, less obedient to familial authority, and less willing to accept discrimination.

Among other things, Los Angeles has a substantial Indian population, growing by leaps and bounds to about 25,000 in 1970. The lot of the urban Indian, often living in poverty, drifting from place to place, frequently afflicted by alcoholism, is not a happy one. But it is in the cities, rather than on the reservations, that one today finds the cutting edge of new Indian nationalism.

## *All Around L.A.*

Once one has accounted for the limited area of "downtown," the geographic ordering of Los Angeles becomes a nightmarish puzzle. The city itself, 469 square miles of territory in a county of 4,068 square miles, is laid out in a crazy-quilt pattern that starts high in the San Fernando Valley, jumps over the Santa Monica Mountains, goes through downtown, and then plunges down an 18-mile-long corridor, just a half-mile wide, so that the city limits can reach the harbor at San Pedro without interruption (much like the corridor that linked ancient Athens and Piraeus.) Enclaves are carved into every edge of the city, and in fact independent cities like San Fernando (254,413) and Beverly Hills City (33,416) are completely surrounded by it.

Los Angeles County, on the other hand, is shaped normally enough, with the ocean on its western and southwestern flanks (offering miles of still magnificent beaches), the desert over the hills to the east (in the direction of San Bernardino and Riverside), an unobstructed opening to Orange County on the southern flank, and the massive San Gabriel Mountains rising to the north. Some 700 square miles are urbanized and built up, but forests and federal lands comprise more than 1,000 acres, and in the late 1960s there were still more than 600 acres devoted to agriculture.

Perhaps Los Angeles' ultimate urban sprawl can be visualized by imagining downtown L.A. as the center of a great clock and the great hunks of land as hour segments, with 12 o'clock due north, 6 o'clock south, etc. We can start clockwise at 9 o'clock:

9 TO 10 O'CLOCK. The most dominant feature as we start out from downtown is Wilshire Boulevard, frightfully stretched out (15 miles in all) but still the most elegant street in the California Southland and one of the U.S.A.'s most sumptuous. Sleek high-rise apartment and office buildings line mile after mile of Wilshire where beanfields still abounded in the 1920s; the Wilshire Corridor also has Los Angeles' finest stores, the excellent County Museum of Art, and such adornments as Beverly Hills and the new Century City (six million square feet of floor space in elegant office buildings, apartments and hotels) along its way or nearby. Until central L.A. began to revive, it appeared that Wilshire would be *the* metropolitan center—fittingly a kind of strip-development downtown dependent on the beloved auto. Still, its prosperous future seems assured. Sadly, many of Wilshire's miles are blighted by billboards; an exception to this is Beverly Hills, which had the sense to outlaw them. And Beverly Hills remains one of America's highest prestige communities, physically spotless, wealthy, disdainful of cooperating with the rest of the Los Angeles community, and heavily Jewish.

Further out on Wilshire one can get a view of one of the world's great Mormon Temples—a reminder that the Latter-day Saints have one of their most powerful outposts in Southern California. And at well-to-do Westwood Village is the 50-year-old campus of the University of California at Los Angeles, fast rivaling Berkeley to the north (of which it was once just the "Southern campus") in prestige and weight in California affairs. The UCLA commitment to solving race and class problems has been strong, and in the 1960s it was becoming increasingly involved in Los Angeles affairs with institutes or study programs in every area from local smog and transit problems to urban planning and architecture. UCLA has risen in the postwar years from middling ranks to be one of the 10 to 20 best universities of the U.S.A. It has excellent graduate schools in such fields as medicine, law, education, and architecture, and reportedly the best geophysics faculty in the country and especially outstanding African and Near Eastern studies centers. With its colossal library and university extension program—the largest in the world—it has become the intellectual focal point of Southern California.

The whole outer flank of our 9-to-10-o'clock belt is dominated by the Santa Monica Mountains, 92 square miles of extremely rugged territory (as big as Pittsburgh and San Francisco put together), intruded into the heart of a heavily urbanized area. Where they meet the sea, one finds famous Malibu Beach. Geologically, the mountains are less than hospitable. One can't go more than a short distance without reaching an earthquake fault; the earth is unstable, grades are steep, earthquake danger is ever present, and all too frequently the chaparral catches fire with disastrous consequences. Yet some Angelenos insist on their mountain homes, feeling they can lead a distinctive way of life in their own little canyons or on the remote hilltops. From the

Mulholland Drive, which snakes its way through the Santa Monicas, the fortunate traveler on a clear night can catch one of those sparkling views of the Los Angeles Basin, when suddenly the urban conglomerate seems to hold together.

10 to 11 O'CLOCK. close-in, there's Hollywood; out further, the San Fernando Valley; in between, more of the Santa Monica Mountains. Sunset Boulevard, hugging the southern exposure of the mountains, meanders out through this time segment and then veers south and west to reach the sea. The close-in part called the Sunset Strip only a few years ago glittered with restaurants and nightclubs of the stars; then it became the title of a television show; presently it is a jumble of office buildings, topless-bottomless clubs and amateur strip joints, psychedelic shops and hippie ghettos. Physical Hollywood (as opposed to the broader celluloid center) has been declining as a shopping center for some time, has mixed housing and commercial neighborhoods, and harbors some 15,000 sexual deviates, according to one local official with whom I spoke. Unlike Beverly Hills, Hollywood itself is not a separate city, but just a neighborhood of the city of Los Angeles.

Out beyond the Santa Monicas is the San Fernando Valley, which was mostly farmland in the 1930s, accommodated only 112,000 people in 1940, and today has a population exceeding a million—a vast slurb which covers 235 square miles (the size of the city of Chicago). Its center is deadly flat; around it are mountains which seal it off from the ocean and the rest of Los Angeles like an immense football stadium. The worst damage of the 1971 earthquake was felt here; more than 40 people died when a Veterans Administration hospital collapsed, and tens of thousands of homes would have been obliterated if the Van Norman Dam, holding back a 100-foot-high wall of water, had not barely held together. The valley is no longer so much a bedroom for L.A. as its own commercial and industrial base, providing jobs for 85 percent of its workers within its own confines. Many San Fernando Valleyans never see downtown Los Angeles.

11 TO 12 O'CLOCK. Close-in, there is the Los Angeles Dodgers' Stadium; then, with the Golden State Freeway the connector, the cities of Glendale (population 132,752, site of gaudy Forest Lawn Memorial Park) and Burbank (88,871), both filled with middle-to-upper-middle-income families.

12 TO 1 O'CLOCK. This segment starts with a jumble of freeways, then encompasses the eastern portion of Glendale and moves on out into the mountains until 35 miles from downtown (as the crow flies), one comes on the dusty town of Palmdale (pop. 8,511) in the Antelope Valley. Here, in flat, high-desert country studded with spiky Joshua trees, one of the world's great airports will be built during the 1970s. According to William Pereira, the L.A. architect-planner for the project, Palmdale will be one of the world's major metropolitan centers, "grand in dimension as well as population," with 2.5 million or more people living in a metropolis centered on the idea of fast and

efficient air and ground travel. The environmentalists, however, are now fighting the Palmdale plan.

1 TO 2 O'CLOCK. Here the dominant feature is the smog-plagued city of Pasadena (1970 population 113,327—down 2.6 percent from 1960), long a household word in the U.S.A. for its dazzling New Year's Day Tournament of Roses, the outgrowth of a village flower fete and sports tourney of 1890. Pasadena embellishments also include the CalTech campus and close to 200 plants in the fields of scientific, pharmaceutical, and cosmetic products; Pasadena's chief problems revolve about race, specifically the influx of blacks, Mexican-Americans, and other minorities, who now represent about a quarter of the city population—and more than 45 percent of the public school enrollment. Amid intense controversy, a radical school busing plan went into effect in 1970. The plan involved busing of some 12,000 children an average of 3.5 miles a day, at an annual cost of about $1 million. About a fifth of the white children left the school system, but the pressures of middle-class parents for good facilities resulted in a marked upgrading of the physical plants and cafeteria and library services in schools in black neighborhoods. Interracial clashes, fairly frequent the first year, dropped significantly in the second year of busing. Especially in the lower grades, teachers noted an amazing degree of "color blindness" among children of the various races.

CalTech, L.A. *Times* writer Robert B. Young notes, "has shown a surefooted instinct for traveling the most promising paths of 20th century science." Whole new technologies and industries have emerged from it, along with 13 Nobel Prize winners among its graduates and faculty. CalTech professors swing a real weight in the country through their myriad consulting arrangements and membership on Presidential, other federal and state committees, and the boards of scientific organizations. During the "fat years" of the '60s, Young observes, CalTech avoided "growth for growth's sake," thus husbanding its resources so that it could easily weather the downturn in science funding that occurred nationally around 1970. Expenditures for teaching and research grew about 10 percent annually during the 1960s, but even today enrollment is only 1,400 and the institute has one of the nation's most favorable faculty-to-student ratios.

Once a place where "hard," natural science ruled absolutely supreme, CalTeach has begun to broaden its view to social applications of science. Among the recent innovations have been an environmental quality laboratory which is trying to identify options in pollution control from such diverse vantage points as chemistry, economics, and law, and a disaster research center focusing its investigations on seismology, floods, landslides, tidal waves, and firestorms (an extremely appropriate California undertaking).

Out beyond Pasadena is the famed Mt. Wilson Observatory and the huge Devil and Bear Canyon Primitive Areas, again underscoring L.A. County's fantastic diversity.

2 TO 3 O'CLOCK. Now our orientation moves to the east of downtown

L.A., and for the next 180 degrees, we must deal mostly with characterless suburbia. First in this segment is the San Gabriel Valley. One town there polled its citizens and discovered, to its horror, that fully one-third of the population moved each year. (One writer's comment: "That isn't a town—it's a gypsy encampment.")

If one sticks it out far enough on the San Bernardino Freeway, the way leads up over the hills, out of the L.A. Basin, and into the desert and the city of San Bernardino (pop. 104,251). Impelled by heavy military and aerospace employment, healthy agriculture (it is host city to the National Orange Show), and aggressive local leadership, San Bernardino has advanced by leaps and bounds since 1940, when it had less than half as many people. Recently it built a $100 million Central City Project, including an enclosed, air-conditioned shopping mall and a cultural center.

3 TO 5 O'CLOCK. Now we come to East Los Angeles and the Mexican-Americans—so many of them, in fact, that only Mexico City has more. But first a quick review of what lies beyond them, starting with Whittier (pop. 72,863), a spot of dullsville suburbia where Richard M. Nixon spent his boyhood. After Whittier come the Puente Hills, a barrier of no mean proportions, and beyond them, the city of Pomona (pop. 87,384), site of the Los Angeles County Fair (largest in the U.S.A.) and a distinguished modern shopping mall. And several miles further in the desert comes the city of Riverside (population 140,089), a citrus center of long standing, the site of an agriculturally inclined University of California campus, and a town expanding with aggressive industrial development programs.

The sprawling Mexican barrio (or ghetto) of East Los Angeles, some 40 percent of its territory in the city of L.A. and the remainder in unincorporated area of the adjoining county, is the biggest single concentration of L.A. County's 1.1 million Mexican-Americans. The classic conditions to fill a people with clotted rage are to be seen in East L.A.—insensitive schools, abhorrent housing, inadequate health care, few decent job opportunities, constant police harassment. Fearful of rising militancy in the barrio (which they attributed to "known dissidents"), the police by 1970 appeared to have adopted a policy of "preemptive strike"—to smash independence before it could take hold. Predictably, the Brown Power movement of young militants, led by the Brown Berets (a sort of Mexican-American equivalent of the Black Panthers), began to sway increasing numbers of the normally quiescent Latins.

Writing in the spring of 1970, Los Angeles *Times* columnist Rubén Salazar, a native Mexican and one of the foremost interpreters of his people, warned that the truculent mood in the barrio was "not being helped by our leaders who are trying to discredit militants in the barrios as subversive or criminal." Just a few months later, 20,000 young militants engaged in a Chicano Moratorium to protest the disproportionate loss of Mexican-American lives in Vietnam. Rioting broke out, and newsman Salazar, covering the scene, was suddenly struck dead by a tear gas projectile designed to pierce barricades but fired by the police into a bar. It would not be the last violent conflict between Chicanos and the police, a problem which drew in U.S. Senator Cranston and other respected figures in an effort to sooth tensions and get the police to adopt a less truculent attitude.

By developing stronger leadership and more political finesse, the Mexican-Americans might get many more concessions from local and state governments in California. Numbering about 3.1 million statewide, they could be the balance of power in a close election. Yet through the 1960s, the Mexicans' ostensible political friends, the Democrats, saw to it that the areas of Chicano population concentration were gerrymandered to bolster Anglo Democrats in nearby districts, not to elect Mexicans. Thus there was no Mexican-American state senator, city councilman, or county supervisor, and only one member of the state assembly and one Congressman (Edward R. Roybal, a Democrat). Shortly before his death in 1970, Rubén Salazar wrote an article entitled "Chicanos' Long Love Affair with the Democratic Party Ends," noting that "the trend in the barrios right now is Chicanos first, party second. And the emphasis is on organization more than election." That fall, Ricardo Romo ran for governor on the Peace and Freedom Party ticket and received the endorsement of several prominent Mexican-American organizations; his vote was 65,954, only 1 percent of the total but a potentially decisive figure in a close election. Tunney, running for the Senate, was shouted down by angry Chicano demonstrators when he tried to speak in East Los Angeles; one of the disrupters said the reason was that Tunney had always sided with the "power structure—the farmers" in his Riverside and Imperial County congressional district. A new party, La Raza Unida, began to form and late in 1971 was responsible for defeat of the Democratic contender in a special East Los Angeles assembly election when it diverted about 8 percent of the vote to its Chicano activist candidate.

5 TO 7 O'CLOCK. This "two-hour" segment, defining a broad arc of land running south from downtown, encompasses L.A.'s black ghettos, big bland suburban cities, and then, at the ocean's edge, the thriving submetropolis of Long Beach and posh Palos Verdes Estates.

Close to 700,000 Negroes now live in Los Angeles, almost ten times the figure at the eve of World War II. What L.A.'s Negroes call "Watts" is actually a fairly small area of some 65,000 people; whites sometimes substitute the term "curfew area" (in honor of 1965) and mean a sprawling south L.A. area, larger than all of Manhattan, including both Watts and other heavily black communities like Huntington Park and now areas further and further west, in the process of white-to-black transition. Just a few miles south is the city of Compton (78,611), heavily middle class and for several years known as the "Beverly Hills of the Black Belt." Compton was 4 percent black in 1950, 40 percent black in 1960, 72 percent in 1972. In recent years, some of its more affluent blacks have begun to move on to more choice communities, and Compton is suffering from a high crime rate and deterioration of its downtown. Blacks took control of the city government in 1969, electing a highly respected member of their race, Douglas F. Dollarhide, as mayor.

Watts' spread-out, palm-lined streets are in such vivid contrast to the stark tenements of South Side Chicago, Harlem, and Bedford-Stuyvesant that no one would ever have imagined this area as the one where the spark of black riots, later to spread to Newark, Detroit, and across scores of American cities, would be ignited. But what looked good in comparison to other ghettos was hardly adequate in comparison to the "good life" of Southern California —and especially the opulent, flashy world of Hollywood and the Miracle Mile reported regularly to Watts by television. Employment, the commission appointed by Governor Brown would later report, was a key factor; only 14 percent of the people in Watts had automobiles; the closest employment agency was an hour and a half away on three separate bus lines. Added to this were strained relations between the black community and the police, high welfare dependency, and a crazyquilt net of county and local welfare agencies, substandard schools where 40 percent of the girls dropped out because of pregnancy, and the highest disease rates in Los Angeles County. The area had no hospital—the nearest public hospital was two hours away by bus.

For the four days of the 1965 riot, the Los Angeles ghetto was convulsed by a sickening orgy of destruction and death, interspersed with carnival-like looting. The toll: 34 killed (mostly Negroes), 1,034 injured, close to $40 million in damage, some 4,000 arrested in a one-square-mile burned-over area. On the worst hit street, 103rd, so many of the businesses burned out that it would be called Charcoal Alley thereafter. Of the blacks arrested, many charged they had been treated with brutality at the hands of the Los Angeles Police. As the riots tapered off, the late William H. Parker, then L.A. police chief, went on television to announce, with typical tact: "Now we're on top and they're on the bottom." One observer's comment: "Many Negroes felt this represented no change."

What has happened to Watts since the '65 riots? In some respects, it has deteriorated. Many shops and restaurants were frightened away, leaving a surfeit of pawnshops and bail-bond offices. Joblessness, by 1970, had soared 61 percent over the 1965 rate, and little was done to correct the woeful transportation situation. Housing remains poor, most of the schools abysmal, and welfare is a way of life. Racial antagonism still simmers below the surface.

Still, there is a residue of progress that has come to Watts to stay. An especially bright development is the Watts Labor Community Action Committee (WLCAC), a true effort at a locally run and controlled community union. WLCAC's chief sponsor is the United Auto Workers, that union again demonstrating its advanced social creativity.* In running WLCAC, major help comes from other unions, foundations, and federal grants and loans. WLCAC has a dazzling variety of activities—comparable probably only

* With 60,000 to 70,000 workers in California auto assembly plants and aircraft factories, the UAW is a significant liberal voice in the state's labor and politics. The regional UAW chief was Paul Schrade, a bearded, highly articulate man who was once a personal aide to Walter Reuther. He is an advocate of aligning the labor movement with student groups, and under his leadership the UAW went all-out to help Robert Kennedy in the 1968 Presidential primary. Schrade was with Kennedy at the Ambassador Hotel and was grievously wounded by Sirhan Sirhan's bullets, though he did recover. Later, he incurred criticism from UAW dissidents who said he should devote more time to union business and less to politics. In 1972, he was ousted in an internal UAW power move.

to Operation Breadbasket in Chicago and OIC in Philadelphia. It has acquired a chain of supermarkets operating within Watts, operated a string of highly profitable local gas stations, offered vocational training in several fields (especially the skills required at a new community hospital) and built a score of vest-pocket parks, constructed hundreds of units of low-cost housing, and scheduled 40 high-rise apartment buildings and a modern shopping and convention center for the near future. The budget rose to $30 million in 1972, with 1,000 minority persons on the payroll. The man chiefly responsible for WLCAC's success is a husky, barrel-chested ex-Mississippi farm boy, Ted Watkins, who took the program over in 1966 and soon distinguished himself as a master orchestrator and bargainer. Watkins' salary is paid by the UAW, for which he had previously been an international representative. UAW leaders believe Watkins' outside salary gives him an independence that other community leaders involved in government and foundation-supported programs simply lack. The UAW and AFL-CIO are also able to provide political back-stopping for Watkins in the L.A. City Council or other public bodies. Following the same pattern, the UAW also pays the salary of Ed Torres, head of the East Los Angeles Community Union, a younger organization which also sponsors economic enterprises, although its thrust is mainly cultural and political.

Private enterprise deserves high marks for a serious effort in Watts. The first big firm to move into the area after the riots was Aerojet-General, which set up a subsidiary, the Watts Manufacturing Company, with a staff of all black executives in control. Watts Manufacturing went to work making tents for the military and survived principally on federal contracts for crates, post office equipment, and electronic assembly items.

The plant of Watts Manufacturing is in a series of low-slung structures strung out along El Segundo Boulevard; as one moves through the shops, the *esprit de corps* of the workers—mostly black, with a scattering of Mexican-Americans and whites—is clear to see. From the outset, Aerojet-General intended to turn over Watts Manufacturing to the subsidiary's employees when the operation became profitable. The subsidiary moved into the black in 1969, and A-G sold the company to Chase Manhattan Capital Corporation, a minority-enterprise subsidiary of the New York bank, which in turn placed 80 percent of the company's stock in a trust fund for purchase by employees (then numbering about 200) over seven years. But Watts Manufacturing continued to have its problems, including the necessity for repeated capital investments to gear up for a succession of one-shot government and private industry equipment orders. Many costs were underestimated, and in 1970 the company had an operating loss of $500,000. The federal government, however, was determined that this showpiece of black capitalism survive. Thus the Economic Development Administration not only provided a guarantee for a major loan but also helped to recruit a new chief operating officer: Mark E. Rivers, a black West Point Graduate, former Air Force lieutenant colonel with a master's degree in engineering, and former executive for TRW. He took over from Watts Manufacturing's first president, Leon Woods, 28, who was admired for his salesmanship and leadership but lacked the depth of managerial skill required. Rivers, the new chief, said: "There's a remarkable work spirit around this place. . . . Now it's time to put that work spirit into the parameters of a profit-making company."

Nartrans, a subsidiary of North American Rockwell set up in central L.A. to draw workers both from Watts and heavily Mexican-American East Los Angeles, scored a success in machining, wood and plastic products, drafting, and keypunch operations. A very tangible sign of new hope in Watts is the 470-bed Martin Luther King Jr. Hospital, the largest of several medical facilities that have come into a section of the city that had virtually none at the time of the riots.

The bulk of southern Los Angeles County, divided by the rather ludicrous commercial strip of L.A. city territory that goes south to the harbor, is filled with instant cities of the 1940s and '50s, many now turning into practically instant slums or close to it—Gardena (1970 population 41,021), Torrance (134,584), Carson (71,150), and Lakewood (82,973). The scene is overwhelmingly one of little frame houses, set on monotonous straight-line streets, mile after mile after mile. In the files of the L.A. *Times* I discovered some yellowing World War II-vintage clips announcing the birth of these cities to house workers at the nearby aircraft and shipbuilding plants. For Lakewood, for instance, there is a quote of the 1942 orders of a government defense housing official: "Build homes, build for permanency, and build faster than ever before!" To this day, these cities lack discernible character; they contract many of their municipal services to the county, the people work elsewhere, and they show little interest in their neighbors or local government.

Moving still further south in the 5-to-6-o'clock segment, we finally reach Long Beach and the oceanside. With 358,633 people in the 1970 Census, Long Beach is California's sixth largest city. The booming port, and especially the great oozy oil field underlying its city, port, and harbor, make Long Beach one of the U.S.A.'s richest cities. With the tidelands oil royalties, which it shares with the state, Long Beach has spent millions on recreational development in the harbor area and begun to bill itself as a major convention center —a little Miami Beach.

Oil also brings its problems, which Long Beach has been trying to meet. Oil rigs still mar the landscape and contribute to depressing stretches of waterfront, but in the harbor they have been camouflaged to look like high-rise buildings, surrounded by waterfalls and trees. As for Long Beach's people, they are a fair prototype of Middle America. The Iowa picnic each year draws tens of thousands from the heartland. Blacks are less than 10 percent of the population. The vote each election is overwhelmingly Republican. For employment, Long Beachers look first to Douglas Aircraft, then to the harbor facilities. California State College, Long Beach, has a phenomenal enrollment of 28,000 students, the largest of any state college in the United States. Recently my friend Stephen Horn, a political scientist and former assistant to Senator Kuchel, took over as president there, hoping to create some communication and understanding among administration, faculty, and the gigantic student body.

Moving westward from Long Beach, one passes the Los Angeles Harbor area and settlements like Wilmington and Harbor City—an ugly hodgepodge of workers' houses, stores, warehouses, oil wells, and storage tanks. Then there is the fishing village of San Pedro, and suddenly one has left the flatlands and come again to ragged mountain and canyon country on the Palos Verdes Peninsula, a quiet and beautiful spot inhabited by the rich and the very rich.

7 TO 8 O'CLOCK. Here we pass through the western extremities of the black ghetto, encounter another one of those bland, sprawling suburban cities —Inglewood (population 89,985)—the Los Angeles International Airport, and finally the ocean and a string of middle-class beach communities.

The L. A. International Airport has developed into a very unwelcome neighbor on its site between Inglewood and the sea. The jet roar, vibrations, air pollution, and congestion of local roads by airline passengers and workers have surrounding communities up in arms—so far that they and their citizens have sued the city of Los Angeles for more than $1.5 billion in damages. Local protests are only one reason, however, that the Los Angeles airport planners are starting the huge new facility at Palmdale.

8 TO 9 O'CLOCK. In this final segment, we move westerly through nondescript commercial and residential sections of the city and the University of Southern California campus, through Culver City (31,035), of M-G-M fame, and finally to the coastal region, rich in aerospace firms, the art community of Venice, and proud, successful Santa Monica (88,289).

Venice, set by magnificent Pacific beaches, was the personal creation some 65 years ago of Abbot Kinney, a wealthy Easterner who had made a fortune from Sweet Caporal cigarettes. From 160 acres of sand dunes and salt marsh, Kinney fashioned a seashore town with 100 miles of canals, just like old Venice. But then oil developments ruined the area and most of the canals were filled in, leaving an unhappy residue of moldy bridges and weeds; Venice, in effect, became a slum. In recent years a major city effort (Venice is within L.A. city borders) has begun to reclaim the canals and bring Venice back to its feet. The ethnic combinations are fascinating —older Jewish people, hippies, artists, blacks, browns, and old-time Bible Belters (many of them Okies). The section toward the beach is developing rapidly into a Greenwich Village, with the familiar succession from poor young artists to decorators and antique dealers to high rents and not so poor artists and assorted hangers-on of the art world. A decade from now, some Angelenos believe, Venice will be an important cultural part of their city. It already has a juice and vitality so missing in most of bland L.A.

Santa Monica, on the other hand, is a town that has never really seen bad times. Like Long Beach, it has many older houses dating back more

than half a century; many were built by the same kind of sturdy Midwesterners. Both cities also share a conservatism and solid middle-class image.
Santa Monica in the 19th century tried to get the Los Angeles Harbor,
but fortunately for it, it failed. The offshore breezes provide cool, clear
weather, even when central L.A. is overlaid with smog. Several streets have
been closed off to create a pleasant shopping mall. Again, this is aerospace
territory—and home of the Rand Corporation.

And now we are back to 9 o'clock and the Santa Monica-Wilshire axis,
from which we started; our long day's swing around the spokes of Los Angeles is finished.

## *The Multicultures of Los Angeles*

"With all our tough problems," Los Angeles *Times* publisher Otis
Chandler said in an interview, "it is easy to forget that Southern California
still offers the good life for most people, and they are enjoying it in their immediate environs." The problems of smog, transportation, education, or taxes,
he said, will all have to get a lot worse before people are forced to look for
solutions. In the meantime, life offers the warm climate, informal style,
nearby beaches and mountains, the backyard swimming pool, the tennis
court, the camper or boat for the weekend—the world glorified in *Sunset*
magazine (a journal that so scorns the East that it charges two dollars extra
a year for any subscription addressed to the other side of the Mississippi).
Southern California life somehow bypasses most community groups and
confines itself largely to the millions of little islands that make up individuals or small family groups; as Christopher Rand has pointed out, this
is the "nuclear" family of father and/or mother (perhaps divorced) and
small children, specifically *not* the European or Oriental "extended" family
that mixes three or more generations. For every 12 marriages in Los Angeles,
there are 10 divorces. The cohesion that might be called true community
is a still-to-be-delivered characteristic.

The greatest asset of this way of life, as many have testified, is the sense
of freedom it gives the individual. A typical newcomer, the New York *Times*'s
Steven V. Roberts, has described that asset as "the lack of community structure, or hoary institutions looming over you psychologically as well as physically, of rules and traditions and expectations." No more fluid society has
ever existed, nor one in which impermanence, rootlessness, lack of belonging
seems so strong. Many fight loneliness through the "singles only" apartment
complexes (described as "a sort of perpetual freshman mixer"), or through
senior citizens' retirement villages with their multiple activities to keep the
aged active and in contact.

The same culture seems to breed materialism and hedonism faster, or at
least more obviously, than the rest of the U.S.A. In large measure, materialism
is what Hollywood "culture" has always stood for. Sexual permissiveness—the

body-conscious society—flourished first and foremost in Southern California, first in Hollywood's purveyance of the single female sex symbol (and God rest the soul of poor, troubled Marilyn Monroe), then in the beach-and-auto society of unfettered, bronzed young bodies, the golden California girls and their swains. The universality of sexual tastes and opportunities is amply illustrated in the remarkable classified section of the Los Angeles *Free Press.* For instance:

> SEXUAL FREEDOM PARTY—This Sat. nite 8 pm—Limit 15 couples. Call for res. 660-0500.
>
> SWINGERS—Dial-A-Soulmate: Guys—Low Fee—655-5377; Chicks-Free—752-3711.
>
> INTERRACIAL LOVE—Meets Wed., Fri. & Sun. 9112 S. Western. 957-1808.
>
> BLONDE GIRL WANTED to share cabin in canyon with generous young man. Must be between 21 and 30 for romantic & steady relationship. Preferably European. Please write Dennis, Rte. 2, Box 110, Saugus, Calif. 91350.

For all such aberrations, the Southern Californian tells a visitor, there are hundreds of examples of normal families of children who grow and date and marry and carry on their lives in very normal ways—an assertion doubtless true. Yet the journalist's attention is seized again by the bizarre, which flourishes here so openly. For example, the gangsterish young motorcycle gang, Hell's Angels, sprang to life first in Fontana, in the L.A. hinterland, the cyclists spreading across California on their big Harleys, sowing terror as they went, fast men with weapons and drugs.

Within this same Southern California flourishes every type of cult, religion, life style imaginable. Part of the disparity, as *Los Angeles* magazine has suggested, is that while Los Angeles by all outward appearances is an overwhelmingly middle-class community, there are in fact two very different kinds of middle-class communities. There is one which is older (not so much chronologically as culturally), whose members work at jobs they mainly dislike, watch television, take their kids to Disneyland, and worry about being correct. There is another which is younger (especially in its culture), which feels both free and alienated and attempts to resolve its paradox by creative acts, uncommon thoughts, and a strange variety of innovative life styles.

Among the "straights," for instance, one could classify most members of Los Angeles' Protestant churches and certainly all but a few of the flock of 1.6 million built up over 21 years (until his 1970 retirement) by James Francis Cardinal McIntyre of the Roman Catholic Archdiocese, the first Prince of the Church to be elevated from a see west of St. Louis.

Yet it is Protestantism, not Catholicism, that sets the tone of Los Angeles; as Christopher Rand has remarked, the city "is the last station . . . of the Protestant outburst that left northern Europe three centuries ago and moved across America." In Los Angeles, the Protestant component covered not only every standard denomination—a sampling from low Baptist to high Episcopalian, accurately reflecting the population mix—but an assortment of kooky cults such as the world has rarely seen. From Thomas Lake Harris (California's first self-proclaimed Messiah) to Sister Aimee Semple McPherson, from the leaders of Theocracy to the fascistic Christian Nationalist Crusade of Gerald L. K. Smith and the modern Sky Pilot Radio Church, where a reader can pursue truth in the I Am Accredited White Temple Reading Room, Los Angeles has had a bit of everything. Some say the cultism is more sedate than it once was, but it is still there. Today there are fervid evangelistic faith healers from the South, and an absolute first in the U.S.A., a church (the nondenominational Metropolitan Community Church) which openly identifies itself as a church for male and female homosexuals. It has several hundred members and, according to reports, probably a truer Christian spirit than thousands of the world's "straight" churches.

To Los Angeles, too, one must travel to find the greatest American flowering of fad and the phenomenon of astrology, enthusiastically practiced witchcraft, and such occult arts as palmistry, numerology, and fortunetelling. And somewhere far out beyond these, at the demonic edge of a troubled and rootless society, stood a figure like Charles Manson, Rasputin-like leader of a band of hippies convicted of having murdered actress Sharon Tate and four others in an orgy of hacking, stabbing, and shooting at the end of the 1960s. Sex, drugs, hypnotism, communal living, hallucinatory thinking—all seemed to have played a role in the events leading up to this murder, perhaps the bloodiest and most senseless of our century. Yet it was not an isolated instance of violent crime in Los Angeles; the area crime rate vies with New York City's as the highest in the U.S.A., with alarmingly high levels of murder, forcible rape, and aggravated assault, in addition to the various forms of property crime. Not all of this is amateur stuff: the Mafia has thrived in Los Angeles since early in the century, prospering today on drugs and a variety of other sidelines as it did on illegal booze about a half-century ago.

A huge nonestablishment, underground community does thrive in the Los Angeles area, but like everything else it is so spread out—from artist communes in the canyons to hippies' beach pads or semiresort hideaways—that it fails to make an impact like the action along Telegraph Avenue in Berkeley. The underground gets a lot of its "bread" from the entertainment scene —Los Angeles is a major recording industry center, and companies specializing in rock music often hire people close to the underground scene. A second important source of support is dope pushing—from the seemingly omnipresent marijuana (grown in vast quantities in nearby Mexico) to LSD and speed and occasionally heroin or opium. (The Mafia would like to make drugs its exclusive commodity, but the stuff is just too prevalent to permit that.)

A major unifying force in the underground world is the Los Angeles *Free Press*, written distinctly for the young, uncommitted, and turned off. Editor Art Kunkin tells how he started the *Free Press*, up to 90,000 circulation at the time of this writing, with a total initial investment of $15 in 1964. Journalistically, it is somewhere between the advocacy papers of the standard underground press (the 200-odd papers in the U.S. which cater mostly to young people of hippie or radical leanings) and more sedate but leftish organs like New York's *Village Voice*. Editor Kunkin, who was a tool-and-die maker before he got into journalism, insists the sex ads had never been planned but turned up unsolicited and eventually became a financial mainstay of the paper. "I suppose they do reflect some sickness in the urban community," Kunkin says. "But boys do have the right to meet boys, boys to meet girls, or whatever."

A discussion of the L.A. multicultures, and especially the drug scene, must include mention of the remarkable Synanon movement, begun at Santa Monica in the late 1950s by Charles E. Dederich. Synanon began, almost spontaneously, as a self-help organization for alcoholics, then expanded to take in heroin and other drug addicts, and finally became a haven for almost anyone in trouble or looking for a new order in his life. Founder Dederich, a lusty iconoclast and former alcoholic, has been variously described as a latter-day Socrates, a madman, a perpetrator of self-glorification, and a herd of one elephant. His movement has now spread to centers at Oakland and Tomales Bay north of San Francisco, to San Diego, and even as far east as Detroit and New York, and has provided a temporary home for more than 10,000 narcotics addicts and other "misfits." Synanon officials, however, insist they are not in the rehabilitation business but are a social movement, "a small model for a better world." The central technique is still the "Synanon game," a free-wheeling discussion—sometimes called "attack therapy" for the verbal brickbats thrown—which is intended to discover and correct the "hangups," or behavioral disorders that may cause a person to turn to the needle or alcohol or otherwise fail to come to terms with society. Men and women are admitted to Synanon to live full time at its facilities, with ground rules of no drugs, no alcohol, no smoking, no violence. New arrivals are taken off narcotics immediately—"cold turkey." The course is a rigorous, demanding one, which works wonders for many human beings. Probing to define a new society, reacting to drugs and confused personal lives, Synanon is completely the child of Southern California; in its movement to a rigorously controlled new life order, forbidding many of life's pleasures, it is quite the opposite or, one might say, an inevitable counterreaction to the society around it.

## L.A. Arts and the Press

Until a very few years ago, Southern California seemed to all the world to be a brash and shallow place, preoccupied with its roads, bridges, hotels, and dams.

Two developments of the past generation, however, have elevated Los

Angeles into a first-rate cultural center. First, in the immediate pre–World War II era, there was the arrival of talented European refugees, some but not all of them Jews fleeing the Hitlerian onslaught, a group that included figures like Bertolt Brecht, Igor Stravinsky, Arnold Schoenberg, Artur Rubinstein, and Jascha Heifetz. As Christopher Rand points out, they were attracted by the climate, the movies, and eventually, each other's presence; almost without exception they chose to settle in the Santa Monica mountains, between Hollywood and the sea. The exiles made Los Angeles into a music center second only to New York in this hemisphere, and stimulated the growth of bookshops, art dealers, and the like. Los Angeles is now the nation's second largest painting and sculpture market, the galleries along La Cienega Boulevard inferior only to Madison Avenue's. The exiles also helped inspire UCLA to inaugurate the best extension courses in the U.S.A. and broadened the professions in Southern California, especially psychoanalysis.

The 1950s and especially the 1960s brought, for the first time, a determination on the part of Los Angeles' old and leading families to make their city a High Culture leader of the country. Rising like an acropolis on a hill in the center of downtown Los Angeles is the massive Los Angeles Music Center, opened in 1964, the home of the Los Angeles Philharmonic (considered one of the country's greatest symphonies), the Center Theatre Group (an ambitious regional theatre), and the Civic Light Opera and Choral Society. Designed by California architect Welton Beckett, the Music Center adds the one touch of true elegance and style to downtown L.A. Some seven miles to the west, on Wilshire Boulevard, is the strikingly designed County Art Museum, opened in 1965. Neither of these projects would have been possible without the extraordinary fund-raising activities of Dorothy (Mrs. Norman) Chandler, mother of the L. A. *Times* publisher and wife of his predecessor.

Yet it would be unfair to say that Los Angeles is preoccupied with top-level culture to be enjoyed principally by the upper classes. Los Angeles teems with amateur musicians and artists, community orchestras (there are 60 symphony orchestras in the area), and chamber-music societies. San Diego and Santa Barbara offer much more of the same; in San Diego, for instance, four to six playhouses are busy at a time, including Coronado Playhouse, California Western University, the Old Globe Theater, and the Art Center in La Jolla. And if anyone tires of the standard fare, he can always make a trip to see the intriguing Watts Towers built by Italian immigrant Simon Rodia, a set of three spires almost 100 feet high and composed of everything from pipes, broken bottles, and cement to iron rods, tiles, and seashells, the fruit of 33 years of labor by the lonely man who died in 1965.

Culture is not the only area in which Los Angeles has grown up. Today its dominant newspaper, the Los Angeles *Times*, competes closely with other great dailies like the New York *Times* and Washington *Post* for the honor of being considered the finest in the U.S.A. Until 1960, when Otis Chandler succeeded his father Norman as publisher, the paper was a fat mediocrity—highly provincial (a Washington bureau of three, a foreign staff of exactly one), slanted in coverage, uncrusading, the safe and sound voice of the Republican party in California and the Wasp community of Los Angeles. Otis Chandler and his editor until 1971, Nick B. Williams (an intellectual Southerner considered one of the best U.S. postwar editors) decided to go first class, with spectacular results in content, style, and editorial direction.

The *Times* has protected its vital flank in Middle America by building or developing excellent sports and financial, entertainment, and women's features. Even black and Mexican-American community news is now covered with care. But the paper has also been able to appeal to Southern California's highly literate leadership community—university and aerospace and think tank people—with a strong diet of national and foreign news and carefully developed interpretive stories. Williams hired many expert reporters—not a few of them from the defunct but still warmly remembered New York *Herald Tribune*. The *Times* correspondent network was widened to 18 in Washington, 16 abroad (from Mexico City to Moscow), and a half-dozen in major U.S. cities (including some of the very best regional reporters in the business). Some of the most important national news breaks of the late 1960s and early 1970s emerged from the *Times*; locally the paper unearthed such corruption in the Board of Zoning Adjustment and the Los Angeles Harbor Commission (including influence peddling and personal profiteering) that Mayor Sam Yorty became a mortal enemy.

Slowly at first, then more rapidly, the *Times* broke loose from its old conservative editorial moorings. Formerly, it had called itself a Republican newspaper; now this was changed to "independent Republican," and finally just to "independent." In 1964, the paper supported Goldwater for President (after backing Rockefeller in the California GOP primary and promising to support the winner in the fall), but in 1970, Chandler told me that under similar circumstances the *Times* would *not* again support a candidate like Goldwater, and that in fact its endorsement in any future electoral race should be considered doubtful.

Part of the wonder of the *Times*'s modern-day success has been that Otis Chandler, who came upon his position by sheer rank of family succession,* should have turned out to be such a skilled publisher. To the casual visitor, Chandler looks like a typical young California businessman—tall, blond, svelte, athletic, genial. But as *New York* magazine summed him up: "California, yes. Beach boy, no." The record shows that Chandler has proven no one's fool in coping with the built-in obstacles to a successful newspaper business in Los Angeles—readers who commute in autos, not trains where there's time to read; the soft outdoor life, competing for attention; fiercely competitive suburban dailies; disparate, farflung and often indifferent communities; and top-drawer local news programming by NBC and CBS outlets, which operate on budgets way over even New York locals and go in heavily for original news and editorials. Between 1960 and 1970, the *Times* increased its daily circula-

---

* Otis is the son of Norman Chandler, who had followed his father, Harry Chandler, who had stepped into the publisher's slot to succeed his father-in-law, Harrison Gray Otis, a Civil War veteran who acquired a quarter-interest in the paper 90 years ago.

tion from 500,000 to almost a million, its Sunday circulation from 900,000 to 1,400,000. In daily circulation, it is now second only to the New York *Daily News*, on Sunday behind only the *News* and the New York *Times*. Its advertising linage *and* its line count of editorial content is by far and away the greatest of any U.S. newspaper. As for the suburban competition problem, the *Times* has gotten a strong early hold on that situation with its Orange County edition, published since 1968 in its own complete plant in the county with 350 employees and separate editorial, sales-service, and production departments.

The horizons of the *Times* and its parent Times Mirror Corporation (1968 gross $352 million) are not limited to the California Southland. Early in the 1960s, the *Times* began to "go national" through its successful joint news service with the Washington *Post* (a service now subscribed to by many other papers). As the decade progressed, several moderate-sized book and magazine operations were purchased. Then, in 1969, came acquisition of the Dallas *Times Herald* (a paper that needed a lot of improving) and CBS affiliate KRLD-TV in Dallas–Fort Worth. And in 1970, it was announced that the *Times* had purchased perhaps the finest afternoon paper of the U.S. today, Long Island's *Newsday*. What was Chandler aiming at? He himself said: "We looked at growth and population figures and concluded that there are four states we should be in—California, Texas, New York, and Florida. . . ." Commented Edward Diamond in *New York* magazine: "The evidence suggests that he is out to create nothing less than the biggest, best communications complex in the nation."

Searching for motivation to explain the expansionist and perfectionist drive from the Chandler empire in Los Angeles, as it now begins to take control of parts of the nation that once treated L.A. as a colony, multiple motives are suggested. One is simply the drive to excel of Otis Chandler, born of two highly ambitious parents. A second is "the Eastern thing"—the Westerner's desire to prove himself equal or superior on the very home grounds, by the very rules, of the Eastern Establishment.

## L.A. Power and Politics

There is scarcely any American city where the question "Who holds the power in this town?" evokes such unsatisfactory answers as Los Angeles. Officials at the Rand Corporation told me that when they wanted to identify the major business and other leaders with influence on city and state governments, they found the task almost impossible. Their net impression: Los Angeles is so diffuse that no one knows what's going on, let alone controls it. There is simply no "establishment" comparable to New York, Chicago, or even San Francisco. Scarcely any "old families" qualify. Otis Chandler's own name automatically goes on any tentative list of Los Angeles leaders, but he told me: "There is no power structure here—only people who think they are."

Even when one looks to the holders of great wealth as natural holders of power, no strong "establishment" comes into focus. Aerospace, big oil, and what's left of Hollywood play little role in local affairs. Fortunes are rarely more than a generation old, and at least until recently, their holders were distinctly disinclined toward politics. The business establishment, such as it is, includes bankers, real estate men, merchandizers, some oilmen, and not a few wealthy owners of savings and loan associations who saw their investments balloon into billion-dollar enterprises during the postwar housing booms.

In recent years, Los Angeles has begun to register a growing number of major contributors to political and civic causes, representing at least an embryonic power structure. The L. A. *Times'* Bill Boyarsky, in a 1970 magazine article written jointly with his wife, Nancy, reported that a careful observer could notice the same names appearing as major donors to big L.A. cultural, charitable, and medical projects. Among the major names the Boyarskys reported were these:

▪ Asa Call, in his late seventies, conservative and successful businessman, ex-president of the state chamber of commerce and the Southern California Auto Club (largest in the world), a position in which he successfully lobbied the state legislature to adopt California's huge freeway system.

▪ Leonard Firestone, chief of Firestone Tire and Rubber Co., a moderate Republican who initially opposed Ronald Reagan and was cochairman of the 1964 Rockefeller for President campaign in California. In 1969, Firestone raised money for black City Councilman Thomas Bradley's unsuccessful campaign. He gives freely to such projects as the Boy Scouts.

▪ Taft Schreiber, a moderate Republican, Jewish, big in the philanthropies, who was Ronald Reagan's old movie agent and helped launch Reagan's political career. Schreiber is an executive of Music Corporation of America, the giant show business combine that controls Universal Studios.

▪ Mark Boyar, chairman of the board of Metropolitan Development Corporation, a land development firm. He is a big Democratic contributor who, along with oilman Ed Pauley, raced up to San Francisco in 1948 to rescue Harry Truman's campaign train, which had been stalled by railroad officials who demanded cash to pay for it. Boyar was also a big Humphrey contributor in 1968. He says: "The hacks like myself have just about had it. The younger men coming up, Democrats and Republicans, worry about social problems and the environment."

▪ Eugene Wyman, former Democratic National Committeeman and state chairman and big fund-raiser for his party, head of the prestigious law firm of Wyman, Bautzer, Finell, Rothman and Kuchel. A "regular" Democrat, Wyman is one of many important Jewish contributors to the Democratic party. According to *Newsweek*, Wyman "is usually good for a $100,000 personal contribution to the Democrat of his choice in a major campaign, . . . but his main clout as a fat cat derives from his network of other major contributors—by which he means $10,000 and up—who are willing to follow his judgments."

▪ Martin Stone, president of Monogram Industries (a manufacturing combine that grosses $150 million a year). In his early forties, Stone is a big money-raiser for the liberal wing of the Democratic party, as opposed to what he calls "traditionalists" like Wyman and Boyar. He has served as president of the Los Angeles Urban Coalition and is candid about his interest in running for governor in 1974.

■   Holmes Tuttle, in his late sixties, a successful owner of five Ford-Lincoln-Mercury dealerships; he is described by the Boyarskys as "the single most influential Republican contributor and money-raiser in the state." Tuttle has been a Reagan friend since 1945, helped launch Reagan's political career, and directed fund-raising in the Reagan gubernatorial campaigns.

A name many would place close to the top of the L.A.-California money-power structure is that of Henry Salvatori, son of Italian immigrant parents, self-made multimillionaire in oil geology, confidant and major fund-raiser for President Nixon, Mayor Sam Yorty, and especially Governor Reagan. (Salvatori is one of a group of businessmen who bought the house Reagan lives in in Sacramento. First they leased it to Reagan, who personally paid $15,000 a year in rent until the state took over payments in 1970.) Salvatori's big interest is in fighting Communism, and he has given heavily to groups like the Christian Anti-Communism Crusade and to conservative politicians who make opposition to Communism a chief talking point.

Los Angeles politics have a turbulent and sometimes violent history. There were many Confederate sympathizers in town at the time of the Civil War who dealt harshly with Negroes and in turn were subdued by Union troops. Public hangings of criminals used to be commonplace near where the Federal Building now stands. Afflicted by a political boss system and the machinations of power-hungry corporations, Angelenos some 70 years ago rose up in a great municipal reform movement that resulted in the recall of the mayor, who was involved in sugar company stock speculation; it was the first use of the recall method in U.S. history. Los Angeles politics turned non-partisan, but up to the 1930s it was known as an open town, with gambling, prostitution, and other diversions. But in January 1938, a couple of police officers planted a bomb in a private investigator's car. The explosion blew the mayor of the moment out of office (again via the recall route). The captain of police went to San Quentin. The new mayor, Fletcher Bowron, closed up the town, reorganized the police and other public boards, and proved so popular he was reelected for three terms. The 1950s brought Mayor Norris Poulson, a pleasant spokesman for GOP business interests running under a nonpartisan banner. During these years the L. A. *Times* came close to dictating the exact course of municipal government. Then, in 1961, Sam Yorty became mayor.

Sam Yorty had come to California from Nebraska when he was 17, first dabbled in politics as a local secretary of the Technocracy movement, and in 1936 went to the state assembly, where he was considered a "flaming liberal" in his first term but then turned sharply to the right. Remaining a Democrat, he alternated the practice of law and occasional runs of public office (winning two terms in Congress). In 1960, he bolted his own party to endorse Nixon for President, authoring a pamphlet, "Why I Cannot Take Kennedy," a tract that did not leave the issue of Kennedy's Catholicism unmentioned. The next year, Yorty got elected mayor, capitalizing on his neopopulist image as a gutsy politician for the little guy against the "bosses" and the politicians.

Came the 1969 election and the *Times*, previously friendly to Yorty, refused to support him (largely because of the scandals its reporters had unearthed). In a first primary, with 14 candidates on the ballot, Yorty picked up only 26 percent of the vote. But the man he was forced to face in the runoff election, Thomas Bradley, a quiet, bright, moderate city councilman who had served 21 years on the L.A. police force, was a Negro. Yorty took the issue and exploited it to the hilt, suggesting that Bradley was linked to radicals, that he would ruin the police (a patently absurd charge in view of Bradley's own police background), and that somehow Reds and blacks and long-haired students and criminals would all "take over" Los Angeles if Bradley were elected. The tactic worked, and Yorty won with 53 percent of the vote. (Of equal significance, however, was the fact that Bradley, a Negro, almost did win in a city where the Negro population is only 17 percent, and that most of the downtown white establishment backed Bradley. Yorty has done much more poorly in statewide Democratic primaries; in 1972, to general amazement, he declared himself a Presidential candidate and ran in the New Hampshire preference primary. Granite Staters gave him 6 percent of their vote.)

Racist and emotional politics in Los Angeles necessarily hamper the formulation of creative policies to ameliorate tensions within the city and deal with its fundamental long-term problems—fiscal insufficiency and irrational boundaries. The fiscal problem seems forever without solution as the population expands, over a vast physical area, faster than government services can catch up. The city simply cannot afford enough police for the population and area it must protect. There are still huge sections, including some in the San Fernando Valley, where the city has yet to provide sewers, storm drains, and paving for new communities. The city's boundaries are so far-flung that many small, independent towns are entirely within it or make deep indentations. A city fire truck, for instance, may have to go through Beverly Hills, right past the fire department of that independent city, to respond to a call in another part of Los Angeles city. A relatively limited Model Cities area picked out for special help by the federal government turned out to lie in three separate jurisdictions—Los Angeles City, Los Angeles County, and the city of Compton. The federal department was obliged to make its grants to the three separate governments, not to mention the coordination with the same area's six autonomous school districts, two Community Action Program agencies, two library service areas, three urban renewal agencies, and three public housing authorities.

It may be argued that the identity of the mayor of Los Angeles is of little importance—a position which Mayor Yorty took indirectly a few years ago when he was testifying on the problems of U.S. cities before the Senate Sub-committee on Executive Reorganization:

*Senator Abraham Ribicoff:* This morning you have really waived authority and responsibility in the following areas of Los Angeles: schools, welfare, transportation, employment, health and housing, which leaves you as the head of the city basically with a ceremonial function, police and recreation.

*Yorty:* That is right, and fire.

*Ribicoff:* Collecting of sewage?

*Yorty:* Sanitation, that is right.

*Ribicoff:* In other words, basically you lack jurisdiction, authority, responsibility for what makes a city move?

*Yorty:* That is exactly it.

The obvious alternative to weak city government would be a strong metropolitan government—a not novel idea which has been justified by Councilman Ernani Bernardi in these words:

We ought to face the fact that we simply can't solve the really big problems —race relations, smog, rapid transit, crime—within the present structure of city government. Urbanization has made city governments obsolete. None of these problems can be contained within municipal boundary lines. Before we can even begin to solve them we will have to have one, integrated countywide government.

There is a chance that county government may fill the void. In California, the counties handle "people problems" like health, welfare, criminal justice, pollution, and housing—the very functions that have grown so rapidly in recent years. The cities are left with fire protection, street sanitation, municipal planning, and zoning. An evolution to stronger county power—fighting the inevitable opposition of cities anxious to preserve prerogatives—may be in the making. Already, L.A. County government has multipurpose citizen service centers spread all around the county. In the area of federal grants, L.A. County has an extremely effective lobbyist, James M. Pollard, in Washington. The county's weaknesses are its multiheaded leadership (five supervisors instead of a single executive) and the fact that so many California government functions (education, rapid transit, etc.) are fulfilled by special-purpose districts. Just a sample of the problems was the imbroglio that followed a 1969 court ruling which required racial balance in the 650,000-student Los Angeles School District. The school board first chose higher court appeals rather than resort to busing, which it estimated would cost $42 million a year in the 714-square mile area of 600 schools. But it did little to investigate or implement the alternative proposed by Wilson Riles: setting up intra-district specialized schools and instituting expanded academic, cultural, and athletic exchange programs.

## *L.A. Economy: Overview and Hollywood*

It seems difficult to believe today, but not many decades ago Los Angeles was just emerging from its drowsy, Arcadian era of citrus groves, exotic shrubbery, and resort life. As a harbinger of things to come, oil was discovered in 1890 and the first movies filmed soon after the turn of the century. But serious growth began only after World War I, as the movies made Hollywood a fashion and scandal center of the world, the aircraft business grew toward major-industry status, and the first large residential subdivisions appeared. In World War II, the big aircraft plants (Douglas, North American, Northrup, Hughes, and others) manufactured a hefty chunk of the planes that fought the war. Millions of dollars also poured into California's new steel mills and into her shipyards as Southern California, for the first time, became really important to the entire U.S. economy.

The postwar story is one of superlatives. Just in manufacturing, for instance, the value of goods produced went up from $2 billion in 1940 to $9 billion in 1963. Personal income soared from $3 billion in 1940 to $48 billion in 1970. Los Angeles County is not only the economic center of the Southwestern U.S.A., but one of the world's largest industrial, financial, and commercial complexes. With the exception of agriculture, every major industry has participated in the area's growth since World War II. In 1965, L.A. surpassed San Francisco as the financial center of the West by forging ahead in three critical measures—total loans, deposits, and savings. Tourism, with only a shadow of the relative importance it had a half-century ago, nevertheless adds more than $1 billion to the Southland's economy each year.

A normally perspicacious San Francisco businessman tells a visitor, "I for one can't see how L.A. can be so damned affluent. There are so many people down there they must just take in each other's laundry." The comment may not be too far from the mark. Jane Jacobs, in her *Economy of Cities*, shows how Los Angeles defied the normal laws of export and import by growing immediately after World War II, even while her exports (wartime ships and planes) fell catastrophically. With Hollywood about to begin its decline and oil eliminated as an export because of local need, many people predicted severe economic distress and depression for Los Angeles. Instead, employment grew. What was happening was that Los Angeles was beginning to replace the goods it used to import with local manufactures, and accommodating the pent-up consumer demands of the war years. It was a period of immense entrepeneureal enterprise, as Jacobs explains:

> The new enterprises started in corners of old loft buildings, in Quonset huts and in backyard garages. But they multiplied swiftly, mostly by the breakaway method. And many grew rapidly. They poured forth furnaces, sliding doors, mechanical saws, bathing suits, underwear, china, furniture, cameras, hand tools, hospital equipment, scientific instruments, engineering services and hundreds of other things. One-eighth of all the new businesses started in the United States during the latter half of the 1940s were started in Los Angeles.

Many of the new companies themselves became successful exporters, and many national firms that used to export to Los Angeles opened branch plants there to produce the goods close to the burgeoning Southern California market. The national auto makers expanded their assembly plants in the city and soon made it the leading exporter of autos in the territory west of the Rockies. L.A. the exporting center might have boomed even more if Japan had not cut into its Pacific basin sales in steel and autos.

A revived and expanded aircraft and general aerospace business was to provide the vigorous export base on which much of L.A.'s modern day prosperity is based, starting with important production during the Korean war. In addition to its new banking power, the city and region forged continuously ahead as corporate headquarters locations, widening a lead over San Francisco and the Bay region. Just a brief sampling of the L.A. area industrial firms, with latest annual sales figures available in 1971, would include North American Rockwell ($2.4 billion), Litton Industries ($2.4 billion), Lockheed Aircraft ($2.5 billion), Occidental Petroleum and Union Oil (each about $2 billion), Norton Simon Inc. ($1 billion), and Dart Industries ($703 million). Among banks, the list is headed by Security Pacific National Bank (assets $8 billion); in the insurance field, Los Angeles has California's largest (Occidental Life, with assets of $1.7 billion) and two of the other four largest; in transportation it has Continental and Western Airlines (with combined revenues of about $590 million).

Los Angeles trade not only dominates western U.S. markets, but is internationally important as well. Both Los Angeles and Long Beach have magnificent, side-by-side, and highly competitive sea harbors behind nine miles of breakwater (actually the world's largest man-made harbor). Scores of freighters can be handled at a time, and the tonnage handled (36.6 million tons in 1967) ranks eighth among U.S. ports if one counts the two rivals as one. Famed San Francisco Harbor handles only a ninth as much tonnage. By some estimates, one worker out of four in Los Angeles is substantially dependent on foreign trade for his livelihood. Out of the ports move oranges, cotton, potash, coke, iron-ore pellets, and thousands of other commodities; in come everything from bananas and Mexican salt to Scotch whiskey, petroleum (which Los Angeles must now import to satisfy its fantastic demand), crude rubber, and foreign autos. One of the most astounding port sights is the acres of Volkswagens awaiting delivery to the auto-hungry Southland market.

The diversity of Los Angeles' economy makes rapid summation hopeless. The city is at once a foremost fishing port and the number two garment manufacturing center in the world; in design and production of sportswear, it has no peer. L.A. also has a higher proportion of small businesses than any other U.S. metropolitan center, more savings and loan associations than any other, and the home offices of some 90 insurance companies. And of course the city was and is the home base of many of America's most daring and successful business tycoons, ranging from highly socially conscious men like the late Dan Kimball of Aerojet-General and multimillionaire industrialist Norton Simon to Reagan's self-made friend Henry Salvatori, wheeler-dealer attorney Sidney R. Korshak (one of the best-connected men in the American West), and the flamboyant, tough, highly successful president of Continental Airlines, Robert Forman Six.

The saddest Los Angeles story is the decline and fall of Hollywood movie-making, the city's great seminal industry and its most unique contribution to American culture. Writing some 25 years ago in *Inside U.S.A.*, Gunther began a few pages on the movie industry with these words:

I would like nothing better than to describe Hollywood at length—that fabulous world of profit, hunger, agents, ulcers, all the power and vitality and talent and craftsmanship with so little genius, options, dynastic confusions, the vulgarization of most personal relationships, and 8,000 man hours spent on a sequence that takes three minutes to see. . . . Or its preoccupation with gossip, personality, dramatic nuances, "entrances." . . . Or on the quasi-theological aspects of the star system. . . .

Today the temptation to write of such things is less, or nonexistent. So much of what was called "Hollywood" (always a euphemism for the studios and lots scattered from Burbank to Culver City) has faded away; in fact the decline has been rather steady since the mid-1940s, when the industry was grossing $1.5 billion and making almost 400 movies each year. The villains in the decline have been, most obviously, television; secondly, foreign competition; third, rising costs (up 50 percent in the 1960s); fourth, the industry's own antediluvian economic practices (overpaid stars, huge lots, overinvestment in individual films, an archaic distribution system); fifth, the unions and "runaway" film production; and, finally, American youth, who are simply turned off by the old ballyhoo, extravaganzaitis, and superficiality.

No one questions that movie-making will continue to be a vital industry in the 1970s and beyond; the question is whether the big Hollywood studios will show enough flexibility to hold a major piece of the action. While the big producers boast they possess the ultimate in technical movie-making skills, some of their most successful ventures are simply to bankroll young, independent producers who know how to turn out the almost psychedelic imagery —split screens, images flashing on and off, images that remain on the screen like stills—popular in the McLuhanesque generation. By 1969, a majority of the big Hollywood studios were losing money, including the once titanic Metro-Goldwyn-Mayer, Paramount, and 20th Century Fox. (Exceptions to the losing rule: Columbia Pictures and the hard-headed successors of Walt Disney.) Inevitably, the conglomerates and proxy challengers moved in: Gulf & Western Industries bought Paramount; Kinney National Service acquired Warner Brothers–Seven Arts; Distillers Corp.–Seagrams and Time Inc., bought control of Metro-Goldwyn-Mayer. M-G-M in 1969 was obliged to hold a monstrous $5 million auction of properties ranging from famous stars' costumes to an 1878 train; also sold were three warehouses packed with tapestries, chandeliers, and furniture of past centuries, picked up during the 1930s when the studios followed authenticity; the auction was a kind of farewell to an era.

Other notes on the movie industry: As anyone could see by a glance at movie marquees around the U.S.A., the day of the nudie and/or pornographic film had arrived in full force by the late 1960s, making mincemeat of the film industry's traditional codes and upsetting local communities. But it was still "family" pictures, and not the sex, that brought in most box-office dollars. Movies for television, once hailed as the industry's salvation, failed to bring prosperity, partly because of Hollywood's lack of talent in producing them, partly because the networks drove the price down to what Hollywood considers a pauper level. The era of the superstar was definitely waning; at the start of the 1960s, Elizabeth Taylor, Marilyn Monroe, and several others could still be classified as superstars, but by 1970 there were scarcely any. Many films, in fact, demonstrated an antistar syndrome by casting only unknown actors.

## *Aerospace, Think Tanks, and Systems Analysis*

The 60-year-old aviation industry and its lively offspring, aerospace, have represented the most dynamic element in Southern California's postwar economy. Through aerospace, California became the leading defense contracting state.

Earnest aircraft production got underway in California soon after World War I, led by Lockheed and Douglas, and later, Northrup, Hughes, North American, and Ryan Aeronautical Corporation. By 1937, California led the U.S. in aircraft production. When airplane factories expanded spectacularly during World War II, California made fighters and bombers (20,000 by Lockheed alone) which were a cornerstone of American air power.

Immediately after the war, defense contracts sagged, depressing aircraft employment. But strong ties had been formed between government, the California aircraft plants and the state's scientifically oriented university communities. When the Korean War arrived, escalating aircraft demands, and the important shift to missiles and spacecraft occurred, California was ready to seize the business. Complementary defense installations (the Air Force's Space Technology Laboratory, the Pacific Missile Range, Vandenberg Air Force Base with its rocket-launching capabilities) also gravitated to California. By the 1960s, people were talking of Los Angeles as a "federal city" because of the close relationship between its economy and that of Washington. Some 40 percent of the area's manufacturing employment was tied directly or indirectly to defense and space spending. In 1962, about 24 percent of all U.S. government military contracts (close to $6 billion worth) went to California, and for several years about 40 percent of contracts for military R & D work were let to Golden State firms. The state's advantage in space agency contracts was almost as great. Congressmen from other regions complained hotly about alleged preference shown California, but the fact was that a huge proportion of the firms and personnel with appropriate R & D and aerospace manufacturing backgrounds were on the coast, plus universities turning out a disproportionately large share of the country's new scientists and engineers. The multiplier effect of research, development, academic, and manufacturing facilities, all in California, would prove hard to break. By 1970, federal military prime contract awards to California were down to 19.6 percent of the U.S. total, but the dollar amount—$5.8 billion—was still close to twice the amount in second- and third-ranking New York and Texas.

While San Diego, Sacramento, and the San Francisco Bay Area have a share of aerospace factories, the great concentration is in Los Angeles County. Here they are dotted about, Christopher Rand points out, in a discernible pattern. Some are grouped around Pasadena, northeast of center L.A., near CalTech and its spinoffs. Others are in the San Fernando Valley, miles to the north and northwest of central L.A.; here, for instance, is the long-time home of Lockheed, the biggest of them all. But the major concentration is down along a 20-mile stretch of L.A.'s West Side, close to the ocean. The coastal strip is home for Douglas, North American, TRW, and Hughes, as well as the nonprofit Aerospace and Rand corporations, and innumerable electronics suppliers and computer firms. Los Angeles International Airport is close to this coastal complex; the cool sea breezes drive away most smog; and a close-knit aerospace community has developed to exchange ideas, do business together, and raid each other's personnel. There are pleasant coastal housing developments nearby for the executives and engineers. In all, some 10,000 Southern California factories serve the aerospace industry.

At the end of the '60s and the start of the '70s, events took a menacing turn for the long-prosperous aerospace industry and the hundreds of thousands of Californians employed by it or related defense industries. A deescalation of the arms race with the Soviets became a distinct possibility. The once-sacred defense budget came under close congressional scrutiny and there was mounting criticism of the huge cost overruns that had led the government to pay two or three times first estimates for several weapons systems. Then came a sharp tapering-off in NASA orders for rockets and space equipment as the Apollo moon-landing program reached its completion. Finally, it became clear that there were simply too many airframe manufacturers for the available volume of business, either military or domestic. As the missile age advanced, many legislators viewed the military plane as an anachronism—and an intolerably expensive one. The airlines, already well stocked with jets and facing a dollar pinch themselves, cut back on their orders.

Between 1967 and 1971, California slipped from 616,000 aerospace jobs to about 450,000. By autumn 1971, the state had an unemployment rate of 7.1 percent—compared to 6.0 percent in the country as a whole. San Francisco and Oakland, the least dependent on aerospace, were the best off (5.9 percent); Los Angeles and Orange County were among the worst off (7.7 and 8.0 percent respectively). "This is now the worst period of unemployment in this state in the last 20 years," the *California Journal* reported. But there were indications that the slump in aerospace employment might finally have bottomed out.

Even Lockheed—the General Motors of aerospace—found itself in serious trouble at the start of the 1970s. Threatened by inflation and public doubt about its capacity to deliver on promises, the company was in a severe dollar-delivery-performance crisis on four big programs—the Air Force C5A cargo jet, the Army's Cheyenne helicopter, the rocket engine for the Air Force's short-range attack missile, and 22 Navy ships. It was obliged to take a loss of $480 million in a negotiated settlement over four of these disputed government contracts. And its first entry into the field of commercial jet aviation, the L-1011 TriStar, was dealt a staggering blow when England's Rolls Royce, the company that made the engine, went bankrupt in February 1971. Threatening, as it were, to die, Lockheed went hat-in-hand to the government and appealed for a federal loan guarantee of $250 million to stave off bankruptcy. Congress reluctantly approved. Another firm with less than a guaranteed future was North American Rockwell, which had 106,000 workers and yearly sales exceeding $2 billion in the mid-1960s. By spring 1970, it was down to 50,000 workers and faced with near disaster when McDonnell Douglas took away the contract for the F-15 fighter plane in which NAR had invested years of engineers' time, at a cost of millions. Finally, North American did land the Pentagon contract for the proposed B-1 bomber, causing cheers and open joyous weeping at its El Segundo headquarters. But there was a danger that Congress might scuttle the whole B-1 program long before its fruition. The projected cost, from official sources, is around $12 billion, but with the industry's typical cost overruns, some fear the price tag could approach $50 billion. Even then, the plane might well be made obsolete by improved Soviet antiaircraft equipment by the time it becomes fully operational (around 1980).

How can aerospace avoid the disarmament blues and survive? Its brightest future would logically lie in fields like mass transit design, environmental control, or information systems—those areas which require systems analysis and a high technological component. Several firms in the industry have ventured into these fields in recent years. Overall, the success has not been great. The basic problem has been aerospace's unfamiliarity with building inexpensive systems. The industry has been accustomed to rapid work in a high-cost environment where it could afford tremendous redundancies, all on rather generous federal patronage. The social fields, performing for tight-budgeted state and local governments, permit no such luxuries. And most aerospace companies are deficient in personnel trained in the social sciences.

Under Governor Brown, an ambitious "California Experiment" to harness aerospace skills was begun in 1965, with four firms paid $100,000 each for special studies. The goal, as *Missiles and Rockets* reported, was "to show that the aerospace industry is uniquely qualified to help solve some pressing and large-scale civilian problems." Crime and delinquency were assessed by the Space-General Corporation, government information systems by Lockheed, transportation systems by North American, and waste management by Aerojet-General. Predictably, the best quality appeared in the reports on specific technical problems like waste management and information systems; the least enlightening results were in the subjective area of crime and delinquency. The state government apparently did little to implement the reports after they were turned in, but several firms' interest in social-economic areas was stimulated.

Dr. Ernest R. Roberts, a talented scientist who heads Aerojet's environmental systems division, speaks enthusiastically of what his firm has undertaken in water and solid waste pollution technology. "But it's a wrong concept to see our environmental work as a replacement for defense work—the magnitudes simply can't be compared," Roberts says. And he adds: "Only profitable hardware manufacture will attract and hold companies like Aerojet in this field at more than token levels. The profit motive is eventually decisive, the motivation from social consciousness only temporary."

Of all the aerospace firms, the most active in the social field has been TRW, Inc., a far-flung, diversified manufacturer of spacecraft, electronics, automotive parts, jet engine components, and defense systems. TRW has its headquarters in Cleveland but its heart and spirit in California. The scientific-social genius of the firm (his name corresponding to the R in TRW) is Dr. Simon Ramo, a Utah-born electrical engineer who picked California as the land of golden opportunity after the war—figuring, quite simply, that the atomic age would require a greater electronic than aerodynamic component in its weapons, and that a great technological industry could be built on the coast. As head of electronics for Hughes Aircraft, and later in his own firm (Ramo Wooldridge), Ramo became the foremost expert in the guidance and control system of airborne weapons and then the chief scientist of the United States' ICBM program. In 1958, Ramo Wooldridge merged with Thompson Products, an auto-and-aviation firm from Cleveland, to make TRW; in the succeeding 12 years, sales of the new firm increased 337 percent to $1.5 billion and it became the 57th largest industrial corporation of the U.S., with more than 80,000 employees and 300 plants. At one time TRW depended on the federal government for 70 percent of its sales; by the late 1960s, that figure had dropped to 36 percent.*

Ramo, now in his late fifties, is a charming, voluble, self-confident and farsighted man, adept not only in science but also in business, sociology, urban problems, and music (he is an accomplished concert violinist)—about as close to the "universal man" as the confused and complex latter 20th century will permit. Speaking of TRW, Ramo explains: "Our life's work is that part of technology which requires interdisciplinary science. We concentrate on putting together the social and the economic with the technological —combining software or systems analysis or analytic thinking, creative and mathematical work, with hardware." Despite the "spacecraft" image of TRW, Ramo insists, "we're involved in information handling more than spacecraft —the sensing, accumulation, storage, deliberation by automatic techniques. Those same techniques can be used to run an airline or a hospital or manufacturing operation, or to examine the resources of an area."

As examples, TRW has in recent years developed integrated, cost-effec-

---

* Even in the recession year of 1970, TRW held its total sales virtually steady and increased its earnings slightly.

tive operational systems for hospitals in the U.S. and Canada; explored a systems analysis of national and regional air pollution as a basis for a national air pollution control information system; led in developing major-city police command and control systems designed to get more efficient control with less forces; employed automatic data processing techniques to show how the multiplicity of data available about local land use can be correlated for intelligent evaluation of governments in land use planning; established the country's only computerized nationwide credit information system; performed detailed engineering studies and systems analysis of transportation requirements in the northeast (Washington to Boston) corridor; and worked on plans for complete "new cities" set far apart from existing urban areas. Ramo sees the systems analysis method as one of great promise in every field from housing and education to transportation and urban development.

Like a Renaissance man, Ramo takes an optimistic view of the world, believing that sufficient information and analysis will eventually lead to right decisions and the better society. He acknowledges that application of the systems approach in the social arena is still at an embryonic stage, and that no example can yet be cited of a completed systems approach application to a problem primarily social in character. He also confesses that any complete systems approach will raise questions many would like to ignore—to wit, in an urban rapid transit system, which city communities should prosper and which wither by the selection of transit right-of-way. But he insists that crises in U.S. life, especially the inner city, are too explosive to permit long delays.

Set close by the glistening Pacific at Santa Monica are the buildings of the Rand Corporation—the name stands for R(esearch) AN(d) D(evelopment)—foremost think tank of Los Angeles and perhaps the world. Rand was born at the end of World War II when high Air Force officials wanted to maintain and develop a civilian brain trust well removed from Washington. Air Force contracts, originally close to 100 percent of Rand's project load, declined over the years to about 50 percent, with another 10 percent for other defense agencies and 40 percent of the nonprofit corporation's work devoted to domestic programs. Some 1,000 mathematicians, chemists, physicists, social scientists, computer experts, and other scholars work for Rand at Santa Monica, another 100 in a Washington office, and a like number in New York.

Rand's specialty since its first days has been to take a clear-eyed look into the future. A 1946 paper clearly outlined the possibilities of satellites circling the earth and returning human passengers through the atmospheric shield. (The worst mistake of the paper was its estimate of the cost of orbiting a man: a paltry $150 million.) Rand studies revealed possible obliteration of the Strategic Air Command's planes in the late 1950s under then-programmed strategic basing (leading to more concentration on stateside bases), predicted the launching of the Soviets' Sputnik I within two weeks of the actual date, encouraged the start of the country's ICBM program, and influenced almost all Air Force strategic weapons over a quarter of a century. And many alumni of "Mother Rand" rose to high national security positions in the federal government.

War gaming has been popular at Rand since its early years, leading some critics to call Santa Monica "the most famous casino of fun-in-death games in the country." Rand, however, insists that war gaming makes up a small portion of its work, although a vital one in analyzing and synthesizing information for broad strategic or tactical studies. But the very sweep and depth of Rand's work, and its isolation from congressional scrutiny, led by the early 1970s to substantial Capitol Hill sentiment for cutting back Rand and its fellow think tanks in favor of increased in-house research at the Pentagon.

A semimilitary aura hangs over the Rand buildings at Santa Monica, with guards, security passes, and big signs on files indicating whether they hold classified material—all underscoring the secret and sensitive nature of Rand's work for the defense establishment over the years. But a talk with officials of Rand's domestic component—on my visit, Anthony Pascal, director of human resource studies, and John Pincus, chief of Rand's California program—quickly dispels the weighty military-industrial complex feel. The ebullient Pascal, in his late thirties and possessed of what must be the handsomest handlebar moustache west of Milwaukee, quickly launched into a description of a Rand project to aid a large school district like Los Angeles' in meeting court requirements that it reassign pupils to end de facto school segregation. A solution would require a fantastically complex balancing of factors like busing, boundary changes, costs, population forecasting, and other devices to prevent resegregation.

The first stage of Rand's California program was directed at education, intergovernmental relations, and air pollution. Within elementary and secondary schools in several California locations, for instance, Rand experimented with methods to develop a new education information system as a tool for economies in scarce tax dollars, better management, and accountability in terms of just what quality of education is delivered. In 1971, Rand's California program broadened with the opening of a Sacramento office to perform broader research and analysis tasks for the state in cooperation with state universities. Some specific state contracts were granted and Rand began to move into new policy areas like health, manpower, and energy problems in relation to the environment. But its biggest domestic contract was far away—a $2 million study for New York City.

By 1970–71, the recession had hit major think tanks in California and other spots across the country. Like the aerospace companies, the think tanks found themselves victims of government spending cutbacks, public disenchantment with technology (a trend that upsets aerospace and think tank officials more than anything else, as they look to the 1970s), and their general isolation from political and economic realities. Some companies lost so much business they had to pare their staffs by as much as 50 percent. Rand's cutbacks were much less (around 10 percent) but the firm in 1971 faced an uncertain future in the wake of the disclosure that its copy of the top-secret Pentagon study of the Vietnam war, released to the press by Daniel Ellsberg in 1971, was obtained by him during the time that he was a Rand researcher. An ominous first sign came when Defense Secretary Melvin Laird ordered the Air Force to assume physical custody of all top-secret documents retained at Rand headquarters. Late in 1971, Rand president Henry S. Rowan resigned his post, and it was authoritatively reported that among the factors leading to his departure were the objection of some of Rand's military clients to Rowan's growing interest in domestic policy research and the fact that he was in charge when the Pentagon Papers were released to the press.

## Setting Records in Orange County

To reach Orange County, they say in Los Angeles, "You go down the freeway and turn right." In all America, there is no greater bastion of conservative voting strength. Goldwater got 56 percent of its vote in 1964, Nixon 63 percent in 1968, Reagan 72 percent in 1966 and 67 percent in 1970. The last time Orange voted Democratic for President was 1936. For 16 years, the county sent to Congress James B. Utt, a man who once said: "Government is like a child molester who offers candy before his evil act." When Utt died in 1969, he was replaced by John Schmitz, an avowed member of the John Birch Society. The Birchers have their largest California chapter here (some 3,000 members). One of the county's most influential citizens is Walter Knott, founder of Knott's Berry Farm and one of the biggest donors in the country to right-wing causes.

For 35 years prior to his demise in 1970, Orange County was home for Raymond Cyrus Hoiles, publisher of the Santa Ana *Register*, who spurned the Presidential candidacy of Robert A. Taft because he considered Taft not conservative enough and wanted to abolish the public schools because he thought their financing a form of compulsory taxation. "Teachers can't discuss tax-supported schools intelligently because they are victims of the system," Hoiles once said. "How can an inmate of a house of prostitution also discuss chastity?" Hoiles also opposed the post office, publicly supported parks, tax-supported police, and child labor laws ("Give him a pick and shovel and let him get started").

There is a lot more to Orange County than its ultraconservatism, of course. It has Mission San Juan Capistrano, where the swallows unfailingly depart every St. John's Day (October 23) to return on St. Joseph's Day (March 19); 40 miles of magnificent beach and choice surfside communities like Newport Beach and Laguna Beach *; world-famed Disneyland; oil wells; mountains; remnants of the orange groves which gave the county its name; the birthplace of Richard M. Nixon at Yorba Linda and his western White House at San Clemente; the Irvine Ranch, six times as big as Manhattan; hundreds of aerospace-defense firms, which account for half the employment rolls; pockets of affluence and wretched slums; but above all, endless suburbia and the great middle-class society.

* Of Laguna, with its rocky headlands and sweeps of clean, white sand, *Holiday* wrote: "The hippies have caused some strange new vibrations but it's still California's grooviest beach resort." I agree.

Orange has also been the fastest-growing big county in the United States, up almost 1,000 percent from a 1940 Census count of 130,760 to 1,420,386 in 1970. Just in the 1960s, the population went up by 716,461. And while this vast suburb lacks a metropolitan heart, it has four cities with more than 100,000 souls—Anaheim (1970 population of 166,701), Santa Ana (156,601), Garden Grove (122,524) and Huntingdon Beach (115,960). The population is 92 percent Caucasian, 7 percent Mexican-American (mostly old field hands and their descendants), and less than 1 percent Negro.

The homogeneity of Orange County is about the best explanation I have ever seen for its conservatism. Engineers, technicians, aircraft workers account for a large share of Orange County's population, a class with a high technological but low humanistic education. It is an eminently middle-society, with middle-class fears: Will taxes take away one's hard-earned prosperity? Will a black move in next door and spoil property values? The flame of resistance to taxes and big government burns bright, even though the county has exceptionally low property taxes and federal spending accounts for so much of the income. Big government outlays for social welfare are bad, but for weapons systems, they are good. Yet even in the ordered world of Orange County, there are now major intrusions of the drug traffic, hippies, campus disorders, smog. All are distinct threats to a people who want to be left alone to coast along.

The anomalies in Orange County attitudes are clear to see. The flame of resistance to taxes and big government burns bright, even though the county has exceptionally low property taxes and federal spending accounts for so much of the income. Big government outlays for social welfare are bad, but for weapons systems they are good. And curiously, along with its diet of rightists, the county sends to Congress from one district a Democratic moderate, Richard Hanna, whose personal charm seems to preserve him in the most hostile territory a Democrat could imagine.

President Nixon's selection of San Clemente (17,063) on the Orange County seacoast as the site of his western White House (and prospective retirement home) seems to be highly symbolic. After seven years as a registered voter in New York City, Nixon shifted his registration to Orange County in 1970. Nowhere in America do Nixonian politics find greater acceptance than in the overwhelmingly white, middle-class, rightward leaning precincts of Orange County. Nixon brings large numbers of his staff to San Clemente for substantial chunks of time. He makes no attempt to hide his visits there and seems almost anxious to convey the message that he no longer regards the White House as exclusively an Eastern institution and that Californians may rightly regard the Nixon compound at San Clemente as coequal to his residence at 1600 Pennsylvania Avenue.*

According to James R. Polk, a former Associated Press investigative reporter working under a grant from the Fund for Investigative Journalism, the man who set up the purchase of the San Clemente estate for Nixon—

* Report of Robert B. Semple, Jr., in the New York *Times*, Jan. 9, 1970.

with a special $1 million mortgage that can await repayment until after the President's term is over—is a little-known Newport Beach attorney, Herbert W. Kalmbach. Kalmbach, whose identity was a close-kept secret in White House politics until Polk's report in February 1972, reportedly travels as Nixon's personal agent throughout the U.S. and as far as Europe to collect campaign checks from big Republican party donors. In 1970 he helped to raise nearly $3 million in covert campaign funds for key Republican Senate candidates, under an operation directed from the White House by Presidential Assistant H.R. (Bob) Haldeman. Kalmbach is also secretary of the Nixon Foundation, created to build a Nixon Presidential library. His law firm grew dramatically after Nixon became President, adding such clients as United Air Lines, Travelers Insurance Company, the Marriott Corporation, and MCA, the giant of the entertainment industry, according to Polk's report. Shortly thereafter, Everett Holles of the New York *Times* reported that Kalmbach was a key figure in the Lincoln Club of Orange County, a group of businessmen (largely millionaires) who boast that without their broad financial support, Nixon would not have been elected President. The Lincoln Club's membership is secret, but the *Times* said it was headed by Arnold O. Beckman, founder of Beckman Instruments of Fullerton, and that its members included the President's brother, Donald Nixon of Newport Beach, actor John Wayne, and many real estate brokers, land developers, and bankers, many of them old friends of the President.

A word about the world that lies behind the 20-foot-high wall of the late Walt Disney's Magic Kingdom at Anaheim. It is all in the furtherance of fun, of course, but overwhelmingly the image of Disneyland is cleanliness and well-scrubbed Americanism. Horse dung disappears in a whisk, mules are sprayed to make them odorless and insect-repellant. Any disreputable types of visitors are turned away at the gate. There is an electronically operated figure of Abraham Lincoln that seems almost human on the Disneyland Opera House stage. The figure speaks selected passages, such as defending the spirit of liberty, but it is a bleached-out history in which nothing is said about the Civil War or slavery. It was here at Disneyland that Ronald Ziegler, later to become President Nixon's youthful press secretary, got his start as a tour guide. ("Welcome aboard, folks, my name is Ron and I'll be your skipper and guide down the rivers of adventure. . . . Note the alligators. Please keep your hands inside the boat. They're always looking for a handout.") Not until 1968 did Disneyland hire its first Negroes in such "people contact" jobs.

Whatever its social implications, Disneyland has been a fantastic financial success, easily overshadowing the once-dominant Disney film operations, which have prospered ever since the founder introduced Mickey Mouse to the world in 1928. The investment at Disneyland has grown from $17 million to $126 million, and the parent company moved from $11.6 million gross in 1954 to $176 million in 1971. The profits would have been even greater if Disney had had the money in the early 1950s to buy up enough perimeter land to avoid development of what he later called a "second-rate" Las Vegas-type strip of motels and bars, mostly along adjacent Harbor Boulevard.

Disneyland could scarcely be anything but the event of the century for the host city of Anaheim. In 1950, the city had 14,556 people; by 1970 166,701. In the first decade of Disneyland, it generated some $560 million in local business, not to mention millions paid in taxes. At the same time, the city attracted many electronic industries, built an $8.5 million convention center across the street from Disneyland, got a big league baseball park (for the American League Angels), and revived its declining "downtown" with a $300 million development of apartments, theaters, medical offices, and a commercial center virtually superimposed on the old core. Local writers described Anaheim as Orange County's "Cinderella City" and speculated on what could ever make the bubble burst.

While Anaheim boomed, the county's long-time leading city, Santa Ana, increased a mere 239 percent in population. By the late '60s, it was suffering from severe growing pains. Despite studies showing Santa Ana would need more than $100 million to meet sewer, park, and other capital improvement needs through 1980, its voters (egged on by Hoiles's newspaper) rejected $25 million in bond issues to finance the first five years' improvements. With a great wrench of their conservative consciences, civic leaders were just beginning in 1970 to accept their first aid funds from the federal government.

The great city in Orange County's future scarcely exists yet. It is Irvine, a projected metropolis of 430,000 people on the vast expanses of the greatest piece of undeveloped urban land in America, the Irvine Ranch. The story of the Irish immigrant James Irvine, I, and the four generations that followed him, the last in open rebellion against a foundation that now controls the ranch, is quintessentially American—of the self-made founder and the first great acquisitions (once totaling 110,000 acres), sheep-herding, fighting off the Southern Pacific Railroad crews at gunpoint, irrigated farming over great swaths of land, commercial reversals, the unhappy and morose later years of James Irvine, II, before his death in 1947, the takeover by the charitable foundation he created (headed by his former accountant), and the spunky, headstrong fight of young Joan Irvine Smith, last of the famous line, to take control of the ranch away from the foundation. An enigmatic, strikingly beautiful, thrice-divorced woman now in her late 30s, Mrs. Smith used her 21.1 percent interest in the company to become the only family member on its board of directors in the late 1950s. Since then, she has fought bitterly in the board room, the courtroom, and the legislature to wrest total control away from the foundation—whose officers she accuses of deliberate mismanagement of the company and conflicts of interest. Partly through her pressures, the company has indeed moved forward to develop the great 100-square-mile ranch, covering some fifth of Orange county. And in 1969 Congress passed legislation which may eventually force the foundation to divest itself of control of the Irvine Company.

As in so many stories Californian, the University of California plays a key role in the modern Irvine story. Master planner-architect William Pereira of Los Angeles, commissioned by the UC board of regents to find a new campus site in the South L.A. County–Orange County area, settled on Irvine as the best possibility. With what must have been masterful tact, he won over the members of the board of the Irvine Company to the idea of donating 1,000 acres to the University of California. As Pereira planned UC Irvine, it would be the focal point for a European-style university community of 100,-000 people living on 10,000 acres of that part of the ranch. University and town government would be closely tied together.

In time, the Irvine Company officials took over more and more of their own planning and decided they ought to have not just another city of some 100,000, but a great metropolis that would dominate Orange County. It would stretch across 82 square miles, the full 53,000-acre central valley of the ranch. Within the city, there would be 40 residential villages, 33 miles of aesthetically landscaped "environmental corridors," recreation facilities, and carefully planned commercial and industrial centers. By the year 2000, it would have a population of 430,000. By the start of the 1970s, in fact, the first glistening high-rise structures had gone up at Irvine's Newport Center, the office towers providing an instant landmark for motorists driving along the coastal highways and even ships at sea.

Not everyone was delighted by the shape of the new plan. Writing in the Los Angeles *Times* in 1970, writer David Shaw said there was a question whether Irvine would become a true "new town" free of congestion and socially integrated, or whether it might "be just a mammoth subdivision"—or, in the words of one USC critic, "a white, upper-middle-class, sterile, suburban ghetto." * Comparing Irvine to new-town developments like Reston in Virginia and Columbia in Maryland, Shaw said the Irvine plan showed none of the other developments' social innovation—single religious buildings in each village to promote ecumenicism, voluntary citywide health insurance, small and responsive governmental units, intervillage minibuses, racial integration, and allowance for low- and moderate-income housing. He quoted a UC Irvine professor as saying: "They've got everything going for them. They own the land outright. They're in the middle of the fastest growing county in the country. They have ideal weather, proximity to prime relaxation facilities, freeway access from all sides. But where Columbia was meant to be socially and spiritually stimulating and Reston was meant to be socially and architecturally stimulating, Irvine is meant only to be profitable."

The compromise in values is already appearing. While many of the first housing developments at Irvine allowed a felicitous treatment of the land,

* Santa Ana is already developing its own shabby and forlorn racial ghettos with 66 percent of Orange County's 10,000 Negroes and many of its Mexican-Americans. City Manager Carl Thornton fears that unless Irvine developers can be persuaded to include substantial amounts of low-income housing in their plans, "our city will look like downtown Kansas City, downtown Detroit." Santa Ana tried, without success, to annex 938 acres of the new city of Irvine. To prevent annexation, the city of Irvine in December 1971 voted to incorporate itself.

with wide-open spaces, more recent developments have a density pattern reminiscent of the worst slurbs. It is not only the profit motive, but fear of the market, that may hold the Irvine planners back from a socially imaginative community. In short, as writer Shaw himself asked, is there a large enough "liberal" market in conservative California? The cosmopolitan, liberal atmosphere of new cities like Reston (Virginia) and Columbia (Maryland) is almost tangible. A similar "liberal" market, only four or five times larger, might be hard to find in Southern California—or at least so the planners of Irvine say. One looks at the temper of the California university generation of today and wonders whether the planners are not planning for an already mature generation, not the one that will be occupying their new community as it is completed over 50 years. But one thing is sure: Irvine, as it is now being planned, will fit right in with the rest of Orange County.

## San Diego: City of Promise

Gunther wrote well of San Diego as "a shining plaque of a city, built around a great park with glorious views of hill and harbor." Here, at the southwestern extremity of the continental U.S.A., we come on one of the world's great natural harbors, set off by shining hills and mesas, and, in winter, snow-capped mountains. Seaward lies the steep-sided, wind-swept promontory of Point Loma, that last point of land for the hundreds of thousands of sailors who have ridden out and back with the fleets for more than a century now.

San Diego's role in California history was vital, for it was on a parched, sun-bleached hill overlooking her harbor that Father Junípero Serra stood in 1769 to proclaim the founding of the first permanent Christian settlement of California. Through the mission years, Mexican rule and the American ascendancy, little changed; the city's age-old rival, Los Angeles, started ahead and stayed ahead in population and wealth and power. Set at a far extremity of the state, with mountains to block off transcontinental travel, San Diego had little but tourism plus the growing commerce generated by the Navy (a constant caller since 1846).

The pace quickened with World War I, the coming of the early aviation companies (Convair and Ryan Aeronautical) in the '20s and '30s, and finally, with the onset of World War II, America's first great Pacific conflict. The Navy-dominated "Dago" of the war years was prosperous but incredibly crowded; suddenly San Diego found itself in a boom-and-bust cycle not yet broken. A postwar dip was followed by salad days for the big aircraft and missile builders (Convair, Rohr, Ryan Aeronautical) in the 1950s, then a cruel recession in the early '60s, strong recovery in mid-decade, and finally, around 1970, a new but not so serious recession. The experience has made San Diego determined to break free of its stepchild relationship to the Navy and Pentagon contractors, and in fact its widened economic base—in tourism, research, and educational complexes—has carried it far beyond its old dependency status.

Once San Diego was literally the end of the line; now it is a gateway, seeking direct air connections to Hawaii and beyond, pressing into new areas of scientific exploration. On America's Pacific coast, only two cities are larger—Los Angeles and San Francisco. In 1970, the Census takers found 1,357,854 people in San Diego County, 696,769 in the city itself. The area total was more than four times what it had been just before Pearl Harbor.

The road to economic diversification was not easily found, and only sought after some hard knocks. Despite a big postwar housing push, the only thing that really saved San Diego from the ravishes of peace was the Cold War. Convair (now a subsidiary of General Dynamics) was then locally owned and progressive and eventually built a forerunner of the Atlas missile along with many fighter planes. But near-disaster struck in the early 1960s, after a merger with General Dynamics, when its 880 and 990 commercial jets failed to score significant sales with the airlines. The Convair work force plummeted from 22,000 to 6,000 as hordes of "tinbenders" —semiskilled aircraft assembly workers—were laid off. For the company, the news was just as grim—loss of a cool $1 billion, according to reliable reports, the largest single corporate loss in history, at least until Lockheed's facilities of the early 1970s.

San Diego's city fathers were determined the same would never happen to them again, and they began to work through their newly formed San Diego Economic Development Corporation to prevent a recurrence. More tourists were attracted through a promotion program based on a 4-percent hotel room tax. A community center for downtown San Diego, to include an income-generating convention center, had been turned down by the voters in five referendums. But Thomas W. Fletcher, then city manager (he later served as deputy mayor of Washington, D.C.) conceived the brilliant idea of borrowing the money from the city employees' retirement fund and giving them a mortgage on the buildings. EDC guaranteed the first funds. It worked, and a concourse with five buildings went up: a splendidly designed civic theater, a government office high-rise, the convention center, and a parking garage. All this sparked a private building boom in downtown San Diego, adding some 16 major high-rise buildings by 1970.

In addition, creation of some 16 industrial parks and the arrival of 150 new manufacturers brought a dramatic expansion of the economy, almost all in the nondefense sector. Between 1964 and 1968, total employment rose 38 percent to 433,000, but the number of workers directly involved in aircraft and missile production edged up only 4.8 percent. A decade before, three out of every four manufacturing employees had been making aircraft and missiles; by the late 1960s, the figure was two out of four. Thus when the national recession and defense cutbacks of the late '60s came, they hurt San Diego but not fatally. Along with Convair, the other big aerospace firms were Rohr Corporation (manufacturers, among other things, of the transit cars for the Bay Area Transit in San Francisco), Solar division of International Harvester, and Ryan Aeronautical Company, a subsidiary of Teledyne Inc. It was Ryan who helped put San Diego on the map between the wars by building Charles Lindbergh's *Spirit of St. Louis.*

Headquarters of the Eleventh Naval District, San Diego ranks with Norfolk as one of the two biggest Navy cities in the U.S.A. One out of four San Diegoans works for the Navy or Marines as serviceman or civilian employee or is a military dependent. Ironically, after San Diego gave a military-minded Californian native, Richard Nixon, 59 percent of its vote in 1968, there were severe military cutbacks that had a domino-like effect on the area's economy. Nevertheless, the Navy and Marine Corps still spend about $1 billion a year in the San Diego vicinity, including outlays for the Navy and the Marines at nearby Camp Pendleton, civilian payrolls, retired service pay, and school "impact" funds. Real peace in Asia, of course, would be bad for San Diego. The town has been the embarkation point for most of the Navy's ships and Marine troops en route to Vietnam. When not working in aerospace factories or tending the military, San Diegoans have three basic sources of income—agriculture, science, and tourism. The least of these is agriculture, but there is still major activity in the growing of citrus trees, avocados, and even flowers not too far from the city.

Science is everywhere, from Scripps Pier to Palomar Mountain, the fulfillment of a prophecy made by a city official about a decade ago: "Rosie the Riveter is leaving town but Sammy the Scientist is coming in." San Diego is becoming a national center in oceanography, a development perhaps preordained by the founding, in 1912, of the Scripps Institution of Oceanography at La Jolla. Now more than 80 companies, military units and universities in the area are in oceanographic research ranging from potential fishery sources and developing underwater instruments to sea-floor topography and possible exploitation of its natural resources. The Scripps Institution has been involved with the National Science Foundation's Deep Sea Drilling Project. Also in the area are the Salk Institute (headed by Dr. Jonas E. Salk, who developed the vaccine for poliomyelitis), Lockheed's oceanographic facility, Gulf General Atomic and Western Behavioral Sciences Institute. Not to be overlooked is the big business of higher education—perhaps worth $100 million annually to the San Diego economy. More than 70,000 students are enrolled at local colleges and universities, including the University of California at San Diego, San Diego State College, United States International University (formerly Cal Western), the University of San Diego, and a variety of junior colleges. Since the moment of its inception, stemming from 1968 campus agitation in which Angela Davis played a prominent role, controversy has swirled around UC San Diego's "Third World" campus, a semiautonomous institution set up to give Negro and Mexican-American students a special break. Conservatives are up in arms about the revolutionary flavor of campus rhetoric while academic traditionalists are alarmed that the Third World experiment, giving students a major role in faculty selection and accepting students unprepared for UC-level work, will result in a fatal lowering of academic standards.

In 1971 San Diego became the surprise choice as the site of the 1972 Republican National Convention—apparently because President Nixon found it so congenial and convenient to his digs at San Clemente. The city had initially declined to bid for the convention because of a lack of necessary facilities, but after the Presidential word was passed, the city fathers assembled a $1.5 million bid in cash, goods, and services. The biggest chunk of this was a $400,000 pledge, which originated with the Sheraton hotel chain, a subsidiary of International Telephone and Telegraph. Columnist Jack Anderson and others later charged there was a direct link between the $400,000 bid and the Justice Department's favorable settlement of antitrust suits against ITT—an allegation heatedly denied by the administration, but one which delayed Senate confirmation of Richard Kleindienst, who had allegedly played a role in the ITT case disposition, as Attorney General. But a lack of needed convention facilities in San Diego, plus embarrassment over the ITT case, prompted the Republicans to move in late spring 1972 toward shifting their convention to Miami Beach, Florida.

Irrespective of GOP convention politics, San Diego is an old hand at accommodating visitors; in fact it welcomes tens of thousands of visitors each day, who spend some $400 million a year. The tourist tradition goes back to highly successful expositions in 1915–16 and 1935–36, and one can see their physical legacy in 1,400-acre Balboa Park, which houses theaters, galleries, and museums. Neil Morgan, the Western writer who makes his home in La Jolla and writes for the San Diego *Evening Tribune*, notes that while competitive San Diegoans of past decades "glowered while Los Angeles became a runaway megalopolis," it is now apparent that San Diego's failure to burgeon like L.A. was a blessing. "Lacking crowding and smog and the other badges of industrial triumph, San Diego has become the playground for Los Angeles' millions, a kind of weekend patio for the Southwest."

The listing of San Diego's tourist attractions can all too easily descend into travelogue. But, in truth, the county does have 70 miles of public beaches, sport fishing and sailing, Palomar Observatory, 65 golf courses, the Light House and Cabrillo monument on Point Loma, and historic missions including California's first, San Diego de Alcala. (Of the mission, a sad story must be told: A freeway constructed in the 1960s makes it almost impossible to reach without special instructions or a guide; officials refused to put in a special exit ramp because a sports stadium is close by.)

Balboa Park is home of the celebrated San Diego Zoo—128 acres with 5,000 specimens, the largest collection of mammals, birds, and reptiles in the world. The climate is so temperate (summer average 67 degrees, winter 55) that most of the animals can be kept outside all year, living in natural-style enclosures. I am particularly fond of the children's section, where youngsters can actually pet and sometimes play with tortoises, fawns, lambs, or exotic animals. It is perhaps the most *natural* experience for children anyone in Southern California has devised.

Just as unique is the city-financed Mission Bay development, just north of the ridgeline of Point Loma. Up to the 1940s, Mission Bay was a gassy, odoriferous tidal mud flat that had lain dormant ever since early explorers bogged down there and named it False Bay. Engineers then made plans to turn the swamp into an aquatic wonderland of peninsulas, islands, roomy channels, and spacious bays. With some $60 million—most of it from the city—the work went forward, involving the moving of more than 27 million cubic yards of bay materials. Today Mission Bay has its own resort hotels and restaurants, marinas, picnic grounds, golf courses, campgrounds, police force, and an exceptionally good oceanarium (Sea World). Various sorts of water activity are carefully zoned, so that sailing, powerboat racing, swimming, waterskiing, and fishing can all go on simultaneously and safely. Mission Bay is simply the most dramatic, all-at-once evidence of the fantastic boom in small water craft which has gripped California (and virtually all U.S. coastal and lake areas) since World War II.

San Diego has also become a major sports center with its 50,000-seat stadium (with American Football League and National League baseball teams). But in terms of drawing tourists, Mexico and its border city of Tijuana (just a 15-minute freeway ride from central San Diego) may be an even greater attraction. Some 12 million *Americanos* visit Tijuana each year, well described as "a wide-open city, dirty and unattractive to many visitors, that offers every sensual indulgence so far conceived by man." But it is Mexico, and does have pockets of interest and charm.

Tijuana's residents and Mexicans from farther down the dusty stretches of Baja California spend almost $100 million a year shopping at San Diego. About 5,000 Tijuanans commute daily to work in the United States. Altogether, some 500,000 Mexicans live in the San Diego-Tijuana area. Their goings back and forth, combined with those of the American tourists, make it small wonder that the illicit drug traffic is growing by leaps and bounds.

San Diego Bay is a sparkling crescent some 15 miles long and a quarter to two and a half miles wide. On a weekend the bay waters flash a thousand white sails and the white wakes of countless powerboats; on the beaches opposite the Naval Station there are swimmers and water-skiers, and fishermen line the sea-walls of the harbor. All this might not be, however, if San Diego's people had not voted in 1960 to indebt themselves for $42.5 million to build a sewage treatment and offshore dispersal system to save the bay from encroaching pollution. Each day, some 60 million gallons of inadequately treated sewage from San Diego and its suburbs were flowing into the bay, plus millions more from Coronado, the Naval Amphibious Base, and local canneries and commercial ships. From its primeval blue, the bay had turned to a brownish-reddish cast, imparted by the proliferation and death of phytoplankton. Along one harbor stretch in the central city, solids had formed a sludge mat along the bay floor 900 yards long. Threatening health, high densities of coliform bacteria were noted. Several beaches were quarantined.

An earlier bond issue for treatment and dispersal of sewage had been rejected by the San Diego voters in 1953, but by 1960 the problem was so egregious that overwhelming approval went to the proposal for a monstrous set of interceptors, carrying the sewage to a plant on the seaward side of Point Loma. There it would be treated and then conveyed more than two miles out under the ocean by two Y-shaped diffuser legs. Construction started in 1961, and was finished in 1965 at a final cost of about $60 million. And then, as if there had been a series of great tidal flushings, the bay quickly cleared, and what had been brown and red became blue and sparkling. Back into the bay swarmed the sea-life it had once known—sculpin, sole, sand bass, steelhead trout, silver salmon, bonefish, baracuda, octopus, shark, seal, and porpoise. The sludge beds began to shrink and the coliform density dropped, permitting reopening of the beaches. With the possible exception of Seattle's Lake Washington, it is difficult to think of a more dramatic victory of an American city in the battle against water pollution.

Another new thing in San Diego Bay is the blue arc thrown against the sky by the superstructure of the Coronado Bridge, completed in 1969 to make a linkage (previously possible only by ferry) between San Diego and the sleepy little city of Coronado. A town long famous for its great, lumbering, white Victorian wonder, the Hotel del Coronado, Coronado is populated by many of the retired Navy brass who give San Diego County its distinctively conservative political coloration.

Lack of early and sound city planning has been San Diego's most serious failure and poses the gravest threat to its future. The city's central growth has turned its back on the magnificent harbor; once-beautiful Harbor Drive has become a heavily traveled airport service road (the airport is set down squarely in an anachronistic center-city location with jets swooping past the high-rises); haphazard commercial development was permitted in Mission Valley; the community of Lemon Grove was allowed to cut down *all* its lemon trees and to put up a huge and atrocious looking concrete lemon at its entrance. The metropolitan concentrate now sprawls 15 miles south of Broadway to the Mexican border and 20 miles north, past wealthy La Jolla on its lovely hill beside the sea, towards Orange County. San Diego's closer-in suburbia, architect Richard Neutra wrote, "is blighted by a kind of elephantiasis." Blacks and Mexican-Americans generally fail to share the middle-class affluence, and the Mexican-American ghetto community of San Ysidro is a forgotten pocket of misery that relates about as well to greater San Diego as Anacostia does to metropolitan Washington, D.C.

Yet there is so much positive—the harbor, parks, and fine colleges and universities; the wonderful climate; the canyons that separate the metropolis into relatively distinct communities on a very human scale. In contrast to most American metropolises, San Diego is less hurried, angry, or intense; though part of Southern California, it blessedly lacks Los Angeles' bedlam and the igloo-shaped ice cream palace culture. The city is still young and malleable, and may well mature into one of America's finest in times to come. What it needs in physical terms, according to Dr. Harry Antoiniades Anthony, a professor of urban planning at Columbia University, is rapid transit to stem the auto blight and a regional plan that will preserve the open spaces between communities "for the pleasures of the eye and the spirit." The county government, once drowsy and rural-oriented, has perked up in recent years and sponsored numerous planning studies. Out of one of these grew a multimillion-dollar open spaces program, voted by the people in 1970. Also approved was a bond issue to acquire a wilderness area near Escondido where the San Diego Zoo plans a vast enclosure in which wild animals can roam free.

Virtually every researcher into the city's power structure has concluded that influence is exerted primarily through the business-financial community, not through the politicians. (The development of powerful political machines nourished by patronage is stymied because of the nonpartisan nature of local politics.) The two businessmen long considered most powerful in San Diego have been C. Arnholt Smith, who controls the U.S. National Bank of San Diego, and John Alessio, a big race-track developer and sometimes associate of Smith. Smith's holdings, many through his own mini-conglomerate (West-gate-California Corp.) include insurance companies, two small airlines, taxi-cab, bus and limousine services, ranches, food processors, a luxury hotel, and the Padres baseball team. According to the New York *Times*, Smith in 1968 raised more than $1 million for the Nixon-Agnew ticket, including $250,000 of his own money; on election night he joined Nixon in the latter's hotel suite to watch the returns come in. One of his employees is chairman of the county Republican committee; the *Wall Street Journal* estimates his wealth from multitudinous business undertakings at more than $20 million. Alessio, likewise a big GOP contributor (to the Nixon-Agnew 1968 campaign in the tens of thousands, for instance), has race-track interests in Mexico, with an inevitable gambling tie-in through his Mexican operations. Early in 1970, the federal government indicted him for evading income tax payments over several years. He entered a plea of guilty and began a three-year prison sentence in 1971. But it was later reported that he enjoyed unusual privileges in a minimum-security federal prison, including "nights off" to conduct personal business and meet women friends in a motel.

In 1970, San Diego was shaken by a series of indictments against eight local officials—including Mayor Frank Curran—on bribery and conspiracy charges surrounding a fare increase for the Yellow Cab Company, which enjoys a near-monopoly position in the city. All but one of the men were exonerated, but the trials left lingering public suspicions about political corruption. Then, in March 1972, investigative reporters Denny Walsh and Tom Flaherty of *Life* magazine revealed there had been much more to it all than met the eye:

The Nixon administration has seriously tampered with justice in the city of San Diego. In an effort to protect certain of its most important friends there from criminal prosecution, the administration has in several instances taken steps to neutralize and frustrate its own law enforcement officials. . . .

An investigation by *Life* has revealed that:

(1) In 1970 a federal organized crime strike force in Southern California was

putting together a case against several San Diegans, including C. Arnholt Smith, for conspiring to violate federal tax law and the Corrupt Practices Act. . . . The investigation was squelched, largely through the United States attorney for the Southern District of California, Harry Steward, a man Nixon had appointed on Smith's recommendation. . . .

(2) A company controlled by Smith . . . was conduit for the expenses of political candidates, and Nixon's 1968 campaign [was] a beneficiary of this. Again investigation was shut off through the administration's U. S. attorney. . . .

(3) When San Diego's Democratic mayor, Frank Curran, was indicted in 1970 for taking a bribe from the president of the San Diego Yellow Cab Company to help raise taxi fares, the administration refused to let a federal investigator—a key witness—testify for the prosecution. Until shortly before the fare increase, Smith had been a part owner of the cab company. . . .

*Life* also charged that White House officials had sought to frustrate the tax fraud indictment of John Alessio, and might well have succeeded without the "timely intercession" of FBI Director J. Edgar Hoover.

Curran was decisively defeated when he ran again for mayor in 1971; his successor was Pete Wilson, 38, an attractive three-term state assemblyman who had distinguished himself in pressing for environmental protection legislation and chairing the legislature's first committee devoted to housing and urban affairs. The youth and reform theme was carried a step further when the voters elected Maureen O'Connor, a 25-year-old high school physical education teacher, to the city council. Miss O'Connor, whose interest in government had been activated when she couldn't get anyone in City Hall to respond when she lodged a complaint about the treatment and pay of some of her Mexican friends, said she owed her victory to the young persons who campaigned and voted for her.

Except for Dallas, San Diego is the largest city of the U.S.A. which retains the city manager form of government; some believe that power brokers like Smith and Alessio prefer having a single powerful city official to deal with. But there has never been a suggestion of impropriety in the manager's office, as there has been with the mayor, the council, and the police. An especially outstanding manager was Thomas Fletcher (1961–66), who pioneered in the creation of neighborhood planning councils to give citizens a maximum voice in their government. Fletcher also helped San Diego avoid the hang-ups of neighboring Orange County cities about accepting federal urban assistance grants.

Well-to-do Republicanism, aided and abetted by the predictably military orientation of those who sup at the Navy-aerospace table, makes San Diego County a disaster area for most Democratic candidates. The prevailing Republican conservatism and militarism of San Diego is reflected and relentlessly reinforced by the San Diego *Union*, the "flagship" of James S. Copley's string of 29 California and Illinois newspapers (including the Sacramento *Union* and the evening San Diego *Tribune*). The loyalties of the San Diego *Union* are amply illustrated by some of its chief executives. Editor Herb Klein regularly took time off from his job in San Diego to handle Richard Nixon's press relations in various campaigns of the 1950s and '60s, finally getting his reward as communications director in the Nixon Presidential Administration. In 1968, the *Union* chose as its editorial and news director retired Lt. Gen. Victor Krulak, a peppery ex-Marine officer (nickname: Brute) who quit the service after heading the corps in Vietnam and being passed over for commandant; it was Krulak's first newspaper job. James Copley himself is a former Navy captain; and the head of his Washington bureau is a retired admiral. "Hawkish" in the extreme, the *Union* is also strong for fiscal conservatism, hostile to students and dissent, and predictably Republican. But its election coverage is now fairer than it was in 1960, when it ran heads like this: "Election of Sen. Kennedy Would Please Russians."

In 1970, the *Union* found itself under fire within its own journalistic profession. *Newsweek* ran a bitterly critical (though not wholly accurate) attack, followed up by a full-scale critique by the liberal, muckraking *San Diego Magazine*. The *Union-Tribune* zapped back with a full-scale defense of its policies and professionalism, but the critics' message about the paper's distorted coverage and tedious moralizing was likely to be remembered.

Neither television nor outside newspaper competition provide any real alternative or counterforce to the *Union* in its home town; an underground newspaper, the *Street Journal*, has mounted blistering attacks on the ethics of the power machinations of Copley, Arnholt Smith, and the entire San Diego establishment, but its readership is not wide and its journalistic standards open to question. San Diego moderates dream of the day the *Union* may go centrist, just as the Los Angeles *Times*—not dissimilar from the *Union* until the late 1950s—has done. And in fact, the "new" L. A. *Times* has been besieged with requests to set up a satellite edition in San Diego.

## Santa Barbara: Trouble in Eden

Our tour of Southern California now ends with gardened Santa Barbara, 100 miles up the coast from Los Angeles, a city set in a crescent-shaped valley between the honey-colored Santa Ynez Mountains and the Pacific. Santa Barbara is so imbued with quiet gentility and tradition that its real soul sister is San Francisco, not the flashy new urban creations of the Southland. No California city is so close, in architecture and life style, to the ancient Spanish. Here is the Queen of the Missions, where the altar candle flame the Padres lighted in 1786 has never been snuffed out.

Nor is there any California city so Eastern; as the social historian Cleveland Amory noted, Santa Barbara is the Western front of the Eastern establishment. The Los Angeles *Times* commented in a review not long ago: "Color it Boston, little Back Bay West with blooming begonias, a New England style blueblood community with two social registers, a court house which looks like a Moorish palace and the third oldest polo playing club in America." The polo is symptomatic of the proper Santa Barbaran's favorite sport—

horsemanship; even more than yachting, the chosen pastime is riding over the brown, rolling hills which sweep to canyon crests over the surf.

Mr. Santa Barbara of the 20th century was Thomas M. Storke, who became editor and publisher of the Santa Barbara *News-Press* in 1901; prior to his death at the age of 94 in 1971, he was the oldest native among Santa Barbara's 70,215 people * and still the city's guiding spirit. Wearer of a vest and a Dakota sombrero, Storke was a direct descendant of José Francisco Ortego, the Spaniard who founded Santa Barbara. Over a long and illustrious lifetime, he was a college classmate of Herbert Hoover at Stanford, a U.S. Senator, a delegate to five national political conventions, a winner of the Pulitzer Prize, and a major benefactor of the University of California at Santa Barbara. A staunch Democrat and liberal in a wealthy and Republican town, Storke helped it advance in the arts and also become a place for the free exchange of ideas—symbolized by the Center for the Study of Democratic Institutions, which he helped attract to the city. I well remember a 1961 interview with Storke in which he brought to my attention, for the first time, the inanities in Birch Society founder Robert Welch's *Blue Book*.

The Center for the Study of Democratic Institutions is quite a different proposition from California's other "think tanks." What happens at the center's Grecian mansion on a hill overlooking Santa Barbara is basically the process of dialogue between noted scholars on pressing issues of the day; the idea is not to produce hard recommendations for change in public policy as much as to educate and influence. As founder Robert M. Hutchins has put it, "We seek only the truth." Criticism of the center has come from right-wingers who see a Communist plot behind the project and alternatively from moderates and other liberals who doubt the relevance or practicality of the center's issue studies.

The most cataclysmic event in Santa Barbara's modern-day history occurred on January 28, 1969. Workmen on Union Oil's "Platform A," drilling for oil six miles off the Santa Barbara shore, cut a hole into a high-pressure deposit of oil and gas. The huge oil bubble boiled up to the surface of the channel at the rate of almost 1,000 gallons an hour, spreading across the blue water for 11 days. Finally, 400 square miles of the ocean were affected and 40 miles of beach front covered with acrid, tarlike slime. Birds diving through the oily swells for fish failed to surface alive. Along the mucky shoreline, thousands more birds lay dying, unable to raise their oil-soaked wings. Oil which had been emulsified by the surf sank to the bottom to kill lobsters, mussels, clams, and some fish.

For Santa Barbara, it was like a horrible dream come true. There had been strong local resistance in 1968 when the U. S. Interior Department auctioned off nearly 600 square miles of channel leases for $603 million—a decision then-Interior Secretary Stewart Udall would later call his own "Bay of Pigs." The city had every reason to be unenthusiastic. Drilling activity brings

* 1970 Census figure for the city alone; including all of Santa Barbara County, the figure was 264,324.

little money into a community, and even without accidents, Santa Barbara's azure channel view is marred by the unsightly drilling platforms and the attendant bustle of oil activities along the waterfront. For most cities, a nearby oil spill would be a scandal; for Santa Barbara, living basically off tourism, it can be a near disaster. Within a year of the 1969 spill, the city's tourist business fell off seriously. Smaller leaks followed, and the channel remained geologically unstable. As drilling continued, the danger of newer and possibly even worse oil spills remained.

The oil industry considers the risks well worth taking. The Santa Barbara Channel happens to cover one of the world's richest oil fields, right beside the world's biggest market for oil—auto-happy Southern California. The loss of some birds and sealife, oilmen maintain, is a small price to pay for the oil that human "progress" demands; anyway, there have been small normal oil "leaks" in the strata near Santa Barbara for as long as the white man can remember. One study of the 1969 blowout showed remarkably little long-term damage.

Santa Barbara citizens see it differently; in fact they are almost unanimous in wanting all oil drilling stopped (a step the federal government refuses to take). Immediately after the big blowout, a community organization called "GOO"—standing for Get Oil Out!—sprang into being. The issue, in fact, "radicalized" a wealthy and conservative community with amazing rapidity. Two years after the big blowout at Santa Barbara, despite temporary suspensions of drilling and heated protests by Californians in Congress, the oil activity at Santa Barbara was still going ahead at the rate of more than 30 million barrels (value $100 million) a year. But the environmentalists took heart from the legislative proposal of President Nixon to buy back 35 of the 70 existing leaseholds to establish a marine sanctuary and from Interior Secretary Rogers Morton's denial of permits for two new oil drilling platforms for "overriding environmental considerations."

An account of the Santa Barbara scene written before 1970 could easily have brushed off the University of California branch there. The school's image, in the words of one writer, was "that of the fun-loving school where blond, sun-tanned youths romped on surfboards and at fraternity parties." Yet suddenly, California and the nation were hearing that these "golden" California youth were engaged in massive rioting and had actually *burned a bank*. These were not the offspring of liberal, intellectual families like those at Berkeley or Madison or Columbia; they were predominately products of conservative, business-oriented homes. How could disorders happen *here*? *

The physical setting and a diabolically unfortunate chain of events appeared to be responsible. The UCSB branch is outside the city of Santa Barbara, separated by 10 miles of airport, swamp, and freeway. And where the students mostly live is not the campus, but the adjoining, unincorporated area of Isla Vista, a mile-square community built for the sole purpose of housing students. Isla Vista, in fact, is a ghetto, set in total isolation, suffering

* Some details of this account are drawn from excellent accounts by UCSB sociologists Richard Flacks and Milton Mankoff in *The Nation* and Leroy F. Aarons in the Washington *Post*.

from constant harassment by the police, afflicted by minimal municipal services, crowded and cheap housing, high rents, and the like. With students thus isolated from the outside world, the conditions were perfect for creation of an alien youth culture—of rock music, widely available drugs (marijuana usage estimated at well over 50 percent), extravagant hippie dress and hairdos, and sex both free and frequent.

Alienation alone, though, does not lead to bank-burning. Within a very few months, these other things happened: the oil spill in the channel, imperiling the students' beaches, followed by much rhetoric but no corrective action from Sacramento or Washington; formation of a radical union which briefly took over the university center; the continuing Vietnam war and President Nixon's disdain for moratorium demonstrations; the draft lottery, highly advertised, but turning out not to be "safe" for anyone anyway; new movies like *Easy Rider* and *Alice's Restaurant*, which reinforced the basic lessons of insecurity and impotence; and finally the early 1970 dismissal by UCSB of Professor William Allen, an unorthodox but popular anthropology teacher. A protest against Allen's firing was signed by 7,776 students (well over a majority), but totally ignored by the university. Then came massive but peaceful student demonstrations over the issue; they likewise were ignored by the university. Instead, university officials called in the police, questionable raids were staged, and the groundwork was set for violence. Police harassment got increasingly worse, students one night beat up a policeman, Chicago Seven lawyer William Kunstler came to speak, police unjustifiably attacked a youth carrying a bottle of wine—and a night of rampage had begun, during which the Isla Vista branch of the Bank of America was burned to the ground.

The students who participated that night later gave such reasons as: "To teach the police that they cannot keep harassing us at will"; "to force the university authority and politicians to recognize us"; "to force people to think about the system." As for the attack on the Bank of America, some students criticized it for making loans to war industries and working through a dummy farm corporation that refused to deal with César Chávez's union. But perhaps most enlightening were these words of a nonrioter, Cecile Currier, from a wealthy Los Angeles suburb, who was "radicalized" by the Bill Allen incident:

It's made me a lot more aware of how interwined the power structure is—the university, the police, politics. At one time we had 5,000 students demanding an open hearing. It wasn't even something illegal, and the 5,000 students meant absolutely nothing. It made me realize how insane people are. You can march publicly and write letters and nothing happens.

Even the bank-burning failed to burn out the passions; in the next weeks came more riots, constant clashes with the police, the accidental killing of a student by a stray bullet from a policeman's gun, and then, in June 1970, one of the most frightening police rampages of modern times, in which officers kicked down apartment doors, dragged students out of bedrooms and bathrooms, menacing, gassing, and clubbing, and arresting hundreds. It was the police's way to "teach the kids a lesson." Perhaps they remembered what Governor Reagan had said earlier in the spring about campus violence: "If it takes a bloodbath, let's get it over with. No more appeasement."

Incredibly, this was happening in progressive and tolerant California, land of golden opportunity, and within the greatest state university of America. Showing a frightful lack of originality, violence-prone agitators attacked the 990 California branches of the Bank of America some 39 times in the 15 months after the Santa Barbara incident, 22 times with explosive devices and 17 times with fire bombs or other forms of arson.

But violence was not to have the last word at Isla Vista. The bank-burning, as Norman Cousins reported in the *Saturday Review* in June 1971, had the effect of undermining the influence of extremist student factions and bringing to the fore a new type of student activist—"intellectually sophisticated, politically adroit, less concerned with ideological sloganeering than with the dynamics of change." Out of regular student fees, these new activists were able to launch a food cooperative where students can buy meat and groceries (some organically grown); a credit union; a legal assistance office for students; a unit providing psychiatric, drug, and contraceptive services; and a facility akin to the Travelers Aid Society, to assist itinerant, homeless young "floaters." Most of these activities were run out of a Service Center made possible in part by a $25,000 contribution from none other than Louis B. Lundborg, chairman of the board of the Bank of America. Lundborg decided after the Santa Barbara bombing that even while violence was to be condemned, it mirrored wells of deep-lying discontent with the Vietnam war and other practices of society, and that "a new value system" was coming to the country, starting with its youth, which the older generation would ignore at its peril. Lundborg's leadership and the emergence of a more mature and self-confident group of student leaders helped open new avenues of communication between the community and campus at Isla Vista. As a result of a special commission's report, the university itself was working to improve student conditions and effect local police reforms.

The 1970-71 academic year witnessed another amazing event: a decision by the Student Body Residents Council to hire a lobbyist to represent student views in Sacramento—on issues of students' rights, but also low-cost housing, equal opportunity for women, minority rights, and environmental protection. After a spirited debate, the regents approved the new lobbying—in large part because several members (including Norton Simon and Lt. Gov. Reinecke) had visited Isla Vista and held personal meetings with the students.

A throwback to the times of violence remains a distinct possibility in California, and probably will for years to come. But out of the valley of discord, new forms of social organization, and responsive forms of intergenerational dialogue, begin to emerge. California, where America gets the signals of what is about to happen to it, may be in trouble. But it is not dead or frozen. It yearns and grows and changes, and it may yet be our best hope.

# OREGON

## "FOR GOD'S SAKE, DON'T MOVE HERE"

MY FIRST INTERVIEW in Oregon was with Glenn L. Jackson, chairman of the board of the Pacific Power and Light Company and chairman of the state highway department, a man many believe to be the state's most influential power-broker. I had been prepared for a hard sell of Oregon's virtues and the desirability of growth and more growth. The message was quite the opposite. "In the Northwest for awhile, everyone was hell-bent for development," Jackson said. "But were we worshipping a false God at the expense of our environment? There's some of this feeling now—much more of it now, in fact."

Governor Tom McCall feels the same way. In an address to conventioneers at the Portland Hilton Hotel, he wound up his remarks this way: "Welcome to Oregon. While you're here, I want you to enjoy yourselves. Travel, visit, drink in the great beauty of our state. But for God's sake, don't move here."

One quickly learns that Governor McCall and Glenn Jackson are not alone in wanting to keep the lid on Oregon's population influx, and especially on the tourist flow from exploding California to the south. Bumper strips proclaim "Oregon for the Oregonians" or "Keep Oregon Green, Clean—and Lean." There is a whimsical group, the "James G. Blaine Society," named for reasons obscure after the losing Presidential candidate from Maine, which tries to discourage newcomers with statements like these from its president, ex-newsman Ron Abell: "You can tell when it's summer in Oregon because the rain gets warm. . . . Did you know that the state animal is the earthworm and the state bird is the mosquito?"

One of the Blaine Society's suggestions is to build no off-ramps on the freeway between California and Washington. And with good reason. Interstate 5, being opened clear from Canada to Mexico, is an open invitation to Californians, whose own recreational facilities are packed to capacity and beyond, to head north with trailers and campers for a quick, cheap vacation. Nine or 10 million tourists come to Oregon each year now, most of them from California, and Oregonians hold them responsible for gauche manners, crowding of the parks, littering and vandalism along the incomparable Oregon coast, and bumper-to-bumper traffic.

Many visitors, despite Governor McCall's admonition, decide to stay, accounting for a major share of Oregon's 56 percent population growth in the postwar years. (The 1970 Census total: 2,091,385 people, compared to 1,338,000 in 1946.) The prevailing migration pattern is said to be from the East or Midwest to California, and thence to Oregon. One of America's most interesting commuting patterns shows up in the pleasant little city of Medford, in the Rouge River Valley, where a number of airline pilots live and jet quickly down to San Francisco in 50 minutes to start their transcontinental or international flights. In quiet Medford, like so many Oregon towns, transplanted Californians seem to find the stability and livable environment they crave. Only a few find the action perhaps too slow, or the rainfall oppressive, and head back to earlier points of origin.

Now receding into the mists of history, and of little import to modern Oregon, are such dates as 1543, when Spanish seamen first sighted its coast, or the 1778 visit of the great English captain, James Cook, or the day in 1792 when the Boston navigator, Robert Gray, discovered the great waterway of the Northwest and named it after his ship, the *Columbia*. Next came the era of the maritime fur traders, the visit of Lewis and Clark in 1805, and the 20-year period when the real governance of the "Oregon Country" * came from the Hudson's Bay Company and its illustrious factor of operation beyond the Rockies, John McLaughlin. Sporadic settlement by Hudson's Bay employees was followed up by opening of the Oregon Trail in 1841, rapid settlement of the Willamette Valley, the treaty with Great Britain resolving the boundary dispute, and territorial government in 1848. Little gold rushes and Indian conflicts enlivened these years, but Oregon had few of the Indian battles, mineral bonanzas, range wars, or colossal cattle drives that punctuate the history of so many Western states. Statehood came in 1859 and Oregon settled down to a process of calm growth that continues to this day.

---

* The massive and ill-defined tract called the "Oregon Country" encompassed not only what is modern Oregon but also all or substantial parts of Washington, Idaho, Wyoming, Montana, and British Columbia.

Conventional wisdom has it that Oregon's prim and conservative manners spring from a strong, early infusion of New England stock. Place names like Portland and Salem and the profusion of church spires and tidy white houses in the Willamette Valley all seem evidence of this. In 1845 a toss of a coin decided the name of a 640-acre tract on the Willamette River, near its junction with the Columbia; Amos Lovejoy of Massachusetts wanted the town called Boston, while Francis Pettygrove of Maine held out for Portland. Pettygrove won the toss, and Portland it has been ever since. The state has always had a fairly homogeneous, overwhelmingly white and Protestant population; Roman Catholics still make up only 11 percent of the state, less than half the national average. But the New England roots may have been exaggerated. The first Census ever taken, in 1850, discovered 13,294 white people in Oregon, of whom only 556 had been born in New England, compared to 2,291 natives of Missouri, 1,057 from Illinois, 906 from Ohio, and 749 from Kentucky.

As they had done in Kansas, New Englanders did set their mark on Oregon in public education, which was pushed so hard in the early days that the *Oregonian* complained in 1879 that "the laboring classes are the real sufferers for the extravagant expenditures in the name of free education, which would otherwise seek investment in organized industries." Literacy and educational levels in Oregon remain high to this day. But one looks in vain for flashes of brilliance—great writers, musicians, or artists, or for any significant social innovation.* Instead, Oregon leads the West in its interest in genealogy; to be descended from one of the early pioneers is a real mark of distinction. In California, by contrast, talk of one's ancestral roots generates a wide yawn in most circles.

The most decisive factor in molding Oregon's character may have been less the regional origin of its people than the predilections of its settlers, from whatever region. During the heyday of the Oregon Trail, a choice of immense future consequences was made by the settlers at a juncture near the Snake River in southeastern Idaho. Wagon trains of farmers and merchants chose the northern extension of the trail, over the Cascades into Oregon's Willamette Valley; the gold seekers and other more adventurous types picked the southern spur, over the Sierra Nevada toward Sutter's Mill and the El Dorado known as California. As time went on, more and more sturdy farmers and loggers found their way to Oregon. Quietly, they lived out their lives, content to be members of an inward-looking community, isolated from the swirling currents of California or Eastern life.

The 20th century has brought new waves of immigrants, altering the old patterns to some degree. During both the world wars and the 1930s, there was a new influx of conservative border-state Southerners, moving into the area of southern Oregon that runs from Salem down to the Cali-

* In the performing arts, however, the Oregon Shakespeare Festival in Ashland draws tens of thousands of theatergoers from all over the United States. The festival was founded some 35 years ago by Angus L. Bowmer, a professor at Southern Oregon College; critics say it presents the most authentic Elizabethan-type performances in the Western Hemisphere.

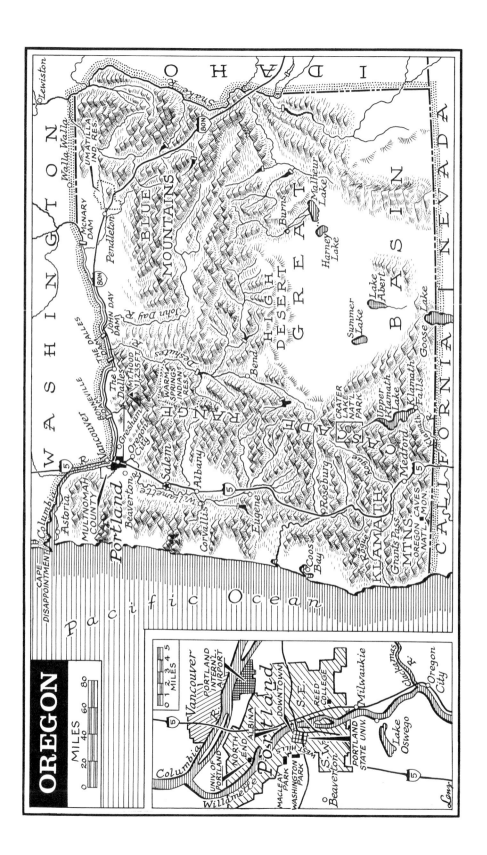

fornia border. The thousands of workers who moved in during World War II were a polyglot bunch certainly less conservative and predictable than the denizens of old, Republican, rural Oregon. From a remarkably strong Ku Klux Klan effort in the 1920s, which could claim 9,000 adherents in the Portland area alone,* to outbreaks of virulent right-wing activity (pro-gun, anti-sex education, etc.) in recent years, Oregon has shown itself not totally immune to political extremism. But it also became the home base of the brilliant and cantankerous Wayne Morse and the state that gave Eugene McCarthy his most important 1968 Presidential primary victory. On the cultural fringe, Oregon turned out to be the state where, strange to tell, Vortex I, the first government-condoned and protected youth-rock-pot-sex festival in America's history, took place in 1970. But no matter what the agitations of the moment, Oregonians seem quickly to return to their middle-of-the-road senses. Above all, Oregon's compulsion seems to be to remain calm and stable. And at that, it succeeds.

### *The Natural Environment—and Its Protection*

On a winter day in December 1843, John C. Frémont and his party ascended to an altitude of 7,000 feet amid snows and howling winds in south central Oregon. Suddenly, from a rim, they looked down 3,000 feet on a lake, warm and smiling and margined with grass and green trees. Down they went into the declivity, from winter into summer. Frémont named the two points Winter Rim and Summer Lake. The episode aptly illustrates the geologic diversity of Oregon, one of the most beautiful of our states. Here is a land of frosty, high mountain peaks, of an incomparable coastline with high bluffs and sandy beaches, of broad and productive river valleys, of upland plains cut by deep gorges of rushing rivers, heavily timbered ranges, and gaunt desert.

Measuring some 280 miles from north to south, and 380 miles from east to west, Oregon is split down its middle by the imposing barrier of the Cascade Mountains, a chain crowned by volcanic peaks of which the greatest and most illustrious is perpetually snow-clad Mount Hood, clearly visible from the city of Portland.

Two-thirds of Oregon's land area lies east of the Cascades, but the region is home for only 12 percent of the population. Here the mountains have cut off most of the moisture coming in from the Pacific, and aridity spells the terms of existence. This is tough, hard uplands terrain of mountains and plateaus. The great pine stands and undulating wheat country closer to Washington give way to the brutal wasteland of high desert,

---

* The Oregon KKK was so strong that it staged parades through the streets of the major cities and got one of its sympathizers elected governor. But it was not so much a racist type Klan as a small-town, busy-body Klan.

with its sagebrush, dry lakes, and lava beds, in the southeast. Distances are immense, the population sparse in the extreme, and a living eked out through wheat, lumber, or livestock.

Moving westerly from the Cascades, one comes immediately on the Willamette Valley, the heartland of Oregon. The valley stretches 180 miles south from Portland and some 60 miles across, abutting the Coastal Range on the west; within it is Oregon's breadbasket and some of its great timber stands. Moisture is plentiful (not excessive) and the climate relatively mild. Again, as so often through the West, we find the overwhelming majority of a state's people packed together in one region. The three large cities of Oregon—Portland, Eugene, and Salem—are here; in fact, no Oregon city of more than 30,000 people is located outside the valley. Oregon's factories, universities, and communications are all centered in this single region.

Alfred T. Goodwin, a state supreme court justice since advanced to the federal bench, told me that between subdivisions and freeways, he foresaw that "the Willamette Valley will one day look like the stretch from San Francisco to San Jose does today." One shudders at the thought and takes comfort in the fact it is not yet so. The morning after I talked with Goodwin at Salem, I drove on south through the placid, rural valley and was attracted by the "World Championship Timber Carnival" near Albany. It turned out to be a kind of reminder of rustic U.S.A. with he-man logging competitions that included such arcane arts as log rolling, speed climbing, standing block chop, and log cutting. The hosts were the Albany Jaycees, the atmosphere old-time American carnival, complete with ferris wheel, barkers, cotton candy, and bright red candied apples. In rural Oregon, a lot of the old lives on.

About halfway down the state, the Willamette Valley stops, and one is in rough territory of mountains, timber stands, and farm valleys between the Cascades and Coastal Range down to the California border. Close by, in the Cascades, is Oregon's great natural wonder: Crater Lake, with its deep blue waters resting in the cone of a massive, collapsed volcano. Oregon naturalists derisively speak of Crater Lake with its heavy tourist load as "the Disneyland of Oregon," but I reject the appellation and find it one of the natural phenomena of the country worth visiting again and again.

Over the relatively modest barrier of the Coastal Range, one comes on coastal Oregon, a strip averaging 25 miles in width that runs along the Pacific coast. High rainfall brings on luxuriant vegetation, and the area is prime farm, fish, and foresting territory. But the real fascination lies with that coastline, which has been well described as the most scenic marine border in the world. Oregon is busily at work eliminating all private beaches, so that the state will own the whole coastline, and each section will be open to the public (with planned access points, parking, and trails to the beach every three miles). Slashes of pure white beach with the surf foaming over, high promontories, battered headlands, secret coves and little inlets, gaunt rock shapes in the water, sea lion herds, lighthouses, dramatic waterfalls—such are the images of this long stretch of land's end by the Pacific.

U.S. Route 101 makes its traffic-choked way along the entire coast, offering incomparable coastal views. In a fit of uncommon candor, the *National Geographic* in 1969 described the coastal strip as "a long, winding avenue of motels, pizza parlors, salt-water-taffy stands, and rock-hound shops that too often hide the seashore's natural beauties." Against the fervent opposition of the owners of such establishments, the state is moving to limit the use of cars and other vehicles on the beaches, obtain zoning to improve land use, and take other steps to protect the coast as a recreational area. But highway commission chairman Glenn Jackson, who is taking the lead in trying to redeem and save the coast, told me somewhat ruefully that on the issue of sign controls, there was scant hope of early reform. "The sign interests are still pretty powerful in the legislature," he said. But he was wrong: a year later, legislation was passed banning billboards outside of cities.

Before departing coastal Oregon, note should be taken of Astoria, set just inside the mouth of the Columbia in extreme northwest Oregon. Astoria advertises itself as the "oldest American city West of the Mississippi," known to white men since 1792 and founded by Jacob Astor's fur traders in 1811. It is also remarkable in being a heavily ethnic city in an otherwise homogeneous state. Finnish immigrants started migrating to Astoria shortly after the Civil War, and in Finland the town is known as the Finnish capital of America. Half of Astoria's 10,244 people are said to be of Finnish descent, including some 300 recent arrivals from the old country. They make their living from the sea, from which they have been drawing magnificent catches of salmon and tuna for 75 years. Sauna baths abound in Astoria, and restaurants daily feature such Finnish specialties as lox loda and salmon stew.

Over 50 percent of Oregon's boundaries are water—the Pacific to the west, the Columbia to the north, and the Snake along much of the eastern border. The reader should consult the Washington state chapter of this book for background on the Columbia and the Idaho chapter of *The Mountain States of America* for discussion of the controversial middle Snake River, a water flow long fought over by the dam builders and the conservationists.

On the whole, Oregon has done a good job in protecting its environment and guarding against destructive natural calamities. It was fortunate not to have been logged-over in the preconservation era, the fate that befell Michigan, Wisconsin, and Minnesota. By the time the axes fell in Oregon, there were some more advanced ideas about the dangers of erosion and need for reforestation. In 1933 a great forest fire—the Tillamook Burn—wiped out 311,000 acres of timber west of Portland in a spectacular blaze that could be seen from Seattle to Medford and 100 miles out to sea. But the reforestation has been so complete that new harvests out of the same lands will soon be possible. The great federal dams along the Willamette and Columbia have done a great deal to prevent erosion and flood damage, once the curse of Oregon. Around Eugene and Springfield there are large tracts of land, now filled with homes, that used to be flooded every two or three years. The last great disaster came in 1948 at the town of Vanport, a temporary World War II city built to house workers at the Kaiser shipyards on the Columbia River. At one point, Vanport had 40,000 inhabitants, making it Oregon's second largest city. But on Memorial Day 1948, the dikes of the flooded Columbia gave way. Vanport simply disappeared. Warnings of the impending disaster, however, held the death toll to eight.

Few states have a park program comparable to Oregon's. There are presently well over 200 state parks with close to 4,000 campsites and 6,000 picnic sites, scattered all over the state with a special concentration along the seashore. Alarmed about out-of-staters' preemption of the choicest campgrounds, Governor McCall in 1970 announced that 1,200 campsites in 10 parks, including several on the coast, would be set aside for "Oregonians only." And in 1969, the legislature empowered the governor to draw up a comprehensive state land-use and zoning plan to go into effect in 1972.

One of Oregon's most persistent air pollution problems—the fallout of solids from the loggers' wigwam burners, especially acute in air inversion areas—is slowly coming under control as the lumber industry uses more and more of what used to be its waste materials. Even bark and sawdust are now used in pulp and paper and various board-like materials.

The most startling progress, however, has been in water pollution, a fight led by McCall, an ardent conservationist. The chief water purity problem has been with the Willamette and smaller rivers that have a greater concentration of use and people in relation to their flow than the Columbia. The Willamette, with Oregon's four largest cities on its banks, was so inundated with municipal sewage, heavily organic industrial wastes from pulp and paper mills, plus the runoff from farms and meat-packing plants, that the Izaak Walton League in 1967 described it as a "stinking, slimy mess" and a "biological cesspool." The oxygen supply in the water reached such a low point that in 1965 only 79 Chinook salmon, instead of the historic number in the tens of thousands, made the run up the Willamette to spawn.

Soon after taking office in 1967, McCall appointed himself temporarily as chairman of the state's environmental quality authority and ordered hearings across the state on water quality standards. As soon as Congress passed the Water Quality Act of 1967, requiring states to set standards, Oregon rushed in with a proposal so effective that the federal government quickly accepted it. Then the state authority published an enforcement plan covering every stream and every city and industry on each Oregon waterway. McCall stepped down as chairman of the control board and was succeeded by John D. Mosser, his former director of finance and administration, who turned out to be one of the country's most persuasive, tough water pollution control officers. Pulp mills by 1969 had installed primary treatment plans, removing 100,000 pounds of settleable solids each day, and they were under state orders to complete secondary treatment plants by 1972. Municipalities were on an even faster schedule. Gradually the salmon began to return to the ancestral spawning grounds. By sometime in the early 1970s, it was predicted, the Willamette River's burden of municipal and industrial waste would be cut by more than 90 percent.

In the meantime, more than 54,000 signatures were gathered for an initiative petition to create a state scenic rivers system controlling development along the Owyhee and Minam Rivers in eastern Oregon, the Rogue and Illinois Rivers in the southwestern part of the state, and the John Day and Deschutes Rivers in central Oregon. Only one of these, the Rogue, a famous fishing stream, had been protected by the National Wild and Scenic Rivers Act. The people approved the initiative by popular vote, 406,315 to 214,243.

The environmental thrust seems destined to endure in Oregon. Occasionally it suffers a setback, as in 1966, when a ballot initiative to divert gas money to preserve beaches for public use was defeated after an expensive oil industry campaign that warned ominously, "Beware of Tricks in Number Six" (the number of the proposition in the ballot).* But an impressive body of conservation legislation has passed under McCall, including conversion of the old state sanitary authority into the very powerful department of environmental quality. Even new Oregonians are interested in the environment; in fact many sacrificed better-paying jobs to come to unsullied Oregon, and they are vehemently protective of it. Late in the 1960s, a coalition of Oregon conservation and sportsmen's groups formed the Oregon Environmental Council (OEC) to lobby actively for causes like an Oregon Cascades Park, a good nuclear siting law, protection of the beaches, and a land-use study and plan for the entire state. The OEC became an early and fervent opponent of the plans of the power companies to build as many as 20 nuclear plants in the state, starting with Portland General Electric's 1.1 million kilowatt facility being constructed 40 miles northwest of Portland. A court suit by OEC charged that the Atomic Energy Commission approved the site without giving sufficient consideration to the danger of radioactive leaks near a metropolitan area, the possibility of earthquake, and overuse of water from the Columbia. McCall supported the project, albeit somewhat reluctantly, confessing to his own nightmare "of having a Hiroshima in your back yard." But he considered the alternatives—more fish-killing dams or a polluting fossil fuel plant—less palatable. "God help me if I'm wrong," he said.

Newborn resistance to Oregon's environmental movement was signaled late in 1971 when industrial and labor union leaders formed a unique

* In 1971, by contrast, the legislature passed a bill channeling 1 percent of all state gas tax revenues for building bicycle lanes and footpaths.

alliance—the first of its kind in the country—to fight what they called the "environmental hysteria" they said was harming the state's economy. The chairman of the new organization, titled Western Environmental Trade Association, was Phil Bladine, a newspaper publisher and board chairman of Associated Oregon Industries; the vice chairman was Ed Whelan, AFL-CIO president in the state. Whelan charged that "hundreds of millions of dollars" of business and many jobs had been delayed in Oregon because of "environmental McCarthyism employed by various self-proclaimed groups."

## Politics: "Oregon System" and Presidential Primaries

Throughout its history, Oregon has received more national political notice than its size warranted. The theme runs from Oregon's status as a pawn in the free state-slave state dispute of the 1850s, its central role in the disputed 1876 Hayes-Tilden election, the drive of reform around the turn of the century which won Oregon the title of "political experiment station of the nation," to decisive votes in several recent Presidential primaries.

After the Civil War, Oregon's Republicans appropriated to themselves a "monopoly on respectability" that was pleasing and appropriate to the staid, middle-class state and paid off constantly in elections. But the corruption that marked the "Gilded Age" across the nation became a special problem in Oregon in the 1880s and '90s, when powerful monied interests took control of political organizations and nominating conventions and filled the legislative halls, according to one account, with "briefless lawyers, farmless farmers, business failures, barroom loafers, Fourth-of-July orators, and political thugs." The legislators at Salem sidetracked popular reform measures and busied themselves with passage of special interest laws or interminable wrangles over election of U.S. Senators. Drunkenness and debauchery surrounded the legislative sessions.

The venal established order came under attack in the 1890s from the Populist movement, feeding on farmers' dislike of the monopolistic out-of-state control of the economy in which bankers, railroads, and land speculators rigged interest rates, farm prices, and land sales to their private gain. The Grange movement, strongly antimonopoly and antirailway, gained strength, and in 1894 the Populists seized several seats in the legislature and found themselves in a balance-of-power situation. Eventually the major party leaders reluctantly agreed to the first great reform—initiative and referendum (approved by a phenomenal 11–1 ratio in a statewide vote in 1902). This, in turn, opened the door to the great reforms of the "Oregon system," in which the people of all the state appropriated to themselves, for a number of years, the final decision on virtually all momentous issues.

The power of the established and graft-ridden political parties was broken, never again to be reasserted; also diminished in great measure was the influence of the special monied interests. In six elections, starting with 1904, Oregon voters expressed their will on 107 specific constitutional or statutory proposals. They instituted direct primary elections in the state and approved a Presidential primary law, prohibited railway passes (a favorite method of corrupting government officials), authorized municipal home rule and local direct legislation by the people, controlled freight rates, placed taxes on public utilities, formed an industrial accident commission, limited the working day for women to 10 hours, and put a corrupt practices act on the books. Political scientist Frederic C. Howe in 1911 described Oregon as "the most complete democracy in the world," where "every . . . community is being trained to a knowledge of politics." Woodrow Wilson, then governor of New Jersey, said Oregon's new laws seemed "to point the direction which we must also take."

Not until the 1914 and 1916 elections was the power of the broadly based "People's Power League," which sponsored many of the most controversial initiatives, finally broken by reversals at the polls. To this day, it is the rare public policy question affecting broad masses of people—be it taxes or environmental controls, daylight saving time or the regulation of fishing—that does not end up on the ballot. This does not mean that Oregon is by any measure a radical or left-wing state; as John Gunther pointed out, "Oregon has, indeed, as good a setup for liberal government as any state—but it makes comparatively little use of it." Indeed, it would be quite surprising if Oregonians, once having appropriated to themselves the final voice in how their state will be run, were to use that power towards overly liberal ends. Radicalism and extremism are simply not part of the sturdy Oregonian character.

Oregon was once called the "Vermont of the West" for its staunch Republican voting habits. Even before World War I, however, the appellation was hardly correct, as Republican splits permitted the Democrats to win almost half the gubernatorial elections. Moreover, Oregon Republicanism through the state's early and middle years was often tinged with the liberal hues of the Populist-Progressive movement. Even in the 1930s, party leaders like Senator Charles McNary (later nominated for Vice President on the ticket with Wendell Willkie) pressed for Columbia River development and similar programs.

In the late 1940s, however, conservatives in the stripe of Douglas McKay and Guy Gordon symbolized Oregon Republicanism. The Republicans' long-term registration edge was fading (finally to disappear in 1954), and aggressive Democrats like Richard L. Neuberger were pointing out that Oregon had not elected a Democratic U.S. Senator since 1914, that it had chosen Republicans in nine of the 10 past governor elections, and not had a Democratic legislature since 1878. Neuberger used to say there were so few Democrats in the legislature that they could caucus in a phone booth or, when his wife got elected to the House along with him, "in bed."

In 1950, however, the top level of GOP leadership in Oregon—including Governor Earl Snell, the secretary of state, and state senate president —were killed in a plane crash. The GOP leadership gap, plus rising Democratic registrations, enabled the Democrats, led by Neuberger, national committeeman Monroe Sweetland, and state chairman Howard Morgan, to effect a major party revival. Neuberger was elected to the U.S. Senate in 1954, and Edith Green the same year was elected to be Oregon's first Democratic House member in a decade. In 1956 the redoubtable Wayne Morse, just turned Democrat, defeated former Governor McKay (who stepped down as Secretary of the Interior to make the race) in the nation's most-watched Senate race of that year; simultaneously the Democrats won the governorship and two more U.S. House seats.

Unlike Oregon's old-time Democrats, many of whom were agrarian and Southern conservative, Neuberger and company were modern, urban-oriented liberals. In 1958 their movement was strong enough to win Democratic control of both houses of the legislature for the first time in the century. But the Democrats suffered from a split personality between Portland liberals and conservative agrarians from southern Oregon. Starting in 1961, a coalition of the Democratic conservatives and like-thinking Republicans took control of the state senate. Eventually the Democrats' strongest statewide candidates—Morse, former Congressman Robert Duncan, state treasurer Robert W. Straub when he ran for governor—fell because they were either too liberal for the downstate conservative Democrats or too conservative for the Portland area left wing. Neuberger himself might have had enough personal strength to buck the trend, but he died in 1960 and his wife, elected to succeed him, tired of the Senate after a term and retired.

Oregon's Republicans, in the meantime, effected a strong comeback, not so much through organization—never strong in either Oregon party—as through the appealing personality of their major candidates, all of whom represented a moderate and sometimes downright liberal Republicanism that was close to the winning Oregon mainstream. The first of the new breed was Mark Hatfield, a political science professor projecting the image of the bright, aggressive young man going places. In 1956, Hatfield won election as secretary of state; in 1958, despite the Democratic sweep of that year, as governor. With the brightest Democratic leaders off in Washington, Hatfield could—and did—dominate the state scene for the next eight years. In 1966, running as a "dove" on the Vietnam issue against Democratic Representative Duncan, who defended Johnson Administration policy, Hatfield was elected to the Neuberger Senate seat. Tom McCall, another liberal Republican, succeeded him as governor.

In 1968 the Democratic rout was completed with the defeat of Wayne Morse by Robert Packwood, another young Republican of moderate-to-liberal persuasion. And while politicians like Hatfield and McCall nurse deep personal antagonisms, and the Republican right wing occasionally rises up in wrath (as it did in winning some local races in the 1970 primary), the basic fact about Oregon Republicanism is that it is moderate, winning, and dominant in its state. The GOP's appeal must remain broad, for Democrats continue to enjoy a registration edge of about 56 percent. And Republicans need the superior financing and organization they enjoyed through 1970—plus the normal number of Democratic dogfights—so that the potential majority won't coalesce against them.

Oregon voters rank consistently among the highest in the nation in the percentage turning out for elections. They may also be the best informed, as a result of the substantial *Voters' Pamphlet* issued by the state government each election time. In it, all of the candidates, as well as proponents and opponents of major initiatives on the ballot, are given a chance to state their case. After the election, the state government publishes a booklet completely documenting reported campaign receipts and expenditures of candidates for public office—again, a unique practice among state governments. In recent years there has been a serious attempt to enforce Oregon's 60-year-old corrupt practices law (the type of legislation ignored in most American states). A state senator who was defeated in the primary got himself declared the winner by claiming in court that his opponent, a former holder of the office, had falsely used the slogan "re-elect" when in reality the opponent had been out of office for two years. The Republican candidate for attorney general in 1968, Lee Johnson, won the election by some 79,000 votes but was prevented from taking office for five months until the courts finally cleared him of charges that he had spent more than the permissible campaign funds and falsified his election expense accounts.

Through its Presidential primary, held in May each four years, Oregon tries to force the major candidates to present their case within the state—and, as the authors of the primary law frankly acknowledged, to make Oregon more important to the rest of the country. Oregon's Presidential preference primary, passed in 1910 by vote of the people, was the first of its kind in the U.S. It provided for a preference vote between Presidential candidates, plus election of delegates who had to pledge to support the preference primary winner. In 1959 the law was revised to give the Oregon secretary of state the power to place on the preference ballot all "generally advocated" Presidential candidates. A potential contender could have his name removed from the ballot only by filing an affidavit saying he did not intend to be a candidate for the Presidency; but in the wake of the 1968 primary, when Nelson Rockefeller filed the affidavit of noncandidacy but shortly thereafter emerged as an active candidate, the law was revised to force inclusion on the ballot of all candidates picked by the secretary of state, regardless of their wishes. Since 1959, several other states have copied the Oregon open-field system. No one seems to have invented a better way to flush out likely contenders for the Presidency and force them to undergo a primary contest.

The most decisive Presidential primary in the state's history was in

1948, when Harold E. Stassen and Thomas E. Dewey competed on the Republican side. Stassen had won a number of earlier primaries and seemed to be gathering momentum for a real blitz at that year's Republican National Convention. Dewey, who had lost to Franklin Roosevelt in 1944, determined that he needed a clear-cut victory to stop Stassen. In a nationally broadcast radio debate from Oregon, the two men tangled on the question of outlawing the Communist Party. Stassen, the liberal, argued for outlawing; Dewey defended legal status for the party and handled himself better in the debate. With a margin of only 9,608 votes, Dewey won the primary. It was enough to erase Stassen as a major contender and enable Dewey to win the nomination. American history might have taken another turn if Stassen had been nominated, for it is very likely he would have avoided Dewey's errors in the general election—and thus defeated Harry Truman that fall.

In 1952 Dwight Eisenhower easily defeated Robert A. Taft in the Oregon primary, and Estes Kefauver swept the Democratic side. But in 1956 Adlai Stevenson defeated Kefauver in Oregon, helping to obliterate the Tennessean's Presidential chances. John F. Kennedy won the 1960 Democratic competition over Senator Wayne Morse, who was making what turned out to be an ill-advised "favorite son" bid. And in 1964 Nelson Rockefeller campaigned hard in Oregon with the slogan "He Cared Enough to Come." For one reason or another, none of his major competitors— Henry Cabot Lodge, Barry Goldwater, or Richard Nixon—considered campaigning in Oregon worthwhile. When the returns were in, Rockefeller had 94,190 votes, 33 percent of the total, compared to 28 percent for Lodge, 18 percent for Goldwater, and 17 percent for Nixon. The outcome should have made it clear enough that Goldwater's extreme form of Republicanism was unwelcome in Oregon; the autumn election proved it when he lost the state to President Johnson with only 36 percent of the total vote. In 1968 right-wing Republicanism was again repulsed when Ronald Reagan permitted his name to stand on the Oregon ballot against Richard Nixon's; Reagan ended up with only 20 percent of the vote, compared to Nixon's 65 percent. That autumn, Oregon was still on its normally careful, moderately conservative course, giving Nixon a 6-percentage point margin over Hubert Humphrey.

The 1968 Democratic preference primary made political history of a sort: it resulted in the first election defeat for a member of that illustrious political clan, the sons of Joseph P. Kennedy. Minnesota's Senator Eugene McCarthy defeated Robert Kennedy in the Democratic preference vote, 163,990 to 141,631. Kennedy was handicapped both by his much later start and the fact that Oregon, comparatively, has few of the blacks and the poor who provided his margin of victory in other states. So Oregon, by conventional political standards, was a bad place for Bobby. But even though the scene was staged for political reasons, somehow the memory flickers back to the young candidate walking barefoot along the magnificent

Oregon beach, touching nature a last time before the tinsel world of California, a few days later, would swallow him up and kill him.

## Governors, Legislators, and Power Base

The two strongest and, by general agreement, best Oregon governors of recent decades have been Mark Hatfield (1959–67) and Tom McCall (1967 to the present). Though both represent moderate-to-liberal Republicanism, they head rival and antagonistic party factions and differ markedly in personality and background.

Hatfield was born in 1922 in a small Oregon town where his father was a railroad blacksmith. He has always been a strong Baptist, a non-drinker and nonsmoker and embodiment of the clean, upright young man. Hatfield first graduated from Willamette University in Salem, then did graduate work at Stanford, where he carefully laid out his prospective political career in talks with his fellow student and Oregonian, Travis Cross.* Seemingly contradictory traits are intertwined in the Hatfield personality. On the one hand, he seems the smooth, anxious-to-please, polished, and tactful politician ready with the proper sentiment on any occasion. Some have charged him with opportunism, as in 1968, when he endorsed Nixon for the GOP Presidential nomination, apparently in hope of being selected for Vice President himself, even when he was known to differ fundamentally with Nixon's general philosophy, most particularly on Vietnam. Yet Hatfield is not always accommodating; in dealings with state legislators during his eight years as governor, for instance, he often acted in a cool, aloof manner, going about the business of administering (which he enjoyed) but letting few men close to him. Finally, there is the element of strong religious belief, which appeared to impel Hatfield, as early as 1965, to thorough opposition to the U.S. role in the Vietnam war. (In a 1971 book, *Conflict and Conscience*, Hatfield recounted a sudden realization in 1954 that he was "a very silent and comfortable Christian." His decision then: "Either Christ was God and Savior and Lord or he wasn't; and if he were, then he had to have all my time, all my devotion, all my life.")

Hatfield's record as governor has been widely praised, especially a major economic development effort which resulted, during his administration, in 138,000 new jobs, a 75 percent boost in foreign trade, and rapid advances in interstate highway construction. He was also credited with an exceptional record in education (including several new community colleges) and civil rights (including refusal to extradite a black prisoner to Mississippi). Hatfield stoutly opposed a sales tax as "regressive," and none

* Cross, one of the most charming and able political professionals of the country, became Hatfield's chief campaign aide and press secretary as governor. In 1969 he was appointed to the sensitive and difficult job of vice president of the University of California for university relations, a post he finally resigned in 1972.

was adopted. His record in the U.S. Senate has turned out to be far more controversial and, as we shall note later, politically risky.

Tom McCall, in a throwback to some of the state's first settlement, is New England born (Egypt, Massachusetts, in 1913). His grandfather, Samuel W. McCall, owned the Boston *Adviser* and served three one-year terms as governor of Massachusetts. But his parents spent their adult lives in Oregon, developing a 640-acre ranch on the eastern side of the Cascades. McCall went into journalism, became known to Oregonians for many years as a leading state television newscaster (from Portland), and made his first break into elective office as secretary of state in 1964, running on an avowedly anti-Goldwater platform. In 1966, when Hatfield moved on to the Senate, McCall won the governorship with a 72,338-vote plurality (three times Hatfield's edge of 24,017 in the Senate race); in 1970 he won again with 76,072 votes to spare.

McCall is as warm and trusting in his approach to people as Hatfield is cool and detached; in fact my Oregon reporter friends tell me McCall often embarrasses them with his utter candor. No one misses McCall in a crowd; at six feet, five inches in height, he is the tallest of the U.S. governors. McCall started out by surrounding himself with a young, eager staff and then instituted the planning program budgeting approach with a first step asking each division of the state government to define its functions and goals—a real shocker for some. McCall's first love and best press coverage has been in the environmental field, alluded to earlier in this chapter; among other things, he got the legislature to approve the permanent state department of environmental quality, fought hard against the Pentagon's shipment of war gas for storage in remote northeastern Oregon, and won approval of the country's first state law to put a price on the head of every beer and pop can or bottle sold (to stop the litter problem). No cause seemed too risky to take on; thus in 1969 he boldly called for abortion law reform, terming antiabortion statutes "callous tools of shame instead of useful tools of society." In 1970 he called for purging Vice President Agnew from the 1972 Republican ticket.

McCall's efforts in the field of state government reorganization were capped by passage in 1969, after a long legislative battle, of the most thorough revamping of state agencies in this century. For the first time, the governor was given exclusive control over almost all state agencies, eliminating archaic devices like an old "board of control" that made him share power, equally, with a three-man board of control also including the state treasurer and secretary of state. One reform created a department of transportation as a kind of umbrella agency over all divisions dealing with air, sea, and land transport. The new department subordinates, at least to some degree, the once-almighty highway department.

In contrast to many of his liberal positions, McCall was quite "hawkish" on the Vietnam war and took a stiff line against campus disorders. In spring 1969, after some outbreaks at Portland State University, he told the members of the state board of higher education, "You are in big trouble" if major disturbances should be repeated. "We simply must," McCall said, "assuage outrage and anxiety of many citizens," adding that public officials who missed the point could risk "banishment to private life."

Oregon's most basic and hard-to-believe problem, however, is taxes. The state has one of the highest U.S. personal and corporate income tax schedules, and on occasion after occasion the people have voted down proposals for a sales tax. The last vote was in June 1969, when a 3 percent sales tax, the proceeds to be used in part to reduce property taxes, was thrashed by a 9–1 vote of the people even though McCall had proposed it and the legislature approved. Despite the relatively high income tax, Oregon's overall tax effort has dropped from one of the highest to one of the lowest positions among Western states; likewise the percentage of local school costs covered by state grants-in-aid has gone down precipitously, to 47th rank among the states. Local property taxes, already quite high, had to be escalated to take up the slack. In 1970 the budget squeeze also forced Oregon to cut its welfare payments, which were already 20 percent below federal standards.*

McCall personally preferred increases in the state's progressive-form income tax, but conservative legislators would hear none of it, leading to the impasse of 1969 and the early 1970s. Increased property tax levies for schools were being rejected everywhere in the state, leaving a dark shadow over one of Oregon's most prized achievements—high quality, public education. The problem, incidentally, might be a little less severe if there were more Catholics in Oregon. As it is, the school population is overwhelmingly Protestant, so that parochial schools divert little of the enrollment as they do elsewhere.

Oregon's legislature has never gained status as a great and independent policy-making body, if for no other reason than because the people are always looking over its shoulder and correcting or adding to its work in referendum and initiative votes. Legislators' working conditions are said to be nothing more than miserable, staffing woefully inadequate (one secretary per member, often his wife), and sessions are still on a biennial basis. Oregon used to have what Gunther called "the rotten borough system *in excelsis*," a result of the state's failure to redistrict, decade after decade, after 1910. Finally the entrenched power of lightly populated eastern Oregon was broken when urban forces, by initiative action in 1952, forced a kind of "automatic reapportionment." Thus Oregon's seats met equal population requirements about a decade ahead of the other states, which waited until the federal courts forced them to act. But reporters who cover the legislature insist that eastern farm representatives still exercise power way out of proportion to their numbers, demonstrating legislative skill and ex-

---

* Adequate welfare payments and new forms of state aid to the sick, aged, and youth were among the chief demands of 2,000 poor Oregonians who met in September 1970 to set up a new Council of the Poor, a nonbureaucratic organization of the underprivileged themselves.

perience that urban lawmakers simply have not matched. The rural lawmakers and those from the state's small cities tend to throw in against Portland, the only metropolis of serious size.*

Party discipline in the legislature is virtually nonexistent, with each party divided into conservative and liberal blocs; in fact, the senate since 1961 has been controlled by a coalition of conservative Democrats working in concert with like-thinking Republicans, even though the Republicans have a technical majority with which they could take complete control if they wished. Whether the people approve of all this is another matter; in 1970 a proposed new state constitution was put on the ballot and endorsed by many leaders; one argument was that a slightly increased legislature would allow a few more seats for the scattered eastern reaches. But that was enough to upset groups like the Oregon AFL-CIO, which feared a diminution of their power at Salem. Even though the new constitution was fundamentally little more than a careful rewrite of the hundred-plus-times-amended 1859 charter, the proposal went down to defeat.

Compared to an average legislature, a populace voting directly on state issues turns out to be as much, if not more, swayed by emotions and whims of a moment. In 1970, for instance, the people not only rejected the carefully drafted new constitution but turned down a proposal to let 19-year-olds vote, a clear reaction to student disorders that same spring. But "ecology" was "in" in 1970, so the voters heartily approved a formidable $200 million state bond issue to underwrite antipollution projects, plus several locally oriented bonding and authority questions related to the same end.

Before we end our review of Oregon government, mention should be made of an especially innovative program of prisoner education instituted at the state penitentiary in the late 1960s, following a suggestion by Thomas Gaddis, a psychologist and author of *Birdman of Alcatraz*. Called NewGate, the program had a federal poverty grant and was backed by Governor Mc-Call. Convicts were given college preparatory classes inside prison and, on parole or school release, were enrolled in college to attend regular classes. With the help of consulting and group therapy services, the rate of rearrest and reimprisonment among NewGate program participants was cut to 20 percent, compared to the normal 75 percent.

The most powerful groups in Oregon politics and government include private utilities (Pacific Power & Light, Portland General Electric), the big lumber companies, public school teachers (organized in the Oregon Education Association), railroads and truckers, organized labor (AFL-CIO, Teamsters, Longshoremen). The power companies invest so heavily in politics,

---

* The reapportionment plan for the 1970s, ordered by Secretary of State Clay Myers after the legislators themselves stalemated on producing a new plan, further increased metropolitan (especially Portland suburban) representation at the expense of lightly populated eastern Oregon. A still more significant shift was provision for single-district rather than at-large legislative elections in metropolitan areas. The result may permit the Republicans to elect more legislators from their pockets of strength in heavily Democratic Multnomah County (Portland).

I heard, that at a campaign headquarters you can see the same 10 secretaries you may have seen at power company headquarters a month earlier. Organized labor performs much the same service for the Democrats and select liberal Republicans; this is, in fact, one of the few states where labor does not automatically line up behind every Democratic candidate. Some 33 percent of Oregon's nonfarm workers are organized, the 12th highest rate of unionization among all states.

In agriculture, the Oregon Farm Bureau and Oregon Agricultural Association are both powers to be reckoned with. But in 1971, when their lobbyist drafted and pushed through the legislature a bill to regulate farm worker unions, they came a cropper. César Chávez's United Farm Workers Organizing Committee claimed that the bill was designed to thwart its organizing efforts in the state and organized a nationwide campaign to pressure Governor McCall to exercise his veto. Chávez threatened "a boycott against all Oregon products" if the bill were signed, and McCall received letters and telephone calls from all over the country urging a veto. McCall said he had never seen comparable pressure against a measure in his 22 years as a state official and political commentator. Finally he did veto the legislation, in part because the state attorney general said it was probably unconstitutional because it would stop workers from ever holding a valid election.

The Portland *Oregonian*, in continuous publication since 1861, remains Oregon's most widely read newspaper, even though its role as great oracle and arbiter of the state's politics has certainly faded. The *Oregonian* describes itself as "an independent Republican newspaper," and its editorial policies bear out the description. Some believe that the *Oregonian*'s golden age was under editor Palmer Hoyt, who retired just after the war to go to Denver, where his services were even more direly needed. But if the paper has lost flair, it has not lost its broad circulation, still going into 245,000 Oregon homes each day, plus areas of Idaho, southwest Washington, and even northern California. In 1971 the *Oregonian* made history of a sort by making William Arthur Hilliard, who had been with the paper for 19 years, its city editor. Hilliard was the first black to reach a position that high in a major U.S. daily newspaper.

The *Oregonian* and its afternoon counterpart, the *Oregon Journal*, experienced one of the longest newspaper strikes on record after newspaper chain magnate S. I. Newhouse bought them in 1959. The four-year struggle was marked by arson, dynamiting of delivery trucks, the attempted assassination of Newhouse's nephew, a union-backed daily, and laws to bar importing of strikebreakers. It was a strange episode, so totally out of character for the state.

The most outstanding of the downstate papers are the Eugene *Register-Guard* and Salem *Statesman*; like most Oregon papers, they lean toward the Republican and conservative side. Recent years have provided a new and influential voice in public affairs reporting through the Portland television stations, especially KGW-TV, where Tom McCall used to be news analyst. KGW is owned by KING-TV Seattle, the Northwest's most prestigious public affairs station.

## Oregonians in the U.S. Capitol

By any measure, Wayne Morse is the most remarkable man Oregon has sent to Washington. Like so many famed Westerners, he was not born there at all, but in the staid Midwest. But Morse's birthplace was a hotbed of Midwestern liberalism, Madison, Wisconsin, and the maverick Wisconsin strain remained with him through a long public career. Born in 1900, graduated from the University of Wisconsin in 1923 and Minnesota Law School in 1928, Morse moved out to Oregon (a state he had never seen before) to become a professor of law at the University of Oregon. His skill in labor relations and his intellect—friend and foe agreed he had one of the finest minds of the times—won Morse a number of federal appointive positions, including the National War Labor Board. In 1944, as a Republican, he ran for the U.S. Senate, upsetting a reactionary incumbent in the primary and winning the general election with ease.

The mutations that carried Morse from party identity as a Progressive to Republican to Independent and finally to Democrat are too complex to recite here; perhaps it suffices to say he always had the courage of his convictions, always felt he was taking a stand for the little man, and never saw the need to compromise. As A. Robert Smith, writer of the excellent Morse biography, *The Tiger in the Senate*, wrote just after Morse's return to private life in 1969:

A hero he was, but not a saint. His faults were as monumental as his virtues, and in time the Legend [of Morse the man of guts, of brilliance, the champion of Everyman] acquired considerable tarnish as Wayne Morse, his rapier never sheathed, hacked a bloody swashbuckling trail through both the Republican and the Democratic parties, beheading old friends and allies faster than he could recruit replacements.

The fatal flaw of Wayne Morse, Smith and others have recorded, was arrogant pride, the kind that tolerated not even the slightest deviance from Morse's own beliefs, even in the closest of friends. The classic case was Morse's feud, on what now seems rather inconsequential grounds, with Richard Neuberger in the late 1950s. A once warm relationship degenerated into an exchange of vitriolic letters.

In the 1950s, Morse became a point of intense controversy when he repudiated Eisenhower midway through the General's first Presidential campaign and in 1955 gave the Democrats the one extra vote they needed to organize the Senate. Those were the same years when Morse, in his prime, could deliver a record 22-hour filibuster speech in an attempt to defeat the oil tidelands bill, fight against exempting natural gas producers from Federal Power Commission regulation, or violently oppose the Landrum-

Griffin labor reform bill. Past his 60th birthday in 1960, some thought he might mellow. But far from it. In 1964 Morse and Senator Ernest Gruening of Alaska were the only two Senators to oppose the Gulf of Tonkin resolution that authorized President Johnson's enlargement of the war. At first as a lonely fight, then with increasing allies, Morse fought vehemently against the American involvement in Vietnam, calling the war there illegal, immoral, and against the national interest. Only time—and events like the 1971 publication of the Pentagon papers—would vindicate him.

By 1968, the opposition to Vietnam that Morse and Gruening had begun reached such proportions that President Johnson was forced to retire. But the battle had taken its toll of Wayne Morse. No new cause to arouse general righteous indignation seemed at hand. His opponent, 36-year-old Robert Packwood, differed little from Morse on the war. And Morse made what Robert Smith later described to me as "the basic tactical error" of running, for the first time in his career, on a platform stressing his congressional seniority and what he could achieve for Oregon in Congress. Morse's image was thoroughly muddied by this effort to identify himself as a member of the Senate power elite he had previously scorned; it also gave Packwood an opening to challenge the cantankerous incumbent's effectiveness in Congress.

The initial vote count that November showed Morse trailing by only 3,445 votes out of more than 800,000 cast. But a recount failed to get Morse as many as 200 new votes, and he ended up at the losing end of a final vote of 408,646 and 405,353. So a turbulent quarter of a century in Congress was ended, and instead of installing Morse as chairman of the Senate Education and Labor Committee in Washington (a post he was in line to take over), Oregon retired the old tiger to his ranch near Eugene —or so it seemed. But then, after four years on the sidelines, Morse entered the political wars again at the age of 71 in 1972, seeking election to the Senate seat held by Mark Hatfield, announcing: "I'm going to run as a young people's candidate. You are only as young as your ideas."

Packwood, the man who succeeded Morse, has such a youthful appearance that he could easily be mistaken for a Capitol Hill page boy or staffer. But he made more than a normal splash in Washington by proposing, in startling rapidity, (1) legislation to legalize abortion, (2) a bill to ban income tax exemptions for more than two children in a family, as a way to stem population growth, and (3) an amendment to abolish the hoary Congressional seniority system in favor of election of their chairmen by members of each committee. Later he became the favorite of the environmentalists (and ruffled the feathers of some other Western Senators) by becoming the outspoken and leading Senate advocate of legislation to put the wild middle Snake River forever beyond the reach of the dam builders.

The seniority system, Packwood argues, is an undemocratic device that often elects committee chairmen out of tune with their times, men whose average age is 65.4 years—beyond the normal retirement point for most men. "Even the law of the jungle operates on the principle of survival of the fittest," Packwood maintains. "Congress operates only on the principle of survival, period." Packwood's causes seemed far out, but perhaps not so impossible as it had appeared, early in 1968, for a newcomer to statewide politics to upset wily old Wayne Morse. How had he done it, outside of the specific issues? As Oregon political analyst Floyd McKay tells the story, Packwood simply discovered and made beautiful use of a cardinal principle of the new politics: that for a large number of people, especially middle-class white suburbanites, the very participation in politics is an end in itself. Packwood was able to harness thousands to work in his campaign, many of whom had little idea of what he stood for. And it was that unlikely army that simply marched all over Wayne Morse.

If the U.S. Senate lost an outspoken "dove" when Morse was defeated, it gained one in Mark Hatfield. Again and again, Hatfield spoke out against Nixon administration policy on the war in Indochina, and in 1970 he even cosponsored, with South Dakota's George McGovern, an "end the war" amendment to compel total withdrawal of all troops within a year and a half. Hatfield also accused the Nixon administration of "wild spending" on weapons systems. This caused some loss of normal GOP strength for Hatfield in Oregon, but the situation was exacerbated further when he openly denounced the administration's "Southern strategy" and the pro-vocative speeches of Vice President Agnew. Following the 1970 elections, for instance, Hatfield said his party had practiced "the politics of revulsion" in that year's campaign, including "guilt by association" and an effort to "identify honorable men with extremists"—a policy Hatfield said could lead "to political disaster in 1972." At home, some Republican leaders suggested that Hatfield switch to the Democratic party.

Oregon's most influential representative in Washington, however, is neither a Senator nor a man, but rather Mrs. Edith Green, nine-term Representative from the Portland area, second-ranking Democrat on the House Education and Labor Committee, and chairman of its Subcommittee on Higher Education. Mrs. Green, now in her early 60s, wields such power in the education area that many regard her as the most powerful woman in Congress. A schoolteacher herself, she got her political start as an education lobbyist in the Oregon legislature. She earned an early reputation in Congress as an unabashed liberal and was one of the first to oppose the Vietnam war.

In later years, however, Mrs. Green became anathema to the very liberals with whom she was once identified. One factor was her strained relations with organized labor; she developed a distaste for the way that other liberals on the Education and Labor Committee invariably followed the will of the AFL-CIO, and for a five year period ending in 1971, not a single AFL-CIO lobbyist entered her office. Increasingly, she seemed to take politics and issues very personally and to resist any kind of ideological tag. Specific issues on which she broke with other liberals were her amendments establishing state and local control over federally aided education projects and poverty programs and her support of a controversial antibusing amendment. Her statements accusing campus liberals of encouraging student anarchists and her proposals for "combat pay" for teachers in schools with a high incidence of violence also led some liberals in her own party to apply such terms as "the liberal racist." For Mrs. Green, these complaints all missed the point. She was concerned that violence on the campuses might cause countermeasures by Congress, that the middle class could be alienated from the educational establishment, and that the schools were being expected to solve an impossible array of racial and class problems, at the expense of good education. For any longtime liberal in her age group, Mrs. Green's worries seemed normal. And if she could find any federal-level solutions to the problem she saw, she had a superb opportunity to get them enacted into law. This was because no one else in Congress had a comparable grasp of education problems or equal skill in committee and floor debate on the subject. Oregon had sent the ultimate schoolmarm to Washington.

Less illustrious but highly competent Oregon Congressmen include Al Ullman, third-ranking member of the Ways and Means Committee, and Republican Wendell Wyatt, who has served on Interior and Appropriations. Ullman has a voice in national tax legislation and was advocating national wage and price controls two and a half years before President Nixon finally imposed them in 1971. As the *Oregonian* pointed out in 1970, Ullman "takes care of his fences around the wheat, cattle and timberlands of eastern Oregon." Wyatt has been effective because of his entree to high Nixon administration officials—a role that Hatfield, in particular, is in a poor position to carry out.

Since the 1940 Census apportionment, Oregon has had four seats in the U.S. House. In 1970 it was only 235 people short of picking up a fifth seat under the national apportionment system. The "near miss" permitted Oklahoma to retain all its six seats, even though its population increase was far below Oregon's. Now Oregon will have to wait until the 1980s for more representation.

## *Timber!*

One of the most awesome sights of the primordial American continent must have been the great stands of virgin timber in the Pacific Northwest—spread from the oceanside up onto the flanks of the Cascades, rolling blankets of Douglas fir laid across the land, some of the trees as high as 280 feet, interspersed with hemlock and cedar; and then, on the eastern slope, millions of ponderosa pine, aspen, and cottonwood. Timber enough there was to build millions of ships or house hundreds of millions. (Oregon is still said to have enough timber to rebuild every home in the 50 states.)

Not surprisingly, lumber became the mainstay of the Northwest's economy. Perhaps because the federal government so early got control of so much timber land, and perhaps because the loggers themselves saw the folly of what their industry had done in the Midwest, the Northwestern lumbermen never inflicted the unspeakable damage that was done in the northern Great Lakes states. But this is not to say that billions of board feet of lumber can be extracted from the forests each year without profound effects. The everyday environment is filled with great trucks thundering out of the forests with massive logs headed for sawmill or pulp plant. Douglas fir, which constitutes 80 percent of the forest stand, cannot be cut selectively out of a forest, but has to be harvested in big patches —usually 50 to 100 acres—which make a lot of Western forest lands look like huge checkerboards from the air. The theory is that uncut areas of the tree, surrounding the cuts, will scatter seeds, though reseeding by man (sometimes done by helicopter) is a more desirable alternative. The practice is also defended by people like Edward P. Cliff, chief of the U.S. Forest Service, as the most efficient method of harvesting mature or overage trees and of assuring maximum sunlight for the growth of the next stand of trees.

But clear-cutting is not a pretty sight. The waste materials left behind are not only unsightly but highly flammable, increasing the danger of forest fires. Debris frequently clogs streams and erosion can occur on the watershed, especially where clear-cutting has been effected on steep grades. The land is excluded from recreational use for many years, and even when new trees grow, they are so uniform that they lack the diversity needed for a good mix of wildlife.

In recent years the U.S. Forest Service (USFS), an arm of the Department of Agriculture, has been under increasing criticism from conservationists for excessive clear-cutting and other land-destructive practices in the 97 million acres of commercial timber it administrates, the source of 40 percent of the country's timber production. The charge, in essence, is that the USFS, once a proud and conservation-minded organization dedicated to preservation of the nation's woodlands, has become obeisant to the economic wishes of the timber companies it permits to log on public land. In the words of Brock Evans of the Sierra Club, the Forest Service has become "a classic case of a regulatory agency being governed by the industry it should be regulating." The controversial University of Montana report on the Bitterroot National Forest in Montana asserted that "consideration of recreation, watershed, wildlife and grazing appear to be afterthoughts."

The Forest Service has not taken the criticism lightly, insisting that it has followed closely the multiple-use standard mandated by Congress—that the national forests shall be administered for outdoor recreation, range, timber, watershed, and fish and wildlife programs, all for the public benefit. In addition to timber, Chief Cliff points out, the Forest Service administers

9.9 million acres of the 10.1 million acres in the national wilderness preservation system, innumerable natural beauty and recreation facilities, including most of the major ski areas of the nation, management programs for 29 endangered species of wildlife, and the like.

It is clear that blame for various alleged abuses does not lie entirely with the Forest Service. In the eight years ending in 1970, USFS received 95 percent of the money it sought from Congress for timber sales activities in the nation's forests but only 40 percent of the funds it requested for reforestation and timber stand improvement and only 4 percent of what it asked for recreational facilities. The Public Land Law Review Commission, chaired by Colorado's Representative Wayne Aspinall, said logging should become the "dominant" use of certain national forests, especially the best timber stands of the Pacific Northwest, in order to meet the projected (though disputed) timber needs for home construction in America in the 1970s and 1980s.* Following a policy laid down by President Nixon, the USFS has announced a goal of increasing the timber yield from national forests by 60 percent. But at the same time, the attacks of conservationists have prompted the Forest Service to tighten up its controls on the size of clear-cuts and the way in which the timber is removed—so much so that timber production from the national forests has leveled off. New national parks, like the Cascades National Park in Washington—and now a similar park is proposed for Oregon —are nibbling away at the acreage controlled by the Forest Service. And finally, USFS officials are fully able to read the political tea leaves of an era of ecologic concern, and they are putting increasing emphasis on recreational uses of the forests.

Northwest boosters will tell one their region "is the best place in the world for growing quality softwood timber." What about the South, I asked? "Sure, it grows faster there, but the quality is just what you'd expect from a conversion of weed." The truth is that most of the great timber firms active in the Northwest—Weyerhaeuser, Crown Zellerbach, Georgia-Pacific, Boise Cascade, St. Regis, International Paper, Scott—are also involved deeply in the Southland. There has been a rapid concentration of ownership into a few large, diversified firms, most now publicly owned and operating across the U.S. and often abroad as well. For the public, this may not be all bad, simply because the big firms have names and reputations to protect and are less likely to resort to unconscionable cut-and-run devastation of the land.

While more and more land has been set aside for wilderness, primitive, or park lands, a process that arouses fervid opposition in the industry, some of the big companies have seen the need for sophisticated reforestation on their own lands. Experts say that good forestry techniques can increase the yields of land by as much as 50 percent. In 1941 Weyerhaeuser started the country's first tree farm near Aberdeen, Washington, a model for some 30,000 later operations across the country. A unique degree of corporate farsighted-

* The same timber companies that complain of potential shortages often export some of their best lumber from the Pacific Coast to Japan.

ness must be involved, since tree farms are often being maintained that could not feasibly be cut within the lifetime of anyone presently in the company's management. Too often, critics say, lumber companies fail to undertake expensive reseeding of their own property, turning instead to the government with the request for opening of more national forest lands. But privately reforested areas do, of course, add to a company's long-term worth, and their care and preservation is a deductible tax expense.

The ways of forestry, and the men who man the industry, have changed fundamentally with time. A century ago, loggers hacked away at the base of trees with axes; later they went to high platforms so they could use a two-man saw; more recently they have worked at the base again, with power saws. Mechanization has arrived with devices like an automatic chipper that can move out in the forest, move a log up its central belt, strip it of bark and branches, and then cut it into convenient small pieces from which to make pulp. Logs are often brought out of remote areas by balloon to avoid road construction costs and scarring of the landscape. And massive log movers can pick up as many as 65 tons of wood in a single motion. Thus the need for workers is less, both in the woods and in the semiautomated factories that turn out paper or plywood (a product invented in Oregon in 1905) or manufacture sophisticated new products like chipboard. Even waste products, including sawdust, bark, and chips, are used in these new processes that literally consume the "whole tree."

Despite automation, a thorny problem for the timber companies—except in times of recession—is to get eager and able young loggers, the kind that poured in during generations past from Norway, Finland, Sweden, Italy, and Eastern Europe. "Today we're logging with gray-haired men," an official of Simpson Timber in Seattle told me. "How do you get young men on the job? Too many of the kind we would like to have as choker-setters, rigging slingers, hook tenders, donkey punchers, truck drivers, fallers, or buckers are now off in Vietnam—or looking for an easier job. Now our best manpower supply is Arkansas, Missouri, and Appalachia. We need individualistic people, often working alone, out in the weather." But the days of the company town and single men living in bunkhouses and eating in cookshacks are gone. Today most loggers are married and drive to work, sometimes long distances from their own rural "stump ranches."

One reason new loggers may be hard to locate is the economic uncertainty of the job. Whenever the national economy hits a downturn, or interest rates go beyond a set point, new housing starts decline—and layoffs face the loggers as their mills close down for weeks at a time. Thousands were unemployed in Washington and Oregon in the last such economic squeeze, 1970–71.

Lumber remains central to both Oregon and Washington economies. Almost half the country's entire production is located on the Pacific coast. Until 1937 Washington ranked as the nation's top producer of forest products. Since then, it has been Oregon. Georgia now ranks first in pulp production, with Washington second. But Oregon leads in plywood, with about 70 percent of U.S. production.

## *Oregon Economy Today*

Despite the mercurial characteristics of its timber industry, Oregon has not developed the superheated economy of California or the rapid takeoffs (and crash landings) of Washington state. Nor has the state become dependent, in any significant way, on federal spending; in fact it ranks 48th among the 50 states in the percentage of its population employed in defense-related industries, getting only a quarter of the military contracts which go to Washington or $\frac{1}{64}$ of those for California.

From its traditional resource-oriented economy—one highly dependent on timber, agriculture, and fishing, with all the cyclical problems those industries entail—Oregon has moved to a highly diversified base. In 1950, 30 percent of all employment in the state was furnished by the combination of the lumber and farm industries. By the end of the 1960s, that figure had shrunk to 17 percent. The growth in new industries was especially strong in the 1960s, when Oregon's job rolls grew at an annual rate of 2.7 percent, compared to 1.1 percent in the 1950s. The '60s brought a doubling of employment in metals and machinery, for instance, and a two-thirds growth in finance, industry, realty, and services. By 1970, jobs in the lumber industry were down to 67,100, some 26,000 less than in 1950. The new figure represented less than one-twelfth of the work force and still falling, an achievement all the more remarkable in light of Oregon's continuing capability to supply most of the nation's plywood and a quarter of its softwood lumber.

The new industrial fields were diverse in the extreme: exotic metals, freeze-dried foods, women's sports clothes, one factory making an Oregon-designed chain saw modeled on the pattern of an insect's ability to chew foods, and electronic industries. Among the latter is Portland's biggest employer, Tektronix, which keeps more than 6,000 workers busy assembling oscilloscopes. Outside of forests and water, Oregon is devoid of significant natural resources; thus its appeal to new factories has to be based in major part on the availability of a well educated work force, known for its high productivity. By 1970, wages paid Oregon workers were up to $5 billion a year, from $2.5 billion in 1960 and $1.5 billion in 1950—impressive, even in the light of inflation.

Among American states, Oregon is one with the most to gain through trade with the Japanese, who are interested in its wheat, aluminum, cattle, and timber. But Japanese trade experts complain privately that Oregon businessmen have shown little ingenuity and competitive instinct in bidding for the Nipponese market, a disservice both to Oregon and to the national balance of payments problem.

Oregon's gross state product is just below $10 billion a year. In terms of single industries, timber still leads (value added $1.8 billion a year), followed by agriculture (over $560 billion in farm sales) and tourism ($325 million in 1970). Of this "big three," the industry that has failed to keep pace is agriculture. Just after World War II, Oregon farm income was $246 million a year and represented 18 percent of all salaries in the state; by 1970 it was down to $174 million, representing a scant 2.2 percent. Increased farm productivity accounted for a sharp drop in the number of farm workers and farm payrolls, but even in the inflationary 1960s farm sales rose less than 20 percent.

Oregon harvests over a million acres of wheat each year (traditionally the major crop), with hay, tree fruits, nuts, many varieties of berries, truck crops, potatoes, and seed crops all runners-up; a thriving greenhouse and nursery business has also made the state first in the U.S.A. in Christmas holly and Easter lily bulbs. Livestock production, however, brings just as much income as the crops combined. Except for a few exotic products in which it excels—ryegrass and red fescue seeds, for instance, or strawberries, loganberries, gooseberries, and raspberries—Oregon ranks only middling among the states in agricultural production. Some critics say that if the state would press harder and faster to get more land under irrigation, especially in its eastern reaches, it could take a much larger bite of the huge agribusiness centered just to the south in California. Irrigation has already meant huge potato crops by Ore-Ida and others in the sagebrush-strewn country of eastern Oregon and a three-fold increase in some crops along the Columbia River Valley. The more Oregon farmers move to draining, irrigating, and fertilizing properly, the more they can turn to high-income row crops that bring enough return to create the capital for more processing industries. The Willamette Valley, it is said, has the potential of feeding up to 12 million people, and agribusiness there is already so successful that Salem is claiming it has bypassed San Jose, California, as the biggest single food-processing center of the U.S.A. Rounding out the food picture, commercial fisheries bring in a harvest of salmon, tuna, crabs, clams, and shrimp worth about $22 million a year.

Tourism, that mixed blessing to which we referred at the start of this chapter, is rapidly accelerating toward a projected level of $380 million in 1975; some believe it may be the state's largest industry by 2000. Along with the people influx, writer Ellis Lucia has pointed out, there's an alarming touch of California life style in swank resorts and condominiums with adjacent golf courses, swimming pools, lodges, and fancy trappings. In the early 1960s, a full-scale land scandal broke out when developers advertised lots in desolate eastern Oregon with brochures giving illustrations of another and more scenic part of the state. The names of the spots for which gullible investors were being asked to lay down hard dollars for their dream lots: Stinking Water River and Jackass Mountain.

## The Portland Scene

If any West Coast city could be said to have a monopoly on propriety and an anxiousness to "keep things as they are," it is Portland, a town of quiet old wealth, discreet culture, and cautious politics. In many ways it is a lovely city, set in the green valley of the Willamette just below its juncture with the Columbia; a city with 7,000 acres of parkland including wilderness areas and miles of rustic trails within its very borders; a city where, on a clear day, Portlanders get an almost magic view of Mt. Hood to the east. Often the mist settles in a band below Hood's summit, leaving the top floating, as it were, on the horizon. More concretely, the mountain feeds an unusually pure lake from which Portland's water supply is drawn. In the moist coastal climate zone, vegetation flourishes, and each June since 1909 there has been the famous Rose Festival.*

The 1970 Census found 382,619 people in Portland, almost identical to 1960; at the same time, however, the suburbs, including those across the Columbia River in Clark County, Washington, had increased 39 percent to 626,510. The portion of the metropolitan area in Oregon accounted for 42 percent of the total state population. The fast-growing counties were Clackamas, to the south of Portland, which grew by 47 percent in the 1960s to a new total of 166,088, and Washington, to the west, which went up 71 percent to 157,920 in 1970. Some form of regional or metropolitan government has long been backed by the influential *Oregonian*, and in 1970 a major step was taken in that direction when the people approved formation of a metropolitan service district which was authorized to operate sewage treatment and disposal plants, solid-waste disposal, mass transit, and flood control. The metro government—if it may be called that—has the power to levy taxes after specific voter approval. Now an 11-member charter commission has begun plans for a single city-county government for Portland and Multnomah County. The result, if approved, would be a metropolis of about 550,000 people, the largest in the Northwest, covering an area of 450 square miles, about the size of Los Angeles.

As for the municipal government of Portland itself, it still functions under a comfortable, honest, but quite inefficient commission form of government. Five elected commissioners act collectively as a city council but also are assigned specific departments of the city government to administrate. The mayor's power is not much greater than that of the commissioners, though he can assign or reassign administrative portfolios among them. The system results in much log-rolling among the commissioners, plus an inability to implement long-term plans and reallocate resources. With nonpartisan elections, commissioners often stay in office for decades. The chain of longevity was rudely broken in 1969–70, however, when death, retirement, and elections opened the way for three aggressive young commissioners to sweep into office. One of the newcomers, legal aid service attorney Neil Goldschmidt, had told me a few months before that he considered the entire city

---

* The heavily publicized Rose Festival is big business in Portland, and there is intensive publicity each year about the selection of Rose Festival princesses in each of the city's 14 high schools. In 1971, however, the students at two schools refused to select princesses; at one school the student body government adopted a resolution questioning the "relevance" of Rose Festival princesses to "the educational purpose of a high school" and charging that "the primary purpose of the Rose Festival is to increase tourism and profits for the businessmen of Portland."

government old and out of touch with real problems. The term of longtime Mayor Terry Schrunk, a spokesman of the older order in his late 50s, would run out in 1972, but regardless of the election, the outlook seemed to be for increasing change over time.

Portland in 1970 made a startling breakthrough in municipal pay scales when it agreed to pay its policemen $10,525 a year. But it also took a pace-setting step toward professionalism by requiring two years of college in all its recruits and forbidding policemen to hold outside jobs. Just a few months later, those police seemed headed for the ultimate test of their professionalism. The American Legionnaires, some 20,000 strong, were coming to town for their annual convention, and so, it was suddenly learned, was a "people's army" of youthful non-establishmentarians to confront the Legionnaires or to join rock festivals. Fearing the very worst, planning began months in advance by city, county, and state police, together with Governor McCall and Portland officials. To avert any real confrontation, McCall made the politically risky decision to give official sanction to Vortex I, a rock festival suggested for McIver State Park about 30 miles south of Portland. And more than 2,000 Portland citizens were mobilized to act as "people for Portland" monitors of all the parades and rallies within the city, backing up local police.

If the essential goal was to prevent confrontation and violence, the plan had to be rated a magnificent success. Only the most minor fracases took place, to everyone's vast relief—excepting, perhaps, some hard-core radicals who had hoped to amass crowds of young people in Portland and then induce the police to attack them, thus unwittingly carrying out the process of political radicalization. But for the young people, the action was not in Portland, but at McIver Park, where up to 32,000 gravitated at one point. Reporter Gordon Bowker of *Seattle Magazine* summarized the scene this way:

> Tuesday, twilight along the Clackamas. It is the fifth day of Vortex I, the first rock festival in history to be sponsored by the governor of one of the 50 states. Beneath the huge stage and the Gothic Speaker system, thousands of young people writhe, stagger, dance and sit motionless as the unnamed band above them plays a 1970 version of "Sexy Ways," written and first performed by Hank Ballard and the Midnighters in 1954, before most of the audience was born. On stage, a blond ingenue of 16 with beautifully formed bare breasts undulates to the rhythm 'n' blues. In the air: dust, music, and pot—lots of it.

Vortex I raised a bevy of new thoughts and problems. What were the implications of official sponsorship of an event at which the laws against drugs and nudity were openly violated? Had a model been discovered for sidetracking violent demonstrations at future times and in other places? Could the hard-core radicals be thwarted by another means than repression? The group to benefit most from Vortex I, a local writer reported in the *Oregonian* a week later, was "the local peaceful longhairs" who "won numerous straights over to admiration, or at least acceptance, of their alternate life style." If true, what could *that* mean for the West Coast's most conservative city?

Portland is economic capital of its state, with the big banks and law firms and corporate headquarters of giant lumber firms; it is also a great port city and home of many electronic component companies, textile firms (notably specialty woolen mills), big aluminum factories (drawing on the abundant supply of hydroelectricity), logging-lumbering equipment plants, lumber mills, and chemical plants. Its entrenched business leadership has often been criticized for negativism, for failing to go after the big aerospace and military-related companies. But in late 1970, when Seattle's unemployment had hit an alarming 12 percent, Portland's was only half as great—a problem, but of much smaller magnitude. "Nobody in Portland lies in bed worrying about tomorrow's cataclysm," one of the editors of the *Oregonian* told me. "We know nothing very bad or very good is going to happen to us." Seattle, he pointed out, "has always been a boom town, built on the Alaskan Gold Rush and still a boom town because of Boeing. Portland is more steady—a place that used to live on lumber, fish, and agriculture. We never had any great gobs of money coming into fatten local payrolls. By not getting on the merry-go-round of federal hand-outs, we may be a lot better off."

The Port of Portland is a great export point for heavy cargoes like wheat, lumber, and wool, bringing in, by contrast, petroleum and ores. The value of foreign imports and exports handled broke the $1 billion mark in 1969. Big docks and terminals line the Willamette River, and the Port of Portland owns a gigantic ship repair facility including the second largest floating drydock in the U.S. It also operates the largest dredge in the Northwest, part of keeping open and deepening the 110-mile channel through the Willamette and Columbia to the open sea. The earth churned up by dredging has created prime new industrial land, which is being turned into an extremely well planned industrial park on the North Portland Peninsula. Usually severe environmental controls are being written into the contracts and deeds of participating industries.

Portland promoters hope that the city's big International Airport, with facilities completed in 1958, can be expanded with a large new terminal and dual runways creating a capacity of 35 million passengers a year (instead of the present 2.5 million). With several times as much airport land as Seattle, Portland could become the air center of the Northwest. Washington state Senators fought tooth and nail against federal appropriations for the airport enlargement, allegedly on environmental grounds (noise pollution over nearby Vancouver, Washington, and the like). Many Portlanders believed they were simply spoil sports, worried about competition to the Seattle Airport and jealous about letting their neighbors to the south get a foot in the federal trough. But then the airport's planned $110 million expansion, which would involve dredging and filling a one-square-mile section of the Columbia was blocked (at least temporarily) by three lawsuits brought by an alliance of conservationists and homeowners from the Washington side of the river.

Running on a north-northwesterly course right through the heart of the city, the Willamette River creates distinct east and west bank communities that are frequently at loggerheads about planning and funding of city projects. The west side has the gleaming high-rise structures of a revitalized downtown, most of Portland's immense, rambling parklands, and well-to-do West Hills, which encompass several handsome residential sections with hilltop views. The west side's ethnic concentrate is white Protestant, but there are pockets of wealthy Jews and even some small groups of Gypsies. Much of the suburban growth has been toward the west, inflating the population of a town like Beaverton, for instance, by 213 percent (to a new total of 18,577) just in the single decade of the 1960s.

The east side of the river contains a great polyglot of neighborhoods, ranging from poor black * to wealthy white Protestant and a number of Oregon's relatively few Catholic communities. Portland has one of the most flourishing beer-drinking pub cultures of the U.S.A., a leftover of the days before 1952 when liquor by the drink could not be served. And wherever the pubs appear, the working class is sure to work or live—in such areas as the North End with its hardy blue-collar class that finds work at the big ship terminals, or high-poverty, white semislums like "Slabtown" and Southeast Portland. Many elderly people live on the east side—old residents of the city, too poor to join everyone else in the rush to the suburbs, even if they wanted to. Out beyond the east side are some thriving suburban towns like Gresham, a gateway to Mt. Hood with a large Japanese farm element and Oregon's biggest strawberry crops, or Oregon City, the old territorial capital, more recently a mixed industrial-farm community, where the original plat for San Francisco is stored in the Clackamas County courthouse.

Portland's cautious personality has not deterred many civic improvements and private capital investment in the postwar era. These included an impressive Memorial Coliseum, new bridges, docks and schools, the excellent but now outmoded air terminal built in the late 1950s, a quality freeway program, and a new zoo. The $100 million Lloyd Center shopping complex features a 20-story office building, walks, and flowered malls. For most of the 1960s, work was underway in a large area of southwest Portland where a mixture of blighted housing and ramshackle business establishments persuaded the planners that major surgery was required. The result was a spurt of shiny new buildings for the telephone company, Blue Cross, the local labor center, Boise Cascade, and others. Interestingly, the big mover and shaker in all this has not been an old Portlander, but rather Ira Keller, an Eastern "carpetbagger" in the city for only two decades. Keller, who is president of the Western Kraft Company, has chaired the Portland Development Commission.

Within and without urban renewal areas, the process of building and

---

* Portland has 21,572 Negroes, most of them in the northeastern Albina section, a small community with all the familiar transportation, job, and housing problems of inner-city blacks, including a history of some firebombing and violence in the late 1960s. The National Alliance of Businessmen made one of its strongest efforts across the country in Portland, getting more than 400 firms to make jobs available. But many Oregon labor unions stoutly resist making more jobs available for blacks, and in 1971 the state's most promising black capitalism venture, the Albina Corporation, which manufactured items for the Defense Department, went bankrupt.

rebuilding the city continues—a Hilton Hotel 23 stories high, three clustered apartment buildings at 25 stories or 240 feet, a Georgia Pacific structure soaring to 375 feet, and last planned—at this writing—a 536-foot contribution of the First National Bank of Oregon, which its architect's press agent ominously promises will rise "40 stories into the air, a towering challenge to Mount Hood." Architectural critics have pointed out that virtually all these new megastructures lack sophistication and create such fantastic parking space demands that vast stretches of the city are given over to parking lots and garages. Where they should bring life to downtown, they tend to do just the opposite with solid marble and concrete street-level exposures broken by nothing more romantic than a corporate entrance and a parking garage.

Sadly, the postwar planners permitted an ugly freeway to slice right along the downtown waterfront, decisively separating water and city. But there are signs of taste and culture. In the Skidmore Fountain area near the river, some of the "old" Portland has been preserved in a handful of Victorian commercial buildings. And in June 1970, the water started flowing in the fountains of a remarkable block-square combination of park, grotto, and public plaza within one of the Portland Development Commission's urban renewal projects. The New York *Times'* Ada Louise Huxtable, one of the sternest critics of Portland's renewal architecture, called the plaza "one of the most important urban spaces since the Renaissance." It consists of a series of man-made "waterfalls" in which 13,000 gallons a minute cascade over rock-like cliffs into a sunken pool. There are terraced steps and platforms that enable the visitor to walk anywhere, even behind the falls. The architect, Lawrence Halprin of San Francisco, had earlier tried a similar water idiom in Portland's Lovejoy Park; the spot became an immediate haven for hippies (who staged a wedding there) and squares alike.

Portland has a cautious middle-class city's standard interest in the arts, but no public subsidy or major corporate backing; the symphony, it is said, is forever hanging by its eyelashes. Universities do enliven the scene, especially Reed College, known nationally for its intellectual freedom and high quota of Rhodes Scholars, and Portland State University, begun after World War II to take care of former soldiers studying under the GI bill. PSU, then known as Vanport College, saw its campus wash away in the Columbia River flood of 1958, but it came back to become one of the country's fastest-growing institutions of higher education; by sometime in the 1970s it is expected to have the largest enrollment in the Oregon state system of higher education. Oregon's older, more established institutions are Oregon State at Corvallis, once purely an agricultural college but now strong in science and engineering as well, and the University of Oregon at Eugene, a respected liberal arts institution with an open atmosphere and notably strong student government.

(In 1971, the state board of higher education took a highly innovative step by authorizing the various public campuses to set up chapters of a so-called Oregon Student Public Interest Research Group, the financing coming from an add-on to mandatory student fees or special student contributions. The idea had first been advanced by consumer advocate Ralph Nader as a way to translate student discontent into effective and lawful action through research programs and appearing before courts, legislative committees, and regulatory agencies for what the students see as the public interest. Oregon students responded more favorably to the idea than those in any other state, and backers of the plan, including education board member Robert Holmes, a former governor, suggested that student involvement for change in society through lawful means would "result in a better form of higher education.")

After Portland, Eugene and Salem are the only two Oregon cities of more than 50,000 souls. Eugene, located 110 miles south of Portland in the upper Willamette Valley went up from 20,838 inhabitants in 1940 to 50,977 in 1960 and 76,346 in 1970, a phenomenal growth of 266 percent over three decades. The metropolitan area (Lane County) now has 213,588 people. But Eugene still maintains the atmosphere described in the WPA book years ago—that "of a landscaped park, with comfortable houses and long lines of shade trees bordering its streets." On Friday and Saturday nights, old farmers still head into town to shop in their bib overalls, white shirts, and ties. This is also a university town, and one with some intellectual ferment. The 14,000 students, plus hundreds of faculty and support personnel, add to the local economy.* But especially, Eugene benefits from its location in the heart of great fir and cedar forest belts, its lumber mills, and new industries springing up from diversification of timber use. Some see the city as becoming one of the major metropolitan centers of the Northwest.

Salem (pop. 68,296) relinquished second-place status to Eugene about a decade ago and finds itself disadvantageously placed so close to Portland (some 45 miles distant) that it cannot acquire facilities—major retailing, a jetport, or whatever—of a truly independent big city. It lives off the state government, a very prosperous fruit and vegetable canning industry, and timber. The generally low-slung white marble State Capitol, built in the 1930s after a predecessor was destroyed by fire, is eye-arresting—but I find hard to say beautiful. Atop the cupola stands an imposing statue of "the pioneer," the work of Ulric Ellerhusen. If the pioneer could see, he might be discouraged by the scene developing between Salem and Portland: wall-to-wall subdivisions across that once inviolate valley of the Willamette.

---

* In May 1971, Eugene voters approved a referendum calling for withdrawal of all U.S. troops from Vietnam by the start of 1972. The voting power of the newly enfranchised students was clearly reflected in the 5,470 to 3,957 vote.

# WASHINGTON

## EVERGREEN AND PUZZLING

WASHINGTON is a puzzling state. We think of it as cool, pristine, and ever-green. Yet the civilization around Puget Sound is industrial, cosmopolitan, intense, wracked by economic boom and bust. There are little towns in Washington as staid and conservative as anything the Midwest can offer, but the same state has a strain of feisty radical politics unrivaled in the American West. In population, Washington trails only California among all states beyond the Rockies. Yet only 120 years separate the prairie schooner and the Boeing 747, an 1850 population count of 1,201 (Indians excepted) and a 1970 tally of 3,409,169 (Indians this time included—exactly 33,386, to be precise).

Is Washington destined to be a junior-sized California, careening into its second century with waves of exploitive growth that carelessly devour landscape and fledgling traditions? Or will there be found here, in the geographically remote northwestern extremity of the coterminous U.S.A., a civilization which more happily balances man and nature, cultural innovation and social stability? The ingredients for all possible outcomes can be seen in the Washington mix. Washington seems forever to be in a state of becoming. But what it is becoming, no man seems to know.

Washington's modern history goes back to 1792, the year that Captain George Vancouver sailed into an exquisite estuary he named Puget Sound.

Vancouver also sighted and gave names to landmarks such as Mount Baker and Mount Rainier. It was in the same year that Captain Robert Gray explored the lower reaches of the Columbia River. Next came the era of the great trading companies. Early in the 19th century, the Northwest Fur Company established Spokane House, the first white settlement, and it is recorded that between 1834 and 1837 some 405,000 pelts—mostly beaver—were received by the Hudson's Bay Company's post at Fort Vancouver. In 1845 the provisional government of Oregon turned away a train of 80 overland wagons because they bore one Negro, free-born George Bush; the party then made its way to a site near what is now Olympia, and Washington had its first permanent American settlement. In 1851 the settlers north of the Columbia started a clamor for separate territorial status from Oregon, a request Congress granted two years later.

The next decades brought explosive growth. Thousands of Midwesterners, plus an influential leavening of New Englanders, came to homestead and to found and run the new cities of Seattle, Tacoma, Spokane, Walla Walla, Vancouver, and Olympia. In 1857 there was a gold rush on the Fraser River; in the 1860s the young territory sent men to fight for the Union; the first railroads arrived and in 1889, having grown to 350,000 souls, Washington gained statehood. The economy was dominated by lumber, and the woods soon filled with Swedes and Norwegians whose lifeblood was logging—indeed many came by way of timber-stripped Wisconsin and Minnesota and probably found Washington's mountains and sounds even more like the "old country." The Alaskan Gold Rush of 1897 brought a ton of gold on a single ship arriving at the Seattle docks, and by 1910 more than a million people inhabited the state. The Scandinavian element remained strong and with it an affinity for the Populist-Farmer-Labor politics of the Upper Midwest. Washington remains today one of the most Protestant of American states (only 14 percent of the people are Catholic or Jewish), and it is no accident that the two United States Senators are named Warren Grant Magnuson and Henry Martin Luther Jackson.

Depressions in Washington's mercurial economy and the wretched living conditions in company-owned towns, where loggers were fed poorly and forced to live in barracks with vermin-infested bunks, fed the fires of radical unionism around the turn of the century. From the Populist movement, many Washington workers and their sympathizers fed into the Socialist party and then between 1905 and 1910 became the spearhead of the new Industrial Workers of the World—better known as the "Wobblies." In 1916 the Wobblies struck lumber mills in Everett. Infuriated Everett industrialists broke the strike and ran about 40 Wobblies out of the town, forcing them to run a gauntlet where they were beaten as they departed. The Seattle IWW retaliated by sending a steamboat with 250 protecters to Everett, where they were met by gunfire from deputies and several died. In 1919 Seattle shipyard workers triggered a general strike that paralyzed that city for several days and aroused fears of a genuine revolution on American soil. A pitched battle broke out in Centralia between IWW members and American Legionnaires, with fatalities on both sides. After that, the IWW declined in strength, but a seed of radicalism, scarcely known elsewhere in America, had been planted.

The left-wing specter rose again in the depression of the 1930s, when the erratically led Unemployed Citizens' League of Seattle came close to seizing control of the Democratic party and frightened businessmen and property owners. California-model movements sprang up left and right, including Townsendites, Technocrats, and a movement to End Poverty in Washington (EPIW), echoing Upton Sinclair's EPIC in the Golden State. Several radically inclined men were sent to Congress, including Hugh De Lacy, a Representative in 1945–46. Fresh fuel for the radical fires came from "blowed-out, burned-out" dust bowl farmers who drifted into the state during the Depression years, occupying miserable shanty towns on the edge of Seattle and other cities, scrounging farm jobs where they could and helping to build the Grand Coulee Dam.

Thus it was that more than a little credence could be given to James Farley's celebrated remark about "the 47 states and the soviet of Washington." But it should be recalled that the radicals were stoutly resisted at every turn, both by the propertied interests and the more cautious Midwesterners and downright conservative border state folk who were an important part of the migration pattern from the 1850s right through the 1940s. Postwar prosperity has banked the fires of extreme radicalism. Even the issue of public versus private power, which raised temperatures to a boiling point in the 1930s and 1940s, has subsided to virtual invisibilty. The young engineers and other sophisticated workers employed by Boeing, the big employer, have been about as unconventional as a country square dance in Walla Walla. Even when Boeing employment takes a roller-coaster-like dive, its new technocrats accept their sudden unemployment as a result of hideous circumstances, nothing one can blame government, or even the company, for. No one takes the ramparts in Washington anymore.

But the old politics have left a legacy. Washington's ideological center is a few degrees to the left of most mountain and Pacific states; in 1968 it was the only one of them (except for Hawaii) that went for Humphrey. Republicans sometimes win, but only if they are moderate or liberal, and then rarely by more than 55 percent of the vote. Democrats may win by as much as the incredible 83.9 percent of the vote Senator Jackson scored against his Republican opponent in 1970. Birchers and other right-wingers make a lot of noise in Washington politics and actually control some important Republican county organizations, but they rarely win real elections. Democratic ultraliberals are at a similar, if not quite so complete, disadvantage. What Washington really likes to elect these days are men of moderation. In its eyes, Senators Jackson and Magnuson stand for just that. And so does the present governor, Republican Daniel J. Evans, who would be in the running, if there were such a thing, for the prize of being the best governor in

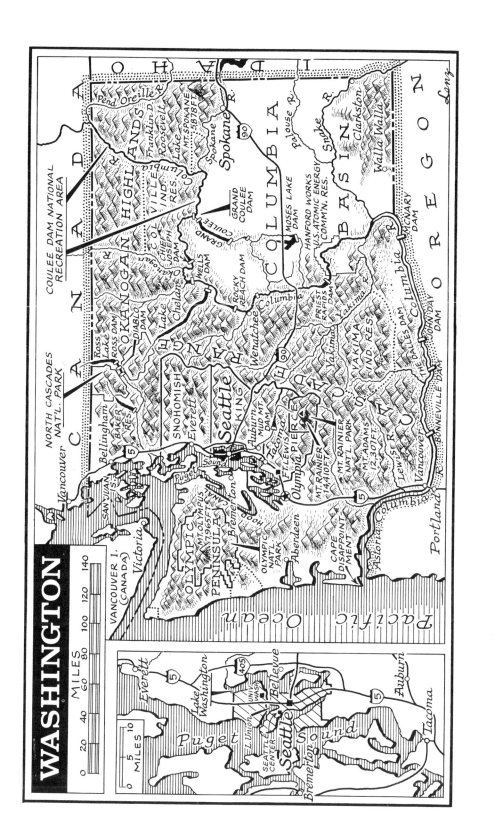

all the U.S.A. today. But we said Washington was puzzling, and Evans perhaps proves the point, because his policies are more progressive than those of his chief Democratic protagonists.

## A Geographic Overview, and the Indians

The borders which Congress finally settled on for Washington state make it the West's smallest, shaped roughly like a rectangle with the northwestern corner nibbled away by the ocean. The measurements are 340 miles east to west and 230 miles north to south. Within that space, one finds every topographic feature from dense rain forest to arid interior uplands, from river basin to alpine heights. In many respects, the geography is a carbon copy of Oregon's to the south, with the same Cascade Mountain Range slicing north to south and creating two entirely different life zones.

West of the Cascades, a temperate, moist climate is assured by the Pacific Ocean breezes, warmed by the Japan Current. The rainfall averages 36 inches a year, though it goes as high as 142 inches on the southwestern slope of the Olympic mountains (the wettest spot on the continent). By the time Pacific clouds reach the Cascades, however, they have lost most of their moisture. Eastern Washington is semiarid, with 10 to 20 inches of rain in a year; nor is there a barrier like the Cascades to protect the east from severe storms originating in the interior and from extremes of temperature.

Predictably, most of the people (about three-quarters) live west of the Cascades, and there one must also look for the seat of political and economic power. One finds it along the shores of 80-mile-long Puget Sound, bordered by cities and towns that hold more than 50 percent of the Washington population, from Bellingham and Everett on the north to Seattle and then Tacoma and Olympia at the south. The State Capitol at Olympia, in fact, sits on a height with a commanding view of the sound, perhaps the loveliest Capitol site in the country. Despite the rapid urbanization, there are still tree-lined and unspoiled stretches along Puget Sound's 1,800 miles of shoreline—reminiscent of the times, little more than a century ago, when a dense forest of Douglas fir, spruce, cedar, and hemlock swept down from the Cascades to the coast, unbroken except for Indian trails and occasional lowland valleys. The beauty of water, islands, and shores is enhanced by the view—whenever the mists clear enough to see them *—of Rainier and other Cascade peaks to the east and the Olympic Mountains to the west.

The Olympic Peninsula, close by Washington's most thickly settled area, is also its most remote and mysterious. A native, Betty McDonald of *Egg and I* fame, has called it "the most rugged, most westerly, greatest, deepest, largest, wildest, gamiest, richest, most fertile, loneliest, and most desolate" in all the world. Virgin evergreen rain forests are so thick that sun-

---

* Seattle may not be the rainiest city in America, but it certainly seems that way. It actually rains there some 163 days a year, in comparison to 54 days in San Francisco and 35 days in Los Angeles.

shine rarely reaches the ground and dark green ferns grow to the height of small trees. In their midst are the Olympic Mountains, alpine and beautiful.

The Cascade Range, shaped somewhat like an hourglass with a width of 100 miles on the Canadian and Oregon boundaries and 50 miles at midstate, has multiple peaks in the 8,000-foot range and then a series of great volcanic cones of which Mount Rainier (14,410) feet is the highest and most breathtaking. Rainier is, in fact, not only Seattle's most startling backdrop but the leading tourist attraction of the Northwest. Twenty-six live glaciers adorn its slopes, fantastic wildflower fields abound in summer, and wildlife includes bear, deer, mountain goats, and elk. Great stands of timber rise to their maximum altitude on Cascade slopes, making the mountains not only a barrier but an important timbering and recreation asset to the state.

Responsible geologists fear that Rainier and the other volcanic peaks of the Cascades might one day become active again, with catastrophic consequences. "The threat," according to Dr. Ian M. Lange of Fresno State College in California, quoted in *Newsweek*, "is not so much from lava flows—although these cannot be ruled out—as from massive mud slides caused by melting snow and ice. Mount Rainier, for instance, has about four cubic miles of snow and ice on its slopes. If volcanic temperatures inside the mountain began to rise, the melted water, mud and assorted rock debris that would flow off those slopes could inundate the Green River Valley." The last peak that erupted in the Northwest was California's Mount Lassen, in 1914. But geologic evidence indicates that some 5,000 years ago a massive wave of mud rolled down from Rainier and inundated 125 square miles of Puget Sound lowlands.

Last, we touch on the area east of the Cascades, some two-thirds of the land bulk of Washington. Where western Washington, in one writer's view, "is moist, heavily timbered, open to the chanting tides of the sea, volatile," eastern Washington "is continental in climate, sparsely wooded, locked by mountain ranges, cautious." Symbolic of the east is its big city, Spokane, which claims the whole region (plus parts of Idaho and Montana) as its "Inland Empire." Spokane not only harbors a strong contingent of John Birchers, but is so conservative that until the very recent past it would not dream of accepting any kind of federal aid.

The east's big interests are wheat, fruit, and cattle, plus scattered industry (especially around Spokane). Actually, the east consists of two major subregions. Along the Canadian and northern Idaho borders, and stretching toward Spokane, are the Okanogan Highlands, marked by gently rising hills, parklike forests, and a booming timber industry along with orchards and cattle ranches. Then, ranging from midstate down to the Oregon border, is the extensive Columbia Basin, in large part flat, arid desert land, though there are some rolling and even hilly portions. Covered with sagebrush, dull and uninviting, the basin area is without doubt Washington's least attractive. Only in its southeastern section is there somewhat more adequate rainfall, thick fertile soil, and diversified agriculture. Otherwise, the Columbia

Basin, except for specifically irrigated stretches, is limited to dryland wheat farming.

A word should be said about Washington's Indians, who live on three comparatively large reservations near Yakima, Spokane, and Colville, and 19 smaller reservations in the western part of the state. As writer Mike Layton observed in the *Argus*,

> Ever since territorial governor Isaac Stephens forced the Medicine Creek Treaty on the Nisquallys, Payallups and other tribal groups in 1854, Indians have been taking an official rooking from the state.
>
> The poorest of the state's poor, their life expectancies little more than half the white man's, their homes hovels, their children forced out of the schools and driven into alcoholism by shame, they are victims more of indifference than discrimination.
>
> Proud to the point of disdain, but shy and fearful of the busy, heedless world of the white, Indians too often refuse to compete. Their passivity looks like laziness to the go-getting white. But they work hard at those pursuits their heritage fits them for. "Try net-fishing some time," suggests Bruce Wilkie, college-educated manager of the Makahs at Neah Bay. "It's tough work and it doesn't bring in a whole lot of money."

A new militancy has appeared among the Indians in the past several years. The Yakima Indian tribe, for instance, is fighting hard for recovery of land it claims whites occupy in violation of treaty agreements, including 21,000 acres inside the Gifford Pinchot National Forest. An even more publicized fight is that of Indians in the state's coastal regions to maintain the fishing rights guaranteed them in the 1854 treaty—rights they claim are aboriginal but which state authorities say can be restricted in the interests of conservation. In the face of state regulations prohibiting net-fishing off the reservations, a practice said to endanger the supply of steelhead trout prized by sport fishermen, the Indians have openly defied the law. As they see it, fishing is not only a livelihood for them but a part of what they are as a people and what it means to be alive.

## The Economy and the Special Case of Boeing

Washington has shifted rapidly from an old wheat-timber-extractive industry base to a manufacturing economy. Before World War II, three-quarters of employment was in agriculture and forest products; now it is one-third, while aerospace and other businesses account for two-thirds of the jobs. One major industry—lumber, which employs some 45,000 Washington workers—is discussed in its Northwest-wide context in the Oregon chapter.

The diminished but continuing role of agriculture should not be overlooked. Annual farm income is about $800 million a year. Washington ranks fifth in U.S. wheat production, and in recent years has been first in apples, a $50–$75 million crop grown chiefly in the valleys running down the eastern slopes of the Cascades. (New York state took first place in apples in 1971, however.) Washington is first in hops and red raspberries and big in potatoes, pears, cherries, and asparagus. Many of these crops are grown in truck farms in the Puget Sound lowlands. Livestock and dairy products account for about a third of the farm income. Still a factor, though not a big one, is an annual fish catch (salmon, halibut, shellfish) valued at $31 million. Mining for a miscellaneous group of ores brings in over $90 million. With its three national parks—Olympic, Mount Rainier, and the newest of them all, North Cascades (established in 1968) *—plus Seattle and other attractions, Washington does a brisk tourist business of almost $400 million a year.

The Port of Seattle, closest on the West Coast to the Orient and capable of handling the deepest-draft ships, has been booming of late and passed its arch rival, Portland, in total tonnage. The port also runs the Seattle-Tacoma Airport, which has been expanded to accommodate rising passenger loads, including the big traffic to Alaska and the Great Circle Route to the Orient that goes out by the Aleutians and then down to Tokyo. Port activity generates some 17,000 jobs and hundreds of millions in annual payrolls, and it could get even bigger if the Alaskan oil pipeline from the Northern Slope is built and quantities of big oil tankers begin to deliver oil from the pipeline terminal on the Bay of Alaska to Puget Sound. But Edward Wenk, science adviser to President Nixon, has warned that if that happens, there would be a high danger of a tanker collision that "could turn Puget Sound into a Dead Sea."

Manufacturing, however, is the volatile and significant part of the Washington economy, with value added each year of more than $3 billion. In peak years, aerospace has accounted for almost $1 billion. Food and wood products, metals, chemicals, machinery, and ship-building are all important. The cheap power from the hydroelectric dams along the Columbia is responsible for a $400 million-a-year aluminum reduction industry, all new since the first plants were built in World War II.

The Boeing Company, its plants set in a string from Auburn south of Seattle to Everett in the north, dominates the economy of a large metropolitan region and a state as no other industrial firm in America. When Boeing is prospering, half of the manufacturing plant workers in the entire Puget Sound area are on its payroll. Then it is that Seattle and the satellite towns glow with economic health, population booms, and the future seems forever assured. But when Boeing's orders begin to dwindle seriously, as they did at the start of the 1970s, the result can be widespread unemployment.

Boeing's fortunes are tied to two mercurial markets—the demand for civilian aircraft and the demand for military weaponry. It was primarily in the commercial market from its founding in 1916 to the eve of World War II, when it had built to about 4,000 employees. Then came a wartime

* Still largely undeveloped for all but the sturdiest hikers, North Cascades is a wilderness of more than 1,000 square miles with jagged peaks, 150 active glaciers, and a remarkable abundance of wildlife. It would never have become a national park had it not been for one man, Patrick Goldsworthy, a professor of biochemistry at the University of Washington medical school. He founded the North Cascades Conservation Council and devoted almost every waking minute not on his job to the park idea. Senator Jackson sponsored the national park bill.

boom and a payroll peak of 48,000 as the company built Flying Fortresses and Superfortresses to defeat Germany and Japan. William Allen, who became president of Boeing in 1946 (and is still its board chairman and guiding light), recalls the day he was celebrating his new job and his 50th birthday at the Rainier Club. A telephone call came from Washington, and Boeing suddenly lost practically all of its government contracts. Employment declined precipitously to about 13,000 around 1947, but then came gradual recovery, the upturn of the Korean War, building of the successful B-52 bomber, and a decade of prosperous years. In the '50s, Boeing made the crucial, brilliant decision to plunge heavily into the commercial jet transport market with the first of its "700" series. From an also-ran in the civilian transport business, Boeing eventually came to produce more commercial jets than the rest of the free world combined. Despite some big disappointments about loss of weapons contracts in the late 1960s, Boeing was enriched by ICBM (Minuteman) and NASA orders (including first stage of the Saturn rockets), and by 1968 the firm reached an all-time high of 101,500 employees in Washington state.

But success, as it turned out, had its dangers. In 1966, Boeing decided to build the gigantic, 350-to-490 passenger 747 jetliner.* The investment ran into so many hundreds of millions of dollars that Boeing's resources were seriously taxed and Allen acknowledged the 747 "was really too large a project for us." Such problems, of course, are often solved by snappy sales, but the 747 went on the market just as the airlines were flying into stormy weather occasioned by spiraling costs, tight credit, overcapacity, and a slowdown in the growth of air travel. The 747 was marketed, but much more slowly than Boeing had hoped for. And while Boeing concentrated on the big plane, two old competitors, McDonnell-Douglas and Lockheed, were getting the jump on it with a somewhat smaller, more versatile "airbus."

In 1966, Bill Allen and his colleagues made another crucial decision: to go ahead, with federal backing, in development of a supersonic transport plane (the SST), capable of flying at nearly three times the speed of sound. Boeing had been studying the possibility of an SST ever since 1952. President Eisenhower had opposed the idea, but in 1961 President Kennedy urged that the federal government agree to pay 75 percent of the cost of designing and building two prototypes. The government had a duty to help pay for the development, Kennedy said, "because the national interest demands it." For its time, the commitment seemed normal; up to then the United States had never hesitated at the challenge of a great national project or an attempted technological breakthrough.

Kennedy had promised that "in no case" would the taxpayers' subsidy for development exceed $750 million, but in typical aerospace style, Boeing's request by 1970 was up to $1.3 billion for building two prototype aircraft

---

* The 747 plant, located at Everett, is as big as 10 Houston Astrodomes and has 35 more million cubic feet than the NASA assembly building at Cape Kennedy. (The structure is so large that clouds form inside and it may rain.)

and subjecting them to 100 hours of test flight. One official of the Transportation Department, which was enthusiastically backing the project, hinted that another $3 billion in federal help to Boeing might be necessary to finance actual production of the SST.* By this time, a full-scale debate had broken out over the SST, vividly reflecting the shift in national concerns and priorities over the decade of the 1960s. Supersonic transports, critics said, would lay down an infernal sonic boom, detracting from the quality of life on earth. Vapor trails from the plane at high altitudes, they charged, would accumulate until sunlight was blocked and the earth's climate affected. And worst of all, SST's enemies insisted, massive government aid for a plane that would benefit only a fraction of the people, getting them from one continent to another in a few less hours, was an unconscionable expenditure in relation to other, crying national priorities. Dr. Simon Ramo of TRW, a pioneer aerospace thinker and exponent of a systems approach to solve complex technical and social problems, told me he considered the SST a horrible example of piecemeal analysis, spending billions to get people between continents in two or three hours without looking at the crucial problems of landing capability, baggage access, or distance of SST airports from major cities.

To the criticisms, SST's defenders ducked, bowed, and fought back with skill. The sonic boom would be no problem, they claimed, because the aircraft would not be allowed to fly over land at supersonic speeds (a reversal of earlier expectations of SST enthusiasts). The vapor trails of a possible world fleet of 500 SSTs, at least according to one set of scientists, would be no greater than that of a single thunderstorm cloud. Anyway, it was said, the U.S. could not afford *not* to build the SST, because the French and British were building the supersonic Concorde and the Soviets had their own version and the U.S. could suffer a big balance-of-payments problem by not being early into the international market for the new generation of aircraft and, what's more, our national prestige would be hurt. The latter argument was apparently decisive in lining up President Nixon behind the SST, even after a blue ribbon committee he appointed concluded, in a secret report, that the SST would be economically wasteful and environmentally harmful.

After a long, bitter fight, Congress in 1970–71 finally decided *not* to give President Nixon the required next installment of $290 million to keep the SST project alive and moving. The decisive congressional vote came in the Senate in November 1970, a decision reconfirmed by both houses, in spring 1971. It was a stunning defeat, not only for Boeing, the Nixon Administration, and the Washington congressional delegation, but for the whole aerospace industry and its strong allies in the AFL-CIO. The policy reasons for killing the SST had been well summarized in a *Christian Science*

* Theoretically, all government payments would eventually have been reimbursed by Boeing, but only after it had sold several hundred SSTs—at a unit cost estimated at $40-$50 million or higher. The financial stakes were illustrated by the fact that airlines would have had to lay out close to $25 billion for the SST, compared to a total free world investment in existing jets of only $18 billion.

*Monitor* editorial in July 1970, which conceded, for purposes of argument, most of the SST camp's arguments about potential economic advantages and lack of a serious environmental threat. "There remains one potent, unresolved argument," the *Monitor* said. "It is simply whether, somewhere along the line, mankind must not put more effort into the quality of life, aid to the downtrodden and repair of the cities—and call a halt to prestige and materialist expenditures, to flying faster and to rushing around so smartly. Are we at the halt-calling place yet?"

To that question, Congress seemed to be saying yes, with consequences either frightening or exhilarating (according to one's point of view) for the United States' international position, for its economic development, and most important, for its self-image and character.

There was less ambiguity about the response in Seattle, however. The SST reversal caused loss of some 5,000 jobs at Boeing, but that was only a drop in the bucket compared to the company's overall loss of 71,500 jobs between the 1968 peak and December 1971. The Boeing optimist in those days, workers said, was a fellow who brought his lunch; a realist, the man who left his motor running in the parking lot. Thousands of highly trained engineers and administrators, men never before unemployed in their lives, were among those thrown out of work. Suddenly, as a report of the U.S. Senate Select Committee on Nutrition and Human Needs pointed out, a class of the "new poor"—people well educated and highly skilled but unable to find any kind of satisfactory employment—was created. The irony of their situation, the committee pointed out, was that the accumulated assets of such a family "have only bargain-sale value on the open market, and therefore, could only be sold at staggering losses. Yet these assets render many of the new poor ineligible for the benefits of the state's public assistance program and for the federal food stamp program." (Of the 71,500 people laid off by Boeing, however, only 10.7 percent—about 8,000—were professional and technical; the vast majority were blue-collar and clerical personnel.)

The area's economic statistics were nightmarish indeed. The Seattle-Everett metropolitan area, which had had a minuscule unemployment rate of 2.5 percent in 1968, had 10.7 percent unemployment by June 1970 and, by the end of 1971, 13 percent—the worst figure in the entire United States. By June 1971, over 103,000 persons were receiving unemployment insurance—but a high proportion of them were approaching the legal end of their unemployment benefits, and the state's unemployment insurance fund was in danger of going broke by mid-1972. By mid-1971, there were 234,000 people in the state on some form of welfare, up 45 percent from just a year before. Food stamps were going to 263,000 people in the state, up from 93,000 two years before. Seattle was dubbed the "food stamp capital" of the country, but even at that, there were also 34 heavily utilized emergency food banks. (The emergency food program, organized by area churches under the title of Neighbors in Need, at one point was raising thousands of dollars a day and feeding an average of 15,000 people a week—one of the most impressive church efforts for the needy ever seen in the U.S.) The general downturn of the national economy played some role in Seattle's plight, but Boeing was the main culprit; as publisher Philip Bailey of the Seattle weekly, the *Argus*, wrote in autumn 1971: "Boeing really did us in when it brought more than 50,000 employees into the area to build the 747, which resulted in too much home-and-apartment building, too much money for schools, too many new taxes, and now too much unemployment."

Oregonians, viewing the economic shipwreck up the coast, recalled Seattle's condescending ways during the good old days at Boeing and rejoiced that their own unemployment rate was only half as high. "Now Seattle," the Portland *Oregonian* editorialized, "is paying a terrible price for allowing a single industry to so dominate its economic structure."

The charge had more than a little validity. Except for its aggressive renewal of port facilities and a light scattering of industrial parks, Seattle did little through the 1960s to diversify its industry in the way Portland did. Part of the blame lay with Boeing itself, which has not encouraged development of many offshoot suppliers within Washington—firms which might then begin to diversify themselves, adding to the economic mix of the area. Nor had Boeing made much of an effort to diversify within itself, though there were hopeful signs by the early 1970s in programs like a computer services division, work on hydrofoils, rapid transit, air cushion vehicles, desalination, and agricultural-industrial site developments. But in dollar terms, the diversification was not yet substantial, and some predicted the company might be forced to merge with another, in a more stable line of industry, within the decade.* Through its rapid employee dismissals and other economies, the company was able to sustain a profit margin, even on a vastly reduced gross. But its backlog of jet orders was being rapidly depleted, and responsible economists saw nothing on the horizon to suggest a major comeback for the company in the foreseeable future. Bill Allen, in his early 70s and still a rugged individualist brooking no criticism of his leadership, continued to lay down the law at Boeing (where some employees call him "God"). But each new wave of layoffs encouraged new doubts in Seattle about who was really running the store.

As serious as the Seattle situation was for the people thrown out of work, it was packed with anomalies. In 1970–71, as the unemployment rolls ballooned, the average wage for people holding jobs in the Seattle area actually went up several percentage points. For the 87 percent of the people still holding jobs, times were not bad at all. There were no street breadlines, no shantytowns reminiscent of the Great Depression. Unless one visited the unemployment and welfare offices, downtown Seattle looked like a thriving place. Retail stores, at first hit by a nervous wave of nonbuying, bounced

* Another criticism of Boeing is that it has shown little initiative or leadership in the fields of poverty, unemployment, race relations, and the like—certainly not on the scale of many other leading U.S. corporations, including other aerospace leaders, or commensurate with its preeminent role in its home state. Partially, Boeing escapes criticism because its plants are environmentally "clean," spewing forth none of the noxious smoke or water pollutants that give people a chance to attack industrial goliaths elsewhere.

back, many with all-time records in sales and profits. Professionals like doctors, lawyers, accountants, and dentists, it was reported, never had it so good. The banks had plenteous funds to lend for new businesses or houses. The pleasure-boat business boomed.

And despite a widely lamented lack of sound planning by business and government to create new jobs to employ Boeing's castoffs, there was a chance that by the natural forces of economics, Seattle might eventually emerge with a healthier economy. The *Argus* reported the interesting observations of a newspaper publisher from eastern Washington, who suggested that Seattle should forget about huge new manufacturing concerns and concentrate instead on developing into a "headquarters city" for the entire state (and perhaps the entire Northwest), a nerve center for banking, trade with Alaska and Japan, insurance, stock brokerage, and distribution facilities. "It is possible that we should avoid growing much larger. A city of around 500,-000 may be the ideal size," the *Argus* suggested. "It might be far wiser to improve the quality of life here than to increase the quantity."

## *Power on the Potomac*

To protect its long list of federal interests—aerospace, military, farm price supports, shipbuilding, fisheries, water—Washington needs some powerful spokesmen in the nation's capital.* It has them. The remarkable Senatorial duo of Henry Jackson and Warren Magnuson, both Democrats, has more than half a century of accumulated seniority and provides a "clout" for Washington state that most other states could envy. Both men head major committees—Jackson the Interior Committee, Magnuson the Commerce Committee plus the powerful Appropriations Independent Offices Subcommittee. Both are skilled power dealers and, until the SST reversal of 1970, had never met defeat on an important issue for their state. (Jackson and Magnuson demonstrated their usual keen legislative skill in fighting for the SST, backed up by lobbies that ranged from Boeing and other aerospace lobbyists to AFL-CIO president George Meany. But a shifting set of national priorities, plus the ad hoc lobby campaign of a group including the Sierra Club, Friends of the Earth, National Wildlife Federation, and Zero Population Growth, proved their undoing. The crucial Senate vote against the SST was 52 to 41.)

There are interesting parallels between the Jackson and Magnuson careers. Both men were born of immigrant parents from Scandinavia (Jackson's

* The list of activities dependent on the national government seems never-ending. Boeing, despite its success in making commercial jets, still utilizes a third of its Puget Sound employees on various defense contracts. There are big military installations at Fort Lewis (an Army training and staging area), McChord Air Force Base, and Whidbey Island Naval Air Station, employing together 50,000 men and bringing about $300 million annually into the area. Price supports for wheat, plus government-sponsored irrigation projects, are vital to Washington farmers. Fisheries depend on federal protection, and shipbuilding on federal subsidies and regulation. And it was the federal government which built and maintains the great series of dams along the Columbia River.

from Norway, Magnuson's from Sweden), both became lawyers and prosecuting attorneys at an early age, both have been in Congress since their twenties, and both (except for a brief early marriage of Magnuson) remained bachelors until their fifties—and then got married.

After that, the personalities diverge. Magnuson has something of the image of an old-style pork barrel liberal, though he has in recent years surrounded himself with a bright, idealistic staff that helps him reflect to some degree the concerns of youth on the Vietnam war and similar issues. Magnuson's easy bachelor life won him a not-always-savory playboy image, almost causing his defeat about a decade ago, even though the activities subject to criticism had already begun to bank down. Since his marriage in 1964, everyone in Washington state will tell you, Magnuson has begun to work a lot harder. Home-state businessmen may not always warm personally to Magnuson, but they hold him in considerable awe for his skill at getting federal money.

Jackson, one of his longtime associates explains, is "a living embodiment of the Puritan ethic, a man to whom work is a virtue and pleasure is sin." Jackson is familiarly called "Scoop," a nickname that goes back to his boyhood when he delivered newspapers and was already proving his affinity for hard work. He is the soul of integrity, the only U.S. Senator I've ever heard of who does not own any stocks or bonds in any private corporations whatever and thinks a Senator shouldn't. He owns only U.S. Savings Bonds. His friends insist that Jackson has softening qualities not apparent to the outside world—tremendous loyalty to friends and care about the unfortunate. But his compassion is shown by private deeds, not worn on the sleeve.

Magnuson's chief congressional interests, outside of getting more money for his home state, have centered on consumer protection legislation (auto safety, cigarette warning, truth-in-packaging), health research, and public broadcasting. He has also sponsored national no-fault auto insurance legislation. But eyebrows were raised in 1971 when Magnuson agreed to introduce legislation that would enable the El Paso Natural Gas Company to continue its control of the Pacific Northwest Pipeline Company, which it had acquired in the 1950s in violation of federal antitrust law.

Jackson's interests have ranged further. In the conservation field, he has steered many important bills through the Senate, most memorably the wilderness bill in the early 1960s, the Redwoods National Park Act, the landmark 1969 Natural Environmental Quality Act, and the North Cascades National Park Act of 1968. He has also pushed hard for a bill to establish a national land-use policy and virtually force all the states to zone their land, allotting sections for future industry, recreation, homes, and natural preservation. (Hawaii is presently the only state with a complete statewide land plan.) But in 1971 Jackson asserted that the U.S. was in danger of becoming a "technological Appalachia" and attacked "environmental extremists" who would sacrifice economic growth on the altar of ecology.

The policy field for which Jackson has won the most attention, however, is national security. His concern with external threats and domestic subversion goes all the way back to his first years in Congress; in spring 1943, for instance, more than a year after West Coast Japanese had been herded into detention camps, he warned that "Pro-Japanese influence still exists in the United States, having gone underground temporarily." For the past two decades, he has been a leading apostle of U.S. military superiority to contain international communism, often warning of a "nuclear Pearl Harbor."

Jackson's fears about the Soviets may well be backed up by the data he receives as a member of the Armed Services Committee, the Joint Committee on Atomic Energy, and the Government Operations Subcommittee on National Security and International Operations, the latter under his chairmanship. He is often referred to jocularly as "the Senator from Boeing," suggesting that his concern about weapons systems is motivated by a role as Boeing's military-industrial agent in Washington. Former Senator Eugene McCarthy once said: "You can't have enough security for Henry. If he had his way the sky would be black with supersonic planes, preferably Boeings, of course." The Boeing part of the charge is unfair, because Jackson's personal integrity is simply too great to let himself be "used" by any private corporation. The long-term shift of Boeing to commercial jets means that the company is presently much less of a defense producer, in terms of its total orders, than it once was anyway. Still, one wonders how the frugal Jackson can—in the words of one Seattle journalist I spoke with—"bear the kind of people he's in bed with on the armaments issue. He must find many of them personally repellent."

Jackson's stature was already so great in 1960 that he was many liberals' choice to be John Kennedy's Vice Presidential running mate, and the Kennedys actually made him Democratic national chairman for that year's campaign. (In those days a strong defense stand and being a liberal Democrat were considered quite consistent. Jackson easily associated himself with Kennedy's warnings of a "missile gap" and view that in matters military, "America should be first—not first, if; not first, when; not first, but; but first.")

After the 1964 election, when Jackson garnered an unprecedented 72.2 percent of the vote, it was clear he had become the most popular political leader in Washington state history. In 1969–70, it seemed his position might be imperiled by his continued defense of the Vietnam war, the leading role he took in defending the Nixon administration's antiballistic missile program (an issue on which even Magnuson broke with him), and finally his general identification with the military-industrial complex. In 1968 McCarthy camp insurgents had upset the regular Jackson-Humphrey faction to take control of the Democratic party machinery in several large counties. And at the 1970 Democratic state convention at Spokane, the left-wingers embarrassed Jackson by pushing through highly controversial resolutions calling for amnesty for draft resisters and Army deserters, support of the Hatfield-McGovern amendment on the Vietnam war, and recognition of

Red China. Carl Maxey, an articulate black lawyer from Spokane, ran against Jackson in the 1970 Democratic primary and seemed for a while to be an almost serious opponent.

But as it turned out, Jackson was never in the least danger. He beat Maxey in the primary with 84 percent of the vote and won the general election by a similar margin, setting another statewide record. Lined up in Jackson's camp, it turned out, were all the regular Democratic politicians of the state, organized labor, *and* many of Washington's wealthiest, most conservative Republican businessmen, including Boeing's William Allen and William Reed, the multimillionaire head of Simpson Timber Company. (Jackson admires and seems to revel in the company of successful businessmen, who, like him, have succeeded in life. I heard the story of a dinner at Jackson's new home in Everett in the late 1960s, when men like Allen and Reed and others, who would have scorned Jackson a few years past as a socialist, were present. Jackson happily announced he was dedicating the great new dining room table to all his "old friends" present. His close ties to Republican business circles are symbolized by John Salter, his chief political operative in the state. Salter runs a Seattle public relations firm which has two chief clients: Boeing and Weyerhaeuser Company).

What makes Jackson such a phenomenally successful politician in his home state? The best explanation I heard came from Congressman Thomas S. Foley from eastern Washington, who used to work for Jackson. Jackson, Foley said, does communicate, quite honestly, a conviction that every American ought to have a decent break in life, a real opportunity—and votes accordingly for social programs. This picks up the support of most liberals and moderates. But Jackson's economic liberalism is mitigated, in the eyes of conservatives, by his own hard-work principle and personal Horatio Alger story. Secondly, Jackson's call for a foreign policy that looks first after *American* interests undercuts the fear of conservatives about "squishy-soft" liberals who would trust the Russians too far. "Instead," Foley points out, "Jackson ends up giving *them*—the conservatives—the lecture about not trusting the Russians. So the conservatives feel for the first time, 'here's a Democrat we can trust' with great national security issues. Again and again, you hear Washington Republicans saying, 'By God, there's one Democrat I'd vote for if he ran for any office, and that's Henry Jackson—even for President."

And thus it is that a Washington state Democrat, with an unblemished liberal record on social issues, can achieve such stature that President Nixon offered to make him Secretary of Defense, that he can win the vast majority of Republican votes in his own state (to the consternation of regular Republican party leaders there), and could become a serious contender for his party's Presidential nomination.

The Jackson Presidential platform set him clearly apart from his mainstream Democratic rivals. For one thing, he took a position on school busing very close to George Wallace's. He also diverged sharply on the issue of the environment, law and order, and of course national defense. Ultraliberals, Jackson alleged, were poor-mouthing America and demanding pure environmental controls that could put workingmen on the jobless rolls. He attacked "absolutists of the Left" who he said were "telling working people that liberals aren't interested in protecting them from crime and disorder, from disruption and muggers and dope addicts." Jackson aligned himself closely with the leadership of organized labor, put Old Guard Democratic leaders in control of his campaign organization, courted big business financial support, and refused to flinch when party figures like Oklahoma's Senator Fred R. Harris suggested that a Jackson nomination would make a liberal fourth party inevitable. "A new party on the left," Jackson said, "would help sharpen the issues." It would draw workingmen back into the fold and "give the Democrats a shot in the arm." But by its polarizing effect, the Jackson candidacy foreclosed the broad base of party support that a man usually needs to win a major-party Presidential nomination.

Washington tends to keep its U.S. Representatives, like its Senators, in office for a long time, but none has achieved the prominence of a Magnuson or Jackson. In 120 House elections since 1932, incumbents have been defeated only 13 times. The last big turnover was in 1964, when Democrats riding Jackson's coattails, and with his man John Salter guiding the campaign, switched the delegation from 6–1 in the Republicans' favor to 5–2 for the Democrats. (In 1970, with Jackson running again, the Democrats gained another seat to leave the GOP with only one district). Two of the young Democrats who came into office in 1964 are potential future Senators—Thomas Foley, a moderate-liberal whose personality and skill in handling tricky reclamation and farm issues enable him to win in the extremely conservative Spokane-eastern Washington district,* and Brock Adams, a bright, articulate Seattle liberal with good ties to blacks and the young Left. Magnuson will be 69 when his seat is next up for election in 1974, and there is some speculation he may step aside.

The men of Congress pay unusual deference to Washington's Congresswoman Julia Butler Hansen, and not just for reasons of male chivalry. She is chairman of the Appropriations Subcommittee on the Interior, which handled $2.2 billion in funds in 1971 alone, including pork barrel projects that are sometimes essential to her colleagues' political survival.

## Free-style Politics

Washington politics have settled down a lot since the turbulent days of the 1930s and before, but the state is still given to an unusually free, open style of politics. Voting participation is high, political "machines" are unknown, party conventions erupt into knock-down, drag-out fights, and almost everyone splits his ballot. (In 1970, for example, while the voters reelected

* Foley has another interesting distinction: he is the only Roman Catholic in living memory to have represented Washington in Congress.

Senator Jackson with 83.9 percent of the vote, they still retained Republican control of the state house of representatives. They turned down a progressive tax reform package but simultaneously voted in favor of legalized abortion—the first voters of any state to do so.) Another hallmark of Washington politics is the ease of lateral movement by new people into political activity, without the expectation of long apprenticeship in precinct party work.

One factor undermining normal party operations is the "blanket" or "jungle primary" ballot, unique to Washington and Alaska, which permits a voter to cast his primary vote for either a Republican or Democratic contender for each office on the ballot, regardless of his own normal party affiliation. The blanket primary is the people's own creation, having been voted by them as an initiative proposal in the 1930s. This power to legislate by initiative, in turn, sprang from the Progressive era when Washington was one of the national leaders in reforms like referendum and initiative, the direct primary, recall of officials, women's suffrage, and economic reform. In 1912 Washington was the only Western state to vote for Theodore Roosevelt and his Bull Moose movement, and in 1924 it gave an exceptionally strong though minority vote to Robert LaFollette's Progressive party candidacy for President.

Fights over control of the party organizations generate a lot of attention but really have significance only once every four years when a structured process of national convention delegate selection goes into operation, functioning on a stairway of precinct caucuses and county conventions leading to a state convention. In 1964 Republican right-wingers exploited the system to get a convention slate for Goldwater, and in 1968, over the fierce opposition of Senator Jackson and the "regular" Democrats for Humphrey, the McCarthy movement took control of several large counties and ended up with about a third of the votes at the Democratic National Convention.

On other occasions, political influence devolves on a set of greater or smaller political warlords and their factions, whose interests may run from patronage to extreme political philosophy. Each of the U.S. Senators has his own personal organizations (and sometimes lends it to his colleague), as does any governor, the Republican right, the Democratic left, and the like. Candidates get minimal financial assistance through regular party channels, and in fact campaign finance remains a dark continent in Washington state because of the lack of any reporting law.

The unusual ways of Washington politics have led to strange anomalies. At several points during the 1960s, it appeared that the right wing, abetted by its control of the King County (Seattle) Republican organization, would take control of the entire state GOP.* King County is key to Washington politics, since it has 34 percent of the population. The right wing has another bastion of strength in eastern Washington, where many border state

* Much of the bankrolling of the GOP right-wing effort was done by Bill Boeing, a third-generation member of the aircraft family. He neither works for nor has discernible influence with the company.

and Southern people arrived during the depression. But Governor Evans and other Republican state officeholders, their base of strength in the open primary, have held the upper hand with the sole exception of national convention delegate choice in 1964. In 1965 Evans openly condemned the John Birch Society and its attempt to infiltrate the Republican party, and his ally, state Republican chairman Montgomery ("Gummy") Johnson, adroitly maneuvered to hold the right wing in check. Since 1965, Evans told me, "the right wing has won some organizational elections while we've been winning the real elections." Despite their ultrarightists, both King County and eastern Washington vote overwhelmingly for Evans in general elections. A rightist Republican national committeewoman, Mrs. Albert Cooper, was ousted by Evans forces in 1968, and the right wing failed to control the Washington delegation to the 1968 Republican National Convention. In 1970, GOP wheelhorse and long-term incumbent Charles O. Carroll was defeated for renomination as King County prosecuting attorney by Christopher T. Bayley, an Evans ally. The election left the county's right-wing Republican leader, Kenneth Rogstad, and his equally conservative successor, Dennis Dunn, without a power base.

Evans and his friends represent a modern, pragmatic form of Republicanism so progressive in tone, and the prevailing control on the Democratic side had drifted so far to the right, that the Republican party today appears to be the more progressive party of the state. Democratic liberals of the McCarthy stripe, in actual elections, have turned out to be a distinct minority in their own party, and the prospective 1972 Democratic candidate for governor, state senator Martin Durkan, is a fiscal conservative whose tax-cutting, hold-the-line budget policies would warm the hearts of many Republicans.* Democratic liberals consider Durkan and the group controlling the state party to be rank opportunists, and at least in private, they express warm approval of Evans and other Republicans like Attorney General Slade Gorton (a prospective successor to Evans praised in the *Argus* as "the most intelligent and best-informed public servant in the state"), Secretary of State A. Ludlow Kramer (who is thoroughly identified with youth and liberal causes), and state senator Joel Pritchard (a progressive and leading contender for a GOP-dominated congressional seat in the Seattle area).

The Democrats' conservative turn stems in part from the decline in liberal militancy in the state's labor unions. The unions have been strong in Washington for many decades, having organized the lumber, fishing, and maritime industries at an early point and worked closely with the Scandinavian-influenced co-op movements, the Grange, and the public power camp. Since the 1930s, Washington has ranked first or second in the nation in the

* Durkan is not conservative on all issues, however. In 1971 an alliance of big farming interests and organized labor wanted to put farm unions under restrictions that would have effectively barred farm labor organization and farm strikes. When Dolores Huerta, vice president of César Chávez's United Farm Workers Organizing Committee, came to Olympia to oppose the bill, Durkan lent his strong support.

percentage of its nonfarm work force in unions (41.4 percent in 1968, trailing only West Virginia with 41.9 percent). Production workers' average earnings, before the latest recession, ranked fifth highest in the country.

This was and is a banner state for the Teamsters. It was in Seattle that Dave Beck made his start as a laundry truck driver, later climbing to the presidency of the International Brotherhood of Teamsters before his high-living ways and free use of union funds finally sent him to federal prison in 1962 for falsifying union tax returns. (Beck's tumultuous career, in which he virtually fulfilled his pledge to unionize "everything on wheels," the "goon squads" in raiding, charges of strikebreaking, the "labor temple" he built for the Teamsters in the national capital, his Fifth-Amendment-riddled appearance before the McClellan committee, and the $850,000 in legal defense fees now fade into history. But Dave Beck, in his late seventies and his 30 months behind bars long since finished, prospers on in Seattle with a $50,000 annual union pension and some $75,000 from other holdings.)

Among Washington's most powerful unions today are government employees (who earn sixth highest average wages among the states) and school teachers (14th highest wages). Neither of their organizations operates very openly in the political arena, however. The Longshoremen, now numbering 7,500, used to be a radical factor in Harry Bridges' heyday but are settled down to respectability. Within the AFL-CIO, the biggest individual union is the Machinists, who number 45,000 at Boeing alone when the big company prospers. The Machinists are about the closest the labor movement comes to a militant industrial union, but they never got a union shop at Boeing, and their political influence is limited. They are tied in closely with military-industrial complex thinking. Lacking from the union mix is a politically assertive, issue-oriented union playing the kind of role that United Auto Workers do elsewhere. (State AFL-CIO president Joe Davis recalls that when the UAW pulled out of the AFL-CIO, his organization lost only 35 members.)

The unions do have a legislative program, and they push it strongly through a United Labor Lobby which includes practically every union in the state. But the issues the lobby pushes—unemployment compensation, protection of favorable provisions in the workmen's compensation fund law, against the Evans tax reform package—seem to be more oriented to protection of the narrow interests of unions and their members than to broad social reform. Labor's biggest election-time victories were in 1956 and 1958, when it beat down right-to-work proposals on the state ballot, helping many Democratic candidates in the process. In 1968 the unions got 147,000 signatures on petitions for an initiative to reduce maximum interest charges in the state from 18 to 12 percent, a victory won over fierce opposition from the financial community.* But the same unions couldn't even produce a man to serve on the governor's committee on causes and prevention of

---

* Davis is especially proud of this achievement, saying it will provide a yardstick for interest charges just as public power provided a yardstick for electric power costs in general.

civil disorder, and discrimination is so rife that numerous cases are brought before the state discrimination board. The unions were a hotbed for Wallace sympathy in 1968, but they take few positions on civil rights or urban problems.

Washington's weak political parties and the consequent lack of disciplinary power in party caucuses make interest groups enormously important in the Washington legislature. Shelby Scates of the Seattle *Post-Intelligencer* reports that "Washington's state legislature pays less heed to the poor and minority groups than to unions and industry. Highway interests—oil, asphalt, contractors, car builders—have the run of the place. Urban mass transit interests barely have a foot in the door." Other interests which maintain especially active lobby operations include teachers, timber, aircraft, trucking, banking, commercial fishing, pinballs, public and private power, gravel, wine and beer (Washington is an important beer-exporting state). The Grange is active in behalf of rural interests and, until overridden by initiative votes of the people, kept the legislature from acting to approve daylight saving time, colored oleomargarine, or reapportionment.

Between 1901 and the 1950s, the legislature failed to reapportion once of its own volition; when the people took the matter in their own hands and enacted a population-based apportionment in 1956, the legislature quickly amended it to retain the control of rural counties and undo the work of the League of Women Voters and others who had pushed through the initiative. (One-man, one-vote reapportionment followed in the 1960s on insistence of the federal courts, but by then, in the familiar pattern, the suburbs had grown so much that the long-deprived cities failed to benefit very much.) Most observers agree the legislature suffers from a surfeit of often overlapping committees, too many committee assignments for each legislator to act effectively, inadequate pay for legislators, and lack of constitutionally mandated annual sessions.

When the legislature is in session at Olympia, a marble corridor running from House to Senate and nicknamed "Ulcer Gulch" teems with lobbyists. They perform the traditional functions of information-supplying for a greatly understaffed legislature, plus the wining and dining techniques of lobbyists everywhere. But their real clout comes through campaign money where, again, the Washington political parties are weak. "Campaign contributions," Scates observes, "are to lobbying what wheat is to bread."

On the "public interest" side, a new and exceptionally effective lobby is the Washington Environmental Council, formed in 1967 by the Sierra Club, Audubon Society, and Washington Roadside Council and numbering 50 organizations by 1970. The conservationist amalgam arose, in the words of Seattle attorney John Miller, who directed the council's lobbying, when "we had run into the real estate, agriculture, and timber interests and failed abysmally because we had no muscle." Brigades of volunteer lobbyists organized by the council were instrumental in getting through a major package of environmental bills in 1970. Years before then, however, Washington had made some major strides in conservation legislation. Most notable was one of America's earliest and strongest anti-billboard laws, passed in 1961 after an almost singlehanded campaign by Jack B. Robertson, founder of the Washington Roadside Council.

As often as not, however, "public interest" legislation is rejected. In 1971 a broad reform program was pushed by the Washington State Coalition for Open Government—a bipartisan coalition including county municipal leagues, the Environmental Council, the League of Women Voters, and the Washington branch of Common Cause. Pressure was put on the legislature to pass a five-point package of reform bills on campaign funds disclosure, conflict of interest, open public meetings, freedom of information, and lobbying disclosure. Most of the proposed bills were defeated, but under a threat by the Coalition to launch an initiative, the legislature did open all legislative committee hearings to the press and the public.

The Boeing Company, perhaps because almost everyone realizes how synonomous its economic interests are with those of the state, fails to play the heavy role in legislative politics or campaign financing that oil, for instance, does in Texas and Oklahoma, or coal in West Virginia, or copper until recent years in Montana. But while the company steers clear of exerting direct political influence commensurate with its power, it does have its lobbyists at Olympia, does run practical politics courses for its employees, and has encouraged scores of them to run successfully for public office. Boeing President Wilson in 1971 fired a right-wing-leaning lobby staff the company had maintained in Olympia and installed a new group headed by Bud Coffey, a veteran of the SST fight in Washington. This may signal a change from the company's policies of a few years before, when a distinguished state senator was fired from his job with a law firm that had a major Boeing account a week after a legislative session in which he crossed the company by voting against a limitation on the property tax.

## An Extraordinary Governor

Daniel Jackson Evans broke into politics from the unlikeliest of all professions—civil engineering. A tall, shy man with a clean-cut, Dick Tracy look, he still has the aura of the eagle scout he was in his boyhood. His personal integrity is so obvious that the nickname "Straight Arrow" has stuck with him. But Evans is tough-minded, has an unusual grasp of the intricacies of state government, doggedly pursues idealistic goals, and is faulted only for not being as gracious to his opposition as a politician is expected to be.

Evans made his political debut in 1956, at age 31, when he was elected to the state house, where he eventually became the Republican floor leader. Eight years later, he took on and defeated two-term Democratic Governor Albert Rosellini by a 148,564-vote plurality in the midst of the 1964 Democratic landslide. The contrast in candidates could scarcely have been greater. Rosellini, Washington's first Catholic and first Italian governor, had a natural politician's warmth but governed in a mediocre way, surrounding himself with a coterie scarcely designed to generate public trust. (Cocktail parties of the Rosellini inner circle and friends, I heard from one Democratic source, "were filled with guys that looked like, if perhaps they weren't, Mafioso—all decked out in dark suits with white ties and diamond rings on their pinkies.")

Running for a second term in 1968, "Straight Arrow" lucked out again when his managers discovered, and leaked to the press, the fact that his opponent, Attorney General John J. O'Connell, was so enamored of gambling that he had a multithousand dollar line of credit in Las Vegas. The Evans camp made the revelation not because it feared losing; polls had shown the governor in the lead, but the gambling issue dried up O'Connell's campaign finances, so that the Republicans had to spend less themselves. Evans coasted to victory with a plurality of 132,116 votes.

One can only say of Evans' gubernatorial service that the office has ennobled, rather than compromised, the man. With courage and tenacity, he has fought for what he believes in, the most important thrusts coming in the fields of tax reform, government organization, the environment, and social issues. Of these, he has had perhaps the least success with taxes, the most success with the environment. The tax structure in Washington is a mess, tied to a regressive 4.5 percent sales tax, no income tax, and the problem of rapidly escalating property taxes and special levies to keep the schools going. In 1970, despite Evans' backing, the voters rejected a single-rate tax reform package. But he kept on trying, appointing a diverse citizens committee that produced a proposal for a graduated net income tax which was praised in many quarters but still unapproved by the legislature at the end of the 1972 session.

Washington has long had one of the strongest state governments in its support of local education—ranking seventh among the 50 states in its share of support (56.6 percent of local costs) in 1970—71. School attendance rates are exceptionally high, expenditures per pupil rank sixth in the country, illiteracy is very low, average educational attainment of the population very high. But all this could be endangered by escalating school budgets which localities lack money to finance. The existing tax structure is also open to criticism because an inordinate share is paid by the elderly and others on fixed incomes.

After several years of disappointment on environmental legislation, Evans finally made a big breakthrough in 1970. Riding the wave of public concern in that year, he won legislative approval of a package of bills that thrust Washington, almost overnight, to the fore among the states in ecology legislation. A state department of ecology was set up to combine air and water pollution control, solid waste management, and water resources functions—all of which had previously been split among many departments.*

---

* Other states with similar "environmental departments" include Arkansas, California, Delaware, Hawaii, Illinois, Maine, Michigan, Minnesota, New Jersey, New York, Oregon, Vermont, and Wisconsin.

One of the country's first councils was set up with power to approve or reject all proposed nuclear and fossil-fueled power plant sites, with help from a "council for the environment." Anyone who spills oil on state waters was placed under unlimited liability for clean-up costs (along the lines of a similar 1970 law in Maine). Gravel pit operators and other surface miners were required to get a license for each excavation, submitting a plan for restoring the site later and posting a performance bond. Water pollution control was tightened to regulate the discharge of pollutants at their source, rather than requiring state officials to prove eventual harmful effects some-where downstream, as previously. Owners of open spaces, farmland, and timberland were allowed to apply for taxes at "current-use" rates rather than at the highest-potential-use rate that encourages rapid sellouts and urban sprawl. Only a proposed seacoast management act was pigeonholed in the legislature, but it was passed a year later—contingent on voter approval in the 1972 general election.

Most of the Evans environmental bills were met by cynical sneers at the start of the 1970 session. But the day-in, day-out lobbying of the conservationists helped, and so did a television speech in which Evans appealed over the heads of the legislators and lobbyists to the people for aid in passing his package. The legislature was inundated with 5,111 telegrams in three days and soon acted affirmatively.

Washingtonians hope the new ecology department may move rapidly to correct their most serious pollution problem—the effluent from pulp and paper mills. Federal officials have also been trying to force Scott Paper, Simpson, Weyerhaeuser, and other giants to stop corruption of the state waterways. All three have actually closed some pulp plants because of added investment that would be needed to stop pollution, or because of weak markets.

Evans' efforts at modernization of the state government, which began his first year in office with creation of a "Little Hoover" project, have met with only limited success. The legislature turned down many of his proposals to modernize by creating "superagencies." Among the casualties was his proposal for a department of transportation that would bring the high-way department under executive control and thus check indiscriminate roadbuilding and shift some emphasis to mass transit needs. But Evans did succeed in making Washington, as he explained in an interview, "the first state in the U.S. with combined budget and planning functions. We have a continuous flow from issue planning and our concepts into long-range development, breaking down into shorter range targets. And our budget system carries through on the goals, and we have some measurements to test our performance."

Evans' deep social consciousness comes out when he approaches areas like youth, race, juvenile delinquency, and mental health. Washington, he says, ranks only 22nd among the states in population but has an urban, sophisticated civilization more akin to the top 12 states than some of the

Midwestern and border states immediately ahead of it in size. In the mid-1960s, as Boeing and the general economy boomed, the Seattle area experienced a sharp increase in Negro population but lacked either the housing or facilities to cope with it. Many people believed Seattle was about to "blow," and there were rumors of an organized black insurgency. Informing the black community but not the press, Evans one hot day traveled to the Central Area of Seattle, where most of the city's 37,868 blacks are concentrated, to talk to 12 angry and upset young militants at the YMCA. As Evans tells the story,

> One youngster pulled his chair right around in front of me and said, "Governor, I'd like to take a gun and shoot you." That's pretty spooky. I said, "What good would that do?" And he said, "It would be one more white bigot gone." I said, "That really doesn't solve anything, does it? After all, what are you going to do about it?" There was some hesitation, and I went on, "Look, why don't you right here form a committee and you go out and find out what ought to be done, and you tell me. Come and see me whenever you're ready."

The young militants did, in fact, form their committee, drew up a list of demands that centered on improved government services in their community, and took the list to Evans. Out of the exchange grew the idea for and reality of a multiservice center in the Seattle ghetto, bringing government services closer to the people instead of sending them out into a hostile, distant world of white-run offices downtown. The center started out with six state agencies involved, and it succeeded, in Evans' view, not only in humanizing state government in the eyes of the needy but in getting people in state government to talk with each other—public assistance and employment security workers, for instance, comparing notes on the same clients and cross-referencing to provide better services.

In an attempt to generate new ideas and wide citizen involvement, Evans appointed an urban affairs council which set up task forces delving into myriad aspects of housing, education, health, the physical environment, and justice. (Evans acknowledges that he criticized Rosellini for appointing too many citizen boards and commissions, but that "subsequently I've probably appointed more committees than any two governors in history. You need people—first for their expertise; second, to sell whatever solutions you do come up with.") Areas of significant progress have included mental retardation, where the focus has been shifted from big state institutions to day-care centers, group homes, halfway houses, and sheltered workshops on a community basis, and a juvenile correction program under which the state subsidizes communities to work with youngsters locally, instead of sending them to a state institution, in return for a subsidy. "The community," Evans insists, "is the most natural and best place to treat all these problems if possible."

What Evans would really like to accomplish is a "massive involvement of people and industry and government in a three-way partnership" to solve local problems. He believes that a university architecture school, for instance, should really study slum area rehabilitation instead of unreal theoretical problems, and that medical students should study better methods of health care delivery to those who really need it. As a pilot program, the students of oceanography at Washington State College in Bellingham got together with the Lummi Indians, a tribe that has long eked out a meager existence by fishing and clam digging, to develop new and better ways of enhancing shell fish production. The students and faculty thus succeeded in helping a tribe that desperately needed to improve its economic base.

Evans' eyes light up, in fact, when he tells other stories of individual volunteers going into mental hospitals, picking lonely inmates they can relate to on a person-to-person basis, and succeeding after months in giving patients a new orientation and even arranging for some to leave the hospital for foster homes. (Lifetime tenancy in a state institution costs about $400,000.) Young people and the retired both offer great pools of volunteer help that could be tapped, Evans believes. "It is difficult to generate this type of activity," he acknowledges. "But it is not impossible."

In 1970, Evans was insisting that state government departments increase minority employment to a minimum of 5 percent at all levels. The same year, when student disorders plagued the country, he went on television to acknowledge he had received many demands for broad retaliation against student violence in Washington. But instead of a tough law-and-order speech, he delivered a plea for toleration, compassion, and patience in dealing with youthful rebellion. Shelby Scates depicts Evans' speech, like his venture into the Central Ward, as a "morally brave action" that a "lesser man" would not have made. Evans also resisted strong appeals to turn out the National Guard on the University of Washington campus during disturbances just prior to the Kent State tragedy in 1970. His action may well have spared lives; he also ended up being probably the only popular politician among the students.

Evans also gave his seal of approval to a remarkable reform program at the Washington State Penitentiary at Walla Walla—a change that made it, starting in 1970, the country's most liberal and innovative maximum security institution. Convicts were given the right to choose their own inmate government in elections held each six months; now guards at Walla are called "correctional officers" and the inmates are called "residents." Prisoners sit in on disciplinary committee meetings, may dress as they please, may make unlimited outside telephone calls, and can send and receive as many letters—all uncensored—as they please. There is even a program under which prison staff members occasionally invite lifers to their homes for dinner. The program is not without its critics, who charge that the convicts now run the prison by intimidation and that prison officials and guards are in danger. But in 1971, Evans was able to tour the prison accompanied only by two inmates. A few months later, the revolt at Attica and killings at San Quentin ensued. The enthusiasts of the Washington system suggest they are on the only track to insure that no Attica or San Quentin ever occurs at Walla Walla.

Evans' brand of politics is as forthright as it is liberal. In 1964 and

1968, he supported Rockefeller for the Republican Presidential nomination, and he insisted even after Nixon's election that he was still glad he had come out for Rockefeller, "even when his chances were only one in a thousand, because I felt the heart of our problems was domestic, and Rockefeller could cope with them." Little love was originally lost between Evans and most of Nixon's political operatives. In 1970, the Evans camp made no effort to hide its disgust and anger when Nixon and the national GOP aided and abetted Senator Jackson's reelection campaign at the expense of the Republican ticket in Washington state. Subsequently, however, Evans made a successful effort to improve relations, an endeavor in which he was helped by his firm friend and supporter, Presidential aide John Ehrlichman, who comes from Seattle.

## *Seattlescape*

For day after day, the dark, moist clouds may come scudding in over the Olympic Mountains, across Puget Sound, and onto Seattle, cutting visibility to fierce minimums and leaving one wondering just what kind of city surrounds him. And then the cloud cover recedes, and the scrubbed Seattle air glows like that of few cities on earth. Everywhere, brilliant waters surround this isthmus city of half a million people: Puget Sound on the west, Lake Washington on the east, and a canal tying them together. In the distance, icy mountains stand sentinel on every side, Rainier the greatest among them. And then there are the hills of the city itself: shockingly precipitous, omnipresent, and offering, as in San Francisco, ever shifting city- and waterscapes. Of all American cities, there are few—perhaps none—more beautiful.

My friend Bruce Chapman, a progressive Republican who was elected to the Seattle city council in 1971, took me on an extended tour beyond the generally familiar downtown-Seattle Center axis. One is impressed by how verdant a city this is, the Pacific moisture forever nurturing the growth, and how overwhelmingly middle class it is, with almost everyone in a single-unit house; not only apartment houses but even townhouses are stoutly resisted. No one goes far in a straight line in Seattle, for there is always a lake, an insurmountable hill, or a twist in the land to throw you off. Personally, I find the city one of the hardest in America to get around in, a cartographer's nightmare, but one of delightful variety.

Among Seattle's unusual sights are Lake Washington, with its varied shoreline of marinas and parks and many homes of architectural excellence, and smaller Lake Union, where some 6,000 to 7,000 people live permanently on houseboats. Lake Washington, threatened by a build-up of planktonic algae and loss of water clarity, was subjected in the 1950s and '60s to a vigorous clean-up that required legislative approval of a 10-city form of limited metropolitan government and issuance of municipal bonds for more than

$140 million in new water treatment facilities. But the price was doubtless well worth it. As Seattle civic leader James R. Ellis said at a 1966 dedication of a major treatment plant, "We are transients on these hills and shores, and the waters are not ours to spend. Here we mark some proof that urban man can live and work in a beautiful land without destroying beauty."

Later a very strong citizens' movement was launched to stop indiscriminate commercial construction along the shores of Lake Union, to get a 12-acre city park built along its banks, and to protect the quality of its water. In addition to these and other lakes, Seattle has the University of Washington in its pleasant, wooded, tightly packed campus; the sequestered, sylvan-like setting of the Seattle Research Center, part of the nationally operative Battelle Memorial Institute for scientific research; and some jewels of parks, including the university arboretum. Now authorized is a 300-acre new park to be constructed on the site of the Army's mostly abandoned Fort Lawton, on a peninsular bluff overlooking Puget Sound. The city has neighborhoods of every income description up to the most patrician housing settlement, Broadmoor, with its own protective guardhouse.

Seattle has made two quite successful efforts to establish its place in the sun by means of fairs—first the Alaska-Yukon Pacific Exposition in 1909, and secondly the Seattle World's Fair of 1962. The modern-day fair was a key turning point in bringing Seattle out of its provincial shell. Seattle auto dealer and attorney Joseph Gandy sparked the effort to make the fair a reality. Amazingly, the affair turned in a cash surplus (in stark contrast to the New York fiasco a few years later). And since most of the buildings were constructed for permanent use, the city was left with a grand, cost-free (to the taxpayer) $90 million legacy—the Seattle Center, which became the cultural and recreation center of the city. The center includes the illustrious Space Needle, a 3,100-seat Opera House, the 750-seat Repertory Theater that has inspired the founding of several others nearby, a Modern Art Pavilion which has also led to the founding of almost a dozen galleries in the area, and an excellent Science Center which is housed in the building the U.S. Government had built for itself at the fair.

The Seattle Center also includes a coliseum used chiefly for sports events. City voters decisively rejected a proposal for an elaborate domed stadium there, and a possible downtown stadium site later emerged. The related subject of professional sports is a sore one in Seattle. In 1970 the American League Seattle Pilots pulled up stakes to become the Milwaukee Brewers, after Seattle refused to put up extra millions to keep the club in town. Baseball pitcher Jim Bouton commented sardonically in his best-selling book, *Ball Four*: "A city that seems to care more for its art museums than its ball park can't be all bad."

Another vestige of the 1962 fair, Seattle's monorail, takes one from the Seattle Center to downtown Seattle in 95 seconds. Little of the architectural excellence of the Seattle Center appears in the plethora of new high-rise office buildings that have been filling downtown since 1958, most of them seemingly products of package builders exclusively concerned with cost. Only a scattering of the new structures, including a Yamasaki-designed IBM building, have real quality; I heard it said that the best-designed building downtown was still the 40-year-old Northern Life tower. Looming above the present scene is the bronze 50-story First National Bank building, so mammoth that it is destructive in scale of the other buildings around it. The architects were so determined to get a pure and pristine effect that they created a cold, sloping ground-level approach, instead of terracing, and kept off the ground floor restaurants or bars or shops or anything that might have made the building truly attractive to people. Some in Seattle now hold out more hope for the new federal building and world trade center, being built on a 9-acre waterfront tract with a design by Fred Bassetti, a creative Seattle architect with a strongly humanistic approach.

I had a chance to visit with Bassetti in his charming studio in a converted old single-story business structure beside the monorail. The studio itself, with wide working spaces for the staff, tapestries, plants, an interior balcony and outside terrace, has won an award from the Seattle chapter of the American Institute of Architects as "a warm, pleasant and busy place" and an example of restoration that gives "new life to the city." Bassetti harbors a nostalgia for the lusty, colorful Seattle of yesteryear, and bemoans much of the "progress" that has come to town:

Downtown Seattle 30 years ago was a dynamic, active urban center. The streets and sidewalks were alive with people. One could go anywhere from almost everywhere cheaply and quickly, on trackless trolleys, with little noise and no fumes. Shopping in town was convenient and the choice of stores was excellent. Small shops throve on every street from First Avenue to Eighth and from Yesler Way to Stewart Avenue. Good restaurants, serving every type of food, could be found in all quarters. Remember Manca's, Rippe's, Blanc's, and The American Oyster House? Each reflected the personality of the owner, each had integrity—not claiming the hollow titles "gourmet" or "cuisine."

Entertainment could be had in any form, from opera in the lovely old Metropolitan Theatre to bawdy shows along the waterfront or gambling in dozens of Chinese lottery houses on Washington and Main Streets, to say nothing of the young man's instant education up the Hill.

Today we have Batman. We also have daily traffic jams because although the traffic network has been adapted to cars instead of to people, it is not successful. Downtown, 40 percent of the major department stores we once prowled in have died a lingering death. [Shopping has gravitated to] shopping centers as faceless and homogenized as the products they sell. The wonderful diversity in restaurants is no more. Pious campaigns by well meaning civic leaders have ended Seattle's lusty seaport character. No more gambling, no more Rose Rooms . . . half the essence of a great city gone because some want to regulate the behavior of others.

Bassetti sees a lot still worth saving in Seattle. He would have one listen or look for the boat whistles, the thump of frozen fish being unloaded on the waterfront, the floating bridges and ferries, Woodland Park Zoo, and Pioneer Square (early center of Seattle's business life, the scene of Skid Road—a loggers' term corrupted into "skid row" elsewhere.) Skid Road was long in deep decay, the place where most of the winos and derelicts congregated; now, however, it is becoming a fashionable shopping-dining area, and art galleries and tastefully restored buildings are appearing. And then there is the Pike Place Market, where a roughness reminiscent of Seattle's beginnings, "an honest place in a phony time where young people who have never known anything other than precut meat, frozen vegetables, or homogenized milk will discover that milk is really made up of two parts—skim and cream; that tenderloin steaks are the least part of the steer, and that carrots are more green than orange." (The flavorful old market, set in a downtown location of seedy wooden stores and rooming houses, became the object of a major Seattle debate over city planning at the start of the 1970s. The big business establishment wanted to tear it down to permit a rash of new apartment units, a hotel, and a gigantic parking garage; sentimentalists insisted that the setting of farmers, fish dealers, fruit sellers and butchers, dealing directly with a variegated public, should be preserved at all costs. The sentimentalist camp won a big victory in the 1971 city elections by passing an initiative to bar urban renewal in a seven-acre tract including the market. Any development in that area must now be restorationist in character. The city had wanted to preserve only 1.7 acres, so the vote represented a major defeat for urban renewal forces.)

To rehumanize Seattle, Bassetti would save the best of these things and then have the planners and architects build downtown apartments people can afford, work for better public transportation, bury or hide the parking lots, create more open spaces, tiny parks, sidewalk cafe alcoves, intimate public squares. If he could, he would like to demolish the multilane, two-level Alaskan Way Viaduct which was built along the waterfront some 20 years ago to speed traffic past; the viaduct in effect has separated the city from its waterfront and blighted a long two-block section where people don't want to walk because of the noise and dirt. The sacrilege of freeways through the heart of Seattle has been compounded by Interstate 5, parallel to and only a few blocks east of the viaduct, forming a concrete collar around downtown. Sad to say, the highway builders with their seemingly inexhaustible supply of dollars from sacrosanct state and federal tax revenues, have still more in the works—but increasingly, the citizens are resisting.

Mass transit could go far toward relieving the transportation problems of Seattle, which, like San Francisco, is sharply constrained by bodies of water that hem in the available transportation corridors into its downtown section. But as a result of negative votes by the people in 1968 and 1970, it appears that there will be no counterpart to San Francisco's BART on the shores of Puget Sound. These votes came as a bitter disappointment to the dedicated civic leader, James Ellis, who led a courageous battle to get Seattle and its suburbs to build a transit system and construct other facilities to enhance the environment and quality of living in the city for generations to come.

Jim Ellis lacks the flamboyance or color one often associates with great civic reformers; he is in fact a quite ordinary-appearing attorney who if he ran for public office might easily be overlooked by an electorate. But since the early 1950s, much to the peril of his own fragile health, Ellis has been warning of the dangers of rapid growth in Seattle, the possibility that the still relatively unsullied city- and townscape between the Sound and the mountains could become a formless, smog-choked Los Angeles. Twice in the 1950s, Ellis tried and failed to get forms of limited metropolitan government approved for the Puget Sound area—meeting defeat each time at the hands of the voters. "The evolution to metropolitan government," he told me, "has been fought with a blind rage by the right wing." He still believes in the need for rationalized area-wide government, but he decided he would not "sit still and watch the metropolitan environment disappear while we argue over the merits of metropolitan government."

Instead, smaller but concrete steps were taken. By the late 1950s, it was obvious that water pollution was at a crisis point, as raw sewage began floating onto Lake Washington beaches and the oysters and clams disappeared from beaches on Puget Sound. Ellis and his allies won approval of a metropolitan-wide sewerage system, which turned out to be a striking success and a nationally copied model; not only was Lake Washington saved in the nick of time, but Puget Sound became cleaner than at any time in a century.

In 1965, in the wake of the World's Fair success, Ellis made a still-remembered speech before the Seattle Rotary Club in which he called on volunteers to draw up a blueprint for the future of Greater Seattle. This was the beginning of Forward Thrust, a program formulated by 200 of the region's leading public servants, businessmen, lawyers, academicians, clergymen, and conservationists. After thousands of man-hours of work, a broad course of action emerged that included mass transit, the domed stadium, a system of community centers, low-income housing, storm water control, a system of vest-pocket parks, a waterfront park downtown, and acquisitions of vast reaches of green space outside the city. The price tag was to be $819 million—the biggest single improvement plan ever proposed for an American city. With Governor Evans' help, the state legislature passed 18 enabling acts. The proposals went before the voters in 1968. They gave majority support to all proposals. But five of 13 bond issues failed to get the required 60 percent. For Ellis, the greatest disappointment was rejection of the proposed $385 million for mass transit (a sum that would have been matched, it was hoped, by twice the amount in federal subsidies). A sudden, skillful opposition campaign by the highway lobby was one reason it failed to pass.

Undaunted, Forward Thrust went back to the voters in 1970 with mass transit, plus the domed stadium. By this time, Seattle was in the early grips of recession, and taxpayers' revolt was in full flower. Both issues lost decisively.

Nevertheless, Ellis had succeeded in the important clean-water campaign, and as a result of Forward Thrust, Seattle would have a magnificent park program with additions double in acreage to those ever undertaken by any county or city in the U.S.A. Few indeed are the men, in America or elsewhere, who have done so much for their city as Ellis. A small reward came to him in 1970 when he was chosen as the first man from the Pacific Northwest to serve on the board of the Ford Foundation. He is also president of the University of Washington board of regents.

If Seattle today were made up exclusively of the descendants of gold rushers and swashbuckling seamen, the cautious votes which thwarted so much of the Forward Thrust program might never have been cast. But again, the heavy Scandinavian element should be remembered. Scandinavians may rise up against dishonest government or oppressive economic powers, as indeed they have in the past. But they are also noninnovators, a stolid and unimaginative folk. To expect them to indebt themselves to the tune of $25 a family a year for mass transit, for example, may have been simply unrealistic.

But a caution about typing Seattle's people: This placid city of trim homes also has the second highest alcoholism and suicide rates in the U.S. (after San Francisco), and the highest divorce rate of any American urban county, bar none. No one has yet explained these phenomena, except that the divorce rate could reflect the low Catholic population.

Another caution about Seattle: After a flamboyant era in the 1930s and '40s, when two mayors were recalled and a band leader named Victor Aloysius Meyers was catapulted into public office, the city seemed to settle down to a plodding normalcy. In virtually every election, the candidate of a cautious downtown "Establishment" emerged the winner. The nonpartisan city council, afflicted by galloping senility, was not about to rock the boat. And this was a town, one was told, where the frugal Scandinavians, even if a numerical minority, would never permit major corruption.

The old image, if ever true, is shattered now. First, on the issue of honesty, a roaring police scandal erupted in 1969–70, including revelations that the cops had been shaking down prostitutes, operators of card rooms, taverns with pinball machines, and homosexual bars to pay huge amounts of protection money to stay in business. In some instances, resisting establishments found their premises smashed. Estimate of the annual payoffs to police ranged as high as $144,000. And all of this, it turned out, was not simply a police phenomenon, but the outgrowth of a 30-year-old "tolerance policy" fully condoned by public officials. Under the system, certain forms of gambling—pinball machines and card rooms—were allowed to exist and even licensed as a way, some said, to keep Mafia-connected crime out of Seattle.*

In August 1968, the Seattle *Post-Intelligencer*—at considerable risk to

---

* Gambling is strictly and totally prohibited under state law. But in the late 1960s, the Internal Revenue Service reported Washington first in the U.S. in revenues collected from "occupational wagering stamps," behind only Nevada and Indiana in collections from the 10 percent wagering tax, and fifth in the nation in collection of taxes off coin-operated machines. In 1969 there were 1,500 multiple-coin operated pinball machines in King County, grossing hundreds of thousands of dollars each month.

itself—ran stories showing ties between high public officials and pinball tycoons, followed in 1969 by stories of alleged bribe attempts in the Seattle police department. Then U.S. Attorney Stan Pitkin, an aggressive young Nixon administration appointee, began a full-scale investigation and won initial conviction of a high-ranking police official. In 1970 the King County prosecutor of 22 years standing, Charles O. Carroll—a former All America football player for the University of Washington, who had been a key figure in the "tolerance policy"—was defeated for reelection by Christopher T. Bayley, a 33-year-old Harvard graduate and leader of the Ripon Society. Within a year, Bayley had brought indictments against 19 persons, including his predecessor Carroll, the former city police chief, a former sheriff, and the president of the city council. They were charged with conspiracy to permit illegal pinball, prostitution, and gambling rackets in return for bribery payments.

A corrupted police force, flaunting some laws while it is supposed to enforce others, inevitably suffers from declining professionalism. The black community charged continual harassment and unnecessary police violence, and there were accusations of heavy-handed tactics against University of Washington students engaged in antiwar demonstrations. And, somehow, the police seemed unable to cope with a rash of bombings, numbering 115 just between January 1969 and June 1970, more per capita than any other U.S. city. (Among those generally suspected were the Weatherman factions of Students for a Democratic Society, plus black radicals interested in driving whites out of the Central Area.) By 1971, however, the rate of terroristic bombings and general crime was in sharp decline.

Seattle government today has shaken off its complacency of the 1950s and early 1960s. Though most of the impetus for change in the city came from movements like Forward Thrust, the last of the establishment mayors, Dorm Braman, did rise above his background as a hard-nosed businessman and penny-pinching city councilman to push for model cities and transportation reform. In 1969, City Hall got a new image when a distinctly nonestablishment candidate, 34-year-old Wes Uhlman, put together a coalition of labor, black, Catholic, and young voters to win election as mayor. Uhlman received a highly favorable national press, being described by many as the "John Lindsay of the West." He appointed a city ombudsman,* turned down a proposed police raid of Black Panther headquarters, and dashed around the city in his personal Fiat 124 sports car. But among the Seattle electorate, he began to lose a major portion of his liberal and black constituency by backing the scandal-ridden police on most issues (his Panther stand being an exception), backing freeways, and failing to identify with the increasingly strong environmentalist movement in the city. Organized labor remained in Uhlman's corner, however, and he maintained a strong liberal Democratic stance on state and national issues. An intensely partisan man, he has high hopes of one day being governor or U.S. Senator.

* King County had voted an ombudsman earlier in the 1960s, the second government in the U.S. to do so. Hawaii was the first.

From the press, Uhlman got initially quite favorable treatment but then more criticism from the Hearst-owned *Post-Intelligencer;* the Seattle *Times,* locally owned and more establishment oriented, remained severely critical of him. Generally, the *P-I* is the better written, more reform-minded, and more topical of the two big city dailies. The *Times* provides more comprehensive local news coverage, and its reporters, many believe, may actually understand the city better.

Of equal or possibly greater significance than the Uhlman election was the formation in 1967 of a coalition of young Republicans and Democrats and junior chamber of commerce types called CHECC ("Choose an Effective City Council"). The objective was to move the aging and complacent council off dead center. (Among the celebrated obstinacies of the old council was refusal to regulate outdoor signs even when it was pointed out that Rainier Beer billboards were obscuring the view of Mount Rainier at certain locations in the city.) CHECC scored several successes at the polls and in 1972 had seven members or allies on the nine-man council, including the aforementioned Bruce Chapman, who won against Uhlman's strong opposition. Like Christopher Bayley, he is a prominent Ripon Society member. CHECC remains a vital force in the city.

After a glance at some unique journalistic undertakings, it will be time to take our leave of Seattle. One of America's best independent weeklies on a region's government, politics, and culture is the *Argus,* born in Seattle in 1894. Publisher Philip W. Bailey and his writers provide incisive commentary without strong ideological bias and are widely read by community leaders. The *Argus* is not self-sustaining but gets support from Prentice Bloedel, a Seattlean who owns a fortune in lumber, including vast tracts of British Columbia.

On the television scene, KING-TV, an NBC affiliate, provides some of the best public affairs programming in the United States, including a weekly discussion show led by Roberta Byrd Barr, a Negro, looking into problems of both the Negro and Indian minorities. Unusually fine election and public affairs programs are offered by the less well known KOMO-TV, the local ABC outlet. And for six years, King Broadcasting sponsored a delightfully muckraking, high-quality monthly, *Seattle Magazine,* beloved of everyone except conservatives and advertisers. With its last issue in 1970, *Seattle Magazine* died a lamented death, the projection sheets showing no hope for a profit, even in another five years.

## Spokane and Pugetopolis

After Seattle, there is scarcely a Washington city—except the delightful state capital at Olympia—that one would want to travel far to visit.

Spokane (population 170,516), to which we previously alluded for its right-wing politics, is the only city of any size outside the Puget Sound area. Uniquely for Washington, it has a strong segment of Irish Catholics, descendants of railway builders and miners. Physically, Spokane is like warmed-over 1930s except for one very modern parking garage. Two railway lines slice right through the middle of town. The city is terribly ingrown, insular by definition, and has historically been dominated by the most reactionary business groups (especially mining and the railroads). Seattle people hold Spokane in unkind contempt; one told me, "If you could just move a couple thousand interesting people into Spokane, it would be a pretty fine place to live." A Seattle economist in 1969 referred to Spokane as a place "with no real growth elements, even though it has tried to lift itself by its bootstraps with a reasonably successful industrial park." But as Seattle slid into deep recession in 1970–71, Spokane's more diversified agricultural-mining-manufacturing economy continued to hum, raising the question about whom the last laugh might be on.

Spokane may make a vital contribution to the Northwestern economy through its Expo '74, approved late in 1971 by the Bureau of International Expositions. The theme will be "Progress Without Pollution," implemented by returning the Spokane River watershed to trout-water quality and rebuilding and beautifying 3,800 acres along the Spokane waterfront. The Expo is expected to draw five million visitors and generate at least 4,000 new jobs in the state, pumping $125 million into the Washington economy when it will be most helpful. But there is strong opposition to Expo in Spokane itself, where the idea was revived by the city fathers after the voters had specifically rejected it at the polls. After the city council cut heavily into the city budget late in 1971, an irate citizen wrote in a letter to the editor: "There must be something wrong with a city government that can find a source of revenue to raise $5.7 million for a phony trade fair but must lay off 22 policemen and close a fire station because of budget problems."

Seattle's mild climate is unknown in Spokane, where summers are hot, winters cold. Someone spotted these three headlines in the Spokane *Daily Chronicle* and sent them to the *Columbia Journalism Review*:

> January 11, 1969: Snow Siege Due to Tighten Grip
> January 27, 1969: Snow Tightening Grip on Region
> January 28, 1969: Winter's Snowy Grip Tightening

While Seattle's population actually declined during the 1960s by 4.7 percent, to a new Census total of 530,831, the Seattle-Everett metropolitan area as a whole added over 300,000 people for a new total of 1,421,869— largely by virtue of a 64.3 percent population increase in the suburbs. The most spectacular growth was in Bellevue, on the eastern shore of Lake Washington, which shot up a phenomenal 377 percent, from 12,809 to 61,102, making it the fourth largest city in Washington. Seattle attorney Irving Clark, former MC of a KING radio talk show, calls Bellevue "almost an unmitigated disaster, where the tasteless tract architecture and the bad shopping centers have affected the quality of thought too." This is station-wagon land, where a third of the population goes to school, sex education is a big issue, and at least for a while in the 1960s, the John Birch Society flourished. The dreary tracts are broken from time to time, however, by architect-designed houses of quality, following a nature-oriented style loosely classified as "Northwest Contemporary." And the dull horizon is now being punctuated vertically by a number of apartment complexes for singles and couples, young and old, and by some office buildings which may permit the city to compete with Seattle as a location for regional office headquarters of national business firms. Bellevue is rapidly shucking its old reputation as "Boeing's Bedroom"; in fact, it continued to grow and prosper even in the midst of the 1970–71 Boeing depression.

On the other side of Seattle, hugging the western shore of Puget Sound, is big, exurban Bainbridge Island, still without a bridge to the mainland and filled with farms and lots of wilderness and the homes of a few thousand people. It is the antithesis of Bellevue, and its people hope not too many will take the delightful half-hour ferry ride from Seattle to invade their sylvan sanctuary.

North of Seattle on the Sound, the biggest place is Everett (pop. 53,622), chief city of that county of delightful old Indian name, Snohomish. Everett is really just an overgrown old mill and fishing fleet town, enriched in recent years by Boeing. There are a scattering of new downtown buildings and some pleasant residential areas, but basically the city is quite unattractive and fast losing business to nearby shopping centers. A little megalopolis—some call it Pugetopolis—is forming from Everett southward through Seattle to Tacoma near the foot of the Sound, a stretch some 60 miles in length. All of this is on the eastern shore; on the west the only settlement of any size is Bremerton (pop. 35,307), where the Naval Shipyard provides important employment.

Tacoma, the state's third largest city with 154,581 people (metropolitan area 411,027), is perhaps the dingiest, most polluted, divided, and perplexed city along the entire West Coast today. A sort of cruel joke is to recall its slogan, "the city of destiny," a relic of the days before the Alaskan Gold Rush when Tacoma hoped to be larger than Seattle. But shipping, railroads, shipbuilding, banking, and aircraft all gravitated to Seattle and Tacoma was left with aromatic raw industry—wood processing plants and a great copper smelter. Tacoma is still a great lumber center, the headquarters city of the giant Weyerhaeuser Corporation, a center for furniture making, a pulp mill, plywood plants, and sawmills; offshore on Commencement Bay there is a huge log dump.

The smelter of the American Smelting & Refining Company (ASARCO) has been humming along since the turn of the century, benefiting from the low power rates of the city-owned electric system. Every hour, ASARCO discharges 22.2 tons of gases into Tacoma's atmosphere, heavily loaded with offensive sulphur dioxide. ASARCO airily brushes aside suggestions that it rebuild its old and outmoded equipment to effect a drastic reduction in the sulphur dioxide discharge, but the regulators are hot on its heels and may yet bring the company into compliance with state law. With smelters all across the West coming under stiff air pollution controls, ASARCO's threat to move away, depriving Tacoma of 850 jobs and a $4 million annual payroll, may not have the credibility it once enjoyed. And the city's economy is much more diversified than it once was, benefiting both from a broad assortment of industries (fishing, concrete, food processing, clothing, chemicals, candy), big military installations, and its excellent deepwater docking facilities.

Tacoma was plunged into turmoil again in the 1960s as the city council found itself torn apart on issues of race, urban renewal, Model Cities, participation in a regional council of governments, crypto-Birchism, and about every other problem one could dream of. A cantankerous and reactionary mayor, Slim Rasmussen, inaugurated an era of "government by uproar" in 1967 and was in turn dismissed by the voters two years later. But ultraconservatives took 5-4 control of the city council, slashed the city budget to pieces, installed a 73-year-old former Army colonel of right-wing views as city manager, and let some suspect contracts for cable TV. That, in turn, triggered a 1970 recall election in which all the conservatives were ousted from office by a 2-1 margin. Some quiet moderates were installed in the vacated council seats, and the council and a new manager seemed to be trying to get back to the serious business of governing.

But no one knew when the next political explosion might occur in Tacoma or, for that matter, in any Washington city. Mellowness and respectability may one day come to the Evergreen State. But the tumult of roller-coaster economics and feverish political passion seems unlikely to abate for quite a while.

## Northwest Water and Power: Harnessing the Columbia

The elemental power and force of the Columbia and its tributaries is a source of continual wonder. In its circuitous 1,207-mile course, from headwaters in a mountain lake in remote British Columbia to the Pacific 100 miles west of Portland, the river drops 2,650 feet, creating a third of the total hydroelectric capacity of the United States. The volume of its flow—1.9 million gallons a second, or 180 million acre-feet a year—is second only to the Missouri-Mississippi system and 14 times as great as the Colorado, lifeline of the Southwest. The Columbia's watershed, counting the powerful Snake (itself 1,000 miles long) and other tributaries, is 259,000 square miles, covering two-thirds of Washington and Oregon, virtually all of Idaho, corners of Wyoming and Montana, and of course the Canadian headwaters region.

To no state is the Columbia more important than Washington, which it flows across or borders for 750 miles. From an entrance point in the northeast, the river courses in a huge bow around eastern Washington, then moves southerly to a juncture with the Snake, and finally forms the border with Oregon for its final westerly plunge to the sea. At Portland, the Willamette, Oregon's great interior river, joins the Columbia. Both states depend heavily on the flow of cheap electricity from the great hydroelectric projects and on the irrigated farmland made possible by the dams.

In the bonanza of benefits from the big federal multipurpose dams, the virulent early opposition to them is often forgotten. A man who faced the enemies of public power, and finally won over them, was Rufus Woods, a poor farm boy from Nebraska who landed in Wenatchee, in eastern Washington, after coming back broke from the Alaskan Gold Rush. Woods eventually bought the local paper and turned it into an evangelizing voice for construction of the Grand Coulee Dam. Private power interests fought him at every turn, for 13 years not a single daily newspaper in Washington except Woods' favored the dam, and one Congressman called the proposed Grand Coulee Dam "the most colossal fraud in the history of America." But gradually public support was won, and then President Roosevelt smiled on the project as a way to create new jobs, and in 1933 construction began. Daily some 9,000 men, from steeplejacks to deep-sea divers, swarmed over the site; its base alone spread over an area three times that of the Great Pyramid in Egypt. When Grand Coulee was finished, as high as a 46-story building and 12 city blocks across, it was the largest concrete structure on earth. Not only did it provide more than two million kilowatts of power, but it provided the principal source of water for the far-reaching Columbia River Basin reclamation project and was the key structure in flood control along the waterway.

Even before Grand Coulee went on line in 1941, the massive Bonneville Dam some 50 miles east of Portland was completed and the Northwest was well on the way to construction of the more than 20 great federal multipurpose dams along the Columbia and its tributaries. (The possible sites are now all exhausted, except for the disputed High Mountain Sheep Dam on the Snake, discussed in the Idaho chapter of *The Mountain States of America*.) Together with 134 hydroelectric projects owned by private utilities or nonfederal public power districts, these dams provide the cheapest electric power in the nation. The Bonneville Power Administration, marketer for federal power in the region, sells vast quantities of energy to municipalities, publicly owned electric cooperatives, industries, and even those private local utilities which initially fought so hard to stop any or all public power. The Northwest has, in fact, developed its water resources so well, and integrated the use of all facilities, public and private, that only the Tennessee Valley could be considered comparable. The main concern of the private utilities these days is not about the federal role in Northwest power generation, but the fear that they will get less federal power to market to their customers. The BPA is being obliged to cut back virtually all its supply of power to private utilities in order to meet the increased needs of its priority customers under law—public agencies and industries.

The intimate daily and hour-to-hour cooperation of the federal and private hydroelectric producers along the Columbia and its tributaries is a source of constant amazement to those who remember the fights of the 1930s. The Bonneville Power Administration is the principal coordinator, with its power dispatchers in virtually constant communication with the dispatchers of the rest of the generating systems. As demands for electricity shift, or reservoir levels shift, the dispatchers rapidly agree which of the 150-odd public and private projects on the river and its tributaries should curtail or expand operations to meet area requirements. A complex coordination agreement sets up basic rules stipulating that all the hydroelectric projects will be operated to provide optimum benefit to the entire area. If operation with that goal functions to the detriment of an individual system, it is compensated accordingly—either in energy or in money. Power can be rapidly shifted from one locality to another by the 15,000 miles of high transmission lines in the Northwest. And now it can even be interchanged with Southern California through the Northwest-Pacific Southwest Intertie, approved by Congress in 1964 as the largest single transmission program ever undertaken in this country. There are 500,000- and 750,000-volt transmission lines, extending from the Columbia to a point near Los Angeles and also to a location near the Hoover Dam on the Nevada-Arizona border. When the Southwest hits peak summertime needs from air conditioning, the Northwest often makes up the deficit; during especially cold winters, the Northwest in turn can import Southwest power for heating.*

Thus, in a way no one anticipated when the idea was up for discussion 20 years ago, the equivalent of a Columbia Valley Authority exists, capable even of trading power with other regions of the nation. The CVA idea, pushed by President Truman, Henry Jackson, and public power enthusiasts in general, was predicated on the idea that a unitary direction was necessary, under a single budget, for optimum development of the valley—along the lines, clearly, of the TVA. But a powerful array of forces, led by the private utilities, blocked CVA in Congress. The Army Corps of Engineers, Bureau of Reclamation, Interior Department, Forest Service, and all the rest remained technically independent in their Columbia Valley operations. But today even liberal politicians from the Northwest will tell you that a CVA would really have made little difference, either in improved organization or, more importantly, in the federal dollars it could have obtained for the valley. So sumptuously has the Columbia region been treated that there were years in the early 1960s, at the height of dam building, when federal outlays for regional development in eastern Washington alone ran well over $100 million—about 10 percent of the national public works budget for an area with 0.4 percent of the national population.

In like fashion, the intense arguments about private versus public power

---

* The Northwest may have no qualms about exchanging electricity to the Southwest, but water is another matter. Trans-basin diversion is opposed in Washington and Oregon because reduced water flow would reduce generating capacity of the dams, would increase the problem of thermal pollution from nuclear generating facilities like those at Hanford, would reduce the navigation potential of the Columbia, and could be harmful to fisheries.

which once convulsed cities and counties of the Northwest have now cooled. In the 1930s and '40s, there were countless referenda on proposed public power districts. The public power people fought on the issue of people's power; the private power forces warned of the dangers of socialism. With exceptions, most Washingtonians went for public power—a natural outgrowth of the Scandinavian love for co-ops. Two early and leading public power cities, for instance, were Seattle and Tacoma. Most Oregonians, by contrast, picked private power. Interesting exceptions: Spokane, Washington, too conservative to dream of public power, and Eugene, Oregon, home of the university and a liberal spot that picked public power.

Today, power costs about 20 percent less in the public power cities, due to the tax-free status of the cooperatives and their priority status in obtaining cheap federal power. But no one seems to agitate any more to change the kind of power his city has.* The directors of a public utility district are likely to convey just as much of an establishment, chamber-of-commerce image as their private utility counterparts in another city—and to be accepted accordingly. More than appearances are involved, because as time goes on, the whole public power establishment begins to think a lot like a private utility's board of directors. The same kind of labor negotiations must be carried on with linemen and workmen, new construction arranged, managers hired, and finally there is the incentive to increase the empire. To do that, PUD directors often negotiate contracts to supply power to nearby private utilities. Armed with those contracts, the public power men may find themselves wined and dined in the bond houses of New York as they work out hundred-million-dollar deals. Suddenly they are closer to being "captains of industry" than "friends of the people."

There are still opportunities for improvement of the Bonneville system. A third power house is being built at Grand Coulee that will eventually hold a dozen 600 megawatt generators; when the last of them is installed around 1990, the third power house will have a generating capacity of 7.2 million kilowatts—compared to 2.2 million kilowatts capacity in the other two power houses, a note on the fantastic technological improvements of recent years. When all this capacity is on line, Grand Coulee will be the largest installed power facility in the world.

Vast stretches of barren landscape in eastern Washington have been transformed into fertile, moist farmland by the great irrigation systems Grand Coulee made possible. By the late 1960s, 460,000 acres were being watered, with a gross average crop value of $221 for each irrigated acre. Neat little towns, blue lakes, and recreation areas began to fill the once dusty

* But in 1971, *Argus* Publisher Philip Bailey suggested, quite seriously, that the city of Seattle sell its long-time pride and joy, Seattle City Light. The city was in desperate need of money, he pointed out, to pull it out of its economic doldrums and to beautify the cityscape. Selling Seattle City Light to a private utility, he said, would bring a windfall of $600 million or more. And electric power, he suggested, would really cost no more. The public utility had become "cumbersome, overloaded and pockmarked with inefficient help," and in Bailey's view, "the myth that publicly owned utilities can operate more cheaply than those privately owned should, by now, be fully exploded." The alleged "savings," he said, were an illusion because of taxes not paid, dividends not paid to stockholders, and the lack of motivation for efficient operation in a public agency.

landscape. The irrigation systems, however, do cost fantastic sums of money. At this writing, another 460,000 acres await irrigation when a great new siphon and tunnel can be built near Grand Coulee, lifting up water from Roosevelt Lake (the dam's 150-mile-long reservoir) to fine soil areas still restricted by dry farming. But the price of doing all this (at 1970 prices) would be $937 million, and Congress is balking. "We have a strange Western water myth," a Northwestern politician told me. "It is the idea that there's a right inherent with citizenship and one's American birthright to be able to march 20 miles into the desert and camp a homesite there and then expect a multibillion-dollar water project to be created so you can have water there. It's as if water and free speech were equal guarantees of the Bill of Rights."

One of the problems that arise as the Columbia system reaches the limits of its hydroelectric capacity is that the water flow is only great enough to use some facilities for occasional "peaking." An important share of the increased capacity at Grand Coulee, for instance, will necessarily be off line a major portion of the time. Thus the region must look beyond hydro-electric power to increase its "base load," and nuclear power is the only logical answer, the region having so few fossil fuels.

Nuclear operations have been underway along the Columbia ever since World War II, when considerations of secrecy led to selection of Hanford, a desolate spot in south central Washington, for the production of plutonium for atomic bombs. The wartime years found a tarpaper city of 50,000 con-struction workers and engineers and their families on the desert stretch; even today thousands still work there for the Atomic Energy Commission's Hanford Project. Several of the more inefficient reactors have closed down in recent years as a result of a dropoff in the military demand for plutonium and an unexpectedly slow rise in the civilian demand. A dual-purpose re-actor, to produce both plutonium and steam for power generation, was completed and put into operation in 1966 at Hanford; though it qualified as the world's largest nuclear-powered steam plant, it proved unreliable, going off line on occasion and disappointing the area's power management. But the future is likely to bring more single-purpose nuclear reactors, and in autumn 1971 the area received a major boost when President Nixon gave a green light to government participation in building two demonstra-tion fast breeder nuclear reactor plants, one of them, he hinted, at Hanford. (The breeder reactor, which will produce more nuclear fuel than it con-sumes, is seen as a solution to a threatened shortage of domestic uranium supplies which the Atomic Energy Commission fears may occur by the late 1980s. By the early 1970s, nuclear power plants accounted for only 2 percent of the country's power supply, a figure expected to increase to 25 percent by 1985.)

All and any ideas for nuclear development seem welcome in Hanford, where a nuclear installation seems as conventional as a water wheel once was in little New England villages. Hanford has yet to develop others' fear of a great explosion or harmful radiation; one might say it can't afford to.

There are, however, serious problems involved. Elaborate 500-foot cooling towers, for instance, are required to prevent reactors from causing thermal pollution of the river that could endanger the varieties of Pacific salmon and trout which make their way each year up the Columbia and its tributaries —even jumping up fish ladders built for them at dam sites—for the ritual of spawning and regeneration.

In a series of articles for Northwestern newspapers in 1971, A. Robert Smith gave the public its first full report on a much more serious danger:

> The Pacific Northwest has become the depository for what is probably the world's most stupendous pile of radioactive waste—surely enough to eliminate human life from much of the continent if it ever got loose in the air or water.

Over 75 million gallons of the lethal chemical, Smith pointed out, are kept stored in the ground at Hanford, "the terrifying residue of a quarter-century of manufacturing plutonium for atomic bombs and nuclear-armed missiles." After a few years, the steel tanks begin to corrode, and between 1958 and 1965 there were leaks in 10 tanks that permitted 227,400 gallons of high-level waste to flow into the ground. A program to solidify the waste, reducing the danger of exposure to the environment, has been underway but will not be completed until the mid-1970s. Even then, there is the grim problem of what to do with waste materials that will remain biologically dangerous for 500,000 years. The AEC is considering burying the waste in lava beds thousands of feet below the Hanford Works, but there is a distinct earthquake danger in the area, so that even deeply buried materials might become exposed to the air or underground water flows. An alternative solution, much safer but likely to cost much more (as much as $1 billion), calls for shipping the materials to Kansas for permanent storage in bedded salt formations. An even more bizarre solution—which the AEC rejected because of the cost and unreliability of rocket transportation—was to load the lethal wastes into space rockets and fire them into the heart of the sun. The eventual solution, Robert Smith wrote, cannot be treated lightly by the AEC, or by the residents of the Northwest. "It could," he said, "be the most vital decision the federal government has made in this region since the Louisiana Purchase."

# ALASKA

## THE GREAT LAND AWAKENS

THE MASTODONIC Great Land of Alaska, which entered the Union as our 49th state in 1959, is of such immense proportions that citizens of the "Lower 48" have difficulty in grasping it. The state sweeps across four time zones, encompassing 586,412 square miles of territory, two and a fifth times the area of once-leading Texas. Alaskans are always telling the joke of their rejoinder to proud Texas: "Stop boasting or we'll split in two and make you third." Superimposed on a map of the contiguous U.S., Alaska's territory engulfs most of the Midwest, its Panhandle extends to the Atlantic near Charleston, South Carolina, and the Aleutian chain reaches out into the Pacific between Los Angeles and San Francisco. Alaska is the northernmost state, the westernmost state, and also the easternmost state—because the last of the Aleutians extend over the 180th meridian into the Eastern Hemisphere. (Attu Island, easternmost of the chain, is due north of Auckland, New Zealand.)

The diversity is just as incredible as the size of this lovely, lonely last frontier. Alaska has great plains, Arctic deserts, swamps, immense forests, the highest mountains of North America, more square miles of glaciers than the rest of the inhabited world, ice fields, broad valleys, fjords, 12 major river systems, active volcanos, three million lakes and countless islands, and 50 percent more seacoast (33,904 miles) than all the continental United States. The coasts are washed by two oceans and three major seas. But the entire state has fewer people than Norfolk, Virginia. In 1970, the Census counted 302,173 Alaskans of whom some 50,000 were native peoples—

Eskimos, Aleuts, and Indians. Theirs is a special and sometimes tragic story to which we will return later in this chapter.

Four out of 10 Alaskans today live around one city (Anchorage). With .5 persons a square mile, the state remains one of the most lightly populated places of the globe where man has ventured at all. There are tracts of interior Alaska, the size of whole states in the Lower 48, where from year to year no living soul may venture. Murlin Spencer, who moved to Alaska a few years ago to become executive editor of the Fairbanks *Daily News-Miner* and later the news editor of the Anchorage *Daily Times,* told me the state reminded him of nothing so much as the South Pacific where he had been stationed in World War II. The South Pacific, he said, is just small islands surrounded by immense distances of water; Alaska is little towns surrounded by trackless wilderness.

The wilderness impinges on normal ways of living in a thousand ways. Long-distance telephoning within the state, always requiring an operator's assistance, is expensive and complicated. Television is available in only a few locations, and the first live programming from outside did not come until 1969, with the American landing on the moon. News pictures are sent to Alaska's papers by airmail instead of wirephoto. Scarcely any radio service at all exists for many native villages, so immense are the distances between them and civilization.* Water transportation is strictly seasonal, with a third of the coastline in solid ice for six months of each year. Few towns or cities are connected by highway because of the immense difficulties of building roads over great distances, often with quaky permafrost beneath and with mountain ranges and glaciers as great obstacles. In fact, the state had only 6,800 miles of highway and trail in 1971, and only 1,300 miles of road were blacktopped. The 320-mile highway between Anchorage and Fairbanks, the two largest cities, was not opened until 1971, and fewer than a dozen of the villages of the native peoples are on the state highway network.

Those who insist on moving about Alaska are obliged to do so by airplane, and in fact there is an aircraft for every 100 residents, ranging from frail float and bush planes to Boeing 737s, from converted World War II-vintage Grumman Gooses and Sikorsky Flying Cranes to modern helicopters. Bankers, oil drillers, physicians, Eskimos on native business, and bishops and politicians spreading their respective words, all must depend on airplanes and not infrequently fly their own. Some of the world's most daring aviators are the Alaskan bush pilots, who presently number about 700. James Bylin wrote in the *Wall Street Journal* that bush pilots "service homesteaders,

* On a September day of 1971 that Governor William Egan called "an historic day and a great day" for the native villages, a satellite terminal was dedicated in Anchorage to facilitate radio contact with remote areas where normal reception is impeded by atmospheric conditions. Utilizing NASA's applied technology satellites and developed by two scientists at the University of Alaska's Geophysical Institute, the program will make it possible for medical personnel in the bush to communicate with physicians in the cities. "It's nothing short of miraculous," Egan said. "It can mean the difference often between prolonged suffering and healing comfort of proper medical care—sometimes the difference between life and death."

miners, trappers, hunters, fishermen, mountain climbers and others with essentials and occasional luxuries, ranging from dogsleds and dynamite to tobacco and tomatoes. Bush pilots will land almost anywhere—on sand bars, glaciers, rivers, ice floes, beaches, lakes, pastures, graveyards, or ball fields. They face the constant danger that each landing may be their last."

On the trail or in large cities, Alaskans are a friendly, outgoing lot, sharing, as it were, their common glory and adversity. But in smaller communities, where few of the people ever travel, a kind of insular, antisocial "garrison life" may develop.

The people drawn to Alaska tend to be hardy individualists, lovers of the outdoors, those with an adventuresome streak in their blood and an itch to escape the constraints of the freeway society in the Lower 48. Roughly speaking, there are two classes of Alaskans: those who think the Great Land is God's Country and swear never to leave, and another group more interested in the fast buck. The latter type—be they oilmen or divers, fishermen or lawyers—strive to make their fortune, great or small, and then retire to Hawaii, or back home, or anywhere that the winters are easier. There is no other state in America so essentially free of class distinctions, no state where a young person can rise so rapidly to the top in business or the professions. (This applies not only to men but women too. Alaska, according to Anchorage newswoman Ruth Edmondson, was "pioneer country" for feminine geologists, lawyers, doctors, dentists, policewomen, taxidrivers, liquor-store clerks, pilots, post(wo)men, and yes—even forest-fighters.) But even those who love Alaska may be driven away once they pass their prime years, by the rigorous winters. The result is a paucity of older community leaders, who, in the words of Richard Austin Smith, "depart from the scene just at the time of life when their counterparts are beginning to lend balance, luster and affluence to the social structure. . . . Think, if you will, of Texas or California or New York being compelled to develop without the money and the experience of its older bankers, lawyers, merchants and other civic leaders."

One of the chief social ills of Alaska is alcoholism, which is tied in part to the raucous frontier atmosphere and wide-open bars. In Anchorage or Fairbanks, or many a smaller town, you can still find bars and taverns sporting names like Silver Dollar, Polar Bear, Gold Dust, Husky, Santa's Cafe, Elbow Room, and Red Dog—and atmosphere to match. Sometimes booze may be a substitute for women; the state ratio is 119 men for every 100 women, a situation aggravated by the high complement of young military personnel. A more fundamental reason for alcoholism may be "cabin fever"—the kind of heavy drinking people are likely to resort to when they are closed indoors for a long, bitterly cold winter, the daylight hours reduced to a handful or so in the shortest days of the year.

Indeed, a kind of weird unreality pervades many things Alaskan. Man and his doings nowhere seem so transient and unsubstantial, like a flash of Northern Lights in the Arctic sky—there now, likely to be gone in a moment.

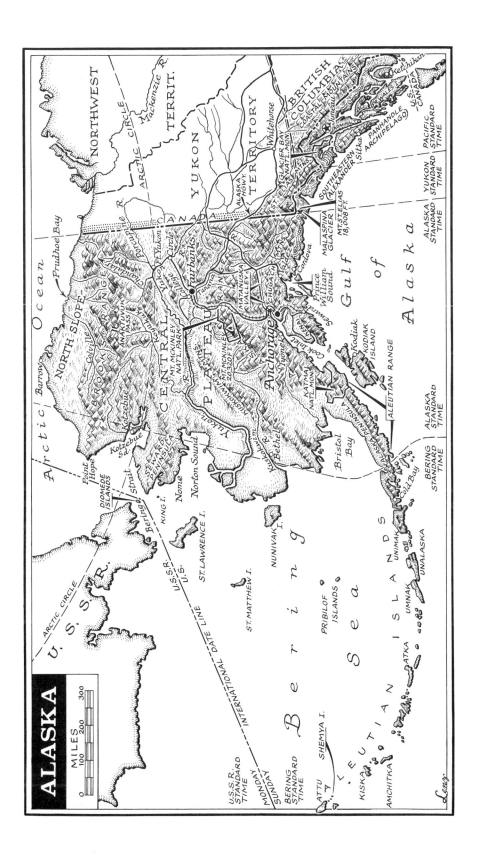

Traditionally, white men have come to exploit Alaska: the Russians to catch furs and suppress the Eskimos and Aleuts they encountered, the Gold Rushers to desecrate the beach and hills at Nome (the scars of their handiwork still apparent), fishermen from the Lower 48 or the Orient to sneak into Alaskan waters and return home wealthy, without so much as a word of thanks.* Today many fear Alaska will once more be plundered and abandoned in the oil development of the North Slope, with irreversible harm done to the delicate ecology of the tundra and the waters of the Bay of Alaska, where gigantic oil tankers will dock. Great stretches of national forest on the southeastern panhandle are endangered. Near the few cities, especially Anchorage, Fairbanks, and Juneau, lakes and waterways are seriously polluted. But for most of the endless stretches of the Great Land, I still find myself compelled to believe that it will be nature, not man, that triumphs. The arctic reaches of continental proportion, the mountains numbering in so many thousands that many still lack names, the coastline stretching on and on before a tiny native settlement pricks the horizon, the river banks untouched by any town or sign of civilization for hundreds of miles—the scale that is so overwhelming, the vastness so awesome, that ultimate desecration is difficult to imagine.

What's more, the Alaskan climate seems deliberately programmed to keep man at bay. Everything about it is extreme. Fort Yukon, in the interior, has reported temperatures as low as 75 degrees below zero, as high as 100 above. It was at Prospect Creek, an oil-company camp in the southern foothills of the Brooks Range, that the lowest temperature record in U.S. history was set in the winter of 1970–71: -79. (The previous low mark, -76, was registered in 1886 at the Tanana River village of Nenana west of Fairbanks.) Soggy Port Walter on the southeastern Panhandle is deluged with 18 feet of water each year, but the wind-dried North Slope has only a few inches of precipitation a year. While Anchorage asserts that it has warmer winters than northern New England or the Upper Midwest, the fact is that in Fairbanks, the only city of the interior, brutal cold of 30 and sometimes more than 55 below zero drives inhabitants indoors for weeks on end. A man or woman who steps outside on the North Slope without proper clothing, at a time when low temperatures and high winds coincide, invites fatal exposure. And for those who could withstand all those perils, it should be remembered that Alaska sits at the midpoint of the great Pacific Basin chain of earthquake and volcanic activity that was subjected to a destructive

* In another form of exploitation, Seattle shippers and merchants long held Alaska as a kind of captive market. Everything eaten, drunk, worn, or used on the Alaskan frontier came through Seattle, and so did all Alaskan goods, for further marketing, in the reverse direction. Seattle's high prices amounted to a kind of tribute exacted of Alaska—even though it had been the rush to the Yukon and Klondike gold fields in the late 1890s that made Seattle as a city. In later years, Alaska chafed under the fact that all its auto distributorships and 13 of 14 liquor distributors were Seattle-owned. There is still a heavy flow of ocean shipping between Seattle and Alaska, but now Alaskans have an air freight option and sometimes ship heavy goods through Portland instead of Seattle to settle the old score. Their reaction in 1970, when officials of the new oil pipeline to the North Slope announced they would set up headquarters in Seattle instead of Anchorage, was extreme and bitter. The Anchorage *Daily Times* rumbled that the choice of Seattle was "a step back to the days of territorialism when Alaskans were some kind of peons, working under controls from distant power centers, not the smallest of which was Seattle."

quake as recently as 1964. On the June night I flew into Fairbanks from Seattle, the air was thick with smoke, the result of huge forest fires raging all over central Alaska. Single areas as large as Massachusetts have burned, and in 1969 an all-time record of 4.1 million acres burned in 520 conflagrations. Fires are often in such inaccessible areas that the Interior Department's Bureau of Land Management, responsible for fire-fighting, simply lets them burn out of their own accord.

## Geographic Alaska

Alaska's continent-sized geography is still something of a mystery to most Americans. Essentially, the state lies in three great climatic belts, separated by barriers of massive mountain ranges. Moving from *south to north*, these are the belts * :

| Region | Climate |
|---|---|
| PACIFIC MOUNTAIN AREA— | |
| Maritime Belt along the Gulf of Alaska | |
| 1. Southeastern Panhandle Largest borough: Juneau (pop. 13,556) | Relatively mild temperatures (by Alaskan standards); very moist, frequent fogs and wind storms. |
| 2. South Central Alaska Largest borough: Anchorage (pop. 102,994) | Medium to cold temperatures, average precipitation. |
| 3. Alaska Peninsula and the Aleutian Islands | Moderate temperatures, very wet, great storms and heavy winds. |
| *Alaskan Mountain Range* Mount McKinley—20,320 feet (highest of North America) | Alpine |
| CENTRAL PLATEAU AREA—from Canada to the Bering Sea, about half of Alaska's land area Largest borough: Fairbanks (pop. 30,618) | Extreme winter cold; not infrequent readings of 50 below zero. Brief, sometimes warm summers. |
| *Brooks Range* Just above Arctic circle, across the breadth of Alaska for 600 miles, all-but-impenetrable barrier 150 miles deep. | Alpine-Arctic |
| NORTH SLOPE Rolling tundra, basically treeless. Largest town: Barrow (pop. 2,104) | Arctic; fierce winter winds. |

With the overall scene in mind, we can fill in some of the geographic details. The Pacific Mountain Area maintains fairly mild temperatures through warming from the Japan Current, which sweeps northward and

* Adapted from a chart in *The Frontier States* (New York: Time-Life Library of America).

eastward beneath the curve of the Aleutians, around the Gulf of Alaska and then down the Panhandle and the coast of British Columbia.

The Panhandle, starting some 500 miles north of Seattle, nevertheless has the moist climate and thick forests associated with coastal Washington. It consists, on one side, of a 30-mile strip of mountainous mainland bordering British Columbia and, on the other, of the countless islands of the Alexander Archipelago—really the remnants of ancient mountains submerged at the end of the ice age. The result is one of the world's most beautiful fjord areas, seen easily from ferries from Seattle which ply the famed Inland Passage along this coast. Towering forests of spruce and hemlock cover most of the lands, and the region holds the bulk of Alaska's pulp and timber industry in its 550-mile length. The Sierra Club has instituted court action to try and prevent a $100 million timber-cutting project in the vast Tongass National Forest, a magnificent wilderness along the region's glacier-capped fjords and waterways which includes 100-mile-long Admiralty Island, packed with wildlife (salmon, bald eagles, and brown bears), virtually the only island in the archipelago still largely in its primeval condition. The U.S. Forest Service has committed itself to clear-cutting practically every marketable stand of spruce and hemlock in the Tongass National Forest. The lumber would not relieve any U.S. housing shortage but would be for export to Japan.* Outside of lumber, the major income of the Panhandle is from fishing (especially salmon) and tourism (scenery plus the colorful Tlingit totem pole culture).

About a sixth of Alaska's people live in the Panhandle region, 13,556 of them in the vicinity of Juneau, the remainder scattered through little fishing and lumber towns like picturesque Sitka (once capital and a great center for the Russians, now proud to have a $66 million Japanese-financed paper mill), Ketchikan, and Skagway (still breathing some of the spirit of the Klondike Gold Rush).

No American state capital is more removed from the geographic or population center of its state than Juneau, which made its start as a gold camp in 1879 and became territorial capital in 1900, years before the first tent went up at Anchorage. Towering mountains dominate the little city, which is set on narrow, precipitous streets, and not far away are huge glaciers, magnificent waterfalls and great, untracked forests where it is best not to tangle with bear coming down to fish in the rivers at salmon spawning time. Some of the state legislators allege claustrophobia as a result of the domineering mountains and the perennial clouds and precipitation (56 inches of rain, 92 of snow in a typical year).† But Juneau does have friendly townspeople (the

---

* Forest Service Chief Edward Cliff offers this defense of the planned harvesting of the timber in the Tongass National Forest: Of the 15 million acres in the harvest, only 4.5 million acres are capable of growing commercial crops of trees, and of these, only 2.8 million acres will be harvested. Cutting the timber will (1) make an important contribution to the Alaskan economy, including the employment of Alaskan natives; (2) reduce Japanese competition for wood and fiber in Canada from which the U.S. imports much timber; (3) contribute to the country's balance of trade; and (4) make use of a deteriorating resource—the timber in mature forests. Opening up virgin timber stands, Cliff says, will increase food production for wildlife and create the "edge effect" necessary for deer and other animals.

† Temperatures are usually much milder than in the rest of Alaska, but sometimes dip to −5 to −10. Combined with a week of 60-knot winds, gusting to 100 knots, in the winter of 1970–71, the temperatures produced a "chill factor" of −90 degrees.

old-time Alaskans), and even though much of the city is weatherbeaten and decrepit, no one can accuse it of being totally out of tune with the times; squarely in the middle of the town now rises a gigantic steel-and-glass rectangle, the new federal building, dwarfing every other structure in sight.

The Panhandle is effectively severed from the main body of Alaska by the spectacular St. Elias Mountains, with 18,000-foot Mount St. Elias itself and the massive Malaspina Glacier precisely at the point where the jutting corner of Canada's Yukon Territory almost reaches the ocean. South Central Alaska, site of Anchorage and home for over half the state's people, fronts on the broad Bay of Alaska, profits from the oil-rich Kenai Peninsula and Cook Inlet beside it, and is marked by stands of spruce and birch, great chains of glacier-packed mountains, and protected harbors (Anchorage, Seward, Valdez, and others). This was the area where the great earthquake of 1964 caused such horrendous damage.

Around the Gulf of Alaska, the most exciting modern development has been oil development on the Kenai Peninsula and in the waters of Cook Inlet. The University of Alaska *Monthly Review* called the first oil strike at Kenai on January 19, 1957, "perhaps the most important date in all of Alaska's colorful history." This strike, not to be confused with the still greater find on the North Slope a decade later, did trigger $1 billion in investment by oil companies, generating income for the state which publisher Robert Atwood of the Anchorage *Times* told me "saved Alaska from bankruptcy." As the oil companies developed the area, new roads were built and chains of lakes and streams opened up, touching off a big recreation boom. In 1969 a $200 million ammonia and urea and gas liquefaction plant opened in Kenai.

So hostile is the general environment that areas suitable for farming number only three and look like flyspecks on the map. Alaska in fact produces only 10 percent of its food supply—less than any other state; as one report put it, much of the soil is either "too thin, too steep, too cold, or too wet for economical production." And production costs are so high that Alaskan farmers have difficulty competing with the prices of foods imported from the Lower 48.* The only truly successful area is the Matanuska Valley at the head of an inlet some 50 miles northeast of Anchorage. Measuring some 10 by 60 miles, the valley is protected by mountains and is famed for its luscious growths, including cabbages that grow to bushel size because daylight in June and July lasts about 20 hours. And though the growing season is short—10 weeks between the last spring frost and the first in the fall—the valley prospers through dairy herds, livestock and poultry, garden and grain crops. Like many things in Alaska, the federal government is responsible for

* Iowa State University is helping University of Alaska scientists with a unique experiment to increase farm production. As reported in the *National Observer*, the plan works this way: Fast-growing, high-yielding barley is planted in Alaska's short growing season. The grain is fed to hogs housed on the bottom floor of a bizarre, two-story "pork palace" to protect them from the subzero temperatures outside in winter. Then carbon dioxide exuded by the hogs' breath and manure is piped upstairs to the second story. The second story is a greenhouse filled with plants whose growth requires carbon dioxide. High-intensity lights substitute for the sun during long winter nights. The plants then produce excess oxygen, which is cycled downstairs and has a "supercharger" effect on swine growth.

development of the Matanuska Valley. Starting in 1935, under the Roosevelt administration, 202 farmers were brought to the valley from drought areas of the Midwest, and most did very well for themselves. Then a connecting road had to be built to Anchorage, and for the first time Anchorage people could move by highway an appreciable distance from their city.

The Alaska maritime belt, stretching from the Panhandle out into the Aleutians, is home of an enduring and leading Alaskan industry: fisheries. In most years, the value of fish caught in Alaskan waters by U.S. fishermen has exceeded that of any of the other 49 states. The $90 million annual catch, in order of descending importance, includes salmon, the illustrious Alaskan king crab, halibut, Dungeness crab, shrimp, and herring. The state's salmon industry was almost destroyed by overharvesting in the 1930s but with careful conservation practices has recovered nicely in recent years. In 1968 the Fish and Wildlife Service boasted that since the inception of the Alaskan fish industry a century before, the cumulative value of Alaska fishery products had reached an estimated $4 billion—more than 550 times the $7.2 million purchase price of Alaska from Russia.

The westernmost edge of the Bay of Alaska is anchored by big Kodiak Island, where the town of Kodiak, once the headquarters of the Russian fur trade (1792–1804), takes in one of the two or three largest fish catches of all American cities. The island and neighboring sections of the Alaska Peninsula have a pleasant maritime climate, many spruce-covered and statuesque mountains. The greatest threats come from inside the earth. Mount Martin on the peninsula was the site of one of the greatest volcanic explosions of recorded history in 1912. The tidal wave from the 1964 earthquake hit brutally at Kodiak. The entire Aleutian Island chain is the site of some of the world's most intense volcanic activity.

The Aleutians, which take up where the Alaskan Peninsula ends, include 14 major islands, 40 lesser ones, and countless islets in their 1,400-mile arc out across the Pacific. Climatically, they have a relatively narrow temperature range. Little else positive can be said of the weather. The skies seem forever leaden with low-flying stratus clouds that hold the sunshine to no more than 25 days a year. At Cold Bay, cloudiness averages nine-tenths of the sky cover the year round; at Shemya Island, it rains or snows or sleets three days out of five. Added to this, there is the wind, averaging some 17 to 20 miles an hour all year round, with gale force blizzards in the winter months. The winds, indeed, are so strong that it is practically impossible for trees to grow. Soldiers planted half a dozen small firs on Amchitka Island in 1943; since then they have grown nine inches. But with the fogs and moisture, the islands sustain a lush growth of grass, shrubs, and moss.

Thousands of ex-GIs can still recall the cold rain and fog and high seas that accompanied their assault on Japanese-held Attu Island, westernmost of the chain, in May 1943—the only ground fighting of World War II in North America. Of an American assault force of some 15,000 men, 549 died; of the 2,379 Japanese on the island, only 29 were taken prisoner. The rest either died in the course of the first 17 days of raw and muddy battle or met their end on the 186th day when the remaining Japanese stormed the American lines in a final *banzai*, or suicide, attack. Even the Aleutian-stationed GIs who never saw a Japanese have few fond memories of the islands; most have little to look back on save a time of grim loneliness, of cursing the angry seas and barren landscape and sodden skies.

Today Attu is uninhabited save for a small Coast Guard station. The litter of wartime embattlements still scar this and other Aleutian islands— miles of rusted barbed wire, unsightly oil barrels, heaps of empty Spam cans and smashed bottles of Japanese *sake*. But this was neither the first nor the last desecration of the Aleutians. The Russians came first, starting in 1741, slaughtering the native Aleuts and pillaging the waters of fur-bearing animals—especially sea otters and seals. The surviving Aleuts were wracked by western diseases, ranging from alcoholism to syphilis. In 1913 President Taft proclaimed most of the Aleutians a national wildlife refuge.

On Amchitka Island, almost 300 miles eastward of Attu, men from the Fish and Wildlife Service began a great wildlife reclamation program after World War II. The sea otter population was restored to its natural levels, the almost extinct Aleutian Canada goose returned, and bald eagles prospered once more. But then, starting in 1964, the Atomic Energy Commission moved in to drill holes thousands of feet into bedrock for the testing of nuclear weapons. In 1969 a 1.2-megaton bomb was exploded with no apparent environmental damage, but the 5-megaton giant planned for 1971 seemed like another matter—possibly the largest nuclear bomb ever tested. (It was a prototype of the warhead for the Spartan missile of the Safeguard antiballistic missile system, which if developed would intercept and destroy hostile ballistic missiles.) Environmentalists feared the test would trigger an earthquake and a gigantic tidal wave, called a tsunami, that could inundate the shores of Japan and Hawaii; they also feared that radiation would escape and contaminate migrating salmon. The protesters included not only conservation groups but the governments of Japan and Canada, the governor and entire congressional delegation from Alaska, the American Federation of Scientists, and the Aleut League. The blast went off on schedule and caused the largest earth tremor ever produced by man—7.0 on the Richter scale. There were numerous cliff falls and rock slides along the island's shoreline, but no earthquakes or tsunami, and the radioactive material was sealed in place by rock compacted by the great explosion in its 5,875-foot-deep shaft. The AEC said the test was so successful that no further tests at Amchitka would be necessary.

Swept by wind and fog, surrounded by fierce tidal currents and treacherous shoal waters, shaken by earthquakes and harboring 27 volcanic peaks, the Aleutians can scarcely be called a place hospitable to man. But man can hardly boast about what he has done to them.

Now our focus must shift northward, across the Alaskan Range that rings off and protects South Central Alaska, and into the vast interior, the

Central Plateau. On the way, one passes the rugged display of nature's handiwork in the icefalls, glaciers, ridges, and the high mountain peaks around Mount McKinley. An unforgettable experience, I hear from those who have done it, is to fly in a small plane around the precipices and along the glaciers, virtually into the bowels of McKinley. Some day I swear to do that, but still one of the most vivid recollections of travels for these books is the sight I caught one morning, on a flight between Anchorage and Fairbanks, of that monarch among mountains rising white and serene above the mists of an Alaskan morning.

The Central Plateau, bigger than all of Texas, is a vast, rolling upland spotted with mountains. It rolls from the Canadian border to the Bering Sea, from the southern wall of McKinley and other peaks of the Alaskan Range to the northern barrier of the Brooks Range. The mighty Yukon River and its tributaries, dotted with native villages along the banks, flow out of Canada and through this region to the Bering Sea. Alaska's big-game hunting centers here—for moose, caribou, bear, sheep, and, along the Bering Straits, for polar bear.

Alaska's most brutally cold winters, and likewise its hottest summer temperatures, are registered on the Central Plateau, the pattern shifting near the west coast to winters with high winds and humidity and summers of cool, rainy, and foggy weather. What all of northern Alaska holds in common, and which stunts its growth now and perhaps forevermore, is permafrost. This is subsoil frozen solid to depths of 1,000 feet or more by eons of freezing weather. The summer warmth is simply insufficient to thaw more than a few feet of topsoil, and that turns into a gooey sludge while the earth below remains frozen solid. Even buildings constructed with the greatest care may begin to crack, heave, and buckle after a few years; in the town of Nome I went poking through a large federal building which had to be abandoned completely for this reason.

Outside of Fairbanks, to be treated later in this chapter, there are no towns of significant population in all of central Alaska and the barest of civilized enclaves along the western coast. West, southwest, and north of Fairbanks is the homeland of Alaska's 28,000 Eskimos, most of whom are scattered through little villages. Two west coast towns have larger concentrations: Kotzebue (just above the Arctic Circle) and Bethel (farther south). Together with Nome, these population centers total 6,600 people on a coastline longer than the entire stretch from Seattle to San Diego.

No place in America has given me such a total feeling of otherness as Kotzebue. The 546-mile air flight from Anchorage is quickly made, but suddenly one is in an alien world, both ethnically and geographically. The Eskimos, those proud yet gentle people, have about them a primordial timelessness, a quality that reminds one that they and their ancestors were surviving in this incredible environment for countless centuries before the white man ever came. Across the Bering Straits, there are Soviet Eskimos whose language and culture are the same as those of their now-American cousins, except that the white man's 20th-century conflicts have closed off their ancient routes of commerce.*

Nor is the geography familiar to any that one knows. The tundra, a blanket of moss, sedges, lichens, bunch grass, and berry plants, soft and mushy in summer and frozen hard in winter, stretches off to an unpeopled horizon. Not a tree breaks the monotony (except one forlorn pine someone coaxed into growth, which is surrounded by a fence and a sign that reads "Kotzebue National Forest"). Dark clouds come scudding in low over the horizon. Along the beach, fish and seal skins hang drying on racks, and caribou hides too. Fishing dinghies with large outboard motors are pulled up on the beach, and dog-sled teams languish in the cool summer sun. A little gravel road separates the beach from the houses, most of which are ramshackle wood and tarpaper shacks, plus a few log houses. All about one sees the same accumulations of junk—old barrels, pieces of broken furniture, rusted hulks of old trucks and autos—that can be seen in the rural Mississippi Delta, so many miles away. The housing in Kotzebue and other Eskimo villages is the worst I have seen, the Delta perhaps excepted, anywhere in the U.S. Yet the Eskimo people, warm and outgoing, with a wonderful sense of humor, are some of the most delightful Americans one can meet anywhere.

By objective standards, Kotzebue is "progressing" mightily. As townsman Harvey Vestal (president of the Northwest Native Association) puts it, "Our centuries of isolation from the world are ending, and our way of living is changing from a subsistence to a cash economy." Electricity, generated locally by oil brought in by ship, arrived in the late 1950s, though its price—$50 a month for a home—is no mean obstacle. Well over 150 telephones are now hooked up in this town of 1,696 souls. A sewer and water system is gradually being installed to break the age-old dependence on the honey bucket and water delivered door to door (at 7 cents a gallon). It may be decades before a road ever reaches Kotzebue, but contact with the outside world is no longer restricted to one or two supply ships each year. Kotzebue has a modern air strip, recently converted from gravel to paving with a styrofoam layer to keep the permafrost from melting. Big Alaskan and Wien Consolidated Airlines jets offer regular service to Fairbanks, Anchorage, and Nome. This service has brought with it a thriving tourist business. Bush pilots also fly prop planes out of Kotzebue to 16 isolated Eskimo villages scattered over a territory of many thousand square miles.

Many Kotzebue natives make their living at the traditional calling of hunting and fishing. Salmon fishing provides a livelihood for some, with Japan and Seattle the chief markets. Delightful native handicrafts, sold directly to the tourists, are another source of income. Kotzebue advertises itself as the "Polar Bear Capital of the World," and some of the natives are professional big-game guides. (For an average fee of $2,000, a hunter is

* The division is most poignant at Little Diomede Island in the Straits, where the Eskimos can look across a mere three miles of open water to Soviet-held Big Diomede, with which they once had such close blood ties. The international date line runs between the two islands; they say one can literally look "from today into tomorrow."

guaranteed a bear. Piper Cubs with skis are used to fly the hunting parties out to the ice packs. Some, it is reported, illegally cross the international dateline into Soviet waters in search of a catch. Eskimos are unhappy that most of the guides in this lucrative business are nonnative. Conservationists are even more alarmed. They charge that indiscriminate killing by "sports-hunters" has so reduced the polar bear population that the remarkable species —so adapted to a land and water environment, to extreme cold and blizzards, the long arctic night and prolonged periods without food—may soon become extinct. The polar bear population has dropped drastically; trouble for the species is indicated by the increasingly younger age of the bears shot and examined; if the numbers drop low enough, the few remaining bears will be unable to find mates in the arctic expanses. There are some indications that the U.S. has killed off all its polar bears, so that the annual Alaskan "take" of over 600 comes completely from animals that are migrating across the state from Canada or the Soviet Union. The number of bears shot by Eskimos for fur and food is only a tiny fraction of the kill of the trophy hunters.)

Kotzebue's only big source of income, and the only steady employment in town, comes from the federal government. Lucky indeed are the natives who get the few permanent jobs for nonprofessionals at the Public Health Service hospital, the school run by the Bureau of Indian Affairs, the Weather Bureau, or the Federal Aviation Agency. The Arctic Circle Chamber of Commerce warns: "Surplus labor work force in Kotzebue and surrounding areas at all times of year. . . . It is recommended that individuals come to Kotzebue only if employment and housing has been arranged for prior to arrival." The officially recognized unemployment rate has been around 30 percent for the past decade, prices are 85 percent above Seattle, and in 1968 median income, adjusted for inflation, was only $575, compared to $3,412 for the nation as a whole. Anyone thinking of getting away from modern pressures by a move to Kotzebue should also be forewarned that there are 119 days each year when the temperature drops to zero or less. With stiff winter winds, the "chill factor" is something to reckon with. Each October a great ice floe fills Kotzebue Sound, and the ice depth reaches five feet. Not until May or early June does the spectacular ice breakup occur.

Nome (pop. 2,488) set on Norton Sound some 180 miles east of Siberia, has long been in the control of an entrenched white minority. Eskimos from elsewhere go out of their way to point out that Nome never was a native town, and of course they are right. Gold founded Nome. In 1899–1900, 15,000 "stampeders" landed here to set up an unsanitary tent city some 30 miles long and to scrabble for gold along tide-washed beaches that couldn't be staked. If ever there was a poor man's gold rush, this was it. Not less than 500 men extracted gold valued at $2 million, or an average of $4,000 a man in the days when that sum represented a small fortune. Then, as quickly as it had come, the gold rush was over for all but a few who had made good claims inland. Afflicted by periodic killer storms and great fires, Nome has limped along, dreaming that one day gold operations (terminated in 1963) might again be economical. (Present-day dreams include mining the huge fortunes in gold that must have washed down into the ocean over the ages, or thawing the permafrost with laser beams, or nuclear power to get at the billions everyone believes must be in the ground still.)

In the meantime, Nome is getting along on a brisk jet-born tourist trade, an ample complement of saloons, several regional federal offices, and as a welfare center. The native unemployment rate is a staggering 60 percent. Between the Eskimos' shocking slum housing, the grotesque remains of gold-mining equipment that still mar beaches and hills, the treeless and sub-arctic landscape, and the dumpy white man's construction, Nome is about as ugly a town as one can find in North America. "Rome wasn't built in a day but Nome looks like it," goes one local saying; another wag has suggested rather cruelly that one match—"midnight renewal"—might be the treatment Nome needs.

A mile from Nome is King Island Village, populated by Eskimos who have moved from wind-swept King Island, 90 miles distant in the Bering Strait. King Island itself is now deserted except in summertime, when 40 of the 200 villagers return to their island in open hunting boats to get seal and walrus. Before the ice closes in again, they return to their enclave by Nome, once called by Sargent Shriver America's worst slum. The King Islanders' most solid cash income is gathered in by their illustrious dancing group, which entertains tourists at Nome with colorful chanting and dancing to the beat of drums made by stretching a walrus stomach over a hoop.

Finally, our geographic circuit takes us farther north to the massive Brooks Range—a region so huge that its territory equals the size of Italy—and to the North Slope. No one who has ever witnessed the coming of spring to the Brooks Range, a writer for *Time* magazine has reported, is ever quite the same again:

After three dark months of frozen silence, the sun reappears as a long, slanting shaft that illuminates only the highest peaks. Each day the light descends, until finally even the deepest valley is bathed in warmth. The ice breaks, roaring like cannon fire, and the ground explodes with color as wild flowers bloom. Big bears stagger out of hibernation. Rivers teem with salmon, grayling, and char. Caribou march in long single files toward new feeding grounds. Glacial ice glitters like emeralds and sapphires. The world seems reborn.

From the Brooks Range, the North Slope begins as a plateauland with stunted willows marking the course of waterways; then even they disappear as the Arctic Coastal Plain sweeps over thousands of square miles to the Arctic Ocean. Summertime brings bright wildflowers across the tundra; in winter there is nothing but a featureless, hostile white expanse of space. The North Slope has been described as "a true desert—a desert of cold." Winter snowfall is light, but once it touches the ground, it is not likely to melt until the following summer. Winter temperatures average about 17 degrees below zero, made infinitely more severe by the intense wind. The ocean ice pack recedes for no more than four or five months of a year. This is the land of the midnight sun, with two months of perpetual summertime light balanced by 72 days of complete winter darkness, starting November 15 of each year.

The ecology of the North Slope has been repeatedly and well described as "fragile." The tundra, set in a lake- and puddle-studded landscape with extreme surface moisture, takes decades to heal once it is disturbed. Even a single vehicle tread exposes the subsurface to the summer sun, leading to the defrosting of waterways that had been permanently frozen and drastic alteration of the natural drainage patterns. On the Seward Peninsula, several hundred miles to the southwest, one can still see wagon trail marks that an old miner remembers were set down in 1920, half a century ago. A crop of simple lichen may take 100 years to grow to its maturity of just a few inches. An unnamed Alaskan in an Anchorage bar was quoted by Lewis Lapham in *Harper's* as commenting that talk used to be about "the hostile, frozen North. Now all of a sudden it's the goddamned delicate tundra." The first roadway of history to the North Slope was built from Fairbanks to the area of the great oil strikes in the late 1960s. Set on permafrost where the tundra has been scraped away, the road is heavily used in winter but turns into an impassable black quagmire with the spring thaws. It is just such lasting scars on the natural landscape, almost certain to increase despite the best counsel of the oil companies' ecologists, that has conservationists up in arms about further North Slope oil development.

Even with the start of the oil boom, the number of white men on the Arctic Slope is still tiny. A handful of Eskimo villages are situated along the ocean. Barrow (1970 population 2,104) is the northernmost settlement of the United States and largest Eskimo village in the world. Perhaps one should take comfort in the thin population and continued isolation of the North Slope. At Anaktuvuk, a village on the only feasible land pass of the Brooks Range, lives Jesse Ahgood, a Nunamuit Eskimo. He remembers seeing the first white men pass through, on their way to the North Slope, in 1901. So brief is man's hold on this distant land. Along with outer space, it is, in truth, our last frontier.

## *Urban Alaska: Anchorage and Fairbanks*

Anchorage, the metropolis no one anticipated, made its start in 1914 as Ship Creek Landing, a tent city at the head of Cook Inlet for surveyors and workers on the Alaskan Railroad. Historians record that the streets were two feet deep in dust, that water sold for five cents a bucket, and the garbage was dumped on an outgoing tide every 24 hours. A year later, the town was moved up and away from the waterfront and two special reserves established —"Bohunk Village" for the workmen, mostly single men recruited in Southern Europe, and "South Anchorage" for the prostitutes. By 1916, the whole conglomerate held some 6,000 people. But then came World War I, curbing growth on the railroad, and by 1920 Anchorage had just 1,856 people. At the eve of World War II, the city had only grown to 3,495 persons. Then came the impetus of military building during the war and afterwards, as Alaska came to be recognized as what Brigadier General Billy Mitchell, the great evangelist of air power, called "the most central place in the world of aircraft." In 20 years of fantastic growth, Anchorage grew 1,165 percent to 44,237 in 1960. In the 1960s the growth was mainly suburban, the city itself rising to 48,209 in population, the total Anchorage area to 124,542.

Today Anchorage is both the largest and youngest city in the biggest state of the Union. It is also Alaska's only really modern town and the epicenter of financial, political, and governmental power in the state. Juneau and the other Panhandle cities, once the center of influence, have been totally eclipsed—a process arousing no little hard feelings, especially in view of Anchorage's bid, up to now unsuccessful, to make itself the state capital. (Two times, in 1960 and 1962, the voters turned down initiative proposals to shift the capital away from Juneau, but the issue is still open. As federal and state offices gravitate increasingly to Anchorage, it may only be a matter of time. I was amused to read a 1970 editorial in the Anchorage *Daily News* entitled "We Can't Afford a Capital Move." The *News* suggested that the feuding and sectional animosities between Juneau and South Central Alaska could be alleviated by forgetting about an expensive move of the capital and concentrating instead on making state government more responsive through such devices as an ombudsman. But then the paper suggested holding legislature sessions every other year in a city closer to the population center—in either Anchorage or Fairbanks. Juneau must indeed believe that big city speaks with forked tongue.)

Luck and some ingenious civic boosterism have contributed to Anchorage's success. The federal government had first planned to establish headquarters for its railroad, running up from the Gulf of Alaska to Fairbanks in the interior, at the marine terminal at Seward. But one greedy entrepreneur tied up all the real estate in Seward, holding up everyone for high prices, and Washington decided to put the headquarters in Anchorage—giving the town its first permanent economic base.

When Hitler started to act up in the late 1930s, Alaska's total defense was one company of infantry, with a single tug to transport the troops. Then the Soviets began to build military installations on Big Diomede Island in the Bering Strait, practically within sight of U.S. territory, sparking new Navy bases. In spring 1940, with the Nazis occupying Alaska's transpolar neighbor, Norway, Congress authorized the Elmendorf Air Force Base at Anchorage. Anchorage went all-out to persuade the Army to put its Alaska headquarters in the city, pointing to its strategic location, the climate, terrain, and transportation facilities. Robert Atwood of the Anchorage *Daily Times* recalls: "We sold them and they came and we've prospered with them. Servicing the military became our major industry." During the war years, thousands of men flocked north to build and man air, naval, and ground force installations; at one time there were 152,000 men stationed in the territory, more than the entire civilian population. After the war the manpower commitment was drastically reduced, but tensions with the Soviet Union kept a strong military presence, directed by the unified Alaskan Command set up with headquarters in Anchorage in 1947. By 1970, serving as a key relay point to Vietnam among its other responsibilities, the Alaskan Command had 31,000 military personnel, 5,000 Department of Defense workers, and 37,000 dependents in the state. Roughly 64 percent of the total worked in or around Anchorage.

Anchorage boosters made an effort to get into the international aviation field after World War II, taking up collections to send representatives to Washington to testify before the CAB on route hearings. They hit the jackpot, with several domestic and nine international carriers (among them Air France, Japan Airlines, BOAC, and Scandinavian Airlines) making Anchorage a port of call. Anchorage built a huge international airport and calls itself "the crossroads of the world" with scheduled flights to the Orient and major European cities across the North Pole. "From that little isolated town of 3,000 when I came in 1935, when there was just one boat a week and it took a week to get to Seattle," publisher Atwood muses, "we can now boast regular commercial nonstop airline service to the three largest cities of the world—London, New York, and Tokyo. And no other city in the world can boast that." Anchorage, one might say, has literally put itself on the map.

Added to this, it still had its rail connection with the interior, a seaport handling more tonnage than any other in Alaska, 60 percent of the state's bank assets, and every kind of service in transportation, health, government, merchandising, and distribution. More even than Fairbanks, it has profited from the North Slope oil boom, both as a funnel for supplies and as Alaskan headquarters of the major oil companies. "This is the big city and everyone has to come here to get it," the local claim goes.

For a while in 1964, it seemed that Anchorage's Cinderella story might come to an abrupt end. At 5:36 A.M. on Good Friday, March 27 of that year, the most severe earthquake ever experienced on the North American continent and the second strongest ever recorded in the world—hitting 8.4 on the Richter Magnitude Scale—struck Anchorage and other locations in a 500-mile swath along the Gulf of Alaska. Mammoth sea waves, born of the quake, swept down the Pacific to send 9-foot waves onto Crescent City, California, and to lash the beaches of Hawaii. In Anchorage, the shock scythed the ground out from under a row of aging one- and two-story cafes, amusement parlors, and a theater on the north side of the main street, 4th Avenue, forming a trough-shaped depression, or graben. Cars were thrown on top of each other and guests at the top of the 15-story Anchorage Westward Hotel had the fright of their lives as the structure swayed back and forth 12 or 15 feet in each direction. Huge cracks appeared on the sides of high-rise buildings. In one suburb, 77 homes slipped into Cook Inlet, and at one outlying location one can still see an "earthquake park" of big blue clay mountains, where pools have been created and trees continue to grow at weird angles.

Miraculously, only nine people in Anchorage lost their lives. The quake was even more devastating to towns like Seward, Valdez, and Kodiak, located on low ground directly on the waterways of the Gulf of Alaska or neighboring Prince William Sound. William P. E. Graves of the *National Geographic*, who rushed to the scene for interviews immediately after the quake, pieced together these accounts:

Seward. Eyes still reflect the fear inspired by seismic sea waves, tsunamis, that swept through the port. . . . A 30-foot-high wave, covered with burning oil, surged at a speed of more than 100 miles an hour across the railroad tracks and into the port's east end. Locomotives and boxcars, their wheels shorn off by the impact, hurtled ahead of the comber.

Valdez. The town of 1,100 counted 31 dead and 25 homes destroyed or damaged. . . . The wave . . . came up the fjord, just after the earthquake, like some monstrous sea creature. Witnesses differ over its appearance—some say it came as a fearful, instantaneous rising of the tide; others recall a mountainous wall of water. One thing is certain: In the triphammer impact of the wave and its terrible backwash, the pier of Valdez, with 28 stevedores and onlookers, vanished forever.

Kodiak. In moments Alaska's largest king-crab fishing center was wiped out, boats, canneries, and all.

Five years later, the Coast and Geodetic Survey reported that the great Alaskan quake had caused Montague Island, near the center of the quake, to rise more than 30 feet. The Chugach and Kenai Mountains, about 80 miles from Anchorage, shifted to the south by about 50 feet. And mountain passes south of Portage sank almost 10 feet. According to a 1972 report by a panel of the National Academy of Sciences, the quake had a "cataclysmic" effect on the ecological balance of Alaska, especially in the Prince William Sound area, where the tremor destroyed 90 percent of the mussels, up to 40 percent of the clams, thousands of red rockfish and cod, and millions of salmon eggs and fingerlings. Salmon-producing streams were severely disarranged, and to this day salmon runs are still below average.

Anchorage leaders vividly recall the traumatic effect the quake had on their city. Much of the city, it was pointed out, was underlaid by an unstable stratum known as "Bootlegger Cove clay" which compounded the earthquake damage by causing disastrous landslides like the one that caused a wedge of center-city land 1600 feet long and 900 feet wide to sink about 15 feet in a downhill direction. Downtown Anchorage from I Street to Cook Inlet, government scientists said, would be forever high risk.

The possibility of abandoning great sections of center city was raised. Publisher Atwood recalls that in those days of uncertainty, he turned to books on the San Francisco earthquake for precedents, and he found scientists then had made the same horrendous predictions about the possibility of renewed destruction at any time. But, as in San Francisco, the momentum for continued growth of the city was too strong for the panic and indecision to last long. Anchorage simply ignored the recommendation of scientists and federal bureaucrats that the whole center core be subjected to urban renewal with massive replacement of unstable dirt, sand, and clay. Instead, just the worst-hit block on 4th Avenue—the so-called buttress area—was excavated and rebuilt. "We think it was a face-saving device by a bunch of scientists who got themselves boxed in and felt obliged to spend some $14 million," Atwood comments. It was pointed out that properly engineered structures like the big federal building, the Anchorage Westward in its location immediately adjacent to worst-hit 4th Avenue, and even apartment houses on mud on hillsides emerged unscathed from the quake. And so it was not long before a then little known developer named Walter Hickel was building the elegant new Captain Cook Hotel. Primed with generous federal aids totaling some $280 million, Anchorage resumed its rapid growth almost as if the earthquake had never happened. Needless to say, magnificent foundation work, including deep pilings, went into the new structures.

Was the massive government aid misspent? Given the engineering work of new buildings, the answer is most probably no. Anchorage is in so many respects a federal city, with agencies rendering services for national defense, communications, aviation, the electronics for the DEW line and the like, that an Anchorage would have to be created if one did not already exist. If federal aid had not been forthcoming for Anchorage people to rebuild their businesses and homes, the government might have been forced to underwrite the cost of a whole new Alaskan metropolis—at a cost many times higher than what was spent.

Even the smaller cities hit by the quake have rebounded. The residents of Valdez, closest town to the quake's epicenter, moved to a more stable site four miles away and actually numbered 81 percent more people (1,005) in 1970 than they had in 1960. Selected as the sea terminal for the oil line from the North Slope, Valdez can expect an oil company investment equal to 100 times its previous real estate value. Kodiak, prospering from its booming fish industry, increased in population by 44.5 percent, to 3,798, during the 1960s, the earthquake notwithstanding. Seward, long in decline as the port of Anchorage snapped up much of the docking activity for the Alaskan Railroad, lost a net of 16 percent of its population in the decade (down to 1,587). But a new scallop fishing industry was born, together with a dockside processing plant, and there was hope for the future.

Except for the buttress area, there is little hint as one walks along Anchorage's neatly ordered streets that a great earthquake occurred there less than a decade ago. Every other Alaskan city continues to reflect the untidiness of frontier living, but Anchorage could easily be mistaken for an average Midwestern city like Lansing or Rockford—minus the smokestacks. Even the same national chains, like Penney's, line the streets, and there is the same downtown parking crush and arguments about the need for a mass transit system to relieve downtown congestion. (Presently, no bus line at all runs in Anchorage). Outside of town, pleasant upper-middle class suburban areas are springing up. But Anchorage appears to have lost the chance for a unified area government under the advanced borough system authorized in the state constitution, a step wisely taken by Juneau in the late 1960s. An area unification scheme was rejected by popular vote in 1970; then, despite an extremely able rewriting of the proposal and backing from progressive forces and Walter Hickel, voters in 1971 again said no. The price, in disjointed government and lack of area-wide planning for land use, police protection, and unified air and water pollution control, will be felt for years to come.

There are unique aspects to Anchorage, however. It claims to have one of the best school systems in the country, and owns its own telephone and electric systems. Without appreciable industry, it would indeed become a ghost town if the federals pulled out. It does have a small black community, which claims to suffer from discrimination like that practiced in the Lower 48, but the more serious problem comes from Eskimos and other native peoples who drift into the city and face severe problems of adjustment to the white culture. To the dismay of the city fathers, numbers of hippies adorn the scene in the summertime. Gone are the days when visiting journalists could write of the city as one so imbued with "lust, sin, and violence" that "it must be rated the bawdiest community in North America." But 4th Avenue still has a complement of tawdry bars, and 80 percent of the cases in the local courts relate to alcoholism. Despite the warming influence of the Japan Current and the mountains which protect the town from the severest extremes of Alaskan weather, snow covers the ground continually for five winter months and the city averages 35 days with temperatures of zero or below. At Thompson Pass, near Valdez on Prince William Sound some 135 miles to the east, an Alaskan record of 975 inches of snow was recorded in the winter of 1952–53 (the height of an eight-story building).

Fairbanks, presently Alaska's second-largest city, is still a rough-and-tumble frontier town that sits on the edge of one of the world's great wildernesses—and shows it. After a few main arteries, one comes on streets unpaved or in disrepair, churning up clouds of summertime dust. Still to be seen are remnants of the 1902 gold rush, old log houses that are now cracked and tilted at crazy angles by the movement of the permafrost beneath them. Frontier-type swinging-door saloons still adorn a ramshackle main drag, and many of the streets, a visitor finds, simply follow the curvature of the Chena River as it swings through town. When I was there, the story was circulating of a man living near the University of Alaska campus, four miles out of town, who looked out of his window one day and saw a big bear looking in. In especially cold winters, the moose still wander into Fairbanks looking for food. Not until the 1940s did the city get a sewer system, and a still-quite-youngish Chuck Hoyt, managing editor of the Fairbanks *Daily News-Miner*, recalls riding the honey bucket wagon with his grandfather, a garbage collector. Up to the early 1950s, water was still being sold door to door. But paradoxically, this raw frontier town has in the *News-Miner* one of the brightest, best-edited small city newspapers in America, comparing not unfavorably with the excellent dailies published in Anchorage.

After the early rush for gold, Fairbanks subsisted as a trading center for the vast but lightly populated interior, the goods flowing in over the Alaskan

Railroad for which the city was—and is—the northern terminus. The gold-mining dredges closed down years ago and are not likely to move back into business as long as the price of gold remains far below the production costs of $90 an ounce. Big military bases arrived with World War II and the Cold War and still account for about a third of the area population of 45,864. The city itself had 14,771 people in 1970, up from 5,771 in 1950 but still small potatoes indeed by modern population standards.

Fairbanks has great hopes of new boomtimes through the North Slope oil development. Starting in the late 1960s, it became a terminal point for giant Hercules planes carrying drilling equipment to the North. The crews had to fight incredible cold in winter and hordes of mosquitoes in the summer, but they persevered in one of the great equipment airlifts in history. Oil speculators crowded into Fairbanks in an atmosphere of secrecy paralleled only by those that must have attended the first gold rush, or wartime military operations. In the long term, however, rival Anchorage is likely to benefit more with the state headquarters for the major oil companies. Booms for oil construction activity are always short-lived. The impact could be more lasting if recommendations to extend the Alaskan Railroad to the North Slope were approved, but that seems doubtful.

Fairbanks' nemesis is its weather. Located just 120 miles south of the Arctic Circle, the town revels in 24 hours of daylight around June 21, when the sun never sets and it looks like high noon all the time. The illustrious Goldpanners baseball team plays a game at midnight without benefit of artificial lighting, and temperatures frequently soar into the 90s. Winter comes roaring in with opposite extremes. The thermometer may drop to 44 below zero for weeks, the sun is faintly seen on the horizon for as little as three and a half hours, and at night the temperature may dip to 60 below. Cars clump around on "square" tires which have frozen with a flat side to the earth. An eerie "ice fog," not unlike a heavy smog, forms out of ice crystals and settles right down onto the ground, especially in depressed or flat areas, without budging for days. "The only thing that makes Fairbanks livable at that time of year is that there's not a breath of wind," I heard. When the ice fog has held on for several days, according to University of Alaska scientists, the city's air pollution levels exceed those recorded on the smoggiest days in the Los Angeles basin. During one recent winter, there were freak winds that made a 3-foot snowfall airborne again and blew a 707 jetliner off the runway at Fairbanks International Airport.

Fairbanks' fierce winters are not its only cross. In 1967 a rampaging story-high flood on the Chena River buried most of the city in muddy debris. St. Joseph's Hospital, the town's major medical facility, was damaged beyond repair. Only a massive injection of federal aid, plus a remarkably cooperative effort of Fairbanks' hardy individualists to shovel, repair, and share together, saved the city just before the beginning of the winter freeze. But later the cooperative spirit ran dry when the townspeople refused to vote the bond issue that would have made available several millions of dollars of matching state funds to rebuild the hospital.

What makes Fairbanks people—especially the women, for whom the dark, cold, and dust must be the toughest—stick it out in their inhospitable environment? Richard Austin Smith discovered part of the answer in an interview with one denizen, who said the typical Fairbanks citizen "feels like the prospector out in the desert: it's tough but it goes against his grain to pack up and move out." But he might have added that close to half of Fairbanks' people desert the city before the worst of winter sets in.

A word might be added about the University of Alaska, located at nearby College, which provides Fairbanks' sole brush with culture and a durable impetus for its economy. For a small, weak land-grant institution with only 2,000 students, the university has performed miraculously in building itself into a leading world center of Arctic and sub-Arctic research. Its scientists have come to play a role in protecting their state's natural environment unmatched in any other. One of my long-time friends, the late Don Charles Foote, was typical of the skillful young scientists working there. When the Atomic Energy Commission in the late 1950s developed its "Project Chariot" to blast out an artificial harbor in northwest Alaska with nuclear devices, Foote and his associates at the university went to work to show that the radiation, physical destruction, and damage to the hunting economy of the nearby Point Hope Eskimos would far outweight any possible lessons to be learned from the experiment. As part of the university's investigation, Foote and his Norwegian-born wife went to live for three years in the village of Point Hope, gathering the volumes of data necessary to show the impact of the blast on the Eskimos. (Foote's death in 1969, when his automobile skidded against an oncoming vehicle on the sheer ice of a Fairbanks winter street, ended the career of one of the more promising Arctic geographers of his generation.)

Though their achievement went largely unsung in the rest of the nation at the time, the scientists who challenged Project Chariot had invented a new concept in public affairs planning—measurement by scientific means of the potential impact of a major construction program. They won that fight, and Project Chariot was dropped. Some years later, they won again by defeating the ill-conceived plan to build the massive $1.5 billion proposed Rampart Dam on the Yukon River. The engineers would have flooded an area greater than New Jersey, drowned seven villages and forced the evacuation of 1,200 natives, and destroyed the breeding grounds of more waterfowl than are produced in all the other states—to produce hydroelectric power Alaska is never likely to need and to attract industry never likely to migrate to the Arctic North in any event.

## Economic Alaska . . .

To this point in its history, Alaska has had a weak, subsidized, high-cost economy. But the state is an enormous storehouse of resources and energy. It has 40 percent of the nation's undeveloped water power, a huge though undetermined share of its petroleum reserves, 54 percent of the U.S. general coastline, 65 percent of the U.S. continental shelf, and immense timber and mineral resources. Compared to its neighbors, Siberia and the Canadian North, it has yet to benefit from the intense national development effort that could lead to making it one day self-sustaining.

The dependence of Alaska on the federal government is overwhelming. No other state comes close to it in per capita expenditures from Washington. In 1950, 55 percent of the personal income realized in Alaska came directly from federal payrolls, in 1968 still 38 percent, with another 5 percent from state and local payrolls. Counting indirect as well as direct government expenditures, economists calculated that in 1960, seventh-eighths of the workers in Alaska owed their livelihood to federal, state, or municipal governments and only one-eighth to private sector activities like fishing, lumber, minerals, or tourism. The federal share has surely dropped since then, due to oil, a decline in military forces, the growth of tourism, and federal sale to RCA of the Alaska Communication System. (The federals would also like to divest themselves of the prosperous Alaska Railroad, which amazingly turns in a profit even while creeping along at an average 30 miles an hour and stopping to pick up anyone who waves it down, whether at a station or out in the bush. In 1969 revenues were $18.9 million, profits $212,000. Railroads in the Lower 48 should take note.)

One reason, certainly, that Alaska has remained such a stepchild of the federal government is that Washington has owned or controlled 96 percent of the state's land area and has kept most of it locked up for possible development at some future time. Another reason has been Washington's traditional lack of interest in Alaskan economic development, an attitude which has begun to shift since statehood with increased public works projects and pump-priming programs like those of the federal Economic Development Administration.

What has chiefly hampered Alaskan growth, however, is the exorbitant price of doing business there.* "High costs," according to Arlon R. Tussing, an economics professor at the University of Alaska, "are a reflection of the remoteness of much of Alaska, of the winter cold and of permafrost, of managerial inefficiency, and above all else of the small size and fragmentation of Alaska's markets." Other studies emanating from the University of Alaska characterize the state's economy as "insular, nondiversified, service oriented, structurally fragmented, and capital intensive." The economists point out that "because of pervasive leakages to the lower states, Alaska's income mul-

---

* The differential between Seattle and Alaskan prices has shrunken some in recent years, but in 1970 the cost of living in Anchorage was still 18 percent above Seattle, in Fairbanks 30 percent higher. Frozen orange juice cost 65 percent more, gasoline 40 percent more, new autos 13 percent more than in the Lower 48. To compensate, Alaskan production workers earned 41 percent above the national average and all government workers got a flat 25 percent federal tax-free cost-of-living allowance. Supermarket clerks started at $800 a month, while North Slope rednecks could easily make $25,000 a year. Isolated stories of incredible income include electricians earning $5,000 a month, divers $4,000, or a king crab fisherman who netted $95,509 in a year. Alaska's per capita income, $4,592 in 1970, ranked near the top among the 50 states. But the unemployment rate (up to 13 percent) ranked first, reflecting both the problems of the native peoples and the difficulty workers face in moving from town to town to take advantage of job opportunities.

tiplier is very small." Given those conditions, it may be unrealistic to expect that manufacturing activity, which accounted for only 8 percent of the gross state product in the late 1960s (compared to 36 percent from government and 12 percent from trade) will grow appreciably. Alaska must simply wait until world economic conditions create a demand great enough to pay for the use of her natural resources—the kind of demand that is now already great enough for oil and gas, and increasingly for timber. The primitive transportation systems will also have to be improved by such ingenious proposals as one from the Boeing Company to build fleets of 60-mile-per-hour air-cushion vehicles able to carry 100 tons of cargo, moving along corridors from which trees and other obstacles had been cleared.

The greatest markets for Alaska's exports are not the Lower 48 but rather that nation of the Pacific Basin with the greatest shortage of and need for raw materials—Japan. From $6.3 million in 1959, Alaskan exports to Japan rose to $92 million in 1970 and were projected to reach $165 million in 1973. In recent years the Japanese have been consuming between 75 and 90 percent of Alaska's exports and have been marketing in Alaska everything from their Toyota and Datsun autos to all of the pipe for the line to the North Slope. Japanese interests were also welcomed to buy a piece of the action themselves in capital-starved Alaska. By 1971 they had invested at least $200 million in Alaskan pulp and paper, natural gas, urea, mercury, and iron ore industries. And for years, Japanese processors have been purchasers of a big part of the catch of Alaskan fishermen and crabbers. Japanese industrialists in the 1960s formed a club to promote trade with Alaska, and the Alaska Chamber of Commerce followed suit with its own Alaska Nippon Kai ("Alaska Japan Club"). Frequent trade missions have been exchanged, and in 1971 Emperor Hirohito made Alaska his only U.S. stop, meeting with President Nixon on his first-ever travels for a Japanese emperor outside his own country. Since 1970 there has been a Japanese consulate in Anchorage, and Alaska has a trade office in Tokyo.

Some detect real or potential problems in the Japan trade—replacement of Seattle, which used to have a stronghold on the Alaska economy, with a new set of absentee owners, tensions over fishing rights in the Bering Sea, or the possibility of stiff competition with Japan's other potential raw material sources in Australia and Siberia. One federal planning officer in Anchorage voiced private fears in 1971 that the state could become a "second Manchuria." But the Alaskans claim to have encountered none of the traditional Oriental inscrutability in dealing with the Nipponese. Now well suppressed, if not forgotten, is the blood-soaked battle to dislodge the Japanese from Attu Island in 1943.

Alaskan businessmen and officials are forever dreaming of the pots of gold at the ends of assorted rainbows. Inevitably, the focus is on potentiality, not present-day reality. The gigantic continental shelf should one day foster a thriving oceanography industry and perhaps reserves of oil to rival those on the North Slope. Precious metals like gold, silver, and platinum, together with exotic elements such as beryllium, molybdenum, and uranium, commonplace iron ore and rich copper deposits might one day bring untold wealth—whenever ways are found to mine them economically and deliver them to overseas customers at a reasonable price. (Vast areas of Alaska have yet to be prospected for minerals.)

One of the surest bets is that tourism, presently returning an income of slightly more than $30 million on 100,000 visitors a year, will grow by leaps and bounds over the years. The reasons are simple: Alaska has natural scenery of a grandeur few other spots on earth can match, and increasingly affluent Americans, Europeans, and Asians (especially Japanese) are but a few jet hours away. But again, the potential will be tapped only in part until Alaska finds ways to open up its incomparable natural wonders—the fjord lands, glacier-packed mountain ranges like the St. Elias, the flanks of Mount McKinley, the Brooks Range, and the Arctic—not only to inexpensive air access but, wherever possible, to auto and bus access as well.* The Alaska Highway, stretching 1,523 miles from Dawson Creek, British Columbia, to Fairbanks, is still unpaved through Canada. Only a handful of cities offer first-class hotel accommodations (if you are lucky enough to get a room; I vividly recall the flea-bag to which I was consigned in Fairbanks). A federal study in the late 1960s projected a need for at least $70 million worth of new hotel rooms in half a decade, but no one was sure if the risk capital and actual construction would be forthcoming. By the state's most optimistic projections, it will have 220,000 visitors each year by the end of the 1970s. But even that would only be a fifth of what Hawaii already has.

### . . . and North Slope Oil

What may really save Alaska from the prospects of modern-day slump can be spelled in three letters: o-i-l. The boom began in what now looks like a small way with the strike on the Kenai Peninsula, on Cook Inlet, in 1957. It became big time in 1968 with the historic strike on the North Slope near Prudhoe Bay. This was to be the beginning of what W. T. Pecora, Under Secretary of the Interior, has called "one of the greatest mineral discoveries in the history of man." By early 1972, conservative estimates put the amount of recoverable North Slope oil at 10 to 15 billion barrels. Walter Hickel, when he was Interior Secretary, once estimated that 100 billion barrels might eventually be recovered. Before the North Slope discovery, the United States' total reserves were 31 billion barrels, and the total amount ever found in North America 118 billion barrels.

The discovery of major oil reserves on the North Slope did not come

* One of the most intriguing tourist possibilities is the opening up of Siberia to American travel—and hopefully, one day, a return flow of Russians to see Alaska. When I was in Nome, I saw a delegation of sturdy Soviet Intourist types visiting as the guests of Alaskan Airlines officials; a few months later the airline finally got clearance for regular tourist excursions to Siberia. Dr. T.I. Lin of the University of California has proposed a bridge-highway across a 50-mile stretch of the Bering Strait, thus linking Alaska and Russia and making it possible one day for people to drive from Paris to New York.

as a total surprise.* Early explorers mushing across the northern tundra had found places where the oil seeped from the earth in plain view. Early in this century, the Geological Survey regularly dispatched small scientific parties to map the region and explore for oil, and in 1923 President Harding, by executive order, carved out a section of the Arctic the size of Indiana and proclaimed it Naval Petroleum Reserve Number 4. During and soon after World War II, the Navy punched 37 holes down into the frozen earth of "Pet 4," as it is called, discovering some oil and gas but no quantities that would justify the massive transportation problems away from the North Slope. The only immediate use was to ship gas to one of the Navy's own installations on the Slope and to the Eskimos at Barrow. The Navy's exploratory work was not lost on the oil industry, whose geologists and executives remained convinced that great reserves of crude oil lay under the Arctic. A number of highly expensive dry holes were drilled during the 1960s by Atlantic Richfield, Humble Oil, and others, using state-owned land to the east of Pet 4. Then, in 1968, came the great strike.

What happened then is what traditionally occurs whenever oil is found—a mad rush of speculative firms to the general area, immense secrecy, the staking of claims. Except that the North Slope proved to be different in almost every respect from earlier experience:

THE GREAT LEASE SALE. The land on which the first strikes were made had been leased from the state of Alaska in the mid 1960s for $12 million—leases worth $2 *billion* after the Prudhoe Bay discovery. But Alaska had another 450,858 acres to lease. A great sealed-bid auction was held at Anchorage in September 1969. Each envelope had to contain a bid and a check for 20 percent of the proffered amount. A jet stood ready at the airport ready to rush the checks to New York so that not a day's interest would be lost. Eyewitness Ed Fortier later reported to the *National Observer*:

> I was making $425 per hour, and getting more excited as the oilmen poured more millions into the game. By the time the day was over, I had made $3,169, and so had each and every one of my 284,000 fellow Alaskans. That was our share of the $900,220,590.21 that the world's largest oil companies had paid our state government in the biggest oil sale in history.

The largest bid that day was for $72,277,133. At $28,233 per acre, it was the highest price ever paid for oil rights anywhere in the world.

THE ARCTIC OILMAN'S LIFE. "Except maybe for parts of Siberia, it's the worst place in the world to drill for oil. It's as godforsaken a spot as you could find, and as difficult and expensive to supply. It's bleak, cold, isolated and flat. There's no sign of vegetation other than the tundra. No people, no trees. And in wintertime, it's always dark."

Wesley C. Christensen, Alaska-based superintendent for Mobil Oil, was not exaggerating when he described North Slope drilling conditions that

---

* For portions of the ensuing account, I am indebted to articles by George Laycock in *Audubon*, Walter Sullivan in *American Heritage*, Richard Corrigan in the *National Journal*, and other sources cited in the bibliography.

way for a national magazine. In blizzards, men go from place to place by pulling themselves along on cables between buildings; otherwise they may die, since visibility may be one foot or less. Eighty-mile-an-hour winds and temperatures down to 40, sometimes even 60, below zero are not uncommon. Exposed flesh freezes in a matter of seconds, and at such temperatures one cannot touch metal with bare hands without losing some skin. Drillers wear two sets of underwear, insulated boots and overalls, wool and leather mittens, and face masks that become coated with a shimmering mask of their own frozen breath. Shelter is provided by tightly built prefabricated buildings, which have thermopane windows and outer doors like the doors of big walk-in refrigerators. The regimen is 12 hours of work a day, seven days a week. Two weeks off and four on. "No weapons, no booze, no women." But most of the men are too tired for anything but food and sleep.

The oil companies have to offer a lot to get men into this kind of environment. Sleeping quarters are excellent, the food (running to 2-inch steaks) plenteous and excellent. The pay is far above stateside rates. The roustabouts, however, are rarely Alaskan; most of them come from Texas, Oklahoma, and those other places where oil is commonplace.

GETTING THE OIL TO MARKET. For all the riches in black gold beneath the tundra, one could not imagine a more difficult place on earth from which to get the oil to market. Fairbanks, the closest city and railroad line, is 450 miles away over a towering mountain range; even the closest Eskimo villages (Barrow, Barter Island, Anaktuvuk) lie some 150 miles distant. The closest road is hundreds of miles away. There is no natural harbor, and ice seals in the coastline most of the year.

How then, to get the oil out? Several ideas surfaced. It could be shipped by great supertankers through the Northwest Passage or be conveyed by nuclear-powered submarines under the polar ice cap. It might be shipped by rail if the Alaska Railroad were extended north from Fairbanks. Or it could be pumped through a giant pipeline to an all-weather port in Southern Alaska.

Gradually, the pipeline idea emerged as the most economical. But first world attention was riveted on the supertanker idea and an actual test. Humble Oil & Refining in 1969 sent the 1,005-foot *S.S. Manhattan*, the largest tanker flying the American flag, around from the East Coast and through the ice-clogged channels of the Arctic Archipelago above Canada in the hope of achieving what so many earlier mariners had attempted—the Northwest Passage. The going was not easy. The massive ship, displacing 150,000 tons, was twice forced to shift course and take detours to avoid ice-packed straits, but finally it broke through into the Arctic Sea, the first commercial ship ever to do so. There were plans for a fleet of 30 such tankers at a total cost of $1.5 billion, plus up to $500 million for port facilities. But late in 1970, Humble decided that the tanker idea would not be the most economical way to get the North Slope's anticipated daily production of 2 million barrels a day to East Coast refineries. The plans were shelved, at least temporarily.

A railroad extension north from Fairbanks was also turned down because of the danger to wildlife inherent in sending 63 trains of 100 tank cars traveling both ways daily, over what would be the world's busiest rail line. Trucking was also rejected, because it would require an eight-lane highway and 60,000 large semitrailer oil trucks, close to the entire number now driving all American highways. Airborne tankers, perhaps converted Boeing 747s, were considered but rejected because of the danger of large aircraft in almost continuous use, often under treacherous weather conditions.

Less than a year after the 1968 strike, a consortium of the big oil companies—Humble, Atlantic Richfield, and British Petroleum, with others invited to buy in—announced plans to build a gigantic four-foot-wide oil pipeline for 800 miles, from the Prudhoe Bay area to Valdez on Prince William Sound. The pipe would move 413,285 gallons of oil per minute through pipe heated by friction to at least 10 degrees over the 160 degrees at which the oil comes from the ground. Though Interior Department approval would be required, the oil companies rushed ahead with orders to Japanese suppliers for the special pipe for the hotline—to be called the Trans Alaska Pipeline System, later rechristened Alyeska Pipeline System with a total of seven oil companies participating.

But formidable obstacles soon appeared—the still unsettled claims of Alaskan natives, which had led to a freeze on releasing any further federal lands in the state for private use; suits filed by conservationists and native groups, which brought federal court restraining orders against proceeding with the pipeline; and prolonged debate within the U.S. Government, and particularly its Interior Department, on whether and under what conditions to permit the pipeline construction. In the meantime, frustrated Alyeska officials saw practically all of the pipe for the line sitting in storage depots, exposed to the elements, along the proposed route. The participating companies were losing $300 million to $400 million in annual revenues and said that the interest alone on their investment was running to some $90 million a year. They were further upset when Governor William Egan interjected a proposal that the state of Alaska itself should build and own the line, raising the necessary money by the sale of bonds. Egan said a state-owned system would enable Alaska to earn an extra $100 million a year. Finally, early in 1972, the Interior Department seemed ready to approve pipeline construction, albeit with many restrictions on the way the job would be done. Even that approval would be contingent on oil company victory in court suits, brought by diverse groups ranging from national environmental organizations to the fishermen of Cordova, on Prince William Sound. And the eventual price of the line, originally estimated at $900 million, had risen to as much as $3.5 billion in some calculations.

Why, one might ask, would oil companies be willing to lay out such fantastic sums for Alaskan oil? The answers were both economic and practical. Oil prices in the U.S. are maintained at an inflated level by the government's oil import program, which limits importation of cheaper Middle East and other foreign oil to about a fifth of the country's domestic consumption. Alaskan oil could be sold at the same inflated prices demanded for oil produced in the Lower 48 states, but its cost to the oil companies would be substantially lower. An economist for the Federal Field Committee for Development Planning in Alaska suggested that the anticipated rate of return for the big oil companies, counting exploration, development, and production, would be about 43 *percent!* Even if the cost of the pipeline doubled, he calculated the return would be 36 percent. The second reason was purely practical: dwindling oil reserves in the Lower 48, and the constantly increasing curve of demand for oil in the United States. Alyeska estimated that when the pipeline reached a 2-million-barrel-a-day capacity, 1.5 million barrels would be delivered to the burgeoning West Coast market and another 500,000 barrels to the East Coast (by tanker through the Panama Canal). "By 1985," Alyeska president Edward L. Patton said, "the West Coast can take all of it." *

What all such projections left untouched was the legitimate question of whether it was really in the broad national interest to open up the North Slope, at this point in time, to private oil development. The prevailing U.S. Government position was that a "compelling" and "unequivocal" need existed to speed delivery of North Slope oil to U.S. markets; as Secretary of Commerce Maurice H. Stans expressed the case: "It would be an unwise decision on the part of this Administration to voluntarily increase our dependence upon foreign sources of oil at a time when the Middle East oil producing countries are coming increasingly under the political and economic influence of the U.S.S.R." In 1971 the American Petroleum Institute launched a $4 million nationwide advertising campaign on the theme: "A country that runs on oil can't afford to run short."

The case for rapid development had its critics, however. In 1971 the *National Journal*'s Richard Corrigan reported that despite the national security rationale of the oil companies and the federal government, there were "strong indications that a sizable percentage of the oil would be consumed in Japan rather than the United States." Alyeska indicated about 5 percent of the North Slope output, or 100,000 barrels a day, might go to Japan.

As for the national security argument, it was undercut to a degree by the critique of U.S. Rep. John Dingell of Michigan, who observed that the pipeline, storage tanks, and ocean tankers would be "obvious and easy targets" in wartime—making the oil unavailable for national security. An even more caustic view was expressed by author Daniel Jack Chasen in *Klondike '70: The Alaskan Oil Boom*. "The United States," he wrote, "supposedly *needs* oil from the North Slope, but only to perpetuate the smog from the internal-combustion engines, and only because laws passed for the benefit of the oil industry restrict the supply from other sources."

One of the strongest arguments for North Slope oil development was little heard up to early 1972: the fact that the region has a stupendous reserve

---

* Alyeska's projected early West Coast distribution: 190,000 barrels a day to Puget Sound (Seattle) area, 540,000 barrels to San Francisco, and 770,000 to Los Angeles.

of some 26 trillion cubic feet of natural gas, that the country is running perilously short in its supplies of that clean-burning fuel, and that the gas, associated with crude oil reserves, cannot be brought out until the oil is produced. But three oil and gas company consortiums were preparing proposals for a long-distance gas pipeline, to be built from Prudhoe Bay down through Canada's Yukon and Northwest Territories to join existing transmission systems that deliver gas to Midwestern U.S. markets.

THE ENVIRONMENT. More than technical problems of getting oil to market, early exploitation of North Slope oil was blocked by fears about the multiple dangers to the Alaskan environment.

Three principal threats were clear. The first was the chopping up of the tundra at and around the North Slope oil installations. Pipe, rigging, fuel barrels, bulldozers, house trailers, trucks, airfields, roads, and all the rest necessarily make a major impact and, if past experience is a guide, may leave a mess behind that no one will ever clean up. This problem is being minimized, however, by agreement of the oil companies not to move equipment across the tundra during its months of thaw (big helicopters are employed instead) and to drill four to six wells from a single pad, boring obliquely to reduce production costs—and, incidentally, spare the tundra. Worried about their public relations, the big oil companies have to date been scrupulously careful about the neatness of their North Slope facilities and have experimented with a variety of grasses to heal scars made on the tundra.

A second threat involves the pipeline corridor to the south, and here the environmentalists were truly up in arms. As writer Richard Pollak wrote for the Sierra Club's book, *Oil on Ice: Alaskan Wilderness at the Crossroads*:

Eventually, two million barrels of hot oil would sluice daily, from the wells in the frozen north to mammoth tankers waiting at the terminus on Prince William Sound.

En route, this viscous crude would travel the breadth of Alaska's most fragile ecosystems: from the ice-worn coast of Prudhoe Bay, across the lichen-sprinkled tundra of the North Slope, up rolling foothills into the glaciated grandeur of the Brooks Range, through barren, snowbound mountain passes, down to the valleys and forests of the interior highlands, hard by the growing population center of Fairbanks, through the Alaska Range, the Copper River Basin and Chugach Mountains and, finally, to the waiting ships at Valdez. . . . On its way, the oil would cross two dozen rivers (including the Yukon), well over a hundred streams, and border scores of lakes in whose sparkling waters salmon, char, pike and myriad other fish abound. . . .

Safely traversing that territory with a cylinder of hot oil (temperatures of up to 170 degrees) posed immense problems. Laid on the permafrost, the line would melt itself into the ground and form a giant trench, causing erosion and the possibility of line breaks, especially in earthquakes. Buried, as the oil companies originally envisaged, it might melt the ground as deep as 50 feet and convert frozen silt into an impassable canal. Elevated above the ground—a much more expensive alternative, but one eventually selected for a major portion of the line—the line might cause problems like blocking migrating caribou that Eskimos and Indians depend on for their hunt. Elevated pipeline could also be a target for stray gunshots or vandals. Then there are the problems of how to detect and repair leaks in remote locations, how to resist avalanches and glacial flooding, and how to cross rivers (where a line break could send thousands of gallons of oil into a great waterway, contaminating the water and killing fish for hundreds of miles downstream). An alternative proposal to route the oil by pipeline into Canada and down the Mackenzie River encountered many of the same objections—plus the barriers of a projected cost of $4 billion to $8 billion, two to four times the cost of the trans-Alaska route.*

Even the oilmen, it was reported in 1971, confessed that if they had crash-built the pipeline in 1969, as they originally planned, they would have made horrendous mistakes. But under pressure from government and the conservationists, they developed increasingly sophisticated methods to minimize the danger of damage, including aerial surveillance of the line-monitoring devices that would automatically turn off the oil flow minutes after a leak was detected. Interior Department specifications stated that only half the line could safely be laid underground, and that there would have to be crossings for big-game animals on sections above ground.

Even on a large map of Alaska, the pipeline's defenders point out, a true-to-scale line for the pipeline would be so thin that one couldn't see it. Walter J. Hickel, a leading proponent of the pipeline, wrote in 1971:

If nature had to put that oil somewhere, I'm glad it was on the North Slope of Alaska and not in the Tetons, or the Sierras, or Cape Cod. America enjoys a cherished and immeasurable wealth of frontier grandeur and environmental bounty in its 49th state. And within Alaska's vast reaches, I believe we have room to set aside just 15 square miles, out of Alaska's 586,000 square miles, to be taken up by the entire right-of-way for an 800-mile pipeline from Prudhoe Bay to a deep-water port on the Gulf of Alaska.

But still, there was the danger of oil spills at sea. The target port of Valdez, on Prince William Sound, is a leading salmon fishery. Even the cleanest existing oil ports of the world experience a loss of .01 percent in connection with storage, loading, deballasting, and shipping of oil. With two million barrels of oil a day flowing through Valdez, that would mean a daily loss of 200 barrels—or 73,000 barrels a year, more than three-fifths the load associated with the *Torrey Canyon* disaster. There could well be, according to government reports, "a devastating effect on the ecosystems of Valdez Arm and Prince William Sound." Commerce Department scientists say that the potential pollution hazard from an oil tanker wreck is "immense" and that most recorded world tanker wrecks "occurred under more benign climatic and geographical conditions than those found in Prince William Sound. . . . Because of both the nature of known navigational hazards within

---

* The environmental problems of a natural gas (as opposed to hot oil) line would be minimized by keeping gas refrigerated to below freezing, so that the permafrost would not be melted.

Prince William Sound and the lack of data concerning possible submarine pinnacles, uncharted currents, and the absence of suitable holding ground, the risk of collision or stranding is magnified." Winds of near-hurricane intensity often build up in the sound and continue for days, making it a classic shipwreck coast.

In the fact of those problems, the oil companies did all they could short of abandoning their project—they began to develop for Valdez Harbor what may be the most advanced antipollution system in the world.

## Native Alaska

Had this book been written a decade earlier, it would have been easy enough to mention in a few sentences the geographic and ethnic distinctions of Alaska's Eskimos, Indians, and Aleuts, to allude to what was already known about their deplorable living conditions, and leave the subject there. Today, no responsible writer could dream of giving the subject such short shrift—not because white men suddenly "discovered" the Alaskan native, but because the natives of the Great Land discovered themselves. There are certainly few parallels in history of an aboriginal people, occupying a vast part of the earth for millenniums of time with scarcely any contact between each other, suddenly coalescing to define their common heritage, articulate their needs, and mount a program of militant action in common accord. That is what happened in Alaska in the 1960s. The excruciating problems remain. But the docile Alaskan native will never be the same.

As good a place as any to get an idea of what the Alaskan native movement is all about is in the untidy offices of the *Tundra Times*, located in upstairs quarters in one of the buildings along the sleazy main street of Fairbanks. I was greeted there first by reporter Tom Richards, a tall, delicate young Eskimo born 20-odd years ago in Kotzebue. With his father, a bush pilot, he moved to Fairbanks before he was 10 and later studied journalism at the University of Denver and the University of Alaska. (His father now pilots a Wien Consolidated Airlines 737, the only Eskimo pilot flying commercial jets.)

What is underway, in Richards' view, is a concerted effort of the native peoples "to retain their culture and also be an economic and political force." "With all consideration for European man," Richard says, "I'd rather spend four years learning what I am." So he takes a keen interest in politics, writes on subjects of wide interest to the natives, but keeps his Eskimo credentials splendidly intact. When I spoke to him, he had just returned from Point Hope, the most northwestern point of the U.S., where the townspeople had just gathered at an old Episcopal mission to celebrate a whale feast. With real enthusiasm about a culture he shared, Richards told of the elders sitting under a great skin (umiat) and waiting for the whaling captain to distribute huge chunks of whale flipper meat. I asked him if exposure to normal Western food had spoiled his taste for the normal village diet, and the answer was no. "I can eat all the delicacies," Richards said, naming whale heart and liver, walrus liver, miquaq (whale meat naturally fermented in barrels for 10 days), and muktuk (outer skin and inner layer of fat, either cooked or, more commonly, eaten raw).

Up to the 1960s, the only native organizations were the Alaska Native Brotherhood and Sisterhood, founded in 1913 and active exclusively among the Tlingit and Haidas Indians of southeastern Alaska. But the Association of American Indian Affairs, and especially its Alaska Policy Committee chairman, the late Dr. Henry Forbes of Milton, Massachusetts, determined in the early 1960s that the time had come to coalesce the efforts of native peoples all over Alaska. Statehood had just been achieved, and in the offing was the problem of dispensation of the 102 million acres of land the federal government had agreed to give to the new state. At Point Hope in 1961, Forbes made the acquaintance of Howard Rock, an accomplished Eskimo artist who had lived several years in Seattle making a living from his native-style designs in ivory. Both men were intensely interested in conservation of the polar bear, and 1961 was the same year that some Alaskan natives were becoming concerned about the Atomic Energy Commission's Project Chariot to detonate a nuclear explosion on the coast some 30 miles south of Point Hope, creating a harbor. With funding from Forbes' group, the first meeting of Northwest natives was called in November 1961 at Barrow. This meeting was to be the forerunner of hundreds out of which emerged the 20-odd native groups, covering every native people and area of Alaska, which were active by the mid-1960s.

Rock and Forbes had discussed the possibility of a newsletter, or even a newspaper, to tie together the emerging native movement. A few months after the Barrow meeting, Rock got a long distance call from Forbes in Massachusetts. "Howard," Forbes said, "I've decided to back the paper on one condition—you be the editor." Thus was founded the *Tundra Times*, "owned, controlled and edited by the Eskimo, Indian, Aleut Publishing Company, a corporation of Alaskan natives." The paper's great and continuing issue was the question of native land claims, but it also took up the cudgel for better native housing (getting the late Senator E. L. [Bob] Bartlett to sponsor a $10 million native housing project in Congress), sanitation (because of the grave dangers to native health posed by poor water supplies and waste disposal facilities), and employment (with strenuous demands for work training programs). "As we fought on these various issues, a high caliber of the new native leadership appeared," Rock says. A prime example was state Rep. William Hensley, a Kotzebue Eskimo. Quite rapidly, white Alaskans learned that the native peoples could be tough bargainers and knew how to use their vote effectively in a balance of power position between the major parties. The *Tundra Times*, its circulation limited to a few thousand weekly copies but circulating into virtually every native hamlet of Alaska, became the spokesman and unifying force of the native peoples.

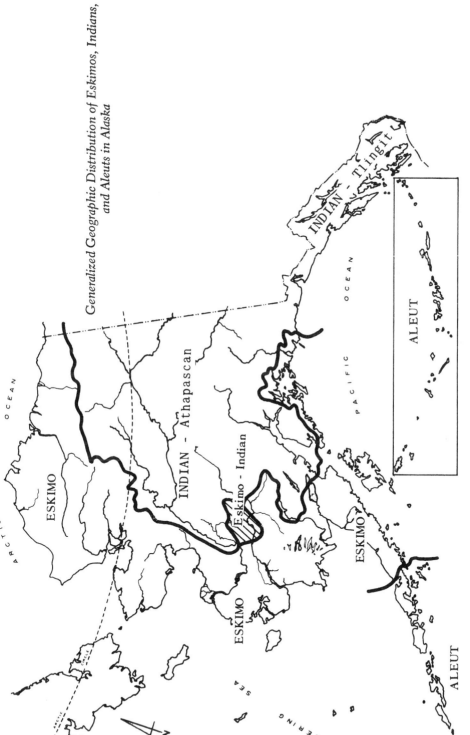

*Generalized Geographic Distribution of Eskimos, Indians, and Aleuts in Alaska*

**Source:** *Alaska Natives and the Land* (report of the Federal Field Committee for Development Planning in Alaska, 1968)

Emergent native power has been most vividly illustrated on the issue of land claims. Under Russia, the native peoples were either ignored or treated as chattels; least fortunate were the Aleuts, inhabitants of the stormbound Aleutians, who numbered some 24,000 before the fur traders arrived. The Aleuts saw their women seized, their furs stolen, and their people massacred and wracked with white man's disease to the point that the population once dropped to little more than 2,000 and an American government report called them a "dying race."

When the United States purchased Alaska from the Russians for $7.2 million in 1867, the native peoples who had occupied the territory for 6,000 years received not a penny of the money. No federal law, with the exception of two small reservations set aside for specific groups, ever recognized native land rights until the 1958 statehood act, which required the state to "forever disclaim all right and title . . . to any lands or other property (including fishing rights), the right or title to which may be held by Eskimos, Indians, or Aleuts." But unlike the Indians of the coterminous U.S., Alaskan natives never entered into treaties with the U.S. defining their land rights, either before or after statehood. Only the remoteness and inhospitality of so many of the lands on which native villages were located, or on which the natives fished and hunted, prevented worse violations of native rights than did occur. Even in the 1960s, natives held legal title to only a few hundred of the thousands of acres they considered their ancestral birthright. An old Alaskan patriarch put the issue well in field hearings on land claims before the Senate Interior Committee: "Did it ever occur to you that maybe you were buying some stolen property when you bought the lands from the Russians?"

The statehood act gave the state of Alaska the right to "select" for its own use 103 million acres of the 375 million acres owned by the federal government. In the 1960s, the state began to exercise that right over a few million acres, running directly into a buzzsaw of angry native protest. Natives began to file stupendous land claims, overlapping both federally held public domain as well as state-selected land and including, significantly, the billion-dollar oil lands of the North Slope. Unable to deal any longer with the conflicts between state land selections, federal withdrawals, and native land claims, Secretary of the Interior Stewart Udall in 1966 ordered a freeze on all federal land transfers. With basic law and issues of rightful land ownership clouded beyond belief, settlement by the courts could have dragged on for years. All eyes looked to Congress for a political settlement—a kind of quit claim, awarding the natives a set amount of land and cash in return for the lands taken from them over the course of history.

Just what that quit claim should involve became the subject of intense debate in Alaska and in Congress, starting in the late 1960s. The Alaskan natives, unified for the first time in 1966 under a statewide Alaskan Federation of Natives (AFN) that included all major regional native organizations, asked for clear title to 40 million acres of land, a cash settlement of $500 million out of the federal treasury (the money to be paid to native development corporations), and a perpetual 2 percent royalty on mineral proceeds from all lands not owned directly by natives.

"To put it bluntly," AFN president Emil Notti told the Senate Interior Committee, "we want to manage our money and our lives, and we must question the fairness of any settlement which does not enable us to do so. . . . Our goal is not merely dollars and cents, but to give each native the opportunity to join the mainstream of American life on equal terms if that is his wish, or the opportunity to continue the traditional way of life while enjoying the full benefits of modern science, if that is his wish." The natives, in other words, wanted both the cash to give them developmental potentiality equal to other Americans and the lands to continue the hunting and fishing "subsistence" patterns of the past. The Federal Field Committee for Development Planning in Alaska reported to the government in 1968 that 60 million acres would be required for the natives to keep on existing that way, and late in 1970 the AFN actually upped its demand to the 60-million-acre amount.

A 40- or 60-million-acre settlement, however, raised stiff opposition among many whites in Alaska, especially state government officials, fishing and hunting sportsmen, oil interests who wanted to exploit as much of the state as possible, and among federal departments like Agriculture and Defense which blanched at the idea of turning over national forest or petroleum reserves to the natives. Senate Interior Committee chairman Henry M. Jackson of Washington became principal author of a bill, which passed the Senate in 1970, to give the natives a cash settlement of $500 million over 12 years for development corporations, and another 2 percent override on mineral royalties (chiefly oil royalties) from federal lands, up to a total of another $500 million. (The natives' mineral royalties would come from payments that would otherwise go into the state treasury, a unique concept in U.S. native claims settlement.) But the 1970 Senate bill guaranteed the natives only 10 million acres of land—a figure they might have gladly accepted some years before but which, in the context of their growing political consciousness, they rejected out of hand. Donald Wright, the affable and extremely able Athabascan Indian who succeeded Notti as president of the AFN, stated his people's case with eloquence: "No one who has not lived in our lands, among our people, can understand the deep emotional—indeed, religious—attachment that our people have to the land. The land is our life. . . . Take our land—take our life!" Wright's impressive presentation in a private meeting with Vice President Agnew and other officials played a major part in getting the Nixon administration to shift from a restrictive settlement recommendation to a quite generous one.

More than an emotional plea was necessary, however, and the natives finally secured a favorable bill because of the unique coalition pressing for an early settlement. This included the oil companies that wanted quick clearance of land claims so they could build their pipeline from the North Slope, the Alaskan congressional delegation anxious to get land and oil revenues for the state, the Leadership Conference on Civil Rights and affiliated church and civic rights action groups, and the Seafarers International Union, whose officials hoped for an early start to oil tanker traffic from Alaska. "The justice of our cause, mixed with oil—that's what did it. . . . Without the pressure from the oil companies, we'd be sitting around debating a bill 10 years from now," said Edward L. Weinberg, an attorney for the natives. Weinberg, former solicitor of the Interior Department, was one of a team of legal heavyweights representing the AFN, a group that included former Supreme Court Associate Justice Arthur Goldberg, former Attorney General Ramsey Clark, and former California Senator Thomas H. Kuchel. (The natives' lobby campaign was financed by a $600,000 interest-free loan from some Alaskan native groups and the Yakima Indian Nation in Washington State.) The most vocal opposition, interestingly, came from conservationists including the Sierra Club, the Wilderness Society, and other groups. They said a big land grant to the natives would constitute "a raid upon the public domain of Alaska" and that the secret force behind the claims settlement was a group of "speculators and exploiters" who would benefit even more than the natives.

The final bill, approved in December 1971, represented what President Nixon called the "last major original Indian claims settlement in American history." The bill was not quite as generous as the natives had come to hope, but in comparison to all prior agreements with the aboriginal people of the continent, it was absolutely unprecedented. The natives were given the right to select 40 million acres of land—the equivalent of 62,500 square miles, an area larger than 30 of the states of the Union. The ultimate cash settlement with them would be $965 million, or $19,300 for each living native.

The complex land provisions of the bill were roughly as follows: The six-year-old land freeze was lifted. The Secretary of the Interior was authorized to set aside a 10-mile-wide corridor in which the pipeline from the North Slope, if approved, might be built. The Interior Secretary was also empowered to withdraw 80 million acres to be designated as national parks, scenic and wild rivers, national forests, and wildlife refuges. (Included, for instance, would be territory like the incomparable Brooks Range.)

Then came provisions giving the natives their chance. Twelve regional native corporations, authorized by the bill, were allowed to designate 22 million of the 40 million acres accorded them—but only from tracts of land adjacent to their existing villages. The North Slope oil lands were specifically excluded. Next, the native corporations and the state of Alaska could select land in a checkerboard fashion from around native villages until the natives had used up the rest of their 40-million acre allotment. Finally, the Alaskan state government could pick land away from the townships until it had received all of the 103 million acres guaranteed it at the time of statehood. The land selection formula caused the most unhappiness among the natives,

because it effectively barred them from picking lands with economic development potential in terms of known mineral resources, timber, or recreation.
Senator Jackson expressed concern that the natives, by receiving an immense
amount of land without high intrinsic value, might end up being land-poor.
While the AFN as a whole agreed to the settlement, the Arctic Slope Native
Association rejected it and said it would press ahead with a court suit to get
control of the entire North Slope, including the oil lands.

The cash settlement with the natives will come in two parts, both paid
to their regional corporations. A sum of $462 million will be paid from the
federal treasury over a period of 11 years. Another $500 million will be paid
from state mineral revenues at the rate of 2 percent.* The natives will
benefit materially, and for years to come, from the settlement. Part of the
money will be used by the development corporations for the natives' own
schools, better housing, roads, and sewers. A substantial amount will filter
down to the individual through employment opportunity. But the only direct cash benefit to individual natives will come in the form of eventual
dividends from the money received by and invested by their development
corporations.

The fascinating story of the next decades, of course, will be how wisely
the native corporations use their new wealth in land and cash to truly improve the lot of their people. But looking back at the long and arduous
process that had brought them a settlement after 104 years of United States
jurisdiction, two facts stand out clearly: Only the ability of the natives to
unify and articulate their demands so well enabled them to receive money
and lands anywhere near the final magnitude. And if it had not been for the
federal land freeze, and then the North Slope oil strike, promising untold
revenues for both federal and state treasuries, there might have been no
settlement at all, or if there had been one, it would have looked like beads
and trinkets compared to what finally emerged. For once, the tides of history converged to produce substantive equity for a large group of America's
native peoples.

That the indigenous peoples of Alaska *need* assistance stands beyond
any reasonable doubt. In its 565-page report, *Alaska Natives and the Land,*
prepared in 1968 at the request of Senator Jackson, the Federal Field Committee for Development Planning in Alaska laid out the problem with poignant and arresting detail.† Alaska's three great native groups—the Eskimos
of the western and Arctic coastal regions, the Indians of the interior and

---

* I asked a Washington attorney representing the natives why a ceiling was put on the mineral
royalties from land that had once belonged to them entirely. "Alaska," he answered, "is a long way away,
and most Congressmen don't really give a damn about it. Moreover, everyone of those Western Congressmen was thinking about what the hell would happen if the Indians of their states were to say, 'All
right, you finally came across and did the right thing by the Alaskan natives, especially by giving them
mineral revenues in perpetuity. How about giving us a fair share of the billions in minerals extracted
from the land we ceded to you so long ago?' "

† This report, available from the Government Printing Office for $16, is well worth the price for
anyone interested in seeing how excellent official reports could be if government administrators were
only willing to hire sufficiently skilled staff people to do the job. The layout and writing are excellent
and provide a unique view of a state and its peoples. The reader is referred especially to the intro-
ductory chapter, "Alaska Natives Today: An Overview," by Robert D. Arnold, of Anchorage.

Panhandle Alaska, and finally the Aleuts of the Aleutians—were found to face similar problems. Seventy percent live in small, isolated villages strung out across the 375 million acres of Alaska, eking out a subsistence living through fishing and hunting, most living in deep poverty. The great majority of native Alaskans are unemployed or only seasonally employed. In 1960 almost seven out of 10 adults had less than an elementary school education. Because they lack cash income, most natives live in small, dilapidated houses in unsanitary conditions. That factor, plus unbalanced diets, makes them prime victims of disease, with a life expectancy of only 35 years—little more than half that of other Americans. The median age of Alaskan natives is only 16.3 years, a result of the short life span and a birth rate *twice* that of the United States as a whole.

There are occasional exceptions to the rule of poverty, the most famous being the Athabascan Indian Village of Tyonek, across Cook Inlet from the Kenai oil fields. Not too many years ago, the inhabitants of the then squalid village were so close to famine that Anchorage pilots flew rescue missions to help feed them. Then oil was discovered on land the village controlled, and in 1962 the Court of Claims awarded them $14 million. The Tyoneks ordered attractive prefabricated ranch houses for themselves, set up a sanitary water supply and sewage system, and built a school much better than the Bureau of Indian Affairs money would normally have permitted. But despite all these advancements, the 232 inhabitants have had difficulty landing permanent jobs. How much more difficult the employment problem is for tiny native villages, separated from urban centers by hundreds of miles, is not hard to imagine.

Harvey Vestal, president of the Northwest Native Association, told me the story of his native village of Deering, some 600 miles south of Kotzebue. Only a handful of families—fewer than 100 people in all—still live there, and Vestal calls it a "ghost town." The people own their own reindeer herds. They sell the meat, providing some cash income, and now the BIA hopes the skins can be marketed for gloves and other novelty items.

A few years ago, there was an expectation that the villages would begin to disappear altogether. But the Field Committee found that while some tiny villages have been abandoned, the medium-sized ones were holding on and the overall population of native places was a third larger than in 1950. Much of the movement has been to regional native centers like Kotzebue and Bethel, where employment possibilities, especially in government jobs, are greater. Bethel, on the southwestern mainland coast where some of the worst poverty conditions in Alaska and perhaps all the U.S.A. are to be found, almost doubled its population in the 1960s and is the site of an ambitious government-subsidized housing program.

Housing efforts, while they create only short-term local employment, may be a key to improvement in the natives' deplorable health status. With the help of the Public Health Service, conditions have already improved since the 1950s when one government report found Alaskan natives to be "victims of sickness, crippling conditions and premature death to a degree exceeded in very few parts of the world." But still in 1966, the Field Committee found, native Alaskans were 10 times more likely than other Alaskans to die of influenza or pneumonia. (They were also twice as likely to commit suicide, and three times as likely to die of accidents.) The death rate among native infants is only slightly greater than among whites during their first six days of life, when they are likely still to be in the hospital. But when a native baby is returned to his village home environment, his chances of death rise as high as 12 times that of whites. A key to village health is the construction of water and sewer systems, but the task in Arctic villages is fantastically difficult and expensive because of the permafrost. Dead bodies are commonly kept outside until summer when the ground has thawed enough for burial.

Funds from the lands settlement may eventually make money available not only for housing and water-sewer systems, but for more adequate local health care and for new schools of superior quality. The Alaskan natives' distaste for the schools run by the BIA, accused of paternalistic and overly regimented ways, is as great as that of stateside Indians. The natives hope that land settlement money will make it possible for them to staff and run their own schools, teaching the indigenous culture with pride and understanding. Already, in schools throughout the bush, the old "Dick and Jane" readers are slowly being replaced by an *Alaskan Reader* that is much more relevant to the real world of native children.

And it is the natives' pride in their own culture that may provide the impetus for a real renaissance. Here one leaves the dollar-and-cents world of housing and employment and health and touches a resilient, very alive native spirit. At the University of Alaska, for instance, skilled native artists like Eskimo Ronald Senungetuk, an associate professor of art, are teaching other natives the carving and molding of silver, soapstone, wood, ivory, and harder stones. Senungetuk insists that the new products will lack the commercialized, cheap quality of a lot of native art work sold today. "The native style of 5,000 years ago," he told me, "has a definite approach to dynamic style. So we concentrate on universal basic design, and our students turn out original works of art, not dead copying of the past." The images and materials of village life and the wildlife that natives know so well shine through in clear, distinct style in some of the work shown at the Alaska Festival of Native Arts—sculptures of whales and masks and seals, ivory carving, silver jewelry, imaginative graphics, dolls and grass basketry, beadwork, and skin-sewing. Together with native music and dance, there is a cultural promise for the whole Alaskan society in which whites may take as much joy as the natives.

Among all the Alaskan native peoples, the most interesting case—unique in the U.S.A. to Alaska, in fact—is that of the Eskimos. Over history, Eskimos have shown an ingenuity that few peoples on earth have matched: to master the forbidding Arctic environment by inventing dogsleds and kayaks, tailoring clothes so that the seams are waterproof, making slit goggles from ivory to protect against the blinding glare of snow. When nature deprived the Eskimos of wood for heating or for light, they invented a smokeless stone lamp that burned seal oil. Their tools and weapons are so beautifully made that they are like works of art in themselves.

Within their own communities, Eskimos are loving and loyal, their culture harking back to the days when arguments might be settled by song and wives shared among friends. Arthur Hippler, an associate professor of anthropology at the University of Alaska, has written that the Eskimo feels a part of the life around him. He is a part of nature. A part of the village. A part of the animal life. A part of the world. He is unique and should not be interfered with and, by the same token, does not wish to interfere with others. "In the old days," Hippler wrote, "if a person became so bossy with others that he could not be tolerated, he was killed or run off. If they couldn't do this, the people who couldn't stand the bossiness then simply moved away." While Eskimos are incredibly tough physically, they are among the world's most permissive child raisers. Eskimo children are rarely spanked. They stay up as late as they like and come and go as they wish.

When these same people are faced by a pushy, competitive, alien culture, they are easily abused. Often they become shy and suffer tremendous indignities in silence. But if they are shown kindness and respect, their native intelligence and ingenuity permit them to prosper. Eskimos, Howard Rock told me, can perfectly well accept radios and outboard motors and snowmobiles and well insulated modern houses and still be fine hunters. His brother Allen, of Barrow, runs a little cafe and makes good money as a cement finisher during the summer. But in winter Allen Rock can still accept the rigors of hunting for walrus, whales, and caribou. "He eats his native food along with bacon and eggs," Rock said. He has spanned two worlds.

Admittedly, the Eskimo youngsters one sees today hanging around barrooms, wearing bellbottoms and smoking pot, hardly conform to the image. But it is the *urban* environment that seems most debilitating. It is in the cities where the great numbers of arrests of Eskimos for drinking in public occur. The intriguing problem of the next decades will be to bring the Eskimo the material comforts of civilization while confirming him in his native culture and his own unique and wonderful skills. Few are the native peoples, anywhere, who have been able to make that adjustment. But if any people has the intelligence and courage to bridge the gap, it may well be this warmhearted race of the distant Arctic North.

## Political Alaska

As history marks the affairs of men, Alaska's arduous battle for statehood was won only yesterday. But the pace of subsequent events in the Great Land has been so rapid—including the earthquake of 1964, the great native awakening, and the discovery of great oil reserves on the North Slope—that the statehood struggle now seems like the affair of another age.

Most of the heroes of that battle, including the revered E.L. (Bob) Bartlett, Alaska's territorial delegate when Congress voted for statehood, are now gone from the scene. Bartlett, a Democrat, became one of the state's first two U.S. Senators, helped Alaska line up millions of dollars of federal aid after the earthquake, and died in 1968. Regarded by many as the state's founding father, his statue now stands in the rotunda of the U.S. Capitol in Washington. The other "first" Senator, Democrat Ernest L. Gruening, is remembered as one of the two U.S. Senators to vote against the Tonkin Bay Resolution. He ran for another Senate term in 1968 at the age of 81 and was defeated by Mike Gravel, an aggressive, somewhat erratic younger Democrat.* Gravel, the son of French-Canadian parents, immigrated to Alaska in 1956, made some money as a real estate developer, became the fair-haired boy of Barney Gottstein (a millionaire contributor to Democratic causes), served with some distinction in the state legislature, and defeated Gruening with a clever media-type campaign. In 1971 he captured national attention by reading from the still-suppressed Pentagon papers at a midnight congressional hearing and breaking into uncontrollable tears because of his horror about the United States' association with "petty warlords, jealous Vietnamese generals, black marketeers, and grand-scale dope pushers."

The most enduring of the statehood fighters, Democrat William A. Egan, became the first governor after statehood, lost out to the colorful Republican, Walter J. Hickel, in 1966, but returned to power in the 1970 elections. Egan, a small-town grocer by trade, is a warm, extremely approachable figure, regarded as honest beyond reproach. No one has ever regarded him as a brilliant administrator, but he was just the kind of fair-minded and accessible governor Alaska wanted after decades of cold, impersonal territorial rule.

The birth of Alaskan statehood took nine decades, from the day in 1867 that Senator Charles Summer, supporting ratification of the treaty of purchase from Russia, made a learned speech in which he dedicated the territory to future statehood. The purchase, historians record, was one where the seller was more eager than the buyer, a well-oiled lobby got the House to approve, and there is a strong possibility that Russian gold eased the way for Senate passage. Secretary of State William Seward saw the purchase treaty he negotiated widely derided as "Seward's folly," and Congress long regarded the territory as a virtual icebox of little value. For years, Alaska had no laws, no government in any form, and its citizens could not even own property or

---

* By the time of his defeat, C. Robert Zelnick wrote later, Gruening "already belonged to history as much as to Alaska." He graduated in 1912 from Harvard Medical School, became editor or managing editor of journals ranging from the Boston *Traveler* to the New York *Tribune* and *Post* and *The Nation*. Under President Roosevelt, he headed the Interior Department's Division of Territories and Island Possessions before being named governor of Alaska in 1939. In that post, he ended racial discrimination in public accommodations and battled against control of the territory by absentee business interests. He became an early advocate of population control and authored books on Mexico and Alaska. In a March 10, 1964 speech on the Senate floor, Gruening called the Vietnam war a "putrid mess" and called for an immediate and complete U.S. withdrawal.

marry. At their own expense, they sent delegations to Washington begging for "any form of civil government." Not until 1906 were they granted a delegate in Congress, and in 1912, when they were finally authorized to elect a territorial legislature, its powers were limited in the extreme. The state's colonial exploiters well into this century were the Seattle- and San-Francisco-owned salmon fish-packing interests, which opposed every step toward self-government and almost got Congress to overturn a small tax on salmon fisheries during the Wilson administration. Not until 1949 did the territorial legislature override the "Alaska Lobby" and enact legislation permitting the territory to impose taxes on incomes and on the value of extracted resources.

The first statehood bill was introduced by Delegate James Wickersham in 1916, but it was effectively opposed by those who said Alaska lacked sufficient resources and that its population was too migratory and sparse (only 55,000 in 1920). Not until the military arrived to revive the lagging territorial economy in World War II did the population go over 100,000. But the War, Navy, Justice, and Interior Departments all resisted statehood for the duration. With peace, an Alaskan Statehood Association was formed, and the first hearings ever on statehood legislation were held in the House. But a coalition of Southern Democrats who opposed any increase in the Union, plus a few Republicans who feared Alaska would forever be a Democratic stronghold, stymied the repeated statehood bills for another decade. The salmon industry continued to lobby against any change in territorial status. In 1954 opponents even suggested partitioning the territory.

By this time, however, the shackles of territorial status were becoming simply unbearable for Alaskans. The governor was still appointed by the President, Congress controlled Alaska's purse strings, and the most important regulations were handed down by federal departments thousands of miles distant in Washington. At home, hundreds of dynastic little boards and commissions made an ineffectual pass at local government. In 1955 the territorial legislature voted to force the statehood issue by calling a constitutional convention. William Egan was president of the convention of wildly diverse characters who agreed on one point: to avoid the divided authority that characterized territorial government. Under the document they produced, author Murray Morgan has written, "the lines of authority stood out as stark as utility poles. They ran straight to the governor's desk." Except for the secretary of state, the governor was the only elected statewide official, with authority to name all other major officials and judges. One of the models the delegates looked to, in fact, was New Jersey's constitution, the ultimate model of complete gubernatorial authority where the governor is the only elected state official.

In all, the constitution was a model of clarity, brevity, and strength, and it seemed to speak well of Alaskans' political maturity. They also showed some political savvy by opting for the "Tennessee Plan" to win statehood. Under this strategy, first used by Tennessee and then by six other would-be states, a shadow delegation of two Senators and a Representative are sent to Washington to lobby for statehood. Alaska's choice of an all-Democratic Tennessee Plan delegation, including Gruening and Egan as the "Senators," rekindled Republican fears about the state's politics. But President Eisenhower backed statehood, and his Interior Secretary, Fred A. Seaton, became a devoted supporter and rounded up needed votes in Congress. Congress voted final approval in July 1958, and the following month 20,000 more Alaskans than had turned out for any previous election went to the polls to approve the statehood referendum by a 5–1 margin.

Not surprisingly, Democrats swept the first state and congressional elections in November 1958. But by 1960 the state was showing its first political independence by going for Nixon over Kennedy in the Presidential election. Republicans gradually built strength in the legislature and in 1966 swept both houses. That was the same year they won their first seat on the congressional delegation and also elected Walter Hickel governor. Two years later, Nixon carried the state for a second time and Hickel flew off to Washington to become Secretary of the Interior. The GOP tidal wave of 1966 began to recede in 1970, with the governorship and the U.S. House seat going back to Democratic control and the legislature shifting in the same direction. But the Republicans' interim U.S. Senator, Ted Stevens, won easily.

Everyone expected Alaska to remain uncertain political territory for some time to come, even though the 1970 party registration figures showed 30,572 Democrats to only 18,217 Republicans. The political balance of power rested with another 55,753 voters listed as independents. Party loyalties may mean little in Alaska anyway, with conservatives and liberals sprinkled freely through both parties. Party organization is notoriously weak. One factor that gives independents a whip hand is the "jungle primary" election ballot, like Washington state's, which lets a voter select either a Republican or Democratic candidate for each office on primary day.

A key swing vote is that of the Alaskan natives. In 1966 the "bush vote" was decisive in electing the state's first Republican U.S. Representative, Howard Pollock, who campaigned tirelessly in the native villages. Four years later, it helped defeat Hickel's lackluster successor, Keith Miller. Native leaders found Miller's position on their land claims obstructionist at best and racist at worst. By 1972, the "political power of the bush" had been demonstrated by the election of natives to two state senate and seven state house seats. And native leaders were laying plans to run one of their own for the U.S. Senate seat of Republican Ted Stevens, a former oil company attorney and defender of the big oil firms, who is considered no special friend of native interests.

Alaskans were immensely proud of Hickel's appointment as the first cabinet member from their state, and not a little dismayed when President Nixon summarily fired him late in 1970. The Hickel story is pure Alaskan. The eldest of 10 children of Kansas tenant farmers, he left home in 1940 and struck out to make his fortune in Australia. But he couldn't get a passport, so he spent his last $40 on a one-way ticket to Alaska, where he arrived on the dock at Seward with 37 cents in his pocket. He got his first grubstake in the boxing ring, then moved into the construction business, hotels, and natural gas, amassing a fortune he estimated at $5 million, "give or take a million." A rough-hewn, outspoken, and often headstrong man, Hickel never shunned controversy from his first day in politics. When he was appointed Interior Secretary, he incurred the ire of the conservationists by remarks saying he was against putting federal lands "under lock and key" just for conservation and that it would be a bad idea to set water pollution standards so high "we might even hinder industrial development." Senate foes held up Hickel's confirmation for several weeks. Within a few days of his taking the oath of office, it turned out that they might have misjudged their man. Union Oil's offshore rig blew in the Santa Barbara Channel. Hickel ordered a temporary shutdown of all federally controlled wells in the channel and eventually a major overhaul of drilling rigs. Later he cracked down severely on offending oil companies in the Gulf of Mexico, acted effectively to protect the Florida Everglades from a proposed jetport, and instigated suits against companies accused of polluting interstate waters with poisonous mercury.

In all, Hickel proved to be the most flamboyant figure to perch on Harold L. Ickes' old roost since the Old Curmudgeon occupied it himself. On several occasions, lacking clear guidance from the President, he was tougher with industrial polluters than the White House liked. Then, in the midst of the May 1970 Kent State-Cambodian crisis, Hickel was turned down by White House staffers when he tried to get an appointment with the President. So he fired off a colorful letter, leaked to the press, in which he called on Nixon to stop alienating American youth. The reaction in the Nixon camp was scarcely disguised fury. Hickel's behind-the-scenes attacks on Vice President Agnew's unfettered campaign tactics were also not taken lightly, and soon he was getting indirect signals that he ought to resign. Hickel would have none of Washington's devious ways. "President Nixon hired me. He will have to fire me," he said. "If I go away, I'm going with an arrow in my heart and not a bullet in my back." So Nixon had to go through with a personal confrontation and the first public firing of a cabinet member in 18 years.

Hickel's comment to the press that day said a lot about the man: "Well, the President personally terminated me about two hours ago and there's really nothing I can say to help the situation and nothing I would say to hurt, given the hostility to me when I first arrived—as you well know—and some of those incredible decisions I had to make immediately thereafter, and trying to do a job for the President and all Americans and still somehow survive as an individual. I had to do it my way." As Spencer Rich and Nick Kotz summed it up in the Washington *Post* the next day: "Here was the essential man—the bluntness, the scrambled syntax, the battler, an Alaskan."

A year later, reviewing Hickel's book, *Who Owns America?*, former Senator Gruening said that by the time of his dismissal, Hickel was no longer a "Nixon Republican," however sincerely he may have been one before:

His varied experience in many fields, his ready absorption of new ideas further developing his own progressive instincts, had lifted him beyond the narrow conservatism and politicking which was increasingly distasteful to him and had come close to making him a Populist. But Nixon's curt dismissal of him after his superlative service was both unjust and stupid, and deprived the Administration and the Republican party of a great asset. Hickel was and would have been the GOP's one viable link with the youth of America whose hero he had become. . . . [His book] is an inspiring story of one man's vision, fearlessness and determination in behalf of the public interest.

Statehood *has* made a lot of difference for Alaskan government. Republican Brad Phillips, then state senate president, told me in 1969 about the "great excitement of being able to develop new institutions from scratch— for instance, the borough system of local government we developed and could watch from abstract conception to implementation." The other factor has been federal aid. "Having some U.S. Senators with juice who can do things for you makes all the difference," state senator Joe Josephson, who had been an aide to Senator Bartlett, pointed out. Specifically, he mentioned federal money for the Alaska Centennial of 1967, more laws to protect against foreign encroachment of Alaskan fishing territory, great hunks of aid in the wake of earthquake and flood, and the land transfers to the state and prospective oil boom profits. Soon after statehood, the state government used its increased powers to develop a "marine highway," or ferry system, that opened up many previously inaccessible areas of the Alaskan Panhandle and was a great boon for tourism. Without statehood, it might never have been possible.

Before the first North Slope oil money came in, Alaska was taxing its people at one of the highest rates in the country and spending more money, per capita, than any other state on education and highways. In health and hospital outlays, it ranked 16th among the states, in welfare 23rd. The entire state tax yield was less than what the federal government sent in grant-in-aid. The problem is that inflated Alaskan prices, plus the high cost of running government in such far-flung territory, minimize the actual level of services that can be delivered. It is difficult to pay enough money to get competent people to fill posts in state government, the state's health and welfare program is substandard, its juvenile program is at a standstill, and there is no penitentiary worthy of the name in Alaska. (Convicted felons are sent on a contract basis to other states, and when matters of parole come up, a member of the parole board has to be sent on a trip around the U.S. to interview prisoners.) Members of the commission supposed to regulate public utilities were unpaid until 1970, with minimal staff, and the utilities have been poorly supervised and municipally owned power systems not regulated at all. The overlay of organized municipal government in Alaska is still so light that less than 15 percent of the state's territory is within organized boroughs. Some of the native villages are simply traditional gatherings, with no incorporation and no equivalent of a county government to turn to for help in solving their problems. Their only appeal is to Juneau or to Washington.

For the hard-pressed Alaskan state government, the Prudhoe Bay oil strike at first seemed to promise an answer to almost every problem. The initial $900 million lease sale would be enough to run the entire state government for several years at the $154 million budget rate prevailing in 1969. It was easy enough to take some of the high estimates of the annual flow of oil in barrels by the mid-1970s, multiply the barrels by the wellhead price, and multiply *that* by the state's 12.5 percent royalty and 4 percent severance tax—and come up with a picture of revenue as high as $500 million a year. If the optimistic expectations of additional discoveries were figured in, Alaskans could see their *entire* state budget covered for up to a century. And thousands of Alaskan boomers entertained visions of immense personal wealth from the plethora of supporting service industries which the oil business would generate.

But the obstacles placed in the way of early construction of the pipeline soon put a crimp in the grand expectations. It was pointed out that the Prudhoe Bay field alone would probably last for no more than 15 to 30 years, solving the state's financial problems for a generation rather than a century. As for economic benefits from the pipeline, the state housing authority prepared a report saying that instead of providing jobs for Alaskans, the pipeline would "attract thousands from depressed regions of other states, causing Alaskan [unemployment] statistics to soar upward." (Unemployment in the state in 1971 was reported in the 10-to-13 percent range.) The state report indicated that the 7,500 workers coming in to build the pipeline would place a severe burden on Alaskan housing, education, and welfare services, but that after two and a half seasons of peak employment, regular employment on the pipeline would fall off to only 300 jobs—"an amount equivalent to employment in one of the department stores in Anchorage."

When the state legislature met in 1970 to decide what to do with its first $900 million, "we discovered," in senate president Phillips' words, "that we had about $3 billion worth of problems." Some people recommended banking all the $900 million and using only the interest; at the opposite extreme there were suggestions to write out checks for $3,000 and give one to each resident as his share of the fossil fuel bonanza, to build roads to every lonely homestead and village, to build a magnificent new State Capitol at the foot of the Mendenhall Glacier near Juneau, or to set up the capitol on a ship so that it could move around. Senator Mike Gravel, in a move some saw as mostly a publicity ploy, flew into Juneau to suggest to a joint legislature session that the $900 million be used on a vast program to meet the state's immediate needs in health, education, transportation and communications, making Alaska a model society virtually overnight.

After the longest legislative session in its history, the 1970 legislature approved a state budget of $314 million, double its predecessor. Aid for local school districts was raised so sharply so that the state would be paying 90 percent of the cost of public education. State-operated schools, mainly in the bush areas, were given a hot-lunch program for the first time in their history, and a $6 million revenue-sharing program was set up to help local communities improve local services ranging from fire and police protection to hospital support. The University of Alaska's budget went up sharply, state employees got a 6 percent pay boost, and legislators gave themselves a 50 percent pay boost, to $9,000 a year, making the Alaska legislature the fifth highest paid in the United States.

By 1971, the fiscal euphoria had passed. The delay in start on the pipeline meant that North Slope oil revenues could not be expected until 1975 or 1976 at the earliest. Despite a handsome annual return of 8 percent on the oil lease money, which was being handled with apparent skill by the Bank of America, interest payments of $114.7 million dollars were not enough to cover state budget increases, and the state dipped into the principal by some $60 million. There was some fear that the oil lease sale money would all be gone by the time regular oil revenues of some $300 million a year began to pour into state coffers from North Slope production. (Under legislation passed in 1970, there will be a 12.5 percent royalty on oil and gas production and a severance tax that ranges from 3 to 8 percent, depending on the productivity of the individual wells.) Governor Egan felt obliged to insist on some reductions in state spending, and the 1971–72 budget was cut back to $292 million.

Computers programmed by the state's department of revenues began to analyze the future—even assuming prompt North Slope oil delivery—and some grim conclusions emerged. Assuming an annual 15 percent budget increase—which many Alaskans believe will be necessary to accommodate inflation and meeting of pressing social needs—even oil royalties eventually reaching $360 million a year would not be enough to prevent annual budget deficits of hundreds of millions of dollars. The only way to prevent the deficits would be a sharp cutback in plans for services—a hard choice, as Anchorage Mayor Sullivan put it, in a state where "we have people living in dirt-floor shacks, two or three families in a shack, in 30-below-zero weather." As Governor Egan put it, in federal hearings on whether the pipeline should proceed: "We cannot lock up all the vast natural resources of the state of Alaska in every corner of the land, ignoring the cry of poverty, of human want, of human ignorance and disease which it is in our power to cure." Without completion of the pipeline by 1976, he warned, the state would face bankruptcy by the middle of that year.*

In the wake of the Prudhoe Bay discoveries, oil lobbyists flocked to Juneau, elbowing aside the salmon, mining, contracting, and labor union lobbyists who had held sway there. In 1970 the oilmen failed to hold the mineral severance tax as low as they would have liked or to get state aid on building the service road along their pipeline to the North Slope. But in 1971, their opposition was reportedly a key factor in defeat of a bill to establish a strong state department of environmental protection; instead a weaker bill, proposed by the governor, was passed.

What Alaskan legislators failed to do in the first years after the oil

---

* Even more dire projections, it should be noted, can be made for many states and cities in the Lower 48, where no oil bonanza awaits. Some localities in the country are already, for all intents and purposes, bankrupt.

strike was to devise an investment program that would bring continuing social and financial prosperity to the state. The political struggle of Alaska's next years, one of the state's leaders told me, "will be between those who have a fairly visionary idea of Alaska's future as far as the quality of life and quality of the environment, culture, recreation, and health are concerned, versus those oriented to quick economic development, to making money as speculators or investors—those who are satisfied to think of Alaska as another California to be exploited rapidly." One of the most striking developments of the late 1960s and early 1970s was the stand of many of the "grand old Alaskans," men who had fought against external domination in the past, against any or all ecological and planning controls of their state. In addition, this group, including chamber of commerce and Rotary Club circles, opposed the native land claims and favored the atomic tests at Amchitka. They claimed that meddling outsiders wanted to turn their vast and resource-rich state into "a national park." Said Robert McFarland, president emeritus of the Alaska State Federation of Labor and a former state labor commissioner: "Most people here are fed up with the ecologists. That ecology is not delicate. It'll eat you up." Referring to many business leaders of like mind, Robert Zelnick told me: "What we may be seeing is that those who won the battle for self-control of the state are now becoming the exploiters and colonizers, and may do to Alaska what they said Seattle was doing to it in times past." But both the exploitive and socially conscious forces are sure to continue, since both lie within the essential Alaska character.

Nothing less is involved than the fundamental question of man's balance with nature in the Great Land. There has never been a cataloguing of the state's vast natural resources, from oil to fisheries to wilderness. Still largely federal- and state-owned, Alaska is a prime candidate, while it is early enough, for careful land and coastal planning so that cities and oil fields, parks and nature refuges can coexist to the maximum benefit of all. Environmentalists point out that Alaska is in many ways similar to the American West of a century ago, and thus a prime candidate for sound land planning to avoid the errors of the Lower 48. A first step in the planning process came in 1971 when the Interior Department, armed with a $350,000 congressional appropriation, began a land-use study for the northern part of Alaska. The same principle, applied to all portions of the state, could have immense benefits for Alaska and the nation. But a really meaningful proposal, to establish a land-planning commission with regulatory and enforcement powers, was opposed by the state and the oil companies and defeated during 1971 debate on the native lands claims settlement bill. (One of the reasons for the defeat was that the conservationists overplayed their hand, trying to use the bill as a device to prevent any pipeline construction.)

With or without planning, there will probably always be fundamental differences between the development of Alaska and the colonization pattern of the American West. As Richard Austin Smith has written: "No waves of people will roll out from the towns to establish permanent settlements in the hinterland, with these in turn becoming the bases for further outward thrusts until the frontier has been swallowed up by towns and farms." Instead, more and more Alaskans are likely to desert the tough wilderness for the comforts of town life, until the state maps show just a few urban centers set in an essentially empty ocean of land. But it is how Alaskans treat and use that land that will make the difference. In the words of Robert Weeden, an Alaskan ecologist:

The world needs an embodiment of the frontier mythology, the sense of horizons unexplored, the mystery of uninhabited miles. It needs a place where wolves stalk the strand lines, because a land that can produce a wolf is healthy, robust, and perfect land. But more than these things, the world needs to know that there is a place where men live amid a balanced interplay of the goods of technology and the fruits of nature.

# HAWAII

## AMERICAN IDYLL—AND IDEAL

SIX HOURS AFTER THE rising sun first touches the tip of Mount Katahdin in Maine, its warming rays filter through the Pacific sky to lighten the summits of fiery Mauna Loa and Mauna Kea, towering almost three miles above the "Big Island" of Hawaii, the 50th of the 50 states, a quarter of the way around the globe. Here is that most improbable of states, a beautiful semitropic archipelago set in the vast void of the Pacific, 2,400 miles from our West Coast. Nowhere else on the globe, in fact, can one find a major island group so far separated from a continent.

And there may be no such idyllic place to live. "The loveliest fleet of islands that lies anchored in any ocean," Mark Twain wrote of them. "No alien land in all the world has any deep, strong charm for me but that one," he continued. "No other land could longingly and so beseechingly haunt me, sleeping and waking, through half a lifetime. . . ." Hawaii is the southernmost state of the Union and lies on a line of latitude with the Saudi desert, Bombay, and the West Indies. But the cooling waters of the sub-Arctic California current, formed just below Alaska, sweep between the Islands. Almost every month of the year, cooling northeasterly trade winds bring moisture and comfort. At the Mauna Loa Observatory, 11,150 feet above sea level, wintertime temperatures of 20 below zero have been recorded, and Hawaii's mountain people live a life with warm wool sweaters and fireplaces. But down near sea level, where most Hawaiians live, the average temperature ranges around 75, varying only 6 degrees or so between the seasons of the year. In the primordial Hawaiian language, there is simply no word for "weather." It is difficult to conceive of a more serene and equable climate.

Of all the 50 states, in the words of Hawaiian writer Frank Sutton, "Hawaii alone has what the French call, with exquisite expressiveness, a *douceur*, a certain sweetness, a smoothness, a fragrance, a softness. It is not only in the air, it is in the people."

The people, of course, are a mix of the original native Hawaiian stock plus Caucasians, Japanese, Chinese, Korean, Filipino, and other minor strains. In Hawaii, every group is in a minority. This is the only one of the 50 states whose principal ethnic roots are Asian, not European. Amazingly, the Islands' polyglot of the world's peoples live together in substantial peace and mutual respect.

Not unrelated is all that lies behind the spirit called "Aloha"—a remarkable word that means hello, good-bye, love, affection, compassion, mercy, and kindness all at the same time. Like a "benign contagion," one writer has noted, the Aloha spirit has spread out from the native Hawaiians, a generous people known for their hospitality to others, to pervade the interpersonal relations of all groups living in the Islands.

I realize that this view of Hawaii is highly romantic and idealized. As we shall see later in this chapter, greedy tourist development threatens the natural beauty of this Pacific paradise. Crass commercialism endangers the Aloha spirit. Deep strains of racial exploitation run throughout modern Hawaiian history and are not entirely expunged today.

But I deliberately chose to go the romantic route first. Why? Because in reaching out to these emerald isles of the distant Pacific to establish its 50th state, the United States did incorporate into the Union that one place under the Stars and Stripes where the realities of place and society so closely approximate what they *ought to be*. Hawaii may be an American idyll. But it is also an American ideal.

## The Creation of an Archipelago and the Neighbor Islands Today

The birth of the Hawaiian Islands has been matchlessly chronicled in the gospel according to Michener,* always a wonder to reread: How in the bosom of the boundless deep, countless millions of years before the first men walked the earth, a massive fissure some 2,000 miles in length suddenly appeared, exuding torrents of white-hot, liquid rock which exploded on contact with the heavy, wet burden of water, sending columns of released

* *Hawaii*, by James A. Michener (New York: Random House, 1959).

steam upward for nearly four miles to break loose on the surface of the sea and form a cloud and signal to an unknowing world the start of what might one day be islands. And for 40 million years, more or less, the dense, volcanic basalt built up, layer after layer; and one day, there was another molten eruption from the earth's core, except that now it reached the surface of the sea, and there was a tremendous explosion as liquid rock struck water and air together, and there was land. And then still more millions of years, the rise and fall of that and myriad other volcanic isles, and wind and water brought the first tenuous plant and animal life—perhaps the seeds of plants and trees, or a coconut washed up against a shore, or a bird from distant realms—and then interspersed ice ages, and finally, in the latter days of time the creation of the Hawaii we know; of lush valley and precipice, of volcanic peaks (some still active) and palm-fringed blue water, and flowers, and white surf, some islands already receding back into the sea, others still growing.

Today you can look at a map of the plateaus and trenches and seamounts of the Pacific Ocean floor, and one feature, between the Aleutians and Australia, stands out. It is the great wall of the Hawaiian Range, set seemingly in the very middle of the Pacific. The range runs in almost a straight line for 1,600 miles, the mountains within it rising as much as 18,000 feet off the floor of the surrounding ocean, but only a few ever reaching the surface. At the northwestern tip are the Midway Islands; then in the central section La Perouse rock and the Gardner Pinnacles, shards of once great volcanic islands which have been worn down, almost to extinction, by the forces of wind and rain and surf. And at the southeastern extremity of the range, there are the 20 islands of the state of Hawaii, seven of them inhabited. The largest of these is the most southeasterly, Hawaii, the "Big Island," bearing the name of the entire chain. It has 4,030 square miles, more than twice the size of Delaware and Rhode Island combined. The most heavily populated island is Oahu, 200 miles to the northwest; it has the city of Honolulu and 80 percent of the people but is only a seventh the size of the Big Island.

Oahu will necessarily dominate much of our chapter, but let us start with the "Neighbor Islands," as they are called, offering us a glimpse of an older Hawaii and perhaps the sites of future growth.

The island of Hawaii not only covers 63 percent of the state's entire land area but is still growing through volcanic activity. I cannot recall any other place where the elemental forces of earth-building are so clear to see. Volcanic fumes leak out from a thousand orifices, and along great sweeps of the coastline one sees immense flows of hardened lava from outbreaks of the last few decades. One flow in 1960 added some 500 acres to the eastern coast. Mauna Loa (13,677 feet above sea level) is the world's most active present-day volcano; it erupted in 1950 for 23 days and produced the greatest amount of lava noted in modern times. This mountain's volcanic activity has been going on over so many eons of time that its land mass of 2,000 square miles above the ocean make it the largest single mountain in the world. Its now dormant neighbor, snow-clad Mauna Kea (elevation 13,784),

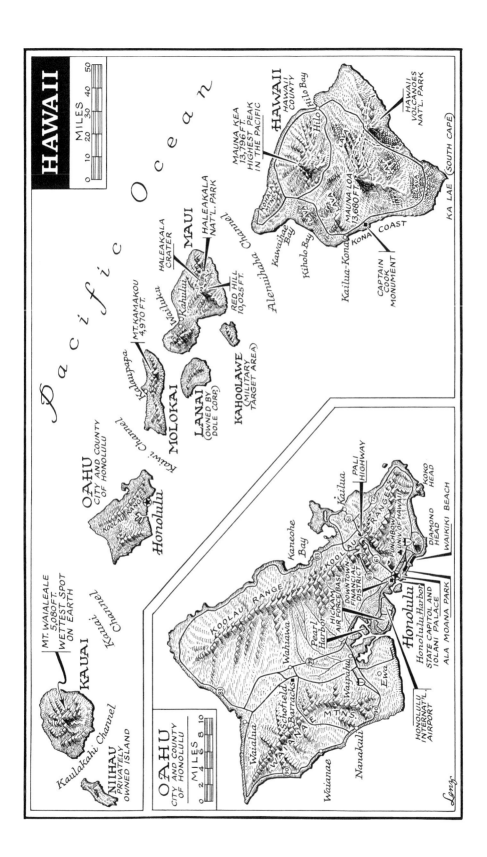

is believed to be the world's largest mountain in height, assuming one counts the rise both below and above the sealine.

While most of the volcanic eruptions pose little immediate danger to human life, they have wiped out villages in recent times, and there are continual fears that the prosperous city of Hilo on Hawaii's east coast could one day be damaged or wiped out by rifts from Mauna Loa's flank. In fact, past performance suggests that a flow will enter Hilo within the next 25 years and one will reach its harbor in the next century, perhaps dwarfing the damage from a great tidal wave which swept over Hilo in 1946 and took some 50 lives. There is little the city can do in defense or prevention. In the meantime, Hilo thrives as a sugar-loading port, county seat, and tourist center. It is a reflection of Honolulu's dominance that this little city of 26,353 souls is actually second largest in the entire state.

In the prevailing pattern of the archipelago, the Big Island has a verdant, moist northeastern side where the trade winds deposit the burden of clouds blown in over thousands of miles of open sea. The southwestern flank, by contrast, is dry and hot. Within a few miles, one can find tropical rain forest and prime agricultural land, misty plateaus and true desert. Sugar cane and cattle ranching are the traditional and still important farm industries, but Hawaii has long been America's leading orchid center and is unique in the U.S. for coffee growing along its eastern Kona coast. Now there is also a prosperous business in macadamia nut growing. Hawaii may make a lot of money over the long run from harvesting of its vast hardwood forests, which began in the 1960s.

The Big Island's two big economic advances of recent years, however, have sprung from tourism. The first was the opening in 1965 of Laurance Rockefeller's $15 million Mauna Kea Beach Hotel and golf course on the arid South Kohola Coast in July 1965. Land for the resort was sliced from the Parker Ranch, outranked in size only by the King spread in Texas. Travel writers who have had the time and money to go there report that the resort may be the most lavish on earth. Mauna Kea's setback architecture blends with rather than dominates the terrain, and the building contains a collection of fine Asian art. The guest is offered "rest, quiet, excellent food and absolute seclusion," and the diversions for the more adventurous range from golf on breathtaking oceanside courses to "women, surfing, skin diving, tennis, wild boar hunting, pheasant shooting, or the great deep-sea fishing only 10 miles away." With my time limited, I chose to visit volcanos and little seashore towns instead; perhaps it was a poor decision.

The Big Island's second big boost came from the start of direct jet flights between Hilo and the West Coast in 1967. A tour pattern developed in which Hilo became a popular exit gateway for tourists on their way back to the mainland, beginning the first major challenge to Oahu's monopoly on tourist days and dollars. Adverse reaction to the overcrowding of Honolulu has also contributed to interest in the numerous resort and land developments on Hawaii and other Neighbor Islands. Aside from Rockefeller, other developers who have been involved on the Big Island include the Dillingham Corporation, Eastern Air Lines, Boise Cascade, and the Bishop Estate (the state's largest landowner).

The 1970 population count of the Big Island was 63,468, just over 10 percent of Oahu's. Should the island begin to play a larger role in Hawaii in the next decades, it would only be a return to historic times. This was the island believed to be first inhabited by the Polynesians, perhaps around 750 A.D. The first European sea captain to set his foot in Hawaii, Captain James Cook, met his death at Hawaii's Kealakekua Bay in 1779. And the first American missionaries landed at Kona, which is the site of the first Christian church in the islands. A few miles to the south of Kailua the Painted Church perches on a flower-decked ocean hillside. The early padres had colorful murals painted on the interior walls to give the native congregation the unconfined, out-of-doors feeling to which they were accustomed. Within the tiny church, a century of history suddenly falls away and one is again at the tender and difficult early juncture point of the Hawaiian and western cultures.

Between the Big Island and Oahu is Maui, the second largest island in the chain, and its three small neighbors—Molokai, Lanai, and Kahoolawe. The county of Maui, which includes all four, noted a 1970 population of 46,156, all but 10 percent on Maui itself.

Maui is called the Valley Isle, for the simple reason that it consists of two volcanic mountains separated by a low isthmus. One of the peaks, West Maui, is ancient in geologic time, but not so Haleakala, the "House of the Sun," a 10,023-foot volcano which last erupted sometime around 1790. Today it is the world's largest dormant (but still very explodable) volcano, with a 33-square-mile crater that the *National Geographic* says could swallow Manhattan Island and all its skyscrapers. Within it are smaller crater cones, caverns, a desert plain, forest niches, green meadows, and rare plants. Haleakala is a national park, and with good reason, for its slopes are also wonders in themselves. Its southern slopes, away from the trade winds, are arid reminders of the mainland Southwest. But on the east side, some 300 inches of rain in a year pound thick forest and dense underbrush. Nurtured by the rainfall, giant tree ferns and ghostly epiphytes enlace towering ohia trees. Ponds and grottos mirror lobelia plants crowned by horizontal sprays of 30 to 60 blossoms. Colorful and sometimes rare native birds feed among the flowers, and wild pigs and goats, which may have been introduced by early Polynesian migrants, root in the upper reaches of the forest. In the late 1960s, a 4,300-acre strip of this land, descending all the way from the crater to the Pacific Ocean, was added to the park by the Nature Conservancy and Laurance Rockefeller.

Maui also offers some 33 miles of beaches, some of black volcanic origin, others of golden sand, many among the most beautiful in all the Islands. The island, it has been reported, still lives on "Hawaiian time," meaning that a relaxed, leisurely, and nonurban pace of life still endures.

Only the past decades have brought major tourist developments, the first big undertaking financed by one of Hawaii's oldest companies, American Factors (now Amfac, Inc.) on the beach at Kaanapali on the leeward west coast. Bigger things are coming with an $850 million development jointly sponsored by Alexander and Baldwin, another old Hawaii company, together with the Grosvenor Estate of Britain. It will be a "City of Flowers," built on a horizontal plan along the slopes of Haleakala with a two-mile ocean frontage; eventually there are to be 11,000 hotel units with a support village for 12,500 employees.

Up to now, though, the Maui economy is still mainly agricultural—sugar, pineapple, cattle. One thriving small "industry" is the "Science City" atop Haleakala, which includes telescopes, air-glow, and zodiacal light observation and a $5 million tracking station and astrophysical observatory for various government agencies and universities.

A "wry little jollity" concerning Maui, Robert Sutton reports, is calling Kahului (pop. 8,280) and its five-mile-distant neighbor Wailuku (7,979) "the twin cities of Maui." Kahului is new and progressive with a large shopping center; Wailuku, its arch rival, is the county seat with official buildings dressed in the architectural dignity of a bygone age, sprinkled in pleasant disarray over the town's hilly and tree-shaded streets.

Maui's neighbor, Molokai, with 261 square miles, is commonly depicted as the Friendly Isle because its inhabitants are thought of as the most affable of all Hawaiians. Until the mid-1960s, it was practically untouched by tourist development and retained a kind of idyllic peacefulness like the dreamy Hawaii of yesteryear. All of that may change soon. Molokai's airport is just 50 miles and 17 air minutes from Honolulu, and there has long been talk of making it into a kind of suburban bedroom for the busy capital city. So far the transportation problem has not been solved, though there are ideas for big helicopters or a giant hydrofoil that would be stable enough to negotiate the rough Molokai Straits between the islands without making passengers hopelessly ill.

In times past, Molokai was known principally to mainlanders—and many other Hawaiians—as the locale of the leper colony on the Kalaupapa peninsula, celebrated in stories like Jack London's tale of Koolau the Leper or James Michener's *Hawaii*. Still revered and honored is Father Damien, the Belgian who arrived at Kalaupapa in 1873 as one of the first white men to work among the patients there. He died there of leprosy some 16 years later. The state's Hansen's Disease Treatment Center (reflecting the more enlightened modern name for the disease) continues on the Kalaupapa peninsula, to which many thousands were exiled to die before the discovery of sulfone drugs brought the dread disease under control in the 1940s. There are still some oldtimers, whose bodies were terribly afflicted by the disease before discovery of the drug, living at the facility. When the last of them die, the center will probably be closed.

Molokai's age-old problem has been water. Its eastern end has rain forests, but the west is dry and barren. Now one of Hawaii's first and the nation's most unique water diversion schemes has been constructed, the project brought to fruition by a resourceful contractor, David F. Wisdom of Wisdom Rubber Industries. A 104-acre reservoir has been built to collect and hold the runoff from the rain forest in the eastern highlands, its bottom covered with a unique nylon-reinforced butyl rubber lining that is cheaper than concrete. The water is then conveyed by a concrete tunnel through volcanic rock to central and western Molokai, thus preserving 14,500 acres of pineapple fields and providing the supply for big resorts like those now being considered or built by big developers on the western tip of the island.

The island of Lanai, just west of Maui and south of Molokai, is the perfect company town. In fact, it is 100 percent owned by the Dole Pineapple Company, and virtually all the 2,204 people who inhabit the island make their living cultivating the 15,000 acres and harvesting 120 million pineapples each year. The island was bought in 1922 by James D. Dole, founder of the company which bears his name. Earlier farmers had failed and cattle grazers had turned the low-lying isle into a virtual dust bowl. In a model of soil conservation, the Dole engineers laid out the central plateau in contours, planted thousands of Norfolk pines to prevent hillside erosion, sowed grass seeds, and developed wells. Today the island is a picture of productivity. One small company-run inn there may be replaced in the 1970s by a contemplated big resort, to take advantage of a fine sand beach and excellent hunting in the cool pine forests.

Last and clearly least in the Maui orbit is pitiful Kahoolawe. This is a 45-square-mile hump eight miles off Maui's west side which the U.S. Navy has been bombing and strafing since 1945. Not a soul lives there; in fact, any trespasser is liable to a $500 fine and six months in jail. The idea, expressed in a 1953 executive order signed by President Eisenhower, was that the Navy should use the island as long as it needed it for target practice and then clear it for human habitation. But in 1969 a Navy admiral responsible for Kahoolawe said that "the ravages of over a quarter of a century of air and surface bombardment have probably irrevocably eliminated the possibility of future, safe domestic use of the land. . . . There may be some 10,000 tons of unexploded ordnance imbedded in the earth, lava, and ravines." The island, Rear Admiral Donald C. Davis told a reporter, "is a barren hellhole" and "a most disagreeable place." There is a dissenter, Mrs. Inez Ashdown, daughter of the rancher who once leased Kahoolawe. The island, she says, is a potential paradise of "gorgeous beaches and spectacular valleys, ravines and cliffs." The county of Maui has been fighting hard to get the Navy to relinquish its hold. But subsequent development might be stunted by lack of water; the island is in the lee of Haleakala and has a very scanty rainfall.

All the Neighbor Islands we have spoken of so far are east of Oahu. There is one major island farther west, some 95 miles out toward Midway. It is Kauai, 551 square miles of lush and tropical beauty, so much the personification of the idyllic South Sea isle that Hollywood has chosen it as the location for *South Pacific* and many other films of like theme.

Kauai was the first of the Hawaiian chain to emerge from the sea, and has been without volcanic activity longer than any of its neighbors. This has permitted the lavas to erode into rich black and red soil that is carved by constant rains into colorful canyons and deep valleys covered with wondrous plants and floral exuberance. Green-carpeted canefields, deserted white beaches lined with clusters of coconut palms, frowning cliffs, swamps and abysmal crevices, areas of utter remoteness, and a central volcanic peak almost eternally surrounded by clouds—these are the hallmarks of Kauai, well named the Garden Island. Mount Waialeale, according to Herman V. von Holt, a leading Hawaiian businessman who helped install a rain gauge there in 1910, has an incredible average of more than 50 *feet* of rain every year, making it the wettest spot on earth. Only a few miles away, by contrast, there is a place where less than one foot a year is recorded.

The 29,524 people who live on Kauai make their living first from agriculture (22 percent of Hawaii's sugar cane, plus pineapple and livestock), second from tourism (a quarter of a million visitors a year, with new resort hotels opened in the 1960s), and third from scientific-military installations. NASA's Kokee Tracking Station has played a major role in Project Apollo and other space programs, and there are key Navy, missile, and AEC installations. All this modernity contrasts with a long history. This was the island Captain James Cook first discovered in 1778; the Russians once built a fort there and withdrew only after warnings from Great Britain; and Kauai was the last independent kingdom of the Islands.

Off the coast of Kauai lies Niihau, the "forbidden island," the private property of the Robinson family ever since King Kamehameha IV sold it to a familial ancestor for $10,000 in 1864. The Robinsons were Scots whose idea was to preserve on the island the gentle life of the native Hawaiians they found there. The 237 people on the 18-mile-long island still speak the old Hawaiian language, and roughly 65 percent of them are still of absolutely pure Hawaiian stock. (Perhaps this has something to do with the fact that Niihau was the only election precinct in Hawaii to vote against statehood in the 1959 referendum.) No visitors are ever permitted, and government officials who go ashore by longboat must leave before nightfall, thus averting dilution of the race. The islanders live a primitive life of raising sheep and shorthorn cattle, keeping bees for honey, and hunting wild pigs, turkey, and peacocks. Movies, alcohol, and dogs are banned.

For many years after World War II, the Neighbor Islands declined in population as agricultural employment declined and little came to take its place. Virtual ghost towns began to appear, and leaders despaired for the future. But with tourism and related activities, the Neighbor Island population rose 5.5 percent between 1960 and 1970. (In the previous two decades, their population had dropped a total of 20 percent.) Now Governor John Burns, with strong backing from his lieutenant governor (and potential successor), George R. Ariyoshi, advocates a system of "population dispersal" from overcrowded Oahu to the Neighbor Islands. (Ariyoshi points out that more than 80 percent of the Islands' people are squeezed together in 595 square miles of Oahu, contrasted to only 8.9 percent on the island of Hawaii, which has 63 percent of the land space.) But "population dispersal" has received an icy response on some of the Neighbor Islands. Mayor Shunichi Kimura of the Big Island told the Los Angeles *Times'* James Bassett: "Let's first discuss population limits for the whole state and do some intelligent master planning for the economy, housing, and all the items we need for population growth."

## *Oahu: Where the Action Is*

Whatever the charm of the Neighbor Islands may be, the island of Oahu and its city of Honolulu are where the people are and where the action is, now and probably for many more decades to come. The reason intensive development started here, rather than elsewhere, is that Honolulu and contiguous Pearl Harbor are the only safe deep-water ports in all the islands.

By 1970, the population of Oahu reached 629,176, up a full 25.7 percent from the previous Census and 144 percent since 1940. The 1970 Census indicated 324,871 people in the city of Honolulu itself, growing more slowly than the remainder of the island but still up 10.4 percent in the decade of the 1960s. Many consider Oahu's development dangerously fast and helter-skelter—a subject to which we will return later—but the fact is that a fantastic amount of human activity has been crowded into this relatively small island (about 40 miles long and 20 miles wide), with the natural environment still largely intact.

One of the pleasant aspects of writing this book, as the reader may have guessed, was to visit some exotic spots I had never seen before, and Hawaii was one of these. Within a few hours, I had been impressed by Oahu's diversity and continuing beauty. My composer-author friend Peter Morse, who met me at the airport, told me there would be time enough to see Honolulu and drove me instead to his remote mountain home above Ewa, some 30 miles to the west of the city. Honolulu could be seen gleaming white in the distance, with the familiar bulk of Diamond Head just beyond it. Ranging from the city northward was the spiny ridge of the Koolau Range, dividing windward Oahu from Honolulu. A constant veil of clouds on the mountains mixed with sunshine splashing across the island's central valley of sugar cane and pineapple fields in their distinctive verdant mantles. More southerly, the three great fingers (lochs) of Pearl Harbor could be seen and, beyond that, the emerald green at ocean's edge leading into the cobalt blue of Pacific sky and water. That afternoon, there was a rainstorm that brought not just a single rainbow but a perfect reflection of itself from the valley floor to the heights. And in the night, Honolulu sparkled below and the stars mirrored their special vividness in the crystal ocean skies.

A drive around Oahu quickly reveals a land heavily touched by civilization but still beautiful and varied in the extreme. Within an hour or two, one can come on smooth white beaches and rocky foam-swept coast, placid lagoons and an anomalous section of "interstate" highways, massive sugar cane and pineapple plantations and smaller farms that grow coconut palms and bananas and avocados, precipitous cliffs and raw jungle, the ominous beginnings of California-style subdivisions and condominium apartments but also flower-bedecked villages on low stilts.

The Honolulu metropolitan concentrate is still largely confined to a 20-mile stretch of Oahu's southern plain, anchored by Pearl Harbor on the west and Koko Head (beyond Diamond Head) on the east. The settlement pokes fingers into the mountains that rim it, but basically the Koolau Range is too massive and craggy to be violated. It may be the very ruggedness of Hawaii's volcanic mountain terrain, in fact, that holds back the worst kind of metropolitan sprawl. (Since statehood, however, subdivisions have filled in the valley at Hawaii-Kai and begun to creep across sections of both Leeward and Windward Oahu. Between 1960 and 1970, the number of housing units on the island increased 48 percent, from 165,000 to 246,000).

Moving west to east along the coastal strip, here are some of the principal features:

Pearl Harbor, a reservation of some 10,000 acres (and $1.5 billion value), combines not only the vivid history of December 7, 1941, but the present-day command of U.S. Naval operations to the westernmost reaches of the Pacific. In Pearl's environs, the Commander-in-chief of the Pacific (CINC-PAC) has directed the massive American military presence clear across to Asia, including the war zones in Vietnam and Korea. (The Pacific Command presently embraces 94 million square miles, from the West Coast of the U.S. to the Arabian Sea, from the North to the South Pole.) Tucked in beside Pearl Harbor are some of the other necessary but not too glamorous facilities vital to the Islands as they exist today: Hickam Air Force Base, where American Presidents and cabinet officers have arrived rather frequently in recent years to plan the Vietnam war; Honolulu International Airport, booming and thriving and cracking at the seams (6.8 million passenger arrivals and departures in 1971); big Naval shipyards, and far to the west, cement and steel plants humming merrily away and providing a major share of the island's needs in their particular fields.

Honolulu Harbor, just a few miles east of Pearl, remains the fulcrum through which passes most of that vast array of goods which Hawaii cannot or will not make for itself. Some 1,700 ships put into the harbor each year. There is still a color and pageantry that no jetliner's arrival can match when one of the big passenger liners steams into port or away, its coming and going punctuated with an outpouring of hula troupes, flowers, and music of the Royal Hawaiian Band. (Modern life seems too short of those moments, with their delicious sentimentality.)

The harbor, still dominated by its colorful old Aloha Tower, is close by the downtown financial district. This area is home still of the Big Five's storied economic power. With other financial giants, the Big Five are housed in an odd combination of soaring modern skyscrapers and placid, squat older buildings so reminiscent of the small, tropical port of yesteryear.

A block or two to the east one comes on Iolani Palace, a wonderful old Victorian extravagance completed by the last of the Hawaiian kings, Kalakaua, at a cost of some $350,000 in 1882. The old palace, all done up in the iron and grillwork considered so elegant in its time, fairly reeks with history. Queen Liliuokalani (1891–93) ruled from its chambers until her autocratic ways led to the overthrow of the monarchy; two years later, after an attempted counterinsurrection, she was held prisoner in the palace for nine months. Sanford Ballard Dole, the son of a missionary who led the republican revolution in the Islands, ruled from the palace first as president of the independent republic of Hawaii (starting in 1893) and then as the first Presidentially-appointed governor of the new territory. (Ceremonies to mark Hawaii's annexation to the United States were held on the front steps of the palace on August 12, 1898, with an emotional moment when the Stars and Stripes were first raised.)

For the next six decades, the territorial Senate met in the onetime royal dining room in the palace, the House in what had been the *throne room!* The old palace was still the chief government building in 1959, when the last appointed governor, William F. Quinn, became the first popularly elected state governor. Not until a decade later, 1969, did John A. Burns, Quinn's successor, sit for one last day as governor in the Iolani Palace and then move to the new State Capitol.

That new Capitol must be considered one of the most exalted public buildings of our times. The strong but airy design by San Francisco architect John Carl Warnecke is rife with Hawaiian symbolism. Like an island, the building stands in a reflecting pool. Its great interior courtyard has openings both to sea and to mountains. And high above, that courtyard is open to the sky through a cone-shaped roof unmistakably patterned after a volcano. Just inside the roof opening, there is a band of deep blue. And up and through that great aperture, one sees the skein of light Hawaiian clouds in constant movement. Suddenly there is unity between sky and viewer, the building of now and the timeless geologic history that it stands for—a remarkable, perhaps unique phenomenon. (On a less ethereal level, I might add that the Capitol has the most spacious offices, California possibly excepted, that I have seen for state legislators anywhere in the U.S. In terms of facilities, staff support, and good management, the Hawaii legislature has been ranked second only to California's in the country.)

Ranging northeasterly from a point not far from the Capitol is the Pali Highway, one of only two roads that pierce the barrier of the Koolau Range. A sign of trouble for Honolulu may be the fact that some lovely old trees along the highway have had to be replaced several times because of auto exhaust fumes; at several Honolulu locations air pollution equivalent to the Los Angeles-Hollywood Freeway has been recorded.

Perched up on the mountainside less than half a mile from the Capitol and close to the Pali Highway is the extinct old volcano, Punchbowl, with its tender burden: the graves of 19,500 American servicemen, 13,000 from World War II, several more thousands from Korea, and since the early 1960s, the graves of a few fallen each week in Vietnam. Most of the new graves hold Hawaiian boys, but there has been a steady stream of mainland families bringing their sons' bodies from the West Coast (where they are automatically shipped) for burial in this "National Memorial Cemetery of the Pacific." What does the Punchbowl, or Hawaii, represent that is important enough for families to fly their sons' bodies back here for burial and pay the great expense of coming themselves? Out of common decency, no one ever seems to ask the bereaved. But it is not hard to imagine.

Most of Hawaii's illustrious educational institutions lie within a one-to two-mile radius east of the Capitol. These include two famous old private preparatory schools (Punahou and Iolani), McKinley High School (which counts among its graduates the first *two* U.S. Senators of Oriental origin, Hiram L. Fong and Daniel K. Inouye), and the University of Hawaii. The university, founded as a land-grant college in 1907, was still regarded as a third-grade farmers' and surfers' school when Hawaii achieved statehood. Then, under the presidency of Thomas H. Hamilton and his successor in 1969, former NATO Ambassador Harlan Cleveland, enrollment tripled and the school began to develop into a first-class regional university, building on its natural bases in geology, oceanography, and Oriental languages and literature.* The campus became home for the East-West Institute established by Congress in the early 1960s. There were plans for major growth in the 1970s, including expansion of a branch at Hilo on the Big Island, a new branch on Oahu but outside Honolulu, and several new community colleges. In line with the Hawaiian economy, the university set up a college of tourist industry management and expanded its adult education programs so far that one in 24 Hawaiians were attending some of its courses in a year.

Directly on the waterfront, between downtown and Waikiki Beach, one comes on the handsome bayside Ala Moana Park, and, beside it, the even more remarkable Ala Moana Shopping Center, built by the Dillingham Corporation on salt marshes that were filled with coral dredged from the Pacific. The center has a 300-foot office tower topped by a revolving restaurant, but the real wonders are nearer ground level where 155 stores are set atop vast subterranean parking spaces. The pedestrian passes art displays and sculpture everywhere, holes cut here and there so that trees may go on through, and broad walkways roofed enough to protect from rain and sun and still leave an open, airy feeling—a shopping center, one concludes, designed the way one ought to be. (Easily, we underestimate the importance of design in shopping centers, where many people have practically their only contact with the outside world.)

---

* By 1970, the university had 19,338 full-time students, plus 13,874 in community colleges or evening courses. Despite its other specialties, it is only now moving to add a medical and a law school.

Ala Moana's customers are as polyglot a group as one could imagine—not only every ethnic strain of the Islands, but every economic class, in every dress. If there is a crossroads of the Pacific, one feels, this must be it. The center is amazingly clean, and people's respect for it is amply demonstrated by a series of open ponds, filled with huge, colorful Oriental goldfish. The opportunities for vandalism—stealing fish, or polluting their water—are obvious. But everyone leaves the fish alone, and one has to think there is some quality in the place, or in the Asiatic character of most of the people, that makes it so.

The stores within the Ala Moana Center range from safe old mainland choices like Penney and Woolworth to illustrious Hawaiian department stores like Liberty House and McInerny's and branches of Japanese department stores. Practically any product or delicacy of the Pacific Basin countries is to be found, with Oriental specialty foods among the most notable. In a store packed with Pacific handicrafts, I succumbed to buying a fleecy-soft owl-face pillow to adorn a couch at home. The tag was a surprise: it was made of llama pelt, and it came from Peru.

Across the Ala Wai Canal and heading now more in the direction of Diamond Head, we reach the economic heart of Hawaii's big tourist industry and its most severe developmental and environmental problem: Waikiki Beach. Behind a narrow, mile-long strip of glittering sand stands an almost solid wall of huge, multistory hotels, jam-packed with 20,000 visitor rooms, the result of a tourist development that began in modest measure with the first hotel in 1901, reached perhaps its esthetic height with the Moorish-style Royal Hawaiian in 1927, was revived by the late industrialist-developer Henry Kaiser in the 1950s, and in the past decade had proceeded at a pace that left Hawaii gasping.

Even Neal S. Blaisdell, who served as mayor of Honolulu during the 14 years that most of the hotel binge was planned or executed, admits serious error on the part of the city fathers in not controlling the growth at Waikiki. In 1956 there was a lost opportunity to realign Kalakaua Avenue so that the beach could have been enlarged and the buildings set further back. (Occupants have an average of 44 square feet of beach space at Waikiki, compared to 57 at Coney Island in August.) Had the buildings been set back, the development could have been in a better sightline of Diamond Head, the number of buildings and size of grounds could have been better controlled, and less construction could have been permitted on small parcels of land. "But the apartment owners balked and it was too much money to afford them," Blaisdell told me.

Others are less charitable about what happened. Horace Sutton has written about a "billion dollar cement mistake" and pointed out that Honolulu never had an architectural review committee, and shied away from any control of what private property owners did. Not until 1970 was a height limitation (a quite generous 30 stories) put on Waikiki buildings. Sutton quotes Aaron Levine, director of the Oahu Development Conference:

The economic pressure was so great, the increases in tourism—20 percent a year, year after year—were so compelling that quality has not mattered. Economically it paid to do it. Engineering and economics predominated, and the idea here was that if you could run a water line to it you could build it. If the zoning, which is to say the public policy, had not permitted such density, then the landowners wouldn't have been able to build so big, so high, and so close. If you expect eleemosynary actions by a builder where everyone else is building to the maximum, you won't get it.

The building was done in part by fast-moving operators who made a business of buying up small lots and building quickly on them. Hawaii's fabulously successful businessman, Chinn Ho, became owner of major hotels like the Ilikai. Sheraton Hotels added thousands of rooms and ran still more for others, and Hilton took a major piece of the action with its Hilton Hawaiian Village. The tourist ghetto they have created is almost tailor-made to isolate the visitor to the islands from contact with the Hawaiian people, from learning what the Aloha spirit is really all about.

Having made that point, I must add: When Hawaiians lament the degeneration of Waikiki Beach into another Miami Beach, they are dead wrong. Compared to Miami, Waikiki is tasteful, pleasant, and beautiful. Its beach, however crowded, is at least open to nonpaying guests and not subject to near disappearance with each high tide. The constant mild climate avoids Miami Beach's oppressively hot summers and sometimes erratic winter weather. Despite the carnival-like atmosphere (which even draws secretive visits from Hawaiian oldtimers), there is little of the disgusting garishness of the Florida competitor. And the scenery, with the azure Pacific and those peaks of Diamond Head and the Koolau Range providing an ever-dramatic backdrop, is beyond compare in all the U.S.A.

Just east and south of Waikiki is the wonderful green tableland of Kapiolani Park, a favorite spot for swimming and watching the magnificent Hawaiian sunsets. Then comes the low-slung profile, a symbol of the Islands around the world: Diamond Head. Diamond Head's hopefully extinct crater is a constant reminder to arriving and departing air travelers, who can see right down into its bowl, of the geologic origin of the Islands. Its history is rich and colorful; at a temple by its base, for instance, Kamehameha the Great placed the heart of King Kalanikupule, whom he had defeated in battle, on the sacrificial altar as an offering to the god Kukailimoku. The illustrious profile came in mortal danger in 1967, when a group of developers proposed erecting high-rise apartment houses around its lower slopes. Forty-some citizen groups banded together in protest, led by the Outdoor Circle, a 54-year-old women's conservation organization whose long list of accomplishments included having purged Hawaii of all billboards. At a now historic meeting of the Honolulu City Council, crowded by 500 witnesses, 40 spoke for making the ground around Diamond Head into a park or retaining single-family residential use, only 13 for zoning that would permit the high rises. The council decided against the developers and for—it would seem—the people.

Since the Diamond Head victory, conservation and opposition to developer usurpation have become the hot issues of Honolulu politics (with big statewide implications we will look at later). In November 1968, the people voted into office a new city council with a majority of members highly dubious about quick tourist development. And for mayor, they chose a soft-spoken but scrappy little Italian, Democrat Frank F. Fasi, who had been defeated in three earlier tries. Fasi personifies antideveloper sentiment, and the whole theme of his campaign was that Honolulu ought to build "for our people first and for the tourists second." His campaign speeches hit what he saw as "the double standards and hypocrisy" and the "developer-oriented government" that had been in office under then-outgoing Mayor Blaisdell. "Even when 99 percent of the people in areas have opposed rezoning to accommodate land speculators," Fasi said, "the rezoning was done." As for himself, Fasi was opposed to "destroying the beauty" of Honolulu "in the name of progress," to "suit the developers."

The theme caught on and Fasi won despite strong "establishment" opposition, especially from the Honolulu *Star-Bulletin*, whose editors consider Fasi an erratic if not dangerous leader. (Later Fasi's Republican opponent in the mayor's race, D. G. Anderson, said of the *Star-Bulletin*: "They hugged me so much I almost died. . . . I think they meant well but they overdid it.") After his election, Fasi—who never shuns a fight—in turn gave the *Star-Bulletin* the back of his hand by actually barring its reporters from his press conferences for close to a year after a dispute over coverage of his administration. In Fasi's view, his struggle with the developers and the newspaper was quite simple: "It all boils down to Chinn Ho, who is chairman of the board of the *Star-Bulletin*. He's a big developer and he knows how to operate. His personal attorney was majority leader of the last city council. . . . I think the *Star-Bulletin* has been used in an unethical manner for Chinn Ho," Fasi said in an interview.*

The local tourist interests have suffered under Fasi. He successfully fought having the city, rather than tourists and other users, pay for a proposed sports stadium. In 1969 he forced Eastman Kodak to give up a little skit of hula girls in grass skirts and boys climbing coconut trees that it had been staging for years on public property at Kapiolani Park for the benefit of camera-wielding tourists. The tour operators were appalled, but most people in the city sympathized with a shutdown of a phony type of show designed mainly to sell Kodak film. Fasi then caused another uproar when he closed the Queen Surf night club, another tourist trap operating on city property. Later, Fasi came up with the unique idea of free bus service in the city, on the basis that money supports highways for those who drive, so why shouldn't tax money support buses for those who don't?

* From other sources I heard that Chinn Ho does not take a great personal interest in the newspaper, which even opposed him on the Diamond Head issue. Both the *Star-Bulletin*, published in the evening, and its morning companion, the *Advertiser*, are of distinctly better quality than the run of the mill of dailies in mainland cities with like populations. Both used to be ultra-Republican, and both are more independent today. The biggest shift may have come in the *Advertiser*, now edited by George Chaplin, an energetic and independent-minded newsman who was editor of the New Orleans *Item* before he moved to Hawaii. Back in the 1930s, the *Advertiser* opposed statehood on the grounds that the Islands held too many Japanese with dual citizenship who were not trustworthy as Americans.

The key to the extraordinary power of a Honolulu mayor lies in the concept of "the city and county of Honolulu" and the modern charter it has operated under since 1959. Under law, the city and county are one and the same entity. The same mayor, city council, police, fire department, and all municipal departments function for the entire county—which is defined as the entire island of Oahu, 608 square miles of territory, half again the size of Los Angeles. This is probably the purest form of metropolitan government in the United States, with business and industrial centers, plantations, farms, and suburbs all falling under the identically same administration. Eighty-two percent of all the people in the state are under this one municipal administration. Historically, it was not done by deliberate intent but because, under the old monarchy, there was a governor for each island. The "mayor" of today exercises authority over the same territory as the old governor. Not infrequently, the rural areas complain that the "city" has little interest in their problems, though in fact the mayor must frequently concern himself with roadways to little villages, country flood control, and sanitation systems, just as he does with port facilities and downtown renewal. His powers are enhanced by the exceptionally strong-mayor form of charter adopted for Honolulu in 1959 and the absence of devices like referendum or initiative to reduce the authority of elected officials.

Oahu will need all the effective government it can get in the 1970s. Mayor Fasi believes the island's population may double to 1.3 million by the end of the decade, with several hundred thousand more vehicles than the present 400,000. Even the once spotless Pacific is being violated by 20 billion gallons of raw sewage pumped each year into the ocean, where it surfaces as an unsightly brown stain some 1,000 feet wide. In 1971 the Federal Environmental Protection Agency recommended a major clean-up program for the island and its waters, including improvements in erosion control, sewage disposal, sugar mill waste disposal, and waste discharge from vessels. The costs were expected to range well over $100 million. Some of the long-range ideas to handle increased population include such devices as "floating" offshore cities to accommodate the population, with the major land mass reverting to "environmental parks" (an idea of Dr. John P. Craven, marine affairs coordinator for the state), and a possible 26-mile rapid transit line from Pearl City to Waikiki.

## The Great Mixing Bowl

The ethnic history of the Hawaiian Islands is thought to go back approximately to the eighth century A.D., when Polynesians in long-distance canoes made their incredible voyages over hundreds of miles of open sea, probably from the Marquesas and Society Islands, to discover and settle the archipelago. Four hundred years later, still more Polynesians came from Tahiti. When Captain Cook's ships first came upon the Islands in 1778, some 300,000 natives lived there. Seventy-five years later, after ample exposure to white man's culture and his diseases (starting with syphilis carried by men off Cook's *Resolution* and *Discovery*), only 71,000 natives remained. In 1872, the combined count of native Hawaiians and *haoles* (Caucasians) in the Islands was 56,897, the lowest population count on record. By the mid-1960s, according to one count, only 9,741 Hawaiians of pure native ancestry remained.

Nevertheless, the ethnic history of Hawaii is considered a model of successful mingling of the world's races—as one Hawaii politician put it in an interview, "the salvation light of civilization." In 1970 the state statistician, Robert Schmitt, listed the nonmilitary population of the Islands this way:

| | |
|---|---|
| Japanese | 34.3% |
| Hawaiian and part-Hawaiian | 21.1% |
| Caucasian | 19.0% |
| Filipino | 8.8% |
| Chinese | 6.2% |
| Other races and mixtures | 10.6% |

Of this unique aggregate of peoples, all save the Caucasians and native Hawaiians are descended from some 400,000 foreign-born laborers who had been brought to Hawaii during the preceding century to man the great sugar and pineapple plantations. In order of introduction, these were Chinese, Japanese, Portuguese, Puerto Rican, Korean, Spanish, and Filipino. At first the native Hawaiians and the *haoles* considered them all "foreigners." But the weight of numbers—and thereby the future—rested with the newcomers.

As early as the 1920s, when the old plantation system still held full sway, it was easy to travel to Hawaii and come away convinced that the ultimate melting pot had been discovered. William Allen White did just that in 1925, reporting after a conference he had attended in Honolulu that Hawaii was the one place in the world where "the so-called race problem is [not] acute," where the eyes of the men of the "brown, black and the yellow [races] of the earth and their mulattoes are [not] looking with suspicion and rage and bitterness into the blue eyes of the men of the northern ruling race of today," and where "race antipathies have disappeared because . . . race injustices are not in vogue."

White was fundamentally wrong. It was true that actual laws of racial discrimination did not exist in the Islands. Both the earlier traders and the missionaries—the former out of a profit motive, the latter because of Christian belief—had treated native Hawaiians with some deference and respect. Plantation life, however arduous, did include an opportunity for the schooling of children, thus giving them the keys for their future emancipation.* But the

---

* Sociologist Arthur W. Lind of the University of Hawaii has pointed out how fortuitous it was that the trader and the missionary, not the plantation owner, set the first rules of interethnic contact. The equalitarian pattern of race relations had 70 years to establish itself in Hawaii before the plantation emerged as the dominant force in the life of the Islands; had it been otherwise, plantation owners might well have turned to slavery, the device so widely used for stoop labor elsewhere in the world, to create their labor supply. As it was, the Hawaiians—a people with a hearty dislike for heavy field labor or repetitive chores—could simply refuse to work in the fields. So the plantation owners had to go overseas to recruit a labor force willing to build the ditches, plant the cane, hoe the weeds, and harvest the crop.

*haole* still dominated Hawaii as a preferred race, straight up to the attack on Pearl Harbor. Governor Burns has written:

> Hawaii of the pre-World War II era was a Hawaii of many social divisions with a superficial frosting of aloha. Americans of Japanese ancestry were considered locally and nationally as an alien people. The Hawaiian people—that marvelous, extraordinary Polynesian society which suffered so much, so patiently, at the hands of the Caucasian—were innocent victims of misguided benevolent paternalism which treated them as valuable children to be used primarily for entertaining tourists or to put away out of sight on poor quality houselots called homesteads. . . .
>
> Our Chinese people were no better off than those of Japanese ancestry, and our newly arrived Filipinos were at the bottom of the ladder of social acceptance.
>
> And the *haole* elite—that glorious old guard, the hegemony, the power structure, the "Big Five," the Republican party—call it what you will, was there with power, money, national prestige and international connections. They ran the Territory of Hawaii as a closed shop, and their policies and opinions had the force and effect of law.

All of this was broken, decisively, by two events surrounding World War II. The first was in regard to the Japanese, who were immediately thrown under a dark cloud of suspicion by the attack on Pearl Harbor. Several hundreds were placed in internment camps, and all were subject to ugly slurs about their patriotism. Then they proceeded to demonstrate their patriotism beyond any shadow of doubt. Not a single act of wartime sabotage by a Japanese was ever reported in the Islands. The Japanese community led in the purchase of war bonds and gave freely to the blood bank. And as soon as Japanese military enlistments were permitted, the all-Japanese 100th Infantry Battalion and the 442nd Regimental Combat Team were formed. Off they went to Italy and France, to fight with great valor and suffer cruel losses. "Those courageous soldiers," George Chaplin of the Honolulu *Advertiser* wrote some years later, "had written in blood the ultimate proof of their loyalty. Tested in the ordeal of combat, they were in no mood to return to a second-class role in the Island structure."

The returning Japanese did indeed prove to be a resourceful group. Many took advantage of the GI Bill to get college and advanced degrees. Today they are among the leading professional men of Hawaii. A few examples: Masato Doi, who grew up as a cane worker's son on a plantation on the Big Island, is now a distinguished circuit court judge. Katsumu Kometani became a dentist and chairman of the powerful state Board of Education. Nadao Yoshinaga, a state senator, has been described by the local press as "Hawaii's single most powerful legislator," and in 1970, George Ariyoshi was elected lieutenant governor. Another veteran of the 442nd, Tadao Beppu, is speaker of the state house of representatives. Spark Matsunaga used his GI Bill to go through Harvard Law School and became a Congressman from Hawaii. Daniel K. Inouye was a member of the 442nd and left an arm behind in Italy. He used the GI Bill to go through the University of Hawaii and George Washington University Law School. Today he sits in the United States Senate.

The "upward mobility urge" of the Japanese has sometimes bordered on the incredible. In 1968 a Buddhist funeral was held in the temple on a plantation in a remote corner of Oahu for a 96-year-old sugar worker named Hamashige. He had spent most of his life on the same plantation, raising a family of seven children with the "picture bride" who came to join him from Japan around the turn of the century. On his pay as a plantation laborer, Hamashige had sent six of his seven children through college. One became a chemical engineer, one the first Oriental WAC officer, one a social worker, and one the head of the pathology department at the University of Southern California Medical School. It is only in the very youngest Japanese generation, the teenagers of the 1960s and early 1970s, that a falloff in this kind of dedication and motivation is being discerned—and decried—by older Japanese.

The experience of the Islands' Japanese in World War II may be one reason that Hawaii was remarkably "hawkish" in its attitude toward the Vietnam war. "The suspicion thrown on our loyalty and patriotism," a leading Japanese politician told me, "left an indelible impression that on such things as military and foreign affairs, one ought not to have opinions contrary to the administration in power." Another factor was that employees of the big military installations were hardly likely to differ much from the government's war policies. But all three Japanese on the Hawaiian delegation to the U.S. Congress, starting with Representative Patsy Mink, turned to a strong antiwar position. In 1971 Representative Spark Matsunaga was sponsor of an end-the-war resolution submitted to the House Democratic Caucus.

A vital element in breaking down Hawaii's racial barriers was the rapid unionization of the state's great sugar and pineapple plantations right after the war, a process which forced plantation workers to collaborate across race lines as they had never dreamed of doing before. Public school education—effected many decades ago despite the fears of some *haoles* about a Yellow Peril—has also worked toward racial assimilation. And so, in amazing measure, has intermarriage. Native Hawaiian mixed with Caucasian or Oriental blood, the so-called "cosmopolitan" mixes of Caucasian with Japanese, Japanese with Chinese, or Caucasian with Chinese, assorted admixtures of Portuguese, Filipino, Puerto Rican—the variations of race are so many that one expert counted 60 separate strains. The process has been likened to Hawaiian flowers, since there are some hybrids that grow only on the Islands.

"Hawaii's greatest strength," George Chaplin told me, "is its people. They have an innate friendliness—perhaps stemming from the Polynesian laissez-faire with a New England ethic laminated onto it. Then you add in Chinese, Japanese, Koreans, and Portuguese from the Azores, and you get a fascinating society. People are proud of their admixture and will tell you they're one-eighth Irish, one-eighth Chinese, etc. It's regarded as an asset rather than something to put behind you." My friend Peter Morse puts it another way—that there are three levels of interaction between people. The first stage is when a person sees that another person is different from him and dislikes him for it—pure prejudice. The second stage is to notice differences in another person but to wipe them out of your mind and try to see him as a fellow human—in other words, tolerance. The third level is "where you look at your neighbor, and you see and are fully aware of differences, and *you are absolutely fascinated by them*. Differences become a really affirmative value in human relations. In this stage, each man has an intense pride in what he is—racially, culturally, intellectually—*not* as something to exclude others, but to share with others. A mixed marriage is not a lowest common denominator, but an addition of factors, when a child may take double pride in his heritages." Morse suggests that this final level is "typical of Hawaii, and maybe, God willing, the whole world will be this way some day."

In 1960 the Census Bureau found that Caucasians made up 32 percent of the Islands' population; 10 years later, almost 100,000 stronger, the Caucasians were 39 percent.* "Perhaps we should refurbish our historical racial balances," Governor Burns said in 1969, referring specifically to the need to create attractive professional openings for non-*haoles*. Under the pattern of the recent past, many young Islanders have looked to the mainland for brighter employment opportunities, while older mainlanders, almost all Caucasians, have sought out Hawaii as a place for their middle or retirement years.† (Hawaii has difficulty holding its young people because its most dynamic industry, tourism, needs only a limited number of skilled workers.) The chances of a *haole* majority in Hawaii, however, are lessened by the fact that the Japanese birth rate is much higher.

Among Hawaii's various ethnic groups today, the Chinese may be the wealthiest, many of their number dominant in the professions and as owners of banks, insurance companies, and large real estate companies. Several are in government, including U.S. Sen. Hiram L. Fong, who made his start as a successful businessman. Low on the totem pole are the Filipinos and Samoans. The Filipinos, the last big group to be imported to work on the plantations, are still the biggest group there, although many have shifted to gardening, or retired, while a younger generation moves more fully into the general life of the Islands. Many of the Filipino plantation workers were single men who came in the 1930s with the thought of making some money and perhaps returning home later. But many who indeed made it back to the Philippines found the life there strange and the weather hot. Often they returned to Hawaii to sit in the park, shoot pool, and wait for the end. Others, aided by the liberalized U.S. Immigration law of 1965, were finally able to bring families to Hawaii and face a happier prospect. The Samoans, fresh arrivals of the 1960s, took menial jobs to start with and mixed with

* Previously cited figures, which showed the present-day Caucasian population at only 19 percent of the 1970 population, did not include the huge and almost all-Caucasian military population on the Islands.

† The 1970 Census found that 25.8 percent of Hawaii's people had been born in another state. But an amazingly small percentage—5.8 percent—were 65 or over. The national average is 9.9 percent.

Filipinos in the poverty-model cities target areas of Honolulu. Unless one counts some 3,000 Negroes clustered in the old Chinatown section, the Filipino-Samoan sections are the only identifiable ethnic neighborhoods in a city that used to be packed with racial enclaves of one description or another. In contrast to the mainland, most Negroes are not ghettoized. Many of them are families of servicemen, in good quality housing. Several blacks, including Charles Campbell, Honolulu Democratic chairman for many years, have risen to positions of prominence.

The saddest story may be that of the surviving original Hawaiians. One hears again and again that the Hawaiian, by basic temperament, loves life and believes man is not made to work. He believes things are put here for us by the Almighty for us to enjoy. The idea of getting out and working and not enjoying life makes little sense—it is, in fact, an alien *haole* idea. In a 1962 study, it was discovered that while Hawaiians and part-Hawaiians then represented only 17 percent of the population, they accounted for more than 35 percent of destitute families, 42 percent of the children arrested, and 51 percent of all illegitimate births. Their school dropout rate exceeded that of all other ethnic groups in the Islands. The situation is not believed to have changed much since. Half a century ago, Congress established a Home Lands Commission to parcel out 200,000 acres of land to families with even a minimal amount of Hawaiian blood. But the commission, in a classic case of governmental slothfulness combined with favoritism to other, more politically potent landholders, has parceled out only a minute fraction of the land and even lost its records on several thousand acres. Even liberal politicians normally for the underdog, including Senator Inouye and Congresswoman Mink, have refused to take an interest in the case. The first substantial protest movement, The Hawaiians, was started in 1970 under a young Hawaiian leader, Pae Galdeira.

The old forms of discrimination by *haoles* linger on, however faintly. Older Caucasians who once lived on plantations remember when the workers couldn't speak English, and they may tend to think of all Orientals the same way. The Oahu Country Club remains snobbish about non-*haole* admissions, although the venerable Pacific Club gave up that old nonsense several years ago. The top business brass is still heavily Caucasian, although there are comparatively more Oriental entries now.*

The main point is that discrimination is simply no longer an accepted public practice, nor is it smiled upon as a private attitude on these Islands. Intermarriage is sure to undermine it more and more, year by year. "Our human relations are not perfect—but they are better than any other place in the United States," George Chaplin believes.

"Or the world," I think he could add. At the East-West Center on the University of Hawaii campus, there may be some 1,000 "students" at any

---

* As if to balance old scores, there are now many major Hawaiian businesses that are practically all Oriental, including Fong's Finance Factors and Aloha Airlines (both Chinese), Filipino banks, and a Japanese supermarket chain.

given time—Asians and Americans in graduate studies, men with advanced degrees working cooperatively on projects, and natives from places like Micronesia, Guam, American Samoa, Fiji, or Tahiti, getting technical training in sanitation or police work or whatever their special concerns may be. Fields range from technological and population problems to "communications" and cultural interchange. Why Hawaii for such a center? Aside from its fortuitous geographic location, Hawaii offers a special atmosphere one could find nowhere else. Consider the reaction of a visitor from Thailand. In Honolulu he will see traffic congestion, the start of air pollution, a few of the frayed nerves that come with Western civilization. But he will also see familiar faces and familiar vegetation. His cultural shock won't be comparable to what it might be on the U.S. mainland. Thus it is that this *Shoal of Time*, as Gavan Daws named his fine book about Hawaii, becomes one of the great "bridge places" of the late 20th century—a place of unique bridges between its own peoples and across the broad Pacific.*

## The Economy: From Feudalism to Tourism

Hawaii's economy grew first on the sandalwood trade, then shifted to whaling, and still later centered around the output of the great sugar and pineapple plantations. With World War II, the federal military role became most important, and since then tourism has grown by leaps and bounds. Economic power in Hawaii until recent years was depicted as swinging on the feudalistic authority of the "Big Five," a tight-knit group of companies who dominated sugar and pineapples and, through those basic industries, the entire economy of the Islands. The companies were held and managed by 30 or 40 families, frequently intermarried, with almost hereditary succession into board chairmanships and presidencies. They successfully manipulated consumer prices through ownership of most important wholesale and large retail outlets and majority ownership of Matson Navigation, the major freight carrier to the Islands. Through direct ownership or interlocking directorates, the Big Five were able to control many of the local banks, public utilities, insurance firms, and hotels. (There were, however, many established and prosperous firms that continued in an independent fashion.)

The same oligarchic relationships symbolized by the Big Five pervaded the ownership of land, and continue in fact almost unabated to this day. The old Hawaiian kings jealously guarded their ownership of land, and the Big Five and the big estates which gained control of it in the 19th century have never let go. In 1967, of all the land in Hawaii, the state government owned 38.7 percent, the federal government 9.8 percent, small landowners

---

* I must add a caveat to the "broad Pacific" idea, which I heard from Governor Burns (who believes in it quite passionately) and many others in Hawaii. Until—or unless—the state can slough off its role as the staging area for U.S. military operations in Southeast Asia, its trans-Pacific cultural role may remain suspect in the eyes of many.

less than 5 percent. The remaining 47 percent was in the hands of only 72 big landowners. Reporting these figures in *The Frontier States*, Richard Austin Smith also pointed out that just considering the privately held land, two-thirds of it was held by a combination of three estates (originally founded by the Bishop, Damon, and Campbell families), two ranches (Parker and Molokai), four of the Big Five Corporations and one other firm—10 holders in all. This is not a clearcut case of *haole* domination, however. A number of the giant land holdings (including the Bishop and Campbell estates) are *Hawaiian*-owned lands, royal and noble, from Hawaiian ladies who married smart *haoles* who managed and prospered the land and got their names attached to it. Such holdings benefit descendants, many of whom the Census would call Hawaiians.

A frequent point of contention arises from the refusal of the big owners to sell their land to new homeowners, insisting on leasing instead. Only a quarter of the housing units in Hawaii are occupied by people who hold title to the land, and land reform was a burning issue in the legislature for years. Even if the major landowners wanted to sell more land, however, they might find it difficult—first because there are some cases in which trustees are forbidden, by a founder's will, from selling, and secondly, because the capital gains tax to be paid on outright sale would be so high as to be punitive. In 1967 a law was passed stating that if the majority of home-owners on a lease-hold voted for the estate to sell their lands to them, the holder could be forced to sell. But many people actually prefer to lease land, avoiding the large capital investment that outright ownership entails. In the legislature, far-sweeping bills to break up the estates and trusts have been consistently rejected.

The Big Five's control of Hawaii's general economy and life continued through World War II. Then, immediately after the war, the ILWU (International Longshoremen's & Warehousemen's Union) staged—and won—great strikes to organize the state's sugar and pineapple workers. To this day, the great plantations are still owned by the Big Five, but the companies' absolute power there is broken. The second major change came with statehood and the tourist explosion. Vast millions were required to finance the new hotels and facilities, but many of the Big Five found themselves timid about using it. They found they lacked managerial manpower to meet the new situation. The only alternative was to recruit managerial talent from the outside, with the inevitable dilution of the clubby patterns of local control that had prevailed so long. It was then only a matter of time until ownership began to slip away from the Islands too.

This does not mean that the Big Five are dead economically—far from it. They have chosen to export their skills in land management and agriculture to far-flung corners of the world and are doing very well. But the oligopoly in Hawaii is gone forever.

The new ownership and activity patterns of the Big Five, plus another giant, the Dillingham Corporation, are a fascinating story in themselves:

■   C. Brewer and Co., Ltd. Founded in 1826 by James Hunnewell, a New England sea captain. In 1954, Oregonian Boyd MacNaughton became its president, the first mainlander without family connections to head the firm. In January 1969, control passed to a Toronto-based conglomerate. The firm is big in sugar, molasses, insurance, ranching. It has sugar management, technology and training contracts from Iran to Taiwan, is a partner in a feed grain pilot project in Australia, and is involved in an $8.5 million, 1,900-acre resort complex in Puerto Rico.

■   Theo. H. Davies & Co., Ltd. Started in 1845 by English merchants and still controlled by a family in Great Britain. Principal income from sugar, merchandising, foreign investment. Philippines-based subsidiary has more than $10 million invested in that country.

■   Amfac, Inc., also still known by its old name, American Factors. Begun by a German sea captain in 1849, as a trading store on the Honolulu waterfront, seized by U.S. in World War I. Majority of shares now held outside Hawaii. Big in sugar and merchandising and has acquired big stateside operations like Joseph Magnin Company, Rhodes Western, and Fred Harvey, Inc. Has worked in almost 30 countries since statehood and has big sugar projects in Puerto Rico and the Dominican Republic.

■   Castle & Cooke, Inc. Started in 1851 by missionaries Samuel N. Castle and Amos S. Cooke, who would probably utter a hearty huzzah if they could see how well their offspring is doing. Gross business passed the $500 million mark in 1970 and is projected at $850 million in 1975—in comparison to the years just before World War II, when the company's total annual business was a tiny fraction of present levels.

The executive officer chiefly responsible for the modern-day growth is Malcolm MacNaughton, brother of Brewer & Co.'s president. Under his prodding, the firm sloughed off its old role of being an agent for others and began to acquire new properties itself. "We're still basically a food company," MacNaughton told me, but he then outlined how diversified the agricultural interests are: sugar plantations in Hawaii; pineapple in Hawaii, the Philippines, and Honduras as owners of Dole Pineapple; second largest banana marketer of the world as owner of Standard Fruit & Steamship, with plantations in Honduras, Costa Rica, and the Philippines; owner of Bumble Bee Seafoods, producing packed salmon, tuna, Alaska and Columbia River shrimp, king crab, and the like; largest coffee producer in the Philippines; grower and marketer of macadamia nuts from a 1,200-acre plantation on the Island of Hawaii. Castle & Cooke is also returning to the retailing trade of the company's first days with a string of discount stores in California, acts as steamship agent in the harbor of Hawaii, and is deeply involved in land development and property management with its 160,000 acres of land in Hawaii.

Why does Castle & Cooke stay in Hawaii? MacNaughton recalls that when he went to the Islands in 1945, it was like emigrating to a sleepy mid-Pacific outpost. It is impossible to think that now when one looks from the windows of his office in the high Financial Plaza of the Pacific, the ragged and verdant mountains now set off by a booming city. But, says MacNaughton, "we probably wouldn't stay here if it weren't for the jet plane and the telephone. Isolation is ended. We can operate from anywhere. I like to live here—I'm as much a reason for our being here as anyone."

If Castle & Cooke did decide to move elsewhere, its stockholders would probably not argue. A clear majority of them are mainlanders anyway.

■ Alexander and Baldwin, Inc. Begun by two missionaries' sons in 1895. Operates the Matson Navigation Company and related docks and warehouses, and has interests in sugar, pineapples, and merchandising. Part owner of a heavy construction leasing company in the Philippines. This company is still largely controlled by owners on Maui, but they are gradually being bought out.

■ Dillingham Corporation. The Dillinghams have been a big name in Hawaii construction since Benjamin F. Dillingham, a New England seafaring man, started in business in Honolulu in 1889. Over the decades, the Dillinghams built dozens of major buildings in Hawaii, opened up its first railway, cleared the channels at Pearl Harbor for big ships, and dredged up the Ala Moana and Waikiki sections of Honolulu from low-lying swamp. But they lacked an entree into the big moneymakers, sugar and pineapple, and therefore remained less than "Big Five" over seven full decades. Then, in the 1960s, two major changes took place. Lowell S. Dillingham, inheritor of the family mantle, merged the two old Dillingham family businesses and began an aggressive course of landing new construction business all over the world and acquiring subsidiaries. At the same time, agriculture's importance to Hawaii, and its profitability, declined. By 1970, the Dillingham Corporation was bigger than any of the Big Five with the possible exception of Castle & Cooke, with which it was competing for the title of Hawaii's largest corporation.

Lowell Dillingham believed that a corporation must grow or face eventual extinction. As a one-man sales force, he flew around the world in a constant search for new construction contracts and new acquisitions. Rather than waiting for construction bids to come to it, the firm frequently thought up projects it considered viable, built them, and often retained them for their cash flow and profitability. (Examples: the Ala Moana Shopping Center, the 43-story Wells Fargo Bank building in San Francisco.) The firm also went into shipbuilding and repair, marine transportation, oceanographic engineering, quarrying, and propane gas distribution. As a contractor, it was busy all along the West Coast and even in isolated eastern locations of the U.S.A., not to mention Australia (where it became the largest contractor), New Zealand, New Guinea, Singapore, Malaysia, Thailand, and Indonesia.

Every big Hawaii firm save Dillingham has turned to hired managers. This may change too, in a few years. Lowell Dillingham is expected to turn over the reins, sometime in the 1970s, to his executive vice president, Herbert C. Cornuelle, whose forte is in operations management and "people development"—a helpful skill in a company trying to assimilate a lot of new subsidiaries. For a while in 1969, it has looked as if Dillingham might succeed in acquiring United Fruit Company, the biggest banana supplier in the U.S. with an annual gross well over Dillingham's own. The deal fell through, with United Fruit going instead to New York's AMK Corporation. But Cornuelle, who had been United Fruit's president and chief operating officer, decided to go to Dillingham anyway. It was, *Forbes* magazine reported that year, "a very nice consolation prize."

Dillingham is not the only new economic giant on the scene. By any reasonable standard, one must count the big mainland retailers (Sears and Penney); the large mainland hotel chains (Sheraton, Western, Hilton); Senator Hiram Fong's "Finance Factors" (insurance, banking, real estate); big developers like Laurance Rockefeller, Del Webb, Boise Cascade, and some of the Japanese investors; the big airlines flying between the state and the mainland (especially United and Pan American, which held a monopoly on the route until 1969); the Hawaii and Aloha Airlines, and finally Chinn Ho.

Mr. Ho, to whom we referred earlier in his role as board chairman of the Honolulu *Star-Bulletin*, is the self-made man of his generation. Starting out as a brokerage clerk, he followed the old Oriental practice of having a lot of small investors pool their capital resources, his financial acumen attracting their support. For almost 20 years he slowly accumulated real estate and capital; in the 1960s he made his first bold stroke by buying out a failing condominium on Waikiki Beach and turning it into the $48 million, 1,600-room Ilikai condominium-hotel complex. Then he undertook a 9,000-acre resort city on the west side of Oahu at Makaha Valley, using old sugar plantation land he had bought several years before for about $1 million; the total investment at Makaha by Chinn and Western Hotels is expected to reach $500 million.

By 1970, Ho's "hui," or Capital Investment Company, also owned big oil holdings in Louisiana, a newspaper in Guam, the Empress Hotel in Hong Kong, and some 2,200 acres in Marin County, across the bay from San Francisco. Ho's image became tarnished in some Islands circles when he became identified with the developer bid to construct high-rises along the flank of Diamond Head. Ho has little patience with criticism of the tourist boom, however. "Anyone who criticizes the tourist industry," he has said, "doesn't begin to appreciate the employment that it produces." He acknowledges that "there have been abuses" at Waikiki but points out that that beach community "comprises a total of 181 acres and yet it pays more property taxes than all the sugar land, pineapple land, and ranch land in the state."

In 1968, when Chinn Ho reached his 65th birthday, there was a big birthday party for him attended by 300 VIP's around the Makaha pool. The guests arranged for a helicopter to deliver Ho's gift—a golf cart with four seats and a four-decanter silver bar. Not without significance was the choice of the man to offer the champagne toasts that evening. It was the governor of Hawaii, John A. Burns.

What was it that ignited Hawaii's economy like a great rocket in the 1960s? The answer seems to be statehood. Up to 1959, there had been a decline in the Islands' traditional agricultural base, and many young people were leaving for the mainland in search of better opportunities. Waikiki Beach was still a low-density spot with lots of calm and vegetation, harboring only a handful of hotels. Travel to the Islands was within the reach of a much narrower group of mainlanders, and those who did come tended to choose a cruise ship and then stay for at least a week or two.

Statehood seemed to change all this, for reasons mostly psychological. The battle to become the 50th state generated reams of stateside magazine and newspaper copy about Hawaii, almost all of it favorable. When the bill passed Congress, Hawaii was suddenly no more some kind of primitive colony but a very real part of the American Union and one most Americans were curious to see. And now all the uneasy fears—that there might be special shots required to go to Hawaii, or that the currency might be different, or other comical concerns of the pre-statehood period—began to drop away. Direct jet service was inaugurated about the same time, and it was only a few hours from the West Coast. And for Hawaii's economic health, the new image also said that it was now a safe place to invest money.

"If one were to pick four items that symbolized what has happened to Hawaii in the first 10 years since statehood," writer Harold Hostetler of the Honolulu *Advertiser* commented in 1969, "he might choose a bulldozer, a construction crane, a cement mixer, and a carpenter's hammer. Combined, those four tools have done more to change the face of Hawaii in just 10 years than has all the activity of man since the Islands were first settled by the ancient Polynesians." In a decade, the construction industry added $3.4 billion in new buildings. The rate for new residential construction was up 55 percent, for government buildings 30 percent, for hotels 600 percent. The number of nonfarm jobholders in Hawaii was up 55 percent to 275,000 in the decade, and the number of people working in hotels by 250 percent. Hawaiians' total income went up 156 percent to $3 billion a year, per capita income up 82 percent to $3,928. Checking accounts in banks were up 138 percent to $632 million. The flow of tourists rose 461 percent—from 243,000 in 1959 to 1,364,000 in 1969. In 1959 the tourists spent $109 million in Hawaii; in 1969 the figure was $576 million. (The contrast to 1949 is even more startling; in that year only 34,000 tourists came to the Islands, and they spent a paltry $18 million.)

The surge of business and inflation of values was apparent in almost every facet of Hawaii life. Retailing receipts, for instance, went up from $707 million in 1959 to $1.54 billion in 1969. The value of property, including both lands and buildings, rose 300 percent in the state as a whole and by nearly 400 percent on the island of Oahu.

All this "progress" did not come without its price. While the business indicators soared, so did the crime rate with burglaries, auto thefts, and petty larceny up 200 percent in the decade.* Taxes soared—from a total of $25.7 million paid by Hawaiians in personal income taxes in 1959 to $86.5 million in 1969. The cost of living in Honolulu was 20 percent above that of the average urban area of the United States, outdone only by Anchorage at 32 percent above average. The inflation in food prices was serious enough, including a celebrated case of No. 2 cans of sliced pineapple selling for 39 cents at a market outside Dole's Oahu cannery, compared to 37 cents for the same item in Baltimore. (Shipping costs are often blamed for higher prices on foods and other goods, but often the price differentials are several times what the actual freight costs could be—suggesting to some that the profiteering ways of yore are still a reality.) Hawaiian families have been so hard pressed to meet the inflationary surge that they have the highest percentage of working wives in the nation.

A wise family can, of course, plan its purchases to avoid some of the high prices—choosing, for instance, more native foods like rice and fish instead of expensive items imported from the mainlands. There are no heating costs, and no one need ever bother to purchase winter wear like overcoats, galoshes, and the like. But unavoidably higher are automobile costs and medical care. Worst of all is housing. In 1970 the Census found the median price of a home in Hawaii was $35,100 and in Honolulu an astronomical $43,200. The U.S. average was only $17,000. Three factors held Hawaiian prices so high: the high demand for construction workers because of the tourist hotel boom, the influx of mainlanders seeking homes that propelled Oahu real estate sales to the $1 billion range by 1971, the shortage of land because of Hawaii's narrow base of land control, and the cost of shipping building materials from the mainland. With a desperate need for thousands of moderately priced homes, the state government in 1970 finally began to invite proposals for low-cost, prefabricated houses. Governor Burns promised that state lands would be made available for mass building of low-cost units.

The issue of the tourist industry and its impact on Hawaii's prices, taxes, and environment expanded from the 1968 Honolulu mayoralty campaign to the governorship contest of 1970, in which Lieutenant Governor Gill unsuccessfully opposed John A. Burns. Gill argued that the high taxes being paid by Hawaiians were being channeled unfairly to building roads, supplying water, and providing other services for the huge tourist resorts. "Who," he asked, "is going to pay the infrastructure bill [for streets, schools, sewers, and other public facilities] if tourism continues to expand? If the estimate [of future growth] is anywhere near correct, we don't have

---

* The property crime rate on the Islands was 131 percent of the national level in 1969, though a large portion of it was confined to Waikiki (locals preying on tourists). Perhaps predictably, in view of the character of the people, the rate of violent crime was only 26 percent of the national average. Hawaii does have a problem with organized crime: between 1962 and 1970, there were 17 confirmed gangland murders in Hawaii. Opinions differ on whether this is Mafioso crime or whether the local syndicates have been successful in keeping out the mainland boys.

the capital-improvement money to pay for it." On occasion, opponents of the tourist inundation even talked darkly of quota restrictions or a head tax. They did campaign openly for a hotel room tax of up to 10 percent.

Burns and others allied with the tourist industry opposed a room tax, either on the grounds that it would "damage the spirit of Aloha" or because they feared it would cut back on business. "We have had enough of pessimistic, poor-mouthing political demagoguery designed to make tourism a dirty word," Burns said. Without tourism, its friends said, Hawaii's economy could be in dire straits. The Hawaii Visitors Bureau estimated that each new hotel room created 1½ new jobs on the Islands.

Nevertheless, critics of the industry continued to pound away on the hotel room tax issue, pointing out—in Mayor Fasi's words—that the "spirit of Aloha doesn't pay the police and firemen nor build roads or clean up the beaches or develop the scenic spots you need." With the financial squeeze on both Honolulu and the state getting tighter, the room tax—similar to one already in effect in resorts like Miami—seemed likely in the 1970s.

The deeper and more difficult issue raised was whether tourism was being allowed to proceed so rapidly that it could devour the very charms that draw visitors to what the Hawaii Visitors Bureau, in its own publicity, calls the "Land of the Golden People." George Walters, a talented Hawaiian planner, has pointed out that the cane and pineapple fields beginning to vanish under spreading asphalt are part of Hawaii's uniqueness. "Why travel," he said, "if it means nothing more than whizzing around in a sealed tourist bus only to sink exhausted in front of a television set in a standard hotel room? We've got to stop paving everything. Modern life demands planning, but at the heart of the plans must be respect for the natural world, the essential mystery of man's fragile survival on this planet, that the Orient knows so well."

To those who wanted to limit the tourist influx in an arbitrary way, however, men like Burns had a strong counterargument. In his address to the legislature in 1968, Burns dwelt on his theme that "We are a free people . . . we are an open society . . . we welcome all visitors to our Island home." In that address he also said:

Provincialism must never get a foothold in these Islands. None of us owns Hawaii. It was passed on to us by others. We, too, have only a transitory claim on this Paradise; and we will pass it on to others. Only the Hawaiian people can rightfully claim it as their own, and it was the Hawaiian people who—with supreme generosity—risked all they posssessed in welcoming Caucasians, Chinese, Japanese, Filipinos, Puerto Ricans, and others to their Islands.

For us to be anything but generous and open to all who wish to come here would be for us to forsake our heritage and our tradition.

The words, as Burns uttered them, make it hard to believe the suggestion of some that he had become simply a tool for developer and tourist interests. In fact, the issue raised by his remarks, of the right of the world's peoples to visit and enjoy the garden spots of the globe—and the concomitant danger to those places which the travel raises—is one I have never seen discussed in depth.

By the start of the 1970s, it seemed that help might await Hawaii in a quite unexpected form. Spurred on by the success of their packaged tours and a constantly increasing tourist load through most of the 1960s, developers committed themselves to a huge wave of construction that increased the visitor plant in 1969–70 by 55 percent, to 35,388 rooms. Then the bloom suddenly left the orchid as the increase in tourists abated for the first time. (The 1971 total of 1,808,215 tourists was only half a percent over the 1970 total, although a substantial increase was projected for 1972.) It appeared that few if any hotels, beyond those already under construction, would be built in Hawaii for some time to come.

Another tourist impetus was also coming to an end: the "rest and recuperation," or R & R trips of American servicemen fighting in Vietnam. The Hawaiian phase of Vietnam R & R was worked out by President Johnson in 1965–66 with the help of his two good friends in Hawaii, Governor Burns and Senator Inouye. One of the aims was to stem the outflow of American gold by inducing GIs, who are entitled to one R & R trip of six days during each year spent in Vietnam, to go to Hawaii instead of the other centers in Sydney, Taipei, Bangkok, Tokyo, Manila, and Hongkong. As it turned out, many of those exotic eastern cities continued to draw the single men, but those with wives or steady sweethearts frequently choose Hawaii for bittersweet reunions. "They drift along on Kalakaua Avenue in Waikiki on Saturday night, wandering with the crowd and watching the hours slip through their fingers," Wallace Turner reported in the New York *Times*. "They have 114 hours, these tanned young soldiers with short haircuts and a slightly haggard look around the eyes. And then it is time to kiss the wife or girl goodbye, and perhaps the baby, too. They owe Vietnam six or seven more months. . . ."

The military flew the R & R men free to Honolulu, while the airlines gave their families reduced rates from the West Coast. To their credit, Honolulu hotel and shop owners granted reduced rates. Of course they had good reason to. Some 10,000 men a month made the trip to Hawaii, and they and their families filled about 15 percent of all the hotel rooms in the state on any given day.

The U.S. military contributes a lot more to the Hawaiian economy than R & R visitors. There is a great weight of installations on Oahu, and this is the place the Vietnam war was run from. So great were the military expenditures in the 1960s, in fact, that outlays crept up toward World War II levels. From $370 million in 1963, Department of Defense expenditures (payrolls, goods, and services) in Hawaii escalated to $660 million in 1969. The state became a temporary home for some 50,000 military personnel plus nearly 60,000 dependents. And direct defense-generated civilian employment kept 9 percent of the labor force busy, a figure second only to Alaska's.

Governor Burns told me he was confident that the military input to Hawaii's economy would continue "As long as we have military forces, they can't be removed from Hawaii." The governor has also been quoted as saying that "if the [Vietnam] war ends it will mean more troops stationed here *permanently*. And if the United States returns Okinawa to Japan, Hawaii would then be a forward base in the Pacific, just as it was years ago."

Not everyone in Hawaii views the military as an unmitigated blessing. It certainly contributes to inflationary pressures and makes the housing shortages on the Islands all that much worse. And many Hawaiians think the armed forces control much more land than necessary. The top secret military depot outside Honolulu, rumored to hold nuclear weapons, is off-bounds for all but a few military personnel, not to mention civilians. The Islands have an incredible concentration of military brass: in 1971, for instance, two full admirals, two full generals, four lieutenant generals, two vice admirals, 11 major generals, 14 rear admirals, and 18 brigadier generals. Yet their relations with people concerned about Hawaii's future leave something to be desired. "You can't reach them," a Honolulu urban planner has been quoted as saying. "They own more land than they know what to do with, but even though we desperately need land for housing, they won't even talk to us."

Sugar and pineapple, onetime leaders of the Hawaiian economy, now rank third and fourth behind the military and tourism. Both crops are fairly static, in part because of the limited land area suitable for agricultural growth—less than a tenth of Hawaii's surface. (Another tenth can be used as forage land for cattle, but 80 percent consists of scenic but unproductive mountains, lava flows, and semibarren deserts.) Gradually some farmlands are lost to new suburbs and towns, but scientific farming methods have effected a dramatic increase in per-acre yields, averting an overall drop in production. Sugar is further stabilized by Congressional production quotas. With a rather constant 220,000 to 240,000 acres planted in cane, the value has risen from $124 million in 1950 to about $200 million today. Compared to 30,000 sugar workers right after the war, mechanization has permitted a reduction to just a few thousand.* "All sugar needs," a local economist told me, "is a few guys to water the cane from time to time, then to burn it at harvest time and operate the cranes to pick up the burned stalks and take them into the plant where the sugar and molasses are extracted and the fibres put aside for building board." (It is difficult to think of any other crop which is most economical to harvest by burning it first. The burning serves two purposes: it consumes all the leaves and chaff, so that countless tons of waste don't have to be picked up, carried to the plant, and laboriously separated; second, it seals the sugar inside the stalk, thus avoiding a huge

---

* Another indication of agriculture's decline as a force in the Hawaiian economy is that in 1930 it accounted for 46 percent of civilian employment, in 1970 less than 3 percent.

waste in leakage between field and plant). Sugar workers, as a result of intense pressure applied by the ILWU, earn up to $25 a day—the highest agricultural wages in the world.

Parenthetically, it might be added that sugar is the only economic activity we have touched on so far in which Oahu does not dominate. The production percentages from a recent year showed: The island of Hawaii 37 percent, Maui 23 percent, Kauai 21 percent, and Oahu 18 percent.

About 6,000 workers produce the Hawaiian pineapple crop, grown on about 70,000 acres and valued at $123 million in the late 1960s. The "pine" industry, as it is called, has faced rough sledding in the past decade because of cheaper labor costs in countries like Taiwan, plus the lack of quotas and regulated markets. Malcolm MacNaughton of Castle & Cooke, whose Dole Pineapple has begun major operations in the Philippines, predicts that "pine will hold its own in Hawaii but won't expand."

After sugar and pine, one drops down to other farm products—cabbage, lettuce, watercress, celery, leeks, papayas, mangos, bananas, melons, and livestock leaders like beef, dairy products, and hogs. They go part of the way toward feeding the Islands' population but are certainly not great enough for export.

Fishing—for bigeye scad, jackmackerel, marlin, tuna, and other varieties —is disappointingly small, only 12 million pounds at a value of a little over $3 million in 1967, for instance. To date, Hawaii's shipping fleets seem to be no competition for the more aggressive and better-equipped Japanese. This may change in time; already a nascent industry in oceanographic research is underway, looking into "sea-farming" and similar techniques. Hawaii lacks a continental shelf but has the advantage of a mid-Pacific position ideal for studying major oceanic currents. There are bands of offshore terraces which simulate conditions of the continental shelf but reach immense depths in a few miles. And Hawaii's clear, warm waters are ideal for divers and other submarine workers. As federal interest in "hydrospace" continues to grow, Hawaii is likely to get some of the business; ready to receive it are the University of Hawaii's developing programs in oceanography and private groups like Taylor A. Pryor's Makapuu Oceanic Institute, which has mounted some imaginative undersea experiments in the last few years. But it may be decades before oceanography makes any real dent on the overall Hawaii economy.

Hawaiians also talk dreamily of their state as an ideal spot for "think tanks" and light-parts electronic assembly, but the distances may simply be too great to make this practicable in the near future, at least on any significant scale. In the same category is the enthusiastic talk of Governor Burns and other officials about the possibilities of great future trade with the Orient. The fact is that Hawaii has little to "export" other than hotel rooms—and the Japanese, in fact, are visiting the Islands in rapidly escalating numbers (25,000 in 1967, 100,000 in 1970). Insularity may be an asset in terms of communications; already Hawaii has one of the world's largest Comsat receiving and transmitting stations. Some economic gain may come from the state's foreign trade zone, opened in 1966, which is used as a drop-off and pick-up point for ships of all nationalities criss-crossing the Pacific and is now the site of a new oil refinery that converts low-sulphur foreign crude oil into fuel for the military, airlines, and ships free of U.S. or state taxes. But the aggregate economic benefit for the average Hawaiian is minimal. Nor is manufacturing ever likely to be a major industry. It has reached an annual level of $350 million in recent years, mostly from food processing. There is some metal products, cement, and furniture manufacture, but for the sole purpose of saving on the inordinate shipping expenses of such heavy items. Only 11 percent of the working force is now engaged in manufacturing—compared to 25 percent working for government.

The fact remains that Hawaii still is, and probably always will be, dependent on the U.S. mainland for the vast bulk of its supplies—from newsprint to gas and oil, from medical supplies to fertilizers, from cars and trucks to electrical machinery. Under federal law, it all has to come on American bottoms, adding to the inflationary pressures. Shipping strikes—like the prolonged West Coast dock strike of 1971–72—can cripple the Islands' economy. Small businesses go under, unemployment rises, sugar and "pine" supplies suffer, goods become scarce, and inflationary pressures are compounded. Burns and many other leading Hawaiians favor an amendment to the Taft-Hartley Act which would recognize the state's unique geographic position by placing it on a provisional "no strike" basis long before the President calls an emergency on the mainland. The outlook for that kind of exception is probably not bright. And there may always be, one feels, some unreal aspects to running an economy for hundreds of thousands of people on islands set in the midst of a great ocean, more than 2,000 miles from anywhere.

## *The Remarkable Longshoremen, or*
## *"How a Communist Turned Establishment"*

Back in 1935, a young seaman and union organizer named Jack Hall left the SS Mariposa in Honolulu Harbor to start organizing the territory's waterfront workers. Hall would never go back to sea again, but he would leave an indelible mark in Hawaiian history. Up to that point, unionism on the Islands had—outside of a few almost all-white trade unions—made scarcely any progress at all. The big mass of workers were on the plantations, but in 1910 AFL president Samuel Gompers had bluntly told striking Isle sugar workers that they couldn't expect any help because they were Orientals. Repeatedly, isolated racial groups among the sugar workers had organized unions, but whenever they struck, the Big Five employers simply imported workers of another race and used every kind of means, including raw physical violence, to break the strikes and crush the unions.

No sooner had Jack Hall arrived in the Islands than he started a weekly newspaper, *Voice of Labor*, to change the climate of workers' fear and create a unified labor movement. Not long afterwards, the CIO Cannery workers got Hall to undertake its Hawaiian organizing work. In 1941, Hall was ready to move with an Islands-wide, interracial sugar organizing drive, and the ILWU had made big strides in organizing the men on the waterfront. Pearl Harbor and martial law intervened, but in 1944 the ILWU picked Hall as its regional director and many of the plantation owners, bowing to what they feared was the inevitable, let the union come in. It was not long, by one account, before the ILWU was moving through the sugar and pineapple plantations "like one great canefield fire." (For years, the ILWU would be the one significant group of organized farm workers in the U.S. By the late 1960s, the ILWU succeeded in moving plantation wages up from a 19-cent-an-hour minimum to well over $2 an hour in 1970, and up to $4 for skilled workers. Longshoremen earn a lot more.)

As the ILWU bid for supremacy and favorable contracts in the late 1940s, Hawaii was wracked by sugar and pine and dock strikes. The ILWU had made 30,000 members by 1947 and had to be reckoned with as a major power point on the Islands. But public patience with the strikes was frayed by a 177-day dock strike in 1949 that virtually crippled the state's economy with losses said to approach $100 million. At the same time the ILWU was moving strongly into Democratic politics. Suddenly charges were raised—often with solid evidence to back them up—that there were many Communists or former Communists, Jack Hall included, in the Hawaiian labor movement. Employers and their conservative allies in Congress used the charges to discredit the ILWU. Along with others, Hall took the Fifth Amendment when the House Un-American Activities Committee asked him if he had ever been a Communist Party member. In 1953 he was convicted under the Smith Act for conspiring to overthrow the U.S. government by violence and force. Even when Hall and six other Hawaiians saw their convictions on that charge reversed,* the image of a dangerously radical and unsavory leader persisted and was encouraged by employers.

Yet, as time went on, Hall mellowed. Still a tough negotiator, he nevertheless showed a willingness to relieve some hard-pressed plantation owners of demands he made on the industry in general. The ILWU, which had made a bid for outright control of the Democratic party in Hawaii in 1948, settled back to a more relaxed game of rewarding friends and punishing enemies in both parties. Democrats got the more frequent endorsements, but Hall and the ILWU actually favored the more *conservative* Democratic faction led by Governor Burns.

Jack Hall, however, remained a tough labor leader—once quoted as saying, "Anybody who plays me for anything else is going to get his pants

* The U.S. Circuit Court of Appeals in San Francisco, in reversing the convictions in 1958, followed the doctrine laid down by the U.S. Supreme Court that abstract preaching of Communist doctrine, even allied with membership in the party, did not constitute a conspiracy to overthrow the government by force and violence.

clawed off." In 1969, when Hall finally left the Islands,* he bequeathed his successors a virile union of 23,900 workers—11,000 in sugar, 6,100 in pineapples, 1,600 longshoremen, 3,000 hotel workers, tour guides, and bus drivers, and 2,100 in general trades that ranged from newspapers and bakeries to scrap iron collectors and tuna canners and workers in cemeteries. Robert McElrath, Hall's successor in Honolulu, told me the union planned an all-out effort to recruit the new hotel workers, rather than letting them slip into the control of the local AFL-CIO Hotel, Restaurant Employees and Bartenders' Union, headed by Arthur A. Rutledge, a longtime and sometimes bitter rival of the ILWU. (Rutledge, a pudgy old scrapper whose "Unity House" also includes the Hawaii Teamsters, calls the ILWU a "dog-eat-dog union" and criticizes it for "raiding" his ranks. The feud has overtones in Democratic politics, with the ILWU in the Burns "conservative" camp, Rutledge behind former Lt. Gov. Thomas Gill and the "liberals.")

In Hawaii today, the ILWU is regarded as a solid part of the establishment. Its interests run to protecting the environment so that union members will have pleasant places to weekend after four-day work weeks, helping with causes like "saving" Diamond Head, and working to protect the government-supported Hawaii Visitors Bureau which promotes tourism (and, in turn, hotel jobs). At an Aloha party held to mark Hall's departure, the business and political establishment of Hawaii turned out to honor him. Lowell Dillingham presented a testimonial from the United Fund and said, "Hawaii is losing its greatest community leader." The same day, the once violently conservative Honolulu *Advertiser* said in a full-page editorial that "more than any other man, Hall helped bring industrial democracy to these Islands as they moved from feudalism and paternalism to the sophisticated and broadly affluent society of today." Hall, a man once so hated by the Big Five business establishments that two attempts were made on his life, found it all a little hard to believe. The nice things being said about him, Hall said, were "almost the exact opposite of the things I heard about myself in 1952 during the six months I spent in Federal Court. It didn't sound like me then, and it doesn't sound like me now."

Hall should not have been surprised. In an interview with Gardiner B. Jones of the *Advertiser* the year before, Hall admitted frustration in a modern labor movement with no further goals than "just more of everything," a $4 instead of a $3 hourly wage or whatever. "This is disturbing for some of us who came into the union movement with some social objectives, to lift the downtrodden and so on. . . . The unions aren't a social force for the general improvement of the community they once were. The radicals are no longer in the unions; they are on the campuses." Hall said the ILWU engaged in community activities so that we can "live with ourselves. It was much easier when we had no friends." Finally, the man once convicted of seeking the violent overthrow of the U.S. government had this to say:

* Hall took on an executive job with ILWU headquarters in San Francisco, where he died early in 1971.

You know, once I wanted socialism but I don't any more. It isn't practical. The American people will never accept it. Most Americans want to be millionaires and engage in free enterprise. Success is measured in dollars. . . .

When I was young, I believed socialism was the answer to unemployment, depression, and poverty. I don't believe that any more.

In 1970 there were signs that the state AFL-CIO, often eclipsed by the ILWU and Hawaii's other feuding unions, might be coming into its own. Its young state president, Walter Kupau, got warring unions together to unite behind a single bill in the legislature to permit collective bargaining and strikes by public employees. This legislation, which became law to almost everyone's amazement, is regarded by its backers as "the most progressive law affecting workers in the nation's history." The governor appoints a five-member public employment relations board with two management level members, two from labor, and a chairman representing the public. Labor unions compete for membership among personnel in 13 bargaining units, ranging from firemen and police to university professors. A union which wins a secret ballot organizational vote then has an exclusive right to negotiate for a contract, working under the agency shop in which union dues must be paid for all members, but membership is optional. The law stipulates fairly long mediation and fact-finding periods in disputes but guarantees the public employees the right to strike except where the government agency can prove that a strike would endanger public health or safety.

## Burns, Statehood, and the Democratic Era

John A. Burns must be called a lucky man. The beginnings were hardly auspicious: a humble birth at the lonely Army post of Fort Assineboine, Montana, where his Sergeant Major father was doing duty in 1909; a difficult youth that bordered on juvenile delinquency; a single semester in college and a single year in the Army; sporadic jobs in the Kansas wheat fields, in Honolulu's pineapple canneries, and as a grape farmer in California. Jack Burns' first solid success was as a patrolman (and later captain) on the Honolulu police force, a job he began in 1934. Not until the years following World War II did he become involved in politics, and then, as Gavan Daws notes in *Shoal of Time*, he "was on the verge of middle age—a common man, without money, quite without social pretensions, and without much claim to depth or subtlety of mind."

Yet within a few years, Burns (1) paved the way for acceptance of the Japanese into the Islands' Democratic party, formed ethnically balanced tickets, and masterminded the smashing of the ancient Republican regime; (2) as a Delegate to Congress, plotted the strategy by which Hawaii won its long-sought statehood in 1959; and (3) three times won election as governor of his Hawaii. The secrets of Burns' phenomenal success have long been debated; among the clues are a plainness and directness of speech that leaves no room for doubts, intense loyalty to friends, the classic skills of a consensus-type politician (who incidentally was a great friend of President Johnson), and a dogged dedication to what it is he believes in, this orbit including the Catholic Church (he attends Mass every morning), racial equality, the desirability of more and more tourism, and Hawaii's role as the center of the Pacific.

This gray-haired and blue-eyed man of handsome, chiseled features, now in his early sixties and showing his age, is thought by some to be extending his hold on Hawaiian government beyond his rightful time and to be too close to business interests he would have scorned two decades ago. But if others entertain doubts, Burns does not. He is a supremely confident and complacent politician, the personification of the old-style liberal made into a centrist and establishment man by the drift of events he himself started in motion.

As Hawaii emerged from its unhappy period of martial law during World War II, it was still ruled by a Republican party which had held unbroken control of the territorial legislature since 1903 and served largely as an agent of the Caucasian business community. The Democrats had all too often been patronage men waiting for a Democratic President for a few plums, like "post office Republicans" in the South. Burns revolutionized all this by reading, quite accurately, the figures showing how many Orientals were becoming naturalized; of course their sons and daughters were American citizens by birth. These were the rejected of the Republican regime; Burns determined to take them to the heart of a new Democratic effort, just as on the mainland, Republicans had given the olive branch to Negroes at the time of the Civil War and the Democrats reached out to foreign ethnic groups in the great cities in the Depression, winning loyalties that might and did endure even beyond their time of historical relevance. The constant theme of Burns' new Democratic party was the election ticket carefully balanced between Japanese and Filipinos and Hawaiians and Chinese and *haoles*. But most important of all was the political role given to the Japanese, who yearned for it so much at this point in history and represented close to a third of the entire voter pool. Labor was brought into the same house, and in 1954 the Democrats won the territorial legislature for the first time in Hawaiian history; after two disappointments, in 1956 the party finally elected Jack Burns as Hawaii's Delegate to Congress.

Our scene now shifts to Washington, where the debate over Hawaiian statehood was moving into its third arduous decade. It was, in fact, more than a century since an 1854 treaty, drawn up between the U.S. Secretary of State and King Kamehameha III, which would have admitted the Kingdom of Hawaii into the American Union as a state "enjoying the same degree of sovereignty as other states, and admitted as such to all the rights, privileges and immunities of a state, on a perfect equality with the other states of the Union." The sudden death of the king had halted negotiations. And the issue lay dormant even when, as a territory starting in 1900, Hawaii had ample opportunity to learn about second-class citizenship: taxation without representation, no protection against sudden congressional abolition of all forms of self-government, Presidential appointment of a governor rather than his popular election, the inability to vote for President, and an obvious disability (despite a nonvoting Delegate to Congress) to get one's fair share of federal money for roads, conservation, harbors projects, or land-grant colleges.

Down to 1934, the leaders of Hawaii's sugar-based oligarchy generally opposed statehood, feeling they could get favorable terms for their product and advantageous concessions on the importation of Oriental labor—all without the risk of local self-government and the possible election of Orientals to office. This changed in 1934 when Congress passed a bill discriminating against Hawaii in sugar allocations; from then on it was not only the Islands' idealists but also its chief capitalists who favored statehood. There was, however, lingering opposition within the territory. Gavan Daws cites Lorrin P. Thurston, part owner of the Honolulu *Advertiser*, "whose family has never endorsed statehood wholeheartedly," and the powerful business leader Walter F. Dillingham, "who in the '40s had been sure that martial law was what the islands needed [and] was equally sure in the '50s that statehood would be a grievous error." And then there was Alice Kamokila Campbell, "an enormously wealthy part-Hawaiian [for whom] every year since the fall of the monarchy had been a bad one, and statehood would bury the past even deeper than before. The thought of a local government dominated by Orientals reduced her to something like desperation."

With historic hindsight, most of the arguments raised in Congress against Hawaiian statehood were specious cover-ups for the gut issue of race. Opposition was led chiefly by Southern Democrats who feared that two Hawaiian Senators would weaken their ability to kill civil rights bills or looked with some horror on the idea of Orientals sitting in the U.S. Senate. Senator Tom Connally of Texas, for instance, announced that he was a better American than anyone who lived in Hawaii. Senator Strom Thurmond pointed to the Oriental majority in Hawaii and suggested that the American body politic might reject it like some unassimilable alien substance. "East is East and West is West, and never the twain shall meet," Thurmond quoted Rudyard Kipling. ("Here," Gavan Daws comments, "was the old fear of the Chinese senator, with pig tail and joss stick, rising from his seat to chop logic with the great lawmakers of the nation. Thurmond wanted the apparition banished forever.")

After that, there was the issue of Communism, stemming from the power of the ILWU, Jack Hall's Smith Act conviction, and the controversy which surrounded it. Senator James Eastland said it was certain that the Islands were "tinctured with Communism." And in the House, a conservative New York Republican, John Pillion, said that giving statehood to Hawaii would be inviting "four Soviet agents to take seats in Congress." *

---

* I often wonder how a man or his family must feel when it becomes clear that on the one issue for which history remembers him, he was so abhorrently wrong.

The pro-statehood arguments, by contrast, were quite simple: It was unfair to keep levying federal taxes on the Islands without representation, and in fact there were nine states already in the Union who paid less taxes. The population of the Islands was greater than any other state on admission, except for Oklahoma. Hawaiians' per capita income was higher than that of 35 states. Its people were literate, had proven their patriotism in the crucible of war, and were ready for first-class citizenship. As for the ILWU, many of its members had fought bravely for the U.S., even in the Korean war against a Communist aggressor, and the number of actual Communists in the territory, as reported by the Justice Department, was minuscule. On the question of noncontiguity from the U.S. mainland, Hawaiians could point out that communications were instant and that when Pearl Harbor was attacked, the country had reacted as if Hawaii were indeed already a part of the Union.

Despite the overwhelming weight of arguments in its favor, Hawaiian statehood was delayed again and again in Congress. Between 1935 and 1958, it was the subject of 20 congressional hearings at which more than 1,000 witnesses appeared. It had passed the House in 1947, 1950, and 1953, only to be killed in the Senate, and it cleared the Senate in 1951 in a joint package with Alaska, only to be killed in the House.

As the problem of which territory took precedence—Alaska or Hawaii —became an increasingly serious obstacle, Delegate Burns in 1958 opted for an unorthodox maneuver: to let Alaska, even though its population and statehood credentials were not as good as Hawaii's, go first. Though his decision drew widespread criticism back home, it made sense in Washington. As Burns later explained:

> It was easier to try and justify Alaska to people. Alaska was the same as every one of the Western states—a bunch of American pioneers went up there and built a country.
> So you could go to Sam Rayburn and point out that Alaska was just like Texas—and he couldn't argue.
> But, at the time, Hawaii was different in people's minds. It had been a monarchy. Two-thirds of the population wasn't Caucasian.

So in 1958, Congress approved Alaskan statehood, and President Eisenhower happily signed the bill. In 1959, with the last serious roadblocks removed, the way was clear for the Hawaiian bill. On March 12 it passed the Senate, 76 to 15, and the next day the House, 323 to 18.

It must have been quite a day in Honolulu. Just after 9:57 A.M., Hawaii time, when the 218th deciding "aye" vote was cast for the bill, William F. Quinn, the territorial governor, went to a telephone booth adjoining the House chamber in Washington and placed a telephone call to Honolulu. At Iolani Palace, Edward E. Johnston, the acting governor, picked up the ringing telephone. Quinn gave him the news, and Johnston declared a two-day holiday. The 52 air-raid sirens on Oahu began to wail. Church bells pealed. Auto horns blew. Ships in Honolulu Harbor sounded their whistles. Mayor Neal Blaisdell began to ring the City Hall's bell and, his eyes brimming with tears, lighted a 30-foot string of firecrackers. The bells began to ring at Kawaiahao Church, and in front of City Hall, the Royal Hawaiian Band began to play "Hawaii Pono'i," the national anthem when Hawaii was an independent nation, now the state song. At the Iolani Palace, some-one put an "Out of Business" sign on the door of the Hawaii Statehood Commission.*

Later, it would be revealed that a public opinion survey taken in the Islands the year before had shown substantial sentiment against immediate statehood, apparently related to hostility toward the increasingly dominant Japanese. The percentages for statehood had been, by ethnic group: Japanese 62 percent, Chinese 44 percent, Filipinos 39 percent, Caucasians 33 percent, Hawaiians and part-Hawaiians 30 percent. But with the bill passed by Congress, almost everyone forgot any reservations and the referendum required by the federal legislation swept to approval by an astounding 17 to 1 margin.

That fall, Burns was persuaded by fellow Democrats to run for governor because of the immense appointive powers the first man to hold that office would have. Giving up almost assured election to the U.S. Senate, Burns agreed—but lost out in the general election to Quinn, a popular Republican liberal who made a major issue out of distributing public lands on a fee-simple basis to Hawaii citizens.

Jack Burns' day came in 1962 when he was able to coalesce all the ethnic and labor factions friendly to the Democratic party and win a strong victory. The Democrats have been in clear control of Hawaii ever since. The state turned in some of the country's highest Democratic Presidential percentages in 1964 and 1968, and at present writing the heads of the four island governments, the city council on each island, the two houses of the state legislature, both U.S. Representatives, the governor, and one U.S. Senator are Democratic. The sole exception is Republican Senator Hiram L. Fong, a political middle-of-the-roader now in his mid-sixties who built up a strong but essentially personal organization that permitted him to win even in the Democratic Presidential landslide year of 1964. In 1970, however, an overconfident Fong, tied too closely to Nixon administration policies for Hawaiian tastes, squeaked to a narrow victory over a virtually unknown opponent. A prominent Democrat, like liberal Representative Patsy Mink, might have defeated him.

The Democrats' dominance has been so complete that they have felt free to engage in sometimes vicious factional politics, symbolized by the unsuccessful 1970 primary challenge against Burns staged by his lieutenant governor, Thomas P. Gill. Gill's liberal and idealistic followers, including some Stevenson supporters from 1960 and McCarthyites of 1968, feel that Burns has failed to grow in office. Suspicious of the growing government-business ties, they recall what was sometimes said of the 19th-century missionaries: "They came to do good and stayed to do well." The Burns camp

---

* Account drawn from "That's How It Was, That Day in '59," by Gene Hunter, Honolulu *Star-Bulletin and Advertiser*, Aug. 17, 1969.

relies on business allies, many old Japanese allies, and not a few state government officials whose jobs depend on Burns. They consider the Gill group naive idealists and Gill himself abrasive and overly ideological.

Gill's defeat in 1970 is not likely to end the tension, since the basic issue of 1970—developer versus environmental interests—is likely to remain around for a long time. As an example, pressure from the environmentalists led Burns, during his 1970 reelection race, to set up a state Environmental Quality Control Center. But his first choice to head the center, announced after the returns were in, was a retired Air Force colonel who had previously attacked conservationists as "instant ecologists." Gill himself remains active in public life as the head of a citizens' lobby. And a new organization, called "Life of the Land," has filed numerous lawsuits to force the state of Hawaii to enforce its own environmental protection laws. It is headed by Tony Hodges, a 30-year-old former airline pilot who ran a surprisingly strong though losing primary campaign for the U.S. Senate in 1970, stressing the ecology issue.

There is great doubt on the Islands about the ability of the Republicans, within a foreseeable future, to capitalize fully on the Democratic divisions. A tremendous disability of the GOP is its continuing image as the "Haole-Big Five" party, harking back to the socially restrictive plantation economy days. Many Hawaiians—and especially the electorally potent Japanese segment of the population—consider the GOP simply out of step with the labor and social revolution that has swept the Islands. The image problem is similar to that of the national Republican party for years after the Depression and coming of the New Deal. On the officeholder level, the Republicans are now relatively well diversified among the Islands' ethnic groups. But, as former Mayor Blaisdell puts it, "When I look around a GOP state convention, the majority of faces are Caucasians—and the same old faces, too." (Something of a new day may be dawning. Mrs. Carla Coray, elected state Republican chairman in 1971, said 70 percent of the Islands' Republicans were actually non-*haole* and that her first job would be to change the "rich *haole*" or "plantation party" image carefully fostered by the Democrats.)

In addition to its respectable old *haole* group, the GOP has a small and vociferous right-wing fringe and also a liberal-to-moderate group in which former Governor Quinn should actually be numbered. Quinn tried to develop a progressive program but was viciously undercut by his own lieutenant governor, and the party pays little heed to him today. (Quinn has done all right personally, however, as president of Dole Pineapple; he has also allowed himself an expression of personal freedom rare among ex-governors and great corporation chieftains: he wears a beard.) There are some aggressive younger Republicans, who under the right conditions could turn their party into an instrument of strong social action on the Islands. Among these is Fred Rohlfing, Republican policy leader in the state senate, who charges that "the Democrats have become the party of the vested interests and the status quo." But getting more Republicans elected will be a problem.

In a 1970 Honolulu *Star-Bulletin* poll, 55.2 percent of a statewide sampling called themselves Democrats, only 27.6 percent Republican. (The remaining 17.2 percent had no party preference.) In terms of actual registration, there are 134,000 Democrats, 120,000 independents, and only 37,000 Republicans. At the Republicans' 1971 state convention, Senator Fong lamented that his party had "gone down in ignominious defeat, election after election" and was at a "nadir or low point in political life in Hawaii." In 1970, he pointed out, only two state Republican parties—those in Louisiana and Mississippi—polled a lower percentage of GOP vote for Congress.

The new ingredient in Hawaiian politics that has everyone fascinated and worried is the mainland immigrants, a bigger segment with each election. The newcomers, or *malihini* in the Hawaiian language, are mostly uncommitted in politics, although there are some radical conservatives and a few ultraliberals in the bunch. As a group, they are likely to find the existing business and political power structure in Hawaii quite confining. What they decide to do in politics could make the difference in the years to come.

For all the talk of political groups, it should be remembered that Hawaii is still a small state, where personal loyalties and antipathies are strong. Ticket-splitting on election day requires no wrench of conscience. The differences within the parties are often as great as those between them. Yet despite the confusion, it is a conscientious electorate, turning out one of the highest percentages of eligible voters among all states. Those voters do not, by most accounts, do much "plunking" (ethnic bloc voting). Among other Hawaiian oddities one can count the 20-year vote approved at the time of statehood (now superceded by the national 18-year-old vote), the latest regular primary election day in the U.S. (the first week in October), and standby authority the legislature now has to enact a Presidential primary law.

## The Most Progressive State?

Finally, a word about the constitution and laws of the Aloha state. Under the very modern constitution that went into effect with statehood, the Islands have perhaps the most centralized government among all the 50 states. In function after function, the lines of responsibility and direction run directly into the State Capitol. The only elected statewide officials are the governor and lieutenant governor (who run together as a team) and the members of the state board of education. In territorial days there had been 104 separate departments, boards, and commissions; in 1959 the new constitution pared the number down to 20, their heads appointed by and responsible to the governor.

The taxing and spending authority is also heavily centralized in the state government, which by one reading in the late 1960s was financing 76 percent of all state and local expenditures in Hawaii, compared to an average of only 51 percent by state governments across the country. The Islanders pay heavily for the kind of government they seem to prefer. Not only must they pay a heavy and steeply graduated personal and corporate income tax, but there is a 4 percent sales tax, called the most broad-based in the nation because it excludes virtually nothing—neither food nor hotel rooms nor agricultural supplies nor industrial equipment. Per capita state government tax revenue ranks first among all states, and the state is third in "tax effort"—combined state and local taxation in relation to personal income. In 1971 the state moved to a planning-program budget in which all appropriations are by program areas rather than by agencies.

Perhaps the most dramatic illustration of Hawaii's centralized government is the school system. Instead of the customary multiplicity of school boards and districts—of which there are still some 22,000 on the mainland—Hawaii has a single, unitary statewide school district. All 215 schools and 180,000 pupils are under the same financing, the same board of education, the same superintendent of education. No child's opportunity to learn depends on whether he lives in a rich or poor community, since all schools are equally funded on a per capita basis. For the same reason, no sullen taxpayer or eroding local tax base can suddenly undermine one of the schools. There is a price to pay, of course: the loss of local control, since community school councils have advisory powers only. Sometimes teachers quarrel about being assigned to remote spots on the Neighbor Islands. But through its unitary state financing and direction, Hawaii has given its schools a stability and manageability that could be the envy of any mainland state. This interest in basic education is matched by one of culture; in fact, Hawaii's state arts council is budgeted for more per capita than that of any other state.

Another Hawaiian breakthrough in the art of government is the statewide land-use classification and greenbelt program, enforced by a statewide zoning board, which was enacted by the legislature in 1961. In that year, former Governor Quinn recalls, the National Governors' Conference met in Honolulu with planning as a chief theme. The Hawaii plan was the envy of many other governors, who went home with hopes of enacting it in their states. By 1970, however, no other state had gone as far as Hawaii. The state land-use commission (or zoning board) sets boundaries for three principal districts to cover all the territory in the Islands—urban, agricultural and conservation. Within each district, the counties continue their normal zoning procedures, but all decisions must coincide with the master state plan.

Like all good ideas, statewide zoning can be open to abuse. The way to overnight fortune in Hawaii, it is reported, is to get the members of the land-use commission to rezone agricultural land for residential use. And in 1970 the Honolulu *Star-Bulletin* and *Advertiser* ran stories charging several members of the commission, all of whose members were appointed by Governor Burns, of making decisions that could or did accrue to their own personal profit in land transactions.

Late in the 1960s Hawaii tried another innovative approach in government by creating the office of a statewide ombudsman—just 160 years after Sweden had hit upon the idea of a single officer to handle complaints and prevent abuses by public officials and agencies. Here one would have to say the Japanese are really coming of age politically in Hawaii. The idea of an Hawaii ombudsman came originally from state senator Duke T. Kawasaki. The man the legislature picked to fill the post first was Herman S. Doi, a third-generation Japanese who had graduated from the University of Minnesota Law School, served as a chief clerk for two legislative committees, been a legal consultant in the process of changing Hawaii from territory to state, and directed the state legislative reference bureau for three years before his appointment.

Just before he started his job in 1969, Doi made a visit to Sweden, Norway, Denmark, and Finland to interview other ombudsmen and find out about the challenges of his job. Then he went to work, handling every imaginable request and complaint in fields including transportation, labor, taxation, health matters, the school system, police abuses—the list seems almost infinite. What makes the Hawaii ombudsman program so impressive is the independence and power given the office. The ombudsman is appointed by the legislature in joint session but then is substantially free of influence even from that sector since his term runs for six years (twice renewable) and he can be removed from office only by a two-thirds vote of the legislature, and then only for neglect of duty, misconduct, or disability. He has the right to go into any state or county government office—excepting only the governor's office, the courts, and the legislature—and demand records and information. He can hold hearings, issue subpoenas, and cause $1,000 fines to be imposed on those who resist his information-gathering activities.

Whether the Hawaii ombudsman experiment would eventually bear out the hope of its sponsors—to provide a last resort to the average citizen struck voiceless by a monstrous and deaf bureaucracy—remained to be seen, but the first years of operation were encouraging. One important source of query referrals, it turned out, were state legislators themselves, a seeming rebuttal to arguments that legislatures would never accept an ombudsman for fear of eclipsing their own political gain from errand running for constituents.

Hawaii has also created an office of legislative auditor, with wide powers to probe the financing, performance, and planning of the state bureaucracy. He and the ombudsman are sometimes referred to around the capitol as "the third house." On a similar plane, the legislature also set up an office of consumer protection, which has wide powers to cope with unscrupulous types who prey on consumers. Each week, a governmentally authorized consumers' food price survey is released, naming and rating Hawaii food markets for price values on various foods. Under another law, tenants in substandard rental units may get emergency repairs done to fix health-threatening defects like poor plumbing and deduct the cost from their rent if the landlord is not willing to undertake the repair himself in the first place. A person injured by a crime or while trying to prevent one can claim injury compensation of up to $10,000 from the state. But there are limits to Hawaii's governmental generosity. In 1971 the legislature set up a one-year residency requirement for welfare recipients to discourage thousands of young people coming in search of a state-supported holiday on the Islands. Lieutenant Governor Ariyoshi said the bill was needed to stop "welfare hippies . . . who have been flocking to our shores in search of the nearest social welfare office."

Abortion reform joined the list of Hawaii firsts in February 1970 as the legislature passed a bill removing all restrictions save two—that abortions be performed by licensed physicians in licensed hospitals, and that they be performed only on women with 90 days' residence in Hawaii. The law was easily the country's most permissive when it was passed. It was vigorously and bitterly fought by the Roman Catholic Church. But the bill's sponsor, Senator Vincent H. Yano, a father of 10, was a Roman Catholic. And Governor Burns, a Catholic, withstood church pressure to veto the bill and let it become law without his signature—even though he was known to be personally opposed and in earlier years had refused an abortion for his polio-stricken wife, even when doctors told him that she might die if she did not have an abortion. (In time the child was born, quite healthy, and Mrs. Burns survived.)

In 1971 the state took an intelligent step toward prevention of un-wanted births by requiring that each applicant for a marriage license be given information on family planning. Consideration was also given to a new criminal code which would legalize, except for prostitution, all forms of sex performed privately between consenting adults—an idea, Wallace Turner of the New York *Times* noted, that would scandalize "the missionaries who put lithesome brown girls into mumuus." But the new code, which would also reduce drastically the penalties for possession of marijuana, did not receive final approval.

What are the forces within Hawaii's legislature propelling it to such liberal and controversial laws? One factor may be the reapportionment of the 1960s, which shifted control from the conservative Neighbor Islands to more liberal Oahu. Related to this may be the liberal outlook of Japanese legislators, who make up about half of each chamber. Having just "arrived," and with fewer vested positions to defend, the Japanese have decided to make their mark with a program that will make Hawaii a model of progressive legislation. Many *haole* and old Hawaiian and other Oriental groups are supporting a number of the new ideas, of course, but the fact remains that the basic impetus is Japanese. Thus it happens, in one of those odd quirks of history, that the very group so darkly depicted a few years ago as incapable of democratic self-government, once having gained power, is building one of the most brilliant and imaginative records of legislators anywhere in the American Union.

# ACKNOWLEDGMENTS

THESE BOOKS had to be, by their very character, a personal odyssey and personal task. But they would never have been possible without the kind assistance of hundreds of people. First there were those who encouraged me to go forward when the idea was first conceived: my wife Barbara (little imagining the long curtailments of family life that would ensue, and whose encouragement was vital throughout); my parents and other relatives; my editor, Evan W. Thomas, vice president and editor of W. W. Norton & Co.; John Gunther; my agent, Sterling Lord, and his assistant at that time, Jonathan Walton; Richard Kluger, editor of my first book, *The People's President;* writer Roan Conrad; editor Joseph Foote (who would later help with many other aspects of the book); William B. Dickinson, editor of *Editorial Research Reports;* Thomas Schroth, then the editor, and Nelson Poynter, publisher of *Congressional Quarterly;* author Michael Amrine and his wife Rene; Richard M. Scammon, director of the Elections Research Center and coauthor of *The Real Majority;* and D. B. Hardeman, professor of political science and biographer of the late House Speaker Sam Rayburn. Later on, those who encouraged or helped me to keep the project moving included F. Randall Smith and Anthony C. Stout of the Center for Political Research; author David Wise; columnist-reporters Bruce Biossat and David S. Broder; and Bernard Haldane. A year's fellowship at the Woodrow Wilson International Center for Scholars provided intellectual and physical sustenance toward the end of the project.

My very warmest thanks go to those who read the draft manuscript in its entirety: Evan W. Thomas; Russell L. Bradley; Jean Allaway; Frederick H. Sontag, public relations consultant of Montclair, N.J.; Kay Gauss Jackson, former critic for *Harper's Magazine;* Donald Kummerfeld of the Center for Political Research; and copy editor Calvin Towle at W. W. Norton & Co. In addition, each of the state chapters was submitted to several persons living in, and having extensive knowledge of, the state in question. The returning corrections and amendments were immensely helpful. The names of those readers appear in the longer list of names below; I choose not to list them here lest someone hold them responsible for something said or unsaid in one of the chapters, and of course the full responsibility for that lies with me.

Various friends and associates helped with many of the details of research, and for that I am especially indebted to Oliver Cromwell, Ursula Lange, Monica and Jason Benderly, Barbara Hurlbutt, Richard Baker, Nancy Nelson, Edith Sontag, James Mulligan, and John Gibson. And without the cheery and efficient services of my typist, Merciel Dixon, the manuscript would never have seen the light of day at all. Rose Franco of W. W. Norton helped in innumerable ways; I am indebted to designer Marjorie Flock of the Norton organization; and credit goes to Russell Lenz, chief cartographer of the *Christian Science Monitor,* for what I feel is the superb job he did on the state and city maps for this book.

Across the country, people gave generously of their time to brief me on the developments of the past several years in their states and cities. I am listing those from the five Pacific states below, together with many people who helped with national and interstate themes. The names of some officials are included whom I had interviewed in the year or two prior to beginning work on this project, when the background from those interviews proved helpful with this book. To all, my warmest thanks.

## PERSONS INTERVIEWED

*Affiliations of interviewees are as of time of author's interview with them.*

ARNOLD, Robert, Development Consultant and former Staff Member, Federal Field Committee for Development Planning in Alaska, Anchorage, Alaska

ATWOOD, Robert, Publisher, Anchorage *Daily Times,* Anchorage, Alaska

BAILEY, Philip W., Publisher, *Argus,* Seattle, Wash.

BAKER, Miner H., Vice President and Economist, Seattle First National Bank, Seattle, Wash.

BARABBA, Vincent, Chairman of the Board, Decision Making Information, Los Angeles, Calif.

BARKDULL, Walter, California Human Relations Agency, Sacramento, Calif.

BASSETT, James, Director, Editoral Pages, Los Angeles *Times,* Los Angeles, Calif.

BASSETTI, Fred, Architect, Seattle, Wash.

BENDERLY, Jason, Economist, Economic Development Administration, Washington, D.C.

BERGHOLZ, Richard, Political Editor, Los Angeles *Times,* Los Angeles, Calif.

BIOSSAT, Bruce, National Correspondent, Newspaper Enterprise Association, Washington, D.C.

BLAISDELL, Neal S., Former Mayor, Honolulu, Hawaii

BOWMAN, Willard L., Executive Director, Alaska Commission for Human Rights, Anchorage, Alaska

BOYD, William J.D., Assistant Director, National Municipal League, New York City

BRENNE, Fred, Former Secretary-Manager, Eugene Chamber of Commerce, Eugene, Ore.

BRODER, David S., Correspondent and Columnist, Washington *Post,* Washington, D.C.

BROWNE, James, Community Relations Officer, Bay Area Rapid Transit District, San Francisco, Calif.

BUNDY, McGeorge, President, The Ford Foundation, New York City

BURBY, John F., Editor, *National Journal,* Washington, D.C.

BURNS, John A., Governor of Hawaii

BURTON, Phillip, U.S. Representative from California

CAHILL, Thomas J., Chief of Police, San Francisco, Calif.

CANNON, Lou, Correspondent, Ridder Newspapers, Washington, D.C.

CARPENTER, Richard, Executive Director, League of California Cities, Sacramento, Calif.

CASSELLA, William N., Jr., Executive Director, National Municipal League, New York City

CAVANAGH, C.J., Executive President, Chamber of Commerce, Honolulu, Hawaii

CHANCE, Mrs. Ruth, The Rosenberg Foundation, San Francisco, Calif.

CHANDLER, OTIS, Publisher, Los Angeles *Times,* Los Angeles, Calif.

CHAPLIN, George, Editor, Honolulu *Advertiser,* Honolulu, Hawaii

CHAPMAN, Bruce K., City Councilman, Seattle, Wash.

CHÁVEZ, César, Director, United Farm Workers Organizing Committee, Delano, Calif.

CLARK, Irving, Jr., Attorney and Commentator for Radio Station KING, Seattle, Wash.

CLARK, Judson, California Research Associates, Sacramento, Calif.

CONWAY, Jack, Director, Center for Community Change, Washington, D.C.

COUGHLIN, Dan, Business Editor, Seattle *Post-Intelligencer,* Seattle, Wash.

COURTNAGE, Clyde, U.S. Economic Development Administration, Anchorage, Alaska

COWLES, Ralph, U.S. Economic Development Administration, Anchorage, Alaska

CROSS, Malcolm, Office of Rep. Edith Green (Ore.)

CROSS, Travis, Vice President—University Relations, University of California, Berkeley, Calif.

DAVIS, Joseph, President, Washington State Labor Council, AFL-CIO, Seattle, Wash.

DAY, Anthony, Editorial Page Editor, Los Angeles *Times,* Los Angeles, Calif.

DEINEMA, J. W., Regional Forester, U.S. Forestry Service, USDA, San Francisco, Calif.

DEMORO, Harre, Transportation Reporter, Oakland *Tribune,* Oakland, Calif.

DEVLIN, Dan, Inspector, San Francisco Police Department, San Francisco, Calif.

DIRKER, W. S., Manager, Special Projects Dept., Port of Portland (Ore.)

DISTEFANO, Robert, Correspondent, Oakland *Tribune,* Oakland, Calif.

DODDS, William, Political Director, United Auto Workers, Washington, D.C.

DOERR, David, Committee Coordinator, Assembly Committee on Revenue & Taxation, Sacramento, Calif.

DROEGE, Richard, Deputy Chief for Administration, U.S. Forest Service, Washington, D.C.

DYMALLY, Mervyn, State Senator, Los Angeles, Calif.

DYSART, Keith, Office of Attorney General Slade Gorton, Olympia, Wash.

EAMES, William, News Director, KNXT-TV, Los Angeles, Calif.

ELLIS, James R., Attorney and Chairman of "Forward Thrust," Seattle, Wash.

EVANS, Daniel J., Governor of Washington

FASI, Frank, Mayor, Honolulu, Hawaii

FELTON, David, Correspondent, Los Angeles *Times,* Los Angeles, Calif.

FISCHER, Victor, Director, Institute of Social, Economic and Government Research, University of Alaska, College, Alaska

FOLEY, Thomas S., U.S. Representative from Washington

FONG, Hiram, U.S. Senator from Hawaii

FOOTE, Joseph, Author, Washington, D.C.

FREEDMAN, Marvin, County of Los Angeles—Dept. of Public Social Services, Commerce, Calif.

FREEMAN, David, Executive Director, Council on Foundations, New York City

GALLEGOS, Herman E., Executive Director, Southwest Council on La Raza, San Francisco, Calif.

GIUGNI, Henry K., Administrative Assistant, Office of Senator Daniel Inouye (Hawaii)

GOLDMARK, John, Attorney and Civic Leader, Seattle, Wash.

GOLDSCHMIDT, Neil, CEP Staff Attorney, Legal Aid Service, Portland, Ore.

GOODWIN, Alfred T., Justice, Supreme Court of Oregon, Salem, Ore.

GORTON, Slade, Attorney General of Washington, Olympia, Washington

GRANT, William A., Assistant Director, Oahu Development Conference, Honolulu, Hawaii

GREENBERG, Carl, Political Editor, Los Angeles *Times,* Los Angeles, Calif.

GUNTHER, John, Author, New York City (deceased)

GUNTHER, John, U.S. Conference of Mayors, Washington, D.C.

HAGGART, Richard, Center for Political Research, Washington, D.C.

HALL, Camden, Attorney, President of CHECC, Seattle, Wash.

HAMILTON, Calvin S., Director, Department of City Planning, Los Angeles, Calif.

HARDING, Kenneth, Executive Director, House Democratic Congressional Committee, Washington, D.C.

HARRIS, Louis, Louis Harris & Associates, New York City

HAYDON, John, Publisher, *The Marine Digest,* Seattle, Wash.

HEREFORD, Peggy G., Public Relations Director, City of Los Angeles, Department of Airports, Los Angeles, Calif.

HICKOK, D. M., Acting Director, Federal Field Committee for Development Planning in Alaska, Anchorage, Alaska

HORN, Stephen, President, California State College, Long Beach, Calif.

HOYT, Charles, Managing Editor, Fairbanks *Daily News-Miner,* Fairbanks, Alaska

HUGHES, Harold, Associate Editor, *The Oregonian,* Portland, Ore.

IKARD, Frank, President, American Petroleum Institute, Washington, D.C.

JACKSON, Glenn L., Chairman of the Board, Pacific Power & Light Company, Portland, Ore.

JAMES, Dave, Vice President—Public Affairs, Simpson Timber Company, Seattle, Wash.

JOHNSON, C. Montgomery, Republican State Chairman, Seattle, Wash.

JONES, Carlisle, Director of Public Affairs, Aerospace Industries Association, Washington, D.C.

JONES, Gardiner B., Associate Editor, Honolulu *Advertiser,* Honolulu, Hawaii

JOSEPHSON, Joe, State Senator, Anchorage, Alaska

KAYE, Peter, News & Public Affairs, KEBS-TV, San Diego, Calif.

KAWASAKI, Duke T., State Senator, Honolulu, Hawaii

KIMBALL, The Hon. Dan. A., Aerojet-General Corporation, El Monte, Calif. (deceased)

KIRKLAND, Lane, Secretary-Treasurer, AFL-CIO, Washington, D.C.

KNEALLY, Don, Inspector, San Francisco Police Department, San Francisco, Calif.

KUMMERFELD, Donald D., Director of Research, Center for Political Research, Washington, D.C.

KUNKIN, Art, Publisher & Editor, Los Angeles *Free Press,* Los Angeles, Calif.

KUSSEROW, Hank, San Francisco *Examiner,* San Francisco, Calif.

LEE, Eric, Legislative Assistant, Office of Senator Daniel Inouye (Hawaii)

LEE, Philip R., M.D., Assistant Secretary for Health and Scientific Affairs, Department of Health, Education and Welfare, Washington, D.C.

LESACA, Reynaldo M., Commissioner, National Water and Air Pollution Commission, Republic of the Philippines

LIPPER, J. J., Corporate Director, Public Communications, Aerojet-General Corporation, El Monte, Calif.

LOORY, Stuart, Correspondent, Los Angeles *Times,* Washington, D.C.

LUNDY, Herbert, Editor, Editorial Page, *The Oregonian,* Portland, Ore.

MacNAUGHTON, Malcolm, President, Castle & Cooke, Inc., Honolulu, Hawaii

MANLEY, John E., General Manager, The Alaska Railroad, Anchorage, Alaska

MARGOLIS, Larry, Executive Director, Citizens Conference on State Legislatures, Kansas City, Mo.

MARQUARDT, Roy, Former President, The Marquardt Corporation, Malibu, Calif.

MARTIN, Louis, *The Defender,* Chicago, Ill., (Former Deputy Director for Minority Affairs, Democratic National Committee)

McCLUNG, David C., State Senate President and Democratic State Chairman, Honolulu, Hawaii

McCOLLUM, A. James, Manager, Advertising and Publicity Dept., Pacific Gas & Electric Company, San Francisco, Calif.

McELRATH, Robert, Regional Director, International Longshoremen's and Warehousemen's Union, Honolulu, Hawaii

McGRATH, Thomas H., Assistant Executive Vice Chancellor, The California State Colleges, Los Angeles, Calif.

McKAY, Floyd, News Analyst, KGW-TV, Portland, Ore.

McLAREN, John, Legislative Assistant, Office of Rep. Lionel Van Deerlin (Calif.)

McMANNIS, Larry, Office of State Senate President David C. Clung, Honolulu, Hawaii

McREADY, Albert L., Editorial Page, *The Oregonian,* Portland, Ore.

MICHAEL, Jay, Special Assistant to the President, University of California, Sacramento, Calif.

MILLER, Bob, Political Writer, Anchorage *Daily Times,* Anchorage, Alaska

MINK, Patsy, U.S. Representative from Hawaii

MORGAN, Neil, Author and Columnist for the San Diego *Evening Tribune,* San Diego, Calif.

MORSE, Peter, Author and Composer, Waipahu, Hawaii

MUCHMORE, Don, Opinion Research of California, Long Beach, Calif.

MUNRO, S. Sterling, Jr., Administrative Assistant, Office of Sen. Henry M. Jackson (Washington)

NARVER, John, Professor, School of Business Administration, University of Washington, Seattle, Wash.

NEUMAN, Robert, Legislative Assistant, Office of Rep. Jerome R. Waldie (Calif.)

NEWPORT, Tuck, Press Assistant, Office of Senator Daniel Inouye, Hawaii

NORRIS, Judy, Anchorage Native Welcome Center, Anchorage, Alaska

NORRIS, William, Attorney, Los Angeles, Calif.

NORWOOD, Gus, Administrator, Alaska Power Commission, Dept. of the Interior, Juneau, Alaska

PACKWOOD, Robert W., U.S. Senator from Oregon

PASCAL, Anthony, Director of Human Resource Studies, RAND Corp., Santa Monica, Calif.

PHILLIPS, Brad, President, Alaska State Senate, Anchorage, Alaska

PINCUS, John, Director, California Program, RAND Corp., Santa Monica, Calif.

POLLARD, Joseph M., Washington Representative for Los Angeles (Calif.) County Government

POTTER, Todd, Director, Bureau of Employment Security, Department of Labor, Washington, D.C.

QUINN, Louis, Louis Quinn & Associates, Los Angeles, Calif.

RAMO, Dr. Simon, Vice Chairman of the Board, TRW, Inc., Beverly Hills, Calif.

RASMUSON, E. E., Chairman of the Board, National Bank of Alaska, Anchorage, Alaska

REES, Ed, Regional Director, Corporate Communications, TRW, Inc., Los Angeles, Calif.

REES, Thomas, U.S. Representative from California.

RICHARDS, Mr. and Mrs. Lawrence, Los Angeles, Calif.

RICHARDS, Tom, Correspondent, *The Tundra Times,* Fairbanks, Alaska

RILEY, Burke, Bureau of Land Management, Department of the Interior, Washington, D.C.

ROBERTS, Dr. Ernest R., Aerojet-General Corporation, El Monte, Calif.

ROCK, Howard, Editor, *The Tundra Times,* Fairbanks, Alaska

RODDA, Richard, Correspondent, Sacramento *Bee,* Sacramento, Calif.

ROHLFING, Fred W., State Senator, Honolulu, Hawaii

RUTLEDGE, Arthur, President, Hawaii Teamsters & Hotel, Restaurant Employees and Bartenders' Union, Local 5, Honolulu, Hawaii

SALTER, John L., Public Relations, former aide to Sen. Henry Jackson, Seattle, Wash.

SCAMMON, Richard M., Director, Elections Research Institute, and Former Director of the Census, Washington, D.C.

SCATES, Shelby, Correspondent, Seattle *Post-Intelligencer,* Seattle, Wash.

SCHRADE, Paul, Director, Region 6, United Auto Workers, Los Angeles, Calif.

SEID, Marvin, Editorial Writer, The Los Angeles *Times,* Los Angeles, Calif.

SENUNGETUK, Ronald, Associate Professor of Art, University of Alaska, College, Alaska

SHORT, Robert H., Vice President, Portland General Electric Company, Portland, Ore.

SMITH, A. Robert, Washington Correspondent, Portland *Oregonian, Argus,* and other Western papers

SMYSER, A. A., Editor, Honolulu *Star Bulletin,* Honolulu, Hawaii

SNEDDEN, C. W., Publisher, Fairbanks *Daily News-Miner,* Fairbanks, Alaska

SONTAG, Frederick H., Public Relations Consultant, Montclair, N.J.

SPENCER, Murlin, Executive Editor, Fairbanks *Daily News-Miner,* Fairbanks, Alaska

SPENCER, Stuart, Spencer-Roberts Associates, Los Angeles, Calif.

STOKES, B. R., General Manager, Bay Area Rapid Transit District, San Francisco, Calif.

SULLIVAN, George, Mayor of Anchorage, Alaska

TANGEN, Eddie, International Longshoremen's and Warehousemen's Union, Honolulu, Hawaii

TAYLOR, H. Ralph, Assistant Secretary for Demonstrations and Intergovernmental Relations, Department of Housing and Urban Development, Washington, D.C.

THIES, Stanton, W., Deputy Director of Information, Bay Area Rapid Transit District, San Francisco, Calif.

TODD, A. Ruric, Manager, Governmental and Political Affairs, Pacific Gas & Electric Co., San Francisco, Calif.

TWIGG-SMITH, Thurston, Publisher, Honolulu *Advertiser,* Honolulu, Hawaii

UNRUH, Jesse, Former Speaker, California Assembly, Inglewood, Calif.

VAN DEERLIN, Lionel, U.S. Representative from California

VAUGHAN, Mr. & Mrs. Samuel, Atherton, Calif.

VINSON, Fred, Jr., Assistant Attorney General, Criminal Division, Department of Justice, Washington, D.C.

VESTAL, Harvey, President, Northwest Native Association, Kotzebue, Alaska

VOEGEL, Elmer, C., News Bureau Manager, Boeing Company—Headquarters Office, Seattle, Wash.

von HOLT, Herman V., Chairman of the Board, First Hawaiian Bank, Honolulu, Hawaii

VORIS, Ed, Washington Democratic Council, Edmonds, Wash.

WALSH, Pearse M., Regional Sales Manager, Alaska Airlines, Nome, Alaska

WALTERS, Robert G., Assistant to the Secretary, California Human Relations Agency, Sacramento, Calif.

WASHBURN, Dr. C. L., Higher Education Specialist, California Council for Higher Education, Sacramento, Calif.

WEBB, Mayfield K., President, The Albina Corporation, Portland, Ore.

WEINBERG, Edward, Attorney and former Deputy Solicitor, Department of the Interior, Washington, D.C.

WILLARD, Robert, Alaska Commission for Human Rights, Anchorage, Alaska

WILLIAMS, Spencer, Secretary, California Human Relations Agency, Sacramento, Calif.

WIRTHLIN, Richard, Decision Making Information, Los Angeles, Calif.

WOODS, Leon, Vice President & General Manager, Watts Manufacturing Co., Compton, Calif.

YELLEN, Ben, M.D., Brawley (Imperial Valley), Calif.

ZELNICK, C. Robert, Anchorage *Daily Times* Columnist, Washington, D.C.

# BIBLIOGRAPHY

Despite the extensive interviews for these books, reference was also made to books and articles on the individual states and cities, their history and present-day condition. To the authors whose works I have drawn upon, my sincerest thanks.

## NATIONAL BOOKS

*Automobile Facts and Figures, 1971.* Automobile Manufacturers Assn., Detroit, 1971.

Barrett, Marvin, ed. *Survey of Broadcast Journalism, 1968–69 and 1969–70* (sponsored by Alfred I. duPont and Columbia University). New York: Grosset & Dunlap, 1969, 1970.

Birmingham, Stephen. *The Right People—A Portrait of the American Social Establishment.* Boston: Little Brown, 1968.

*Book of the States, 1968–69.* The Council of State Governments, Chicago, 1968.

Brownson, Charles B. *Congressional Staff Directory.* Published annually, Washington, D.C.

*The Capitol and the Campus—State Responsibility for Postsecondary Education.* Report and Recommendation by the Carnegie Commission on Higher Education. New York: McGraw-Hill, 1971.

*1969 Census of Agriculture.* Bureau of the Census, Washington, D.C.

*1970 Census of Population.* Bureau of the Census, Washington, D.C.

Citizens Conference on State Legislatures. Various studies including *The Sometime Governments: A Critical Study of the 50 American Legislatures,* by John Burns. New York: Bantam Books, 1971.

*Congress and the Nation, 1945–64,* and Vol. II, *1965–68.* Congressional Quarterly Service, Washington, D.C., 1967 and 1969.

*Editor and Publisher International Year Book—1971.* Editor and Publisher, New York, 1971.

*Employment and Earnings—States and Areas, 1939–69.* U. S. Department of Labor, Bureau of Labor Statistics, Washington, D.C., 1970.

*Encyclopedia Americana,* 1969 Edition. New York: Americana Corporation. (Includes excellent state and city review articles.)

Farb, Peter. *Face of North America—The Natural History of a Continent.* New York: Harper & Row, 1963.

*Fodor-Shell Travel Guides U.S.A.* Fodor's Modern Guides, Inc., Litchfield, Conn., 1966, 1967. (In several regional editions, the best of the travel guides.)

*From Sea to Shining Sea—A Report on the American Environment—Our Natural Heritage.* President's Council on Recreation and Natural Beauty, Washington, D.C., 1968.

Gunther, John. *Inside U.S.A.* New York: Harper & Row, 1947 and 1951.

Hess, Stephen, and Broder, David S. *The Republican Establishment—The Present and Future of the G.O.P.* New York: Harper & Row, 1967.

Jacobs, Jane. *The Economy of Cities.* New York: Random House, 1969.

*Life Pictorial Atlas of the World.* Editors of *Life* and Rand McNally. New York: Time Inc., 1961.

Lundberg, Ferdinand. *The Rich and the Super-Rich.* New York: Lyle Stuart, 1968.

*Man . . . An Endangered Species?* U. S. Department of the Interior Conservation Yearbook, Washington, D.C., 1968.

Marine, Gene. *America the Raped—The Engineering Mentality and Devastation of a Continent.* New York: Simon & Schuster, 1969.

*The National Atlas of the United States of America.* Geological Survey, U. S. Department of the Interior, Washington, D.C., 1970.

Pearson, Drew, and Anderson, Jack. *The Case Against Congress.* New York: Simon & Schuster, 1968.

Phillips, Kevin H. *The Emerging Republican Majority.* New Rochelle, N.Y.: Arlington House, 1969.

*Presidential Nominating Conventions—1968.* Congressional Quarterly Service, Washington, D.C., 1968.

*Rankings of the States, 1971.* Research Division, National Education Assn., Washington, D.C., 1971.

*Report of the National Advisory Commission on Civil Disorders,* Washington, D.C., 1968.

Ridgeway, James. *The Closed Corporation—American Universities In Crisis.* New York: Random House, 1968.

Saloma, John S., III, and Sontag, Frederick H.

*Parties: The Real Opportunity for Effective Citizen Politics.* New York: Knopf, 1972.

Scammon, Richard M., ed. *America Votes—A Handbook of Contemporary American Election Statistics.* Published biennially by the Governmental Affairs Institute, through Congressional Quarterly, Washington, D.C.

Scammon, Richard M., and Wattenberg, Ben J. *The Real Majority—An Extraordinary Examination of the American Electorate.* New York: Coward-McCann, 1970.

*State-Local Finances and Suggested Legislation, 1971 Edition.* Advisory Commission on Intergovernmental Relations, Washington, D.C., December 1970.

*State Government Finances in 1969.* U. S. Department of Commerce, Bureau of the Census, Washington, D.C., June 1970.

*Statistical Abstract of the United States, 1971.* U. S. Department of Commerce, Bureau of the Census, Washington, D.C., 1971.

Steinbeck, John. *Travels With Charley—In Search of America.* New York: Viking, 1961.

Steiner, Stan. *La Raza—The Mexican-Americans.* New York: Harper & Row, 1969.

*Survey of Current Business.* U. S. Department of Commerce, Office of Business Economics, Washington, D.C., monthly. August editions contain full reports on geographic trends in personal income and per capita income.

Thayer, George. *The Farther Shores of Politics.* New York: Simon & Schuster, 1967.

*These United States—Our Nation's Geography, History and People.* Reader's Digest Assn., Pleasantville, N.Y., 1968.

*Tour Books, 1970–71.* American Automobile Assn., Washington, D.C., 1970.

Trippett, Frank. *The States: United They Fell.* New York: World, 1967.

*Uniform Crime Reports for the United States, 1969.* U. S. Department of Justice, Federal Bureau of Investigation, Washington, D.C., 1970.

Von Eckardt, Wolf. *A Place To Live—The Crisis of the Cities.* New York: Delacorte, 1967.

White, Theodore H. *The Making of the President, 1960, 1964, 1968.* New York: Atheneum, 1961, 1965, 1969.

Whyte, William H. *The Last Landscape.* Garden City, N.Y.: Doubleday, 1968.

Williams, Joe B. *U. S. Statistical Atlas.* Elmwood, Neb., 1969.

*The World Almanac and Book of Facts.* Published annually by Newspaper Enterprise Assn., Inc., New York and Cleveland.

## REGIONAL BOOKS AND SOURCES

Among the first informative books covering parts or all of the Pacific states region are two in the Time-Life Library of America series—*The Pacific States,* by Neil Morgan, and *The Frontier States,* by Richard Austin Smith (New York: Time-Life Books, 1967, 1968). There are informative chapters on each state and regional summaries in *Politics in the American West,* ed. Frank H. Jonas, (Salt Lake City: University of Utah Press, 1969). Reference was also made to Neil Morgan's *Westward Tilt—The American West Today* (New York: Random House, 1961). Other sources consulted for the regional introduction included: "Cross-Flow of Capital Is Creating Phenomenal Growth in Pacific," *Pacific Business News,* May 22, 1969; statistical publications of the Aerospace Industries Association; "Hawaii and Alaska Map Plans to Help Each Other," by Barbara J. Fox, *Christian Science Monitor,* Nov. 26, 1969; "The 49th and the 50th," by James H. Shoemaker, Honolulu *Star Bulletin,* Nov. 6, 1969; "Hawaii as Heart of Giant Pacific State Proposed," Honolulu *Star-Bulletin,* Dec. 12, 1969 (based on article by Ernest Gruening in *The Nation,* Dec. 15, 1969); "Pawn in the Pacific," by Donald F. Smith, *The Progressive,* December 1971; "Union Mood Indicates Prolonged Dock Strike," by Leroy F. Aarons, Washington *Post,* Aug. 16, 1971.

## CALIFORNIA

California, as state and culture, has been the subject of more books, and many of them excellent, than any other state. Those which provided the most helpful background for this book included: *The California Syndrome,* by Neil Morgan (Englewood Cliffs, N.J.: Prentice-Hall, 1969); *The Pacific States,* by Neil Morgan (New York: Time-Life Library of America, 1967); *The Last Days of the Late, Great State of California,* by Curt Gentry (New York: Putnam's, 1968); *Dancing Bear—An Inside Look at California Politics,* by Gladwin Hill (New York: World, 1968); *Ronnie and Jesse—A Political Odyssey,* by Lou Cannon (Garden City, N.Y.: Doubleday, 1969); *Big Wayward Girl—An Informal Political History of California,* by Herbert L. Phillips (Garden City, N.Y.: Doubleday, 1968); *The California Revolution,* ed. Carey McWilliams (New York: Grossman, 1968); *California—A History,* second edition, by Andrew F. Rolle (New York: Crowell, 1969); *Beautiful California,* by the editorial staffs of Sunset Books and Sunset Magazine (Menlo Park, Calif.: Lane Books, 1963); *How to Kill a Golden State,* by William Bronson (Garden City, N.Y.: Doubleday, 1968); *California Government—One Among Fifty,* second edition, by C. E. Jacobs and A. S. Sokolow (London: Macmillan, 1970); *The Challenge of California,* ed. Eugene C. Lee and Willis D. Hawley (Boston: Little Brown, 1970); *California Government and Politics,* fourth edition, by Winston W. Crouch, John C. Bollens, Stanley Scott, and Dean E. McHenry (Englewood Cliffs, N.J.: Prentice-Hall, 1967); *California: The Great Exception,* by Carey McWilliams (New York: Wyn, 1949).

*Eden in Jeopardy—Man's Prodigal Meddling With His Environment: the Southern California Experience,* by Richard G. Lillard (New York: Knopf, 1966); *North from Mexico—The Spanish-Speaking People of the United States,* by Carey McWilliams (New York: Greenwood, 1968); *Politics Battle Plan,* by Herbert M. Baus and William B. Ross (New York: Macmillan, 1968); *The Politics and Economics of Public*

*Spending,* by Charles L. Schultze (Washington, D.C.: Brookings Institution, 1968); "California: Enigmatic Eldorado of National Politics," by Totten J. Anderson, in *Politics in the American West,* ed. Frank J. Jonas (Salt Lake City: University of Utah Press, 1969); "California," by Irving Stone, in *American Panorama* (Garden City, N.Y.: Doubleday, 1960); *California: People—Problems—Potential* (San Francisco: Bank of America, 1970); *Western Market Almanac 1969–70* (Menlo Park, Calif.: Sunset Magazine, 1969); *Wells Fargo Country Factbook—California Business Statistics by Counties* (San Francisco: Wells Fargo Bank, Winter 1968–69).

Other sources: Regular news coverage of the Los Angeles *Times,* San Francisco *Chronicle,* Sacramento *Bee, Los Angeles* (city magazine), *San Diego* (city magazine), *Cry California* (publication of California Tomorrow), and the *California Journal,* an excellent monthly digest of California government and politics which began publication in 1970. Listed below, by subject matter and geographic area, are articles from which material was drawn for the chapter.

GENERAL "California: A State of Excitement," *Time,* Nov. 7, 1969; "California: The Rending of the Veil," by Marshall Frady, *Harper's Magazine,* December 1969; "Legally California May Be a .Single State, Actually It is Cruelly Fragmented," by Alan Cranston, Sacramento *Bee,* Aug. 15, 1965; "Theoretical Look at Proposals for Two Californias," by John Pastier, Los Angeles *Times,* July 26, 1970; "California's Top Court Rules System of School Financing Unconstitutional," *Wall Street Journal,* Aug. 31, 1971; "The Welfare Compromise," editorial in Los Angeles *Times,* Aug. 8, 1971; "Nader Task Force Blasts State Officials, Land Use Practices," and "Background on the Report: How It Was Done, What Happens Next," *California Journal,* September 1971; "Water, Land Plundered, Nader Team Says," by Linda Mathews, and "Officials Assail Nader Report as Malicious," by Paul Houston, Los Angeles *Times,* Aug. 22, 1971; "Nader Has Wrong Gun, Right Target," by Lou Cannon, Long Beach *Press-Telegram,* Sept. 1, 1971; "32.3 Million Residents in State Seen by 2000," by Tom Goff, Los Angeles *Times,* Sept. 18, 1971.

POLITICS "Comparing Political Regions: The Case of California," and "The Repeal of Fair Housing in California: An Analysis of Referendum Voting," both articles by Raymond E. Wolfinger and Fred I. Greenstein, *American Political Science Review,* March 1969 and September 1968 respectively; "California Shift Will Help Voter," by Gladwin Hill, New York *Times,* April 26, 1959; "California GOP Faces Task of Reforming Image," by Curtis J. Sitomer, *Christian Science Monitor,* March 5, 1970; "The Palsy of the CDC," by Francis Carney, *The Nation,* May 4, 1970; "Meeting May Determine CDC 'Life or Death'," by Richard Bergholz, Los Angeles *Times,* May 5, 1970; "Pat Frawley: Right-wing Money Bag," by William W. Turner, *The Progressive,* September 1970; "The Bloodiest Ballot in the United States," by Art Seidenbaum, chapter of *The California Revolution* (previously cited); "The Democratic New Guard," by Mary Ellen Leary, *The Nation,* March 8, 1971; "The Political Giant," by David S. Broder, Washington *Post,* May 11, 1971; "Moscone Is Preparing to Run for Calif. Governorship in '74," by Syd Kossen, Washington *Post,* Dec. 26, 1970; "Reagan Spent $2.1 Million on Campaign, Unruh $873,552," by Jerry Gillam, Los Angeles *Times,* Dec. 6, 1970; "Politicians and the Poor," by Steven V. Roberts, New York *Times,* Dec. 30, 1970; "The Legal Battle in California," by John V. Tunney, New York *Times,* May 28, 1971; "Now Is the Time for All Good Men to . . . What's

That?" and "Labor's Changing Role: Unions, Voting Independently," interviews by David Broder and Haynes Johnson, Washington *Post,* Dec. 19 and 14, 1971; "Will the 'Youth Vote' Decisively Affect the Election?" by D. J. R. Bruckner, Washington *Post,* Feb. 14, 1972.

PERSONALITIES, LEADERS "The Hottest Candidate in Either Party" (Reagan), by Paul O'Neil, *Life,* Oct. 30, 1970; "The Public Record of Ronald Reagan," *Congressional Quarterly Weekly Report,* July 28, 1967; "Ronald Reagan: The Man of Parts," chapter of *The Republican Establishment,* by Stephen Hess and David S. Broder (New York: Harper & Row, 1967); "California's Governor Finds Old Issues Work in Bid for a New Term," by Norman C. Miller, *Wall Street Journal,* Oct. 9, 1970; "Senator Murphy Defends Fee He Receives from Technicolor," by Warren Weaver, Jr., New York *Times,* March 13, 1970; "Reagan May Have Found a Tax Shelter in Cattle Breeding Herds," by Wallace Turner, New York *Times,* June 13, 1971; "Taxing Reagan," *Newsweek,* May 17, 1971; "Reagan Signs Bill to Protect Public from Auto Repair Fraud," by Jerry Gillam, Los Angeles *Times,* Nov. 23, 1971; "An Agency in California Is Model in Campaign to Curb Repair Frauds," by James E. Bylin, *Wall Street Journal,* Jan. 11, 1972; "California Commission Is Rapped for Handling of Regulatory Matters," by Herbert G. Lawson, *Wall Street Journal,* Feb. 29, 1972. "Ronald Reagan's Slow Fade," *Newsweek,* Dec. 20, 1971.

"The New Jesse Unruh," *Time,* Sept. 14, 1970; "Unruh: Campaigning on a Shoestring," by Leroy F. Aarons, Washington *Post,* Aug. 24, 1970; *Californians in Congress, 1967, 1968* and *1970* (Reports of the California Congressional Recognition Plan, Claremont, Calif.); "'Pete' McCloskey vs. Richard Nixon," by James M. Perry, *National Observer,* March 22, 1971; "Is McCloskey the McCarthy of '72?," by R. W. Apple, Jr., New York *Times Magazine,* April 18, 1971; "Challenging Rafferty," *Time,* Nov. 2, 1970; "California School Race Touchy," by Curtis J. Sitomer, *Christian Science Monitor,* Oct. 17, 1970; "Cool, Tough and Black" (Wilson Riles), by Tom Wicker, New York *Times,* Oct. 13, 1970.

LEGISLATURE "California Legislature Goes 'Revolutionary'," by John C. Waugh, *Christian Science Monitor,* Aug. 2, 1968; "Unruh Departs, Leaving List of Achievements," by Robert S. Fairbanks, Los Angeles *Times,* Jan. 7, 1969; "Conflict of Interest Law Dying," by Sydney Kossen, San Francisco *Examiner & Chronicle,* April 19, 1970; "Capitol Lobbyists: How They Operate Behind the Scenes," by Tom Goff, Los Angeles *Times,* Feb. 22, 1970; "California Lobbying Undergoes Change," by Robert Fairbanks, Washington *Post,* April 27, 1969; "Why Burns Lost Out in Senate Fight," by Jack S. McDowell, San Francisco *Examiner & Chronicle,* May 18, 1969; "Burns' Long Reign Over Senate Ends," by Tom Goff, Los Angeles *Times,* May 14, 1969; "Sacramento: A Capital Offense," by Myron Roberts, *Los Angeles,* March 1970; "The Secret Boss of California," by Lester Velie, *Collier's,* Aug ⌐13 and 30, 1949; "Black Power: A Political Surge," by Robert C. Maynard, Washington *Post,* May 2, 1971; Legislative Outlook: Same Old Impasses," by Tom Goff, Los Angeles *Times,* Jan. 3, 1972.

MENTAL HEALTH, PENOLOGY "Legislative Initiative in the Mental Health Field," by Arthur Bolton, *State Government,* Summer 1968; *When Governors Change: The Case of Mental Hygiene* (Institute of Government, University of California, Davis, 1968); "California's Soledad Prison: A 'Pressure Cooker' for Rage Among Inmates," by Steven V. Roberts, New York *Times,* Feb. 7, 1971; "The California Plan—How

One State Is Salvaging Its Convicts," *U. S. News & World Report*, Aug. 24, 1970; "Prisons in Turmoil," *Newsweek*, Sept. 14, 1970; "Do California Prisons Lag?" by David Holmstrom, *Christian Science Monitor*, Nov. 4, 1970; "Reforms and Violence in California's Prisons, by Barry Kalb, Washington *Star*, Aug. 29, 1971; "San Quentin Massacre," *Newsweek*, Aug. 30, 1971.

UNIVERSITY "California: University on Trial," *Newsweek*, Nov. 23, 1970; "California Facing Campus Crisis," by John Berthelsen, Washington *Post*, Nov. 9, 1969; "The Governor v. The University," *Time*, March 30, 1970; "Berkeley's Meddlesome Regents," by Bettina Aptheker, *The Nation*, Sept. 7, 1970; "Full Impact of Budget Cut Jolts State Colleges," by Noel Greenwood, Los Angeles *Times*, July 29, 1970; *Confrontation*, NBC White Paper on "The Ordeal of the American City," broadcast April 22, 1969; "Still No. 1," *Newsweek*, Jan. 11, 1971.

CONSERVATION "A Wink at the Environment," by Robert A. Jones, *The Nation*, April 27, 1970; "Conservation Comes of Age," by Scott Thurber, chapter of *The California Revolution* (previously cited); "Sierra Club Mounts a New Crusade," *Business Week*, May 23, 1970; "Private Group Maps Plan for State Growth," by Daryl Lembke, Los Angeles *Times*, Nov. 9, 1970; "Scenic Roads," chapter of *The Last Landscape*, by William H. Whyte (Garden City, N.Y.: Doubleday, 1968); "Lobbying: The Case of the Freeway Establishment," by Bob Simmons, *Cry California*, Spring 1968; "Judge Halts the Building of a Coast Freeway," by Steven V. Roberts, New York *Times*, Nov. 14, 1971; "The Forest Service Versus California's Last Wilderness," by T. H. Watkins and Joan Parker, *Cry California*, Spring 1971; "Oversight," by Joseph Morgenstern, *Newsweek*, May 24, 1971.

GEOGRAPHY "In California, the Earthquake Threat Is Real," by Walter Sullivan, New York *Times*, March 23, 1969; "Waiting for the Big Bump," *Newsweek*, Sept. 28, 1970; "Hopeful Scientists Run a Hard Race to Control Earthquakes," by John Peterson, *National Observer*, Oct. 12, 1970; "A Shock to Seismologists," *Time*, Feb. 22, 1971; "Millions on Coast Ignore Peril of a Cataclysmic Quake," by Sandra Blakeslee, New York *Times*, April 29, 1971; "California: Ordeal by Fire Storm," *Time*, Oct. 12, 1970; "Southern California: Rain . . . Rain . . . and More Rain," by Leroy F. Aarons, Washington *Post*, March 1, 1969; "Southern California's Trial by Mud and Water," by Nathaniel T. Kenney, *National Geographic*, October 1969; "Fires Strip 500,000 Acres —California Studies Flood Problem," by Kimmis Hendrick, *Christian Science Monitor*, Oct. 13, 1970.

NORTH COAST, SIERRA, NEVADA "The New Redwood Park," *National Parks Magazine*, December 1968; "Yosemite Park Serene," by Ron Abell, *Argus*, July 17, 1970; "The People vs. Yosemite: Can Our Parks Be Saved?" by Jack Goodman, New York *Times*, May 3, 1970; "Yosemite: Better Ways to Run a National Park?", *U.S. News & World Report*, Jan. 24, 1972; "Protectionists vs. Recreationists—The Battle of Mineral King," by Arnold Hano, New York *Times Magazine*, Aug. 17, 1969; "Trash Plagues Mount Whitney as Climbers Go into Thousands," AP dispatch in New York *Times*, Aug. 30, 1970; "Old Mining Law Hampers U.S. Agents in California," by William R. Wyant, Jr., St. Louis *Post-Dispatch*, Dec. 16, 1971.

DESERT "Death Valley, the Land and the Legend," by Rowe Findley, *National Geographic*, January 1970; "New Signs of Life in Death Valley," New York *Times*, Feb. 22, 1970; "The Palmy Springs (All that Money Can Buy)," chap-

ter of *The Right People*, by Stephen Birmingham (New York: Dell, 1968); "Ben Yellen's Fine Madness," by Michael E. Kinsley, *Washington Monthly*, January 1971; "The Crooks' Dilemma," *Newsletter from Dr. Ben Yellen*, Brawley, California, April 5, 1971; "Water, Water For the Wealthy," by Peter Barnes, *New Republic*, May 8, 1971; "Land Reform Drive Problem for White House," by Nick Kotz, Washington *Post*, Dec. 27, 1971; "Geothermal Power—Virtually Pollutionless," by Eric Burgess, *Christian Science Monitor*, Nov. 4, 1970; "The Steam Inside," *Newsweek*, June 7, 1971; "Sands of Time Running Out for State's Desert?" by Philip Fradkin, Los Angeles *Times*, Feb. 13, 1972.

CENTRAL VALLEY, CÉSAR CHÁVEZ "New Drive to Cut Subsidies for Giant Farms," *U. S. News & World Report*, July 27, 1970; "Movements: A New Breed of Lawyer, with the Poor as His Client, Is Forcing Basic Reform of the System," by Lisa Hirsh, *City*, October 1969; "Nerve Gas in the Orchards," by Ronald B. Taylor, *The Nation*, June 22, 1970; "The Little Strike that Grew to La Causa," *Time*, July 4, 1969; "Sal Si Puedes," by Steven V. Roberts, New York *Times Book Review*, Feb. 1, 1970; " 'La Huelga' Becomes 'La Causa'," by Dick Meister, New York *Times Magazine*, Nov. 17, 1968; "La Raza in Revolt," by Roy Bongartz, *The Nation*, June 1, 1970; "California Grape Boycott," *Trans-action*, February 1969; "Vineyards Giving in to Once-Hated Union," by Leroy F. Aarons, Washington *Post*, July 6, 1970; "Pacts Bring Labor Peace to Vineyards at Delano," by Bill Boyarsky, Los Angeles *Times*, July 30, 1970; "With the Grape Pacts Signed, César Chávez Looks to Other Crops," by Henry Elliot Weinstein, *Wall Street Journal*, July 31, 1970; "The California Wine Rush," *Time*, March 3, 1971; "Chávez Union Sees Salinas Strawberries Ripe for Boycott," by Curtis J. Sitomer, *Christian Science Monitor*, May 29, 1971; "To Die Standing," by John Gregory Dunne, *Atlantic Monthly*, June 1971; "Subsidy Cuts Hit Big Cotton Farmers," by Herbert Koshtez, New York *Times*, Jan. 10, 1971; "Reshuffled Farm Ownerships Avoid Cotton Subsidy Limit," by Leroy F. Aarons, Washington *Post*, Dec. 20, 1971; "California Law Seeks to Curtail a Heavy Influx of Illegal Aliens," by Everett R. Holles, New York *Times*, Nov. 21, 1971; "Dancing on the Street," chapter of *A Place to Live* by Wolf Von Eckardt (New York: Delacorte Press, 1967); "Bakersfield Schools Get Warning on Integration," and "School System of Bakersfield in Center of New Battleground," by Noel Greenwood, Los Angeles *Times*, July 13 and 20, 1969; "Conglomerates Reshape Food Supply" and "U.S. Policy Handcuffs Small Farmer," by Nick Kotz, Washington *Post*, Oct. 3 and 5, 1971; "Nader Brands San Luis Dam 'Boondoggle' ", by David Holmstrom, *Christian Science Monitor*, Sept. 24, 1971; "Crop Failure Down on the Conglomerate Farm," *Business Week*, Feb. 19, 1972.

SAN FRANCISCO—GENERAL Articles in *Holiday*, special issue on San Francisco, March 1970: "In San Francisco, You Can (Still Just Barely) See Forever," by the editors; "The Light and Color of a Lovely City," by Bruce Davidson; "Who's in Charge Here?" by Nicholas von Hoffman; "God, Gurus and Gay Guerrillas," by Richard Atcheson; "Culture, Counter-culture, or 'Barbaric Intrusion,' There's Something Going on in San Francisco," by Herbert Gold; "The Overheated Campuses of the Bay Area," by Herbert Wilner.

Articles in *Trans-action*, special issue on "Deviance and Democracy in San Francisco," April 1970; "The Culture of Civility," by Howard S. Becker and Irving Lou Horowitz; "The Health of

Haight-Ashbury," by David E. Smith, John Luce, and Ernest A. Dernburg; "Alioto and the Politics of Hyperpluralism," by Frederick M. Wirt; "Red Guard on Grant Avenue," by Stanford M. Lyman; "The Game of Black & White at Hunters Point," by Arthur E. Hippler; "San Francisco's Mystique," by Fred Davis.

"San Francisco Wins, 2–1, As America's Favorite City," by George Gallup, Des Moines *Register,* Sept. 8, 1969; "San Francisco—Plenty of Avant Left in the Garde," by Herbert Gold, New York *Times Book Review,* Jan. 11, 1970; "San Francisco: the City that Enjoys," by George Barmann, Cleveland *Plain Dealer,* March 11, 1969; "San Francisco Suicides," segment of *60 Minutes,* CBS News, Dec. 16, 1969; "In San Francisco's North Beach, the Many Different Worlds and Generations Never Meet," by Steven V. Roberts, New York *Times,* Nov. 4, 1969; *San Francisco— City on Golden Hills,* by Herb Caen and Dong Kingman (Garden City, N.Y.: Doubleday, 1967); " '67 Flower Children Lose Ardor," by Robert Strand, United Press International dispatch in Los Angeles *Times,* Dec. 14, 1971.

PRESS "The Chronicle: Schizophrenia by the Bay," by David M. Rubin and William L. Rivers, *Columbia Journalism Review,* Fall 1969; "The Golden Gate's TV," *U. S. News & World Report,* Sept. 7, 1970.

GOVERNMENT, POLITICS "Mayor with a Flair," by John C. Waugh, *Christian Science Monitor,* June 11, 1968; "Alioto One Year Later," by Russ Cone, San Francisco *Examiner and Chronicle* magazine, *California Living,* Jan. 26, 1969; "San Francisco's Mayor Alioto and the Mafia," by Richard Carlson and Lance Brisson, *Look,* Sept. 23, 1969; "Alioto: A Politician Lands in Hot Water," by Wallace Turner, New York *Times,* Dec. 28, 1969; "Alioto's Woes," *Newsweek,* April 5, 1971; "S.F.'s 10 Most Powerful," by Dale Champion, San Francisco *Chronicle,* April 21, 1971; "San Francisco Tackles Realities," by Marquis Childs, Washington *Post,* Nov. 23, 1971; "The Sheriff of San Francisco," *The Nation,* Nov. 22, 1971; "New Sheriff in Town," *Newsweek,* March 20, 1972.

BUILDING "Skyscraper Plan Debated on Coast," by Lawrence E. Davies, and "High Skyline Opposed on Coast," by Robert A. Wright, New York *Times,* Aug. 24, 1969 and Oct. 26, 1970; "A Love Affair With S. F. Has Its Ups, Downs," by Jerry Hulse, Los Angeles *Times,* May 3, 1970; "Bay Waterfront High-Rises Draw San Franciscans' Ire," by Rasa Gustaitis, Washington *Post,* Nov. 11, 1970; "Slum Clearance Makes Agonizing Gains in S. F.," by Daryl Lembke, Los Angeles *Times,* March 2, 1969; "The Two Most Exciting Cities in the Nation?—Boston and San Francisco, Some Say . . . ," by Ian Menzies, Boston *Globe,* Sept. 27, 1970.

ECONOMY "The *Times'* Roster of California's 100 Top Industrials," "Top Financial Institutions," etc., Los Angeles *Times,* May 10, 1970; "Sibley of Pacific Gas & Electric," *Fortune,* September 1969; "From Dustbowl to Saigon: The 'People's Bank' Builds an Empire," by Michael Sweeney, *Ramparts,* November 1970; various reports of Pacific Gas & Electric Co.

MINORITIES "Chinatown in Crisis," by Min Yee, *Newsweek,* Feb. 23, 1970; "San Francisco's Chinatown," by Mary Ellen Leary, *Atlantic Monthly,* March 1970; Busing Comes to Chinatown," by Min S. Yee; *Race Relations Reporter,* January 1972; "Filipinos: A Fast-Growing U. S. Minority," by Earl Caldwell, New York *Times,* March 5, 1971.

SAN FRANCISCO BAY "Victory on San Francisco Bay," by Judson Gooding, *Fortune,* February 1970; "That Grass May Grow by San Fran-

cisco Bay," *Life,* July 4, 1970; " 'Save' San Francisco Bay Hearings On," and " 'Save Bay' Drive Wins Long Fight," by Gladwin Hill, New York *Times,* March 23 and Aug. 9, 1969; "Powerful Twosome Leads Ecology Campaign," by Evelyn Radcliffe, *Christian Science Monitor,* June 29, 1970; "Canal Plan Stirs Calif. Environmental Fight," by John Berthelsen, Washington *Post,* Feb. 22, 1970; "Quenching California's Thirst," *Time,* July 6, 1970; "The Battle of the Bay," *Newsweek,* Dec. 28, 1970.

BART "The City: A Different Kind of Trip," *Time,* May 16, 1969; "Space Age Commuting," *Newsweek,* June 16, 1969; "BART: Years of Decision," advertisement in *Fortune,* September 1970; "BART—Catalyst for Bay Area Planning," *Going Places* (publication of General Electric), Third Quarter, 1968; various releases and publications of the San Francisco Bay Area Rapid Transit District; "San Francisco's New Transit Era Leaves Driving to Computers," by David Holmstrom, *Christian Science Monitor,* June 11, 1971.

WEST BAY "Marin County: San Francisco's Connecticut," *Holiday,* March 1970; "The End of a California Dream?" by Philip Hager, Los Angeles *Times,* July 31, 1970; "Santa Clara Goes Urban at Expense of Farming," by Daryl E. Lembke, Los Angeles *Times,* Jan. 1, 1964; "Idyllic Valley Now Urban Anthill, Planner Charges," by Wallace Turner, New York *Times,* Sept. 7, 1970; "The Making of Slurban America," by Karl Belser, *Cry California,* Fall 1970.

"Land Bank Urged Instead of Foothill Growth," by Evelyn Radcliffe, *Christian Science Monitor,* Oct. 9, 1970; "Stanford Park Blends Goals," by Robert Cour, Seattle *Post-Intelligencer,* Oct. 12, 1970; "War Research at Stanford—Sidestepping the Militants," by Larry Schwartz, *The Nation,* March 9, 1970; "Stanford's 'Community of Consent,' " by Peter S. Stern, *The Nation,* Sept. 7, 1970; "Tame Spring, Troubled Stanford," *Time,* May 10, 1971; "Felicity Fights Back," *Time,* May 24, 1971; "The Stanford Daily: A Student Newspaper Staff Under Fire," by Leroy Aarons, Washington *Post,* May 24, 1971; "A Radical Departure," *Newsweek,* Jan. 24, 1972.

"Town vs. Gown: A New Battle in Santa Cruz," by Lance Gilmore, *San Francisco Examiner,* Dec. 21, 1969; "Wandering in Steinbeck Country," by John Morton, *National Observer,* Feb. 16, 1970; "Cannery Row Is Gone, but Monterey Remains—in that Genteel State Known as American Picaresque," by William Schemmel, *Atlanta,* June 1970; "Cannery Row," by Sam Zelman, segment of *60 Minutes,* CBS News, Nov. 24, 1970; "Where Do San Franciscans play? Well, for Example . . . ," by Kenneth Lamott, *Holiday,* March 1970; "Fear and Tension Grip Salinas Valley in Farmer Workers' Strike" by Steven V. Roberts, New York *Times,* Sept. 6, 1970.

EAST BAY, OAKLAND, BERKELEY "Is Oakland There?" *Newsweek,* May 18, 1970; "Oakland: That Troubled Town Across the Bay," by Sol Stern, *Holiday,* March 1970; "Leader of Panthers—Bobby George Seale," by Lawrence Van Gelder, New York *Times,* Aug. 22, 1970, "The Transformation of the Panthers," by Ross K. Baker, Washington *Post,* Feb. 13, 1972; "The Gain Mutiny," *Newsweek,* Dec. 27, 1971.

"The Ordeal of a City," by Charles Howe and Charles Raudebaugh in San Francisco *Chronicle,* Sept. 14–18, 1970; "Berkeley, 5 Years Later, Is Radicalized, Reaganized, Mesmerized," by A. H. Raskin, New York *Times Magazine,* Jan. 11, 1970; "Occupied Berkeley," *Time,* May 30, 1969; "Public Schools—Buses Can Travel Both Ways," *Time,* Nov. 8, 1968; "How School Busing Works in One Town," by Gertrude Samuels, New York *Times Magazine,* Sept. 27, 1970; "Berkeley Vote Lesson," by Steven Roberts, New York *Times*, April 9, 1971.

LOS ANGELES—GENERAL *Los Angeles: The Ultimate City*, by Christopher Rand (New York: Oxford, 1967); *Los Angeles—Portrait of an Extraordinary City*, by the editors of Sunset Books and Sunset Magazine (Menlo Park, Calif.: Lane Magazine & Book Co., 1968); "Los Angeles," by Steven V. Roberts, *Atlantic Monthly*, September 1969; "The Forces At Work on Our Next Five Years," by Myron Roberts, John Pastier, and John Haase, *Los Angeles* (magazine), January 1970; "Los Angeles," by Robert De Roos, *National Geographic*, October 1962; "Take Me to Your Power Structure," by Bill and Nancy Boyarsky, Los Angeles *Times West Magazine*, Oct. 4, 1970; "A Clowder of Fat Cats," *Newsweek*, Dec. 13, 1971; "Safety, Solvency, Balance: Los Angeles School Issues," and "School Chief Resents Reliance on Courts," by Curtis J. Sitomer, *Christian Science Monitor*, Sept. 24 and Nov. 22, 1971; "Friendly Administration, Growth of Suburbs Boost Counties' Influence," by William Lilley III, *National Journal*, May 29, 1971; "This Is the Valley," by Michael Fessier, Jr., Los Angeles *Times West Magazine*, Nov. 1, 1970.

CRIME AND CULTURE "Los Angeles Area Is Shaken Over a Series of Violent Acts," by Steven V. Roberts, New York *Times*, May 3, 1960; "Hell's Angels Have Changed a Bit, but the 'People Haters' Are Still There," by Jim Stingley of the Los Angeles *Times* in the Boston *Globe*, July 12, 1970; "For Squares: Open House at Synanon," by Gertrude Samuels, New York *Times*, Sept. 6, 1970; "Synanon City: A New Community Designed for People who Have Been Damaged by Old Ones," by Gail Miller, *City*, August 1969; "Homosexuals in Los Angeles, Like Many Elsewhere, Want Religion and Establish Their Church," by Edward B. Fiske, New York *Times*, Feb. 15, 1970.

AIR POLLUTION "Los Angeles Has a Cough," by Roger Rapoport, *Esquire*, July 1970; "L. A. Area Called Free of Power Plant Smoke," by George Getze, Los Angeles *Times*, July 23, 1969; "Pollution Dims Los Angeles' Lofty Dreams," by Haynes Johnson, Washington *Post*, Feb. 12, 1970.

PRESS "The Los Angeles Times," by John Corry, *Harper's Magazine*, December 1969; "Will Big Otis Try to Cross the East River?" by Edwin Diamond, *New York*, Aug. 24, 1970.

ECONOMY "L.A. in 1970s: Much More of Everything," by Ray Hebert, Los Angeles *Times*, Dec. 29, 1969; "State's Top Companies Grow Larger—Times Roster Shows L. A. Widens Lead as Headquarters City," Los Angeles *Times*, May 10, 1970; "Aerospace Companies, Workers Hurt by Cuts in Government Outlays," by Earl C. Gottschalk, Jr., *Wall Street Journal*, May 15, 1970; "The Withering Aircraft Industry," by Dan Cordtz, *Fortune*, September 1970; "The Aerospace Industry Hits Some Bumpy Air," *Newsweek*, March 2, 1970; "Lockheed's Illness Is Contagious," by Robert A. Wright, New York *Times*, April 12, 1970; "Coming Up Unk-Unks," by Harold B. Meyers, *Fortune*, Aug. 1, 1969; "The 'One More Chance' Bomber," *Fortune*, July 1970; "Cheers and Tears," *The Nation*, June 22, 1970; "The B-1 Bomber: The Very Model of a Modern Major Misconception," by Berkeley Rice, *Saturday Review*, Dec. 11, 1971; "Industry Studies California Problems," by Willard E. Wilks, *Missiles and Rockets*, Feb. 15, 1965; "A Quarter for the Seventies," *Fortune*, January 1970; "Head of Lockheed Offers to Resign," by Robert J. Samuelson, Washington *Post*, June 12, 1971; "Troubled Think Tanks," *Newsweek*, Jan. 25, 1971; Congress Presses Pentagon to Phase Out 'Think Tanks,' Shift Emphasis to in-House R

and D," by John Maffre, *National Journal*, Nov. 12, 1971.

HOLLYWOOD "Hollywood: The Year You Almost Couldn't Find It," by Jack Hamilton, and "Hollywood: Broke—And Getting Rich," by Fletcher Knebel, *Look*, Nov. 3, 1970; "The Last Days of Babylon?" *Forbes*, Nov. 1, 1969; "Hollywood: Will There Ever Be a 21st-Century Fox?" *Time*, Feb. 9, 1970; "The Old Hollywood: They Lost It at the Movies," *Newsweek*, Feb. 2, 1970; "Holywood's 'Dream' Turns to Nightmare," by Michael Kernan, Washington *Post*, March 23, 1970.

ETHNIC GROUPS "The Old Order Passes for L. A. Japanese," by Stanley O. Williford, Los Angeles *Times*, Aug. 24, 1969; "Chicanos Stirring with New Ethnic Pride," by Steven V. Roberts, New York *Times*, Sept. 20, 1970; "Mexican-American Hostility Deepens in Tense East Los Angeles," by Steven V. Roberts, New York *Times*, Sept. 4, 1970; "The Gentle Revolutionaries: Brown Power," by Ralph Guzman, *Black Politician*, July 1969; "Third Party Politics: Old Story, New Faces," by Richard Santillan, *Black Politician*, October 1971; "Urban Indians, Driven to Cities by Poverty. Find Harsh Existence," by Barbara Isenberg, *Wall Street Journal*, March 9, 1970.

NEGROES "Thomas Bradley—Rising Political Star in the West," *Ebony*, June 1969; Watts: Everything Has Changed—And Nothing," *Newsweek*, Aug. 24, 1970; "Watts Is Being Reborn," by Leroy F. Aarons, Washington *Post*, April 16, 1970; "Watts 1970: Despite Changes, Much Remains the Same Five Years After Riots," by Robert A. Wright, New York *Times*, Sept. 13, 1970; "Labor-Aided Enterprise Applies Union Expertise to Ghetto's Problems," by Mitchell Gordon, *Wall Street Journal*, July 7, 1969; "Watts Company, Established After 1965 Riot, Sold," by Jack Jones, Los Angeles *Times*, May 8, 1970; "A West Pointer for Watts Mfg.," *Business Week*, Oct. 2, 1971.

GEOGRAPHIC "Sprawling Los Angeles Gets a New Skyline," *Business Week*, Dec. 13, 1969; "Folks in Pasadena Say Running a Huge Parade Is No Bed of Roses," by Earl C. Gottschalk, Jr., *Wall Street Journal*, Dec. 30, 1969; "Broad Busing Plan in Pasadena Is Implemented With Harmony," and "Pasadena Voters Support School Board Members Who Back Integration Plan," by Steven V. Roberts, New York *Times*, Sept. 20, and Oct. 15, 1970; "Pasadena, After Year, Adjusts to Busing, but Opposition Remains," by Steven V. Roberts, New York *Times*, Nov. 21, 1971; "Caltech Facing a Critical Decision: Which Way to Go," by Robert B. Young, Los Angeles *Times*, Nov. 7, 1971; "San Bernardino Mayor Gets City on Move," by Ken Overbaker, Los Angeles *Times*, July 6, 1969; " 'City' Springs into Being Adjacent to Long Beach," and "Build Homes and Build Fast, Federal Men Urge Angeleans," Los Angeles *Times*, Nov. 2, 1941 and Feb. 22, 1942; "Southland Housing Explosion 25 Years Old Today," by Henry Sutherland, Los Angeles *Times*, June 18, 1967.

ORANGE COUNTY "Nixon Birthplace Safe for G.O.P.," by Gladwin Hill, New York *Times*, Nov. 2, 1968; "Nixon's Native County Viewed as Sample of Wave of Future," by Don Oberdorfer, Washington *Post*, Jan. 8, 1970; "Nixon Among the Oranges," by Ernest B. Furgurson, Baltimore *Sun*, June 9, 1969; "Disneyland: Can It Top 15 Years of Success?" by Herman Wong, Los Angeles *Times*, July 12, 1970; "Anaheim—Cinderella City of the Southland," by Jack Boettner and Don Smith, Los Angeles *Times*, March 20, 1966, and successive articles in same series; "Irvine—City or Super Subdivision?" by David Shaw, Los Angeles *Times*, June 14, 1970; "Irvine Heiress—Two Sides of an Enigma," by Howard Seelye, Los Angeles

*Times,* Feb. 23, 1970; "This Summer It's Laguna Beach," by Frank Riley, *Holiday,* May 1970; "GOP's Kalmbach: The Covert Collector," by James R. Polk, Washington *Evening Star,* Feb. 2, 1972; "Exclusive Coast Club Spurs Gifts of Millions for Nixon and GOP," by Everett R. Holles, New York *Times,* Feb. 16, 1972.

SAN DIEGO "San Diego: 200 but Still a Mover," by Ellen Shulte, Los Angeles *Times,* March 9, 1969; "San Diego: California's Plymouth Rock," by Allan C. Fisher, Jr., *National Geographic,* July 1969; "San Diego Cleans up Once-Dirty Bay as Model for U.S.," by E. W. Kenworthy, New York *Times,* Sept. 25, 1970; "Richard Neutra Looks at San Diego," by George Waldo, *San Diego Magazine,* May 1970; "A Vision of San Diego," by Harry Antoniades Anthony, *San Diego Magazine,* June 1970; "Who's In Charge Here?" by Harold Keen, *San Diego Magazine,* February 1970; "San Diego—City on the Verge of Controlled Growth," by James Bassett, Los Angeles *Times,* Feb. 14, 1971; "California Goes After a Transportation Octopus" (about activities of C. Arnholt Smith), *Business Week,* Sept. 25, 1971; "Wilson Wins Mayoralty," *Ripon Forum,* Nov. 15, 1971; "Young Councilwoman," Associated Press dispatch in Washington *Evening Star,* Dec. 6, 1971; "Tampering with Justice in San Diego," by Denny Walsh and Tom Flaherty, *Life,* March 24, 1972.

"Herb Klein's Old Paper," *Newsweek,* Jan. 5, 1970; "*Union-Tribune,* The Mute Town Crier," by

Ed Self, *San Diego Magazine,* June 1970; "*Union-Tribune* Zaps Back," letter from *Union-Tribune* news director Milford Chipp, and "The Editor Replies," by Ed Self, *San Diego Magazine,* August 1970; "Commissar of Credibility," by Dom Bonafede, *The Nation,* April 6, 1970; "Censorship by Harassment," by Kingsley Widmer, *The Nation,* March 30, 1970.

SANTA BARBARA "Santa Barbara: Old Guard and New Life-Style," by Kelly Tunney, Los Angeles *Times,* Dec. 28, 1969; "Environment: Tragedy in Oil," *Time,* Feb. 14, 1969; "One Year Later, Impact of Great Oil Slick Is Still Felt," by Gladwin Hill, New York *Times,* Jan. 25, 1970; "Santa Barbarans Cite an 11th Commandment: 'Thou Shalt Not Abuse the Earth'," by Ross MacDonald and Robert Easton, New York *Times Magazine,* Oct. 12, 1969; "Oil in Santa Barbara and Power in America," by Harvery Molotch, *Ramparts,* November 1969; "U.S. Bars Permits for Oil Drilling at Santa Barbara," Washington *Post,* Sept. 21, 1971; "Bank Burning Shows New Side of Youth Revolt," by Leroy F. Aarons, Washington *Post,* May 3, 1970; "Why They Burned the Bank," by Richard Flacks and Milton Mankoff, *The Nation,* March 23, 1970; "The Isla Vista War —Campus Violence in a Class by Itself," by Winthrop Griffith, New York *Times Magazine,* Aug. 30, 1970; "California's Isla Vista: 'From Anathema to Dialogue'," by Norman Cousins, *Saturday Review,* June 5, 1971.

## OREGON

There are scarcely any modern books treating Oregon exclusively. Sources most useful in preparing the chapter included: *Empire of the Columbia: A History of the Pacific Northwest,* 2nd ed., by Dorothy O. Johansen (New York: Harper & Row, 1967); "Oregon: Green and Gangly," chapter of Neil Morgan's *Westward Tilt* (New York: Random House, 1961); John M. Swarthout and Kenneth R. Gervais, "Oregon: Political Experiment Station," in *Politics in the American West,* ed. Frank H. Jonas (Salt Lake City: University of Utah Press, 1969); *Oregon: End of the Trail,* rev. ed., compiled by workers of the Writers' Program of the WPA (Portland, Ore.: Binfords & Mort, American Guide Series, 1951); and *Oregon,* a pictorial by Ray Atkeson and Carl Gohs (Portland, Ore.: Charles H. Belding, 1968).

Other Sources: General coverage of *The Oregonian* (Portland) and *Argus* (Seattle), plus the specific named below:

GENERAL "Oregon's Many Faces," by Stuart E. Jones, *National Geographic,* January 1969; *1968 Oregon Presidential Primary* (Political Report for CBS News Election Unit, Robert Richter, Director for Political Research and Analysis, New York, 1968); "Oregon: State Fights Population Explosion," by Peter J. Bridge, Newark *Sunday News,* Nov. 8, 1970; "Please Keep Off the Oregon," by Ellis Lucia, Los Angeles *Times WEST Magazine,* Aug. 23, 1970; "Beset by Immigrants, Oregon Seeks a Halt," by Leroy F. Aarons, Washington *Post,* Nov. 22, 1971; "Oregonians Put Men over Parties, and Like Them Independent," by John Corry, New York *Times,* May 26, 1968; "Slavery in Oregon: A Matter of Personalities and Issues," by Bob Sutton, "They Always Put Their Money Where Their Brains Are," by Malcolm Bauer, and "Oregon's Politics Is Anyone's Guess," by Robert Olmos,

all in *Northwest,* magazine section of *The Sunday Oregonian,* Sept. 20, 1970; "Oregon's New 'Merchant,'" *U.S. News & World Report,* Sept. 7, 1970; "History of Oregon," by Robert Carlton Clark, in booklet, *Oregon,* published by Oregon State Highway Department; "Astoria, Oregon— 'Finland' of New World," by Charles Hillinger, Los Angeles *Times,* Jan. 5, 1970; "Town and Gown for Peace" (about Eugene), *The Nation,* June 14, 1971.

POLITICS AND GOVERNMENT "Two-Party Blues in One-Party State," by Richard L. Neuberger, New York *Times Magazine,* Feb. 1, 1953; "GOP Conservatives Gain in Oregon," by Harold Hughes, Washington *Post,* July 13, 1970; "1909 Election Law Stirs Oregon Politicians," by Wallace Turner, New York *Times,* Jan. 27, 1969; "An Outspoken Governor: Thomas Lawson McCall," New York *Times,* July 13, 1971; "New Oregon Districts Bring Major Changes," *National Civic Review,* October 1971; "Oregon Legislative Windup," by Malcolm Bauer, *Christian Science Monitor,* June 6, 1969; "Oregon to Vote on New Constitution," by Ron Abell, *Argus,* Oct. 10, 1969; "Oregon Primary Hints U.S. Trends," by Malcolm Bauer, *Christian Science Monitor,* June 2, 1970; "Oregon: Sweeping Reforms but with Some Loose Ends," *Ripon Forum,* July 1969; "Making Prison a Beginning, Not an End," Washington *Post,* Nov. 4, 1969; "New Gate Plan Gives Prisoners Opportunity to Get College Degree," by Joann S. Lublin, *Wall Street Journal,* Oct. 4, 1971; "Oregon May Be First to Try Nader Scheme," by A. Robert Smith, and "Campuses Win Vote on OSPIRG," by John Guernsey, *The Oregonian,* Oct. 29, 1970, and March 16, 1971; "Governor of Oregon Vetoes Bill Regulating Farm Labor Unions," New York *Times,* July 3, 1971.

CONSERVATION "Conservationists See Hope, At Last," by Ron Abell, *Argus,* July 10,

1970; "How Many Tourists Is Too Many?", editorial in Medford (Ore.) *Mail Tribune,* June 27, 1969; "McCall Announces Plan to Reserve Campsites for Oregon Residents," by Marcia Lieurance, *Idaho Statesman,* March 29, 1970; "Tough Rules Saving a Dying Oregon River," by E. W. Kenworthy, New York *Times,* Sept. 8, 1970; "Oregonians Argue Over Beaches," by Ron Abell, *Argus,* May 15, 1970; "The Nation Debates an Issue: the Economy vs. the Environment," by Stanford N. Sesser, *Wall Street Journal,* Nov. 3, 1971; "Waterways in Oregon Preserved," by Malcolm Bauer, *Christian Science Monitor,* April 13, 1971; "Oregon Coalition Wary on Ecology," New York *Times,* Dec. 26, 1971.

CONGRESSIONAL DELEGATION "An Old Tiger Resting," by A. Robert Smith, *Northwest,* magazine section of *The Sunday Oregonian,* Jan. 12, 1969; "Biography of . . . Wayne L. Morse," *Congressional Quarterly Weekly Report,* July 26, 1968; "Wayne Morse Runs Again," *The Progressive,* November 1971; "Morse Returns," *The Oregonian,* Sept. 29, 1971; "The Public Record of Mark O. Hatfield," *Congressional Quarterly Weekly Report,* Aug. 18, 1967; "Nixon Accused of Neglecting Needs at Home," by S. Robert Jacobs, Philadelphia *Evening Bulletin,* June 2, 1969; "Hatfield Says GOP Practiced the 'Politics of Revulsion,' " by David S. Broder, Washington *Post,* Nov. 6, 1970; "Oregon Party Raps Hatfield for Criticizing National GOP," by Malcolm Bauer, *Christian Science Monitor,* July 9, 1970; discussion of Hatfield in *The Republican Establishment,* by Stephen Hess and David S. Broder (New York: Harper & Row, 1967); "Youngest Senator Attacks Seniority," by Peter C. Stuart, *Christian Science Monitor,* Aug. 24, 1970; "Sen. Packwood Wants More Youth in Politics," by Richard Bergholz, Los Angeles *Times,* Feb. 15, 1969; "The 'Kaffeeklatch' Constituency," by Floyd McKay, *The Nation,* Feb. 17, 1969; "Edith Green: 'A Smiling Corbra' or 'Mrs. Education'?" by Gayle Tunnell, *Potomac,* magazine of the Washington *Post,* Aug. 9, 1970; "Liberals Linked By Edith Green to College Riots," by Alvin P. Sanoff, Baltimore *Sun,* Feb. 19, 1969; "Rep. Green Sees 'Disenchantment' with All Education," *Argus,* July 25, 1969; "Strong, Balanced Teams," editorial in *The Oregonian,* Oct. 8, 1970; "Al Ullman Smiles an 'I Told You So,' " *Business Week,* Sept. 4, 1971.

ECONOMY "Oregon Economy Shifts Priorities Away from Lumber, Agriculture," by Ron Abell, *Argus,* April 17, 1970; "Oregon Grows Slowly, Surely with Diversified Industries," by Gerry Pratt, *The Oregonian,* Feb. 2, 1969; "Governor Sums Up 1968 as 'Vintage' Growth Year," by Robert Landauer, *The Oregonian,* Jan. 5, 1969; "State's Real Gross Product to Drop in '70," New York *Times,* Jan. 3, 1971; "Oregon Poor People Organize State Council," by Robert Olmos, *The Oregonian,* Sept. 21, 1970; *Oregon the Growth State—Fact Summary 1969, and 1970* (Portland, Ore.: State of Oregon Economic Development Division); *Background on Oregon's Agriculture* (Corvallis, Ore.: Cooperative Extension Service, Oregon State University, 1969); "Loggers in Oregon Feel Money Market Squeeze," by Robert A. Wright, New York *Times,* April 5, 1970; "Wasting the Wilds," by James Risser of the the Des Monies *Register and Tribune,* series condensed in Washington *Post,* April 4, 1971; "Forest Service Smarts Under Critics' Claim It Allowed Damage to Public Timberlands," by Burt Schorr, *Wall Street Journal,* June 4, 1971.

PORTLAND "Oregon Districts to Merge," *Christian Science Monitor,* June 16, 1970; "Portland, Ore., Readies for City-County Merger," by Malcolm Bauer, *Christian Science Monitor,* Dec. 2, 1971; "New Blood in Municipal Races," by Ron Abell, *Argus,* Jan. 23, 1970; "Portland, Ore., Policemen Win Pay Increase to $10,525 a Year," New York *Times,* Feb. 1, 1970; "Oregon Averts Legion-youth Conflict" by Malcolm Bauer, *Christian Science Monitor,* Sept. 14, 1970; "Bacchanal on the Clackamas," by Gordon Bowker, *Seattle Magazine,* October 1970; "Paranoia—Portland Style," by Art Chenoweth, *Northwest,* magazine section of *The Sunday Oregonian,* Sept. 13, 1970; "Only Exports Bolster Portland," by Art Pine, Baltimore *Sun,* Aug. 17, 1970; "In Portland, Ore., Urban Decay Is Masked by Natural Splendor," and "Coast Fountain Melds Art and Environment," by Ada Louise Huxtable, New York *Times,* June 19 and 21, 1970; "U.S. Culture Moves West," *U.S. News & World Report,* Sept. 7, 1970; "From Token to the Top," *Time,* May 17, 1971; "New Jetports Held Up by Protest Movements," by Robert Lindsey, New York *Times,* July 11, 1971; "Fading Roses," *The Nation,* June 7, 1971.

# WASHINGTON

Books providing valuable background on the statewide scene included *Washington: A History of the Evergreen State,* 2nd ed., by Mary W. Avery (Seattle: University of Washington Press, 1965); *Empire of the Columbia: A History of the Pacific Northwest,* 2nd ed., by Dorothy O. Johansen (New York: Harper & Row, 1967); "Washington State: Free Style Politics," by Hugh A. Bone, chapter of *Politics in the American* West, ed. Frank H. Jonas (Salt Lake City: University of Utah Press, 1969); "Washington," by Nard Jones, chapter of *American Panorama* (Garden City, N.Y.: Doubleday, 1960); "Washington: The Gentle People," chapter of *Westward Tilt: The American West Today,* by Neil Morgan (New York: Random House, 1961); and *Washington: A Guide to the Evergreen State,* compiled by writers of the Writers' Program of the WPA (Portland, Ore.: Binfords & Mort, American Guide Series, 1941).

Other Sources: General coverage of the Seattle *Post-Intelligencer,* the Seattle *Times, Argus,* Seattle *Magazine,* plus the specific articles named below:

GENERAL, ECONOMICS *Introducing Washington* (joint publication of Oregon Department of Commerce and Economic Development, Department of Public Instruction, and Secretary of State, 1969); "The Volcano Watchers," *Newsweek,* Sept. 27, 1971; "Indians Are Poorest of This State's Poor," by Mike Layton, *Argus,* Nov. 8, 1968; "Yakima Indians Claim Land," by Eldon Barrett of United Press International, Washington *Post,* Dec. 10, 1970; "Indians Claim Fishing Rights," by Frye Gaillard, *Race Relations Reporter,* Feb. 16, 1971.

"Seattle Payrolls Fattened by War," by William E. Ames, *Christian Science Monitor,* May 23, 1969; "The Boeing Depression in Washington State," *Intermountain Observer,* May 30, 1970; "William Allen Marks 20th Year at Boeing; No Immediate Plans for Retirement," by Shelby Scates, *Argus,* Aug. 20, 1965; "SST Will Boom Area's Economy," Seattle *Post-Intelligencer,* Sept.

23, 1969; "Boeing Does It Again," editoral from *The Oregonian* reprinted in *Argus*, Oct. 9, 1970; "In a Stunned Seattle, Only Radicals See Good in Rejection of SST," by Herbert G. Lawson, *Wall Street Journal*, Dec. 7, 1970, and reply, "Seattle Deserves a Correction," editorial in *Argus*, Dec. 11, 1970; "Boeing Sees 32,500 Jobs by End of 1971," by Al Watts, Seattle *Post-Intelligencer*, Oct. 1, 1970; "The Big Squeeze," by Patrick Douglas, *Seattle Magazine*, May 1970; "Company-Town Blues," by James E. Bylin and Richard Immel, *Wall Street Journal*, July 6, 1970; "Should SST Go Forward?", editorial in *Christian Science Monitor*, July 28, 1970; "New Doubts Shake the Supersonic Airliner," by Wesley Pruden, Jr., *National Observer*, July 27, 1970; "The SST: A Turbulent Journey," by David Hoffman, Washington *Post*, Nov. 10, 1970; "U.S. SST Commitment May Increase by $3 Billion," by Christopher Lydon, New York *Times*, May 12, 1970.

GOVERNMENT AND POLITICS "Sponsor of Pollution Control Bill: Henry Martin Jackson," New York *Times*, Jan. 2, 1970; "SST Lost Despite Push by Jackson," by James Doyle, Washington *Evening Star*, Dec. 4, 1970; "Sen. Jackson Gets Help from GOP Rivals in Washington Race," by Albert R. Hunt, *Wall Street Journal*, Sept. 15, 1970; "How Scoop and Maggie Met Their Match," by Robert Smith, *Intermountain Observer*, Dec. 12, 1970; "War Is Hell for Senator Jackson," by Bernard Weiner, *The Nation*, Aug. 31, 1970; "Bill by Magnuson Would Permit El Paso to Keep a Pipeline It Acquired Illegally," by Wallace Turner, New York *Times*, Feb. 25, 1971; "The Scoop on Candidate Jackson," *Newsweek*, Oct. 11, 1971; "Sen. Jackson, Running Hard, Woos the Media in Quest for 'Exposure,'" by Arlen J. Large, *Wall Street Journal*, Nov. 19, 1971; "The Candidacy of Senator Jackson," by Joel Connelly, *The Nation*, Nov. 15, 1961; "The Controversial Candidate," by David S. Broder, Washington *Post*, Oct. 3, 1971.

"The Public Record of Daniel J. Evans," *Congressional Quarterly Weekly Report*, Aug. 18, 1967; "Evans Gave Tax Reform His Best Efforts," by Worth Hedricks, *Argus*, Nov. 13, 1970; "Wn., Ore. Governors React Differently to Campus Violence," by Melvin B. Voorhees, *Argus*, July 10, 1970; "Evans Moves to Hire More of Minority Groups, Set Quotas," by Worth Hedrick, *Argus*, Sept. 18, 1970; "Washington State Pollution Controls Prize for Governor," by Daryl Lembke, Los Angeles *Times*, March 14, 1970.

"Lobbyists Find Olympia Their Happy Hunting Ground," by Mike Layton, *Argus*, Feb. 13, 1970; "Lobbying: An Integral Lever in the Machine," by Shelby Scates, Seattle *Post-Intelligencer*, March 8, 1970; "115 Measures Find Passage in Legislative Session," Associated Press Dispatch in Seattle *Post-Intelligencer*, Feb. 14, 1970; Politics: The Game of Ecology—A box Score of the Legislature's Runs, Hits and Errors," by David Brewster, *Seattle Magazine*, April 1970; "Durkan: No New Taxes, Cut Costs 'To The Bone,'" by Philip Bailey, *Argus*, Dec. 11, 1970; "Rightists To Take Over Republican Party?" by Mike Layton, *Argus*, Aug. 14, 1970; "Slade Gorton: Best GOP Candidate for Governor," by Philip Bailey, *Argus*, July 16, 1971; "Farm Workers and City Unions," by Richard P. Gibbons, *The Nation*, July 24, 1971; "Self-Governing Inmates of Walla Walla Prison Find Life Easier," by Wallace Turner, New York *Times*, Oct. 18, 1971; "Prisons Take a Giant Step," *Newsweek*, Nov. 1, 1971.

SEATTLE "In the Last, Idyllic Trading Post, the Blight of Real Depression—Seattle," by Paul O'Neil, *Life*, Oct. 2, 1970; "The Lord Helps Those Who Help Themselves," 'Time to

Stop Crying: Things Not That Bad," and "Seattle of Tomorrow: What Should It Be?" by Philip Bailey, *Argus*, April 9, July 23, and Oct. 29, 1971; "The New Poor of Seattle," editorial in Washington *Post*, Dec. 2, 1971; "Lake Washington," *The Progressive*, April 1970; "Argus Salutes the Leaders of the 1960s," *Argus*, Jan. 2, 1970; "Seattle's Modern-Day Vigilantes," by John Fisher, *Harper's Magazine*, May 1969; "Seattle Fights Complacency," by Bruce K. Chapman, *Reporter*, March 21, 1968; "Thrust Toward Quality," by James R. Ellis, *National Civic Review*, February 1969; "Seattle's Winking at Gambling Finally Pays Off in Black Eye," by Daryl Lembke. Los Angeles *Times*, July 27, 1970; "Criminals in Blue," by Joseph Kraft, Washington *Post*, Aug. 9, 1970; "City Had a Good Thing Goin,'" by Shelby Scates, Seattle *Post-Intelligencer*, Oct. 5, 1969; "Seattle Is Jolted by Disclosures of Police Payoffs," by Shelby Scates, Washington *Post*, Sept. 24, 1970; "Seattle: An End to Tolerance," *Newsweek*, Aug. 9, 1971; "Police Bribe Ring Charges Studied by Jury in Seattle," by Wallace Turner, New York *Times*. Aug. 8, 1971.

"What Kind of a Guy Is Braman," by Mike Conant, Seattle *Post-Intelligencer*, March 23, 1969; "Uhlman Stuns with Victory over Frayn-'Establishment,'" *Argus*, Nov. 7, 1969; "Uhlman Fails to Give City Dynamic Leadership," by Philip Bailey, *Argus*, Dec. 4, 1970; "The Perils of A Swinging Mayor," by Mike Conant, Seattle *Post-Intelligencer*, March 22, 1970; "You've Come a Long Way, Wes," by David Brewster, *Seattle Magazine*, September 1970; "Oil Spills Could Make Puget Sound 'Dead Sea,'" by Philip Bailey, *Argus*, Feb. 26, 1971; "The Battle in Seattle" (about Pike Place Market), *Newsweek*, May 17, 1971; "Where Are They Now?—The Wheel Rolls On" (regarding Dave Beck), *Newsweek*, Feb. 23, 1970; *Race and Violence in Washington State* (Report of the Commission on the Causes and Prevention of Civil Disorder, February 1969).

OTHER CITIES, SUBURBS "Spokane Economy Is Humming, Not Affected by Recession," by Ellen Ewing, *Argus*, Aug. 14, 1970; "Spokane's Expo '74 Right on Schedule," and "Expo '74 Hit by Critics," by Ellen Ewing, *Argus*, April 23, 1971 and Jan. 14, 1972; "Bellevue: The Good Life Begins at Home," by Rosella Broyles, Seattle *Post-Intelligencer Northwest Today*, Nov. 29, 1970; "Bellevue Moves Ahead, in Spite of Bust at Boeing," by Edward Trimakas, *Argus*, Oct. 22, 1971; "Tacoma Fortissimo," by Gordon Bowker, *Seattle Magazine*, May 1970; "Tacoma Politics Baffle Even Natives in 'City of Destiny'" and "New Tacoma Council Staid and Sober," by Murray Morgan, *Argus*, March 27 and Oct. 23, 1970; "A City that Mingles with Nature," by Jack Ryan, "Washington's First Boom Town," by Murray Morgan, and "Diversification Pulls a City Out of the Woods," all in Seattle *Post-Intelligencer Northwest Today*, Nov. 15, 1970; "Getting Sick of Sulphur in Tacoma," by Herbert G. Lawson, *Wall Street Journal*, Oct. 14, 1970; "Tacoma's Tall Stack," by William H. Rodgers, Jr., *The Nation*, May 11, 1970.

NORTHWEST WATER AND POWER, HANFORD "Rufus Woods' Magnificent Pipe Dream," by William M. Greene, *Country Beautiful*, 1962; *A Ten Year Hydro-Thermal Power Program for the Pacific Northwest* (Bonneville Power Administration, Department of the Interior, January 1969); *Operation of Pacific Northwest Electric Systems* (working paper of Portland General Electric Co., 1969); "State's Vital Columbia Basin Project Is 'Stalled'; Food Needed, Half Million Acres Under Water," by Phil Peterson, *Argus*, Oct. 11, 1968; "$937 Million to Finish Columbia Basin Project," by Melvin B. Voorhees,

*Argus,* April 14, 1970; "Seattle's Money Problems Easily Solved: Sell City Light," by Philip Bailey, *Argus,* April 30, 1971.

"U.S. to Build Second Fast Breeder Unit for Atomic Power," *Wall Street Journal,* Sept. 27, 1971; "Hanford Has Huge Mass of Radioactive Waste," by A. Robert Smith, *Argus,* April 9, 1971; "The Search for an Atomic Burial Ground," "AEC Glosses Over Hanford's Earthquake Danger," and "Safety Takes a Back Seat," by A. Robert Smith, *Intermountain Observer,* April 10 and 17 and May 1, 1971.

# ALASKA

Alaska has fascinated writers over many decades. Some of the books I found most helpful were these: *The Frontier States—Alaska, Hawaii,* by Richard Austin Smith (New York: Time-Life Library of America, 1968); *The State of Alaska,* by Ernest Gruening, rev. ed. (New York: Random House, 1968); *Alaska,* by Bern Keating (Washington: National Geographic Society, 1969); *The New States: Alaska and Hawaii,* ed. William P. Lineberry (New York: H. W. Wilson, The Reference Shelf, Vol. 35, No. 5, 1963); "Alaska: Empire of the North," by Herman E. Slotnick, in *Politics in the American West,* ed. Frank H. Jonas (Salt Lake City: University of Utah Press, 1969); *Klondike '70—The Alaskan Oil Boom,* by Daniel Jack Chasen (New York: Praeger, 1971); and *Alaska Survey and Report,* ed. Stephen Brent and Robert Goldberg (Anchorage: Anchorage *Daily News,* 1970, 1971).

OTHER SOURCES General coverage of the Anchorage *Daily Times,* the Anchorage *Daily News,* the Fairbanks *Daily News-Miner, Argus* (published in Seattle), and the specific articles listed below.

GENERAL "The Great Land: Boom or Doom," *Time,* July 27, 1970; "Alaska's $50-Billion Boom," *Forbes,* Nov. 15, 1969; "The Giant Sleeps No More," by Murlin Spencer, and other articles in the *Daily News-Miner,* 19th Annual Progress Edition (1969); "The Oil Rush of '70," by Bob Zelnick, New York *Times Magazine,* March 1, 1970; "Anticipation of Boom from North Slope Oil Spurs Alaska Economy," by James E. Bylin, *Wall Street Journal,* Oct. 20, 1969; "On Alaska—b-r-r-r," by Thomas M. Brown, *Christian Science Monitor,* Feb. 12, 1971; "An Alaskan Bush Pilot Risks Life and Limb to Help Rescue Others," by James E. Bylin, *Wall Street Journal,* March 17, 1971; "Women's Lib Really Works in Alaska," by Ruth D. Edmondson, *Argus,* July 9, 1971; "Gravel, Egan Dedicate New Satellite Program," Anchorage *Daily Times,* Sept. 4, 1971; "Unfreezing Alaska," by Peter Barnes, *New Republic,* Sept. 11, 1971.

GEOGRAPHIC AREAS, CITIES "Earthquake!" by William E. Graves, *National Geographic,* July 1964; "The ABM, an Accomplice in the 'Rape of Amchitka,' " by Philip D. Carter, Washington *Post,* April 13, 1969; "Is This Blast Necessary," *Newsweek,* Nov. 1, 1971; "Autopsy on Cannikin," *Time,* Nov. 22, 1971; "Elated A.E.C. Planning to Quit Aleutians," by Wallace Turner, New York *Times,* Nov. 8, 1971; *City of Kotzebue, Alaska,* (publication of Arctic Circle Chamber of Commerce, 1969); "Visiting Nome Via Jetliner and Dog Team," by Shari L. Wigle, New York *Times,* July 7, 1970; "The Polar Bear Nears Extinction," by Lewis Rogenstein, Washington *Post,* Oct. 21, 1971; "Warning: The Chain Saw Cometh," by Paul Brooks, *Atlantic Monthly,* November 1971.

"Anchorage Celebrates 50th Birthday; Already Has Many Urban Problems," by Ruth D. Edmondson, *Argus,* Nov. 27, 1970; "Alaska's Largest City is Modern," by Tommy Holmes, Newark *News,* Aug. 9, 1970; "An Action Plan for 1990—Operation Breakthrough's Report on the Anchorage Area's Next 20 Years," supplement to Anchorage *Daily News,* Sept. 26, 1970; "Slump and Rough Weather Depress Alaska," by Ruth D. Edmondson, *Argus,* Dec. 18, 1970.

ECONOMY "The Moose Gooser: Tiny Alaska Railroad Battles the Elements," by James E. Bylin, *Wall Street Journal,* Aug. 4, 1970; "Alaska Taking in Japan as 'Partner,' " by Thomas W. Bush, Los Angeles *Times,* Jan. 26, 1969; "Japan's Foothold in Alaska: 200 Millions—and Growing," *U.S. News & World Report,* Sept. 27, 1971; "Farm Researchers Set Out to Raise Hot-House Hogs in Subzero Alaska," by Edward J. Fortier, *National Observer,* Dec. 14, 1970; "Alaska Airlines Gets Final Soviet Approval for Siberia Flights," by William McAllister, *Wall Street Journal,* March 9, 1970; "Alaskans Fired Up Over New Boeing Craft," by Ruth D. Edmondson, *Argus,* Jan. 29, 1971; "State Government and Economic Development in Alaska," by Thomas A. Morehouse and Gordon Scott Harrison, *State Government,* Autumn 1970.

OIL "Our Last Great Wilderness," by Walter Sullivan, *American Heritage,* August 1970; "Alaska—The Ecology of Oil," by Barry Weisberg, *Ramparts,* January 1970; "Kiss the North Slope Good-by?" by George Laycock, *Audubon,* September 1970; "Alaskans Fear Boom in Oil Perils the Land," by Steven V. Roberts, New York *Times,* Aug. 23, 1970; "Alaska's New Strike," *Time,* Dec. 13, 1968; "Alaska Pipeline Puts Nixon on Spot," by A. Robert Smith, *Argus,* May 22, 1970; "But Tract 57 Woke Up with a Gasp," by Ed Fortier, *National Observer,* Sept. 15, 1969; "The Deadly Land on the Polar Bear Yields a Rich Discovery," *Denver Post Empire Magazine,* June 8, 1969; "Alaska's Black-Gold Rush," *Newsweek,* Jan. 6, 1969; "Billions of Barrels at 50° Below," by Jordan Bonfante, *Life,* Feb. 14, 1969; "Oil Workers Meet Alaskan Challenge," by Wick Temple, Associated Press dispatch in Washington *Post,* Dec. 10, 1970; "Tanker's Voyage Caps Five-Century Search," by Robert C. Jensen, Washington *Post,* Sept. 16, 1969; "Alaskans 'Offended' and 'Furious' as Seattle Selected for TAPS Pipeline Headquarters," by Ruth D. Edmondson, *Argus,* Sept. 25, 1970; "Alaska's Big Worry: Getting Oil to Market," *U.S. News & World Report,* June 8, 1970; "Is Pipeline Really Necessary?" by Daniel Jack Chasen, *Argus,* Jan. 1, 1971; "Costs to Keep Northwest Passage Shut; Jersey Standard Unit to Focus on Pipeline," by Roger W. Benedict, *Wall Street Journal,* Oct. 22, 1971; "Fishing Town Joins Legal Fight to Stop Trans-Alaska Pipeline Project," "Alaska Considers Regulatory Scheme to Maximize State's Share of Oil Bonanza," and "Japan May Get Some Alaskan Oil; Foreign-flag Shipping of Exports Is Likely," by Richard Corrigan, *National Journal,* July 3, 10, and 31, 1971; "Alaska's Frustrating Freeze in Oil," *Time,* July 26, 1971; 'Stalling of Alaska Pipeline Sparks Arrays of Ideas, Most of Them Impractical, to Protect Environment," by James E. Bylin, *Wall Street Journal,* Sept. 27, 1971; *Oil on Ice: Alaskan Wilderness at the Crossroads,* by Richard Pollak (Sierra Club Battlebook, 1971); "Alaska's North Slope Waits as Pipeline Is Debated," by Carroll Kilpatrick, Washington *Post,* Oct. 14, 1971; "Alaska Pipeline Is Upheld by Interior Agency Study," by David E. Rosenbaum, New York *Times,* Jan. 14, 1971; "The Alaskan Pipeline Is Essential," by Walter J. Hickel, New York *Times,* March 24, 1971; "The Cordova Fishermen," *The Nation,* Dec. 6, 1971; "Alaska: Oil vs. Wilderness," series by Roberta Hornig, Washington *Evening Star,* Aug. 24, 25, and 26, 1971; "State, Private Reports Score Alaska Pipeline," by Elsie Carper, Washington *Post,* May 5, 1971; "Gas Now Becomes an Issue in the Arctic," *Business Week,* Aug. 28, 1971; "Dealing with a Northern Sheik," *Time,* Nov. 29, 1971.

NATIVES *Alaska Natives and The Land,* report of the Federal Field Committee for Development Planning in Alaska (Anchorage, Alaska, October 1968); various editions of the *Tundra Times;* "The Case of the Alaskan Native," by Deborah Movitz, *Civil Rights Digest,* Summer 1969; "A Far-Flung People" by Peter Farb, *American Heritage,* October 1968; "The Eskimo Search for Identity," by Slim Randles, Anchorage *Daily News,* Dec. 11, 1970; "No More Dick and Jane Readers for Them!" by Lansing R. Shepard, *Christian Science Monitor,* April 15, 1971; Alaska's Natives Uneasily Await House Action on Land Claims," by Steven V. Roberts, New York *Times,* Sept. 9, 1970; "Alaska Natives Scorn $1 Billion Land Offer," by Richard Harwood, Washington *Post,* Aug. 9, 1970; "Alaska Natives Want Big Piece of Oil Action," by A. Robert Smith, *Argus,* March 6, 1970; "AFB Ups the Ante as Slope Natives Return to Fold," by Allen Frank and Linda Billington, Anchorage *Daily News,* Dec. 12, 1970; "The Natives May Win One: The Great Alaskan Real-Estate Deal," by Thomas M. Brown of the Anchorage *Daily News* in New York *Times Magazine,* Oct. 17, 1971; "Alaska Natives Criticize Bill," by Steve Nickeson, *Race Relations Reporter,* Nov. 15, 1971; "Proposed Land Gift in Alaska Opposed," United Press International dispatch in St. Louis *Post-Dispatch,* Oct. 3, 1971; "Hill Weighs Alaska Natives' Claims," and "Alaska Native Land Payment Passed," by Elsie Carper, Washington *Post,* Oct. 18 and Dec. 15, 1971; " 'Bush Power' Wins Alaskan Land Claims," *Business Week,* Dec. 18,

1971; "Alaska Natives Win Landmark Claims Case; Attorney Cites 'Justice . . . , Mixed with Oil,' " by Richard Corrigan, *National Journal,* Dec. 18, 1971.

GOVERNMENT, POLITICS "Alaska's Struggle for Statehood," by Robert B. Atwood, *State Government,* Autumn 1958; "Alaska Charter Set for Signing," by Lawrence E. Davies, New York *Times,* Feb. 5, 1956; "The Most Powerful Governor in the U.S.A.," by Murray Morgan, *Harper's Magazine,* October 1965; "We Can't Afford a Capital Move," editorial in Anchorage *Daily News,* Sept. 12, 1970; "Alaska: Politicians and Natives, Money and Oil," by Lewis Lapham, *Harper's Magazine,* May 1970; "Alaska Spends Newfound Wealth," by Gerald E. Bowkett, *Christian Science Monitor,* June 18, 1970; "Oil Lag Hits Alaska Pocketbook," *Christian Science Monitor,* July 16, 1970; "What Do You Do With $900,000,000?" by Dale Wittner, *Life,* April 10, 1970; "Master Blueprint for Alaska," by A. Robert Smith, *Argus,* July 31, 1970; "Alaska Legislators Spend Oil Money with Abandon," and "Alaska Primary Gives Independents a Whip Hand," by Ruth D. Edmondson, *Argus,* June 26 and Aug. 7, 1970; "Oil Windfall Aids Alaska Revenue," by Wallace Turner, New York *Times,* July 11, 1971; "Alaska Faces Prospect of Fiscal Hard Times Despite Huge Oil Find," by Herbert G. Lawson, *Wall Street Journal,* Nov. 16, 1971.

Also: "Hickel Turned Dream into More than $1 Million," Anchorage *Daily Times,* Dec. 11, 1968; "Walter Hickel Is an Endangered Species," by Paul O'Neil, *Life,* Aug. 28, 1970; "Hickel Was Shooting for Veep Spot in '72," by A. Robert Smith, *Argus,* Dec. 4, 1970; "Exit Walter Hickel . . . ," editorial in New York *Times,* Nov. 27, 1970; "Hickel Departs Just as He Arrived—in a Swirl of Controversy," by Spencer Rich and Nick Kotz, Washington *Post,* Nov. 26, 1970; "The Man Who Let Down the Side," by Ernest Gruening, *The Nation,* Oct. 18, 1971; *Who Owns America?* by Walter J. Hickel (Englewood Cliffs, N.J.: Prentice-Hall, 1971); "What Makes Mike Gravel Run" by C. Robert Zelnick, Washington *Post,* June 21, 1971; "Late Late Show," *Newsweek,* July 12, 1971.

## HAWAII

There are two excellent histories of the Islands: *Shoal of Time: A History of the Hawaiian Islands,* by Gavan Davis (New York: Macmillan, 1968); and *Hawaii Pono: A Social History,* by Lawrence H. Fuchs (New York: Harcourt, Brace & World, 1961). Other books which provided background for the chapter included *Aloha, Hawaii,* by Horace Sutton (published as United Air Lines Guide to the Hawaii Islands by Doubleday, 1967); *The Hawaiians,* a superb picture and impression book by Robert B. Goodman, Gavan Daws, and Ed Sheehan (Australia: Island Heritage Ltd., Norfolk Island, 1970); *The Frontier States,* by Richard Austin Smith (New York: Time-Life Libary of America, 1968); *Hawaii,* by James A. Michener (New York: Random House, 1959); *The New States: Alaska and Hawaii,* ed. William P. Lineberry (New York: W. H. Wilson, The Reference Shelf, Vol. 35, No. 5, 1963); "Hawaii: The Aloha State," by Norman Meller and Daniel W. Tuttle, Jr., chapter of *Politics in the American West,* ed. Frank H. Jonas (Salt Lake City: University of Utah Press, 1969); "Hawaii," by Frank J. Taylor, chapter of *American Panorama* (New York: Doubleday,

1960); *1969–70 Annual Almanac and Government Guide of Hawaii* (Honolulu: Republican State Central Committee of Hawaii, 1969); *The Neighbor Islands—The Other Hawaii* (published by Counties of Hawaii, Maui, and Kauai and Hawaii Department of Planning and Economic Development, 1969). A new view of the Islands' culture is provided in *Hawaii: An Uncommon History,* by Edward Joesting (New York: Norton, 1972).

Other Sources: General coverage of the Honolulu *Star-Bulletin* and Honolulu *Advertiser,* plus the specific coverage cited:

GENERAL "Hawaii: From a Mid-Pacific Feudal Society . . . ," by George Chaplin, Honolulu *Advertiser,* Sept. 28, 1969; "Hawaii: Too Much Prosperity," *Newsweek,* April 8, 1968; "Paradise in Peril?" by Gereon Zimmermann and Frank Trippett, *Look,* April 29, 1969; "The 50th State: Still Soaring, But—," *U.S. News & World Report,* Nov. 10, 1969; *Hawaii Facts & Figures,* 1969, 1970, and 1971 editions (Honolulu: Chamber of Commerce of Hawaii); "Running Against Growth in Hawaii," by Louise Campbell, *Washington Monthly,* September 1970; "The Erosion of

Eden," by Horace Sutton, *Saturday Review,* June 6, 1970; "Hawaii: A State Seeking Identity," and "Hawaii Future: Hub of Pacific Understanding," by James Bassett, Los Angeles *Times,* Dec. 6, and 17, 1971.

NEIGHBOR ISLANDS "The Outer Hawaiian Islands," by Robert Carson, *Holiday,* October 1969; "Paradise Isn't Quite Enough," by Kathryn Hulme, *Holiday,* April 1969; "Rockefeller Center West: Hawaii's Mauna Kea," by William Price Fox, *Holiday,* May 1969; "Kipahulu from Cinders to the Sea," by Peter Matthiessen, *Audubon,* May 1970; "Maui Revisited," *Seattle Magazine,* March 1969; "Battle of Kahoolawe: Hawaiians Blast Use of Island as a Target," by James E. Bylin, *Wall Street Journal,* April 29, 1970; "The Land Blooms in Molokai," *Fortune,* January 1970; "Say Aloha to Your Cash, Mainlander," by Richard L. Coe, *Washington Post,* June 7, 1970; "Hawaii Implored to Retain Island," AP distpatch in New York *Times,* Feb. 15, 1970; "The Beach Leads Way in Boom on Island," by Earl A. Selle, New York *Times,* Sept. 26, 1971; "Cleanup Ordered at Pearl Harbor," New York *Times,* Sept. 26, 1971; "Pollution in Paradise," *Newsweek,* March 1, 1971; "Hawaiian Leper Colony Afflicted by Fear of Change," by Wallace Turner, New York *Times,* April 28, 1971.

OAHU "Look What's Happened to Honolulu," by Jim Becker, *National Geographic,* October 1969; "Between Mountain and Sea," *Time,* March 21, 1969; "Ten Long Minutes in Punchbowl," by Joan Didion, *Life,* April 10, 1970; "Hawaii U. Pledges New Role in '70's," New York *Times,* Jan. 11, 1970; "Battling to Save Historic Places . . . Diamond Head," *National Observer,* Oct. 6, 1969; "Hula Dancers' Show Is Closed in Honolulu and a Storm Gathers," by Norman Sklarewitz, *Wall Street Journal,* June 20, 1969; "The Outdoor Circle—These Conservation-Minded Ladies Are the Conscience of Hawaii," by Chester Collins, *San Francisco,* February 1970; "The Beach Leads Way in Boom on Island," by Earl A. Selle, New York *Times,* Sept. 26, 1971; "Cleanup Ordered at Pearl Harbor," New York *Times,* Sept. 26, 1971; "Pollution in Paradise," *Newsweek,* March 1, 1971.

ECONOMY "Bulldozer, Crane, and the Hammer," by Harold Hostetler, Honolulu *Advertiser,* Aug. 17, 1969; "Economy of Islands Has Soared in 10 Years Since Admission," by Donald Boswell, Honolulu *Advertiser,* Aug. 17, 1969; "Hawaii Finishes Decade as State," New York *Times,* Aug. 24, 1969; "Isles' Boom Out of Perspective," by Gene Sherman, Los Angeles *Times,* May 20, 1963; "Hawaii's Economy: It's as Lively as the Hula," by Martin Rossman, Los Angeles *Times,* June 29, 1969; "Castle & Cooke Sets the Pace in the New Pacific Era," by John D. Ramsey, *Pacific Business News,* May 22, 1969; "Dillingham Deals from Strength in Hawaii," *Engineering News Record,* Sept. 5, 1968; "Bring on the Big Five," *Forbes,* Dec. 1, 1968; "Lure of the Islands," *Forbes,* Oct. 5, 1969; "Chinn Ho —From Bean Picker to Waikiki Millionaire," by Lloyd Shearer, *Parade,* Nov. 1, 1970; "Hawaii's Visitor Industry—A Friendly Giant Who's Still Growing," by A. A. Smyser, Honolulu *Star-Bulletin,* June 2, 1969; "Burns Rebukes Critics of Tourism," Honolulu *Star-Bulletin,* Dec. 11, 1969; " 'R & R' in Honolulu a Six-Day Moment of Peace for Soldiers and Their Wives," by Wallace Turner, New York *Times,* April 13, 1970; "R and R: Biggest Single Factor in Isle Tourism Today," *Pacific Business News,* May 22, 1969; "Hawaii Gets That Empty Feeling," by Jerry Hulse, Los Angeles *Times, May* 3, 1970; "Hawaiians Vexed by Top

U.S. Costs," Associated Press dispatch in New York *Times,* June 8, 1969; "Hawaii: America's Window on Asia," by Robert A. Wright, New York *Times,* Oct. 24, 1971.

LABOR *Raising Cane—A Brief History of Labor in Hawaii,* by Victor Weingarten (published by International Longshoremen's and Warehousemen's Union, Honolulu, September 1946); *Jack Hall-ILWU* (published by ILWU, Honolulu, 1952); "The Old Jack Hall—The New Jack Hall —The Real Jack Hall," by Robert McElrath, *Voice of the ILWU,* June 1969; "The Right to Strike in Hawaii," by William L. Abbott, *The Nation,* June 22, 1970.

RACES "Race Relations Frontiers in Hawaii," articles by Andrew W. Lind in *Race Relations: Problems and Theory, Essays in Honor of Robert E. Park,* ed. Jitsuichi Masuoka and Preston Valien (Chapel Hill: University of North Carolina Press, 1961); "Japanese Joining Hawaii's Elite," by Wallace Turner, New York *Times,* Oct. 24, 1970; "The First Decade of Statehood," by John A. Burns, Honolulu *Star-Bulletin,* Aug. 18, 1969; "Hawaiians Begin to Stir from Apathy," by James Bassett, Los Angeles *Times,* Dec. 14, 1971.

GOVERNMENT AND POLITICS "The Long Struggle for Statehood," by Gerald R. Corbett, Honolulu *Star-Bulletin,* Aug. 18, 1969; "Burns Recalls Statehood Bill Strategy," by Gerry Keir, Honolulu *Advertiser,* Aug. 17, 1969; "That's How It Was, That Day in '59," by Gene Hunter, Honolulu *Advertiser,* Aug. 17, 1969; *Centralization of Government in Hawaii,* by W. Brooke Graves (Library of Congress, Legislative Reference Service study, March 30, 1962); *With an Understanding Heart: Constitution Making in Hawaii,* by Norman Meller (New York: National Municipal League, 1971); "The Constitutional Convention of Hawaii of 1968," by Hebden Porteus, *State Government,* Spring 1969; "Quinn Recalls Days of Transition," Honolulu *Star-Bulletin and Advertiser,* Aug. 17, 1969; "Hawaii Leads Way in Advanced Legislation," by Ed Meagher, Los Angeles *Times,* Aug. 23, 1970; "Hawaiians Avoid School Problem," by Wallace Turner, New York *Times,* April 11, 1970; "New Ombudsman on Job in Hawaii," by Lawrence E. Davies, New York *Times,* Oct. 26, 1969; "Ombudsman Has Good 1st Year," by Ed Meagher, Los Angeles *Times,* Aug. 30, 1970; "Ombudsman Calls the Office Sound," by Wallace Turner, New York *Times,* Sept. 27, 1970; "The Hawaii Ombudsman Appraises His Office after the First Year," by Herman Doi, *State Government,* Summer 1970; "Hawaii Passes Bill to Legalize Most Abortions," by Birch Storm, *National Observer,* March 2, 1970; "Abortion Unlimited," *Newsweek,* March 9, 1970; "Hawaii Expected to Ease Sex Laws," by Wallace Turner, New York *Times,* April 4, 1971; "Hawaii Votes Law Curbing Welfare," Associated Press dispatch in New York *Times,* June 13, 1971; "Hawaii Returns to Biennial Budgeting," *State Government News,* December 1971.

Also: "Young, Newcomers Seen Holding Key to '70 Vote," by Tom Coffman, Honolulu *Star-Bulletin,* Dec. 9, 1969; "Politics: Where Do We Stand?", series of 16 articles by Gardiner B. Jones in the Honolulu *Advertiser,* January 1968, including quoted interview with Jack Hall; "The 1968 Election in Hawaii," by Marshall N. Goldstein, *Western Political Quarterly,* September 1969; "Fong Blasts Role of Isle GOP," and "New GOP Chairman Will Seek To Restore Balance in Politics," by Duck Donhan, Honolulu *Star-Bulletin,* May 22 and 26, 1971.

# INDEX

Page references in **boldface** type indicate inclusive or major entries.

THE AUTHOR

NEAL R. PEIRCE began political writing in Washington in 1959 and is author of the definitive work on the electoral college system, *The People's President*, published in 1968. He was political editor of *Congressional Quarterly* for nine years and became a consultant on network election coverage, initially for NBC News and after 1966 for CBS News. In 1969 he became a founding partner of the Center for Political Research and subsequently politics consultant for its weekly publication, the *National Journal*. In 1971, he became a Fellow of the Woodrow Wilson International Center for Scholars.

A native of Philadelphia, Mr. Peirce graduated from Princeton University, Phi Beta Kappa, in 1954. He lives in Washington with his wife and their two daughters and a son.

Scale of Miles
0 100 200 300 400 500

C A N

WASH.
Seattle
Olympia
Spokane

MONT.

N.D.

Helena
Butte
Billings

Bismarck

Portland
Salem
ORE.
Eugene

IDAHO

Boise

S.D.
Aberdeen

YELLOWSTONE
NATIONAL
PARK

WYO.

Pierre

CALIF.

NEV.

Great
Salt Lake

Pocatello

Casper

Ogden

NEB.

Reno

Salt Lake City

Cheyenne

Oakland

Carson City

UTAH

Sacramento

COLO.

Denver

KA

San Francisco

YOSEMITE
NAT'L. PARK

Colorado
Springs

Mt. Whitney

GRAND
CANYON
NAT'L. PARK

Las Vegas

Wich

Santa
Barbara

Farmington

Los Angeles

ARIZ.

Santa Fe

Okla
C.

San Diego

Albuquerque

Amarillo

Pacific
Ocean

Phoenix

N.M.

Wichita
Falls

Tucson

Lubbock

Fort Wort

El Paso

TEXA

Austi

San
Antoni

U. S. S. R.

Kotzebue
ALASKA
Nome
Fairbanks

CANADA

U.S.S.R.
U.S.

Anchorage

MEXICO

Bering
Sea

Juneau

MILES
0 200 400 600

Lon